Nietzsche

Nietzsche

PHILOSOPHER, PSYCHOLOGIST,

ANTICHRIST

BY WALTER KAUFMANN

Third Edition

PRINCETON, NEW JERSEY

PRINCETON UNIVERSITY PRESS

1968

The author wishes to thank the Manuscript Division
of the Princeton University Library
for permission to reproduce the Nietzsche letter
that appears on pages 464-466, and the Houghton Library
at Harvard University for permission
to reproduce the Nietzsche letter that appears on pages 470-473.
The other two letters that are reproduced
are from the author's own collection.

TO MY WIFE AND CHILDREN
HAZEL, DINAH, AND DAVID

PREFACE TO THE THIRD EDITION

I

A man who has published six books, all of them about Nietzsche, says on page 431 of the fifth of them: "This compelled the author once again to occupy himself intensively not only with Nietzsche, which in any case is not one of the pleasant things in life, but also with the Nietzsche literature, which is, with few exceptions, insufferable." [1]

Over twenty years have passed since I submitted my doctoral thesis on "Nietzsche's Theory of Values" to the Department of Philosophy at Harvard, and since then I have written extensively on Nietzsche (though nothing like six books) and translated ten of his books, if I may for the moment include *The Will to Power* under this heading; but if anything "compelled" me to occupy myself so intensively with Nietzsche it was my love of his books.

Agreement rarely involves love, and love does not necessarily entail agreement. Most of my books are not about Nietzsche, and over the years I have developed my own views on many of the problems with which Nietzsche dealt.

The literature about Nietzsche is another matter entirely. In 1952, when I visited C. D. Broad at Trinity College, Cambridge, he mentioned a man named Salter. I asked whether he was the Salter who had written a book on Nietzsche, to which Broad, one of the most eminent British philosophers of his generation, replied: "Dear no; he did not deal with crackpot subjects like that; he wrote about psychical research." (Broad had been President of the Society for Psychical Research.)

---

[1] Erich Podach: see section II of the Appendix, below.

All sorts of men, including some crackpots, have written about Nietzsche, but among those who have contributed to the literature are Thomas Mann and Camus, Jaspers and Heidegger, and leading poets as well as renowned scholars. No other modern philosopher, at least since Kant and Hegel, has been so highly esteemed by so many illustrious writers. Yet many studies, including some by very honorable men, are based on scholarship so shoddy it almost defies belief. This does not mean that the Nietzsche literature is worse than secondary literature on other fascinating men and subjects.

If Erich Podach, who finds the Nietzsche literature, "with few exceptions, insufferable," had not concentrated exclusively on Nietzsche but had also done research on Kierkegaard or Christianity, on Judaism or the Bible, he might have found most of the literature no less repellent. Whoever digs for gold must clear away a lot of rubbish.

Or must he? Would it not do to bypass the accumulated errors and confusions, concentrating solely on the primary materials? This advice could mean two different things. Those who *ignore* the secondary literature usually fall into scores of errors and confusions from which some of their predecessors might have saved them. And if one reads the literature but does not refer to it in print, where are readers to find guidance, confronted with a wealth of studies many of which are quite uninformed?

Obviously, the thing to do is to lose little time over incompetent writers who are unlikely to be taken seriously by many readers, but to be firm and forthright, faced with "men of position and fortune." And to allude to another Aristotelian formulation: one should not sacrifice the truth to friendship.

This book is about Nietzsche, but it is also a guide to much of the Nietzsche literature. If one is not content to offer just another view of him, there is no alternative. Sound method requires that we do not merely marshal the evidence for our own views: we must go out of our way also to confront evidence that on the face of it contradicts our views (in the present case, passages in Nietzsche that do not seem to fit our image) and alternative constructions (those proposed by other writers on the subject).

If no other study of Nietzsche deals so thoroughly with rival interpretations, demonstrating why they are untenable, it is also true that most other writers on Nietzsche tend to fasten on a few snippets from his works, heedless of the fact that scores of other snippets might be used to support very different exegeses. They treat Nietzsche the way most theologians treat Scripture—or the way many theologians gerrymander the writings of rival faiths in order to come up with bogeymen.

It was the surpassing merit of Karl Jaspers' *Nietzsche* (1936) that he counseled Nietzsche's readers never to rest content until they had also found passages contradicting those found first. This should have spelled the end of the theological era of Nietzsche exegesis, but of course, it did not: some recent studies are as arbitrary as any. Alas, Jaspers' own interpretation rests content with superficial contradictions and ignores the context of the snippets on his file cards, the development of Nietzsche's thought, and the difference between Nietzsche's books and notes.[2]

In sum, these are some of the differences between this book and most other studies of Nietzsche: (a) I love Nietzsche's books but am no Nietzschean. (b) The development, the context, and the interrelations of Nietzsche's views are given an unusual amount of attention. (c) So are apparently negative evidence and rival interpretations.

II

A fourth point might be added. When I was working on the original edition, a young colleague in another department expressed surprise: "I thought Nietzsche was dead as a doornail." Today few philosophers are more alive, and millions are discussing his pronouncement that "God is dead." But it would be a mistake to associate Nietzsche primarily with a few theologians. After all, they are making news not because they echo Nietzsche's words more than fourscore years later, but because, while doing this, they insist on remaining Christian theologians. It is plain what Nietzsche would have thought of that: as little as he would have thought of most movements that have sought the sanction of his name.

By 1950 Nietzsche had been linked in turn with evolution, with depth psychology, and with the Nazis; but in the English-speaking world he had not come into his own as a philosopher. In the United States, my book probably did its share to get Nietzsche to be taken seriously as a philosopher; but soon it be-

---

[2] See Chap. 2, section I, below.

came fashionable to see him as a precursor of existentialism. In 1961 Heidegger's two-volume *Nietzsche* appeared in German, and in 1965 an American translation of Jaspers' *Nietzsche* appeared. R. J. Hollingdale's *Nietzsche,* the first decent biography in English, also came out in 1965; and so did paperback reprints of George A. Morgan, Jr., and Crane Brinton, originally published in 1941, and Arthur Danto's attempt to link Nietzsche with analytical philosophy.

Obviously, Nietzsche can be, and has been, linked with a vast variety of intellectual fashions—movements as well as men—but it is clear that any attempt to define his significance and meaning mainly in terms of one such juxtaposition is bound to be misleading. This is not to say that all "Nietzsche and *X*" titles are worthless, but it may help to restore perspective if one notes that *X* has been, among others—and I confine myself to items listed in the bibliography at the end of this volume—Bachofen, the bourgeois spirit, Burckhardt, Carlyle, Christ, Christianity, Dostoevsky, Emerson, the French, the German future, Goethe, Hitler, Kierkegaard, the labyrinth, Luther, Thomas Mann, National Socialism, nihilism, the pre-Socratics, Schopenhauer, Tolstoy, the transformation of man, Wagner, Wittgenstein, and women.

Even so, there is still room for good monographs on Nietzsche's relation to the Greek philosophers, to French literature, and to linguistic philosophy. But no study of that sort could possibly provide the key to Nietzsche. His house has many mansions, and any attempt to find the clue to everything in some nook, or in a similarity between a detail here and a trifle in another edifice, or in a guest glimpsed in the parlor, is simpleminded.

The subtitle of my book still seems right to me: Nietzsche was a philosopher above all, but not only that; he was also a psychologist; and he defined his own significance very largely in terms of his opposition to Christianity. To do him full justice, one might add that he was a poet as well; and the first edition of this book did have an "Appendix: Nietzsche as a Poet." Two men who spoke very generously of the book convinced me that even so I had not done justice to Nietzsche as a poet and writer: Thomas Mann and A. J. P. Taylor. No wonder: I had been reacting against the view that Nietzsche was primarily a great stylist, and the burden of my book had been to show that he was a great thinker.

Meanwhile I have tried to make amends, but let me first conclude that this book differs from many other studies of Nietzsche in this way also: it is not a study of "Nietzsche and *X*" or a study of "Nietzsche as *Y*" but an attempt to do justice to Nietzsche's thought as a whole. And from most other books that have tried to do that, it differs in the three respects mentioned.

III

How does the present edition differ from its predecessors? (A) I have brought it up to date by taking account of works published in recent years. (a) Two German editions (1956 and 1961) of Nietzsche's late works and notes—especially of *The Antichrist, Ecce Homo,* and *The Will to Power*—created an international sensation, though they are unsound: a detailed critique of both is offered in a new Appendix. (b) No book about Nietzsche has caused an equal sensation. Comments on various studies will be found in the notes, the Appendix, and the Bibliography—the Index shows where. (c) Two discoveries have a bearing on Nietzsche's biography and character. Karl Schlechta's demonstration[3] that the few late letters in which Nietzsche complimented his sister were not genuine is grist to my mill. Rudolph Binion's imposing study of Lou Andreas-Salomé shows that she, too, tampered with the truth and with some documents, and throws new light on Nietzsche's relationship to her. I read Binion's book before publication, studied scores of unpublished letters and drafts for letters that are relevant, and then revised and greatly enlarged my account of Nietzsche's friendship and break with Paul Rée and Lou, in Chapter 1.

(B) Previously unpublished letters are not only cited in Chapter 1; four more are reproduced in facsimile near the end of this volume and discussed at length in another major addition. Nietzsche was a fascinating human being as well as a great philosopher, and this new edition provides an opportunity to do justice to the man no less than the thinker.

(C) There are many smaller additions throughout the book, including a new section at the end of the Epilogue.

(D) My own publications pose special problems, but did not require any expansion of the book. On the contrary, there is no

---

[3] Nietzsche, *Werke,* III (1956), 1408 ff.

need now for the Appendix on "Nietzsche as a Poet," already omitted in the second edition to save space. For in my *Twenty German Poets: A Bilingual Collection* I included all the poems from the old Appendix, along with some of Nietzsche's other poems and several poems about him, and tried to relate him both to his predecessors and to those influenced by him. I have also dealt with Nietzsche as a poet in three essays that at first appeared separately but eventually found their way into my *From Shakespeare to Existentialism* (Chapters 12–14). Nor was there any need to duplicate the introductions and commentaries written for my new translations of Nietzsche, or other relevant essays and book reviews: they are listed in the Bibliography to this volume. But in many cases I have substituted my new translations for the old ones.

(E) The Bibliography, omitted in the second edition, has been very greatly expanded and brought up to date; the Index, truncated in the second edition, has been expanded, too; and the footnotes, collected at the end of the book in the second edition, are once again printed on the pages to which they refer. In the original edition each chapter had a motto. Although I pleaded that I had often placed the most crucial quotations at the beginning, these mottos were deleted in the second edition to save space. They are now restored. Finally, I have made hundreds of minor changes, mostly stylistic.

I am delighted that the Princeton University Press and Vintage Books have agreed to publish this third revised edition of my *Nietzsche* simultaneously in hard covers and in paperback. I want to thank Herbert S. Bailey, Jr., and Miriam Brokaw of the Princeton University Press, and Jason Epstein and Berenice Hoffman of Random House for having made this possible.

My father, Bruno Kaufmann (1881–1956), helped me with his comments on parts of early drafts. To begin with, his view of Nietzsche had been very different from mine; perhaps he was my first convert. As I said in the original Acknowledgments, his faith in my work was an inspiration.

PREFACE TO THE SECOND EDITION (1956)

Nietzsche has grown on me since this book was first published. I still do not agree with him, but more than ever he seems to me one of the most interesting thinkers of all time. Few, if any, since Plato can match the breadth, depth, and passion of his mind.

To find fault with Nietzsche is easy. As Hegel has said in the Preface to his first book: "Nothing is easier than to judge what has substance and quality; to comprehend it is harder; and what is hardest is to combine both functions and produce an account of it."

To swim against the stream is fun in any case; in a conformist age it is a duty; and in writing about Nietzsche any other attitude would be sufficient proof that the author is basically uncongenial to his subject. In this book I have tried to buck the current prejudice against Nietzsche. If any further justification is needed, I can only express the hope that those who do likewise will find him richly rewarding.

For this new edition I have made hundreds of minor changes, none greater than striking out about a page early in Chapter 3 because I no longer see much point in it. The Appendix which offered some of Nietzsche's poems in the original and in translation has been omitted for reasons of space; the Index has been abridged; and most of the Bibliography has been omitted; but the notes contain ample references to the literature. Both text and notes are offered unabridged.

The Viking Press has kindly granted me permission to substitute the improved wording of my translations in *The Portable Nietzsche* for some of the quotations in the original edition. The sixty-odd pages of editorial matter in *The Portable Nietzsche* supplement the account of Nietzsche given in the present volume, as do some of my other recent publications which are listed at the end of this volume, in lieu of substantial additions.

What I have written in the following pages I see no need to retract or alter further. I should not say precisely the same things, or say them in exactly the same way, today; but the book may stand as an invitation to read Nietzsche and, above all, to think. Its message is essentially the motto which Socrates in his Apology inscribed over all subsequent philosophy: "The unexamined life is not worth living."

PREFACE TO THE FIRST EDITION (1950)

Nietzsche, more than any other philosopher of the past hundred years, represents a major historical event. His ideas are of concern not only to the members of one nation or community, nor alone to philosophers, but to men everywhere, and they have had repercussions in recent history and literature as well as in psychology and religious thought. Yet Nietzsche's way of writing—his reputation as a great stylist notwithstanding—and the excessive freedom of most translations of his work make it difficult for the contemporary reader to find out what Nietzsche himself stood for. One knows of his anticipation of psychoanalysis, of his decisive influence on Spengler and existentialism, and of the problem posed by his relation to the Nazis; but the details remain something of a mystery, and Nietzsche's thought has been obscured rather than revealed by its impact.

The present book aims at a comprehensive reconstruction of Nietzsche's thought and is addressed to the general reader no less than to scholars. It is not a monograph, but seeks to capture something of the fullness and the wealth of Nietzsche's philosophy without forcing it into a Procrustean system.

Nietzsche is here assigned a place in the grand tradition of Western thought and envisaged against the background of Socrates and Plato, Luther and Rousseau, Kant and Hegel—not, as has often been done, as Schopenhauer's wayward disciple or a lone epigone of the pre-Socratics. The cliché of his romanticism is rejected, and his debt to Goethe and Heine emphasized. And it is suggested that he was not a Darwinist, but only aroused from his dogmatic slumber by Darwin, much as Kant was a century earlier by Hume; and Nietzsche, too, sought to counter the posi-

tivistic challenge from across the Channel (which seemed nihilistic to him) by developing a new picture of human dignity.

A bird's-eye view of the book at this point may prove helpful. The Prologue on "The Nietzsche Legend" is intended primarily to show, in a few large strokes, why yet another addition
to the Nietzsche literature is needed. And since many readers
have some fairly definite ideas about Nietzsche, it seemed advisable to make clear at the outset what the author considers mere
"legend" and on what issues he would like the reader to suspend
judgment until he has read further.

Part I seeks to furnish the background required for an understanding of Nietzsche's thought. It begins with a chapter on
"Nietzsche's Life as Background of His Thought" because some
aspects of his life are admittedly relevant to a study of his philosophy. The presumption, however, that his ideas—unlike those
of other philosophers—are altogether reducible to biographical
or psychological data, is rejected. The second chapter seeks to
show how Nietzsche's literary style reflects a way of thinking—
indeed, a method which has philosophic significance. And the
third chapter offers an interpretation of Nietzsche's conceptions
of "The Death of God and the Revaluation"; for the proclamation that "God is dead" marks the beginning, just as the revaluation is generally considered the end, of Nietzsche's philosophy.
Throughout Part I, the perspective is dictated less by historical
considerations than by the needs of the contemporary reader who
seeks an approach to Nietzsche. Part II, on the other hand, traces
"The Development of Nietzsche's Thought" in its actual sequence, from his first book to the proclamation of the will to
power in *Zarathustra*.

Most interpreters either consider Nietzsche's notion of power
central and construe it in terms of ruthless self-assertion or, when
Nietzsche is presented in a more appealing light, minimize the
will to power. It is the contention of the present book that the
will to power *is* the core of Nietzsche's thought, but inseparable
from his idea of sublimation. The third and main part of the
book begins with a comprehensive discussion of Nietzsche's conception of sublimation, and the conclusions of the first two chapters of Part III constitute the center of the book—not only
spatially. The next chapter examines Nietzsche's opposition to
the pleasure principle, both as a psychological postulate and as
an ethical norm, while his relation to the Nazis is presented in a

new light in the following chapter, "The Master Race." A demonstration of the mutual compatibility and close interdependence of Nietzsche's conception of the superman—or better, overman[1] —and his doctrine of the eternal recurrence of the same events concludes Part III, "Nietzsche's Philosophy of Power."

Part IV offers a "Synopsis" of Nietzsche's thought in the dual perspective of his repudiation of Christ and his admiration for Socrates. The temptation to eschew any extended treatment of Nietzsche's attack on Christianity had to be resisted because he himself defined his historical significance in terms of this issue, and his philosophy cannot be understood apart from it.

All translations from the German are the author's, and all quotations have been rendered into English. In view of the great freedom of the published English versions of Nietzsche's works, it seemed unnecessary to encumber this study with polemics against them. Criticisms of the Nietzsche literature, however, could not be entirely omitted without inviting the charge that this book represents "just another construction" of Nietzsche. On important points, views different from the author's have therefore been referred to, usually in footnotes, and reasons have been given for rejecting them.

To keep down the number of notes, cross references have been avoided almost completely, and references to Nietzsche's writings are given in parentheses in the text. A key to the abbreviations used for this purpose will be found at the end of the book.

The contemporary relevance of Nietzsche's views could be established only by the reconstruction of his problems. This approach involves a measure of *internal* criticism. And to this extent at least, an attempt has been made to throw light not only on Nietzsche—though this is of course the primary intent of every chapter—but also on some of the problems with which he dealt; e.g., in the chapter on "Power versus Pleasure." Moreover, some passages—especially, but not only, in Chapter 8—may also contribute to the understanding of Hegel.

The historical accuracy of Nietzsche's views—whether of Socrates and Rousseau, Christianity or the German people—could not be discussed critically. In each case, another book would have

---

[1] For this translation of *Übermensch* cf. Chap. 11 below and *The Portable Nietzsche*, 115.

been required to give due consideration to the relevant literature, and the understanding of Nietzsche would not have been advanced materially. Suffice it to state here that Nietzsche's historical profiles are rarely realistic and frequently outright caricatures.

In the end one is bound to be asked what prompted the choice of the man to whom one devotes such a study. The Epilogue, "Nietzsche's Heritage," may provide a partial answer, but a few points may be suggested at the outset. First, there is the scholar's interest in correcting what he takes to be misapprehensions. Then certain aspects of Nietzsche's critique of modern man may deserve serious consideration: ever more people seem to realize that their pleasures do not add up to happiness and that their ends do not give their lives any lasting meaning. Properly understood, Nietzsche's conception of power may represent one of the few great philosophic ideas of all time.

The decision to write on Nietzsche, however, was not inspired by agreement with him. What seems admirable is his deprecation of the importance of agreement and his Socratic renunciation of any effort to stifle independent thinking. Without acceding to his philosophy, one may respect his overruling passion for intellectual integrity; and his protestant perspectives are often suggestive and fruitful even when they are unacceptable. Nietzsche's greatest value may well lie in the fact that he embodied the true philosophic spirit of "searching into myself and other men"— to cite the *Apology* of Socrates—and few men could have reiterated the words of the great Greek with more conviction: "if you say to me, . . . you shall be let off, but upon one condition, that you are not to enquire . . . in this way any more, and that if you are caught doing so again you shall die; if this was the condition on which you let me go, I should reply . . . while I have life and strength I shall never cease from the practice and teaching of philosophy."

CONTENTS

NIETZSCHE

A NOTE ON THE CITATIONS

In citations from Nietzsche's books the titles are abbreviated (a key will be found on pages 479–80), and the Arabic figures after the letters refer to sections—the same in all editions, regardless of language. A 4, for example, means: *The Antichrist,* section 4.

Nietzsche's notes are cited according to the *Musarion* edition of the *Gesammelte Werke* (23 vols., 1920–29). The key to the abbreviations and the note following it show how every reference reveals at a glance the approximate date of each passage. Roman numerals refer to the volumes, Arabic figures to the pages. Thus, XIV, 147 means: vol. XIV, p. 147.

In citations from other books, Arabic figures also refer to pages unless otherwise indicated. Dates of first publication are usually given in parentheses because it is interesting to know when something was said. Additional data will usually be found in the Bibliography at the end of this volume.

PROLOGUE

The Nietzsche Legend

The first adherents prove nothing *against* a doctrine.—XI, 143.

One generally mistakes me: I confess it; also I should be done a great service if someone else were to defend and define me against these mistakes.—XIV, 318 f.

Nietzsche became a myth even before he died in 1900, and today his ideas are overgrown and obscured by rank fiction. Divergent evaluations, of course, are not uncommon; but in Nietzsche's case there is not even basic agreement about what he stood for: his admirers are as much at odds about this as his critics. It might seem that one cannot properly speak of a Nietzsche legend where so many different conceptions are current, but it is actually typical of the manner in which legend appropriates historical figures that it takes no offense at generating clearly incompatible accounts. This situation, however, has led to the assumption that Nietzsche lacked any coherent philosophy, and that different readers are bound to come up with different interpretations. In a sense, the present book as a whole represents an attempt at a *constructive* refutation of this view; but the demonstration would not be complete, and it would lack historical perspective, without at least a brief account of the origin of the legend.

I

The legend began to develop shortly after Nietzsche had become insane in January 1889. Until then, his writings had received little attention: he had had to draw on his own funds to see some of his books published, and the first three parts of *Zarathustra* had found so few readers that Nietzsche had despaired of publishing the fourth. Only as his voluntary exile from Germany came to a close and he was brought home, his mind and body spent, did the cycle of his "withdrawal and return" end. In 1888, Georg (Morris Cohen) Brandes (1842–1927) had given the first lectures on Nietzsche, in Copenhagen, and now Nietzsche's fame began to spread like wildfire.

The tragedy was played out, and a satyr play followed. While the author of the *Antichrist* was lingering in his mother's house, hopelessly mad, his sister—under the same roof—employed her considerable propaganda talents in the service of that Teutonic "Christianity" and chauvinistic racism which Nietzsche had loathed as "scabies of the heart" (FW 377) and for which he had bitterly denounced Wagner and—his sister. Her husband, Bernhard Förster, had been one of the leaders of the German anti-Semitic movement, and the couple, inspired by the rising tide of colonialism, had founded a Teutonic colony in Paraguay. Now that Förster had died by his own hand, she divided her time between business activities in South America and propaganda efforts at home. She tried to make a national hero of her husband, but in vain: she only provoked more and more attacks from disillusioned colonists who considered themselves swindled and ruined by the Försters. Then, suddenly, she realized that her brother's star had meanwhile begun its steep ascent—and Frau Förster turned into Elisabeth Förster-Nietzsche, became her brother's chief apostle, and began to fashion the Nietzsche legend.

Her interpretations of her brother's thought were immediately accepted almost everywhere; and right up to the present, books which are violently opposed to her husband's heritage have often failed to question the legitimacy of her fusion of this heritage with that of Nietzsche. Few writers today would cite her as a reliable interpreter, but her influence is still tremendous, if unrecognized.

This situation leads one to ask whether she was well acquainted with her brother's thought when she took up his cause in the eighteen-nineties. Rudolf Steiner, a Goethe scholar and later the founder of anthroposophy, reports that she asked him to give her "private lessons in the philosophy of her brother": "The private lessons . . . taught me this above all: *that Frau*

Förster-Nietzsche is a complete laywoman in all that concerns her brother's doctrine. . . . [She] lacks any sense for fine, and even for crude, logical distinctions; her thinking is void of even the least logical consistency; and she lacks any sense of objectivity. . . . She *believes* at every moment what she says. She convinces herself today that something was red yesterday that most assuredly was blue." [1] In retrospect, one might characterize her work by quoting from Nietzsche's venomous estimate of St. Paul: through a prolific career of writing and editing she "inverted" her brother's philosophy "into a pagan doctrine of mysteries which learns eventually to get along with the State, wages wars, . . . tortures, . . . and hates" (WM 167).

One wonders how her success was possible and why the many learned men who produced monographs on various aspects of Nietzsche's thought deferred so humbly to this woman. Of course, she reaped the belated sympathy which many people suddenly felt for her brother, but it was her handling of Nietzsche's *Nachlass* that constitutes the decisive factor. She jealously established and guarded her authority by first gaining exclusive rights to all of her brother's literary remains and then refusing to publish some of the most important among them, while insisting doubly on their significance. Nobody could challenge her interpretations with any authority, since she was the guardian of yet unpublished material—and developed an increasingly precise memory for what her brother had said to her in conversation. Finally, she blended all these considerations with a shrewd business sense.

She published edition after edition of Nietzsche's "collected works," ever rearranging the material and including something new. Nietzsche's last work, *Ecce Homo,* was withheld for years, while she spiced her introductions to his other works and her own writings with liberal doses of quotations from it. And when it was finally published in 1908, it was brought out only in an expensive limited edition. After this "bank directors' edition"— as it was nicknamed—had been exhausted, *Ecce Homo* was included in an edition of the works. Eventually it found its way into a popularly priced volume, and when the copyright expired

---

[1] "Zur Charakteristik der Frau Elisabeth Förster-Nietzsche" in *Das Magazin für Litteratur,* Feb. 10, 1900. See also Podach's well documented sketch of "Bernhard und Eli[sabeth] Förster" in *Gestalten um Nietzsche* (1932) and, for Nietzsche's relation to his sister and brother-in-law, Chap. 1, below.

Nietzsche's works were made available in cheap volumes which could be bought singly.

The long delay of the publication of *Ecce Homo* was fateful because the book contains explicit repudiations of many ideas that were meanwhile attributed to Nietzsche and have been associated with him to this day. Possibly still more fateful was his sister's decision to patch together some of the thousands of jottings, scribbles, and notes which Nietzsche had accumulated over a period of years, largely on his long walks in the Alps, and to publish this fabrication as his system, under the title *The Will to Power*. The first version (volume xv of the "collected works," 1901) contained some four hundred "aphorisms." Three years later, two hundred pages of further material "from *The Will to Power*" were integrated into the last volume of Frau Förster-Nietzsche's biography of her brother; and in 1906, finally, a second edition of *The Will to Power* made its appearance in a new edition of the "collected works." Now there were 1067 "aphorisms," the new material being mixed in with, and not appended to, that published previously. Some editorial omissions were admitted, but this edition was never augmented. And although a large percentage of the notes included had already been utilized by Nietzsche in the many books written after *Zarathustra,* no attempt was made to distinguish the by-products of these works from the material that Nietzsche had not yet used in any published work.[2]

To arrange the material, Frau Förster-Nietzsche chose a four-line draft left by her brother, and distributed the notes under its four headings. Nietzsche himself had discarded this draft, and there are a dozen later ones, about twenty-five in all (XVIII, 335–61); but none of these were briefer than this one which listed only the titles of the four projected parts and thus gave the editor the greatest possible freedom. (It was also the only draft which suggested "Zucht and Züchtung" as the title of Part IV, and Frau Förster-Nietzsche may have been charmed by these words, although her brother, as we shall see, did not consider "breeding" a function of race.) His own attempt to distribute

---

[2] I.e., J; FW, Book v; GM; W; G; A; and EH. The approximate dates of composition of all the notes incorporated in WM are given in my edition of WM (cf. also XIX, 417–31), and in my footnote commentary I call attention to relevant passages in the later books. Properly edited, many of these notes are fascinating.

some of his notes among the four parts of a later and more detailed plan (XVIII, 347; XIX, 390–402) was ignored, as was the fact that, in 1888, Nietzsche had abandoned the entire project of *The Will to Power*. Some previous drafts had called for the subtitle, "Attempt at a Revaluation of All Values"; and Nietzsche, who now proposed to write a different *magnum opus,* decided on the title *Revaluation of All Values*—and actually finished the first quarter: the *Antichrist*. The similarity of the new title of the projected work to the subtitle of the previous plan led his sister to designate the *Antichrist,* when she first published it, as Book I of *The Will to Power*; and though this error was corrected in later editions, some writers still speak of it as "the only finished part of *Der Wille zur Macht*." [3]

All this may seem academic. Yet it is significant that *The Will to Power* was not, as is so often supposed, Nietzsche's last work; that it was abandoned by him before the *Antichrist* (1895) was written; and that this, like most of Nietzsche's later books, was based in part on notes which were later included, uncritically, in the posthumous edition of *The Will to Power*. Moreover, the *Antichrist,* however provocative,[4] represents a more single-minded and sustained inquiry than any of Nietzsche's other books and thus suggests that the major work of which it constitutes Part I was not meant to consist of that maze of incoherent, if extremely interesting, observations which have since been represented as his crowning achievement. While he intended to use some of this material, he evidently meant to mold it into a coherent and continuous whole; and the manner in which he utilized his notes in his other finished books makes it clear that many notes would have been given an entirely new and unexpected meaning.

The publication of *The Will to Power* as Nietzsche's final and systematic work blurred the distinction between his works and his notes and created the false impression that the aphorisms in his books are of a kind with these disjointed jottings. Ever since, *The Will to Power,* rather than the *Götzen-Dämmerung,*[5]

---

[3] Knight, *Some Aspects of the Life and Work of Nietzsche* (1933), 46. This error is quite common.

[4] Morgan's translation of the title as "The Antichristian"—in *What Nietzsche Means* (1941)—overlooks that Nietzsche plainly means to be as provocative as possible.

[5] "The Twilight of the Idols" is an accurate translation of the title, but does not bring out Nietzsche's polemic against Wagner's *Götterdämmerung.*

Antichrist, and *Ecce Homo,* has been searched for Nietzsche's final position; and those who find it strangely incoherent are led to conclude that the same must be true *a fortiori* of his *parva opera.*

The two most common forms of the Nietzsche legend can thus be traced back to his sister. In the manner just indicated, she unwittingly laid the foundation for the myth that Nietzsche's thought is hopelessly incoherent, ambiguous, and self-contradictory; and by bringing the heritage of her late husband to her interpretation of her brother's work, she prepared the way for the belief that Nietzsche was a proto-Nazi. These two views, of course, are not generally held by the same people, though they do not logically exclude each other.

There are some other misconceptions for which Nietzsche's sister is at least partly responsible. His conception of the over-man—as different from man as man is from the ape—might in any case have supplied a Darwin-conscious age with a convenient symbol for its own faith in progress. The development, however, was aided and abetted by her long delay of the posthumous publication of *Ecce Homo,* which contains a vitriolic denunciation of this misinterpretation. Around the turn of the century, the legend thus associated Nietzsche with a Darwinistic superman.

When enough of Nietzsche's works and notes had finally been published to make possible a scholarly appraisal of his thought, the First World War broke out. This was not the time for a sober study of such an explosive figure as Nietzsche. Feelings ran high both in Germany, where *Zarathustra* was pushed to new sales records as a "must" for the soldier's knapsack, and in England and the United States, where Nietzsche began to be considered as the apostle of German ruthlessness and barbarism. Yet neither the often misleading parables of *Zarathustra* nor such slogans as "will to power," "master morality," and "blond beast" can beget an understanding of Nietzsche's thought unless they are considered in the context of his philosophy and against the background of his total literary output.

During those war years, the "superman" began to be associated with the German nation; and militarism and imperialism were read into Nietzsche's conception of power, although nothing could have been further from his mind. Again, these misinterpretations were supported, and perhaps partly inspired, by the work of Nietzsche's sister. The French, incidentally, on whom Nietzsche had so frequently lavished his praise, on the whole have retained a far more favorable picture of his thought than have people in the Anglo-Saxon countries where the war-begotten misconceptions have never been eradicated from the popular mind. The advent of Hitler and the Nazis' brazen adaptation of Nietzsche have strengthened these misapprehensions. And while the nature and principles of their exegesis will be considered later, Nietzsche's fate in pre-Nazi Germany must be further considered here.

II

The growth of the Nietzsche legend in Germany is so inextricably involved in, and so symptomatic of, the development of German thought during the last decades that no summary account may seem possible. A study of "Nietzsche: The History of His Fame" or "Nietzsche in the Twentieth Century" might grow into a cultural history of twentieth-century Germany, seen in a single, but particularly revealing, perspective. For our purposes, however, it will be sufficient to concentrate on only two further phases. The first is represented by Stefan George (1868–1933), a poet whose influence at first eclipsed that of Rilke. He is best known as the founder of a literary circle, the *George Kreis,* which made important contributions to modern German poetry, criticism, and cultural historiography. Some of its members became professors at various German universities, and it was primarily as an educator of educators and writers that George made his influence felt. And as Nietzsche became one of the heroes of the *Kreis,* the poet's influence on the Nietzsche legend was considerable.

The *Kreis* was united by a common sorrow over the desecration of the German language, its progressive degeneration into journalese, and the impossibility of using this profaned medium for the expression of deep feelings or great thoughts. At the same time, George and his Circle were convinced that no established scripture, myth, or philosophic system could spell salvation now, and that no return was possible to a bygone age. While George translated Dante and inspired Rudolf Borchardt to render Dante and the great troubadours into the minnesingers' German, these were only excursions from which one must return, enriched, to a more genuinely creative task.[6] A new German language and a new mythology had to be generated; and the language-creating genius of Dante or Goethe, while an inspiration and a model, seemed too distant to dispel the doubt that such feats were still possible. There was a need for one who could show that a heroic life was still possible in the modern world, and for a predecessor to bridge the temporal gap between Goethe and George—in short, for Nietzsche. Also wanted was a scripture to reveal how one might approach the past without becoming subservient to it, and how the study of history could be used to inspire new creation; and the *Kreis* found such a book in Nietzsche's "untimely" essay on history. (See Chapter 4 below.)

Nobody could have recognized more clearly than George that Nietzsche's message was unalterably opposed to many of the fashionable notions associated with his name; but the poet's own conception of Nietzsche was not free from legendary touches either. Nietzsche's idea of power may have been grasped intuitively by the poet who declared, *"j'aime l'art comme pouvoir"* [7] —but the power-craving poet was not one to look into the past dispassionately: his picture of Nietzsche was highly personal and clearly determined by his own aspirations. He envisaged Nietzsche as the incarnate repudiation of modern vulgarity—a prophet driven insane by the blindness and deafness of his contemporaries. Nietzsche's philosophic endeavors had been heroic but essentially futile: what was needed was the creation of a small *Kreis* as a nucleus for a future regeneration. Some lines from George's poem, "Nietzsche," written in 1900 on the philosopher's death and published in *Der Siebente Ring,* give expression to this vision:

> Dull trots the crowd below, do not disturb it!
> Why stab the jelly-fish or cut the weed?
> For a while yet let pious silence reign,
> and let the vermin that stain him with praise
> and are still fattening in the musty fumes
> that helped to stifle him, first waste away!
> But then, resplendent, thou wilt face the ages
> like other leaders with the bloody crown.

---

[6] Cf., e.g., George's poem "An Gundolf" in *Der Siebente Ring* (1907).
[7] George's retort when he was told of Napoleon's *"j'aime le pouvoir comme artiste."* Cf. R. Boehringer in *Corona* x (1942), 587 f.

Redeemer thou! thyself the most unblessed— . . .
Didst thou create gods but to overthrow them,
never enjoying rest or what thou built?
Thou hast destroyed what in thyself was closest
to tremble after it with new desire
and to cry out in pain of solitude.

He came too late that said to thee imploring:
There is no way left over icy cliffs
and eyries of dread birds—now this is needed:
constraint within a circle closed by love.

One of George's critics, whose polemic takes the form of a sixty-
page commentary on this poem, remarks apropos the poet's en-
treaty, "There is no way left . . .": "A romantic implores the
shadow of a skeptic: turn back!" And the critic further insists
that the phrase "Didst thou create gods?" is highly misleading.[8]
To be sure, George projected himself into his Nietzsche picture;
and he lacked a sympathetic understanding of what mattered
most to Nietzsche. In a second poem on Nietzsche, on the eve
of the First World War, George no longer takes Nietzsche to task
for his philosophic flights, but gives expression to his own
prophetic disillusionment. No regeneration is to be hoped for.
And Nietzsche, in reality the proponent of *amor fati* and the
eternal recurrence of the same, is now credited with another feat
of incredible daring: an attempt to arrest history and avert the
inevitable catastrophe.

One man arose who, sharp as lightning, cracked
open the clefts and, steel-like, severed camps,
creating a Beyond, inverting your old Here—
who roared your madness into you so long
with so much force that his throat burst. And you?
Some dumb, some clever, false or genuine,
perceived and looked as if nothing had happened.—
You go on speaking, laughing, and conspiring.
The warner went—the wheel that hurtles down
toward emptiness no arm attempts to tackle.[9]

---

[8] Thiel, *Die Generation ohne Männer* (1932), 334 and 349 f. In this book,
Shaw, Freud, Rathenau, George, Thomas Mann, and Spengler are criticized
in turn from what Thiel takes to be Nietzsche's point of view.

[9] "Einer stand auf . . ." in *Der Stern des Bundes* (1914). The complete
German texts and my translations of both poems are included in my
Twenty German Poets.

All the above mentioned criticism of George's two poems may be utterly irrelevant aesthetically—and if the Circle had broadened George's poetic vision of the "untimely" and aristocratic Nietzsche, the true outlines of Nietzsche's thought might well have been recovered eventually. George, however, like Richard Wagner, received the unswerving obedience of his followers who called him "Master"; and instead of transcending him, his disciples accepted his every word religiously. Their many studies of Nietzsche re-echo untiringly the lines of the two poems cited, and not one went beyond the master's vision to give an exposition of Nietzsche's philosophy. Nietzsche, himself "most unblessed," was but a voice in the wilderness preceding the master's advent. One disciple explains the break with Wagner thus: "Nietzsche's . . . apostasy . . . was . . . but a sign that the god whose arrival he had hailed had not appeared yet. . . . Thus he followed his law and his fatality: to sit in judgment over all that existed, to move the goal beyond all that had been achieved into the unachievable, and to strive for the infinite out of a finitude which he could not bear any more." And another disciple concludes: "Only George *is* what Nietzsche convulsively coveted to be." [10]

III

It is against this background that we must consider the Circle's first and most successful contribution to the literature, Ernst Bertram's *Nietzsche: Versuch einer Mythologie*. With this "Attempt at a Mythology" the Nietzsche legend enters another phase, and our account need not extend beyond it. Bertram entitled his Introduction "Legend," and we may say in retrospect that it is here that the legend first appears fully grown and an author frankly admits that this is what he is offering.

Bertram's conception was partly inspired by the George Circle's need for a new mythology. He, too, is concerned with Nietzsche's "most unblessed" individuality, not with his philosophy; and he not only agrees that Nietzsche's collapse is not to be

---

[10] *Nietzsche als Richter unserer Zeit* (1923), 31 f. and 102. (See also 33, 48, 61.) The book consists of two essays, the first by Ernst Gundolf, the second by Kurt Hildebrandt. Hildebrandt's other three Nietzsche books agree in not doing justice to their titles because they all stop short of Nietzsche's philosophy.

explained in terms of any disease, but actually envisages his pitiful insanity as an "ascent into the mystic" and a "proud transition" which calls for comparison with Christ's Crucifixion.[11] Beyond this, Bertram develops George's idea of Nietzsche's self-laceration into the claim that Nietzsche perpetually contradicted himself; and his "attempt at a mythology" may be said to typify the legend as a whole. These two points require at least a brief elucidation.

What had hitherto been the largely unintentional result of the many hundred volumes of the Nietzsche literature, contributed at random by philosophers, literary critics, journalists, poets, psychiatrists, and others who often lacked any thorough knowledge of Nietzsche's works, Bertram sought to achieve deliberately through the cultivated incoherence of his chapters and a willful disregard for the sequence of Nietzsche's thought—even for the immediate context of his utterances. In his Introduction, Bertram renounced the very possibility of historiography: because it must needs involve a measure of interpretation, we cannot hope for more than "legend." The element of truth in this contention had of course long been recognized by historians and philosophers, including Nietzsche. What distinguished Bertram's book, which first brought this idea to the attention of many thousands, was the author's evident satisfaction with this half-truth and the way in which he used it to justify an open break with previously accepted standards of scholarship. Thus he counters in advance any criticism of his interpretation: "Suffice it that the figure of Nietzsche was at least once envisaged thus." [12] From such utter relativism it was but one step to the Nazis' "subjective" historiography; and one may note in passing that Bertram himself proceeded in this direction, and that, during World War II, he published a defense of the Nazis' suppression of free speech—and the motto of this tract sums up its gist and its essential dependence on ambiguity: ". . . the most genuine freedom is a holy imprisonment of the heart. . . ." [13] It would seem that, like many other Nietzsche interpreters, the author projected his own personality into Nietzsche's when he proposed to consider him as "the typically ambiguous one." [14]

---

[11] Bertram, *Nietzsche* (1918), 361 f.
[12] *Ibid.*, 10.
[13] *Von der Freiheit des Wortes*, Inselbücherei, n.d.
[14] *Nietzsche*, 8.

What Bertram meant was actually not so much a predilection for equivocal statements as constant self-contradiction, for he failed to see that this self-contradictory quality is merely the characteristic of legend and not typical of Nietzsche. And the alleged contradictions can generally be resolved in one of two ways. The utterly superficial inconsistencies dissolve as soon as one checks the quotations and recognizes the meaning they had in their original context. Bertram makes this difficult by withholding exact references. His work is full of phrases in quotation marks that are integrated into his own prose, though this sometimes involves an alteration of both text and meaning; e.g., "What a strange picture, this radical and revaluer of values for whom 'duration on earth' is 'a first-rate value'!" [15] No reference is given. In fact, Nietzsche says (FW 356) that medieval society had at least "durability (and duration is a first-rate value on earth)." Surely, Nietzsche's view of the value of duration cannot be determined on the basis of an altered quotation from a parenthesis.

The apparently more profound contradictions can be resolved by the discovery of a larger context, namely that of Nietzsche's philosophy, his development, and his basic intentions—all of which are ignored by Bertram and in the legend generally. Nietzsche, we are told, was in some ways more Christian than pagan although he attacked Christianity so bitterly; he valued not only health but also suffering and sickness; he both loved and hated Socrates and Wagner. Why can one not ask in Nietzsche's case, as one would in any other, what he opposed in Christianity and to what elements he shows an affinity? How he defined health and why he valued suffering? What, more precisely, was his relation to Socrates? And what made him break with Wagner?

We shall seek the answers to these questions in the following chapters, but may anticipate even now that any attempt to "experience him as he experienced the romantic: 'as the typically ambiguous one' " [16] means identifying Nietzsche with what he fought. Indeed, he had jotted down in a draft: "the type of the romantic: ambiguous" (xviii, 356). When he utilized this draft

---

[15] *Ibid.,* 12: *"dem 'Dauer auf Erden ein Wert ersten Ranges' ist"*—while Nietzsche writes: "Dauer ist auf Erden. . . ." All this remained unchanged in the 7th rev. ed. (1929; 21,000 copies).
[16] *Ibid.,* 8.

later (G IX 8), however, he omitted this point; and he himself
sought to avoid any ambiguity by distinguishing sharply between
the "romantic" and "Dionysian" (FW 370; WM 843 ff.)—and the
"romantic" was precisely what he opposed.

It would be idle to attach so much significance to Bertram's
"mythology," had it been less influential or representative. Except
for Frau Förster-Nietzsche's popular biographies, however, no
other book on Nietzsche left so decisive a mark on the literature.
E. Gundolf, for example, relies on "Bertram's brilliant book"
and its "most perfect instruction" [*vollkommenste Belehrung*]
rather than on any direct acquaintance with Nietzsche, and is
thus led to assume that it was Kurt Hildebrandt who, in 1912,
first used the term "romantic as a contrast to the Dionysian." [17]
And Thomas Mann not only hailed Bertram's *Nietzsche* as "the
most beautiful book about him," but also accepted the conception of Nietzsche as a "late son of romanticism." [18] Parallels
between Nietzsche and the German romantics can of course be
found,[19] and it is also possible to define the notoriously equivocal
word "romantic" in a sense which would permit its application
to Nietzsche; but, especially where no precise definition is given,
any interpretation of Nietzsche as the typical representative or
the late son of a movement that he consistently opposed seems,
to say the least, highly misleading.

Nietzsche defined his own position in terms of his crucial
break with Wagner; and in *Nietzsche Contra Wagner* (8) he
says expressly that it was in part Wagner's "ambiguity" that he
could not "bear." Nietzsche may have been more similar to
Wagner than he admitted when he spoke of "We Antipodes,"
but any writer is misunderstood fundamentally when his intentions are ignored and he is identified with the forces he fought.
And the "ambiguity" of the romantics—their protest "against
reason, enlightenment, taste, and the eighteenth century" (WM
849)—is just what Nietzsche denounced. Bertram, like Frau
Förster-Nietzsche, belongs to the many interpreters who ignore,
or are loath to accept, Nietzsche's break with Wagner. And in the

---

[17] *Op. cit.*, 4, 31, 13.

[18] "Rede über Nietzsche" in *Bemühungen* (1925), 335.

[19] Cf. Joel, *Nietzsche und die Romantik* (1905) and—influenced by Bertram
—Langer, *Das Problem der Romantik bei Nietzsche* (1929). Joel was one
of George's friends (cf. Bondi, *Erinnerungen an Stefan George*, 1934, 8),
and George had admired both Nietzsche and the romantics even in the
eighteen-nineties.

face of attempts to claim his sanction for facile resignation and
relativism in matters of truth, it seems important to remember
that Nietzsche himself was a fanatical seeker after truth and
recognized no virtue above intellectual integrity.[20] His intentions
are singularly unequivocal, and he was not one to sit on both
sides of the fence at once. Insofar as he had a "dual nature," [21]
he was seeking to overcome it: "My *strongest* characteristic is
self-overcoming" (XXI, 102). Self-overcoming, not ambiguity, is
the key to Nietzsche.

In a way, this is recognized by Jaspers, but he treats Nietzsche
as a precursor of *Existenzphilosophie* and introduces us not to
Nietzsche's philosophy, but to Nietzsche's "philosophizing." [22]
The process of self-overcoming, as conceived by Jaspers, tends to
lose all content and lapses into endless, aimless self-destruction.
Nietzsche's problems, in the sense of clearly defined questions
capable of being answered, are neglected, and Jaspers may be said
to revert to Stefan George's poetic vision:

> Didst thou create gods but to overthrow them,
> never enjoying rest or what thou built?
> Thou hast destroyed what in thyself was closest
> to tremble after it with new desire
> and to cry out in pain of solitude.

Thus one may find the two fountainheads of the legend in Frau
Förster-Nietzsche and George; and Bertram may be said to have
accomplished a synthesis of their views, for his interpretation of
Nietzsche's "most unblessed" individuality in terms of ambiguity
automatically makes room for the sister's misconstruction—as
well as for any other one—and in that sense Bertram represents
the legend as a whole.[23]

---

[20] E.g., M 91, 164, 456, 556; FW 2, 319, 335; Z IV 13; J 227, 229; XXI, 78; A
36; EH-W 3.

[21] Bertram, *Nietzsche*, 8.

[22] *Nietzsche: Einführung in das Verständnis seines Philosophierens* (1936).
This and the following comments apply equally to Jaspers' *Nietzsche
und das Christentum* (n.d.). Cf. my essay on "Jaspers' Relation to Nietzsche" in *The Philosophy of Karl Jaspers,* ed. P. A. Schilpp, reprinted in
my *From Shakespeare to Existentialism.*

[23] Jaspers, *op. cit.,* justly criticizes Bertram for overlooking the process of
Nietzsche's philosophizing, but nevertheless follows Bertram in speaking
often of Nietzsche's "ambiguity." What he means will be considered in
Chap. 2.

There is no need here for tracing the growth of the legend further. We shall later have occasion to consider the Nazis' use of Nietzsche. For the present we may conclude that his alleged ambiguity as well as his supposed affinity with Nazism—indeed, that the whole legend—depends on the failure to ask: What did Nietzsche oppose? What did he seek to overcome? What were his problems? The answers can be found when these questions are recognized. And in this manner mere legend can be transcended, and the element of subjectivity which besets any effort of interpretation can be minimized. One need not resign oneself to the complete relativity of historical truth, abandon the discipline of scholarship—and fall prey to the doctrines of totalitarian propagandists.

To crystallize Nietzsche's own problems, and to understand his attempts to cope with them, one must forgo any temptation to picture him as the precursor of one of the many contemporary movements that identify him with their own causes. What is needed, to make possible an adequate analysis of *Nietzsche's Philosophy of Power* (attempted in Part III of this book), is a historical sketch of *The Development of Nietzsche's Thought* in its actual sequence. Since the exact dates of his works and most of his notes are known, such a sketch is possible. (Part II represents an effort in this direction.) The *Background,* finally, which Part I seeks to furnish, is not that of Nietzsche, but rather the background that we require today to understand his thought. Thus the third chapter inquires in some detail whether Nietzsche was truly a philosopher rather than, say, a would-be prophet and value-legislator; and the second chapter aims to show that his thought cannot justly be charged with ambiguity, basic inconsistency, or incoherence. First of all, however, we shall consider "Nietzsche's Life as Background of His Thought" (Chapter 1), concentrating on particularly pertinent aspects. Special emphasis will be placed on three points: the break with Wagner, which Nietzsche himself experienced as the capital event of his life and which crystallized his basic intentions; his relation to his sister, which throws light both on Nietzsche's thought and on her interpretation of it; and finally the possible relation of his eventual insanity to his work—for one must know at the outset whether some of his writings ought to be discounted as the creations of a madman. Incidentally, the diagnosis of Nietzsche's disease throws an interesting sidelight on the claim that it was the stupidity of his contemporaries that drove him mad; an analysis of his relation to his sister discredits the major source of the Nietzsche legend; and his repudiation of Wagner, correctly understood, explodes the very core of the legend itself.

I

Background

A very popular error: having the courage of one's convictions; rather it is a matter of having the courage for an *attack* on one's convictions!!!

—XVI, 318.

1

NIETZSCHE'S LIFE AS BACKGROUND OF HIS THOUGHT

Here the ways of men part: if you wish to strive for peace of soul and pleasure, then believe; if you wish to be a devotee of truth, then inquire.—LETTER TO HIS SISTER, June 11, 1865.

I am *impassioned for independence;* I sacrifice all for it . . . and am tortured more by all the smallest strings than others are by chains.—XXI, 88.

I

Nietzsche's family background offers a striking contrast to his later thought. It is tempting to construe his philosophy as a reaction against his childhood: his attitudes toward nationalism, Luther, Christianity, small-town morals, and the Germans may seem easily explicable in such terms. Yet this approach, while frequently adopted, bars any adequate understanding of Nietzsche's philosophy. The thought of a philosopher may be partly *occasioned* by early experiences, but the conception of strict causality is not applicable here. A problem, once suggested, carries its own impetus; and the thinker is driven on by it to new problems and solutions. To understand these, we must follow the development of his thought—and that is best done separately from the survey of his life, as any joint treatment will almost inevitably suggest a false notion of causal relationship between life and philosophy.[1]

---

[1] In the next few paragraphs I have made use of my article on Nietzsche in *The Encyclopedia of Philosophy,* New York, Macmillan and The Free Press, 1967, vol. 8, 504 ff., which also contains some additional material on Nietzsche's medical history and on the events preceding his call to the chair of classical philology at the University of Basel.

Nietzsche was born in Röcken, in the Prussian province of Saxony, on October 15, 1844. His father, Ludwig Nietzsche, a Lutheran minister and the son of a minister, was thirty-one, and his mother, the daughter of a Lutheran minister, was eighteen. His paternal grandfather had written several books, including *Gamaliel, or the Everlasting Duration of Christianity: For Instruction and Sedation* . . . (1796). Many of Nietzsche's ancestors had been butchers; none of them seem to have been Polish noblemen, as he believed. His father christened him Friedrich Wilhelm after King Friedrich Wilhelm IV of Prussia, on whose birthday he was born. The king became mad a few years later, and so did Nietzsche's father. Nietzsche later shed his middle name, along with his family's patriotism and religion, but in January 1889 he, too, became insane.

In an early autobiographical sketch Nietzsche wrote, "In September 1848 my beloved father suddenly became mentally ill." When Elisabeth Förster-Nietzsche published this sketch in her biography of her brother (1895), she changed the wording to read, ". . . suddenly became seriously ill in consequence of a fall." In fact, the doctor's diagnosis was softening of the brain (*Gehirnerweichung*), and after Ludwig Nietzsche's death in 1849, his skull was opened, and this diagnosis was confirmed. Nevertheless, most experts agree that the philosopher's later insanity was not inherited.

In January 1850, Nietzsche's widowed mother lost her youngest son, born in 1848, and moved her family to Naumburg. Here Nietzsche spent the rest of his childhood as the only male in a household consisting of his mother, sister, father's mother, and two maiden aunts.

In 1858 he entered the old boarding school of Pforta on a full scholarship. For six years he was subjected to the exacting discipline and traditions of the school which Klopstock and Novalis, Fichte and Ranke, as well as the brothers Schlegel, had attended before him. He did exceptionally good work in religion, German literature, and classics, and poor work in mathematics and drawing.

In 1861 he wrote an enthusiastic essay on his "favorite poet," Friedrich Hölderlin, "of whom the majority of his people scarcely even know the name." Hölderlin had spent the last decades of his life in hopeless insanity, but sixty years after Nietzsche wrote his essay, Hölderlin was widely recognized as Germany's greatest poet after Goethe. The teacher wrote on the paper, "I must offer the author the kind advice to stick to a healthier, clearer, *more German* poet."

The medical records of the school contain an entry, recorded in 1862: ". . . shortsighted and often plagued by migraine headaches. His father died early of softening of the brain and was begotten in old age [actually, when his father was fifty-seven, his mother thirty-five]; the son at a time when the father was already sick [most experts deny this]. As yet no grave signs are visible, but the antecedents require consideration."

In 1864 Nietzsche graduated with a thesis on Theognis. Before he left for the university of Bonn, he stated in his *curriculum vitae* that Plato's *Symposium* was his *Lieblingsdichtung*.

At Bonn he joined a fraternity but soon found himself revolted by its lack of sophistication and the very unclassical, beer-drinking patriotism of his fraternity brothers. He made a quixotic attempt to raise their level to his own—and then resigned. It was also as a student at Bonn that Nietzsche, in June 1865, wrote his sister a letter that is noteworthy because it anticipates the temper of *Human, All-Too-Human* and the other works written after the break with Wagner.

> . . . As for your principle that truth is always on the side of the more difficult, I admit this in part. However, it is difficult to believe that 2 times 2 is not 4; does that make it true? On the other hand, is it really so difficult simply to accept everything that one has been brought up on and that has gradually struck deep roots —what is considered truth in the circle of one's relatives and of many good men, and what moreover really comforts and elevates man? Is that more difficult than to strike new paths, fighting the habitual, experiencing the insecurity of independence and the frequent wavering of one's feelings and even one's conscience, proceeding often without any consolation, but ever with the eternal goal of the true, the beautiful, and the good? Is it decisive after all that we arrive at *that* view of God, world, and reconciliation which makes us feel most comfortable? Rather, is not the result of his inquiries something wholly indifferent to the true inquirer? Do we after all seek rest, peace, and pleasure in our inquiries? No, only truth—even if it be most abhorrent and ugly. Still one last question: if we had believed from childhood that all salvation issued from another than Jesus—say, from Mohammed—is it not certain that we should have experienced the same blessings? . . . Every true faith is infallible inasmuch as it accomplishes what the person who has the faith hopes to find in

it; but faith does not offer the least support for a proof of objective truth. Here the ways of men part: if you wish to strive for peace of soul and pleasure, then believe; if you wish to be a devotee of truth [*ein Jünger der Wahrheit*], then inquire.

At first Nietzsche had studied theology and classical philology, but in 1865 he gave up theology and followed his favorite teacher, Friedrich Ritschl, to Leipzig.

His friend Paul Deussen (1845–1919), who later acquired fame as one of the foremost translators and interpreters of Indian philosophy, had shared Nietzsche's experiences at Pforta and at Bonn; but now he went on to Tübingen. Even so, he remained close to Nietzsche and shared the latter's enthusiasm for Schopenhauer. It was in Leipzig that Nietzsche accidentally picked up a copy of Schopenhauer's *Die Welt als Wille und Vorstellung* in a second-hand bookstore—not to lay it down again until he had finished it. Deussen remained more faithful to Schopenhauer than did Nietzsche: he dedicated his *System des Vedanta* to the great pessimist who had been one of the first to try to draw the attention of Europe to the wisdom of the Upanishads; and Deussen crowned his monumental history of philosophy, which takes the reader from ancient India to modern Europe, with an elaborate presentation of Schopenhauer's thought in which he found the ultimate synthesis of Orient and Occident. Though Nietzsche later outgrew his early infatuation with Schopenhauer, Deussen remained his faithful friend until the end.[2]

Less fortunate in this respect was Nietzsche's friendship with Erwin Rohde (1845–1898). As fellow students at Leipzig

---

[2] Deussen later published *Erinnerungen an Friedrich Nietzsche* (1901). A minor episode reported early in the book has attained some literary importance: Deussen describes how the young Nietzsche, arriving in Cologne one day, asked a porter to take him to a hotel and was unexpectedly taken to a brothel. Horrified at the sight of flimsily clad women, the youth first froze, then walked over to a piano, which seemed to him the only live thing in the room, struck a chord, found the spell broken, and hastened out. H. W. Brann, *Nietzsche und die Frauen* (1931), cited this incident as possibly significant—and Thomas Mann, finally, incorporated it into his *Doktor Faustus,* where precisely the same story is told of the hero, Leverkühn. (This name contains a conceptual allusion to Nietzsche's famous phrase, "Live dangerously.") Cf. Mann's essay on "Nietzsches Philosophie" in *Neue Studien* (1948) where this experience is also considered crucial, inasmuch as Mann supposes that Nietzsche could not resist the temptation to return to a brothel a year later and then infected himself. Cf. note 37 below.

they were drawn to each other by a common enthusiasm for ancient Greek culture and became the closest of friends. Professor Ritschl called them "the Dioscuri," and they seemed inseparable. It was not a shift in interests that finally led them apart: Nietzsche never renounced "Dionysus"; and the work which later established Rohde's fame as a classical philologist, *Psyche,* dealt with Greek conceptions of the soul in the same light in which the "Dioscuri" had approached antiquity at Leipzig— yet Rohde's many pages about Dionysus were not to contain a single reference to the author of *The Birth of Tragedy.* It was a divergent development of character that precipitated the end of the friendship. Nietzsche's publication of the enlightened and critical *Human, All-Too-Human* struck Rohde as a scarcely credible betrayal of their youthful and romantic Wagner worship. Later Rohde married and began to raise a family, while Nietzsche turned to *Zarathustra.* Now Rohde felt increasingly provoked by his friend's excessive self-esteem, and some of his letters suggest that his annoyance may have cloaked doubts whether it was not he himself who had undergone a change rather than Nietzsche, whose fire seemed to feed on itself. Having settled down, the successful professor could not share the loneliness in which his uncomfortable twin conducted his persistent inquiries and uninhibited attacks in book after book. One of Rohde's letters to Franz Overbeck, occasioned by the publication of *Beyond Good and Evil,* shows especially well how utterly unsympathetic Rohde had become. The final break, a year before Nietzsche's collapse, was little more than a formality. But much later, when Nietzsche had become famous, Rohde made a belated and impossible attempt to make up with his former friend. He yielded to the insistent entreaties of Frau Förster-Nietzsche—who probably played on cherished memories—and, without actively collaborating, he gave his backing and sanction to her work. If this action was typical of others who had had no sympathy for Nietzsche in his later years, it seems clear that Rohde did not consciously betray a trust: he had never understood Nietzsche's books after the break with Wagner. The professors at Basel, however, kept better faith with Nietzsche.

His call to the university of Basel came as a surprise to Nietzsche, who had not yet received his doctorate though he had published some fruits of his research in a scholarly journal. He had actually considered giving up philology for science when, on Ritschl's recommendation,[2a] he was appointed a professor of classical philology at Basel, and Leipzig hurriedly conferred the doctorate without examination. Thus Nietzsche was a professor at twenty-four, and his unusual success does not seem to have humbled him.

At Basel he taught for ten years, from 1869 till 1879, when he retired because of poor health. This illness may have been connected with his brief military service in 1870, during the Franco-Prussian War. His previous military training in 1867 had been cut short by injuries contracted through a fall from his horse, and by 1870 he was a Swiss citizen. When the war broke out, however, he volunteered for service as a medical orderly. While ministering—in a boxcar, and unrelieved for three days and nights —to six men who were severely wounded and also sick with dysentery and diphtheria, Nietzsche caught both diseases and, after delivering his charges to a field hospital, required medical attention himself. "Moreover"—he wrote his friend Gersdorff— "the atmosphere of my experiences had spread around me like a gloomy fog: for a time I heard a sound of wailing which seemed as if it would never end." One gathers that he may have had a physical and nervous breakdown. Yet a month later he is back at the university in Basel, perhaps quite eager to drown in a double load of work his recent experiences and the uncomfortable knowledge that the war is still going on and that other men are still being maimed and disfigured in ways of which he has inextinguishable memories. Thus he plunges into two new lecture courses as well as seminars and the Greek lessons which he has agreed to give at the local *Pädagogium*. He also writes of committee meetings and a social life—and all of these matter much less to him than his work on his first book and his frequent visits to the house of Richard Wagner. The relation of a possibly incomplete recovery from his illness to the continued spells of migraine headaches and painful vomiting which made Nietzsche miserable during the next ten years has never been clarified conclusively. His last disease will be considered later.

In 1872 Nietzsche published his first book, *The Birth of Tragedy*. It was not what a university would expect from a young philologist who has yet to establish his reputation as a scholar:

[2a] For the original text see Johannes Stroux, *Nietzsches Professur in Basel* (1925); for a translation of most of Ritschl's amazing encomium, see *The Portable Nietzsche*, 7 f.

there were no footnotes, references, or Greek quotations; Schopenhauer's philosophy had tinged some of the contentions; and the style was, where not beautiful, flamboyant. Moreover, as Nietzsche himself recognized in his preface to the second edition, he had weakened his case by appending to the fifteen sections which comprised his main thesis about ancient tragedy another ten which utilized these considerations for a poorly written eulogy of Wagner. This conclusion gave the entire work the appearance of a none too well considered but impassioned editorial. Among the many critics of the book who were entirely blind to its merits was Wilamowitz-Moellendorf (1848–1931), who later became an outstanding philologist, though his translations of Aeschylus and Sophocles into colloquial German hardly demonstrate the most subtle understanding of tragedy. Rohde, then still Nietzsche's closest friend, countered Wilamowitz's criticisms with a deadly polemic to which Wilamowitz replied. All three pamphlets are nasty to the point of being funny.

Not entirely sympathetic with Nietzsche's tone and quite contemptuous of Wagner, but nevertheless in accord with much that Nietzsche had to say of ancient Greece, was Jacob Burckhardt (1818–1897), who was Nietzsche's elder colleague at Basel. In his maturity, his outward sober calm and dignity, and his Olympian reserve, he reminds one of the old Goethe—and like Goethe he did not share the enthusiastic notions of some of the younger men of genius who came within his orbit. Perhaps Burckhardt, like Goethe, looked back upon the storm and stress of his own youth, sensed in himself a still dangerous medley of passions that could be controlled only by maintaining a subtle equilibrium, and deliberately refused to become involved in the younger man's comet-like career which for Burckhardt could mean only destruction. While Goethe, however, deeply wounded men like Hölderlin and Kleist—the poets whose meteoric lives, ending respectively in insanity and suicide, invite comparison with Nietzsche's—Burckhardt managed to let Nietzsche feel his sympathy; and the younger man was frequently less struck by the ironical reserve of Burckhardt's letters to him than we are today.

Nietzsche attended some of Burckhardt's lectures at Basel, though not regularly; and in some of his letters to friends he refers to them with great enthusiasm. Occasionally he met the great historian socially, he even took a few walks with him, and the two men had some long conversations. The similarity of some of their ideas has inevitably raised the question, who influenced whom—especially as regards their interpretations of classical Greek culture.[3] This problem has never been solved conclusively —but it is hardly very important: for it appears that neither of them was detracted from his own path or greatly helped by the other, and the ideas of each can be explained in terms of his own background. Nietzsche's *juvenilia* which plainly contain the seeds of much of his later thought are of special value in this respect.[4] One may conclude that the two men, who differed so widely in age and temperament, were probably attracted to each other— insofar as Burckhardt may be said to have been attracted to Nietzsche—by common conceptions and perspectives no less than by their common interest in ancient Greece and Renaissance Italy. Agreement may be due less to any influence than to an affinity. There is thus no need for digression into Burckhardt's ideas about ancient Greece, Christianity, or history.[5]

Nietzsche—and this seems noteworthy—never relinquished his veneration for the old historian who was so remarkably free from most of the prejudices of his time, such as narrow nationalism or glib faith in relentless progress. Long after he had

---

[3] Burckhardt's posthumously published *Griechische Kulturgeschichte* (vols. VIII–XI of the *Gesamtausgabe*, 1930–31) was written much later than Nietzsche's parallel efforts. The following sections invite comparison: vol. II, "Greek Envy" (335), and "Greek Pessimism" and "Suicide" (343– 92); vol. III, "The Free Individuality" (342–81) and vol. IV, "The Colonial and Agonistic Man" (61–163, especially 87 ff.). The section on Greek Tragedy (III, 190–239) does not associate Socrates with its demise, but describes its development out of the chorus and its ultimate origins in the Dionysian cult—and here Burckhardt, unlike Rohde, gives express credit to Nietzsche. In the section on Socrates (III, 352–57), his optimism, irony, and dialectic are emphasized, and Burckhardt insists that Socrates wanted death and forced the death sentence upon himself. Burckhardt's *Weltgeschichtliche Betrachtungen (Force and Freedom: Reflections on History)*, though also published posthumously, were known to Nietzsche as lectures.

[4] These *Jugendschriften* comprise vol. I of the *Musarion* edition of the collected works. The first volumes of the "Historical-Critical" edition contain even far more *juvenilia*, including many trivia.

[5] Cf. Löwith, *Jacob Burckhardt* (1936); Salin, *Jacob Burckhardt und Nietzsche* (1938); von Martin, *Nietzsche und Burckhardt* (3rd rev. ed., 1945). Andler's long section on Burckhardt as Nietzsche's *précurseur* (in vol. I of *Nietzsche: Sa vie et sa pensée*) is not very specific; but Felix Stähelin's few pages on the subject of any possible influence are very good, though admittedly quite inconclusive. (Introd. to *Griechische Kulturgeschichte*, ed. cit., xxiii–xxix.)

broken with Wagner, whom Burckhardt had always disliked, Nietzsche still revered the old professor and paid his respects to him in his last works. And it was to Burckhardt that he sent that last four-page letter in which he explained that he would rather have been a Swiss professor than God, but had not dared to push his private egoism so far.[6] The older man's reaction seems typical: sympathetic and yet without relinquishing his customary reserve, he took the letter to Nietzsche's friend Franz Overbeck, stating that he believed it was something of concern to Overbeck.

Overbeck (1837–1905) was nearer Nietzsche's own age, though still seven years his senior, and he was closer to Nietzsche than anybody else in Basel. For a time, the two men lived in the same house; and even after Nietzsche left Basel, Overbeck kept in close touch with him. His disposition, wholly lacking in flamboyancy, was even more different from Nietzsche's than was Burckhardt's. For while the older man liked to rise above the level of mere scholarship to the inspiring and inclusive visions of genius, Overbeck could not, with a good conscience, leave the plain of dry and solid research. This inhibition was aggravated by his calling: he was a professor of church history without religious faith. While he also wrote a work on the Scholastics, his main interest was directed toward the New Testament and the Early Church Fathers—and he was deeply impressed by the profound differences between ancient and modern times, and particularly between Early and contemporary Christianity. Lacking Nietzsche's or Kierkegaard's temperament, he shrank from communicating any major conclusions to his students, and preferred to dig deeper into ancient documents.

Again the question arises whether Overbeck exerted a decisive influence on Nietzsche—and it is plain that he did not. Nietzsche had early been impressed with what he took to be a deep contrast between modern theology and early faith, and he would hardly have formed a friendship with a church historian who had felt differently. Overbeck may have called Nietzsche's attention to helpful passages in early writers. Finally, one may mention that Burckhardt, Overbeck, and Nietzsche shared the conviction that asceticism was one of the most decisive features of early Christianity—but again one should not infer rashly that Nietzsche's

---

[6] A facsimile of this letter is appended to Podach, *Nietzsches Zusammenbruch* (1930); a translation is included in *The Portable Nietzsche* (1954).

profound concern with this phenomenon was derived from the interests or studies of a friend. Overbeck was important to him as a humane and faithful friend.[7]

II

Nietzsche's most famous friend was Richard Wagner (1813–1883). As a student, Nietzsche had been enamored of *Tristan;* he loved much of Wagner's music; and he considered the composer Germany's greatest living creative genius. Nietzsche's discernment in such matters was generally good, and he believed that Schopenhauer, Heine, and Wagner were the most important men in German arts and letters since Goethe's death. (Later he included himself in this group.) Schopenhauer and Heine were dead, whereas Wagner lived in Tribschen, not far from Basel.

It was Wagner's presence that convinced Nietzsche that greatness and genuine creation were still possible, and it was Wagner who inspired him with the persistent longing first to equal and then to outdo his friend. Again, Nietzsche did not require Burckhardt to suggest to him the agonistic interpretation of classical Greek friendship. Even after his break with Wagner, Nietzsche frankly admitted how much he owed to the early inspiration of this friendship—and one may safely follow his judgment in this instance. The relation to Wagner was indeed crucial. Yet it would be a serious mistake to assume that such a relation must necessarily be construed in terms of an *intellectual* influence, or that its importance consisted in Nietzsche's acquisition of sundry ideas or opinions: what he received along those lines he was soon to outgrow and abandon. Some of the lasting

[7] Overbeck's *Über die Christlichkeit unserer heutigen Theologie: Streit- und Friedensschrift* (1873) came out simultaneously with Nietzsche's "untimely" essay on Strauss—and the friends considered their two attacks on the *Zeitgeist* as twins. Overbeck's later works were scholarly rather than polemical, but some of his most controversial notes were published posthumously by C. A. Bernoulli: *Christentum und Kultur: Gedanken und Anmerkungen zur modernen Theologie* (1919). Here one finds frequent references to Nietzsche, but they were written after Nietzsche had become insane. Cf. also Löwith's section on "Overbecks historische Analyse des ursprünglichen und vergehenden Christentums" in *Von Hegel bis Nietzsche* (1941), 514–29; Overbeck's *Selbstbekenntnisse*, ed. Fischer (1941); and of course *Friedrich Nietzsches Briefwechsel mit Franz Overbeck* (1916).

elements of Nietzsche's thought, however, are inseparable from these personal experiences: the friendship with a man of great creative genius; the jealous aspiration to excel the friend and, begotten by it, the deep insight into the artist's soul—the starting point of Nietzsche's depth psychology and one of the decisive inspirations of his later conception of the will to power.[8] And above all, this friendship first raised the sights of the young philologist to distant and not very philological dreams of greatness.

Of course, Wagner attracted Nietzsche not by his greatness alone: Nietzsche had a profound love for music; he admired the revolutionary character of Wagner's work; and they shared a passion for Schopenhauer. *Tristan,* moreover, celebrated not only Schopenhauer's ceaseless, blind, and passionately striving will but also a drunken frenzy which suggested to Nietzsche's mind the ecstatic abandonment of the ancient Dionysian cults. Even that part of *The Birth of Tragedy* which deals with the Greek drama could probably never have been written without Wagner's work. And even years after his break with Wagner, Nietzsche admitted how much *Tristan* had meant to him:

> All things considered, I could not have endured my youth without Wagner's music. For I was *condemned* to Germans. If one wants to rid oneself of an unbearable pressure, one needs hashish. Well then, I needed Wagner. Wagner is the antitoxin against everything German *par excellence*—a toxin, a poison, that I don't deny.
>
> From the moment when there was a piano score of *Tristan* —my compliments, Herr von Bülow—I was a Wagnerian[8a] . . . older works I deemed beneath myself—still too vulgar, too "German."
>
> To this day I am still looking for a work of equally dangerous fascination, of an equally gruesome [*schauerlich*] and sweet infinity as *Tristan*—and look in all the arts in vain. All the strangenesses of Leonardo da Vinci emerge from their spell at the first note of *Tristan.* This work is emphatically Wagner's *non plus ultra* . . . The world is poor for anyone who has never been sick enough for this "voluptuousness of hell"; it is per-

---

[8] From the posthumously published notes which Nietzsche penned while working on his "untimely" essay on Wagner, one can trace a direct development to the section on artists in his next work, *Human, All-Too-Human.*

[8a] For a detailed discussion of this claim, see my commentary on *Ecce Homo.*

mitted, it is almost imperative, to employ a formula of the mystics at this point.

I think I know better than anyone else of what tremendous things Wagner is capable—the fifty worlds of alien ecstasies for which no one besides him had wings; and given the way I am, strong enough to turn even what is most questionable and dangerous to my advantage and thus to become stronger, I call Wagner the great benefactor of my life [EH II 6].

One may add that Wagner thought well of the young Nietzsche and, for obvious reasons, highly praised his first book. Wagner also had a fascinating wife—and though her importance in Nietzsche's development can be overestimated, some clarification seems necessary.

Cosima Wagner, illegitimate daughter of Franz Liszt, and the wife of Hans von Bülow before she eloped with Wagner, was—so at least it seemed to Nietzsche—the first woman of stature with whom he came into close contact. The difference from the small-town women who had dominated his childhood was indeed striking. Nietzsche never outgrew her fascination: in his late notes and poems she appears as Ariadne, while he increasingly identifies himself with Dionysus—and Wagner must occasionally fill the role of Theseus. It was not until the first days of his insanity, however, that he sent out several notes that revealed who Ariadne was. Cosima herself received a sheet of paper with the sole inscription: "Ariadne, I love you. Dionysus." And on March 27, 1889, in the asylum at Jena, Nietzsche said: "My wife, Cosima Wagner, has brought me here."

Frau Förster-Nietzsche assures us that it is fantastic that Nietzsche loved Cosima (he loved only his sister)—and she "explains" the matter. Hans von Bülow, deserted by Cosima, visited Nietzsche in March 1872 and in their conversation likened himself to Theseus, and Cosima to Ariadne, who had now abandoned him for the superior and godlike Wagner-Dionysus. (In the legend it is Theseus who abandons Ariadne.) In Nietzsche's earlier notes, says Frau Förster-Nietzsche, Dionysus is Wagner.[9]

---

[9] Cf. Frau Förster-Nietzsche's forty-page postscript to Paul Cohn, *Um Nietzsches Untergang* (1931)—a feeble reply to Podach, *Nietzsches Zusammenbruch* (1930). Brinton, *Nietzsche* (1941), 71, is thus in error when he refers specifically to this postscript claiming that Frau Förster-Nietzsche "continues to deny that the Ariadne story relates to Cosima." In the earlier writings, moreover, Dionysus *is* often associated with Wagner. The last important passage in which the god still bears some of Wagner's

Assuming that all this is perfectly true, it remains a fact that Nietzsche—who in *The Birth of Tragedy* may still be playing Apollo to Wagner's Dionysus and later, when he breaks with Wagner, determines to express himself in Apollinian aphorisms —in the end makes Dionysus his own god, while claiming that Wagner really was not Dionysian but only "romantic." In the later notes, Nietzsche presents himself as Dionysus; and when he lets Ariadne say: "This is my last love of Theseus: I bring about his downfall" (xvi, 428)—he seems to have in mind the influence of the formerly Catholic, religious, and anti-Semitic Cosima on Bayreuth and *Parsifal*. When he adds: "Last act. Marriage of Dionysus and Ariadne," he puts on paper the fulfillment of his own wish fantasy. And when madness breaks down all his inhibitions, he frankly signs his last letters and notes as "Dionysus." Certainly his last note to Cosima did not mean that the long dead Wagner loved her.

Even so, Nietzsche's love of Cosima was but a secret reverie, impossible of fulfillment—a forbidden wish of which not even the object herself knew. Its prime significance must be sought in the light it sheds on Nietzsche's attitude toward Wagner. It so happens that the composer was born in the same year as Nietzsche's father: 1813. His father had died when Nietzsche was four, and it is known how Nietzsche felt about being condemned to live in a fatherless household, alone with five women. He resented his mother and frequently made unrealistic references to his father, whom he pictured as more wonderful than he had actually been. As a child, Nietzsche sorely missed the father who might have redeemed him from his almost intolerable situation; and he evidently fastened on Wagner as a father substitute. One might add that he belatedly experienced Oedipal feelings:

---

characteristics, though other lines indicate that Nietzsche is steering toward a deliberate contrast with Wagner, is J 295: he "whose mastership [*Meisterschaft*] includes the knowledge of how to seem—not what he is but what is to those who follow him one *more* constraint" might yet be Wagner; but he "from whose touch everyone walks away richer, not having found grace nor amazed, not as blessed and oppressed by the goods of another, but richer in himself . . . opened up . . . less sure perhaps" —that is Wagner's antipode: Socrates. Nietzsche occasionally refers to both men as "pied pipers"—an expression used in J 295 and later (G-V) applied to Nietzsche himself. Nor is Frau Förster-Nietzsche's claim that eventually "the name Ariadne appears as a symbol of the human soul" (*op. cit.*, 134 f.) as disingenuous as it seems at first glance. An explanation will be ventured in the text.

Nietzsche loved Cosima impermissibly without daring to confess his feelings; any indulgence or marriage was as thoroughly out of the question as if she had been his own mother; and his love of Wagner became more and more ambivalent.

His days in the Wagners' house in Tribschen were as close as he ever came to having a home in which he belonged and of which he could feel proud. In his last book he still recalls "Tribschen—a distant isle of the blessed" (EH–MA 2) and confesses: "I'd let go cheap the whole rest of my human relationships; I should not want to give away out of my life at any price the days of Tribschen" (EH ɪɪ 5).

Thus Ariadne meant more to him than just the flesh and blood Cosima Wagner, whom he does not seem to have in mind when he writes: "A labyrinthian man never seeks the truth but always only his Ariadne—whatever he may tell us" (xɪv, 22). His sister is not entirely wrong when she claims that he is speaking of the human soul, though today we have perhaps a somewhat more accurate term in C. G. Jung's conception of the *Anima:* originally dependent on a "mother image," it grows into the ideal which a man pursues through his adult life.[10]

In the end, one may cite some sentences from the postscripts to *The Case of Wagner* in which Nietzsche was undoubtedly referring to Cosima:

> One cannot serve two masters, when one is called Wagner. Wagner has redeemed the woman; the woman has in return built Bayreuth for him. All sacrifice, all devotion: one has nothing that one would not give him. The woman impoverishes herself for the sake of the master, she becomes touching, she stands naked before him. The *Wagnerianerin*—the most charming am-

---

[10] Nietzsche's Oedipal feeling for Cosima seems to have eluded the many psychologists who have examined Nietzsche's life and loves. Even W. Stekel, the psychoanalyst, is no exception. In an article on "Nietzsche und Wagner" in the *Zeitschrift für Sexualwissenschaft* (vol. 4, 1917), he argues: "I see in the love for Cosima only a leaping over of the love for Wagner to the creature loved by him" (26). The love for Wagner is construed homosexually, and Stekel suggests that Nietzsche was a homosexual without himself knowing it. This claim, justly repudiated or ignored in the rest of the literature, seems based on the flimsiest knowledge of Nietzsche. His intellectual celebrations of male friendship notwithstanding, the overheated and strained heterosexual imagery of *Zarathustra,* especially in its poems, and Nietzsche's later requests for women in the asylum seem proof that his dreams were of women. Cf. Brann, *Nietzsche und die Frauen.*

biguity that exists today; she *embodies* Wagner's cause—in her sign his cause becomes *victorious*. Ah, this old robber! . . . he robs even our women. . . . Ah, this old Minotaur!

If Wagner was a Christian, well, then Liszt was perhaps a Church father!

Liszt had retired to Rome in 1861, joined the Franciscan order in 1865—and eventually joined the Wagners in Bayreuth, where he died in 1886.

It is not here intended to create the impression that Nietzsche's break with Wagner can be adequately explained in such terms alone. What has been suggested is merely a bare framework. Some passages in Nietzsche's later notes and books cannot be fully understood without such an account, which also supplies the necessary overtones for the symbolical slaughter of the father in *Der Fall Wagner* and for some of the *Dionysos-Dithyramben*. Of greater importance, however, is Nietzsche's experience of what might be called another adolescence: the story of how he left his new-found home, the painful process of emancipation from his "father" Wagner, and his eventual declaration of independence.

Nietzsche did not come fully into his own until he broke with the beloved tyrant who made him change the ending of his first book and then also of the third *Meditation*,[11] the man who frowned on the second *Meditation* because it had no special reference to himself and who demanded frequent visits and exertions for his own cause, though they interfered with the work and ideas of the younger man. To the end, Nietzsche conceded Wagner's greatness. He considered it the best sign of Shakespeare's genius that Shakespeare had realized how "the height at which he places Caesar is the finest honor which he could bestow on Brutus: thus alone he raises Brutus' inner problem, no less than the spiritual strength which was able to cut *this* knot, to tremendous significance" (FW 98).

---

[11] Nietzsche's *Unzeitgemässe Betrachtungen* have been translated as "Thoughts out of Season." Even more literal translations of the title have missed the meaning of *Betrachtungen* which distinguishes these "contemplations" from Nietzsche's other, generally uncontemplative, works. The fact that his next book, *Menschliches, Allzumenschliches*, was, in its first edition, prefaced with a long motto from Descartes' *Meditations,* suggests that Nietzsche's *Betrachtungen* were probably named after Descartes' work.

> Independence of the soul—that is at stake here! No sacrifice can
> then be too great: even one's dearest friend one must be willing
> to sacrifice for it, though he be the most glorious human being,
> embellishment of the world, genius without peer . . . [FW 98].

In the man whose passion for philosophy was praised even by
the ancients, in Brutus whose Stoic persuasion Nietzsche, who
called himself "the last of the Stoics" (J 227), stressed persistently,
in the hero who sacrificed Caesar though he himself had been
spiritually Caesar's adopted son (and, according to Plutarch,
perhaps actually Caesar's natural son)—Nietzsche (as he himself
says of Shakespeare) finds the "symbolism" of a "dark event and
adventure out of" his "own soul of which he wants to speak only
in signs" (FW 98).

The battle with Wagner, as it turned out, was only the first
and greatest in Nietzsche's long war for independence; but it
should not be viewed merely as an instance of Nietzsche's "transcending"—and certainly not as proof of his incapacity for any
lasting human attachments. Nietzsche retained Overbeck's friendship until the end; few philosophers have written more eloquently
in praise of friendship than Nietzsche; and while he was surely a
"difficult" person, the inference that he was incapable of lasting
friendship seems unwarranted. The break with Wagner cannot
be understood as long as Wagner is treated as a mere occasion,
as the man who accidentally played the role of the friend at this
particular juncture.[12] His personality and ideas must not be
ignored. What is wanted, however, is not the kind of portrait
that we should expect from a historian primarily interested in
the composer and his music: the decisive question in the present
context is how Wagner appeared to Nietzsche when he felt that
the friendship had to be ended.

Legend has it that Nietzsche, the pagan, broke with Wagner
because he turned Christian in *Parsifal*. It has already been
mentioned that Cosima had helped to inspire this opera. When
Bülow had finally divorced her, after she had given birth to
three of Wagner's children, she turned Protestant; but she did

---

[12] Bertram's treatment of the break with Wagner under the chapter heading "Judas" (*op. cit.*) suggests—no less than his insistence on Nietzsche's
"ambiguity" and "romanticism"—how Bertram, then himself the disciple
of another "Master," projected his own problems into his *Nietzsche*. His
evaluation was accepted by E. Gundolf, *op. cit.*, 31: "apostasy."

not take religion lightly, and her cast of mind helped to suggest to Wagner another way of salvation when the theme of redemption seemed all but exhausted by his previous music dramas: there was yet Christianity, and Wagner wrote *Parsifal.*

Nietzsche never ceased respecting that sincere and "genuine Christianity" which he considered "possible in all ages" (A 39)—but Wagner's *Parsifal* clearly did not seem to him to belong in that category. In the *Antichrist* Nietzsche called it a lack of "decency and self-respect" that the Kaiser, Bismarck, and their generals, "anti-Christians in their deeds," should publicly profess their Christianity (A 38). How much more sickening to him was the spectacle of Wagner, obviously burning with worldly ambition, making this ostentatious obeisance to Christian otherworldliness; Schopenhauer's foremost disciple writing the great Christian music drama; the self-styled modern Aeschylus celebrating the very antithesis of all Greek ideals—"the pure fool." That Nietzsche was revolted by Wagner's *Parsifal,* though not necessarily by its music, seems plain—but the break with Wagner was merely sealed in this way. It had come about long before Nietzsche received the opera with a note from Wagner.

The breach developed gradually, as Nietzsche became increasingly aware of the impossibility of serving both Wagner and his own call. Instead of coming out into the open, his aversion first cloaked itself in migraine headaches and vomiting which served Nietzsche as an excuse to stay away from Wagner after he had moved to Bayreuth. Not that the spells were faked: Nietzsche was truly miserable; but there is reason to believe that his misery was psychogenic—and there is no doubt that it was at least made more acute by his profound mental anguish.[13] Nietzsche seems to have hoped that the whole Bayreuth scheme might fail; and while his first three *Meditations* appeared at intervals of about six months, he abandoned the fourth and last one, *Richard Wagner in Bayreuth,* to turn to other plans, stalled again and again, and finally brought it out after a two year interval. Meanwhile he had accumulated many notes which anticipate some of the most basic points of *The Case of Wagner.* Nietzsche, however, had not yet clearly decided in his own mind whether he should

---

[13] The best account of Nietzsche's illnesses during this period and the best argument for their psychogenic character is to be found in Hildebrandt, *Gesundheit und Krankheit in Nietzsches Leben und Werk* (1926).

continue to conceal his objections. The breach was finally precipitated "not by Wagner's art, but by Bayreuth." [14]

Bayreuth was becoming a "cultural" center of the new empire which Nietzsche had so bitterly denounced in his first *Meditation* for its predominant "cultural philistinism." Wagner's Bayreuth was developing into a symbol of the "extirpation of the German spirit in favor of the 'German *Reich*'" (U 1 1): the Holy City of anti-Semitic "Christian" chauvinism. Now this was just what one might have expected of Wagner, who clearly was not another Aeschylus and who had never made a secret of his fanatical bigotry and Germanomania. Yet Nietzsche, moved to the depths by much of Wagner's music, first convinced by it that greatness was still possible in his own time, and then, offered the friendship of this genius, had evidently been quite eager to ignore misgivings about Wagner's personality and opinions. The same attitude is after all still adopted by some of Wagner's greatest admirers who claim that "it was wholly natural and permissible for him, as a German fanatically convinced of the superiority of the 'German spirit' to all other national spirits, to hold these views." [15] Nietzsche may have had similar feelings as long as Wagner was in Tribschen. The canonization of such views at Bayreuth, however, was a different matter.

Perhaps Nietzsche had all-too-innocent expectations when he went to Bayreuth for the first great festival, though he certainly did not expect—Newman's insinuations notwithstanding—that the crowds at the opening night might conform to his own fanciful picture of ancient Athens. His first *Meditation,* years before, had given impassioned expression to his disillusionment with the victorious German Empire; and his inevitable disappointment at Bayreuth merely meant the final recognition of what Wagner stood for.

What did I never forgive Wagner? . . . that he became *reichsdeutsch* [EH II 5].

---

[14] Ernest Newman, *The Life of Richard Wagner,* IV (1946), 525. Newman treats Bayreuth as the cause rather than the occasion of the breach. This whole question is one of the major topics of Newman's volume IV, and his treatment is the most complete and scholarly one available in English; but the interpretation to be offered here differs decisively from Newman's. Under the circumstances, it seems best to refer freely to Newman and to make clear the reasons for the disagreement.

[15] *Ibid.,* 271.

Looking back, we cannot consider this disillusionment the result of naïve expectations: what Nietzsche decided to break with was not a dream impossible of fulfillment but a mass movement and a *Weltanschauung* with which he could not compromise.

Ernest Newman, foremost authority on Wagner, feels that "if the indulgence in sham-intellectual maunderings of this sort helped Wagner in any way to write the *Ring* and the *Meistersinger* and *Parsifal* . . . it did . . . enough to make us look upon it with a tolerant eye. . . . His heart was in the right place, as was proved by the energy with which he threw himself into the campaign against vivisection." [16] (Hitler later copied Wagner's anti-vivisectionism and enforced it by law.) Nietzsche, who was then championing the ideals of Voltaire and the Enlightenment, advocating intermarriage between different races, and propagating the vision of the "Good European"—views which, as we shall see, he never repudiated—considered intellectual integrity one of the cardinal virtues. No campaign against vivisection could reconcile him with "the fanatical vegetarian" [17] who in "his insatiable lust for domination" wanted to be "an undisputed dictator," [18] who considered all other people, including the French in particular, inferior to the Germans, and who "worked himself into a paroxysm over Bismarck's tolerance towards the Jews." [19] Even while working on his pro-Wagner essay, *Richard Wagner in Bayreuth*, Nietzsche had realized how dangerous Wagner was, and "Nietzsche's notebooks were packed by that time [June 1874] with memoranda that show how far he had diverged by now from Wagner";[20] but then Wagner still was a lonely genius. Now Bayreuth became the center of political

---

[16] *Ibid.*, 601.

[17] *Ibid.*, 192.

[18] *Ibid.*, 297.

[19] *Ibid.*, 598.

[20] *Ibid.*, 435. Newman's searching scholarship, his exposure of Frau Förster-Nietzsche's many inaccuracies, and his minute attention to detail are more impressive than his memory for some of the more important points. Thus we are told (494) that "nothing is more certain than that in 1875 Nietzsche was still heart and soul with Wagner in all essentials." Nor does Newman's elaborate proof that Nietzsche felt too ill to hear much of the music at Bayreuth rule out the possibility that his severe headaches and upset stomach were connected with his shocked realization of what Wagner stood for. Newman, however, is surely right that it was not Wagner's music that drove Nietzsche away.

propaganda no less than of the new music drama. Wagner's "sham-intellectual maunderings" were becoming popular:

> Blood crossings have led to the nobler races being tainted by the ignoble. There is no virtue in, no hope for, any but a "pure" race of which the German could be the shining exemplar if it would only rid itself of the Jews. . . .
>
> The Germans, of course, are by nature the flower of humankind: to fulfill their great destiny they have only to restore their sullied racial purity, or at all events to achieve "a real rebirth of racial feeling."
>
> The Jewish race is "the born enemy of pure humanity and everything that is noble in it." [21]

It is only fair to mention that Wagner's admirers see Nietzsche's break with the master in a different light. Thus Newman's unbounded enthusiasm for Wagner's music leads him to attach little or no importance to the composer's "maunderings." Yet though he seems quite sold on Wagner's personality, he does not permit his love to interfere with his superb and scholarly presentation of the evidence—and thus he indirectly indicts his hero more forcibly than any less well documented accusations could. His picture of Nietzsche, on the other hand, is largely based on "Mr. Knight's valuable book" and on Bäumler's "masterly epitome of Nietzsche's thinking, *Nietzsche, Der Philosoph und Politiker*." [22] Alfred Bäumler was the professor whom the Nazis called to Berlin to "interpret" Nietzsche. His exegetic principles —including the premise that Nietzsche did not mean what he wrote in his books—will be considered briefly in the next chapter, and some samples of his "interpretations" will be encountered later. Suffice it here to say that he followed Frau Förster-Nietzsche in discounting completely the three works which were the fruit of Nietzsche's break with Wagner, i.e., *Human, All-Too-Human, Dawn,* and *The Gay Science,* as well as the two anti-

---

[21] *Ibid.,* 616, 617, 639. This is Newman's paraphrase of Wagner's *Religion and Art.* The quote within the last quotation is from one of Wagner's letters to King Ludwig.

[22] *Ibid.,* 498 and 335. Of course, Newman does not always agree with Knight or Bäumler, but he shows no equal familiarity with other recent studies of Nietzsche; and he is apparently unaware of the full extent of Knight's indebtedness to Frau Förster-Nietzsche, Richard Oehler (her nephew), and Bertram, of Knight's many "original" factual errors, and of Bäumler's near-perfect perversion of Nietzsche.

Wagner polemics of 1888; that he accepted her edition of *The Will to Power* as Nietzsche's *magnum opus;* and that he approached Nietzsche with preconceived ideas (Nazism) that he was determined to read into Nietzsche's work. Newman, while detesting Nazism, takes Bäumler's word for it that Nietzsche was a Nazi—and concludes: "Could fifty Wagners have led the nation into worse disasters than one Nietzsche has done?" [23]

Hitler, of course, knew fifty times as much about Wagner as he did about Nietzsche, and Wagner's essays, unlike Nietzsche's, did not have to be expurgated by the Nazis before being used in schools. One is reminded that another English Wagner enthusiast, a generation ago, also considered Bayreuth the greatest of all monuments of German art and culture, moved there after Wagner's death, asked Frau Cosima for the hand of Wagner's daughter, married her, and was entrusted by the Frau's *Meisterin* with the task of propagating Wagner's heritage. This was Houston Stuart Chamberlain, who abominated Nietzsche, preached the gospel of Teutonism and a new "Aryan" Christianity, and wrote *Die Grundlagen des Neunzehnten Jahrhunderts,* a two-volume work to which the Nazis' Alfred Rosenberg later wrote the sequel in *Der Mythus des Zwanzigsten Jahrhunderts.* Now it might seem that the real Wagner was perhaps as different from the Wagner legend as Nietzsche was from his. Thus Newman says that "the true founders of Wagnerism as a 'faith,' a religion, were Cosima and Houston Stuart Chamberlain." [24] Yet nobody has submitted more evidence to show how Wagner himself founded this faith than has Newman himself, and one fails to see how or in what respects the Nazis altered this faith or disagreed with Wagner. That he was a musical genius is a different matter.

It may seem idle to attach so much importance to Nietzsche's break with Wagner, but no other episode in Nietzsche's life has excited more public interest and comment; Nietzsche devoted two books to Wagner; and their break illuminates Nietzsche's thought and his historical position. Before long, Nietzsche was once more confronted with a man who, owing to his lack of genius, was an even more typical proto-Nazi than Wagner.

---

[23] *Ibid.,* 530.
[24] *Ibid.,* 103.

III

Nietzsche's relation to his sister always evidenced a powerful ambivalence. It is conceivable that his passionate love of her as a boy had something to do with his later remark: "To Byron's Manfred I must be profoundly related: I found all these abysses in myself—at thirteen, I was ripe for this work" (EH II 4). His love, however, alternated with a hatred no less passionate. As in the case of Wagner, Nietzsche came to realize that her character and outlook were basically opposed to what he wanted his own to be. Yet even though she embodied the narrowness, the chauvinism, and the deeply unchristian Christianity which he loathed, she loved him devotedly and had faith in him for a long time. That was more than he experienced from any other woman and therefore humanly more important to him than the patent fact that she could not understand nor follow his ideas. "What does he know of love who did not have to despise just what he loved!" (Z I 17).

In 1885, his sister was married to Bernhard Förster, a prominent leader of the German anti-Semitic movement which Nietzsche loathed. His contempt for anti-Semitism was not prompted by the man who took his sister away from him: Nietzsche's position had been established unmistakably about the time of his breach with Wagner, and *Human, All-Too-Human* (1878) leaves no doubt about it.

Förster's ideology, briefly, comprised "partly racial notions of Gobineau's, received second-hand from Wagner . . . partly Förster's own conceptions, such as . . . the notion of Christ as Aryan with which he secures for himself the honor of having been the predecessor of Julius Langbehn, Ernst Haeckel, and H. St. Chamberlain. . . ." Christ appeared among the Jews—to cite Förster himself—because "on the dark background of the most depraved of all nations, the bright figure of the Savior of the world would stand out the more impressively." And "in the emphasis on the special predestination of the religious make-up of the Teutonic tribes for Christianity, Förster could scarcely satisfy himself. At the same time, however, he thought with sorrow and not without consciousness of sin of the faithlessly abandoned cult of Wotan." [25] Nietzsche, on the other hand, had

---

[25] Podach, *Gestalten um Nietzsche,* 134 f.

written, even before his sister fell in love with Förster: "If one wants to claim that the Teuton was preformed and predestined for Christianity, one must not lack impertinence"; he had called "Jesus [whom he respected without believing in the Incarnation] and Saul [St. Paul] the two most Jewish Jews perhaps who ever lived"; and he had insisted that "Christianity *issued* from Judaism" (xi, 73). The full meaning of these statements, especially the last one, will be discussed later, when Nietzsche's thought is examined in detail. The contrast with Förster speaks for itself. Nevertheless, Förster—typical in this respect, too—blandly admired Nietzsche.

A scandal which ensued when Förster insulted and manhandled Jewish streetcar passengers helped to precipitate his emigration to Paraguay, where he founded a Teutonic colony, *Nueva Germania*. It was there that Elisabeth went to live with him during the years when her brother wrote his last, and probably most important, works.

Nietzsche's attitude toward his sister's marriage and the issues involved in it is of at least as much interest as the facts themselves; and it seems best to quote some of his reactions from the second volume of his letters to his mother and sister:

> You have gone over to my antipodes. . . . I will not conceal that I consider this engagement an insult—or a stupidity which will harm you as much as me [#377].[26]

> To an enthusiasm for *"deutsches Wesen"* I have indeed attained very little so far, but even less to the wish to keep this "glorious" race *pure*. On the contrary, on the contrary [#402].

> The whole affair [the marriage] went *through and through me*. And since your son is in poor health, he was consequently sick all the time; this spring was one of the most melancholy springs of my life. . . . For my personal taste such an agitator [Förster] is something impossible for closer acquaintance. . . . Vegetarianism, as Dr. Förster wants it, only makes such natures still more petulant [#409].

---

[26] In 1956, Schlechta showed in his edition of Nietzsche's *Werke*, III, 1409 ff., that at least thirty-two of the letters printed in *Gesammelte Briefe*, V (1909), are inauthentic; also that this does not mean that all of these letters to the sister were invented by her: in composing these epistles to herself, she made abundant use of letters and drafts of letters to others. Among these "forgeries" are two of the letters quoted in the text: #377 above and 479 below. Plainly, the quoted passages were not made up by the sister, though the possibility cannot be ruled out that she may have toned down some parts.

One may note that Förster was the first, but not the last, anti-Semitic rabble-rouser in Germany to have copied both Wagner's ideology and his vegetarianism. Förster, like Hitler, was an admitted Wagner disciple.

When he heard that Förster had decided to concentrate on his colonial work and give up his racist propaganda—a report which later turned out to have been false—Nietzsche wrote: "Since he has stepped back from his agitation, which like every negative striving contains the danger of corrupting an originally noble character most easily, I am full of sympathy" (#417). This, however, did not prevent him from confessing to Overbeck, in October 1885: "I have not yet laid eyes on my brother-in-law, Herr Dr. Förster— . . . that suited me excellently just that way" (#418). Loath to break entirely with his sister, yet quite unwilling to leave any doubt about his position, he writes to her in Paraguay in 1886, calling himself an "incorrigible European and anti-anti-Semite" and suggests that Förster should abandon his ideology and come back to Germany to become the head of "an independent educational institution that would actively oppose the drilling of State slaves," which Nietzsche considers characteristic of German schools (#430). While he thus suggests to his sister that he might like to have her back in Germany, he writes his mother that he is glad that Förster left Germany before getting involved again in his anti-Semitic movement (#431). Speaking of anti-Semites generally, he writes: "You see, because of this species of men I could not go to Paraguay: I am so happy that they voluntarily exile themselves from Europe. For even if I should be a bad German—in any case I am a *very good European*" (#443).

Most interesting, however, are two letters in which Nietzsche expressly takes a stand concerning his beginning "influence." The first is dated one week later than the four line draft which his sister later used for her edition of *The Will to Power,* partly because the title of the fourth part contained a reference to "Breeding":

> I have somehow something like "influence." . . . In the *Anti-Semitic Correspondence* (which is sent out only "to reliable *Parteigenossen*") my name is mentioned almost in every issue. Zarathustra, "the divine man," has charmed the anti-Semites; there is a special anti-Semitic interpretation of it which made me laugh very much [#460; cf. letter #271 to Overbeck].

By the time Nietzsche writes the second letter, Christmas 1887, he is no longer in a laughing mood. He has discovered that his sister's colony has after all an essentially anti-Semitic character. Now he decides to speak his mind to her:

> One of the greatest stupidities you have committed—for yourself and for me! Your association with an anti-Semitic chief expresses a foreignness to *my* whole way of life which fills me ever again with ire or melancholy. . . . It is a matter of honor to me to be absolutely clean and unequivocal regarding anti-Semitism, namely *opposed,* as I am in my writings. I have been persecuted in recent times with letters and *Anti-Semitic Correspondence* sheets; my disgust with this party (which would like all too well the advantage of my name!) is as *outspoken* as possible, but the relation to Förster, as well as the after-effect of my former anti-Semitic publisher Schmeitzner, always brings the adherents of this disagreeable party back to the idea that I must after all belong to them. . . . Above all it arouses mistrust against my character, as if I publicly condemned something which I favored secretly— and that I am unable to do anything against it, that in every *Anti-Semitic Correspondence* sheet the name Zarathustra is used has already made me almost sick several times [#479].

In a similar passage in his last book, Nietzsche is horrified that anyone should have associated him with the political Right, and especially with the nationalistic and anti-Semitic *Kreuzzeitung,* the Junker newspaper:

> Would you believe it? The *Nationalzeitung*—a Prussian newspaper, as I might explain for the benefit of my foreign readers—I myself read, if I may say so, only the *Journal des Debats*—actually managed to understand the book [*Beyond Good and Evil*] as a "sign of the times," as the real and genuine Junker philosophy for which the *Kreuzzeitung* [an ultra-right newspaper] merely lacked the courage? [EH III, 1].

Anti-Semitic Teutonism—or proto-Nazism—was one of the major issues in Nietzsche's life, if only because his sister and Wagner, the two most important figures in his development, confronted him with this ideology. In both cases Nietzsche's attitude was uncompromising—and if his suggestion to "expel the anti-Semitic squallers out of the country" (J 251) might seem a mere literary flourish, one may recall that this idea so possessed him that, when madness began to break down his inhibitions, he scrawled across the margin of his last letter to Burckhardt: "Abolished [Kaiser] Wilhelm, Bismarck, and all anti-

Semites"—while the last note to Overbeck ends: "Just now I am having all anti-Semites shot." [27]

If one wanted a symbol of his sister's unfitness for her later role as his apostle, one might find it in the name which she assumed in this capacity: Förster-Nietzsche. The irony of this name suggests almost everything that could be said against her: the gospel she spread was indeed Förster first and Nietzsche second. Like her husband and the party men who so troubled Nietzsche, she never accepted Nietzsche's break with Wagner and attempted throughout to reconcile their irreconcilable heritages. And it is perhaps pertinent to observe, though it takes us beyond the actual span of Nietzsche's life, that his sister doggedly persuaded the Nazis to accept her brother as their philosopher, and that it was in response to her insistent invitations that Hitler eventually visited the *Nietzsche-Archiv*—on a trip to Bayreuth. Years before, she had written, in *The Young Nietzsche,* in her comment on his letter which was cited near the beginning of this chapter: "the most difficult task of my life began, the task which, as my brother said, characterized my type—i.e., 'reconciling opposites.'"

Some other figures, though less important for Nietzsche's life than Wagner and Elisabeth, must still be considered. First, there is the "disciple" Heinrich Köselitz (1854–1918), an unsuccessful composer, whom Nietzsche preferred to call Peter Gast or even Pietro Gasti. From him Nietzsche received in his last years that unswerving devotion and complete faith in his greatness which even his sister—whom he also occasionally called a "disciple"—had not been able to give him. Yet while Gast was invaluable as a human being who was willing to share Nietzsche's loneliness and as a clerk who copied manuscripts, he was not the kind of pupil Nietzsche wanted most. Elisabeth and Gast were, in the end, "undesirable disciples": "This one cannot say No, and that one says to everything: 'Half and Half'" (FW 32). Gast applauds

---

[27] Cf. the last note to Fräulein von Salis: "The world is transfigured, for God is on earth. Do you not see how all the heavens rejoice? I have just now taken possession of my kingdom, am casting the Pope into prison, and am having Wilhelm, Bismarck, and Stöcker shot." Adolf Stöcker, a Protestant minister, was the prime exponent of anti-Semitism in Germany. The text of this note was first published in *Neue Schweizer Rundschau,* April 1955, p. 721.

the master's every whim, while Elisabeth would like to blend half of his ideas with those of Wagner or Förster—or Hitler. She is the type who "will fabricate a mean out of every cause he represents and thus make of it something mean—such a disciple I wish my enemy!" (FW 32). The young Elisabeth and Gast may also have been in his mind when he wrote in a key passage at the end of the first part of *Zarathustra*, quoted again in the preface to *Ecce Homo*:

> You say you believe in Zarathustra? But what matters Zarathustra! You are my believers—but what matter all believers! You had not yet sought yourselves, and you found me. Thus do all believers; therefore all faith amounts to so little.

What Nietzsche wanted desperately was a disciple who would be more than a disciple. Thus he said in the passage from which we have just quoted: "One repays a teacher badly if one always remains a pupil only. And why will you not pluck at my wreath?" Nietzsche wanted to be different from Wagner, who had appeared to him tyrannical and unwilling to permit contradiction. Wagner had taken pleasure in the most uncritical adulation of his Wagnerians. Nietzsche, loath to be another such "master" in search of disciples, gradually came to regard himself as another Socrates who had no system of his own and encouraged intellectual independence—and Nietzsche's search for a Plato was fraught with heartbreak.

Lou Salomé came closest to being accepted by Nietzsche for the role that neither Elisabeth nor Gast could fill. In fact, the only other serious candidate was Heinrich von Stein, who never ceased being a Wagnerian—and Nietzsche quickly abandoned hope. The three days the two men spent together in the Engadin, when von Stein came to visit Nietzsche, may have meant much to both; but in a letter to his sister, only a few months later, Nietzsche refers to the youth with cutting condescension. In *Ecce Homo,* the episode is mentioned twice:

> This excellent human being, who had waded into the Wagnerian morass (and even into the Dühringian one [i.e. anti-Semitism]!) with all the impetuous simplicity of a Prussian Junker, was, during these three days, quasi changed by a gale of freedom, as one who is suddenly lifted to *his own* height. . . . I kept saying to him that this was due to the good air up here . . . and that one was not 6,000 feet above Bayreuth for nothing—but he would not believe me [EH 1 4].

Once when Dr. Heinrich von Stein complained quite honestly
that he did not understand a word in my *Zarathustra,* I said this
was quite in order . . . [EH III 1].

Nietzsche's relationship to Lou Salomé (1861–1937) had been
far closer and meant much more to him. She was, he thought,
of very unusual intelligence and character, and she had written
a "Hymn to Life" which he considered magnificent and set to
music. Later, long after his break with Lou, he had the poem
published with the score and still referred to it with high praise
in *Ecce Homo* (EH-Z 1). He had found a person to whom he
could speak of his innermost ideas, receiving not only intellectual
understanding but a response based on Lou's own experience.

Nietzsche met Lou through two friends: Malwida von Meysenbug (1816–1903, the author of *Memoiren einer Idealistin,* which
was at first published anonymously in 1876, and was in its third
edition by 1882) and Paul Rée (1849–1901). Rée and Nietzsche
met in Basel in the spring of 1873, when Rée, who had been
wounded in the Franco-Prussian War, was still working on his
dissertation. He wrote on Aristotle's ethics; and in 1875 he received his doctorate and published *Psychologische Beobachtungen.*
Nietzsche liked these "psychological observations" and wrote the
author a very cordial letter (October 22); Rée replied October
31; and a genuine friendship developed that lasted seven years.

Rée's *Der Ursprung der moralischen Empfindungen* (1877)
owed a great deal to discussions with Nietzsche. The twenty-six
extant (but hitherto largely unpublished) letters Rée wrote
Nietzsche up to April 20, 1882, show how asymmetrical a relationship it was, and that Rée was conscious mainly of his own
debt to Nietzsche. Rée's letters are of exceptional charm—including the twenty letters he addressed to Elisabeth Nietzsche during
that period and the twelve he addressed to Nietzsche's mother.
During the same period, Nietzsche sent Rée twenty-six letters,
still extant and mostly shorter than Rée's; and all these documents suggest that this friendship was among the best things
that ever happened to Nietzsche. There was something heavy
about Overbeck and Gast, and neither of them could stimulate
Nietzsche philosophically. Rée had a light touch and was interested in some of the very same problems that occupied Nietzsche.

It was Rée who wrote Nietzsche about Heinrich von Stein

and later about Lou. Lou, incidentally, was not Jewish, as many writers have claimed. Rée, much to his own regret, *was* a Jew.

The relationships between Nietzsche, Lou, and Rée have been a matter of controversy ever since Nietzsche broke with Lou and Rée. Until 1967 there were mainly two versions: Elisabeth's and Lou's; and those who had discovered Elisabeth's sovereign impatience with the truth, and eventually that she had even tampered with the documents and forged letters, believed in Lou's unquestionable honesty. It was only in a comprehensive study of Lou's life and works published in 1968 that *her* falsification of the record and her tampering with the evidence were proved.[28] Now we know that *both* women are unreliable witnesses.

---

[28] Rudolph Binion's *Frau Lou* (1968) supersedes all previous accounts. He deserves all the credit for the breakthrough, and at the end of his book he describes how difficult it was to get to see some of the relevant documents. Had it not been for him, I should have left unchanged the substance of my account in the second edition; but my analysis and quotations are now based on the documents themselves, and in some minor ways our interpretations, like our translations, differ slightly.

The original texts of *some* of the letters cited in the remainder of this section have been published. The two letters to Overbeck are included in *Nietzsches Briefwechsel mit Franz Overbeck* (1916), and a few of the drafts I quote are included in *Gesammelte Briefe*, V (1909)— #343, 350, and 361—but the printed versions are not reliable. Four letters are included in *Werke*, ed. Schlechta, III (1956): the second letter to Lou (#155), the letter to Paul Rée (#167), the letter Nietzsche addressed to Lou and Rée together (#169), and the 1882 letter to Overbeck (#171); but the letter Nietzsche wrote Lou the day after he wrote #167, which shows that #167 was not mailed to Rée, is not printed by Schlechta, any more than the draft that shows how #169 ended. Schlechta did not have all the documents at his disposal when he prepared his edition (see III, 1372); his summary of the friendship and break with Lou (1372 f.) is full of errors and betrays a strong bias against Nietzsche; and it is completely dated by Binion's work.

Podach's *Friedrich Nietzsche und Lou Salomé* (1938) includes few of our texts: the draft for the letter to Georg Rée (86 ff.), the letter to Lou and Rée together, with the relevant draft (155 f.), and parts of the draft for a letter to Malwida, July 1882 (159). He also prints (79 ff., 89 ff.), with the express intent to incriminate Nietzsche, two letters to the sister (#364 and 401) which, as Schlechta has shown meanwhile, the sister forged. Podach's book is utterly dated now, but his bias against Nietzsche mars his last two works (discussed in the Appendix, below) to an even greater extent.

Stefan Sonns had no access to Nietzsche's and Rée's unpublished correspondence and actually thought that most of it was lost (*Das Gewissen in der Philosophie Nietzsches*, 1955, 34); but his dissertation takes

Fortunately, we have enough documents beyond April 1882 to reconstruct what happened. Though Lou's letters to both Rée and Nietzsche are largely lost, Lou kept about two dozen letters from each of them (through December 1882); and many relevant letters from others, including Malwida and Elisabeth and the Overbecks, have survived along with Nietzsche's notebooks, which contain many drafts for letters.

Plainly, Lou was a very remarkable woman, even at the age of twenty-one when Nietzsche knew her, in 1882. She soon became a prolific writer, but in spite of her many books her chief claim to fame remains that she was for a few months Nietzsche's friend, that she later became—after marrying F. C. Andreas (1846–1930) —Rilke's mistress, and that, much later, she became a friend of Sigmund Freud. A complete list of her friends approximates a catalogue of German and Austrian literary figures of the period. The photographs that illustrate her posthumously published *Lebensrückblick* (1951) remind us forcefully that in 1882 she still looked more like a schoolgirl than like the stunning woman she had become by 1897. Her first book, *Im Kampf um Gott,* appeared in 1885, three years after her encounter with Nietzsche.

She came "west" with her mother after an early and unhappy attachment to a married man, and we still have a letter she wrote him from Rome in March 1882. Her tone was totally different not only from that of old progressives like Malwida and young reactionaries like Elisabeth, who were Victorian prudes compared to her, but also from the courteous, seasoned manners of Rée and Nietzsche. She was precocious, quick, and brash; eager to meet famous people (if possible, Burckhardt in Basel and the Wagners in Bayreuth); and proud of being free of old-fashioned inhibitions.

After Rée's death, Lou spread the tale that both he and Nietzsche had proposed marriage to her, and that Nietzsche had asked Rée to transmit his proposal. Others embellished the story by adding that, unknown to Nietzsche, she was Rée's mistress even then. Binion has shown that she remained a virgin until more than ten years later and that Nietzsche never proposed

into account Rée's books and shows that, notwithstanding the claims of Lou and of various writers who relied on her, Nietzsche did not adopt Rée's ideas. Incidentally, Rée inscribed a copy of his *Ursprung* for Nietzsche: "To the father of this essay, most gratefully from its mother."

marriage to her, although she was apparently waiting for him to do so.

For years Nietzsche's health had been wretched. If his own comments on his pains should be suspect, consider a passage from Overbeck's letter to Gast, June 25, 1882, which incidentally illustrates Overbeck's rather professorial and pedantic manner:

> I found that N had reached the point which I had expected to see him reach soon, in case his health should allow one to expect anything at all; namely, full of the urgent desire for a new way of life that might remove him less from men and things. Moreover, his appearance made the attempt seem possible; only that it is to be made so far up north fills me with the greatest worry, at least for the winter. . . . Five days like those he recently spent here—with the exception of a few hours, usually speaking or listening enthusiastically until about midnight—also much music [footnote in letter: two long sessions with the dentist are not to be forgotten either]—all this without any real crisis and even a single hour of complete prostration—I have not experienced with N for many years now, during which I was not accustomed to seeing N even for two days without N's spending about half the time in bed. Bad days, to be sure, had gone immediately before and also followed immediately—nevertheless the experience remained most surprising and agreeable . . .

The following day, June 26, Nietzsche wrote Lou to suggest that she spend part of the summer with him at Tautenburg (about fifteen miles east of Weimar):

> My dear friend, half an hour from the Dornburg on which the old Goethe enjoyed his solitude, lies Tautenburg in the midst of beautiful woods. There my good sister has fixed up an idyllic little nest for me, for this summer. Yesterday I took possession; tomorrow my sister is leaving and I shall be alone. But we made an agreement that may bring her back. For supposing that *you* found no better use for the month of August and found it seemly and feasible to live with me in the woods here, my sister would accompany you here from Bayreuth and live with you here in the same house (e.g., the parson's where she is staying at the moment: the village offers a selection of modest but pretty rooms). My sister, about whom you can ask Rée, would prefer seclusion precisely for this period in order to brood over her little novella eggs. She finds the thought of being in your and my proximity extremely attractive.—There! And now candor "even unto death"! My dear friend! I am not tied down in any way and could most easily change my plans if *you* have plans. And if I am

not to be together with you, simply tell me that, too—and you don't even have to give any reasons! I have *complete* confidence in you: but that you know.

If we harmonize, our healths will harmonize, too, and there will be some secret advantage somewhere. I have *never* yet thought that you should read to and write for me; but I should like very much to be permitted to be your *teacher*. Finally, to tell the whole truth: I am now looking for human beings who could become my heirs; I am carrying around a few ideas that are not by any means to be found in my books—and am looking for the most beautiful and fruitful soil for them.

Just look at my *selfishness!*—

When I occasionally think of the dangers to your life, your health, my soul is always filled with tenderness; I cannot think of anything that brings me so close to you so quickly.—And then I am always happy to know that you have Rée and not only me for a friend. To think of you two together walking and talking is a real delight for me.— . . .

> Faithfully your friend
> NIETZSCHE.

That he wished to be her teacher, he had already told her in another letter eight days earlier. He had reached a second great turning point in his career, comparable to the transition from his early works (*The Birth of Tragedy* and the *Untimely Meditations*) to *Human, All-Too-Human*; and a week later he wrote Lou, after mentioning that he was about to proofread *The Gay Science:* "This book marks the conclusion of that series of works which begins with *Human, All-Too-Human:* together, they are meant to erect 'a new image and ideal of a free spirit.' " And less than a week later:

> My dear friend, Now the skies above me are bright! Yesterday around noon things were happening here as if I had a birthday: you sent me your acceptance, the most beautiful present anyone could have given me now—my sister sent cherries, Teubner [the printer] sent the first proof sheets of *The Gay Science;* and, on top of all this, the very last portion of the manuscript had just been finished, and thus the work of 6 years (1876–82), my whole "free-spiriting"!

Around the same time, he wrote in a draft for a letter to Malwida, after remarking again that the new book represented the end of a chain: "The next years will not bring forth any books—but I want to study again, like a student." And:

This year, which signifies a new crisis in several chapters of my life (epoch is the right word—an intermediate state between two crises, one behind me [1876–79?] one ahead of me [which turned out to be the final collapse?]) has been made much more beautiful for me by the radiance and charm of this truly heroic soul. I wish to acquire a pupil in her and, if my life should not last much longer, an heir and one who will further develop my thoughts [*Erbin u. Fortdenkerin*]. Incidentally: Rée should have married her; and I for my part have certainly urged him all I could. But the effort now seems in vain. At one final point he is an unshakable pessimist; and *how* he has remained faithful to himself at this point, against all the objections of his heart and of my reason, has in the end won my great respect. The idea of the propagation of mankind seems intolerable to him: it goes against all his feelings to add to the number of the wretched. For my taste, he has too much pity at this point and too few hopes.

It is interesting to consider against this background the last three aphorisms of *The Gay Science* (not counting Book V, which was added only in the second edition, in 1887). Number 340 bears the title, *The Dying Socrates,* and begins: "I admire the courage and wisdom of Socrates in all he did, said—and did not say." The next section deals with the eternal recurrence and will be quoted and discussed in due time, in Chapter 11. Nietzsche's plan to go back to a university and study was probably inspired in part by the desire to see if the eternal recurrence of the same events could be proved scientifically; but his psychological interests, too, led him to feel that he ought to know more about physiology and the natural sciences generally. The concluding aphorism, finally, is entitled *"Incipit tragoedia"* (the tragedy begins) and describes Zarathustra's decision to leave his mountain and return again among men. Soon this section was used again —as the beginning of Nietzsche's next book, *Thus Spoke Zarathustra.* The plan to go to a university town together with Lou and Rée—first they were thinking of Vienna, in the end of Paris —came to nothing; and so did the resolve to stop writing for a few years. The winter of 1882/83, when the first part of *Zarathustra* was written in Rapallo, and the summer of 1883, when he wrote Part II, in Sils Maria, were among the loneliest and most desperate periods in his life.

The meeting in Tautenburg (August 7–26) got off to a bad start: Elisabeth and Lou had a terrible scene before they ever got there. Our major source for the details of what each of them said is a very long letter Elisabeth wrote a friend not quite two months later. Here she describes Lou as "the *personified* philosophy of my brother: this insane [*rasend*] egoism that knocks down whatever is in its way, and this complete lack of morality." Such was Elisabeth's understanding of her brother's philosophy!

As for the hatred she conceived for Lou, that had a threefold inspiration. First and above all else, jealousy. Elisabeth had been unusually attached to her brother ever since their childhood, and suddenly found herself displaced by another woman whose intellect was far superior to her own and who could talk about philosophy with Nietzsche as she could not. The situation in Tautenburg was bound to be extremely painful for Elisabeth and plainly called for extreme tact, consideration, and maturity on Lou's part. But Lou, at least at twenty-one, did not have these qualities; far from it.

Still, it might have helped if Lou had approached Nietzsche with a certain reverence, showing profound appreciation of his interest: that might have mollified Elisabeth to some extent. But Lou did more nearly the opposite—first at Bayreuth, which she visited with Elisabeth, and then in Jena, on the way to Tautenburg, during the crucial scene between the two women. It was one thing for Elisabeth herself to say near the beginning of the letter to her friend: "Alas, my dear, dear Clara, *don't tell anybody*, I have lived through hideous days here; I had to realize that Fritz has become different; he himself is just like his books." It was another matter entirely for Lou to pooh-pooh Elisabeth's lecturing her about her "pure-minded brother."

This brings us to the last point: Lou was sufficiently annoyed to retort, according to Elisabeth's letter: "Yes, your noble, pure-minded brother first had the dirty plan of a 'wild marriage'!" She also suggested that this was after all what all men want, and said—there seems to be no reason to doubt Elisabeth's word about that: "I could sleep in the same room with him without any rebellious thought." And Elisabeth comments: "Do you consider that possible? [She meant, no doubt, to refer to that kind of talk, but the ambiguity is amusing, and her misspelling of *Hälst* instead of *Hältst* (*halten* means "hold" or "consider," while *halsen* means "neck" or "embrace") adds to the involuntary humor of her query.] I was also entirely besides myself and shouted at her more than once: 'Stop talking so dirty!' 'Pah,' she said; 'with Rée I even talk much dirtier.' She had also told me that it was Rée who had told her that Fritz was thinking of a 'wild marriage.' "

It seems that Elisabeth informed her brother of the gist of this conversation the following morning, although, as she wrote Clara, "of course, I could not tell it to him as dirty as it had been. Ah, for my delicate feelings the whole story was torture! They had it out"—but Lou stayed until August 26 and spent a great deal of time with Nietzsche, while Elisabeth was excluded and had time to nurse an overpowering resentment. Nietzsche commented on some of Lou's manuscripts, rewrote some of her aphorisms, and discussed some of his own ideas with her. When Lou left, they were still agreed to spend the winter in Paris, with Rée, to study there. In the fall the three of them spent some time together in Leipzig, and that was the last Nietzsche saw of either Lou or Rée: the plans for the winter fell through. In November Nietzsche went south again, to Rapallo, estranged from his sister and his mother, lonelier than ever.

Nietzsche liked to call his sister "llama"—a nickname he first gave her when they were children because, as she explained later, they had a book in which this animal was characterized in terms "exactly fitting" her. But the pointless description quoted by her, apparently from memory, is not to be found in the children's biology book, which was preserved in the *Nietzsche-Archiv*. What the book does say is this: "It is characteristic that the llama, as a means of defense, squirts its spittle and half-digested fodder at its opponent." [29]

Her performance was unusually revolting in the present case. Her accusations, recriminations, and gossip did not remain oral only but were also poured out in a stream of letters. It would be tedious to quote from these at any length, but a single sentence, from a six-page postscript that she added to a twelve-page letter about this matter to Overbeck's wife, January 29, 1883, may give some idea of the level to which she could stoop: "[Lou] is rather like an animal in other respects, too, able to move her ears singly as well as her scalp." So much for Lou Salomé!

What all of this did to Nietzsche, and in the long run also to Lou, is not funny. Having given up his sister and mother for Lou's sake, though they did after all love him in their miserable way as nobody else did, he seems to have come to feel more and

---

[29] Quoted by Podach (1938), 112, from F. Schoedler, *Buch der Natur.*

more that Lou ought to have appreciated this, and her lack of "reverence" apparently bothered him more and more. We cannot fully reconstruct the development that finally led him to break with Lou in December, even if we assume that the lost letters he sent her correspond closely to the drafts that have survived in his notebooks, for her letters to him are no longer extant, and his growing annoyance seems to have been due in large part to what she wrote him. In November he was still well disposed toward Lou and Rée and wrote Rée:

> But dear, dear friend, I thought you would feel the *opposite* way and be secretly happy to be *rid* of me for a while! There have been a hundred moments this year, beginning in *Orta,* when I felt that you were "paying too high a price" for our friendship. I have already received far too much of *your* Roman find (I mean, Lou)—and I always felt, especially in Leipzig, that you had a right to become a bit taciturn toward me.
>
> Think as well as possible of me, dearest friend, and ask Lou on my behalf to do likewise. I belong to both of you with my most cordial feelings—I think I have proved this better through my separation from you than through any *proximity.*
>
> All proximity makes one so exacting—and in the end I am after all an exacting person.
>
> From time to time we'll see each other again, won't we? Don't forget that *as of this year* I am suddenly poor in love and consequently very much in need of love.
>
> Write me something *really* definite about what now concerns us most—what "has come between us," as you write.
>
> > Love [*In ganzer Liebe*], Yours,
> > F.N.

And the next day he wrote Lou:

> My dear Lou, yesterday I wrote the enclosed letter to Rée; and just now I was on the way to the post office with it, when something occurred to me and I tore off the envelope again. This letter, which concerns you alone, might create greater difficulties for R. than for you. In brief, *you* read it; and it is entirely up to you whether R. should read it, too. Take this for a token of confidence, of my purest will to create mutual confidence between us.
>
> And now, Lou, dear heart, let there be a pure sky over us! I no longer wish for anything anywhere except for pure, bright sky: as far as everything else is concerned I'll manage somehow,

no matter how hard it may go. But a solitary suffers terribly from any suspicion concerning the few people he loves—especially when it is a suspicion concerning a suspicion they have regarding his whole character. . . .

You know, perhaps, *how* intolerable I find any desire to put to shame, all accusing and having to defend oneself. One does *much* wrong, inescapably—but one also has the splendid *counter*-force to benefit and to create peace and joy.

I feel every impulse of the *higher* soul in you; I love nothing in you except these impulses. I gladly renounce all familiarity and proximity if only I may be sure of this: that we feel *at one* where common souls don't reach. . . .

Forgive me! Dearest Lou, be what you *must* be.

F.N.

Around the same time, also toward the end of November, Nietzsche wrote in drafts for a letter to Malwida: "I beg you with all my heart to retain your tender interest in Miss S— even *to do more*. . . . 'The virtuoso of self-overcoming'—that is what Rohde recently called me. There is an awful lot to *overcome* in my self. . . . My sister considers L. as poisonous vermin that must be destroyed at any price. This is a thoroughly exaggerated point of view and repels me utterly: on the contrary, I should like to profit her as much as possible . . ."

During the next two weeks Nietzsche's drafts suddenly strike some very different notes, evidently in response to some letters that disappointed him deeply. The chronological sequence of these quotations is uncertain:

> M[y] d[ear] L[ou] Don't write me such letters! What is that kind of wretched stuff to me? [*Was habe ich mit diesen Armseligkeiten zu tun!*] Can't you see: I wish you would *raise* yourself up before me so that I need not feel *contempt* for you.

> But L, what kind of letters are you writing? That is how vengeful little school girls write. What is that kind of paltry stuff [*Erbärmlichkeiten*] to me? Do understand: I wish you would *raise* yourself up before me, not that you make yourself still smaller. How am I to forgive you if I do not first rediscover in you the character *for whose sake* one can forgive you!

> No, m. d. L., we are nowhere near "forgiving" yet. I cannot shake forgiveness out of my sleeves after the injury [*Kränkung*] has had four months' time to burrow into me.

Adieu, m. d. L. I shall not see you again. Preserve your soul from sim. actns and make good to others and esp. to my friend Rée what you cannot make good to me any more.

I have not created the world and L: I wish I had—then I alone could bear the guilt that things turned out that way between us.

Adieu, d. L. I haven't yet finished your letter, but I have already read too much.

Part of the last quoted draft is crossed out, and none of it may have been mailed. But he did break with Lou about the middle of December; it was he who broke off the relationship; and lacking her letters to which he responded we cannot tell to what extent he overreacted. Only one of the letters she actually received in mid-December survives; and that shows abundantly in what state of mind he was by that time:

My dear ones, Lou and Rée: Do not be too upset about the outbreaks of my "megalomania" or of my "hurt vanity"—and even if, prompted by some feeling, I should accidentally take my life some day, that, too, would not be reason for too much sorrow. What are my fantasies to you! (Even my "truths" were nothing to you hitherto.) By all means, take into due consideration between the two of you that in the end I am a half-madman who suffers in the head and whom long solitude has confused completely.

This, as it seems to me, *reasonable* insight into the situation I have reached after taking an immense dose of opium—from despair. But instead of thus losing my reason, I seem to have *found* it at long last. Incidentally, I was really sick for several weeks! and if I say that for twenty days I have had Orta weather here, I need not say anything further.

Friend Rée, ask Lou to forgive me everything—she will yet give me an opportunity, too, to forgive her. For so far I have not yet forgiven her anything.

It is much harder to forgive one's friends than one's enemies.

That brings to mind Lou's "defense."

The rest of this letter Lou did not preserve. But there are drafts for this letter, and they provide a conclusion, though we cannot be certain that the actual letter continued precisely the same way:

That brings to mind Lou's defense. Strange! Whenever anybody defends himself before me, the upshot is always that *I* am supposed to be in the wrong. By now I know this in advance; hence I have lost interest.

Should Lou be a misunderstood angel? Should I be a misunderstood ass?

> *in opio veritas:*
> Long live wine and love!

On Christmas day, Nietzsche wrote Overbeck:

This last *bite of life* was the hardest I have chewed yet, and it is still possible that I may *suffocate* on it. I have suffered of the ignominious and tormenting memories of this summer as of a madness . . . I tense every fiber of my self-overcoming—but I have lived in solitude too long, living off my "own fat," so that now, more than anyone else, I am being broken on the wheel of my own feelings. If only I could sleep! But the strongest doses of my opiates help me no more than my six-to-eight-hour marches.

If I do not discover the alchemists' trick of turning even this —filth into *gold,* I am lost.—Thus I have the *most beautiful* opportunity to prove that for me "all experiences are useful, all days holy, and all human beings divine"!!!!

All human beings divine.—

My suspicion has now become very great: in everything that I hear I feel contempt for me.—E.g., most recently in a letter from Rohde. I could swear that, were it not for the accident of our former friendly relationship, he would now condemn me and my goals in the most disdainful manner.

Yesterday I broke off my correspondence with my mother, too: it had become unendurable, and it would have been better if I had stopped enduring it long ago. *How* far the hostile judgments of my family have spread meanwhile and ruined my reputation—well, I'd still rather know it than suffer this uncertainty.—

My relationship with Lou is in its final and most painful throes: at least it seems that way to me today. Later—if there is any later—I'll say a word about that, too. *Pity,* my friend, is a kind of hell—whatever the adherents of Schopenhauer may say.

I am not asking you: "what am I to do?" A few times I thought of renting a small room in Basel, visiting you now and then, and attending lectures. A few times I also thought of the opposite: driving my solitude and renunciation to its ultimate point and—

Well, let that be. Dear friend, you with your worthy and wise wife—you are almost the last foothold I have left. Strange!

May you two fare well!

Your f.n.

All experiences *were* useful for Nietzsche, and he turned his torments into his later books, from *Zarathustra* to *Ecce Homo.*

When he wrote of pity and resentment, solitude and conscience, he knew whereof he spoke. And when, a little over four years later, he discovered Dostoevsky's *Notes from Underground*, he instantly recognized a matchless psychologist.

Yet the end of 1882 did not bring the end of the relationship with Lou and Rée. In March, Nietzsche wrote Overbeck that he had a bad case of influenza, felt physically miserable, and expected it to last for four to six weeks. But the weather was clear, and inside, too, he felt a new clarity. "The detachment from my family is beginning to appear to me as a real blessing. Oh, if you knew what I have had to overcome in this chapter (since my birth)! I don't like my mother, and the voice of my sister grates on me; I have *always* become sick when I was together with them. . . . Another 'liberation' I'll merely hint at: I have refused that Rée's major work, 'History of Conscience,' should be dedicated to me—and have thus put an end to a relationship that led to many calamitous misunderstandings.—Whether my last work [*Zarathustra*, Part I, completed meanwhile] is being printed seems doubtful to me; I neither hear nor see anything of it. Well, there is no hurry. . . ."

Late in April, he received a conciliatory letter from his sister and decided to visit her in Rome in May, apparently with the expectation that there would be no further discussion of Lou. Alas, there was. And the new angle was that Rée had behaved even worse, if that was possible, than Lou.

After six weeks with his sister, Nietzsche proceeded to Sils Maria in late June, and there wrote the Second Part of *Zarathustra*. No sooner had he finished it than his sister sent him a copy of a letter she had written Rée's mother, and convinced him that the previous year she had not told him the worst facts. As he put it in a draft for a letter to Frau Overbeck: "Suddenly Dr. Rée moves into the foreground: having to *relearn* about a human being with whom one has shared love and confidence for years, is dreadful."

There was just barely enough truth in Elisabeth's charges to make them seem justified. Rée had quickly become infatuated with Lou in a way in which Nietzsche had not; while Nietzsche called her *Sie*, Rée called her by the familiar *Du*, and though they made a great point of calling each other brother and sister, and Rée also called her "snailie" and himself her "housie," he did feel possessive about her, and his jealousy of Nietzsche was plain—though evidently not to Nietzsche. Long before Rée put it that way in a letter, Lou had come "between" them, and Nietzsche had ceased to be the friend to whom Rée wrote and had instead become an object about whom he talked and corresponded with Lou. It was not a deliberate intrigue but rather what happened to Rée, and it made him feel guilty vis-à-vis Nietzsche.

It will suffice to quote two passages. The first comes from a letter Rée wrote Lou, probably in late May 1882. "I just thought (I really ought to be thinking about 'the origin of conscience in the individual,' but, dammit, I am always thinking about Lou) that in my relationship to Nietzsche I am not altogether frank and honest, especially since a certain little girl from abroad appeared. But entirely frank, as I am with you, I never was with him, and I am with nobody in the whole world; only with one person besides you, in the past. Now it is true, to be sure, that one can have several friends . . . But with me that is after all not the case. I am wholly friends only with *you*, and that is how it shall remain. It does not offend my conscience when I dissemble a little and behave a little falsely, a little mendaciously and deceitfully against somebody, excepting you. . . ." And on July 29 he wrote her: "Motto: white to myself, false to others (excepting one person)."

The point here is not to place Rée in a bad light: perhaps he was more honest with himself and with Lou than most men are in comparable situations. But by totally ignoring this development, most writers on this matter have given an utterly false account of Nietzsche's eventual reaction and of Nietzsche's character. That Rée had spoken critically and indiscreetly about Nietzsche to Lou, is plain, and evidently Lou had cast up some of these remarks to Elisabeth, admitting they came from Rée. Now Elisabeth convinced Nietzsche that both of them had said terrible things about him behind his back, ruining his reputation and thus discrediting his books.

In August, alone in Sils Maria, during the depression that followed the completion of *Zarathustra,* Part II—Part III was written in Nice the following January, but now he was living through the insufferable lull between books—Nietzsche penned some dreadful drafts for letters that survive in his notebooks: one to Lou's mother, one to Rée that evidently was not sent, and then one to Rée's brother to tell him that henceforth he could no longer write Paul Rée because "behind my back he behaved toward me as a sneaky, slanderous, mendacious fellow." The letter to Georg Rée he actually mailed, but we do not know whether the final version was as bad as the draft, and the letter from Rée to which Nietzsche refers in his draft for a reply has not survived. What we do know is that immediately afterwards Nietzsche wrote his sister how terrible he felt about his own letter.

Georg Rée replied, threatening him with a libel suit, and Nietzsche, more than three-quarters blind, responded by threatening him—as he put it in a letter to Frau Overbeck—"with something else"; no doubt, a duel. The Overbecks often received letters hinting at thoughts of suicide, and once Nietzsche put the point by saying that he found the thought of a pistol pointed at him pleasant.

In a draft of that time he calls Lou and Rée "persons whom I have loved and whom I perh. still love even now: at least I am prepared to throw away at any moment the whole lot of insults and injuries done me if I knew I could really profit them."

The ugly drafts for letters of August 1883 remain. What would almost anyone else have done in a comparable situation? He might have said to his wife or to a friend, perhaps over drinks, that the bastard had evidently double-crossed him. Nietzsche had not a soul to speak to. How was he to get the poison out of his system? Taking Freud's advice before Freud gave it, he wrote down some of his thoughts—and feeling dirty about writing things like these into his notebooks, behind Rée's back, he felt he ought to tell him what he thought. And so he mailed a couple of ugly letters. Eventually, Nietzsche offered his own apology in *Ecce Homo:*

> It also seems to me that the rudest word, the rudest letter are still more benign, more decent than silence. . . . Swallowing things leads of necessity to a bad character . . . If one is rich enough for this, it is even a good fortune to be in the wrong [I 5].

More of this passage is quoted in Chapter 12, section V, below; and there are also—not surprisingly—parallels in *Zarathustra*, above all in the chapter "On the Adder's Bite" (I 19), which is among the finest things Nietzsche ever wrote. He also went out of his way in *Ecce Homo* to speak generously of both Lou and Rée. He despised resentment; he noted at the time, in

1882 and 1883, how sullied he felt by such sentiments; and in August 1883 he purged himself of the poison.

In November 1886, Lou became engaged to—and subsequently married—Fred Charles Andreas (1846–1930). He was much older than she was, but only two years Nietzsche's junior; he had eye trouble and an interest in Zarathustra; he was a philologist and a professor; and though he called himself Charles she called him Fred—and in writing usually "F." [30]

In November 1883, Elisabeth became engaged to—and in May 1885 she married—Bernhard Förster, whom we have already considered; and early in 1886 the couple went to Paraguay. In May 1884, Nietzsche wrote Malwida:

> Meanwhile the situation has changed, and I have broken radically with my sister: for heaven's sake, don't think of mediation or reconciliation—between a vengeful anti-Semitic goose and me there *is* no reconciliation. Otherwise I am as considerate as possible because I know what is to be said in defense of my sister and what lies behind her behavior which for *me* was so ignominious and unworthy: love. It is absolutely necessary that she should sail for *Paraguay* as soon as possible. Later, much later, she will come to see for herself how much she has harmed me during the most decisive period in my life, with her incessant, dirty insinuations regarding my character (this story has been going on for two years now!). In the end I am left with the very uncomfortable task of making good to some extent to Dr. Rée and Miss Salomé what evil my sister has done (soon Miss S's first book is to appear, "On the Religious Affect"—the same topic for which I discovered her extraordinary talents and experience in Tautenberg; it makes me happy that it was not altogether for nothing that I exerted myself so much at that time). My sister reduces such a rich and original creature to "lie and sensuality"—she sees nothing but two "scoundrels" in Dr. Rée and her—and *against that* my sense of justice revolts, however good my reasons are for considering myself deeply insulted by them. It was very instructive for me that my sister eventually behaved just as blindly-insinuatingly against me as against Miss S; it was only *then* that I realized how all the evil I believed about Miss S goes back to that squabble which antedates my closer acquaint-

---

[30] The juxtaposition no less than the information about Andreas comes from Binion's masterly sketch of him. Binion's *Frau Lou* also offers a detailed critique of Lou's book on Nietzsche, a sustained analysis of Nietzsche's impact on her life and works, and proof that her memoirs, which include a chapter on Nietzsche and Rée, are far from truthful.

ance with Miss S: *how much* may my sister have misunderstood and read into what Miss S said! She lacks even the slightest gift for understanding people. . . . Again, forgive me for bringing up again this old story! . . . Extraordinary people, like Miss S, deserve, especially when they are so young, the highest degree of consideration and compassion. And even if *I* am not yet able, for various reasons, to *wish* that she would approach me again—if her situation should become bad and desperate, I would put out of mind any personal considerations. Now I have come to understand only too well, through *manifold* experiences, *how easily* my own life and fate could become every bit as notorious as hers —deservedly *and* undeservedly, as is always the case with such people.

In one of his last letters, Nietzsche wrote Overbeck, Christmas 1888: "I still dare to tell you that in Paraguay things are as bad as can be. The Germans who have been lured over there are in revolt and demand their money back—but there is none. There have already been brutalities; I fear the worst.—This does *not* prevent my sister from writing me for October 15 [Nietzsche's birthday], with the utmost derision, that apparently I also wish to begin to become 'famous.' What a sweet idea that was! And what riffraff I had sought out—Jews who have licked at every pot, like Georg Brandes.—And then she calls me *'Herzensfritz'?* —That has been going on for seven years now!—So far, my mother has no idea of all this—that is *my* masterpiece. For Christmas she has sent me a game: *Fritz* and *Lieschen*."

For all that, Elisabeth (as well as, and even more than, Wagner) was very close to Nietzsche. One may recall *The Brothers Karamazov:* there are four brothers, and the clue to the character of each is that whatever is embodied explicitly in one is implicitly present in the other three. Alyosha's devout soul contains Smerdyakov's wickedness, Mitya's passion, and Ivan's skepticism —nor would Ivan be so troubled if his philosophy had come more easily to him, and if Alyosha were not within him fighting his position. So, too, Nietzsche's sister was, as it were, the embodiment in the flesh of that part of his character which he tried, all his adult life long, to overcome. That he was really not entirely unlike her is true enough but misses the more significant point: because he was cursed with the same heritage that came to full flower in her, his philosophy was a triumph of integrity. "My *strongest* characteristic is self-overcoming. But I also need it most" (XXI 102).

IV

A few words remain to be said about Nietzsche's books and then about his final illness. In 1879, when Nietzsche resigned from the university, his health seemed broken completely. Yet Nietzsche celebrated the new vistas of his freedom in *Dawn.* Upon this followed *The Gay Science,* which seemed to him to mark the consummation of his conquest of death. He had thought that he might die in 1880, at the age of thirty-six as his father had done; but now he felt that he had been restored to life and become capable of a new and halcyon gaiety. Next he wrote *Zarathustra,* spending only about ten days on each of the first three parts, but availing himself of material and ideas which he had accumulated previously. The very rapid composition itself, however, was accomplished in a frenzy of inspiration in which the author felt as if he were a mere mouthpiece of the flood which erupted out of him. The fourth and last part, of which only a very few copies were privately printed and distributed while he was sane, was not originally intended as the conclusion of the work but as a mere interlude.

Because he associated *Zarathustra* with the joy in which he had composed it, Nietzsche loved this book more than any of his others, though he occasionally referred to it as the mere antechamber of his final philosophy. An unprejudiced examination of this work would indicate that it is neither "the most profound book" of world literature (G IX 51) nor "destructive nonsense." [31]

To explain *Zarathustra,* which contains most of Nietzsche's ideas in veiled and symbolical form and is hence a good summary for those who know Nietzsche thoroughly, but hard to understand correctly for those who do not, Nietzsche added first *Beyond Good and Evil* and then the *Genealogy of Morals.*[32] In

---

[31] Brinton, *op. cit.,* 63: "*Zarathustra* is destructive nonsense."

[32] An intelligent reader with an open mind and no false preconceptions about Nietzsche can of course understand a good deal of *Zarathustra* without having read Nietzsche's other books. G. Wilson Knight's "The Golden Labyrinth: An Introduction to *Thus Spake Zarathustra*" (Chap. v of *Christ and Nietzsche,* 1948) is a case in point, for Knight states in the Preface that he did not consult J and that he knows little of Nietzsche's other writings except GT. It seems relevant that he admittedly has little or no acquaintance with the Nietzsche literature, but an un-

1888, finally, he sensed a euphoria unprecedented in his long experience of illness and recovery, and within six months he penned *The Case of Wagner, Götzen-Dämmerung, Antichrist, Ecce Homo,* and *Nietzsche Contra Wagner* (a collection of passages from his earlier works, some admittedly edited a bit, designed to show that *The Case of Wagner* was not the fruit of sudden resentment but rather of long and mature deliberation). *The Case of Wagner* was the last book which Nietzsche himself saw published. When the *Götzen-Dämmerung* appeared early in 1889, he was hopelessly insane. The other three works of 1888 were published many years later by his sister.

These works, which were the fruit of Nietzsche's final efforts, are perhaps his most important. If Nietzsche's repudiation of Wagner as his antipode had been taken seriously—Nietzsche reiterates what fascination Wagner's music holds for him—and if *Ecce Homo* had been understood better, with its vitriolic denunciation of any Darwinistic construction of the overman, of racism, of German nationalism, of almost everything that he has since been associated with—perhaps there would never have been the legend that prevailed so long. There has been a tendency, however, to discount these works as the writings of a madman; the *Antichrist* has been ignored either to "shield" Christianity or to "shield" Nietzsche; and the other books of 1888, too, have rarely been read closely.

The ending of the *Antichrist* and much of *Ecce Homo* certainly show so strange a lack of inhibition and contain such extraordinary claims concerning Nietzsche's own importance that, knowing of his later insanity, one cannot help finding here the first signs of it; and some of his letters show the same symptoms. A study of Nietzsche's earlier letters, however, back to his comments on his first book, or even to his school years, reveals that they contain a great number of similar passages.[33] That they are lacking in tact is clear, but that they are lacking in sanity is a questionable inference—the more so because Nietzsche's conviction that his books, then still ignored, would some day become

---

usually good knowledge of Shakespeare and English poetry generally. In fact, except for Chapter v the book deals rather more with these than with Nietzsche, whose explicit critique of Christianity, moreover, is not considered, the title of Knight's book notwithstanding.

[33] Many of these are listed by Hofmiller, "Nietzsche" (*Süddeutsche Monatshefte,* November 1931).

famous has since been borne out. Evidently Nietzsche had a strong sense of having a mission and little doubt concerning his own significance; and in 1888 his inhibitions decreased rapidly to the point where he freely expressed himself on these subjects not only in more and more letters, but in his books, too. Altogether, the disease can explain no more than his growing lack of any inhibition and, toward the very end, the failing power to fashion ideas into a well designed whole. It certainly cannot explain away Nietzsche's ideas. Large parts of his last books are actually distinguished by a clarity and lucidity that are almost unequaled in German letters, and by a startling depth of insight. And if the preface to *Nietzsche Contra Wagner*—one of the very last things Nietzsche wrote—admittedly ends on a note that lacks relation to the preceding passage, the final sentence warns the Italians "whom I *love*" not to enter into a Triple Alliance with the German *Reich*. It is dated Christmas 1888. Even the notes Nietzsche sent to his acquaintances during the first days of January 1889, signing them "Dionysus" or "The Crucified," throw light on his thought and are meaningful, if mad.

Early that January, he collapsed on the street in Turin, the city where Cesare Lombroso, the author of *Genius and Insanity*, was living even then. As Nietzsche fell on the pavement, he threw his arms around the neck of a mare that had just been flogged by a coachman. He had to be carried home. When he recovered consciousness, he sent the aforesaid notes to his friends.

When Overbeck arrived, prompted by the note he had received and by the longer letter Nietzsche had sent to Burckhardt, Nietzsche recognized him but also visited upon him fitful Dionysian frenzies which Overbeck later preferred not to discuss. He decided to take Nietzsche to Basel—and on the train Nietzsche sang the Gondola Song from his *Ecce Homo*.[34] In Basel, Nietzsche was taken to a clinic—and from there to the asylum in Jena.

Julius Langbehn claimed that he could cure Nietzsche, if given unlimited authority over the patient. He was the author of a sensational book which was then about to be published anonymously: *Rembrandt as Educator* (1890). This title is generally

---

[34] This incident found its way into Malraux's novel, *La Lutte avec l'ange.* An English translation of this episode appeared in *Partisan Review*, Spring 1946.

taken to have been suggested by Nietzsche's *Schopenhauer as Educator,* though the content is anything but Nietzschean. Nietzsche's mother refused Langbehn's suggestion, after consulting Overbeck—and soon after, Langbehn fled, frightened by an outburst of Nietzschean wrath.[35] A little later, Nietzsche was taken home by his mother.

Elisabeth, home from Paraguay after her husband's death, sits under the same roof and pens appeals for money to get a Christian minister for her *Nueva Germania.* Then she returns to Paraguay to liquidate the colony. A while after her return, when Nietzsche's fame has begun to spread rapidly, she climbs on the bandwagon. She acquires the sole rights to all his writings, including even the letters that he had sent to others. She sues those who publish material to which she can claim a right. After her mother's death, she moves the hopelessly insane invalid, whose right side is paralyzed, to Weimar where he lingers on another three years and dies August 25, 1900—in Goethe's city, as planned by his sister. At his funeral, Gast proclaims: "Holy be thy name to all coming generations." In his *Ecce Homo* Nietzsche had written:

---

[35] Cf. the chapter on Langbehn in Podach's *Gestalten um Nietzsche,* and *Der Kranke Nietzsche: Briefe seiner Mutter an Franz Overbeck,* ed. Podach (1937). Langbehn followed up his Rembrandt book with a volume of painfully poor verse, some of it pornographic. When the poems were suppressed, he hung a black wreath on the plaque which he had previously placed on the publisher's house to commemorate the printing of the "Forty Poems by a German." (Cf. Hofmiller, "Der Rembrandt-Deutsche als Dichter" in *Süddeutsche Monatshefte,* August 1931: XXVIII, 11, 819 ff.) Another man who hoped to cure Nietzsche—through a Corybantic dance!—was Alfred Schuler, a close friend of Klages, the famous characterologist. (Both men were then still affiliated with the *George Kreis.*) Schuler studied ancient texts but decided to change the rites freely "according to disclosures which he received through inquiries from his own innermost soul, and contrived preparations for almost two years, but only in—conversation. . . . He . . . used to expect the *practical* steps toward realization from other people; then doubts increased with time whether it would be possible to find suitable youths for the cultic dance; finally, it seemed hopeless to raise the required means. . . . The armor of the dancers would have had to be of pure copper because he credited this above all metals with symbolic contents and magical power. . . ." Klages concludes this account by saying it proves that Schuler's "inner connection with the cultic soul of antiquity was through and through a matter of living experience . . . and by no means a matter of mere objective research which could be presented in theories." (*Alfred Schuler: Fragmente und Vorträge aus dem Nachlass mit Einführung* [119 pp.] *von Ludwig Klages,* 1940, 60.)

I have a terrible fear that one day I will be pronounced *holy:* you will guess why I publish this book *before;* it shall prevent people from doing mischief with me. I do not want to be a holy man; sooner even a buffoon.—Perhaps I am a buffoon [EH iv 1].

During his disease Nietzsche was almost invariably gentle and pleasant, and in lucid hours he engaged in conversation. Sometimes, however, he was wild and frenzied. At no time could he be induced to discuss any of his works or ideas. His last books and letters notwithstanding, his disease was not paranoia but almost certainly an atypical general paralysis. If this diagnosis is correct, it would follow that he must have had a syphilitic infection—but it cannot be claimed that "the fact that Nietzsche did have syphilis may be regarded as proved (as certainly as anything of the kind can be proved)." [36] The certainty that can be achieved today by various tests can never be matched by posthumous conjectures on an atypical disease. All we can say is— and all sober and unsensational medical treatments of the subject seem agreed on this—that Nietzsche very probably contracted syphilis.[37]

---

[36] Brinton, *op. cit.*, 15; the sentence continues: "by the publication of E. F. Podach's book, *Nietzsches Zusammenbruch.*" Podach himself concludes more than once that this diagnosis is "unproved," cf. especially 159 ff.

[37] So far as is known, Nietzsche lived as an ascetic, and very probably had no knowledge of having contracted syphilis. Hildebrandt, *op. cit.*, considers the possibility that Nietzsche might have infected himself without sexual relations—perhaps through a skin wound during the war when he ministered to sick soldiers. Brann, *op. cit.*, suggests that Nietzsche may have visited prostitutes twice in his life, infecting himself both times as a form of subconscious self-punishment. This hypothesis is based on the following entry in the clinical records at Basel, dated the day of Nietzsche's admission in January 1889: "In the afternoon, pat. speaks continually in utterly jumbled confusion [*wirr durcheinander*], at times singing and yelling loudly. The contents of his talk is a variegated confusion [*buntes Durcheinander*] of former experiences; one thought chases another without any logical connection.—Claims that he has specifically infected himself twice." Podach, who published these records (*op. cit.*, 110), attaches no significance to this entry, and one may surely doubt whether it contains more "truth" than does Nietzsche's assertion that his wife, Cosima Wagner, had brought him to the asylum. Thomas Mann's account of the matter in *Neue Studien* (1948) blends *Dichtung und Wahrheit* and is probably to be understood only in connection with his novel, *Doktor Faustus* (1947), which fuses Nietzschean motifs into a vast allegory. (Cf. note 1 above.) To cite Podach (158 ff.) once more: "One can with the best conscience agree with Hildebrandt's judgment: 'For the claim that Nietzsche infected himself with *lues* in 1866, any trace of a proof is lacking.' It should also be noted that later examinations of

What seems important today is mainly whether any of his books can be discounted as the fabrications of a madman. To this the answer is an unreserved No. In his later works we find a steady decrease in tact and a rapidly mounting lack of inhibition, and the form of expression shows signs of the coming madness. The contents of the books, however, cannot be disposed of lightly. There is a decided break in Nietzsche's sanity which comes only later, after his collapse in the street. From then on there is no startling lucidity, no great vision, but only a steadily increasing and unrelieved dullness of mind, a spreading darkness which envelops Nietzsche's mind in hopeless night.

One author—the first to have defended the diagnosis of progressive paralysis in a sensational book which has come in for much criticism from all sides—has claimed that even *Zarathustra* was a product of insanity.[38] This view has been rejected almost universally, and it has frequently been pointed out that even the eleven and a half year period of verified insanity is quite extraordinarily long for a paralysis. Antedating the outbreak of this disease means adding to this figure and also would involve the claim that *Beyond Good and Evil* and the *Genealogy,* as well as the books of 1888, would be the works of an advanced paralytic. As such, they would be unique. Thus we cannot get rid of any of Nietzsche's works simply by referring to his illness.

The diagnosis that has been suggested would eliminate the notion that Nietzsche's insanity was the inevitable outcome of his thought. The fact remains that his life and work suggest an organic unity, and the claim that he was just about to complete his *magnum opus* when his disease broke out[39] has no plausibility. Rather, one feels that he had been unable to fashion the systematic work that would have carried out his promises; he had taken refuge in writing other works instead—by way of pre-

---

Nietzsche for signs and traces of a *lues* had completely negative results." Cf. Hildebrandt, *op. cit.,* 108 ff.

See also my article on Nietzsche in the *Encyclopedia of Philosophy,* 8, 505 f., and section VIII of the Appendix, below.

[38] P. J. Möbius, *Über das Pathologische bei Nietzsche* (1902).

[39] P. Cohn, *op. cit.,* 23. This book, favored with a forty-page postscript by Frau Förster-Nietzsche, seems typical of the literature sponsored by her: Nietzsche was "perhaps the greatest mind of mankind" (23); "Nietzsche was a royal spirit; consequently all he grasped became royal in itself; he was a royal psychologist, a royal philosopher, a royal stylist"—and as for his ironical self-glorification in *Ecce Homo,* "Nietzsche might well have used even much higher words" (50).

paring the public—and as long as he still had anything left in himself to say, it appears as if he had been able to ward off the final outbreak of his dread disease. His disease does not seem to interrupt an otherwise organic development; it gives an appearance of continuity with his active life.

Some will, no doubt, see Nietzsche's final catastrophe as the last act in which the Devil claims his own, while to the more extravagant disciples it appears as a transfiguration. Less spectacular than some of these conceptions, but juster perhaps, is the assertion that few men have fought more heroically against illness and agony, seeking to derive insight from their suffering, utilizing their talents to the last, and making their misery a stepping stone to new and bolder visions. This is not to deny that Nietzsche occasionally resembles Don Quixote,[40] or that—as some of his biographers like to remind us—he came from the middle class and was a *"petit rentier,* at that." [41] Socrates appeared even more ridiculous to some of his contemporaries. Surely, Nietzsche's rank must be determined not by looking at his life—whether devoutly or ironically—but by a careful examination of his thought.

---

[40] Nietzsche loved Don Quixote and tended to identify himself with him. He censured Cervantes for having made his hero look ridiculous—and of Nietzsche's own fear of being no less ridiculous there can be no doubt. Thus he envies Demosthenes the stature of his audience and concludes: "he did not have to consider himself a Don Quixote" (v, 226). And the young professor of classical philology speaks of "the reverence for classical antiquity" as "a magnificent example of Don Quixotism: and that is what all philology is at best. . . . One imitates a mere chimera . . . which has never existed. . . . There can be no imitation . . ." (VII, 208). He jots down: "One of the most harmful books is *Don Quixote*" (VII, 381)—and explains in a later note: "Cervantes could have fought the Inquisition, but he preferred to make its victims, i.e., the heretics and idealists of all kinds, look ridiculous. . . ." Cervantes' attack on the romance of chivalry turned "into the most general *Ironisierung* of all higher aspirations," and the book must therefore be considered a symptom of "the decadence of Spanish culture" and "a national misfortune" (IX, 445). In the same note, Nietzsche protests against the end of the book: "Yes, he does not even spare his hero the dreadful illumination about his own state at the end of his life. . . ."—and in the *Dawn* (114) Nietzsche actually compares "the poor dying Don Quixote's" sudden enlightenment about himself to Jesus' "My God, why hast thou forsaken me!" In another note he again refers to Don Quixote's "horrible end" and comments: "Mankind is ever threatened by this ignominious *denial of oneself* at the *end* of one's striving" (x, 413). Cf. also U II 5; XIV, 293; and GM II 6.

[41] Brinton, *op. cit.,* 50.

2

NIETZSCHE'S METHOD

It is aphorisms! Is it aphorisms?—May those who would reproach me thus reconsider a little and then ask pardon of themselves.—XXI, 80.

Nietzsche's books are easier to read but harder to understand than those of almost any other thinker. If we ignore for the moment the symbolism of *Zarathustra,* we find that practically every sentence and every page of his writings presents far less trouble than the involved and technical periods of Kant, Hegel, and even Schopenhauer. Not even the British Empiricists would seem to have written more lucidly. Yet grave difficulties are encountered when one tries seriously to follow Nietzsche's thought. As soon as one attempts to penetrate beyond the clever epigrams and well turned insults to grasp their consequences and to coordinate them, one is troubled. Other thinkers generally accomplish this coordination for us, and if we follow their arguments, they will show us the connection that leads from one claim to the next. Frequently we may not be convinced, or we detect loopholes or inconsistencies; yet we feel for the most part that we recognize what the author is driving at. Thus it is perhaps easier to form an opinion of the general meaning of Kant's *Critique of Pure Reason* than to grasp the precise significance of any number of sentences in that work—while in Nietzsche's books the individual sentences seem clear enough and it is the total design that puzzles us.

I

The best critique of Nietzsche's style is to be found in *The Case of Wagner.* The great problem with which the book deals is decadence, and Nietzsche—always eager for a historical name that may serve to represent what he has in mind—discusses Wagner as the archdecadent. At the same time he admits that he himself is "no less than Wagner, a child of this age, that is, a *decadent:* but I comprehended this, I resisted it" (W-V). Wagner, on the other hand, chose in the end not to fight his age; he made his peace with his contemporaries and became the high priest of decadence. This is the background of Nietzsche's sketch of the style of decadence:

> What is the mark of every *literary* decadence? That life no longer resides in the whole. The word becomes sovereign and leaps out of the sentence, the sentence reaches out and obscures the meaning of the page, and the page comes to life at the expense of the whole—the whole is no longer a whole. This, however, is the simile of every style of decadence: every time there is an anarchy of atoms [W 7].[1]

The sustained grandeur of the *Iliad* or Spinoza's *Ethics,* of Shakespeare's and Goethe's dramas, Beethoven's music, and Hegel's system seems a matter of the past; and in modern books, whether literary or philosophical, we generally applaud a few great insights or a certain sketch or chapter more than the total work. And Nietzsche himself is perhaps, as he said of Wagner, "our greatest *miniaturist* . . . who crowds into the smallest space an infinity of meaning" (W 7), while apparently lacking the gift to fashion a large fresco.

Now it might give us pause that Nietzsche claims—not only in the preface of his polemic against Wagner, but throughout his later works and notes—that he fought and overcame his decadence. Still viewing this question with an eye to his style,

---

[1] This is a paraphrase of a passage in Paul Bourget's *Essais de psychologie contemporaine,* I (1883), 25; but although Nietzsche praises Bourget elsewhere, he does not state his indebtedness here. Cf. Wilhelm Weigand, *Friedrich Nietzsche: Ein Psychologischer Versuch* (1893), 67 f., and Hofmiller, *op. cit.,* 121 f., who juxtaposes both passages. Hofmiller errs, however, when he claims that "Before Nietzsche gets to see Bourget's book (1883), the word *decadence* is not used by him at all"—and that "the first mention of the word decadence occurs in a letter from Nizza to Dr. Carl Fuchs in the winter 1884–85." Nietzsche says in a note of about 1878 that Cervantes' *Don Quixote* "belongs in the decadence of Spanish culture." (IX, 445) Bourget's chapter, *Théorie de la décadence,* does not introduce an entirely new turn into Nietzsche's thought; it merely strengthens a previously present motif. The generalization seems justified that Nietzsche's "borrowing" is usually of this nature.

we are led to wonder whether the "anarchy of atoms," or the maze of aphorisms, is perhaps integrated into a large design. While the epigrams evidently come to life at the expense of the whole, we should inquire whether behind them there is a whole philosophy. Of course, we cannot hope to find an answer to this question if we adopt the line of least resistance and merely browse here and there, deliberately ignoring the sequence of Nietzsche's thought. Before we offer our own solution of this problem, however, it seems best to consider another approach which was provoked by Nietzsche's unusual style and may have aided the growth of the Nietzsche legend.

In one of the best books yet written about Nietzsche, Jaspers tells us that the true alternative to merely nipping here and there in Nietzsche's works and notes consists in nowhere being satisfied until we have "*also* found the contradiction." [2] This is decidedly not the line of least resistance; and Jaspers, believing that there are fundamental antinomies, sees a virtue in Nietzsche's

---

[2] *Op. cit.*, 8. This program is the clue to Jaspers' development of the "ambiguity" theme which was first struck by Bertram. The word "ambiguity" (*Zweideutigkeit*) is somewhat misleading, and Jaspers uses it in three different senses. *First,* he refers to Nietzsche's own remarks to the effect that an epigram or aphorism often has a different meaning in its proper context from what it seems to mean when considered *per se*. Thus Nietzsche insists (M-V 5; GM-V 8) that his aphoristic style, which invites this illegitimate procedure, may mislead unqualified readers. Yet this sort of "ambiguity" poses no serious problem: to some extent it applies to all writers, and one of the two meanings can always be discounted as purely exoteric, while the other unequivocally represents Nietzsche's position. *Secondly,* Jaspers gives examples of seeming "ambiguities"—meaning, without exception, views that seem to contradict each other: but even where he does not go on to show this, the inconsistencies are only apparent and yield to analysis. Examples will be encountered later. *Finally,* Jaspers speaks of Nietzsche's "irresolvable ambiguity [*Zweideutigkeit und Vieldeutigkeit*]" (368). The last word suggests many meanings rather than two only, and Jaspers is referring not to any statements, but to Nietzsche himself and his philosophizing. In this sense, Nietzsche is surely *vieldeutig*, but the same may be said of Plato or Caesar—indeed of every man and everything. This consideration does not force us back into Bertram's relativism. If we view Nietzsche's thought as we should view any other philosophy, not just as an aspect of his life, we shall *not* encounter contradictions whose clarification "cannot be gained by mere logical insight but exists really only as the amplification of the lighting-up space of possible *Existenz*" (9). Jaspers' position depends on his own *Existenzphilosophie*, i.e., on premises which cannot be discussed here—*not* on the presence in Nietzsche's writings of contradictions that defy reason. That, of course, is not to deny that occasional inconsistencies can be found in Nietzsche's writings, as they can in those of other philosophers.

bold attempt to face such contradictions squarely. This, however, should not blind us to the fact that we are urged to adopt a wholly singular approach. We are to look, as it were, at the twenty-odd volumes of Nietzsche's books and notes and compare statements picked at random: if we do that, we should always find contradictions. Our success, it would seem, depends on how far we carry this approach. If we do not hesitate to break up sentences and carve our looked-for contradictions out of parentheses, we should get far; and while it is perfectly plain that Jaspers does not mean to exhort us to any such unscrupulous procedure, it seems striking that his approach would never have been even considered for, say, the works of Kant. As a matter of fact, the *Critique of Pure Reason* is a happy hunting ground for those who would prove their logical acumen by convicting Kant of inconsistencies; and even such a short and relatively simple work as his *Grundlegung* abounds in verbal contradictions. Were one to spread out all of Kant's works, precritical, critical, and *Opus postumum,* the mass of contradictions would rise to the point of utter absurdity—even before we should resort to the additional expedient of breaking up sentences. Nietzsche's writings, however, have almost invariably been approached in some such manner.

We have already mentioned some of the reasons for this state of affairs: his sister's monopolizing of the manuscript material; her decision to withhold *Ecce Homo* while publishing some random notes as her brother's last and greatest work; and the superficial similarities between the incoherence of the notes and the style of some of the books. The main reason, however, is surely to be found in the fact that Nietzsche's style makes impossible the systematic approach which is usually adopted in the study of other thinkers.

The elusive quality of this style, which is so characteristic of Nietzsche's way of thinking and writing, might be called *monadologic* to crystallize the tendency of each aphorism to be self-sufficient while yet throwing light on almost every other aphorism. We are confronted with a "pluralistic universe" in which each aphorism is itself a microcosm. Almost as often as not, a single passage is equally relevant to ethics, aesthetics, philosophy of history, theory of value, psychology, and perhaps half a dozen other fields. Thus the editors' efforts to arrange Nietzsche's notes systematically under appropriate headings, both in *The Will to*

Power and elsewhere, have been unsuccessful; and Oehler's attempts to subdivide systematically all the more comprehensive reference words in his two volume index to the works often seems grotesque.[3]

It is difficult to find any satisfactory alternative to the systematic approach which fails us in this case. No half systematic anthology of sundry opinions can tell us "what Nietzsche means" —either in the sense of his intentions or in the sense of his significance for us. We might as well scan a digest of the plot of *The Brothers Karamazov* to find what Dostoevsky means. To art and philosophy there is no royal road, and we cannot understand Nietzsche if we deliberately ignore[4] the thought processes by which "he came to think as he did." The opposite attempt to view Nietzsche's ideas as merely biographical data—dissolving them existentially or trivializing them psychologically—seems based on resignation that despairs of finding any coherent body of thought. Yet before a sounder approach can be discovered, and before Nietzsche's elusive "style of decadence" can be understood —and it becomes apparent how Nietzsche also overcame this "decadence"—one must, as a first step, reconsider the relation of his *opus postumum* to the books which he published.

A division of the posthumous material into at least three parts seems obvious. *First,* there are the works Nietzsche completed, but did not publish because he collapsed while still negotiating with publishers. In this category belong *Antichrist, Ecce Homo,* and *Nietzsche Contra Wagner*—and they may be treated exactly like Nietzsche's other books. *Secondly,* there are the notes Nietzsche used for his lectures at the university of Basel: they are an important source of information concerning Nietzsche's relation to the ancient Greeks; they are "full" notes and can be

---

[3] *Musarion* edition, vols. XXII and XXIII; e.g., Passion (*Leidenschaft*) is subdivided into Essence of Passion, The Great Passion, Passion of the Spirit and Cognition, Cult and Value of the Passions, Passion and Life, Passion and Society and Law, Control of Passion, and—inevitably— Miscellany. The index is not according to ideas but according to words, and many a crucial term is omitted, although this is by far the best index of the three which Oehler has compiled for as many editions of the works. It is the fruit of patient labor, but Oehler's understanding of Nietzsche's thought does not equal his thoroughness.

[4] Morgan, *What Nietzsche Means,* viii.

read continuously; and they present no great difficulty, provided one keeps in mind that they represent lectures Nietzsche gave while working on some of his earlier books.

Finally, there is the mass of fragments and notes which includes unfinished essays, long continuous passages, brief notebook scribbles jotted down on Alpine hikes, and outlines for projected works yet to be written. This third part of the *opus postumum* can be further divided into two classes: the material that never found its way into a published work and, secondly, the notes that were eventually put to use and developed in his later works. This last type does not reveal his final views but rather the manner in which he arrived at these views which we find in the finished books. The material, on the other hand, which was not used in the composition of any book was almost invariably held back because it had not yet been fully thought through and was not developed to the point where Nietzsche might have been willing to stand up for it. In either case, whether used or not, all of this material in the third group must be sharply distinguished from the books Nietzsche completed; and a careful examination of the notes of which he availed himself in the composition of his later works furnishes ample evidence for the assertion that he frequently used, or planned to use, them in a context in which they turn out to have a meaning quite different from that which they appear to have in isolation. These notes, including those contained in *The Will to Power,* are of great interest, frequently very suggestive, and distinctly helpful as background material for a better understanding of the finished books. In the past, however, they have been vastly overestimated —and this has prevented a correct understanding of Nietzsche's method, i.e., of the manner in which he deliberately availed himself of the "style of decadence" in an effort to transcend any mere "anarchy of atoms" and to achieve a coherent philosophy.

Thus Jaspers poses an alternative between two current modes of approach: [5] some writers discount the finished books and prefer the posthumous material "as the ground out of which the publications are only scattered and in themselves incomprehensible growths," and they suspect all that Nietzsche says in his published books because there his phrases seem polished for

---

[5] *Op. cit.,* 3.

effect; other interpreters prefer the books and suspect the notes because Nietzsche did not examine them critically—which is a striking understatement. The two suspicions are hardly of equal force. It seems wholly preposterous to ignore the works which a philosopher has published, to claim that he did not really mean what he said in them, and to prefer to them the scattered scribblings which he penned on his walks. To speak concretely, this was the Nazis' approach, frankly maintained by Bäumler. Confronted with books in which Nietzsche quite consistently, from the *Untimely Meditations* to *Ecce Homo,* poured invective on State idolatry, Germanomania, racism, nationalism, and almost the entire Nazi creed, Bäumler resorted to the subterfuge that Nietzsche did not mean it. The Nazis ignored the fact that the notes and letters contain the identical ideas, usually in less polished form, but frequently even sharper. No serious scholar has ever preferred the notes to the books, but most of them consider books and notes on the same plane.[6] While this is, of course, far better than Bäumler's notion that the sister's edition of *The Will to Power* was Nietzsche's "main work" and his "system," it still seems wholly unjustifiable.

II

We are now prepared to understand how Nietzsche employed the "style of decadence" methodically in an effort to overcome "decadence" and attain a philosophy. It is very well to say that it is a sign of the spirit of the age that single passages should be so much more memorable than the whole book in which they occur; and one may even appreciate the fact that Nietzsche, with the possible exception of *Zarathustra,* made no attempt to write in a more epic vein, as so many writers have done since, when only an occasional line in a long poem, or a sketch or idea in a bulky book, sustains the reader's attention. Nietzsche's style can be taken to represent a brutally frank admission that today hardly anyone can offer more than scattered profound insights or single beautiful sentences—and his writings abound in both.

All that, however, tells no more than half the story. Nietzsche's style is more than the "style of decadence," and his aphorisms are

---

[6] This is true even of Jaspers and Morgan—and, of course, Danto.

not only monadologic but also add up to a philosophy. Literary criticism is fruitful up to a point, but Nietzsche was more than a literary figure, and we must now ask questions of a different sort: decadence apart, for what reason or purpose did Nietzsche reject systems and prefer to write aphorisms? The answer to this question will reveal his "method."

It is evident at once that Nietzsche is far superior to Kant and Hegel as a stylist; but it also seems that as a philosopher he represents a very sharp decline—and men have not been lacking who have not considered him a philosopher at all—because he had no "system." Yet this argument is hardly cogent. Schelling and Hegel, Spinoza and Aquinas had their systems; in Kant's and Plato's case the word is far less applicable; and of the many important philosophers who very definitely did not have systems one need only mention Socrates and many of the pre-Socratics. Not only can one defend Nietzsche on this score—how many philosophers today have systems?—but one must add that he had strong philosophic reasons for not having a system. These we must now consider.

Like almost all other philosophers, and unlike Hegel, Nietzsche believed that a system must necessarily be based on premises that—and this is his objection—by its very nature it cannot question. The systematic thinker starts with a number of primary assumptions from which he draws a net of inferences and thus deduces his system; but he cannot, from within his system, establish the truth of his premises. He takes them for granted, and even if they should seem "self-evident" to him, they may not seem so to others. They are in that sense arbitrary and, Nietzsche suggested, reducible to the subjective make-up of the thinker. A strikingly similar view is familiar to American readers from the writings of William James: "A philosophy is the expression of a man's intimate character." [7]

---

[7] *A Pluralistic Universe*, 20. Though James' point seems much like Nietzsche's, he offers us only two possible philosophies to choose from at the end of the book, urging us to accept his—and in a more famous passage in *Pragmatism* he tells us that by choosing one or the other we show whether we are "tough" or "tender." Here the similarity with Nietzsche wanes, and we hear echoes of Fichte's challenge to choose between Idealism and Dogmatism, thus showing whether we have character or not; and beyond that there are the Gospels—whoever is not for me is against me—and Deuteronomy: Choose life or death this day! For James, too, the issue between the "tender" and the "tough" is a moral one—and a critic

While the early Nietzsche suggests that one may "delight in such systems, even if they should be entirely mistaken," because they are after all expressions of the humanity of "great human beings" (IV, 151), it is plain that the same point can be turned negatively—and after thinking the matter over for some years, Nietzsche gave vehement expression to the other side of the question.

> The will to a *system:* in a philosopher, morally speaking, a subtle corruption, a disease of the character; amorally speaking, his will to appear more stupid than he is. . . . I am not bigoted enough for a system—and not even for *my* system [XIV, 313].

What Nietzsche objects to is the failure to question one's own assumptions. The philosopher who boasts of a system would appear more stupid than he is, inasmuch as he refuses to think about his premises. This is one of the recurrent themes of Nietzsche's later thought, and in characteristic fashion he often formulated it in more offensive language: "the will to a system is a lack of integrity" (G I 26). Building systems seems, moreover, to lack ultimate seriousness. It seems playful to elaborate conclusions which must necessarily follow from assumed and unquestioned premises; any child can do that: "building *systems* is childishness" (XIV, 366; XVI, 68).

As Nietzsche ponders the question further, he turns the point positively once more, reconciling his early appreciation of systems with his later insight that they narrow thought artificially:

> The different philosophic systems are to be considered as *educational methods* of the spirit: they have always *developed* one particular force of the spirit best by their one-sided demand to see things just so and not otherwise [XVI, 76].

The development of Nietzsche's view of philosophic systems, as here suggested, is reminiscent of Hegel's dialectic. This, however, does not mean that his statements contradict each other or that he claims that reality is self-contradictory. Only unqualified judgments about reality involve us in superficial inconsistencies:

---

may marvel how "pluralism" is abandoned so suddenly and how radically unempirical is the claim that there are only two philosophies to choose from: James' and Royce's.

When Brinton, *op. cit.*, adapts James' distinction and juxtaposes "gentle" and "tough" Nietzscheans, the moral color is lost; for both are seen to misinterpret Nietzsche to an almost equal degree.

thus systems are good, but also bad. The contradiction disappears as soon as we qualify such statements and specify in what respects systems are good and bad.

Systems, says Nietzsche, are good insofar as they reveal the character of a great thinker—but this goodness is independent of the truth of the system. The system is reducible to a set of premises which cannot be questioned within the framework of the system—and these basic assumptions give expression to the mental make-up of the philosopher. This affirmation of the goodness or value of systems contains, implicitly (*an sich,* as Hegel would say), a negative truth about systems—and Nietzsche proceeds to state this truth explicitly (*für sich*). The thinker who believes in the ultimate truth of his system, without questioning its presuppositions, appears more stupid than he is: he refuses to think beyond a certain point; and this is, according to Nietzsche, a subtle moral corruption. In this sense, systems are bad—but this assertion does not contradict the earlier affirmation that they are good: rather it follows from this very affirmation. They are not good in every way, and their being good in one way involves their being bad in another. *An und für sich,* systems are neither unqualifiedly good nor entirely bad. When we consider them as a whole, we become aware of both their *Nutzen und Nachteil,* their usefulness and their disadvantages. No one system reveals the entire truth, but by surveying a number of them, we can educate our minds. To sum up, they are good for the man who uses them intelligently, but bad for the philosopher who artificially imprisons his thought in one of them.

When we compare this conclusion with Hegel's view, we find a significant area of agreement. Hegel might have subscribed to the assertion that philosophic systems are educational methods of the spirit. There are, however, important differences. Hegel attached supreme significance to the actual historical sequence of the various philosophic systems and proposed to understand it in terms of development.[8] Thus Hegel could have a system of his own in which the previous development was, as he saw it, subsumed. To Nietzsche this seemed objectionable. Against Hegel's system he might have urged, as he did against the philosophizing at the German universities, that Hegel let "concepts, opinions,

---

[8] *Geschichte der Philosophie,* 47 and 59. All page references to Hegel's works refer to the *Jubiläumsausgabe,* ed. H. Glockner, unless otherwise specified.

things past, and books step between himself and things" (U III 7). Hegel, like the university scholars whom Nietzsche criticized, was concerned with the opinions of others—and instead of questioning them rigorously, he felt committed from the start to reconcile them with each other. In their thinking about values, which seemed especially important to Nietzsche, such men would be prone to perpetuate previous prejudices and to rationalize the valuations of their own society or state. Nietzsche himself, while using systems for his education, would employ them only with critical caution as aids to ruthless questioning: "to look now out of this window, now out of that; I guarded against settling down . . ." (WM 410). Previous systems are thus reduced to correctives both for each other's one-sidedness and for possible errors of the thinker who employs them critically.

Thus Nietzsche is, like Plato, not a system-thinker but a problem-thinker.[9] Like every philosopher, he uses premises— but not all men employ these in the manner to which Spinoza aspired in his *Ethics:* deducing a system from a set of unquestioned assumptions. Perhaps it is the most striking characteristic of "dialectical" thinking from Socrates to Hegel and Nietzsche that it is a search for hidden presuppositions rather than a quest for solutions. The starting point of such a "dialectical" inquiry is not a set of premises but a problem situation—and Plato, of course, excelled at giving a concrete and dramatic setting to this. In the problem situation premises are involved, and some of these are made explicit in the course of the inquiry. The result is less a solution of the initial problem than a realization of its limitations: typically, the problem is not solved but "outgrown." [10]

The applicability of this consideration to Socrates and Plato cannot be discussed here; but it seems pertinent that Nietzsche, like Kierkegaard, envisaged Socrates from some such point of view as a fearless questioner who, instead of deducing a system from

---

[9] Cf. Nicolai Hartmann's elaborate contrast of system-thinking and problem-thinking in *Der Philosophische Gedanke und seine Geschichte* (1936). Hartmann's study is not devoted to Nietzsche, though he would be the first to acknowledge that he has learned much from Nietzsche. I do not follow Hartmann in all particulars but consider this distinction fruitful.

[10] C. G. Jung (*Europäische Revue,* v, 1929) has developed a strikingly similar notion on the basis of his psychoanalytical practice. He claims that the normal and healthy way of dealing with psychical problems is "overgrowing" them (*überwachsen*) and thus achieving an elevation of the level of consciousness (*Niveauerhöhung des Bewusstseins*).

accepted premises, was ever engaged in the pursuit of independent problems and helping others with theirs—not by "blessing and oppressing" them with his own solutions but by showing them to their astonishment what they had presumed in formulating their problems.

Hegel's use of the "dialectic" is often a rather academic business—more reminiscent of some of Plato's later dialogues than of the earlier ones in which Socrates still leads the discussion —and Hegel's is also widely, though erroneously, associated with a three-step of thesis, antithesis, and synthesis. That, however, is not what is here meant by the "dialectical" approach. The meaning intended is that which Plato suggests when he contrasts mathematical deduction, which takes for granted its assumptions, with philosophic "dialectic" which questions these assumptions, inquiring what they themselves may presuppose, and thus moves backward, "reductively," to a first principle.[11] In Hegel, the best example of such an approach must be sought in the *Phä-nomenologie:* no premises are explicit to start with; no problems are solved, but each problem is outgrown in turn while—to use C. G. Jung's phrase—the level of consciousness rises. The method here is strictly not deductive, and while spirit is Hegel's ultimate metaphysical principle, he does not employ it as a premise from which he might then derive particular conclusions. Instead Hegel starts out with the apparent certainty of sense experience; he then seeks to uncover the naïve and unwitting assumptions that underlie this supposed certainty; and going back, step by step, he is led at the end of his book to introduce the ultimate reality of the spirit as the final premise—or first principle—of all our experience, thought, and knowledge. The validity of this effort, or of the individual arguments used by Hegel, need not be discussed here. Nietzsche, to be sure, did not accept Hegel's demonstration; nor is it likely that anyone today would care to defend all of the steps by which Hegel reaches his first principle.

Hegel managed to be both a "dialectical" philosopher and a system builder—but his system was *sui generis* insofar as he no-where acknowledged a set of unquestioned premises. The key to this riddle is that he took for granted not a series of more or less arbitrary assumptions, but rather the overwhelming truth of all preceding systems and philosophies. Where they apparently

---

[11] *Republic* 511.

contradicted each other, arbitration seemed to him to be called for; and by introducing qualifications, he effected some fruitful, as well as some rather strained, reconciliations. Nietzsche was more consistently "dialectical"—or to avoid any misunderstanding, he was, like Socrates, a far more rigorous questioner and by no means prepared to admit that the systems of the past are overwhelmingly true. He doubted that the truth was to be found in "things past and books." These had to be subjected to scrutiny no less than any other opinions. *All* assumptions had to be questioned.

It is true that Nietzsche often gave expression to opinions he had not questioned critically. In his writings, as in those of any other encyclopaedic philosopher—whether it be Plato, Aristotle, Aquinas, Kant, or Hegel—we must distinguish between the human and the all-too-human elements. Nietzsche's writings contain many all-too-human judgments—especially about women —but these are philosophically irrelevant; and *ad hominem* arguments against any philosopher on the basis of such statements seem trivial and hardly pertinent. As Nietzsche well knew, the "debauches and vices of the philosopher are always accepted first and made matters of belief" (FW 99) and "his injustices find exaggerators" (XVI, 15).[12] Therefore the unjust and unquestioned prejudices of a philosopher may be of interest to the historian as well as to the psychologist; but Nietzsche's prejudices about women need not greatly concern the philosopher.[13]

Of pre-eminent interest to the philosopher, however, is the problem how even the most ruthless questioning can rid us of the necessity of letting "concepts, opinions, things past, and books step between" ourselves "and things." At this point Husserl's phenomenology and contemporary *Existenzphilosophie* are at one with Nietzsche, and we should not consider his call to philosophers to by-pass concepts and opinions, things past and

---

[12] In both passages, Nietzsche is referring particularly to the influence of Schopenhauer's anti-Semitism on such men as Wagner, Dühring, and Eduard von Hartmann.

[13] H. W. Brann, *op. cit.*, has shown not only how Nietzsche's epigrams about women may have been connected with his own experiences, but also how they were copied from Chamfort, La Rochefoucauld, and— of course—Schopenhauer. One may conclude that, while Wagner and Dühring made Schopenhauer's other injustices matters of belief, Nietzsche copied some of his remarks about women.

books, as a mere personal idiosyncrasy but rather as a significant program that deserves consideration.

III

Viewed in this light, Nietzsche's aphoristic style appears as an interesting attempt to transcend the maze of concepts and opinions in order to get at the objects themselves. The "style of decadence" is methodically employed in the service of Nietzsche's "experimentalism." The key terms that Nietzsche uses time and again are now *Experiment* and now *Versuch;* but it is well to keep in mind that *Versuch,* too, need not mean merely "attempt" but can have the characteristic scientific sense of "experiment": it is quite proper in German to speak of a scientist as making a *Versuch.*[14]

Each aphorism or sequence of aphorisms—and in Nietzsche's later works some of these sequences are about a hundred pages long, and the aphoristic style is only superficially maintained— may be considered as a thought experiment. The discontinuity or, positively speaking, the great number of experiments, reflects the conviction that making only one experiment would be one-sided. One may here recall Kierkegaard's comment on Hegel: "If Hegel had written the whole of his *Logic* and then said . . . that it was merely an experiment in thought . . . then he would certainly have been the greatest thinker who had ever lived. As it is, he is merely comic." (*Journals,* ed. Alexander Dru, 134.) Nietzsche insists that the philosopher must be willing to make ever new experiments; he must retain an open mind and be prepared, if necessary, "boldly at any time to declare himself *against* his previous opinion" (FW 296)—just as he would expect a scientist to revise his theories in the light of new experiments.

---

[14] A few characteristic references: MA I-V 4; M 187, 453, 501, 547; X, 357 f.; FW 7, 51, 110, 289, 319, 324; J 42, 205, 210; GM II 24; GM III 24. Oehler's index contains not one of these references—nor the subtitle of the projected *Der Wille zur Macht: Versuch einer Umwertung aller Werte,* and the subtitle of the *Antichrist: Versuch einer Kritik des Christentums.* Löwith, *Nietzsches Philosophie der Ewigen Wiederkunft des Gleichen* (1935) and Jaspers, *op. cit.,* speak of Nietzsche's experimentalism but overlook its connection with Nietzsche's effort to get at his objects directly. Schlechta's *Nietzsche-Index* (1965) offers only one reference for *Versuch.*

Nietzsche, no less than Hegel, wanted philosophy to become scientific, *wissenschaftlich*—but science did not mean the same thing to both thinkers. To Hegel it meant above all the rigor of a system. This he opposed to the romantics' sentimental enthusiasm which had come into flower since the publication of Fichte's *Wissenschaftslehre*. Thus he insisted that we must elevate philosophy to a science—and this programmatic declaration in the preface of his first book holds equally for all his later works. In fact, the title of each of the four books which he himself published contained a reference to *Wissenschaft*. The *Phenomenology* was published as Part 1 of the "System of Science"; the *Science of Logic* and the *Encyclopedia of the Philosophical Sciences* followed; and finally there was the *Philosophy of Right* which has a long and elaborate title in which we find the word *Staatswissenschaft*. Nietzsche did not want philosophy to be less scientific than this but rather more so; only he had in mind the "gay science" of fearless experiment and the good will to accept new evidence and to abandon previous positions, if necessary.

It may be recalled that Kant, in his preface to the second edition of the *Critique of Pure Reason,* had spoken of an "experiment of pure reason"—meaning the kind of singular experiment whose outcome may furnish the decisive confirmation of an entire world-view. That was not what Nietzsche intended. In fact, he believed that he had to break with the philosophic tradition of centuries on just this point.

> The small single questions and experiments [*Versuche*] were considered contemptible. . . . To solve all with one stroke . . . that was the secret wish. . . . The unlimited ambition . . . to be the "unriddler of the universe" made up the dream of the thinker . . . many had the delusion, . . . at last Schopenhauer, that they were this one being [M 547].

The philosophers of the future, Nietzsche thought, would have no such delusions. They would not shirk small questions but consider them on their own merits and not as corollaries of a previously conceived all-solving system.

> A new species of philosophers is coming up . . . these philosophers of the future might require in justice, perhaps also in injustice, to be called *attempters* [*Versucher*]. This name is . . . only an attempt and, if one prefers, a temptation [*Versuchung*] [J 42].

These "philosophers of the future," and Nietzsche as their "herald and precursor" (J 44), would be more modest and less ambitious than Schopenhauer and his kind. Greatness would consist in "holding one's own in an unfinished system with free, unlimited views" as Leonardo da Vinci did (XVI, 51 f.). Systems are blinders and bar many views; systems keep one from questioning certain premises: by abandoning them, one may also abandon their frequent superficiality. Unimpeded by presuppositions that one may not question, one can penetrate one's subject matter more deeply, diving, as it were, through the haze of prejudices and opinions.

> For I treat deep problems as I would a cold swim—quickly into them and quickly out again. That in this way one does not get . . . deep enough *down,* that is the superstition . . . of the enemies of the cold water; they speak without experience [FW 381; cf. FW 322].

After scorning the ambition of the great systematizers down to Schopenhauer, Nietzsche thus develops a pride of his own. By his fearless questioning he hopes to get to the bottom of problems. The insights which he tries to formulate in his aphorisms will have to be accounted for in any comprehensive explanatory system, just as an honest scientific experiment cannot be ignored by any comprehensive scientific system. While the systems come and go, the experiment—perhaps variously interpreted—remains. This may have been what Nietzsche had in mind when he celebrated his style in the *Götzen-Dämmerung,* using the hyperboles characteristic of his last works:

> To create things on which time tests its teeth in vain; in form, in *substance,* to strive for a little immortality—I have never yet been modest enough to demand less of myself. The aphorism, the apothegm . . . are the forms of "eternity" [G IX 51].

Nietzsche's experimentalism may seem suggestive of pragmatism; and as a matter of fact there are in his writings—and particularly in those of his notes which deal with epistemological problems—a great number of passages that read like early statements of pragmatic views. This will surprise nobody who has considered the historical roots of pragmatism which must surely be sought, above all, in Darwin and Kant. The teachings of evolutionism supplied the decisive impetus that prompted the development of pragmatic doctrines at about the same time—

toward the end of the nineteenth century—in England, France, Germany, and of course the United States.

The intellect, hitherto regarded as essentially eternal, now had to be accounted for in terms of evolution. Instead of having existed before the mountains were brought forth, it now appeared to have originated in time—not all at once, but through the struggle for existence and the survival of the fittest. It was an instrument, a tool, an asset in the struggle; and those possessing it had survived because of its great practical value. Now it was recalled that Kant already had insisted that we cannot apprehend ultimate reality, and that what we know are but phenomena. In other words, the world of our experience is not a likeness of the "real" world. And as Kant's philosophy was fused with Darwin's theory, the doctrine developed that our "truths" are not accurate descriptions of a transcendent reality, but simply statements that "work" and thus fit us for survival—in Vaihinger's provocative phrase, "the most expedient form of error."

There are of course a great variety of pragmatic philosophies, and a description that would come close to doing justice to Bergson's reflections might completely fail to encompass Peirce's. It appears to have been Darwinism, however, that induced philosophers to develop Kant's philosophy along these lines; and thus it is not surprising that various forms of pragmatism were evolved about the same time by a great number of different thinkers, including James, Dewey, F. S. C. Schiller, Simmel, Vaihinger, Ernst Mach—and Nietzsche.

It so happens that Nietzsche's formulations, while barely later than Peirce's, antedate most of the others. For the most part, however, they are to be found in his notes; and—as is the case with so much of the posthumously published material—Nietzsche seems to have withheld them because they were not fully developed. While one could prove his historical priority on a number of points by quoting a considerable number of scattered statements,[15] it seems more important to note that these utterances are really no great asset to his thought: for whatever one may think of pragmatism, Nietzsche did not think it through and

---

[15] Cf. Vaihinger, *Die Philosophie des Als-Ob* (1911), last chapter. This treatment of Nietzsche as a "historical confirmation" of Vaihinger's philosophy seems more suggestive than the same author's *Nietzsche als Philosoph* (1902). Cf. also R. Eisler, *Nietzsches Erkenntnistheorie und Metaphysik: Darstellung und Kritik* (1902).

failed to integrate it successfully with the remainder of his philosophy. We are thus confronted with thought experiments from
which Nietzsche had not drawn any final conclusions when illness
put an end to his deliberations. The main current of his thought
had not yet reached out to embrace these reflections, they lie
outside it; and Nietzsche's theory of knowledge will only be
touched on in this book.

In a later chapter more will be said of Nietzsche's very decided opposition to what James later called "the right to believe"
and to any doctrine of double truth. Suffice it at present to conclude that Nietzsche's experimentalism is not to be equated with
pragmatism. A single passage may crystallize a certain methodological agreement as well as a fundamental distinction:

> I would praise any *skepsis* to which I am permitted to reply:
> "Let us try [*versuchen*] it!" But I do not want to hear any-
> thing any more of all the things and questions that do not per-
> mit of experiment . . . for there courage has lost its rights
> [M 51].

Experiment is for Nietzsche not quite what it is for most other
philosophers or scientists. Its distinguishing characteristic, which
we must now consider, is what we shall call its "existential" quality. The use of the word "existential" is not meant to fix
Nietzsche's position in the history of ideas, to relegate him to
any school, or to imply anything more than we are about to
develop explicitly.

IV

Questions permitting of experiment are, to Nietzsche's mind,
those questions to which he can reply: *"Versuchen wir's!"* Let
us try it! Experimenting involves testing an answer by trying to
live according to it. To many of Hegel's questions, Nietzsche
would thus say that they were of no interest to him because they
were too abstract to be relevant to his way of living. The decision to live according to his answers is, however, not an
afterthought. The problem itself is experienced deeply, and only
problems that are experienced so deeply are given consideration.
Only problems that present themselves so forcefully that they
threaten the thinker's present mode of life lead to philosophic
inquiries. This, of course, means an arbitrary limitation of sub-

ject matter. In his defense, Nietzsche can claim that some such limitation is necessary anyhow. He can add that there are enough problems that do present themselves in this manner to keep his selection from limiting inquiries unnecessarily. As often, Nietzsche feels that he is emulating Socrates. Inquiry must take for its starting point a problem that is concrete and not artificial or merely "academic."

From this point of view, Nietzsche is prepared to question the entire educational system of his day. "A scanty knowledge of the Greeks and Romans" is forced down the students' throats "in defiance of the supreme principle of . . . education: that one should give food only to him *who has a hunger for it!*" Only in the "despair of ignorance" can we come to realize that "we *need* mathematical and mechanical knowledge." Our "small daily life," the common events of the workshop, of nature, and of society, must be seen to give rise to "thousands of problems—painful, abashing, exasperating problems." Only then, feeling a need and thirst for scientific knowledge, we should also feel the proper "awe," and our souls would tremble "with the wrestling and succumbing and fighting on again . . . with the martyrdom that constitutes the history of *strict* science" (M 195).

Again we see that science is for Nietzsche not a finished and impersonal system, but a passionate quest for knowledge, an unceasing series of courageous experiments—small experiments, lacking in glamour and apparent grandeur, yet so serious that we cannot dodge them without betraying the scientific spirit of inquiry. Science and life are no longer wholly separate; science and philosophy are a way of life: "All truths are for me soaked in blood" (xxi, 81).

Questioning means experiencing fully, with an open mind and without reservations; and failure to question seems to Nietzsche more and more synonymous with the desire not to experience possible implications. Where other critics of a philosopher might assume an oversight or error, Nietzsche frequently flies into personal attacks against what seems to him a flaw of character and a lack of intellectual integrity. His attitude is summed up in the epigram: "error is cowardice" (EH-V 3).

More important is another implication of Nietzsche's "existentialism": it obviates the hopeless incoherence to which his experimentalism might otherwise lead. His experiments do not constitute a discrete series, and a new experiment is not a capricious affair or a matter of being bored with, or forgetful of, something begun previously. The coherence is organic. This last term may seem hazy, but a brief reconsideration of Nietzsche's critique of systems may show clearly what is meant.

Nietzsche objects to the solution *en passant* of important problems; he would not deduce answers from a system. If the system's premises were truly beyond question, one need not object to the deduction of new answers. Only because there always are premises that ought to have been questioned and would have been found wanting if questioned, is it an unnecessary vitiation of new answers—and objectionable methodologically—if systematic consistency is allowed to dictate new solutions.

By constant experimenting, Nietzsche hopes to escape such vitiation as far as possible. The ideal is to consider each problem on its own merits. Intellectual integrity in the consideration of each separate problem seems not only the best way to particular truths, but it makes each investigation a possible corrective for any inadvertent previous mistakes. No break, discontinuity, or inconsistency occurs unless either there has been a previous error or there is an error now. Such inconsistencies, however—which should be the exception rather than the rule—should not go unnoticed but should ever become the occasion for revision.

By "living through" each problem, Nietzsche is apt to realize implications that other, non-existential, thinkers who merely pose these problems histrionically have overlooked. His "existentialism" prevents his aphorisms from being no more than a glittering mosaic of independent monads. The "anarchy of atoms" is more apparent than real; and while the word frequently "becomes sovereign and leaps out of the sentence" and "the sentence reaches out and obscures the meaning of the page," we cannot say in justice that "life no longer resides in the whole" (W 7). Life does indeed reside in the whole of Nietzsche's thinking and writing, and there is a unity which is obscured, but not obliterated, by the apparent discontinuity in his experimentalism.

This point is perhaps best illustrated by a reference to the variety of styles that distinguishes Nietzsche's literary output. This will also afford us a welcome opportunity for correcting any impression we may have given that Nietzsche's books are all aphoristic and lacking in continuity of presentation. *The Birth of Tragedy* and the four *Untimely Meditations* represent diverse forms of the essay, more or less richly blended with polemics. In these early works Nietzsche is not yet deliberately experimental. The next three books, *Human, All-Too-Human, Dawn,* and *The Gay Science* offer various treatments of an aphoristic style, and here the experimentalism reaches its climax. Nietzsche is deliberately anti-dogmatic and accumulates his observations with an open mind. He is, as it were, performing the countless experiments on which later theories might be built. *Zarathustra* is, stylistically, an experiment in dithyrambs; philosophically, certain significant conclusions are drawn, often in veiled allegories, from the empirical data of the previous three books. *Beyond Good and Evil* shows Nietzsche turning away from his previous aphoristic style: now most of the aphorisms are quite long and clearly anchored in their context. The *Genealogy of Morals* is aphoristic in appearance, but actually consists of three sustained and continuous inquiries—and the third of these represents a new experiment: the "exegesis" of a single aphorism in about eighty pages (GM-V 8). *The Case of Wagner* displays a new form of polemics, and *Götzen-Dämmerung, Antichrist,* and *Ecce Homo,* though returning to the length of the earlier "*Meditations,*" are each *sui generis.*

Philosophically, the works after *Zarathustra* do not any longer contain series of small experiments but the hypotheses that Nietzsche would base on his earlier works. As such, they may seem less tentative, and the tone is frequently impassioned: but Nietzsche still considers them *Versuche* and offers them with an open mind. Thus he repeats at the end of his career: "One should not be deceived: great spirits are skeptics. Zarathustra is a skeptic. . . . Convictions are prisons" (A 54). And later in the same paragraph he speaks of "conviction as a *means*" and claims that "great passion uses and uses up convictions, it does not succumb to them—it knows itself sovereign." The usual term for such employment of "convictions" is: making hypotheses.

Nietzsche's ceaseless experimenting with different styles seems to conform to the *Zeitgeist* which was generally marked by a growing dissatisfaction with traditional modes of expression. Wagner, the Impressionists and the Expressionists, Picasso and the Surrealists, Joyce, Pound, and Eliot all show a similar tendency. Nietzsche's experiments, however, are remarkable for the lack of any deliberateness even in the face of their extreme diversity. Thus Ludwig Klages, the characterologist who began his literary career as a George disciple, can speak of "the almost peerless uniformity of Nietzsche's style." [16] What is perhaps really peerless is the concomitance of uniformity and diversity. Nietzsche is not trying now this and now that style, but each experiment is so essentially Nietzschean in its strengths and weaknesses that the characterologist experiences no trouble in recognizing the author anywhere. Involuntarily almost, Nietzsche is driven from style to style in his ceaseless striving for an adequate medium of expression. Each style is characteristically his own, but soon found inadequate, and then drives him on to another newer one. Yet all the experiments cohere because they are not capricious. Their unity one might call "existential."

Considering that the aim of this brief account of Nietzsche's method has been to make possible a better understanding of his thought—not to resolve the more intricate problems of philosophic methodology—no detailed critical appraisal of Nietzsche's method seems called for. Since it is our intention, however, to give a more systematic exposition of "Nietzsche's Philosophy of Power" later on, it may be well to offer at least a brief critique of Nietzsche's rejection of systems.

His position seems plausible when one takes into account what it was that he opposed in systems. His attack was aimed at the presumption—common in the Germany of his day—that a system as such has a special claim to truth. Although lacking any thorough training in mathematical or logical theory, Nietzsche realized that the coherence of a finite system could never be a guarantee of its truth. His experimentalism seems sound as a reaction against "the time when Hegel and Schelling seduced the minds" of German youth (W 10), to use Nietzsche's own provocative phrase. The "gay science" which he opposed to the Idealists' conception of philosophy seems fruitful and deserves attention. Nietzsche, however, overlooked the possibility that systematization might be one of the most useful tools of the experimentalism he envisaged.

In the first place, systematization reveals errors. Previously unnoticed inconsistencies become apparent when one attempts to integrate a host of insights into a coherent system. And internal consistency, while admittedly not a sufficient condition of

---

[16] *Die psychologischen Errungenschaften Nietzsches* (1926), 15.

the truth of a system, is surely a necessary condition. The discovery of inconsistencies should prompt not automatic compromise but further inquiry and eventual revision. The same consideration applies to external inconsistencies: the ultimate test of the truth of an observation is consistency with the rest of our experience—and thus systematization of wider and wider areas of knowledge may raise ever new questions. Again, the new insight should not be sacrificed unscrupulously to entrenched prejudice—the great danger of systematizing; rather traditional beliefs should be subjected to ever new questioning in the light of new experiences and ideas. In this sense, a new insight is not exploited sufficiently, and the experiment is stopped prematurely if systematization is not eventually attempted in the very service of the "gay science."

This last point may be restated separately: while offering many fruitful hypotheses, Nietzsche failed to see that only a systematic attempt to substantiate them could establish an impressive probability in their favor. Hence his experiments are often needlessly inconclusive. Though a system may be false in spite of its internal coherence, an unsystematic collection of sundry observations can hardly lay any greater claim to truth.

Nietzsche, unlike Aristotle, Aquinas, or Hegel, did not mark the culmination and conclusion of a long development—as it were, a great harvest. Rather he marks the beginning of a new period, and he was acutely aware of this. Many of his most promising insights were developed after his death by other writers: Freud and Adler, Jung and Klages, F. Gundolf and Spengler, Scheler and Hartmann, Heidegger and Jaspers, Shaw and Sartre, and a host of others. Yet it would be false were one to conclude that Nietzsche was a mere aphorist and a sower of seeds, and not a philosopher in his own right. While he did not follow up *all* his suggestions, he succeeded in fashioning a coherent and noteworthy philosophy that may well surpass the systems of his successors in breadth, depth, and originality.

These brief observations do not, of course, represent a "systematic" treatment: they have purposely been kept down to the minimum prerequisite for a study of Nietzsche's thought. But in his case, some such reflections must be considered indispensable as a prolegomena to any serious philosophic study of his writings. The usual excerpt lifting, always dangerous, is doubly dangerous in Nietzsche's case, however much his style may invite it. The reader is usually so impressed, whether favorably or not, by the expert "miniatures" that he fails to look for any larger context, though this alone can indicate the meaning of a passage.

Indeed, "the sentence reaches out and obscures the meaning of the page" and "the word becomes sovereign and leaps out of the sentence": the "blond beast" is known, and so are the "super-man" and the "will to power"—and perhaps a few sentences in which one or the other is referred to. Their meaning, however, cannot possibly be grasped except in terms of their place in Nietzsche's whole philosophy.

THE DEATH OF GOD
AND THE REVALUATION

Not only the reason of millennia—their insanity, too,
breaks out in us.—Z I 22.

I

Nietzsche himself has characterized the situation in which his
philosophic thinking started by giving it the name of nihilism.
This feature of his age struck him as a challenge he meant to
meet, and we must not ignore the historical juncture at which
he enters the philosophic stage. Speculative philosophy seemed
to have spent itself in the ambitious systems of Schelling, Hegel,
and Schopenhauer; and Darwin's doctrines were conquering the
world. At the same time, Prussian arms established Germany's
political supremacy on the continent; science and technology
were making the most spectacular advances; and optimism was
common. Nietzsche, however, stigmatized this age as nihilistic.

All the material improvements of his time meant as much to
Nietzsche as the luxuries and comforts of their generation had
meant to Amos, Isaiah, and Jeremiah: they disgusted him. Only
one thing seemed to matter, and it was incomprehensible that
anyone could have eyes or ears for any other fact. What else
avails? "God is dead!"

Nietzsche invented a parable from which, some eighty years
later, a few American Protestant theologians derived inspiration
—and this slogan.

> *The Madman.* Have you not heard of that madman who lit a
> lantern in the bright morning hours, ran to the market place,
> and cried incessantly, "I seek God! I seek God!" As many of

those who did not believe in God were standing around just
then, he provoked much laughter. Why, did he get lost? said
one. Did he lose his way like a child? said another. Or is he
hiding? Is he afraid of us? Has he gone on a voyage? or emigrated? Thus they yelled and laughed. The madman jumped
into their midst and pierced them with his glances. "Whither
is God?" he cried. "I shall tell you. We *have killed him*—you
and I. All of us are his murderers. But how have we done this?
How were we able to drink up the sea? Who gave us the sponge
to wipe away the entire horizon? What did we do when we
unchained this earth from its sun? Whither is it moving now?
Whither are we moving now? Away from all suns? Are we not
plunging continually? Backward, sideward, forward, in all directions? Is there any up or down left? Are we not straying as
through an infinite nothing? Do we not feel the breath of empty
space? Has it not become colder? Is not night and more night
coming on all the while? . . . God is dead. God remains dead.
And we have killed him. . . . What was holiest and most powerful of all that the world has yet owned has bled to death under
our knives. Who will wipe this blood off us? . . ." Here the
madman fell silent and looked again at his listeners; and they
too were silent and stared at him in astonishment. At last he
threw his lantern on the ground, and it broke and went out.
"I come too early," he said then; "my time has not come yet.
This tremendous event is still on its way . . . —it has not yet
reached the ears of man. Lightning and thunder require time,
the light of the stars requires time, deeds require time even
after they are done, before they can be seen and heard. This
deed is still more distant from them than the most distant stars
—*and yet they have done it themselves.*"—It has been related
further that on that same day the madman entered divers
churches and there sang his *requiem aeternam deo*. Led out and
called to account, he is said to have replied every time, "What are
these churches now if they are not the tombs and sepulchers of
God?" [FW 125; cf. Z-V2].

Nietzsche prophetically envisages himself as a madman: to have
lost God means madness; and when mankind will discover that it
has lost God, universal madness will break out. This apocalyptic
sense of dreadful things to come hangs over Nietzsche's thinking
like a thundercloud.

We have destroyed our own faith in God. There remains only
the void. We are falling. Our dignity is gone. Our values are
lost. Who is to say what is up and what is down? It has become
colder, and night is closing in. Without seeking to explain away
Nietzsche's illness, one can hardly fail today to consider it also

symbolical. "Not only the reason of millennia—their insanity, too, breaks out in us" (Z I 22). We cannot distinguish what sense he may have had of his own doom from his presentiment of universal disaster.

The prophet Hosea was married, and when his wife became unfaithful to him, he experienced his relationship to her as a simile of God's relationship to Israel. Was not his wife as faithless as his people? Yet he loved her as God must love his people. Who can say if his anguished outcries, his protestations of his love, and his pleading for the loved one to return are meant for his wife or his people? Sometimes prophecy seems to consist in man's ability to experience his own wretched fate so deeply that it becomes a symbol of something larger. It is in this sense that one can compare Nietzsche with the ancient prophets. He felt the agony, the suffering, and the misery of a godless world so intensely, at a time when others were yet blind to its tremendous consequence, that he was able to experience in advance, as it were, the fate of a coming generation.

> If the doctrines of sovereign Becoming, of the fluidity of all . . . species, of the lack of any cardinal distinction between man and animal . . . are hurled into the people for another generation . . . then nobody should be surprised when . . . brotherhoods with the aim of robbery and exploitation of the nonbrothers . . . will appear on the arena of the future[U II 9].

Yet educated people everywhere were surprised when these unholy brotherhoods did appear. It seemed an incomprehensible relapse into the Dark Ages. Nietzsche's writings abound in similar "prophecies"—yet we should lay stress on the conditional character of his visions: "if the doctrines . . . of the lack of any cardinal distinction between man and animal . . . are hurled into the people for another generation," if mankind realizes that the unique worth of the human being has evaporated, and that no up and down remains, and if the tremendous event that we have killed God reaches the ears of man—then night will close in, "an age of barbarism begins" (XI, 120), and "there will be wars such as have never happened on earth" (EH IV 1). Insofar as Jeremiah's criterion of prophecy is valid and the false prophet is he who cries "peace, peace, when there is no peace," while the true prophets have ever spoken "of evils, and of pestilence, and of wars," one may feel inclined to consider Nietzsche a prophet in the true sense.

The content of Nietzsche's message, however, no less than the form it entails, offers the most striking contrast to the Biblical prophets. He lacks their humility which, while defying the judgment of mankind, yet knows itself no more than a mouthpiece of God. Nietzsche seems less appealing than the ancient prophets because his outrageous conceit steps between him and us. Yet if there is any sense in which he seems more appealing, it is that he thus appears more wretched, more forsaken, and more tragic. Perhaps we should go back to the Greeks rather than to the Bible to find his like: Cassandra, prophetess of doom without promise and nemesis without love. Here we are confronted with ineluctable fate, unmitigated by salvation; here, among the Greeks, we find tragedy—and it does not seem strange that Nietzsche should have had such a feeling for tragedy.

Does it follow that Nietzsche was not a great questioner after all? If he proclaimed the death of God, it may be said, he did not question all that is questionable. And Morgan has said that "beyond question the major premise of Nietzsche's philosophy is atheism." [1]

This is often assumed, and authors have not been lacking who have sought to explain Nietzsche's atheism as a reaction against the narrow-minded Christians of his provincial home town. John Figgis, in particular, has given us a moving description of the aunts who shook their heads when the young man took a walk instead of going to church, and the uncles who were shocked to see him read Voltaire and offered him "good" books.[2] One gathers that if Nietzsche had only been confronted with a more liberal outlook, he might have been spared a lot of trouble. Any such psychological trivialization of Nietzsche's ideas —even if less patronizing than this one—quite misses the point. It is generally rather easy to discover a connection between an author's background and his work; but if the author is worth his salt, his own experience has usually become the occasion for

---

[1] Morgan, *op. cit.*, 36.
[2] *The Will to Freedom, or the Gospel of Nietzsche and the Gospel of Christ* (1917), 50. "He was in reaction against his aunts" (51).

a more general insight. Nietzsche is not opposing claim to claim. He is not saying, as it were: you have been told that there is a God, but verily I say unto you, There is no God. What he does say is "God is dead."

This is the language of religion, and particularly of Christianity: the picture is derived from the Gospels; and one may note that Hegel, certainly not an atheist, had frequently spoken and written of the death of God. Nietzsche infuses a new meaning into this old image, while yet implying clearly that God once was alive. It seems paradoxical that God, if ever he lived, could have died—and the solution is that Nietzsche's pronouncement does not at all purport to be a dogmatic statement about a supernatural reality: it is a declaration of what he takes to be a historical cultural fact. "God is dead"; "we have killed him"; and "this tremendous event . . . has not yet reached the ears of man" —that is an attempt at a diagnosis of contemporary civilization, not a metaphysical speculation about ultimate reality.[3]

It may yet seem that Nietzsche assumes as a premise what is merely a growing belief—or disbelief—in Western society. He may appear to accept as an absolute presupposition the claim that there is no God—and in that case we should have laid our hands on a questionable assumption he failed to doubt. This construction, too, is untenable. Because Nietzsche did *not* start with any premises that he consciously failed to question, he *could* not base his philosophy on the assumed existence of God. This is overlooked when it is claimed that he never questioned atheism seriously: "rather he describes himself as an atheist 'by instinct.' " [4] The very passage in which Nietzsche does describe himself in this manner confirms what has been said of his method:

---

[3] Heine, whom Nietzsche admired fervently (e.g., EH II 4), had used the image of the death of God in much the same way in *Zur Geschichte der Religion und Philosophie in Deutschland*. At the end of Book II, Heine commented on the publication of Kant's first *Critique:* "Do you hear the little bell tinkle? Kneel down—one brings the sacraments for a dying God." Beyond this, the conception of "the history of religion and philosophy in Germany" as a unit, and the treatment of Luther as the background for Leibniz, Kant, and Hegel, may have impressed Nietzsche. But Heine's picture of Luther, while ironical, is incomparably more appreciative than Nietzsche's and clearly influenced by Hegel under whom Heine had studied.

[4] Morgan, *op. cit.*, 36.

It is a matter of course with me, from instinct. I am too in-
quisitive, too *questionable,* too exuberant to stand for any gross
answer. God is a gross answer, an indelicacy against us thinkers
—at bottom merely a gross prohibition for us: you shall not
think! [EH II 1; cf. GM III 27].

Nietzsche's atheism is thus a corollary of his basic commitment to question all premises and to reject them unless they are
for some reason inescapable.

The issue has been confused by the invective which Nietzsche
poured on Christianity and the Christian conception of God:
"What differentiates *us* is not that we find no God—neither in
history, nor in nature, nor behind nature—but that we do not
feel that what has been revered as God is 'god-like'" (A 47).
Nietzsche is in revolt against the Christian God and the state of
mind and the moral attitude that seem to him inseparably connected with the Christian faith. His anti-Christianity will be
taken up in detail in Chapter 12.

Nietzsche was more deeply impressed than almost any other
man before him by the manner in which belief in God and a
divine teleology may diminish the value and significance of man:
how *this* world and life may be completely devaluated *ad mai-
orem dei gloriam.* Yet Nietzsche did not proceed to postulate—
as others have done since, partly under his influence—the nonexistence of God or of any divine purpose. We must not attribute
to him "the postulated atheism of seriousness and responsibility"
that is meant to assure human responsibility.[5] The roots of this
attitude can be found quite unmistakably in some of Nietzsche's
epigrams; but while he was keenly aware of the sense in which
the existence of God might diminish the value of man,[6] he was
no less aware of, if not altogether overwhelmed by, the manner
in which the nonexistence of God would threaten human life
with a complete loss of all significance.

This sense of the utter bleakness of life and the "devaluation"
(WM 2) of all values, which is the immediate consequence of
the modern loss of faith in God, is not just a casual insight which
can be illustrated by the parable of the madman or by some other

---

[5] Max Scheler, *Mensch und Geschichte* (1929), 54–60. Scheler claims the
concurrence of Nicolai Hartmann, *Ethik* (1926), 185.

[6] Cf. the entire polemic against otherworldliness; e.g., M 464; G VI 8; WM
243, 245; EH II 3.

scattered aphorisms: most of the drafts for the *magnum opus* envisage as the contents of the first book a development of this theme to which Nietzsche gave the name of nihilism. In fact, one plan would have devoted three out of four books to this conception (XVIII, 345). To escape nihilism—which seems involved both in asserting the existence of God and thus robbing *this* world of ultimate significance, and also in denying God and thus robbing *everything* of meaning and value—that is Nietzsche's greatest and most persistent problem.

When the problem is phrased differently, Nietzsche's experimental attitude becomes more apparent. He opposed the kind of naturalism that he put within quotation marks, i.e., the literary movement associated with Zola (WM 864); and he crystallized his objection in one of his late, and characteristically provocative, epigrams: "Zola, or 'the delight in stinking' " (G IX 1). In philosophy, however, the word "naturalism" has another sense, which J. M. Baldwin defines in his *Dictionary of Philosophy and Psychology* as "a view which simply limits itself to what is natural or normal in its explanations, as against appeal to what transcends nature as a whole, or is in any way supernatural or mystical"—and Nietzsche's problem was whether it might be possible to put "in place of our 'moral values' only *naturalistic values*" (WM 462). This experiment does not require the premise that God does not exist. It demands no more than that we agree not to invoke God to cut discussion short.

The account which has been given above of Nietzsche's method is thus consistent with his proclamation that "God is dead" and with his effort to establish values that are not based on any supernatural sanction. Yet the admission that Nietzsche was something of a prophet, and his opposition to the acceptance of current valuations may still suggest that his works cannot be studied philosophically. To answer this charge, it may be well to consider first Nietzsche's attitude toward the philosophical rationalization of prevalent valuations and then the meaning of his own "revaluation of all values."

II

Nietzsche's difference from other naturalistic philosophers must be sought first in his profound concern whether universally valid values and a meaningful life are at all possible in a godless world, and secondly in his impassioned scorn for those who simply take for granted the validity of any particular set of values which happens to have the sanction of their religion, class, society, or state. He did not consider it the philosopher's task to develop his ingenuity, or his disingenuousness, in "the finding of bad reasons for what we believe on instinct." [7] Nietzsche himself considered his opposition to rationalization a major point of departure from traditional philosophy; and it is undoubtedly the source of many of his most far-reaching differences with Kant and Hegel. Kant's moral philosophy appeared to him a prime instance of the finding of bad reasons for what one believes on instinct—or, in Nietzsche's words: "Kant wanted to prove in a way that would dumfound the 'common man' that the 'common man' was right" (FW 193).

To put it more technically: Kant, as is well known, seems never to have questioned the existence of the moral law as a synthetic judgment *a priori*—i.e., as a proposition which is neither tautological nor dependent on empirical observation, and yet knowable by, and binding on, all rational beings. On the basis of this moral law, Kant sought to establish the freedom of the will, the immortality of the soul, and the existence of God and a moral world-order—all the while assuming the possibility of synthetic judgments *a priori* as an unquestioned premise. His problem was only *how* such judgments were possible. Thus he skipped the very question with which Nietzsche's thinking about moral values started—and this is the clue to Nietzsche's incessant polemics against Kant.

Nietzsche was not blind to Kant's merits: in his first book he spoke of the "tremendous courage and wisdom of Kant and Schopenhauer" (GT 18); and later he sided with Kant against Schopenhauer on other questions (M 132) and admitted Kant's decisive contribution to philosophy (FW 357). His own philosophy even shows many decided affinities to Kant's; but Kant's failure to question the existence of a universal moral law provoked Nietzsche's attacks which further illustrate his reasons for opposing systems and his "existential" identification of any failure to question with a desire not to experience fully. The

---

[7] F. H. Bradley's famous definition of metaphysics to which he himself added: "but to find these reasons is no less an instinct." *Appearance and Reality* (1891), xiv.

merciless personal quality which is thus introduced into Nietzsche's polemics is apparent when he charges Kant with a lack of "intellectual conscience" (A 12) and of "intellectual integrity" (EH-W 2); nor can Nietzsche resist the temptation of making a pun on "cant" (G ix 1). Nietzsche's conception of "intellectual conscience" is explained by him elsewhere:

> *The Intellectual Conscience. . . . By far the most lack an intellectual conscience . . . by far the most* do not find it contemptible to believe this or that and to live according to it, *without* first having become conscious of the last and surest reasons pro and con, and without even taking the trouble to consider such reasons afterwards—the most gifted men and the most noble women still belong to these "by far the most." Yet what is good-heartedness, refinement, and genius to me, when the human being who has these virtues tolerates slack feelings in his faith and judgments, and when the demand for certainty is not to him the inmost craving and the deepest need—that which distinguishes the higher from the lower men. . . . *Not to question,* not to tremble with the craving and the joy of questioning . . . that is what I feel to be *contemptible,* and this feeling is the first thing I seek in everyone: some foolishness persuades me ever and again that every human being has this feeling, as a human being. It is my kind of injustice [FW 2].

Just as characteristic is the manner in which Nietzsche seeks to explain why Kant failed to question the moral law. His first answer is that "Kant clung to the university, submitted to governments, [and] remained within the appearance of a religious faith" (U iii 3). He was, "in his attitude toward the State, without greatness" (U iii 8).

The gist of this argument is that one compromise with the existing order leads to another. *Even* Kant, that is Nietzsche's point, was led to clip the wings of his own spirit. *Even* Kant, whose reasoning power was second to none, stopped short of questioning the moral law, ceased prematurely to think, and thus vitiated his moral philosophy. "A university scholar [*ein Gelehrter*] can never become a philosopher; for even Kant could not do it and remained to the end, in spite of the innate striving of his genius, in a quasi cocoon stage" (U iii 7). A philosopher, says Nietzsche in this context, must not allow "concepts, opinions, things past, and books" to step "between himself and things." He must not rationalize the valuations of his own society. As

Nietzsche sees it, the temptation to do this is particularly great for the German professor who is an employee of the State. Of course, that is a chief reason for his choice of Schopenhauer as his protagonist in the essay in which he attacks the State so fiercely; for Schopenhauer was, unlike Kant and Hegel, no university professor.

As a matter of fact, one may note that Schopenhauer attempted to teach at the university of Berlin, Hegel's stronghold, and that he was a failure—largely because he deliberately chose to deliver his lectures at times when he knew that Hegel would be lecturing, too. In this self-chosen contest he lost out; and his later diatribe *Über die Universitätsphilosophie* (in *Parerga und Paralipomena*) might be considered "sour grapes." Yet the repudiation of universities and of civil life generally as irreconcilable with the life of a thinker is characteristic of the reaction against Hegel. Hegel had taught: "Whoever wants something great, says Goethe, must be able to limit himself"; and Hegel had concluded that political freedom must be sought within the limitations of a responsible role in the civic life of the community. That there was more than this to freedom, he had never dreamed of denying: absolute freedom could be achieved only in the realm of Absolute Spirit, i.e., in art, religion, and philosophy. Such pursuits, however, did not seem to him to involve the rejection of civic life, but only its completion. The living example was Goethe who combined a civic career of public service as a cabinet minister in Weimar with artistic creation of the highest order.[8]

---

[8] Cf. *Rechtsphilosophie;* the quotation is from §13 *Zusatz.* The sphere of Absolute Spirit is the topic of *Phänomenologie,* Parts VII and VIII, and of *Encyclopädie,* §§553–77. The popular view that the political sphere was for Hegel the highest, and that the State was his God, is quite untenable, as any reference to his system as a whole (*Encyclopädie*) shows readily enough. Much damage has been done by an oft quoted sentence which is ascribed to Hegel: "the State is the march of God through the world." The sentence is from Scribner's *Hegel Selections,* represents a plain mistranslation, and was not even in its German form written by Hegel. Though there is no indication whatever of this in the *Selections,* the sentence is taken from a *Zusatz* (addition) to §258; and the *Zusätze* were added by Eduard Gans in the posthumous edition, with the explicit admission: "the stylistic order, the connection of the sentences, and sometimes the choice of words as well are mine." The notorious sentence reads in German: *"es ist der Gang Gottes in der Welt, dass der Staat ist."* The word *dass,* of course, is neither the same gender as *Gang* nor any pronoun at all; and the sentence fragment means merely that it is the

Schopenhauer marked only the initial reaction against this ideal. Ludwig Feuerbach, Arnold Ruge, Bruno Bauer, and Eugen Dühring lost their positions at various universities; Max Stirner struggled along in enforced privacy; Marx, although a doctor of philosophy, did not teach, and spent his life in exile; and Kierkegaard never made use of his theological degree to become a minister.[9] The political views that led to the early retirement of some of these men are, of course, themselves expressive of a historic change. Kant, instead of resigning, got along with a mediocre and impertinent king; and Fichte had an illustrious civic career after the *Atheismus-Streit*.

Nietzsche, who wrote his most important books in privacy, had given ill health as his reason for resigning his professorship at Basel; but his state of health was connected with his inability to reconcile his university career with his writing. The essay on Schopenhauer was published when he was still a professor, and he made it clear then and there that he felt that any compromise with the existing order prevented a thinker from "following the truth into all hide-outs" (U III 8).

Thus we find some methodological significance even in Nietzsche's personal attacks. They are prompted by the same reasons which led him to oppose systems.

> Kant as well as Hegel and Schopenhauer—the skeptical attitude as well as the historical and pessimistic—have a *moral* origin. I saw no one who had ventured a *critique of moral value-feelings*. . . . How is Spinoza's position explainable, his . . . rejection of moral value judgments? (It was *one* consequence of his theodicy!) [WM 410].

The point is as much *ad hominem*, but also as significant methodologically, as the claim that Kant rationalized his personal psychological inclination (WM 424) and that he invented the

---

way of God with this world that there should be the State—i.e., the State is not an accident, and we must seek to understand its "reason" (in a double sense) which Hegel finds in its being a prerequisite of art, religion, and philosophy. Thus Hegel begins his discussion of the State with the definition, "The State is the actuality of the ethical idea" (§257)—this idea being freedom, i.e., the positive and constructive freedom which culminates in art, religion, and philosophy, while depending on techniques, traditions, and education which, according to Hegel, can be maintained only in the State.

[9] Cf. Löwith, *Von Hegel bis Nietzsche* (1941), 95 f.

transcendent world to leave a place for moral freedom (WM 578). Error is spread unnecessarily when moral doctrines, which are vitiated by personal bias or a compromise with State or Church, are allowed to become the basis for metaphysical or epistemological considerations. That this, however, has been the case in almost all philosophies up to now, Nietzsche never tires of insisting (e.g., J 6; WM 413, 428).

One may question Nietzsche's assumption that Kant assumed the possibility of synthetic judgments *a priori* only because he took the moral law for granted *a priori:* while there are passages even in his first *Critique* in which Kant himself suggests that his theory of knowledge was inspired by a moral purpose,[10] Kant also thought of mathematics as presenting us with synthetic judgments *a priori.* He did, however, carry to extremes the solving of problems by reference to conceptual analogies, parallels, and symmetries. One might therefore raise the Nietzschean objection precisely against the *Critique of Practical Reason* and the *Critique of Judgment* which seem indeed unnecessarily vitiated by forcible parallels to the first *Critique.* Reading them, one often feels that Kant abandoned a rigorously questioning attitude and an analysis of actual experience for the sake of symmetry and repetition of the neat schemes of his *Critique of Pure Reason.*[11] We may be far more readily inclined to forgive Kant's belief that mathematics contains synthetic judgments *a priori* than we would be to pardon his failure to question or discuss his assumption that there is an *a priori* "moral law." If this assumption can be established by cogent argument, Kant certainly did not show this.

If some light has been shed on Nietzsche's opposition to any rationalization of current valuations, the question remains what alternative he would offer instead. It is at this point that he is often taken to have presented himself as the legislating "prophet" and revaluer of values. Fortunately, we do not have to rely on

---

[10] E.g., 2nd ed., xxvii ff., 825 ff.

[11] The classical, very detailed and well documented, account of the vitiation of Kant's thought by the desire for symmetry is given in Schopenhauer's *Kritik der Kantischen Philosophie.* (Appendix of *Die Welt als Wille und Vorstellung* 1.)

the stylistic peculiarities of *Zarathustra* to settle this point, for Nietzsche furnishes us with quite explicit statements about the meaning of his "revaluation."

In *Beyond Good and Evil*—the first book he published after *Zarathustra* to explain its often obscure suggestions—Nietzsche argues at some length that we should distinguish "philosophic laborers" from philosophers proper. The laborers' "tremendous and wonderful task, in whose service every subtle pride, every tough will, can surely find satisfaction," consists in compressing into formulas former "value-creations that have become dominant and are for a time called 'truths.' " Thus previous valuations can be more readily surveyed. The task is important, and those who dedicate themselves to it are to follow "the noble model of Kant and Hegel." The real philosopher, however, has another task. He, too, must stand at one time on all the steps "on which his servants, the . . . laborers of philosophy . . . must remain standing." For that matter, however, he must also be a "poet and collector and traveler . . . moralist and seer and 'free spirit' and almost everything to traverse the range of human values and value-feelings and *to be able* to look with sundry eyes and consciences" at all valuations. All these are only "preliminary conditions of his task." *"Genuine philosophers, however, are . . . legislators"* (J 211). This may seem to be an unequivocal statement of Nietzsche's conviction that men like Kant and Hegel were merely his "servants" and "laborers," while he himself had a task even far nobler than theirs: value-legislation. Any such construction, however, would have to be based on a complete disregard for the further development of the argument. The aphorism concludes: "Are there such philosophers today? Have there been such philosophers yet? *Must* there not be such philosophers?" The next aphorism answers these questions; for *Beyond Good and Evil* is much more continuous than its aphoristic form would indicate. Thus the argument in question is continued with the assertion that such philosophers have not existed so far and do not exist yet.

Nietzsche then develops his conception of the utmost that philosophers have achieved to date and can achieve now. For that reason, this particular aphorism (J 212) is of unique importance. The model philosopher is pictured as a physician who applies the knife of his thought "vivisectionally to the very *virtues of the time.*" As a paragon of such a philosopher Nietzsche pictures Socrates whom he would emulate by uncovering "how much hypocrisy, comfortableness," and lack of self-discipline is really "hidden under the best honored type of contemporary morality." [12]

Nietzsche's conception of his own relationship to the legislating philosophers is expressed quite clearly in an earlier aphorism of the same work where he speaks of himself as a "herald and precursor" of "the philosophers of the future" (J 44). Instead of rationalizing current valuations which appear to him as previous "value creations that have become dominant and are, for a time, called 'truths,'" he offers a critique and thus prepares the ground for a new "value-creation" or "value-legislation" in the future.

Now it may be asked: if Nietzsche thus criticizes and helps to destroy prevalent values, does he not hasten the advent of nihilism? does he not seek to shatter our faith in God before he adds his "woe is us"? does he not help to bring about that catastrophic vacuum which he is prophesying? Perhaps the most precise answer to these questions is to be found in a line from *Zarathustra:* "what is falling, that one should also push!" (Z III 12). Nietzsche is not speaking of "mercy" killings of the crippled and insane, but of all values that have become hollow, all creeds out of which the faith has gone, and all that is professed only by hypocrites. The New Testament picture is that one should not pour new wine into old skins, nor put new patches on an old garment.

Traditional morality seems to Nietzsche ineluctably moribund—a dying tree that cannot be saved by grafting new fruit on it. We may recall his conception of the philosopher as a doctor—a surgeon. The health of our civilization appeared to him to be severely threatened: it looked impressively good, but seemed to Nietzsche thoroughly undermined—a diagnosis which, though trite today, was perhaps no mean feat in the eighteen-eighties. Under the circumstances, one could humor the patient and let him die, or put hypocrisy and flattery aside, speak up in behalf of one's diagnosis, and "apply the knife." In other

---

[12] The importance of the ideal of the doctor for the shaping of Socrates' and Plato's conception of the ideal philosopher has been developed by Werner Jaeger, *Paideia* III (1943). Instead of recognizing Nietzsche's kindred remarks, however, Jaeger—like almost everybody else—takes for granted "Nietzsche's hatred" of Socrates (II, *passim*).

words, Nietzsche believed that, to overcome nihilism, we must first of all recognize it.

III

There still remains the question what the "revaluation" amounts to, seeing that Nietzsche speaks of himself as a mere "herald and precursor." Does Nietzsche offer us new values? It would of course be easy to show that the virtues praised by him are all to be found in previous writers. In that sense, however, it would be altogether questionable whether there is novelty in the history of ideas. Hence we should change our question and ask not whether Nietzsche's wine was new, but whether it was his intention and his own conception of the "revaluation" to pour us new wine. The answer is: No.

Those who would make good their claim that our question must be answered in the affirmative have to rely on their imagination to produce Nietzsche's "new" virtues. The virtues he praises are honesty, courage—especially moral courage—generosity, politeness, and intellectual integrity. In his later writings, Nietzsche placed increasing emphasis on self-discipline and hardness—but unlike some of his critics, he knew the Stoics; he did not regard Spinoza as a sentimentalist; and he did not consider Kant's ethics one of softness. It is often charged that Nietzsche exhorted us to be ruthless against others—and up to a point that is true, although he also insisted up to the very end that to treat those who are weaker than oneself more tenderly than oneself or one's peers is "not just a courtesy of the heart," [13] but a *"duty"* (A 57). That one must occasionally be hard against others for the sake of the perfection of one's own soul—though not as hard as one must be against oneself—that is a truth which was not discovered by Nietzsche. Perhaps the command to leave one's father and mother gives symbolic expression to this insight.

The "revaluation" is then still unaccounted for. It does not mean a table of new virtues, nor an attempt to give us such a

---

[13] The phrase "courtesy of the heart" Nietzsche borrowed from Goethe, *Wahlverwandtschaften* (1809), II, 101: "There is a courtesy of the heart; it is related to love. It gives rise to the most comfortable courtesy of external behavior."

table; and it is one of Nietzsche's most serious faults that, in his great loneliness, he injected into his writings elements that aroused such expectations. What he really meant by his "revaluation" was clearly nothing of the sort, as is shown by the few passages in which Nietzsche explains his conception. The notes and the finished works of 1888 present a perfectly consistent picture in this respect.

One of the most revealing characterizations of the "revaluation" occurs in *Ecce Homo:*

> After the Yes-saying part of my task had been solved, the turn had come for the No-saying, *No-doing* part: the revaluation of our values so far, the great war—conjuring up a day of decision. This included the slow search for those related to me, those who, prompted by strength, would offer me their hands for *destroying* [EH-J 1].

In other words, the "revaluation" means a war against accepted valuations, not the creation of new ones. Later in *Ecce Homo,* Nietzsche elaborates:

> *Revaluation of all values:* that is my formula for an act of ultimate self-examination by mankind which in me has become flesh and genius. My lot is that I must be the first *decent* human being, that I know myself to be in opposition against the mendaciousness of millennia [EH iv 1].

Without denying the touch of madness in the uninhibited hyperbole of Nietzsche's phrasing, one can use this statement as a clue to Nietzsche's meaning. The "revaluation" is essentially "a courageous becoming conscious" (WM 1007); in other words, the diagnosis itself is the revaluation, and this consists in nothing beyond what Socrates did: "applying the knife vivisectionally to the very *virtues of the time*" and uncovering "how much hypocrisy, comfortableness, letting oneself go and letting oneself drop, how many lies were concealed under the most honored type of their contemporary morality, how much virtue was *outlived*" (J 212). The "revaluation" is not a new value-legislation but a reversal of prevalent valuations—not from a new vantage point, nor arbitrary,[14] but an *internal* criticism: the discovery of what

---

[14] Almost all of Nicolai Hartmann's criticisms of Nietzsche in his famous *Ethik* (1926) depend on this misunderstanding. Of course, he is not blind to Nietzsche's merits and even suggests in the preface that the task of ethics today consists, at least to a considerable extent, in achieving a synthesis of Nietzsche and Kant.

Nietzsche variously refers to as "mendaciousness," "hypocrisy," and "dishonesty."

The conception of the revaluation is characteristic of the late Nietzsche who never tires of reiterating that his "inmost nature" is *"amor fati"* (EH-W 4), that "nothing that is may be subtracted, nothing is dispensable" (EH-GT 2), and that he "wants nothing to be different, not forward, not backward, not in all eternity" (EH II 10). The revaluation is not the accomplishment of the individual philosopher who enters the arena to tackle ancient valuations and to reverse them as a sport; rather, "the values we have had hitherto thus draw their final consequence" (WM-V 4); *"the highest values devaluate themselves"* (WM 2). This Nietzsche can call the revaluation—in the same note in which he defines it as "a courageous becoming conscious"—a *"saying Yes* to what has been attained" (WM 1007). On the face of it, this contradicts the passage in which Nietzsche associates the revaluation with "no-saying" (EH-J 1); but the contradiction is merely verbal. Thus Nietzsche himself can say: "I contradict as has never been contradicted before and am nevertheless the opposite of a no-saying spirit" (EH IV 1). In Hegelian terms, Nietzsche's attitude is positive insofar as he negates a negation—for he considers Christianity as the "revaluation of all the values of antiquity" (J 46). More judiciously put, he points out how our accepted morality is dying of internal inconsistencies. His No consists in the acceptance of a *fait accompli*. The philosopher only lays bare the cancerous growth.

Against this background one may also understand the title of one of Nietzsche's last works: *"Götzen-Dämmerung oder Wie man mit dem Hammer philosophiert."* It is usually assumed that the hammer with which Nietzsche philosophized was a sledge hammer. As a matter of fact, he had planned to call the book *Müssiggang eines Psychologen* (The Idleness of a Psychologist) and substituted *Götzen-Dämmerung* only after the work was finished—at Gast's insistence; and the simile of the hammer is explained in the Preface:

> There are more idols than realities in the world: that is *my* "evil eye" for this world; that is also my "evil *ear.*" For once to pose questions here with a *hammer* and perhaps to hear as a reply that famous hollow sound . . . what a delight for one who has ears even behind his ears—for me, an old psychologist and pied piper before whom just that which would remain silent

> *must become outspoken.* This essay, too—the title betrays it—
> is above all a recreation . . . the idleness of a psychologist. . . .
> This little essay is a *great declaration of war;* and regarding the
> sounding out of idols, this time they are not just idols of the age,
> but *eternal* idols which are here touched with the hammer as
> with a tuning fork [!]—there are altogether no older ones . . .
> Also none more hollow.

And this was written "on the day when the first book of the *Revaluation of All Values* was completed."

The hyperbolic epithets associated with the revaluation in *Ecce Homo* bear out our interpretation. Nietzsche speaks of "the hammer blow of historical insight *(lisez: revaluation of all values)*" (EH-MA 6); and he calls the three inquiries which constitute the *Genealogy* "Three decisive preliminary studies by a psychologist for a revaluation of all values" (EH-GM). In other words, the *Genealogy* is now viewed as a prelude to the *Antichrist*—and Nietzsche thinks of his account of the genesis of Christianity as a "historical insight." When he speaks of "the smashing thunderbolt of the *revaluation*" (EH-W 4), this picture of the destructive *Blitzschlag* is similarly suggested by what Nietzsche takes to be a sudden and terrifying illumination about the true nature of our traditional values—an illumination which these values cannot survive.

The revaluation is thus the alleged discovery that our morality is, *by its own standards,* poisonously immoral: that Christian love is the mimicry of impotent hatred; that most unselfishness is but a particularly vicious form of selfishness; and that *ressentiment* is at the core of our morals. This view finds further confirmation in Nietzsche's plan for his projected *magnum opus:*

REVALUATION OF ALL VALUES

BOOK I: THE ANTICHRIST:
ATTEMPT AT A CRITIQUE OF CHRISTIANITY.

BOOK II: THE FREE SPIRIT:
CRITIQUE OF PHILOSOPHY AS A NIHILISTIC MOVEMENT.

BOOK III: THE IMMORALIST:
CRITIQUE OF THE MOST FATAL KIND OF IGNORANCE,
[CURRENT [15]] MORALITY.

---

[15] That current morality is meant, and not morality in general, is clear from the half dozen pages of notes for this book which were published

BOOK IV: DIONYSUS:
PHILOSOPHY OF ETERNAL RECURRENCE.

This plan dates from the fall of 1888 and is reprinted in most editions of the *Antichrist*—the first and only finished part of the *Revaluation*. Three of the four parts of the *Revaluation* were meant to be critiques—one should note the attempt to outdo Kant—and we shall see in a later chapter, when considering the eternal recurrence, that the subject matter of the projected fourth book would not have included any new value legislation either. Here, too, it would have been a matter of accepting what Nietzsche took to be a *fait accompli*.

The Preface for the projected *Revaluation,* a single page long, nowhere refers to new values and leaves little doubt about the author's intentions:

> . . . The conditions under which one understands me, and then *necessarily* understands me—I know them only too well. One must be honest in intellectual matters to the point of hardness . . . one must never ask whether the truth will be useful or whether it may become one's fatality. A preference of strength for questions for which nobody today has the courage; the courage for the forbidden . . . A new conscience for truths which have hitherto remained mute. . . .

The enterprise requires a probing intellect that shrinks from no discovery; it consists in an examination of the psychological motivation of religious beliefs, metaphysical doctrines, and morality; and Nietzsche feels inspired by a relentless determination to make this motivation a matter of conscience.

The revaluation culminates in the claim that the so-called goodness of modern man is not virtuous, that his so-called religion is not religious, and that his so-called truths are not truthful. While those who are truly powerful and rich personalities will be kind and generous, spontaneously and instinctively, the weak who insist on conformity to the old standards—says Nietzsche—find in such conformity a mere screen for what is, according to these very standards, petty wickedness. In the weak the law abets and breeds sin.

---

together with the *Antichrist*. The *"Opposite Type"* of the "good" man is described in the first note: "True goodness, nobility, greatness of soul . . . which does not give to take, which does not want to *promote* itself by being good; *squandering* as the type of true goodness, the wealth of personality as prerequisite."

The details of these highly controversial views will have to be considered later. Suffice it for the present if the necessary background for such a discussion has been given. Nietzsche was "prophetic" in the sense that he divined what the mass of his generation was blind to: he anticipated problems that today stare us in the face. He did not, however, consider himself a prophet in any sense that would preclude a philosophic approach to his writings: although Zarathustra, in Nietzsche's most famous book, seems to speak as one having authority, Nietzsche generally developed his points more carefully and patiently— and they may be studied in that manner.

Finally, Nietzsche himself clearly wanted to be a philosopher and not the founder of a new religion. His scorn for the unquestioning disciple is one of the persistent motifs of his thought. In *The Gay Science*—the work that immediately preceded *Zarathustra*—this theme is aired a great number of times, beginning with the Proem (7 and 23).

Since this side of Nietzsche's thought has been unduly neglected, it may be well to quote a few characteristic passages:

> Let us remain faithful to Wagner in that which is *true* . . . in him—and especially in this that we, as his disciples, remain faithful to ourselves in that which is true . . . in us. Let him have his intellectual tempers and convulsions. . . . It does not matter that as a thinker he is so often wrong; justice and patience are not *his* strength. Enough, if his life is justified, and remains justified, before itself: this life which shouts at every one of us: "Be a man and do not follow me[16]—but yourself! But yourself! [FW 99].

Nietzsche recognized his self-portrait no less than we do today. He knew of his own "intellectual tempers and convulsions"; he was aware of the fact that "as a thinker he is so often wrong"; and he had no illusion that "justice and patience" were his strength. Nor did he crave slavish adherence to his pronouncements any more than he could respect such uncritical acceptance of Wagner's ideas. A few pages later we find Nietzsche's picture of the ideal disciple:

---

[16] Goethe added this motto in the later editions of his *Werther* because the hero's suicide had inspired many readers to follow his example.

When he had said that, his disciple shouted . . . : "But I believe in your cause and consider it so strong that I shall say everything, everything that I can find in my heart to say against it." The innovator laughed . . . : "This kind of discipleship," he said then, "is the best . . ." [FW 106].

One may also cite two other passages from *The Gay Science*:

Everybody knows that to be able to accept criticism [*Widerspruch*] is a high sign of culture. Some even know that the higher man invites and provokes criticism of himself to receive a hint about his injustices which are yet unknown to him [FW 297].

A kind of intellectual integrity [*Redlichkeit*] has been alien to all founders of religions and their kind: they have never made their experiences a matter of conscience for knowledge. "What did I really experience? What happened then in me and around me? Was my reason bright enough? Was my will turned against all deceptions . . . ?"—none of them has raised such questions; all the dear religious people still do not raise such questions even now: rather they have a thirst for things that are *against reason,* and they do not want to make it too hard for themselves to satisfy it. . . . We, however, we others who thirst for reason want to look our experiences as straight in the eye as if they represented a scientific experiment . . . ! We ourselves want to be our experiments and guinea pigs [*Versuchs-Tiere*]! [FW 319].

Even so it may seem that when Nietzsche wrote *Zarathustra* a little later, he changed his mind and mood. It is undeniable that—if we are to use Nietzsche's own play on words—*Zarathustra* was not only an experiment and an attempt but also a temptation. Man often craves religious certainty in direct proportion to his profound and tormenting doubts. Like Pascal and Kierkegaard and many another, Nietzsche, too, knew the temptation to let doubt be bygone and to "leap"—as Kierkegaard himself would put it—into faith. What distinguishes Nietzsche is not that he experienced this attraction, but that he felt obliged to resist it to retain his integrity (WM 1038). He did resist it to the end and retained an open mind and the will to hold his own "in an unfinished system with free, unlimited views" (XVI, 51 f.).

Nietzsche knew that he was, "no less than Wagner, a child of this age"; but he insisted that he had "fought against this" (W-V): in the pose of Zarathustra we recognize Wagner's contemporary; but when we see the far more melodramatic notes

(xiv) which were not utilized in the completed version, we see how Nietzsche fought his temptation; and the final speech of the first part—which Nietzsche himself considered so important that he quoted it at length in the Preface to *Ecce Homo*—shows Nietzsche overcoming Wagner in himself and turning to Socrates:

> Go away from me and resist Zarathustra. . . . Perhaps he deceived you. . . . One repays a teacher badly, if one always remains a pupil only. Why do you not pluck at my wreath?

One may agree with Nietzsche that this is not the language of prophets and founders of religions: "he does not only speak differently, he also *is* different" (EH-V).

Even in *Zarathustra* where Nietzsche chooses the founder of a great religion to be his protagonist, and even in *Ecce Homo* where his claims of his own greatness reach their incredible climax, Nietzsche-Socrates overcomes Nietzsche-Wagner. To be sure, in *Ecce Homo* Nietzsche attempts what might be called a deliberate self-mythologization; some of his statements obviously make no claim to literal correctness; and poetic license is in places extended beyond all boundaries of reason and good taste. The mythological mask, however, that Nietzsche seeks to create for himself is not that of a prophet who establishes a new religion; it is the antithesis of Zarathustra and of the legend that his sister and her associates cultivated later while advisedly withholding *Ecce Homo*:

> I *want* no "believers"; I think I am too sarcastic [*boshaft*] *to* believe in myself; I never speak to masses. I have a terrible fear that one day I will be pronounced *holy:* You will guess why I publish this book *before;* it shall prevent people from doing mischief [*Unfug*] with me [EH IV 1].

The bombast is indeed harnessed by irony; the prophetic pathos is employed in the service of Nietzsche's proclamation that he is not a prophet; and the insane pride is based in large part on his triumph over any dogma, on his sense of a new freedom, and on his enjoyment of unprecedented wide and open vistas. A few weeks earlier, in *The Antichrist*, it had not been a new faith that Nietzsche had pitted against Christianity, but the "gay science" of the open mind, a fanaticism for truth, and a new *skepsis* (A 54).

It may be asked whether Nietzsche's *Ecce Homo* was really designed to prevent posterity from using him to bad ends. Was it the kind of book that, if published and read earlier, might have counteracted the growth of the legend or the Nazis' later *Unfug?* If one examines the book with such questions in mind, one cannot help concluding that Nietzsche, who announced in this work "I am no man, I am dynamite" (IV 1), was honestly concerned lest this explosive might be employed in the service of the very things he had fought.

He went to extremes to counteract the potential influence of *Zarathustra*; he denounced, vehemently, those who might interpret his conception of the overman Darwinistically, though his own Zarathustric allegories had plainly invited such misunderstanding; and he missed no opportunity to heap scorn upon German nationalistic aspirations, racism, and the irresponsible reinterpretation of past history which was even then becoming fashionable. For all its obvious and glaring faults, *Ecce Homo* repudiated in advance the forces that were later to claim Nietzsche as their own. The explicit denunciation of his sister, which one might expect to find in the book, was apparently included in the manuscript, but obliterated by her at an early date—because she then expected that he would recover from his madness, and she was eager to save *him* the embarrassment of seeing what terrible things he had written! [17]

The Förster-Nazi attempt to find a new religion in *Zarathustra* or a finished system in *The Will to Power* is as opposed to Nietzsche's own basic intentions as was the hallowing of his name at his funeral and the subsequent attempt to make a saint or a prophet of the new Germany out of him. We need not look at Nietzsche through the warped glasses of those whom he himself dubbed "Zarathustra's apes." The Wagnerian pose of his most famous book, its similes which have struck popular fancy and invited misunderstanding—"those were steps for me, and I have climbed up over them: to that end I had to pass over them. Yet they thought that I wanted to retire on them" (G I 42).

---

[17] Podach, *Gestalten um Nietzsche,* 201 f.

II

The Development
of Nietzsche's
Thought

If this writing is incomprehensible for anybody or will not go into his head, the fault, it seems to me, is not necessarily mine. It is plain enough, assuming—as I do assume—that one has first read my earlier writings and not spared some trouble in doing this—GM-V 8.

The worst readers of aphorisms are the writer's friends if they are intent to guess back from the general to the particular instance to which the aphorism owes its origin: for with this pot-peeking they reduce the author's whole effort to nothing, and thus they only deserve it when, instead of a philosophic outlook or instruction, they gain nothing but—at best, or at worst—the satisfaction of a vulgar curiosity—MA II 129.

4

ART AND HISTORY

All that happens is symbol, and as it represents itself perfectly, it points to the rest.—GOETHE, LETTER TO SCHUBARTH, *April 2, 1818*.

The crown of Nietzsche's philosophy is the dual vision of the overman and the eternal recurrence; its key conception is the will to power. After setting out to question all that could be doubted, Nietzsche wound up with these eminently questionable notions. One is therefore in danger of robbing Nietzsche's ideas of all plausibility and relevance to contemporary thought—and one may indeed fail altogether to understand them correctly—if one ignores how Nietzsche came to think as he did. When it is shown, on the other hand, how Nietzsche came to invoke such extreme conceptions, it will appear that his later doctrines are answers—worthy of consideration, although hardly entirely acceptable as they stand—to problems that still plague us today.

The question arises as to where we are to find the thread of Ariadne to guide us through the labyrinth of Nietzsche's thought: where is Nietzsche's most fundamental problem on which all his philosophic labors are focused? This crucial question is easily overlooked; but asking it almost means answering it—so little doubt does Nietzsche leave concerning his primary concern: values. To be sure, he was less concerned with the academic field of value theory where discussion is apt to bog down in definitions or in analyses of the distinctions between fact and value. Nietzsche attacked the value problem that stares our generation in the face—the dilemma that haunts modern man and threatens our civilization:

> The end of the *moral* interpretation of the world, which no
> longer has any *sanction* after it has tried to escape into some
> beyond, leads to nihilism. "Everything lacks meaning." . . .
> Since Copernicus man has been rolling from the center toward
> "x." . . . What does nihilism mean? *That the highest values
> devaluate themselves.* The goal is lacking; the answer is lacking
> to our "Why?" [WM 1–2].

Modern man finds that his values are worthless, that his ends
do not give his life any purpose, and that his pleasures do not
give him happiness. Nietzsche's basic problem is whether a new
sanction can be found in this world for our values; whether a
new goal can be found that will give an aim to human life; and
what is happiness?

These concerns are plain enough in Nietzsche's later works;
but his answers pose grave difficulties that are best removed by
going back to his early works in which no will to power and
no doctrine of recurrence stump the understanding. It will
appear that even then Nietzsche was seeking to cope with similar problems; that he was not able to solve them to his own
satisfaction; and that he then temporarily abandoned his ambitious project, turned to psychological inquiries, discovered
the will to power in the course of these by a bold induction—and
then returned to his value problem to supplement and strengthen
his earlier efforts by introducing this novel conception. At that
point, of course, a more systematic treatment of Nietzsche's
thought becomes possible. Meanwhile, a study of some of his
early works will furnish the necessary foundation.

I

Among Nietzsche's early books, *The Birth of Tragedy* and the
Meditation on history are by far the most famous, but the *Meditation* on Schopenhauer is of at least equal importance. We
shall consider *The Birth of Tragedy* and *Of the Use and Disadvantage of History for Life* in the present chapter, and discuss
the essay on *Schopenhauer as Educator* in the next.[1] All three
have certain important features in common: they pose the problems and announce the major themes that Nietzsche later de-

---

[1] The first *Meditation* (on Strauss) will also be considered in the present
chapter, but in less detail.

veloped; they are fairly single-minded essays of a little over a hundred pages each; and they are largely unencumbered by the sound and fury of Nietzsche's later polemics.

The only fierce attack in these three books is directed against the State, which is pictured as the very devil. This, too, is an announcement—by drums and trumpets—of a motif that remains characteristic of all of Nietzsche's works. He was not primarily a social or political philosopher, his "influence" and Bäumler's caricature of him as *Politiker* notwithstanding. Nietzsche and Hegel were both primarily concerned about the realm of Absolute Spirit, i.e., art, religion, and philosophy, and both evaluated the State in terms of its relation to these higher pursuits. Hegel had praised the State because he thought that it alone made possible these supra-social enterprises; Nietzsche condemned the State as their archenemy. Each considered customary morality essentially social and hence associated it with the State. Hence Hegel affirmed it, while Nietzsche criticized it, but they agreed in their firm opposition to Kant's doctrine of the primacy of moral values.

This is plain even in Nietzsche's first book. *The Birth of Tragedy* maintains that "only as an *aesthetic phenomenon* are life and the world *justified* eternally" (5, 24); and the Preface, added in 1886, declares militantly:

> Here is announced . . . a pessimism "beyond good and evil" . . . that "perversity of outlook" . . . against which Schopenhauer never tired of hurling his most irate curses . . . in anticipation—a philosophy that dares to place morality itself not only in the world of "appearances" (in the sense of the Idealistic *terminus technicus*) but even among "deceptions," as semblance, delusion, error, interpretation . . . art.

Still later, Nietzsche summarized: *"Aesthetic values"* are "the only values recognized in *The Birth of Tragedy"* (EH-GT 1).

Nietzsche was by no means the first German philosopher to reject Kant's postulate of the moral world-order: Hegel had criticized it while Kant was yet alive;[2] and he elevated art into the realm of Absolute Spirit, while morality was included in that of Objective Spirit. Logically, Hegel had founded his position on his own unquestioned belief in a rational world-order which, as expounded in his system, required social morality as a step-

---

[2] *Glauben und Wissen (Werke*, I), 324 ff.

ping stone for the development of art, religion, and philosophy
—in that order. Historically, he had followed the example of
Schelling's *System des Transcendentalen Idealimus* (1800).

Nietzsche has often been compared both with the German
romantics—among whom Schelling was the leading philosopher
—and with the existentialists, who have drawn inspiration from
Schelling; indeed, Paul Tillich wrote two dissertations on him,
and Jaspers a big book. Hence Schelling's final position is of
interest here. For Nietzsche's early concern with art—and history
—has created, or supported, the presumption that the young
Nietzsche was essentially romantic. In fact, he was anti-romantic,
even in his first three books. This is an important point, and
we shall therefore link our discussions of each of these three
works with a brief contrast with some of the leading German
romantics.

To return to Schelling: in the end, he renounced the primacy
of aesthetic values and turned to religion as Novalis and Friedrich Schlegel had done earlier. Although Hegel had long since
buried Schelling in his history of philosophy, assigning him a
place of honor as his own immediate predecessor, the old Schelling made a spectacular return to public attention after Hegel's
death. Lecturing at the university of Berlin (Hegel's former
stronghold), Schelling now relegated his own earlier system, as
well as any moral or rational world-order, to the limbo of "negative" philosophy. A new "positive philosophy" is—so he claimed
—demanded by the individual "whom ultimate despair overpowers" and who is not satisfied with anything less than God
himself who is "the *really* highest good." God "must come to
meet with his help" the individual who "neither by ethical
action [Kant] nor by the life of contemplation [Hegel] can
eliminate the cleft." Through divine grace alone one may hope
for blessedness "which is *not deserved* and therefore also not
proportional, as Kant would have it, but can only be undeserved
and for that very reason incalculable and surpassing." "Negative philosophy may tell us in what blessedness consists, but it
does not help us to achieve it." [3] One can picture Hegel replying
—as he did when told that with mere thinking one could not
lure a dog away from a hot stove—that this was after all not
the task of philosophy.

---

[3] Schelling, *Philosophie der Mythologie* (*Werke*, II, 1), 566 f.—the transition
to *Philosophie der Offenbarung.*

Nietzsche and Kierkegaard shared Schelling's concern for the "ultimate despair" of the individual—but with a difference. Kierkegaard attended the lectures of the old Schelling and was impressed by his program, though not by its execution; and in his own work he later developed the theme Schelling had suggested. "Infinitely interested in his eternal happiness," Kierkegaard desired to "come into possession of it." [4] The main ideas shared by Kierkegaard and Schelling resulted, of course, from their common Christian heritage; but Kierkegaard followed the older man's approach quite closely, and his frequently unfair polemics against Hegel were based partly on Schelling's rancorous references to his former friend, against whom Schelling had developed a powerful *ressentiment*. And Schelling's contrast of a "negative" and "positive philosophy" has become the point of departure for modern existentialism and its polemics against Hegel's alleged preoccupation with mere essences.

Nietzsche may not have read Schelling's lectures, although Burckhardt, who had heard some of them, may conceivably have told him about them. As is well known, the young Nietzsche followed Schopenhauer rather than Schelling; and while he, too, rejected the conceptions of the rational and moral world-order, he could not follow Schelling and Kierkegaard in accepting an entire revealed religion on faith. Nietzsche's fundamental attitude and method barred him from this course: for Kierkegaard not only failed to question an incidental premise but abandoned philosophy altogether to "leap"—as he himself put it—into religion. While Nietzsche had not read Kierkegaard (Brandes called his attention to Kierkegaard in 1888, too late for him to acquire the works of the Dane), *Zarathustra* anticipates what would undoubtedly have been Nietzsche's reaction:

> Weariness that wants to reach the ultimate with one leap, with one fatal leap, a poor ignorant weariness that does not want to want any more: this created all gods and other worlds [Z 1 3].

In this respect, Nietzsche is closer to the Enlightenment than to Schelling and Kierkegaard: he would establish values without divine sanction; but unlike many of the thinkers of the Enlighten-

---

[4] *Concluding Unscientific Postscript,* transl. D. F. Swenson and W. Lowrie (1944), 20. His initial infatuation with Schelling in 1841 is reflected in the *Journals,* ed. A. Dru, 102, while his disappointment is registered on February 27, 1842 (104).

ment, he begins by doubting that *moral* values can be maintained in this manner. By way of contrast we shall briefly cite Kant's suggestive essay on the philosophy of history,[5] which seems typical of much of the Enlightenment. No extramundane deity makes its appearance, but the whole essay depends on a conception of nature that Nietzsche could not accept unquestioned. At the outset, Kant speaks of a "purpose of nature"; and in the "fourth axiom" the key conception of *"Antagonism"* is explained in these terms: "man wants concord; but nature knows better what is good for his species; she wants discord." In the seventh section, finally, the aim of nature is described more fully: "Nature has used the unsociability of man, and even of . . . large states . . . as a means . . . : by wars, by the overstrained and unrelenting armament for these, by the need which every state must thus feel in the end, even in the midst of peace, she drives first to imperfect attempts and eventually, after many devastations . . . to that which their reason might have told them even without so many sad experiences—namely, to leave the lawless level of the savages and to enter into a League of Nations [*Völkerbund*] in which every state, even the smallest one, may expect its security and rights not from its own power . . . but alone from this great *League of Nations.*" A similar appeal to the purpose of nature appears at the beginning of the *Grundlegung* where Kant seeks to establish moral values—and while it was, of course, Kant's own intention to found such values solely on rationality, we shall have occasion later to note that his conception of reason was as unempirical as his "nature": both rested, in the last analysis, on Kant's unquestioned faith in God.[6]

Though Kant's arguments are far more subtle and seasoned, his position is similar to that in Lessing's essay on the philosophy

---

[5] *Idee zu einer allgemeinen Geschichte in weltbürgerlicher Absicht* (1784).

[6] Vaihinger, *op. cit.*, claimed that Kant—especially in his *Opus postumum* —considered the idea of God a mere fiction. While he backed up this assertion with a number of quotations, E. Adickes showed later that Vaihinger's interpretation of these quotations depended on his considering them out of their context; and Adickes proved that Kant firmly believed in God even in the *Opus postumum. (Kants Opus postumum dargestellt und beurteilt,* 1920, 827 ff.) Vaihinger's interesting collection of quotations from Nietzsche—whom he claims as another "historical confirmation" of his own "Philosophy of the As-If"—also gives a misleading picture to the uninitiate who is apt to overlook the fact that he is sampling widely scattered notes, torn from their context.

of history, which antedated Kant's by four years.[7] Lessing assumed three stages in the moral education of mankind. The first, identified by him with the Old Testament, involved "education by means of immediate . . . punishments and rewards" in *this* life (§16). The second stage, attained in the New Testament, conceives of morality as "an inner purity of the heart, with an eye on *another* life" (§61). The third and highest stage, finally, is reached when mankind learns "to do the good . . . because it is the good, not because arbitrary rewards are offered for it" (§85). While Lessing seems to feel in the end that he has established moral values without supernatural sanction, his noble scheme, which invites comparison with Kant's, did not accomplish anything so spectacular. While man does the good merely because it is the good, he would not know what is good had it not been revealed by God. His valuations are still based on supernatural authority, and one need not be surprised that Lessing speaks in the end of "divine education" (§84) and "eternal providence" (§91).

Neither Lessing nor Kant had seriously questioned the existence of God: perhaps it would be misleading to say that they reintroduced God through the rear door, since God had really been in the back of their minds all along. They had merely tried to do without him and to forget about his existence for a moment—but the idea of God, like a repressed wish in psychoanalysis, was loath to be so forcibly ignored and made its reappearance under a new guise.

Nietzsche's inquiry as to whether values could be maintained

---

[7] Lessing, *Die Erziehung des Menschengeschlechts* (1780), cited according to sections. Two differences between Lessing's and Kant's essays seem noteworthy. First, while Kant, too, views history in terms of progress, he does not believe in progress along a straight line: he emphasizes conflict and strife and lays the foundation for later "dialectical" conceptions of progress. Secondly, while Kant, too, believes in a purpose of nature, this purpose is not external but immanent: thus the purpose of nature in fashioning cork oaks is not to furnish men with stoppers but to develop the cork oak itself. And—closely connected with this—the purpose is not a providential entity which is "known" to exist, but an indispensable *idea* apart from which nature—and history—are incomprehensible. This idea, however, is considered not a fiction (as in Vaihinger) but essentially rational; and rationality has lost none of the absoluteness which was associated with it by earlier thinkers who considered it God-given. (Cf. the second half of Kant's *Kritik der Urteilskraft*—a major source of Schelling's romantic Idealism.)

without supernatural sanctions was based on his "existential" questioning of God's existence: and because he *really* questioned it, he lacked Lessing's and Kant's easy conviction that our ancient values could be salvaged after the ancient God had been banished from the realm of philosophic thought. Even in his early works, he was concerned with the problem of maintaining values without recourse to "eternal providence" or the "purpose of nature"—but perhaps because moral values were so closely associated with transcendent sanctions, whether it be God or Plato's Idea of the Good, Nietzsche began his inquiries with aesthetic values.

The key conceptions of *The Birth of Tragedy* are the Apollinian and the Dionysian. Apollo represents the aspect of the classical Greek genius extolled by Winckelmann and Goethe: the power to create harmonious and measured beauty; the strength to shape one's own character no less than works of art; the "principle of individuation" (GT 1); the form-giving force, which reached its consummation in Greek sculpture. Dionysus, in Nietzsche's first book, is the symbol of that drunken frenzy which threatens to destroy all forms and codes; the ceaseless striving which apparently defies all limitations; the ultimate abandonment we sometimes sense in music.[8]

In *The Birth of Tragedy,* Nietzsche did not extol one at the expense of the other; but if he favors one of the two gods, it is Apollo. His thesis is that it took both to make possible the birth of tragedy, and he emphasizes the Dionysian only because he feels that the Apollinian genius of the Greeks cannot be fully understood apart from it. Against Schiller's analysis of "naïve" art, Nietzsche urges that "the Homeric 'naïveté' is to be understood only as the perfect victory of the Apollinian":

> Where we encounter the "naïve" in art, we have to recognize
> the highest effect of Apollinian culture—which always must

---

[8] In *The Birth of Tragedy,* the Apollinian power to give form is further associated with the creation of illusions, while the Dionysian frenzy carries with it a suggestion of blind will: in other words, both are colored by Schopenhauer's distinction of the world as will and representation. A similar contrast of the Apollinian and Dionysian could already be found in Schelling's *Philosophie der Offenbarung* (*Werke*, II, IV, 25). Following the precedent of Brinton, Morgan, and the English version of *The Decline of the West,* I render *Apollinisch* as "Apollinian."

first bring about the downfall of a Titans' empire and kill monsters [GT 3].

Only a generation that applauded Rousseau's conception of a paradisiac state of nature, says Nietzsche, could believe that Greek culture was a peaceful and idyllic Eden. In fact, culture is born of conflict, and the beauty of ancient Hellas must be understood in terms of a contest of two violently opposed forces. There is the onslaught of the Dionysian "fever" which was rampant everywhere "from Rome to Babylon," and when it was allowed to rage unchecked it led to "sexual licentiousness":

> . . . precisely the most savage beasts of nature were unleashed, including even that disgusting mixture of voluptuousness and cruelty which always seemed to me the real "witches' brew" [GT 2].

Only the Apollinian power of the Greeks was able to control this destructive disease, to harness the Dionysian flood, and to use it creatively.

This picture of the Dionysian, as a most destructive fever, is so far from its alleged glorification at the expense of the Apollinian that one may wonder how *The Birth of Tragedy* could ever have been so thoroughly misconstrued. The explanation, however, is easy enough. It has been overlooked that the Dionysus whom Nietzsche celebrated as his own god in his later writings is no longer the deity of formless frenzy whom we meet in Nietzsche's first book. Only the name remains, but later the Dionysian represents passion *controlled* as opposed to the extirpation of the passions which Nietzsche more and more associated with Christianity. The "Dionysus" in the Dionysus versus Apollo of Nietzsche's first book and the *"Dionysus versus the Crucified"* in the last line of Nietzsche's last book do not mean the same thing. The later Dionysus is the synthesis of the two forces represented by Dionysus and Apollo in *The Birth of Tragedy*—and thus Goethe, certainly not an anti-Apollinian, can appear in one of Nietzsche's last books as the perfect representative of what is now called Dionysian (G IX 49).

In *The Birth of Tragedy,* the Dionysian represents that negative and yet necessary dialectic element without which the creation of aesthetic values would be, according to Nietzsche, an impossibility. True to his method, he does not, to begin with, assume a divine providence or a purpose of nature—and lacking these, he seems to have no sanction for an absolute obligation or a moral "ought." He turns to aesthetic values which are not so firmly associated with a supernatural sanction and are conceivable without any element of obligation. One can speak of beauty without implying that anything ought to be beautiful or that anybody ought to create anything beautiful. Beauty can be construed as a factual quality which either is or is not present, and it can be approached descriptively rather than normatively. Nietzsche would describe it in terms of the two Greek gods: beauty is the monument of Apollo's triumph over Dionysus.

Developing the picture of the Dionysian fever, one can express Nietzsche's point in terms of a dialectical conception of health. It would be absurd to say that the work of healthy artists is *eo ipso* beautiful, while that of the ill must be ugly. Keats was consumptive, Byron had a clubfoot, Homer was blind and Beethoven deaf. Even Shakespeare and Goethe—Nietzsche thinks —must have experienced a profound defect: artistic creation is prompted by something which the artist *lacks*, by suffering rather than undisturbed good health, by "sicknesses as great stimulants of his life" (WM 1003).

> A Homer would have created no Achilles, a Goethe no Faust, had Homer been an Achilles and had Goethe been a Faust [GM III 4].

> I know no more heart-rending reading than Shakespeare: what must a man have suffered to have such a need of being a buffoon! [EH II 4].

> . . . It does not seem possible to be an artist and not to be sick [WM 811].[9]

These quotations are from Nietzsche's later works, but the same idea is developed in *The Birth of Tragedy*. Not only Achilles but the entire Olympian realm was born of a terrible privation: "To be able to live, the Greeks had to create these gods out of the most profound need" (GT 3). Their magnificent tragedies represent to Nietzsche's mind a yet unbroken reply to the vicissi-

---

[9] Cf. the last stanza of Heine's well-known *Schöpfungslieder:*

Disease was the most basic ground
Of my creative urge and stress;
Creating, I could convalesce,
Creating, I again grew sound.

For the complete text see my bilingual *Twenty German Poets.*

tudes of fortune, a triumphant response to suffering, and a celebration of life as "at bottom, in spite of all the alterations of appearances, indestructible, powerful, and joyous." Tragic art was the "comfort" which the Greeks created for themselves and which they needed because they were "uniquely capable of the tenderest and deepest suffering." Nietzsche envisages "the *sublime* as the artistic conquest of the horrible"; and he celebrates the Greek "who has looked with bold eyes into the dreadful destructive turmoil of so-called world-history as well as into the cruelty of nature" and, without yielding to resignation or to "a Buddhistic negation of the will," reaffirms life with the creation of works of art (GT 7).

Instead of proving himself in his first book as an unswerving follower of Schopenhauer—as has so often been taken for granted —Nietzsche discovers in Greek art a bulwark against Schopenhauer's pessimism. One can oppose the shallow optimism of so many Western thinkers and yet refuse to negate life. Schopenhauer's negativistic pessimism is rejected along with the superficial optimism of the popular Hegelians and Darwinists: one can face the terrors of history and nature with unbroken courage and say Yes to life.

In terms of health: Nietzsche—though he does not use exactly these expressions—defines health not as an accidental lack of infection but as the ability to overcome disease; and unlike Lessing's and Kant's conceptions of providence and nature, this idea of health is not unempirical. Even physiologically one might measure health in terms of the amount of sickness, infection, and disease with which an organism can deal successfully (cf. M 202).

Thus Goethe's health consisted in his triumphant weathering of any illness that might befall him. Born so sickly that he was not expected to live, he overcame his sickliness and in later life withstood illness after illness, often being severely stricken but always recovering. That this physical history has a striking parallel in Goethe's artistic career, that his vitality often seemed crushed by profound despair and yet roused itself to ever new creation—is well known and seems to have made a profound impression on Nietzsche, in whose mind Goethe was ever present.[10]

---

[10] The unparalleled impact of Goethe's personality, life, and works on nineteenth-century German thought can hardly be exaggerated. His effect on Nietzsche will become more and more apparent in later chapters. Cf.

We are not presented with an elaborate theory of aesthetic value, but we find that the creation of beauty is envisaged as the response of a fundamentally healthy organism to the challenge of disease. Those who have never faced disease and suffering have no need of producing beauty—on that note *The Birth of Tragedy* closes: "How much did these people have to suffer to be able to become so beautiful." These ideas Nietzsche never renounced, and he even sharpened his point in his later writings: "Whatever does not destroy me makes me stronger" (G I 6). "One must need to be strong, else one will never become strong" (G IX 38, 14). "For the healthy type, sickness may be an energetic *stimulant* to life, to more life" (EH I 2). Here it is assumed that to meet a challenge one must, and does, develop a strength greater than that which one had previously—a hypothesis that is strongly colored by Lamarckism and does not preclude scientific examination, although science might not bear it out.

Nietzsche's theory fits at least some empirical data very well, especially the close relationship between artistic genius and physical or mental disease. Keats and Schiller, Kleist and Hölderlin, Byron and Baudelaire, Homer and Beethoven, and Dostoevsky and Nietzsche himself all possessed that health which responds even to the severest penalization and to nameless suffering with defiant creativity. The premature death of the consumptive poets, the suicide of Kleist and the eventual madness of Hölderlin and Nietzsche bear witness to the final triumph of disease: yet they do not disprove the claim that in the previous struggle the prospective victim showed a strength far beyond that of normal men.

Nietzsche's turn of mind is thus dialectical in two ways. First, in the very limited sense which was developed in the discussion of his method: he refused to accept "rough-fisted" answers and insisted on treating the most venerable dogmas as questionable hypotheses. Secondly, it now appears that his thought is dialectical also insofar as he shows a special appreciation of the negative:

also my "Goethe and the History of Ideas," in the *Journal of the History of Ideas*, October 1949, and in my *From Shakespeare to Existentialism*, and Barker Fairley, "Nietzsche and Goethe," in the *Bulletin of the John Rylands Library*, Manchester, 1934. Fairley says little of Goethe's importance for Nietzsche's later philosophy, but shows how "Nietzsche in his twenties was soaked in Goethe" (302). See also the Index to my edition of *The Birth of Tragedy*: the book is full of Goethe quotations, although Goethe is not always cited by name.

even as his view of philosophic systems was developed through an insight into their dangers and disadvantages, he accounted for the birth of beauty in terms of conflict and a triumph of Apollo over Dionysus. The full extent of the elaborately dialectic scheme of *The Birth of Tragedy* will become apparent only when the role of Socrates is analyzed in the last chapter.

The systematic weakness of this account of aesthetic value is revealed when one asks whether Nietzsche would make value a function of interest. Kant and Schopenhauer had described the aesthetic experience as definitively free from interest—and their main reason must be sought in their conviction that interests are essentially utilitarian, hedonistic, or moral, while the concern for beauty is not. It is also noteworthy that in the relevant passages only the receptive experience is considered and no reference is made to the creation of works of art.[11] Nietzsche, on the other hand, concentrates on the creative aesthetic experience, and he seems to imply that man has a vital interest in the beautiful which is somehow different from the other, "psychological" interests that modern writers have in mind, much as Kant did, when they speak of interest in the context of value theory. Nietzsche, however, fails to elucidate this point.

One might, of course, distinguish "physiological" interests from "psychological" ones, if the latter were defined as essentially involving consciousness. The body needs and requires certain substances and conditions to function normally: it has a "physiological interest" in such things as water, air, calcium, thyroid, and certain minimum climatic conditions. It might further be maintained that these interests are, on the whole, shared by all human beings, while the "psychological interests" differ vastly from one individual to another. If beauty were then considered a function of human interest, it would make a decisive difference whether this interest were "psychological" or "physiological"— in the first case, but not in the second, we should be confronted by relativism, and beauty would be reduced merely to a matter of individual taste. This, however, does not seem to be the view

---

[11] Cf. Kant, *Kritik der Urteilskraft*, §§1–5, 41 f.: Kant's conception of the genius, his contrast of the beautiful and the sublime (to which Nietzsche's contrast of the Apollinian and Dionysian is indebted), and his way of treating art and nature in the same book, which so impressed Goethe— these suggest that Kant had insights that came close to exploding the neat but all-too-narrow confines of his conceptualistic symmetries.

underlying *The Birth of Tragedy*. It might then be maintained
that the human organism, when its normal functioning is interfered with by severe physical defects, disease, or suffering, may
sometimes have a "physiological interest" in making a complex
response that is commonly referred to as "artistic creation," and
that the distinguishing characteristic of the objects fashioned
under such circumstances would be "beauty." Although Nietzsche's later philosophy has sometimes been labeled as "physiologism," the construction just offered seems a caricature of his
final as well as of his earlier philosophy. Nietzsche never defined
his view in terms of interest, but one may anticipate that his
conception of beauty—and indeed of the value of what he was
soon to call culture—depended on a kind of interest that differs
from the two types here suggested. Further elucidation, however,
must wait upon the introduction of the will to power.

II

During the year that followed the publication of *The Birth of
Tragedy,* Nietzsche published the first of his *Untimely Meditations:* a temporary departure from his value problem, yet in
many ways a characteristic anticipation of his later writings. The
object of Nietzsche's polemic is the "pseudo-culture" of the
cultural philistines who seemed to him to have become predominant in Germany after the victorious war against France.
He attacks the smug assumption that the military victory implies
any superiority of German culture—in fact, he derides any *"deifi-
cation of success"* (7)—and he foresees *"the defeat—yes, the extirpation of the German spirit in favor of the 'German Reich' "*
(1). He insists that "strict war discipline, natural courage and
endurance, superiority of the leaders, unity and obedience among
the led . . . have nothing to do with culture" and he explains:
"culture is above all the unity of the artistic style in all the
expressions of the life of a people" (1). This definition was later
taken up and developed by Spengler, though Spengler could be
criticized by quoting the sentence immediately following Nietzsche's definition: "Much knowledge and learning is neither a
necessary means of culture nor a sign of it and, if necessary, gets
along famously with the opposition of culture, barbarism: i.e.,
the lack of style or the chaotic confusion of all styles." This

bedlam, says Nietzsche, characterizes postwar Germany. At the same time, he is convinced that "culture" is the only end which can give meaning to our lives:

> To our scholars, strangely enough, even the most pressing question does not occur: to what end is their work . . . useful? Surely not to earn a living or hunt for positions of honor? No, truly not. . . . What good *at all* is science if it has no time for culture? . . . whence, whither, wherefore is all science, if it is not meant to lead to culture? [8].

As often, Nietzsche chooses a person to represent the outlook he opposes—this time, David Strauss, the author of a celebrated *Life of Jesus,* whose more recent book on *The Old and the New Faith* was just then enjoying a huge popular success. Nietzsche's attack, *David Strauss: The Confessor and Writer* (U 1), while characteristically vehement, was not motivated by any personal feelings; and thus Nietzsche could write his friend, Carl von Gersdorff, on February 11, 1874: "Yesterday David Strauss was buried in Ludwigsburg. I hope very much that I have not aggravated the end of his life, and that he died without even knowing of me." Clearly, Strauss himself had been incidental to Nietzsche's mind, and even the book *The Old and the New Faith* had not been his ultimate target. The motivation of the attack is discussed in Nietzsche's last book, in a passage which represents an important clue to his other polemics as well:

> My practice of war can be summed up in four propositions. First: I only attack causes that are victorious; I may even wait until they become victorious.
> Second: I only attack causes against which I would not find allies, so that I stand alone—so that I compromise myself alone. —I have never taken a step publicly that did not compromise me: that is *my* criterion of doing right.
> Third: I never attack persons; I merely avail myself of the person as of a strong magnifying glass that allows one to make visible a general but creeping and elusive calamity. Thus I attacked David Strauss—more precisely, the *success* of a senile book with the "cultured" people in Germany: I caught this culture in the act.
> Thus I attacked Wagner—more precisely, the falseness, the half-couth instincts of our "culture" which mistakes the subtle for the rich, and the late for the great.
> Fourth: I only attack things when every personal quarrel is excluded, when any background of bad experiences is lacking.

On the contrary, attack is in my case a proof of good will, some-times even of gratitude [EH 1 7].

The irony of Nietzsche's style in *Ecce Homo* notwithstanding, it is surely true that what he had seen in Strauss' book was the incarnation of the *Zeitgeist:* unproductive smugness, intellectual snobbery, superficial assimilation of great works of art and new scientific theories, myopic criticism and patronizing praise of even the greatest genius, comparisons of Haydn with an "honest soup" and of Beethoven's quartets with candy, a mixture of bombastic, didactic periods with coy colloquialisms, and the attempt every-where to strike a pleasant mean, though "between two vices virtue does not always dwell, but all too often only weakness and lame impotence" (11). What enraged Nietzsche most was Strauss' comfortable and untroubled renunciation of Christianity, coupled with an easy conviction that Darwin was one of mankind's great-est benefactors and that—though Strauss gave no reasons for this —traditional values could of course be maintained.

He proclaims with admirable frankness that he is no longer a Christian, but he does not want to disturb any comfortableness of any kind; it seems contradictory to him to found an associ-ation to destroy an association—which really is not so contra-dictory. With a certain tough satisfaction he clothes himself in the hairy garments of our ape genealogists and praises Darwin as one of the greatest benefactors of mankind—but abashed we see that his ethics is quite untouched [7].

Strauss has not even learned that . . . preaching morals is as easy as giving reasons for morals is difficult; it should rather have been his task seriously to explain and to derive the phe-nomena of human goodness, mercy, love, and self-abnegation, which after all exist as a matter of fact, from his Darwinistic presuppositions: yet he preferred to flee the task of *explanation* by a leap into imperatives. In this leap it even happens to him that he also jumps, with an easy mind, over Darwin's funda-mental axiom. "Forget," says Strauss, "at no time that you are a human being and not a mere *Naturwesen*" [7].

These sentences, rather than the protests against the bad taste of Strauss' remarks about Jesus and the early Christians, or Nietzsche's scorn of the ill-chosen metaphors and the miserable style of the man who was then so widely hailed as a German *Klassiker,* establish the importance of this *Meditation* for Nietz-sche's own thought. The problem of the old faith and the new, the challenge of Darwin, and the sanction and derivation of moral values: these are the themes of most of Nietzsche's later works.

While no exhaustive analysis of the first *Meditation* is possible here—and it yields much less, philosophically, than either *The Birth of Tragedy* or the second *Meditation*—it should be mentioned that the essay contains a suggestive self-portrait of Nietzsche, and that he here identifies himself with the great critic, poet, and philosopher of the German Enlightenment, Lessing. The fact, moreover, that Friedrich Schlegel, a leader of the early romantic movement in Germany, wrote a remarkable essay on Lessing, affords us a rare opportunity for a brief comparison of Nietzsche with the famous romantic.

Scorning Strauss' admiration for Lessing, Nietzsche says:

> . . . Not one of the great German writers is as popular with the small German writers as is Lessing; and yet they shall not be thanked for it; for what do they praise in Lessing? [4].

This sounds much like Schlegel, who spends the greater part of his essay insisting that Lessing's popularity goes hand in hand with a complete misunderstanding of the nature of his greatness —but as we read on, we may wonder whether Nietzsche is not perhaps including Schlegel in the mass of "the small German writers." What they admire in Lessing, says Nietzsche, is this:

> First, his universality: he is critic and poet, archaeologist and philosopher, dramatist and theologian. Secondly, "this unity of the writer and the man, of the brain and the heart."

Since these same two points were later applied to Nietzsche by his own admirers, his commentary is of special interest:

> The last point applies to every great writer, sometimes even to the small ones; for even a petty brain gets along famously with a petty heart. And the first point, this universality, is in itself nothing excellent at all, especially since in Lessing's case it was only a necessity.

Thus two of the most characteristic ideals of the early German romantics are rejected as not in themselves admirable—and one may note that Schlegel, in his discussion of Lessing, had emphasized "this *mixture of literature, polemics, wit, and philosophy. It is just this mixture by which* . . . *he enthralls me.*" [12] Nietz-

---

[12] *Friedrich Schlegel 1794–1802: Seine Prosaischen Jugendschriften,* ed. J. Minor (2nd ed., 1906), II, 416.

sche, on the other hand, finds Lessing's excellence elsewhere—
in his courage, enlightenment, and intellectual integrity which
sacrificed the comfort of cherished illusions. His universality—
unlike Goethe's or Leonardo's, which issued from strength as the
overflow of a rich personality—was but a weakness inspired by
want:

> . . . These Lessing enthusiasts . . . have not the slightest un-
> derstanding of that consuming need which drove him through
> life, and to this very "universality"—they have no feeling for
> how such a man burned down too quickly like a flame, no indig-
> nation that the meanest narrowness and wretchedness of his
> environment, and especially of his scholarly contemporaries,
> should have troubled, tortured, and stifled one glowing so ten-
> derly—yes, that just this much praised universality ought to
> awaken profound pity. "Be sorry," Goethe shouts at us, "for the
> extraordinary man that he had to live in such a miserable age
> that he had to exert himself polemically all the time."

This romanticized portrait of Lessing bears a close resem-
blance to the Nietzsche picture which was later developed by
the *George Kreis*—a picture, by the way, which brings to mind
Schlegel's comment on Lessing: *"He himself was worth more
than all his talents.* In his individuality lay his greatness." [13]
Nietzsche, however, is not at all willing to discount Lessing's
enlightened views; and the romanticized features of his portrait
are precisely what Nietzsche did *not* admire and what he considered "nothing excellent at all," a profound weakness—in other
words, what he was later to condemn as "romantic" and distinguish from the "Dionysian."

Schlegel could admire Lessing only after disposing of his
philosophic and critical ideas: in fact, his essay of 1797 remained,
characteristically, a fragment in which he never got beyond the
negative stage of pointing out what was not great in Lessing. In
1801, however, Schlegel attempted to conclude his essay, and he
succeeded in making clear what he did admire in Lessing. He
begins with a sonnet, entitled "Something that Lessing said"—
and now it becomes quite clear that the great proponent of the
Enlightenment is acceptable only insofar as it is assumed that in
the end he renounced his enlightened views. "When even chilly
doubters speak as prophets," we are told,

---

[13] *Ibid.*, 151. For George's conception of Nietzsche, see the Prologue, above.

Then, truly, a new era must begin,
Then shall the dawn yet give us great delight,
Then are the arts renewed to novel height,
And man can break his petty discipline.

"There is a new evangel yet to come."
Thus Lessing said, and yet the stupid herds
Did not detect the portal thus unlocked.
However, of his projects the whole sum,
All that he thought and searched and fought and mocked,
Is not as precious as are these few words.

"*This* it is; this makes him so dear to me; and if he had said nothing of significance, except this one word, I should have to honor and love him on this account. And just *he* had to say it —he who lived entirely for pure understanding, who was almost without imagination, except in his wit; he had to say it out of the midst of the vulgarity which surrounded him so closely—as a voice in the wilderness. . . . I honor Lessing for the *great tendency* [*Tendenz*] of his philosophic spirit and for the *symbolic form* of his works." [14]

It was thus that Stefan George, a century later, envisaged Nietzsche. Again, the "chilly doubter" was admired only because he had also spoken as a prophet; again the interpreter contrasts his own vision to that of the *"blöde Rotte"* (Schlegel's phrase); and again a renewal of the arts is hoped for. The thinker is reduced to a voice in the wilderness; the content of his message is discounted; and only the "great tendency" of his spirit and "the symbolic form of his works" is honored. This parallel is indeed striking—but the contrast between Schlegel and Nietzsche is no less evident. For what Nietzsche admired in Lessing was not the eventual turn to a Spinozistic pantheism for which Schlegel gave him credit[15] and of which Nietzsche knew nothing: Nietzsche revered Lessing as "the most honest theoretical man"—to cite the conception of Lessing already found in *The Birth of Tragedy* (GT 15). And when Nietzsche later discovered Spinoza

---

[14] *Ibid.*, 415 f.

[15] Cf. Johanna Krüger, *Friedrich Schlegels Bekehrung zu Lessing* (1913). She concludes: "The fragmentist Schlegel, who occasionally has lightning-like flashes of insight at his disposal, is not like the fragmentist Lessing, whose seemingly accidental and unsystematic thoughts were backed up by a full spiritual totality" (99). One could substitute Nietzsche's name for Lessing's without detracting from the truth of this statement.

for himself, it was not the pantheism, so admired by the German romantics, that thrilled him:

> I am utterly amazed, utterly enchanted! I have a *precursor*, and what a precursor! I hardly knew Spinoza: that I should have turned to him just *now*, was inspired by "instinct." Not only is his over-all tendency like mine—namely to make knowledge [*Erkenntnis*] the *most powerful* affect—but in five main points of his doctrine I recognize myself; this most unusual and loneliest thinker is closest to me precisely in *these* matters: he denies the freedom of the will, teleology, the moral world-order, the unegoistic, and evil. Even though the divergencies are admittedly tremendous, they are due more to the difference in time, culture, and science. *In summa:* my lonesomeness [*Einsamkeit*] . . . is now at least a twosomeness [*Zweisamkeit*].[16]

Thus Nietzsche, too, admires Lessing and Spinoza; but this superficial similarity cloaks a profound difference—and this is true of most of the parallels between Nietzsche and the German romantics.

Returning to the passage from the first *Meditation* which we have been considering, we find that Nietzsche's thoughts wander from Lessing to Winckelmann, and then to Schiller—and his remark about the latter is aimed, at least in part, at the German romantics who so bitterly attacked Schiller: "And if you took Goethe's friendship out of this famished life which was hunted to death—it would have been your part to extinguish it even sooner!" Then, addressing himself to a wider public, Nietzsche proceeds:

> Not in one of the life works of your great geniuses have you helped. . . . In spite of you they created their works; against you they turned their attacks; and thanks to you they collapsed too early, before completing their work, broken or rendered unconscious by their fights.

The similarity of this last passage to George's previously cited Nietzsche poems raises the question as to whether the young Nietzsche shared George's and Schlegel's romantic dreams of a regeneration of and through the arts. In fact, Nietzsche appended such a vision to *The Birth of Tragedy*—in the concluding paragraphs, which he later regretted (GT-V 6) and which had not been part of the original version. Actually, these passages were a

---

[16] This first ecstatic reaction, on a postcard to Overbeck (July 30, 1881), is at one with Nietzsche's later works and notes.

reflection of Wagner's neo-romantic aspirations, and are not in harmony with Nietzsche's own basic intentions. And one may agree with Josef Hofmiller when he says in a different context: "It is not as if he had deserted *from* Wagner. Rather one could say that he deserted *to* Wagner and returned to himself after a few years." [17] Nor was it only after his break with Wagner that Nietzsche abjured this romantic vision, but already in his second book, the *Meditation* on Strauss. At the moment when the young Nietzsche turns from Lessing to draw a deliberate parallel to his own aspirations, the romantic coloring which forebodes George's poems disappears, the primacy of art and aesthetic values is renounced—and one marvels that Wagner should have loved the essay and failed to sense the threat. Today we cannot help finding here the announcement of the impending break with the composer, and a hint concerning the nature of Nietzsche's later works, from *Human, All-Too-Human* on:

> Indeed, we need a Lessing, Goethe already cried; and woe unto
> . . . the whole aesthetic kingdom of heaven, when once the
> young tiger whose restless strength becomes visible everywhere
> in swelling muscles and in the glance of his eyes, rises to seek
> his prey!

We have already noted that the early romantics, too, later gave up the primacy of the aesthetic realm—to subordinate it to religion. That, however, is not what "the young tiger" has in mind. His comment on a line from Strauss' book foreshadows his ambitions:

> "It does not even occur to me to want to destroy any church."
> —But why not, Herr Magister? What matters is only that one is
> able to do it [3].

III

The second *Meditation* is entitled *Of the Use and Disadvantage of History for Life,*[18] and the Preface refers to it as a "meditation about the value and disvalue of history." Nietzsche's object is

---

[17] "Nietzsche," 96; cf. *Friedrich Nietzsche,* 25. Characteristically, Nietzsche remarks elsewhere in his first *Meditation,* in one of his few early references to romanticism, that "the brewage of fantastic . . . philosophies . . . and the carnival of all gods and myths which the romantics concocted" around the turn of the century deserved to be repudiated (U I 2; cf. VII, 231).

[18] "History" here means the study of history, not the course of events itself.

plainly to gauge this value in terms of use and disadvantage for life. The continuity with *The Birth of Tragedy* becomes apparent when one recalls how the Greeks had there been pictured as creating beauty "to be able to live." In retrospect, one may say that Nietzsche had even then gauged aesthetic worth in terms of use for life—but only now does this standard become fully explicit.

Historically, the second *Meditation* is of special interest because of its decisive impact—already referred to in the Prologue —on the *George Kreis:* for in this essay Nietzsche proposes an approach to history which was later cultivated by George's disciples in their many studies of "great men," of which F. Gundolf's books on Shakespeare, Goethe, and Caesar are probably the best known. The essay, however, is no less important to the student of Nietzsche's development. It is here that Nietzsche unmistakably abandons his previous preoccupation with art to turn to values outside the aesthetic realm, and that he begins to deal with the problems posed by Darwinism. In the essay on Strauss, he had not yet been ready to tackle Darwin: the denial of any cardinal difference between man and animal had not seemed comforting or beneficial to him, but he was not prepared to deal with it *en passant*. In the second and third *Meditation* he returns to this question; and he is taken to the point where he begins to realize the inadequacy of his early philosophy.

The essay on history has some familiar features. At the outset, man is contrasted with a herd of cattle which lives in the moment, forgets, and may thus be happier than we are—a contrast also found in Kant's previously cited essay on history. For Kant, Hegel, and Nietzsche—no less than Schopenhauer and Burckhardt—history is decidedly not the ground of happiness.[19]

While the stress on suffering is familiar, Nietzsche's version of it is distinguished from Kant's and Hegel's by its vivid personal coloring, which gives his philosophy that characteristic unacademic flavor to which his readers react so diversely: to one

---

[19] Cf. Kant's previously cited concept of "antagonism." That Nietzsche was conscious of his affinity to Kant on this point is evidenced by the following quotation: "Kant says: 'these sentences . . . I subscribe to with full conviction: *il solo principie motore dell 'uomo è il dolore.'*" (WM 698) Hegel's remark, in the Preface to the lectures on the Philosophy of History, is well known: "World history is not the ground of happiness. The periods of happiness are empty pages."

author this personal and unconventional quality makes Nietzsche's thought an "oasis of life in the desert," [20] while to another
it is evidence that "Nietzsche . . . was never really house-
broken." [21] Some feel that it is ungentlemanly to make so much
of suffering; others may think that "where all is rotten it is a
man's work to cry stinking fish." [22]

Nietzsche's emphasis on suffering was not due to any *fin de
siècle* infatuation with the sordid. On the basis of his historical
studies, possibly to some extent under Burckhardt's influence,
and on the grounds of his personal experience, he was impressed
with the terrors and "cruelty" of life. Physically, he experienced
ever again "the tortures that go with an uninterrupted three-day
migraine and agonizing phlegm-retching" (EH 1 1). And he was
never able to overcome the fierce anguish he felt when Wagner's
influence turned out to be the opposite of what he had hoped
it might come to be. Whether Nietzsche made too much of his
personal suffering and was led to a serious misunderstanding of
the world, need not be decided at this point. Perhaps we can
today understand Nietzsche where many of his readers and interpreters in the years before 1914 either did not see any plausibility
at all or read into Nietzsche's work a Darwinistic optimism and
a cheerful faith in "evolutionary progress" that is just about the
opposite of what Nietzsche had in mind.

In *The Birth of Tragedy,* Nietzsche emphasized the horrors
of history as a challenge that may lead the weak to negate life,
while it leads the strong to create the beautiful. He might conceivably have asserted in his second *Meditation* that history is
valuable insofar as it plunges us into profound despair and thus
prompts the strong and healthy to counteract their suffering by
creating beauty. The study of history would then be a poisonous
stimulant, a tribulation that will either destroy or toughen the
mind.

Nietzsche, however, does not approach his subject as a province of a previously conceived system, and his open mind saves
him from the absurdities of the position just indicated. Instead
of bringing to his work the presuppositions of his previous work

---

[20] Morgan, *op. cit.,* vii.
[21] Brinton, *op. cit.,* 231.
[22] Bradley, *Appearance and Reality,* xv. Bradley, of course, was not referring
to Nietzsche.

as unquestionable premises, he is ever willing to revise his theories in the face of new evidence. Thus he does not construe the value of history to fit his more or less casual remarks on history in his first book.

The three key concepts of the essay on history are the "historical," the "unhistorical," and the "supra-historical" rather than the more famous categories of "monumentalistic," "antiquarian," and "critical" history; and the lengthy development of the five reasons why the hypertrophy of the historical sense is disadvantageous for life is altogether of subordinate importance. "Monumentalistic" history, to put it briefly, means the concentration on the heroes of the past in an effort to derive comfort and inspiration from the fact that man is capable of greatness, contemporary mediocrity notwithstanding.[23] "Antiquarian" history means the pious and reverent consolidation of our knowledge of the past, which is considered as an object of respect simply on account of its age. "Critical" history, finally, turns the historian into a judge who passes sentence on the course of past events, without illusion or mercy. In each instance Nietzsche dwells both on the use and disadvantage of such history for life. Of more fundamental importance, however, is the question of the value of the "historical" as such—and this is tackled in terms of a contrast first with the "unhistorical" and then with the "supra-historical"; and in the end "monumentalistic" history, though not explicitly recalled by that name, receives a new significance.

The value of the "historical" and "unhistorical" is analyzed at first in terms of happiness and suffering. The study of history does not, *prima facie*, make us happy; rather it tends to make us unhappy. The "historical," in the form of memory, seems to

---

[23] This conception is closely related to Goethe's epigram, which Nietzsche cites twice during this period (U I 2; VII, 5): "The best part of history is the enthusiasm it begets." (*Betrachtungen im Sinne der Wanderer.*) Cf. also Goethe's secular conception of "the 'community of saints' *we* profess." (Letter to K. F. Zelter, June 18, 1831.) The Preface of Nietzsche's *Meditation* on history opens with a quotation from Goethe, and Goethe is cited over half a dozen times in the essay itself. The conception of the "supra-historical," which will be considered below in this chapter, was probably inspired, in large measure, by Goethe. An elaborate discussion of Goethe's attitude toward history (without reference to Nietzsche) may be found in F. Meinecke, *Die Entstehung des Historismus* II (1936), chapter x, "Goethe," 480–631. Cf. also Karl Viëtor, *Goethe* (1949), 484–503.

prevent us from being happy. "In the smallest . . . as in the greatest happiness, it is always the same factor that makes happiness happiness; the ability to forget . . . to feel unhistorically while it lasts" (1). Now it may be objected that memories may be enchanting, and that in dark moments we recall the past to achieve some degree of happiness. This, in fact, is Nietzsche's next point: *"The unhistorical and the historical are equally needed for the health of an individual, a people, and a culture."* In everyday language: men must "know how to forget at the right time as well as how to remember at the right time" (1).

So far Nietzsche is able to apply the standards of life and health. A complete lack of memory would incapacitate man for life. The "historical," in the widest sense of that word, is necessary for life, and this is its value. If man would remember everything, however, if he were only "historical" and not at all "unhistorical," i.e., able to forget also, he would again be incapacitated for life. Both are necessary. The lack of the "historical" in the narrower sense, i.e., of the awareness of one's past history, would similarly constitute not only a statistical abnormality but a defect that, in direct proportion to its extent, would destroy the chances of the organism to survive. A people with absolutely no memory of their past would be unable to govern themselves successfully, to abide by a proven way of life, and to keep the law; a culture with no traditions, with no memory of past techniques or customs, would be similarly incapacitated. On the other hand, a people or a culture without the ability to forget would be unable to make decisions, to act, and to be creative.

Much of this essay is satisfied with various applications of these considerations. Their banality does not deter Nietzsche: he is eager to criticize the monstrous preoccupation of his age with historical research; he offers his polemics against an education that tells man more about the past than he can possibly digest; he shows the disadvantages of what he calls "an excess of history" or, in more nearly physiological language, the "hypertrophy" of "the historical sense in our time" (1).

His own calling he conceives as that of a doctor; for, as he said of Plato, Nietzsche himself also "received from the apology of Socrates the decisive thought of how a philosopher ought to behave toward man: as their physician, as a gadfly on the neck of man" (IV, 404). He first attempts a diagnosis and then tries to effect a cure, if possible. As a mere "herald and precursor" (J 44) of the philosophers of the future, Nietzsche attains greatness through his diagnoses rather than through his prescriptions. His imperatives, however, generally resemble those of a doctor who tells his patients what to do to be cured, and they are thus essentially different from, say, Kant's.

Kant's Categorical Imperative would permit of the following hypothetical formulation, without any injustice to Kant's thought: do this, if you want to be rational! The condition here is of a kind that seemed to Kant sufficiently unique to warrant the name "Categorical Imperative." This imperative depends, of course, on an analysis of reason and rationality; and the most basic and profound weakness of Kant's moral philosophy may be found in his failure to offer such an analysis.[24] As it is, Kant's conception of reason is decidedly not naturalistic. It is not based on any empirical account of the differences between man and the animals, or of what Max Scheler has aptly called the *Sonderstellung*, the exceptional position, of man in the cosmos.[25] Kant's ethics, which depends on his unempirical notion of reason, must be considered equally unnaturalistic.

Nietzsche's prescriptions are, in Kant's language, hypothetical imperatives and do not involve any absolute obligation. If a man does not want to be healthy, the most that can be said against him is that he is diseased to the marrow or, in Nietzsche's later terminology, decadent. The criterion of naturalism should be found in the sanction of valuations or moral imperatives. In Nietzsche's early value theory the sanction is, unlike Kant's, naturalistic. No principles are invoked that are not subject to investigation by the natural sciences. Certain practices will lead to disaster without requiring the intervention of supernatural

---

[24] It would seem that the analysis, had it been made, would have shown that Kant's conception of reason did not bear out his moral philosophy. Three references to the *Grundlegung* may suggest very briefly what is meant. The four "examples," which Kant adduces to show that a breach of the Categorical Imperative would involve a contradiction, do not demonstrate any logical contradiction; and Kant's conception of reason does not make clear what, if any, other kind of contradiction there might be. Secondly, Kant's notion of the "dignity" of the individual is not borne out by his idea that reason is essentially impersonal; rather, it seems to imply the doctrine that reason permits of individuation. The conception of "practical interest," finally, rests on the assumption that reason can "induce" action by becoming a *Bewegungsgrund*—a complete mystery according to Kant's own candid admission.

[25] *Die Stellung des Menschen im Kosmos* (1928), 9 ff.

powers—and the hypertrophy of the historical sense, for example, may well lead us to natural destruction.

Nietzsche's difficulties in this essay arise from his consideration of the "supra-historical." With the "historical" and "unhistorical" he had been able to deal in terms of life and health, not profoundly perhaps, nor brilliantly, but apparently to his own satisfaction. The "supra-historical point of view," however, threatens to upset his entire scheme. What, then, is the "supra-historical"? Nietzsche imagines the question put to a number of people "whether they would wish to live through the last ten or twenty years once more." He is sure that everybody would answer "No" —but for different reasons. From the "historical" point of view, people would decline because to them applies what "David Hume says derisively: 'And from the dregs of life hope to receive / What the first sprightly running could not give.' " [25a] In Nietzsche's words, they "believe that the meaning of existence will come to light progressively in the course of its *process*." The "historical man" has faith in the future. The "supra-historical" man, on the other hand, is the one "who does not envisage salvation in the process but for whom the world is finished in every single moment and its end [*Ende*] attained. What could ten new years teach that the past could not teach?" (1).

The value or disvalue of this "supra-historical" outlook cannot be determined as easily as that of the "historical" or "unhistorical," both of which were evidently required for life and health. Tentatively, Nietzsche juxtaposes it to life as "wisdom" and apparently closes the discussion by intimating that his concern is only with the study of "history for the sake of *life*" and that he can, therefore, afford to disregard the "supra-historical" (1). The problem touched here is, however, of supreme importance and actually nothing less than *the* problem of *Historismus,* which was later to be developed by Ernst Troeltsch, Benedetto Croce, and Friedrich Meinecke. Nietzsche's long polemic against the hypertrophy of the historical sense is not nearly as important as, and receives what significance it has from, this problem in which philosophy of history and theory of values meet: whether there are genuinely supra-historical values or whether all values

---

[25a] The quotation is actually from John Dryden's *Aureng-Zebe,* Act IV, 1, and the original has "think," not "hope."

are merely historical phenomena which are valid only in a certain place and time. The relation of the "historical" and "supra-historical" thus involves the problem of the relativity of values.

In *The Birth of Tragedy,* moral values were evidently not considered "supra-historical," but aesthetic values appeared to be, in a sense, independent of historical change: if the Apollinian power to master suffering and disease was not a supernatural gift, it might be construed physiologically. Now Nietzsche asks whether beauty is perhaps not "infra-historical" but "supra-historical"—not beneath historical change but above and beyond it. If the beauty of Greece is still beauty to us, is not its independence of time rather different from that of the human anatomy? Is there not a decisive difference between biological data and works of art? Approaching this problem with an open mind, without the bias of any previous commitment, Nietzsche could hardly fail to see the plausibility of this distinction. Being a person of aesthetic sensitivity, he was aware of the fact that a work of art elicits a response fundamentally different from anything the human organism produces through its more usual physiological processes. Therefore, it should not be overlooked that Nietzsche, after trying to get away from the "supra-historical" at the beginning of his essay on history, returns to this subject later on in the same *Meditation.*[26]

In the middle of his exposition, where he speaks of the "value of history," we find a sudden recognition of the value of the supra-historical. Nietzsche declares that he "hopes" of history "that its value is just this, to circumscribe . . . an everyday melody . . . , to elevate it, to intensify it into a comprehensive symbol." While this is merely a "hope," it is plain that Nietzsche does not look at history as a naturalistic (biological) sequence: for naturalistic events as such are not "symbols." Instead Nietzsche would look at history as a work of art.

The "wisdom" of the supra-historical point of view thus seems to have been absorbed by the historical attitude no less than the "unhistorical" ability to forget had been absorbed earlier. The

---

[26] Löwith, *Jacob Burckhardt,* 35 ff., dedicates a section to "The Use and Disadvantage of Remembering and Forgetting" and paraphrases the beginning of Nietzsche's *Meditation.* His account, however, ends with Nietzsche's initial remarks on the "supra-historical"; from there the author proceeds immediately to *Zarathustra* and a contrast with Burckhardt.

historian must not only be able to forget and to select from millions of events the few worth remembering: he should also have faith that this knowledge has an additional value inasmuch as these events, or some of them, are "symbols." Yet this point lacks precision. Is this a "hope" only? Nietzsche speaks of sensing "a whole world of deep meaning, power, and beauty" (6), without making clear of what exactly historical events are supposed to be symbols and whether this value of history is still naturalistic. Toward the end of the essay, however, we find a few statements that suggest the course his answers would have to take.

In an extended polemic against the "influence" of Hegel—less against Hegel's own philosophy—Nietzsche denounces "naked admiration for success" and the "idolatry of the factual" as leading to a Yes to "every power, be it a government, public opinion, or a majority of numbers." History does not reveal values in the sense that what succeeds is thereby proven to be valuable; and Nietzsche explicitly disagrees with the optimism of the contemporary Hegelians and Darwinists. Empirical facts do not seem to him to warrant the belief that history is a story of progress, that ever greater values are developed, and that whatever is later in the evolutionary scale is also *eo ipso* more valuable.[27] "The *goal of humanity* cannot lie in the end [*Ende*] but only *in its highest specimens*" (9). Perhaps there is no more basic statement of Nietzsche's philosophy in all his writings than this sentence. Here is the most crucial point of his philosophy of history and theory of values—no less than the clue to his "aristocratic" ethics and his opposition to socialism and democracy.

This sentence also shows how the historical and supra-historical are finally integrated. In the highest specimens of humanity we envisage the meaning of life and history: what can an additional ten or twenty centuries bring to light that we could not find in contemplating Aeschylus and Heraclitus, Socrates and Jesus, Leonardo and Michelangelo, Shakespeare and Goethe, Caesar and Napoleon, or Plato and Spinoza? In them the events of history have truly been "intensified into symbols."

---

[27] Yet "this ethical addition to the theory of evolution" is taken to be "the crucial point of Nietzsche's philosophy" in W. T. Stace, *The Destiny of Western Man* (1942), 221 *et passim*. This book, of course, does not purport to be a study of Nietzsche's philosophy, and Nietzsche is introduced merely as the representative of an outlook which the author opposes—much as Nietzsche himself employed historical figures to add vividness to his polemics.

On what, however, does Nietzsche base his position? His point can be understood only if one keeps in mind his initial nihilism. When God and any supernatural sanction of our values are questioned, the bottom falls out of our values, and they have no basis any more. If the teaching of evolution is correct and man is not essentially different from the apes; if he is, as all appearances seem to indicate, more similar to the monkeys than these are to the "lower" animals; if he is just another of the primates; then it would follow, Nietzsche thinks, that the mass of mankind lack any essential dignity or worth.

No quantitative addition, either of more and more human beings or of more and more intelligence (which man is supposed to share with the chimpanzee, though he has more of it), can give man the unique dignity which the Western tradition has generally conceded him. What is worthless to start with, cannot acquire value by multiplication. If man's value is zero, no addition of such zeros will ever lead to any value. A steady increase of intelligence through history, even if it could be demonstrated, would not change this picture. If man is to have any worth, there must be a "qualitative leap," to use Hegel's apt expression.[28] That there are any such leaps Nietzsche has not shown so far. His statement, however, that "the goal of humanity cannot lie in the end" is thus explained; and so is the addition that, if there is any goal, it can be found only in what he calls "the highest specimens."

Nietzsche looked upon history empirically. He juxtaposed the personalities in the two periods in history that he knew best with those of his contemporaries. How did his contemporaries fare in any comparison with the ancient Greeks or the men of the Renaissance? Being primarily interested in art and philosophy, Nietzsche found that asking the mere question amounted to a condemnation of his contemporaries and a repudiation of any belief that history is a story of progress. What philosophers are living today whom one could even compare to Plato or Spinoza; and what artists, whom one could seriously juxtapose to Phidias or Michelangelo? Has the worth of man increased? Nietzsche concluded that what comes later in time is not necessarily more valuable.

Then Nietzsche looked at the productions of the great artists

---

[28] *Phänomenologie* (1807), xiii; *Logik* I, 459.

and philosophers. Would he gauge the worth of these men by the mass of their productions, by the average excellence of their works—or by their greatest works?[29] Again, the answer cannot be in doubt. Leonardo has left fewer paintings than have most painters; but we should not judge him a poor painter on that account. We judge artists, and also philosophers, by their "master-pieces." We say that if Beethoven had just written some one symphony which we consider his best, then he would be as great a composer as has ever lived, even if he had never written anything else. If Shakespeare had written just *Lear* or *Hamlet*, his place would be secure. If Spinoza had written only the *Ethics*, he would still be one of the greatest philosophers of all time.

There is thus a certain plausibility to Nietzsche's doctrine, though it is dynamite. He maintains in effect that the gulf separating Plato from the average man is greater than the cleft between the average man and a chimpanzee. While Nietzsche may agree with Christianity, as Simmel insists, in ascribing infinite worth to the individual human soul,[30] Nietzsche does not ascribe this worth to every man as such, but only to some men. Whether this is essentially unchristian, need not be decided here. There are some Christian doctrines that resemble his view to some extent: there are, for example, heaven and hell; and there is the cleft between the blessed and the damned. If one adds to this doctrine of hell the dogma that some souls are predestinated unto eternal damnation, the result is perhaps even more disturbing than Nietzsche's need be.

Nietzsche agrees with the Christian tradition and such thinkers as Kant and Hegel that the worth of man must consist in a feature he does not share with any other animal. He believes that the worth of man, and thus the value of his life, his creations, and his acts, depends on his *Sonderstellung*, his unique position, in the cosmos. Darwinism, however, instead of infusing him with optimism, convinces him that empirical facts do not bear out the prevalent view that all men, as such, occupy a unique position

---

[29] This illustration of Nietzsche's "aristocratic" preference of the few excellent ones over the mass of the mediocre is taken from Simmel, *Schopenhauer und Nietzsche* (1907), 226 f. Simmel, however, misses the crucial point that, for Nietzsche, the mass of men has no worth whatever and is essentially continuous with the animal kingdom, and that therefore no quantitative addition can generate any worth.

[30] *Ibid.*, 200 ff.

in the cosmos. Most men are essentially animals, not basically different from chimpanzees—distinguished only by a *potentiality* that few of them realize: they can, but rarely do, rise above the beasts. Man can transcend his animal nature and become a *"no-longer-animal"* and a "truly *human* being"; but only some of "the *philosophers, artists, and saints"* rise to that point (U III 5). The unphilosophic, inartistic, and unsaintly mass remain animals. Hell is, so to speak, man's natural state: only by a superhuman effort can he ascend into the heavens, leave the animal kingdom beneath him, and acquire a value and a dignity without equal in all of nature.

The triad of "philosophers, artists, and saints" recalls Hegel's subdivision of the realm of Absolute Spirit into art, religion, and philosophy. For Hegel, however, the decisive "leap" was that which led from the Philosophy of Nature to the Philosophy of Spirit, and man *as such* was elevated above the animals and all the rest of nature. For Nietzsche, the fatal step is the transition from the sphere of Objective Spirit, in which society, the State, and history are included, to the supra-historical realm of art, religion, and philosophy. World history, like evolution, does not relate the story of progress but only the endless and futile addition of zeros, which does not show us that life can have worth or meaning. It does not teach us to have faith in the future but rather to despair at the sight of our depravation.

At the end of his second *Meditation,* Nietzsche turns away from all faith in progress, admits that the Greeks, three thousand years ago, took a step that raised them above ourselves, and tries to draw comfort from his contemplation by looking at history not as a process but as a timeless allegory. The Greeks, in the beginning of their history, were in danger of being completely overwhelmed by a chaotic flood of "foreign, Semitic, Babylonian, Lydian, and Egyptian forms and concepts": their early religion was a veritable arena in which the gods of the Orient fought each other. Yet the Greeks, imbued with the Apollinian spirit, learned to *"organize the chaos"* (10).

Suddenly one realizes that *The Birth of Tragedy* had already envisaged history from a supra-historical point of view and that Nietzsche, from his first book to his last, considered historical events and figures less with an eye to literal accuracy or correctness than "to circumscribe . . . an everyday melody . . . , to elevate it, to intensify it into a comprehensive symbol" (6). The birth of tragedy, Dionysus and Apollo, Socrates and Goethe, Strauss and Wagner become, in Nietzsche's vision, symbols of timeless themes. The conception of organizing the chaos turns out to be of the utmost significance: introduced in an apparently historical account as the essence of the Apollinian genius, it remains one of the persistent motifs of Nietzsche's thought—and nothing could show more clearly how the connotation of the Dionysian is changed in his later works than the fact that Dionysus is later associated with this very power of integration and self-discipline.

Nietzsche's supra-historical perspective, however, and the initially poor reception of *The Birth of Tragedy* in philological circles, should not blind us to the fact that this book did anticipate a new era in the interpretation of Greek culture. F. M. Cornford, one of the foremost authorities on early Greek religion and philosophy, was to hail *The Birth of Tragedy* as "a work of profound imaginative insight, which left the scholarship of a generation toiling in the rear";[31] and his own, as well as Jane Harrison's, painstaking scholarship has vindicated Nietzsche's intuition of the Apollinian and Dionysian.

Greek culture, according to Nietzsche, was not a function of the paradisiac endowment of the happy Hellenes, as previous generations of German scholars had believed, nor the creation of any fair-haired invaders from the north—"blond beasts," as it were—as later Nazi phantasies would have had it. In fact, Nietzsche notably resisted any temptation to construe the Apollinian and Dionysian racially and viewed them supra-historically as timeless forces that appear elsewhere, too, in different guises, and produce culture through their interplay. Even so, one may recall Nietzsche's later note—the pertinence of which seems confirmed by the most recent scholarship and by the telling fact that Sparta, where the invaders prohibited intermarriage with the native population, did not develop a great culture of her own: "Where races are mixed, there is the source of great cultures" (XVI, 373). One may also recall another note:

---

[31] *From Religion to Philosophy* (1912), 111; cf. xi. Cf. also Harrison, *Themis* (2nd ed. 1927), 476, and *Prolegomena to the Study of Greek Religion* (2nd ed. 1908), 445.

The Germans alternate between complete devotion to the foreign and a revengeful craving for originality. . . . The Germans
—to prove that their originality is not a matter of their nature
but of their ambition—think it lies in the complete and over-
obvious *difference:* but the Greeks did not think thus about the
Orient . . . and they *became* original (for one is not original to
begin with, but one is raw!) [XI, 110; cf. V, 246; VI 339].

The Greeks' originality did not preclude their overwhelming
debt to earlier civilizations, and to the Oriental religions in particular; and it may well be true that Greek culture consisted, to
a considerable extent, in the gradual refinement of the Dionysian
religion, through Orphism and Pythagoreanism, to Platonism:
in other words, in Apollo's harnessing of Dionysus.[32]

Thus Nietzsche, unlike Spengler, did not believe that we are
doomed to be epigoni. The Greeks, too, found themselves at the
end of a long line of magnificent civilizations and were yet able
to develop a culture of their own by integrating what had gone
before. We might appropriate their "conception of culture as
another and improved *physis* without inside and outside . . .
culture as a harmony of living, thinking, appearing, and willing"
(U II 10).

This notion—and especially the tremendous admiration for
Goethe, by whom it is obviously inspired—invites yet another
comparison with the early German romantics. Again, there are
crucial differences. We have seen how Friedrich Schlegel's admiration for Lessing's "individuality" involved a striking abstraction—
namely, an attempt to get around his hero's opinions and ideas.
Similarly, the "tendentious Goethe cult" (MA II 170) of the early
German romantics did not preclude their express opposition to
Goethe's own basic intentions and to his unromantic—frequently
even outright anti-romantic—views.[33]

---

[32] Bertrand Russell seems unaware that his own account of the early Greeks,
which is based on Harrison and Cornford, often reads like a paraphrase
of Nietzsche, whom he caricatures and of whom he says: "Consciously
his outlook was Hellenic, but with the Orphic component omitted. He
admired the pre-Socratics, except Pythagoras." (*A History of Western
Philosophy,* 760 f.) Actually, Nietzsche called attention to the Orphics and
to Dionysus, their inspiration; and the "Dionysian" philosophy of the
eternal recurrence was originally Pythagorean.

[33] For Goethe's relevant views, see Otto Harnack, "Klassiker und Romantiker" in *Essais zur Literaturgeschichte* (1899) and the chapter on romanticism in Viëtor's *Goethe* (1949). For the romantics' attitude toward Goethe
see, in addition, Rudolf Haym, *Die Romantische Schule* (1870), and

Nietzsche's Goethe picture was essentially different from that of the romantics. A note, written in preparation for the second *Meditation,* is characteristic:

> *Goethe* is exemplary: the impetuous naturalism which gradually becomes severe dignity. As a stylized human being, he reached a higher level than any other German ever did. Now one is so bigoted as to reproach him therefor and even to censure his becoming old.[34] One should read Eckermann and ask oneself whether any human being in Germany ever got so far in noble form [VI, 340; cf. U II 8].

Nietzsche never abandoned this conception of Goethe; he merely elaborated it. Not long after, he declared flatly that he considered "the Conversations with Eckermann the best German book there is" (S 109: cf. XVII, 348). Till the end, he preferred it to *Faust* and *Meister;* for what he associated with Goethe was neither the boundless striving that pushes on into infinity, like Schopenhauer's irrational will, nor the dreamlike dissolution of all border lines between illusion and reality (which Schlegel had found in *Meister*)—but the hardness of the creator who creates himself.

In this "supra-German" Goethe (MA II 170) Nietzsche discovers a modern embodiment of Greek "culture." In other words, it is the "classical" Goethe that he admires, and Goethe became for him, more and more, the incarnate triumph over romanticism. Thus it was Goethe's famous pronouncement to Eckermann (April 2, 1829), "The classical I call the healthy, and the romantic, the sick," that inspired Nietzsche's later contrast of the romantic and the Dionysian (S 217; GT-V 6; FW 370). The whole conception of the Dionysian was then revised, as we shall see; and Goethe, as the embodiment of that culture which Nietzsche

---

Victor Hehn, *Gedanken über Goethe* (1887; read by Nietzsche, who found in it confirmation for some of his previously expressed views). While the early German romantics helped to spread Goethe's fame, their aims were decidedly not his. In his enthusiastic essay *Über Goethes Meister* (1798), for example, F. Schlegel read his own intentions into the novel; and the next spring he applauded Ludwig Tieck's *Sternbald* (1798) as much more romantic and "far above *Meister.*" Still later, he extolled Fouqué's *Zauberring* (1813) above both. Novalis also abandoned his earlier admiration for Goethe when he realized that *Meister* was basically not romantic. (*Fragmente der letzten Jahre,* 2840 and 2905) And Schlegel's and Novalis' adulation led Tieck to consider his own romantic efforts as being far greater than Goethe's works.

[34] According to Hehn, *op. cit.,* F. Schlegel did just this.

envisaged at the end of the second *Meditation,* could thus be called "Dionysian" in Nietzsche's last great tribute to him (G ɪх 49). Precisely the old Goethe who had overcome his youthful storm and stress and harnessed his Faustian-Dionysian frenzy is the perfect representative of what Nietzsche later had in mind when speaking of the Dionysian—and that in spite of the fact that Nietzsche still felt that Goethe had not understood Greek culture correctly (G х 4), i.e., that he had failed to interpret it in terms of his own spiritual development.

It was not only in Nietzsche's later works that Goethe served him as a trump against the romantics' opposition to "reason, enlightenment, taste, and the eighteenth century" (WM 849; cf. W 3): a similar contrast will be encountered in the next chapter, when we consider the third *Meditation.* The Dionysian, however, is not yet contrasted with the romantic at this juncture, but with the Apollinian; and the question arises as to whether the two Greek gods represent essentially separate principles, like form and matter, in which case a development of—if not a break with —Nietzsche's earlier naturalism would be necessary. For what Nietzsche now endorses is clearly not biological nature but "culture as another and improved *physis* [nature]." Nature must be transformed, and man must become like a work of art. Apollo must triumph over Dionysus—and if these gods represent truly separate forces, and culture originates only when nature is subdued, then we are led back to an unnaturalistic dualism, not unlike that maintained by Kant and the Christian tradition.

Whence comes Apollo? That is the question. If he "must have descended to us, wrapt in a cloud," as the closing paragraph of *The Birth of Tragedy* suggested somewhat playfully, Nietzsche's early attempt to make the secular the birthplace of the sacred has failed. Yet he seems to be urging against Kant and Christianity that the *physis* is not essentially opposed to our highest aspirations but is only in need of improvement. The conception of "culture as another and improved *physis*" is as yet far from clear; but the chord on which the second *Meditation* ended becomes the leitmotif of the third.

5

EXISTENZ VERSUS THE STATE, DARWIN, AND ROUSSEAU

He will be mistaken for another and long be considered
an ally of powers he abominates.—U III 4.

The third of the *Untimely Meditations,* though not as well
known as the second and *The Birth of Tragedy,* represents nothing less than the consummation of Nietzsche's early philosophy.
As the essential sequence of his thought from book to book is
often overlooked even where the organic unity of his work is
granted in principle, it is significant to note that the major themes
of his earlier publications are here taken up once more. In *The
Birth of Tragedy,* Nietzsche had concerned himself with aesthetic
values and tried to give a dialectical, yet naturalistic, account of
them. In spite of the dialectical analysis in terms of the Dionysian
and Apollinian, a plausible case could yet be made in favor of
the assertion that health, defined as the capacity to overcome sickness, was a naturalistic notion. In the second *Meditation,* a fair
account was given of the value and disvalue of remembering and
forgetting, of the historical and the unhistorical, health was still
quite a sufficient standard, and no supernatural sanctions were
invoked. Then, however, Nietzsche turned to a consideration of
the supra-historical. He suggested that the values of art, religion,
and philosophy were above the flux of history. In the end, he conceived of beauty and self-perfection as "culture" and, apparently
conscious of the etymology of this term, defined it as "another
and improved *physis,*" i.e., as a cultivated *physis.* What gives
man his *Sonderstellung,* his unique position in the cosmos, is
thus conceived neither as a natural endowment nor as a supernatural gift. Man, as such, is an animal. What distinguishes him

is not that he is *eo ipso* superior, but only that he has an additional potentiality and can raise himself above the animals, if he will cultivate his nature—his *physis*.

An ethics of self-realization is thus suggested, and Nietzsche, who attempts to face its problems in his third *Meditation,* cannot escape the inevitable paradoxes of this doctrine. Man need only cultivate his nature to realize himself, but he does not "naturally" succeed—and the vast majority of men never do realize themselves. There is an implicit distinction between man's *true* nature and man's nature; and the crucial question is whether the conception of man's true nature is still empirical.

I

At the outset of the essay, it is assumed that every man is by his very nature unique:

> The man who would not belong in the mass needs only to cease being comfortable with himself; he should follow his conscience which shouts at him: "Be yourself! You are not really all that which you do, think, and desire now" [1].

Culture consists in the overcoming of any discrepancy between inside and outside, and the uncultured man is not really embodied in his acts, thoughts, and desires. A cleft remains in him between appearance and reality, between his nature and his true nature.

The reason why most men fail to heed the voice of their true self is twofold. Nietzsche hesitates to decide which is the most universal human characteristic: fear or laziness. Both keep man from heeding the call to achieve culture and thus to realize himself. Men are afraid of social retaliation and do not dare be their own unique selves. It is for this reason that the State becomes the devil of Nietzsche's ethics: it intimidates man into conformity and thus tempts and coerces him to betray his proper destiny.

Man's task is simple: he should cease letting his "existence" be "a thoughtless accident" (1). Not only the use of the word *Existenz,* but the thought which is at stake, suggests that the third *Meditation* is particularly close to what is today called *Existenzphilosophie.* Man's fundamental problem is to achieve true "existence" instead of letting his life be no more than just another accident. In *The Gay Science,* Nietzsche hits on a formulation that brings out the essential paradox of any distinction between self and true self:

> *What does your conscience say?*—"You shall become who you are" [*Du sollst der werden, der du bist*] [FW 270; cf. 335].[1]

Nietzsche maintains this conception until the end, and the full title of his last work is *Ecce Homo, Wie man wird, was man ist*—how one becomes what one is.

The problem that then arises is how we can recognize our true self, for Nietzsche assumes that we must know it before we can realize it. At the same time, he is aware of the limitations of introspection, which does not reveal all we are looking for. We cannot shed our skin to behold our true self. We can only try to find a clue in our past behavior by examining our life to date, and Nietzsche suggests that perhaps the most revealing question is: "What have you really loved till now?" The answer will show you "your true self [which] does not lie deeply concealed within you but immeasurably high above you, or at least above what you usually take for your ego" (1). As we contemplate the traits we have most loved and admired in our self-chosen educators—as we meditate upon the dearest features of those few men whom we elected from millions past and present to help us shape our selves—we envisage our true nature which we would realize if we were not too lazy and afraid.

There follows Nietzsche's *Meditation* on *Schopenhauer as Educator*, i.e., Nietzsche's attempt to discover his own true self by considering those traits which he has in the past loved and admired most in Schopenhauer. Admittedly, this is not a literally correct historical portrait of Schopenhauer but only a device by which Nietzsche hopes to envisage his own true self—not deep inside, but "immeasurably high above" his present ego. His own later exegesis of this essay in *Ecce Homo* is thus quite sensible, although it has occasionally been considered absurd or disingenuous. Referring to his third and fourth *Meditation*, Nietzsche claimed that he had there pictured "Schopenhauer and Wagner *or*, in one word, Nietzsche" (EH-U 1); and he elaborated:

---

[1] From Nietzsche's correspondence with Rohde it appears that he derived this formulation from Pindar, Pyth. II, 73: *"genoi hoios essi."* Cf. also Hegel: "The spirit is such that it creates itself and makes itself that which it is. [. . . *sich zu dem macht, was er ist.*]" (*Die Vernunft in der Geschichte: Einleitung in die Philosophie der Weltgeschichte*, ed. G. Lasson 1917, 52; cf. 131.) Cf. my *Hegel*, section 60.

> Thus Plato used Socrates . . . in *Schopenhauer as Educator*
> my inmost history . . . is inscribed. . . . *What* I am today,
> *where* I am today . . . I *saw* the land . . . actually not "Scho-
> penhauer as educator" but . . . "Nietzsche as educator" is de-
> scribed . . ." [EH-U 3].

This interpretation hardly does the third *Meditation* any violence, and the reference to Socrates and Plato, too, seems candid
enough. Nietzsche's conception of "culture" is obviously indebted
to them, and the significance that he attaches to the love of
one's educator points in the same direction, especially to the
Symposium, the youth's *Lieblingsdichtung.* Not only his early
curriculum vitae and several explicit references to this dialogue
in Nietzsche's notes (II, 377; IV, 393) testify to the profound impression the *Symposium* made on him; nor need we rely on his
picture of Socrates as the "true erotic" (GT 13; G II 8): Nietzsche's
entire thought was deeply influenced by this Platonic dialogue,
from which he derived many significant suggestions for his later
conception of the will to power.

When Nietzsche proceeds to consider Schopenhauer's honesty and
integrity and—of all things—his "cheerfulness" (2); when he
meditates on the advantages of Schopenhauer's "separation" from
the universities and on the dangers of "loneliness" and of the
"despair in truth" and concludes, "life itself means being in
danger" (3)—one will readily believe that this is not meant to be
an accurate likeness of Schopenhauer but rather Nietzsche's description of the character he himself hopes to develop. Here is
the kind of life he admires and hopes yet to realize. Schopenhauer is viewed supra-historically as a symbol, and Nietzsche
writes not as an "antiquarian" historian but as a "monumentalistic" artist who emphasizes certain traits at the expense of others
because his concern is not at all with the past as such.

> Every great philosophy . . . as a whole says always only: this
> is the image of all life, and from this learn the meaning of
> your life. And conversely: read only your own life and under-
> stand from this the hieroglyphs of universal life. This is how
> Schopenhauer's philosophy, too, should always be interpreted
> first: individually, by the single one [*Einzelnen*] alone for him-
> self, to gain insight into his own misery and need . . . [3].

What Schopenhauer "teaches us," when he is approached in
this supra-historical manner, is "how neither riches nor honors,

nor scholarship can raise the single one out of his profound discouragement over the worthlessness of his existence, and how the striving for these goals can receive meaning only from a high and transfiguring overall aim: to gain power in order to aid the *physis* [nature]." Here the theme on which the second *Meditation* closed is taken up again, and the conception of the "transfigured *physis*" (3) becomes the leitmotif of the new essay.

Riches, honors, and even scholarship are merely futile multiplications of a value that is zero to start with. Not one of them can raise us above the animals, with whom we even share intelligence. "Between a clever chimpanzee and Edison, if he is considered as a technician only, there exists merely a—certainly very great—difference in *degree*." [2] In terms of human worth or dignity, however, this difference in degree is nil, if it is understood that human worth and dignity depend essentially on a cardinal difference between man and the animals. What is required is a goal that only man can reach. Nothing short of the "remaking" of human nature[3] will give it back that dignity which the Bible had bestowed on it and which Darwin took away. This "remaking," however, cannot be accomplished for us by another, whether man or God or evolution—and hence there is no talk of raising all of mankind out of its depraved state. The question Nietzsche puts is essentially *Die Frage an den Einzelnen,*[4] a question for "the single one alone for himself" (3)—Kierkegaard's *hiin Enkelte,* who is the antithesis of the crowd. Individuality, worth, and dignity are—to recall Kant's play on words—not *gegeben,* i.e., given to us as data by nature, but *aufgegeben,* i.e., given or assigned to us as a task.

---

[2] Scheler, *Die Stellung des Menschen im Kosmos* (1928), 46. In this book, Scheler mentions Nietzsche twice to repudiate his will to power (19, 99) and once in agreement on a minor point (52)—and he may not have been aware of the fact that the sentence quoted here is entirely in Nietzsche's spirit. Generally, of course, Scheler was conscious of his debt to Nietzsche and was inspired by him to write a long essay on *Das Ressentiment im Aufbau der Moralen,* which later found its way into a two-volume collection of essays with the somewhat Nietzschean title *Vom Umsturz der Werte.*

[3] Cf. W. E. Hocking, *Human Nature and Its Remaking* (1918).

[4] The title of a book by Martin Buber (1936), included in his *Between Man and Man* (1948) in English translation. In the essay, Kierkegaard, but not Nietzsche, is discussed sympathetically and yet critically. The English volume, however, also contains a critical discussion of Nietzsche's conception of man (148–56).

In a sense, Nietzsche may seem closer to the Greeks than to the Bible: for among the Greeks, too, it was held that not all men as such are superior to the animals and have dignity and command respect; the vast majority was considered as not essentially different from the animals: only the few were rational. For the Greeks, however, the freeborn Greek was *by nature* a member of the elite while the barbarian was *by nature* fit to be a slave. This whole question will have to be discussed in more detail in Chapter 10, but one may anticipate that Nietzsche did not accept any racial setting, in spite of his great admiration for Hellas. For the Protestant minister's son it seems to have been a foregone conclusion that human worth is a function not of blood but of the spirit, and that the question of spiritual worth is a question for the single one.

Unlike Luther, however, and like Kierkegaard, Nietzsche pushes the meaning of being single to its very limits. Kierkegaard had already differed from Luther—who had symbolically and ostentatiously married Katharina—by refusing just as deliberately to marry Regine. In each case, the action marks the attainment of a new spiritual freedom. Nietzsche, of course, remained single, like Kierkegaard; but if one were to search his life for a similarly symbolic breach with society, it would be found less in his refusal to get married than in his resignation from the university and his breach with Wagner.

This neo-Protestant rebellion against the nineteenth century removes Nietzsche even further from the ancient Greeks. Society and the State represent to his mind not the consummation of rationality and justice, of ethics and philosophy, but only the embodiment of mediocrity and the temptation that has to be overcome before the individual can come into his own; and this point of view is characteristic of Nietzsche's writings from beginning to end. It first becomes manifest in the untimely *Meditation* about David Strauss; it reaches a provisional climax in the angry denunciations in the essay on Schopenhauer; then the same theme is taken up again in *Zarathustra,* in the chapter "Of the New Idol"; and, like so many persistent motifs of Nietzsche's thought, it is consummated in the diatribes of the *Götzen-Dämmerung* (G VIII) and *Ecce Homo* (EH-W). This consistent attitude and its motivation have often been overlooked or misunderstood. Thus Brinton supposes,[5] presumably deceived by Frau Förster-Nietz-

---

[5] *Op. cit.,* 227.

sche's propaganda, that the works of Nietzsche's "very latest period" do not contain such vehement denunciations of the State —though both the *Götzen-Dämmerung* and *Ecce Homo* were written during the last five months of Nietzsche's career. Bäumler, fully aware of the fact that Nietzsche's attacks on the State reached their climax precisely in 1888, misrepresents their motivation completely when he tries to explain it biographically.

Nietzsche's views are misunderstood when they are considered no more than personal opinions or preferences which must be explained psychologically. His denunciation of the State should be considered in its context as a corollary of his value theory. The State is depreciated, not because of its "disadvantage for life"— the criterion at the beginning of the *Meditation* on history—but because it prevents man from realizing himself. The standard of valuation is no longer simply life but the improved, perfected, and transfigured life, first envisaged at the end of the second *Meditation*.

Bäumler's many arguments are for the most part too absurd to merit serious refutation. Granting, for example, that Nietzsche did repudiate the State consistently, Bäumler adds that, after all, "the State . . . is an invention of the Orient"; and he quite generally uses "Teutonic" and "how primordially Teutonic!" as arguments.[6] Against this approach one can cite Nietzsche himself, who denounced this very attitude:

> One must first be "German" and have "race," then one can decide about all values and disvalues *in historicis* . . . "German" has become an argument, *Deutschland, Deutschland über alles,* a principle; the Teutons represent the "moral world-order." . . . There is now a historiography that is *reichsdeutsch*; there is even, I fear, an anti-Semitic one . . . and Herr von Treitschke is not ashamed . . . [EH-W 2].

Only two of Bäumler's arguments are apt to seem at all plausible to readers who do not share his Nazi presuppositions. Both are stated together in the following comment on Nietzsche: "He sees Germany become a state before his eyes—but it is a Christian state, led by a Christian statesman. And he sees himself entirely ignored by this state. . . ."[7] What Bäumler overlooks is, first,

---

[6] *Nietzsche der Philosoph und Politiker* (1931), 92, 94, *et passim.*
[7] *Nachwort* to *Kröners Taschenausgabe,* vol. 77, 596.

Bäumler's postscripts to these popular editions of Nietzsche's works, though ignored by English and American writers, have perhaps intro-

that Nietzsche denounced the State vigorously even in his early *Meditations* when he had no particular reason yet to complain of being ignored; and secondly, that Nietzsche attacked the State in his essay on Schopenhauer not because it was Christian but— because it is unchristian. His attack is not a temperamental diatribe against the German *Reich* only but primarily a judgment concerning the State in general. His point of view, in other words, is less historical than supra-historical.

The passage in the *Meditation* on Schopenhauer in which Nietzsche anticipates much of his later attack against Christianity —in terms which are less anti-Christian than his later efforts to be provocative—repays study. This paragraph also explains how Nietzsche could value the "saint" so highly that he placed him with artist and philosopher as the only kind of truly *human* being while, at the same time, he opposed Christianity.

> One should only recall what has gradually become of Christianity under the selfishness of the State. Christianity is certainly one of the purest revelations of this urge for culture and especially for the ever renewed generation of the saint; as it has been used hundreds of times, however, to turn the mills of the State's forces, it has gradually become diseased to the very marrow, hypocritical and full of lies, and has degenerated to the point where it contradicts its original aim [6].

Nietzsche objects to the State because it appears to him as the power that intimidates man into conformity. Christianity, as he sees it, was originally a call to man *not* to conform, to leave father and mother, and to perfect himself. Nietzsche's protest may then seem, at first glance, to be entirely in the spirit of the German Reformation and its attack upon the Catholic Church. Nietzsche, however, includes Luther's Protestantism in his indictment; for Luther impressed upon the new church he founded the fateful words of Paul in whose Epistles he had found what he took to be true Christianity: "Let every soul be subject unto the higher powers. For there is no power but of God: the powers that be are ordained of God. Whosoever therefore resisteth the power, resisteth the ordinance of God: and they that resist shall receive to themselves damnation." (Rom. 13: 1–2.)

Nietzsche's repudiation of Christianity will be discussed in a

---

duced wider circles of the German people to the Nazi approach to Nietzsche than any single book. Since 1945 they have been reprinted with revisions.

later chapter; but one may here anticipate that he discounted Luther's proclamation of the freedom of the individual conscience and believed that Luther had insisted on conformity.[8] Within ten years of Luther's death, moreover, his friends and followers had accepted the principle *cuius regio, eius religio*, according to which the German princes could determine the religion of their subjects. Thus Nietzsche's critique of Christianity cannot be understood on the basis of any equation of Christianity and democracy—with science possibly thrown in as a fashionable third. We shall see later that Christianity and science were to Nietzsche's mind antipodes; and the Christianity he knew from personal experience and from German history was of course not identifiable with the democratic spirit.

Nietzsche's opposition to political liberalism cannot be analyzed in this context either—but one statement that helps to explain his position can be found in the *Meditation* on Schopenhauer: "How should a political innovation be sufficient to make men once and for all into happy inhabitants of the earth?" (4). Nietzsche opposes not only the State but any overestimation of the political. The kingdom of God is in the hearts of men— and Nietzsche accuses Christianity of having betrayed this fundamental insight from the beginning, whether by transferring the kingdom into *another* world and thus depreciating *this* life, or by becoming political and seeking salvation through organizations, churches, cults, sacraments, or priests. He will not put his faith either in a church or in a political party or program, for

---

[8] Luther's attitude toward the Jews furnishes an extreme example, and one may contrast his position with Hegel's, who is often charged with having conceived of freedom merely as the freedom to agree and conform. Under the influence of the Enlightenment, Hegel championed the doctrine of unalienable secular rights to which man *as such* is entitled, regardless of his beliefs—and he included the Jews (for whom he had no special liking) because they are, "first of all, *human beings.*" (*Philosophy of Right* §270) Luther, on the other hand, whose attitude toward the Jews had earlier been remarkably free from prejudice, was so outraged by their refusal to agree to his religious doctrines that he wrote: "What shall we Christians do now with this depraved and damned people of the Jews? . . . I will give my faithful advice: First that one should set fire to their synagogues. . . . Then that one should also break down and destroy their houses. . . . That one should drive them out of the country." (*Sämtliche Schriften*, St. Louis, 1881–1910, XX, 1989 ff.) It was by accident, not design, that the Nazis accepted this "faithful advice" on Luther's birthday, November 10, 1938.

he believes that the question of salvation is a "question for the single one."

Even in his *Meditation* on Schopenhauer, to be sure, Nietzsche recognizes that there is more to the State than its oppressive and intimidating power which makes men conform and thus betray their unique destiny of self-realization. The modern situation, and the Nation State in particular, has another side as well, but according to Nietzsche

> the second side is not a bit more delightful but only more disturbing. There are certainly . . . tremendous forces, but they are savage, primordial, and utterly merciless. One looks upon them with uneasy expectations as upon the seething cauldron of a witch's kitchen: any moment it may flash and lighten to announce terrible apparitions . . . the so-called Nation State . . . is . . . only an increment of the general insecurity and menace . . . and the hunt for happiness will never be greater than when it must be caught between today and tomorrow: because the day after tomorrow all hunting time may have come to an end altogether. We live in the period of atoms, of atomistic chaos. . . . Now almost everything on earth is determined by the crudest and most evil forces, by the egotism of the purchasers and the military despots. The State, in the hands of the latter . . . wishes that people would lavish on it the same idolatrous cult that they used to lavish on the Church [4].

Who will, "in the face of such dangers," serve *"humanity [Menschlichkeit]"* and resurrect *"das Bild des Menschen"*—i.e., an image of man as a *human* being, as not just another animal? Who will return to man his ancient dignity and peerless worth? Nietzsche himself italicizes both *Menschlichkeit* and *Bild des Menschen*. These are the conceptions that seem all-important to him; for the dangers he envisages seem to him inseparably connected with man's loss of faith in his own essential humanity and dignity. Already in his second *Meditation,* Nietzsche had emphasized this point; and one passage in particular shows clearly why he felt that a new picture of man was required to meet the dangers of the immediate future:

> If the doctrines of sovereign Becoming, of the fluidity of all . . . species, of the lack of any cardinal distinction between man and animal—doctrines I consider true but deadly—are hurled into the people for another generation . . . then nobody should be surprised when . . . brotherhoods with the aim of robbery and exploitation of the non-brothers . . . will appear on the arena of the future [U ɪɪ 9].

Even in his first *Meditation* Nietzsche had criticized David Strauss for being blind enough to consider "Darwin as one of the greatest benefactors of mankind" (7). Not that he himself had been prepared to reject the new doctrines either on fundamentalist or on pragmatic grounds, any more than Kant had rejected Hume's fatal attack on ideas he had cherished. Nietzsche was aroused from his dogmatic slumber by Darwin, as Kant had been by Hume a century earlier; and again it was a question of creating a new picture of man in reply to the "true but deadly" nihilism from beyond the Channel.

Nietzsche is impressed with the urgency of this task. The ancient theological picture of man is gone. If we cannot discover a new picture of man that will again give him a sense of his essential dignity, the State, in the hands of military despots, will demand that we should yield to it in idolatry; and eventually men will lose all respect for one another, all social structures will break down, and men will seek only to rob and to exploit one another. The problem is whether it is possible to give man a new image of himself without introducing supernatural assumptions that experience does not warrant and that we cannot, with integrity, fail to question. Looking into the past, Nietzsche proceeds to contemplate three different pictures of man, each of them represented, supra-historically, by a historical figure: Rousseau, Goethe, and—representing his own conception of man—Schopenhauer.

II

Rousseau's man "has the greatest fire and is sure of the greatest popular effect," but he is also the most dangerous: he urges revolution and a return to nature which, when emulated by the masses, leads to the unbridling of the most savage and destructive forces. Goethe's man "is no such menacing power." In fact, the dialectical Nietzsche thinks of this man as an antithesis and a mature reaction against a youthful cult of Rousseau's gospel. The Goethean man embodies the great contemplative type who is essentially unrevolutionary, even antirevolutionary. He is concerned with himself and would like to absorb in his soul all the riches of the world. Again, this picture of man "is misunderstood by the mass" who are simply unable to emulate Goethe. Using an image from the end of *Faust,* Nietzsche writes: "When the German ceases to be Faust, no danger is greater than that he may become a Philistine and fall into the Devil's hands—only heavenly powers can . . . redeem him."

As images of man that might counteract the menace of our age, both Rousseau's man and Goethe's man are insufficient. The individual embodiment of the type may be admirable—Dionysus and Apollo are both gods—but the "followers" represent two antithetical and almost equally objectionable characters: one "can easily become a Catilinarian," while the other is apt to "degenerate into a Philistine." Against revolution and complacency, Nietzsche urges the transfigured *physis,* the cultivated nature—using Schopenhauer as his mythical protagonist.

These pages offer the clue to Nietzsche's attitude toward both Goethe and Rousseau. With Goethe, Nietzsche has, in general, no quarrel. The Olympian embodiment of harmony and measure—the Apollinian perfection which is here pictured as Goethe's most decisive feature—is so utterly beyond the reach of Nietzsche that he could admire Goethe all his life long without being able to equal him. On the other hand, Rousseau's Dionysiac return to nature, his moral pathos, and his abandonment to the elemental forces that make revolutions and may ruin states constituted the very dangers of Nietzsche's own philosophy. Hence, he generally reviled Rousseau.

The discussion of Rousseau and Goethe represents no departure from Nietzsche's main concern and might have been entitled: Of the Use and Disadvantage of the Apollinian and the Dionysian. The Apollinian—if it does not, as in Goethe, thrive upon the fertile ground on which Dionysus has first been subdued—may easily amount to no more than the Philistine's complacency. The Dionysian, if it is not held in check by the god of Delphi, may run amuck and bathe the world in blood.

C. G. Jung, in his chapter on, "The Apollinian and the Dionysian," in *Psychologische Typhen,* has claimed that Nietzsche, throughout his glorification of the Dionysian, forgot that "the urges dammed up in civilized man are terribly destructive and much more dangerous than the urges of primitive man who, to some degree, gives constant vent to his negative urges. Thus no war of the historical past can rival the wars of civilized nations in grandiose sordidness." This criticism of Nietzsche is scarcely justified and depends on the usual, but false, assumption that for

Nietzsche "The Dionysian is a Good Thing. . . . The Apollinian is a Bad Thing." [9] In *The Birth of Tragedy* and at the end of the second *Meditation,* the dangers of the Dionysian are clearly recognized, and Nietzsche admits that it leads only to wantonness and licentiousness unless it is harnessed and transformed by Apollo's intervention. In the third *Meditation,* the night side of the Dionysian is presented still more explicitly, if under a different name: Nietzsche's opposition to Rousseau cannot be understood unless one keeps in mind that Rousseau serves Nietzsche as the representative of the dangers of the Dionysiac frenzy.

To be more specific, Nietzsche offered three criticisms of Rousseau. First, he recognized in the citizen of Geneva one of the main forces contributing to the origin of the modern Nation State. Since it was Nietzsche's profound concern to counteract the influence of the modern Nation State, he was opposed to Rousseau; for the Nation State seemed to Nietzsche the arch-enemy of nonconformity, self-realization, and the "single one's" remaking of his own nature.

Secondly, in spite of his alleged preference for the Dionysian, Nietzsche's basic concern for the individual set him against the abandonment of individuality and the Dionysian drowning in nature or in the brotherhood of man. One may recall that his initial description of the Dionysian in the first paragraph of *The Birth of Tragedy* would invite a comparison with Rousseau, even if Nietzsche had not chosen as an illustration the chorus of Beethoven's *Ninth Symphony,* which is based on Schiller's celebration of the brotherhood of man. Nietzsche, however, did not endorse the Dionysian as such, but only the synthesis of such passion with the Apollinian "principle of individuation."

Finally, and this is only a development of the previous point, Nietzsche did not believe that by "returning to nature" man would become good, or that Liberty, Equality, and Fraternity were close to the state of nature. His view of "nature" was much the opposite: by returning to nature man would only become a beast of prey or a Catilinarian criminal—and a people following Rousseau might find themselves transformed into a revolutionary mob thirsting for blood. The association with the mobs of the revolution colored Nietzsche's attitude toward Rousseau. In the last work he sent to press, the contrast of Goethe and Rousseau

---

[9] Brinton, *op. cit.,* 39.

is offered once more in the characteristic hyperboles of 1888; it is hard to understand without the background of the earlier *Meditation,* and the identification of Rousseau with the revolutionary mobs is complete (G IX 48 f.; WM 1017).[10]

Men, as Nietzsche saw them, were not naturally equal, did not naturally love one another, and were not naturally free. Nietzsche agreed with Hegel that freedom is essentially a product of culture—though he thought, unlike Hegel, that true "culture" could be achieved only through an open break with the State. Primitive man, far from enjoying freedom, lived in constant fear of savage animals, of his barbarian enemies, of his gods, and even of his own dreams (M 5). Thus Nietzsche, instead of wanting man to "return" to nature, thought that we must "cultivate" and "improve," "transfigure" and remake our nature.

Nietzsche's reasons for opposing Rousseau are far clearer than his right to this opposition: there is still the problem of the origin of Apollo, the question as to whether the force that transforms our nature is itself a naturalistic principle. What seems to be needed is a redefinition of nature that would parallel the dialectical definition of health as the overcoming of disease—but this is not yet forthcoming.

Even now Nietzsche realizes certain implications of his own position. While he brands Rousseau's picture of man as dangerous, his own conception of nonconformity is not free of danger either. He quotes Goethe's *Wilhelm Meister:* "You are disgruntled and bitter, that is fine and good; if only you will once become rather evil, then it will be still better"; and Nietzsche adds: "Thus, speaking frankly, it is necessary that we once become rather evil that it may get better"—evil, that is, "for myopic modern eyes which consider negation always the sign of evil" (4).

Nietzsche's insistence that the negative may not be evil from a long-range point of view, but a necessary stage in the development toward something positive, is not a casual point in his thought but one of the characteristic motifs that recur throughout: one must negate, one must renounce conformity,

---

[10] In the aphorism in the *Götzen-Dämmerung* Nietzsche writes: "I too, speak of a 'return to nature,' although it is really not a going back but an *ascent.* . . . But Rousseau—to what did *he* really want to go back?"

one must break the ancient tables of values—in order to prepare for the creation of something positive. The systematic foundation of this notion will be considered later; but one may note that Nietzsche in this passage also refers to Goethe's Mephistopheles, who speaks of himself as a part of that force which ever wants the evil and ever creates the good, as the spirit who ever negates because all that comes to be deserves to perish. Nietzsche might also have referred to God's call to Jeremiah: "to root out and to pull down and to destroy, and to throw down, to build, and to plant."

Nietzsche realized that his breach with conformity, his negation and repudiation of tradition, was certain to be misconstrued; yet he saw no other way to perfect himself, nor any way for others to perfect themselves, but to renounce the Moloch of the state and what he took to be the hypocrisy of a church that had "degenerated to the point where it contradicts its original aim" (6).

> . . . A fiery desire should develop in everybody to become such a Schopenhauerian man: to be in one's quest for knowledge full of a strong consuming fire . . . ever offering oneself as the first sacrifice to the truth one recognizes. . . . Certainly, he destroys his earthly happiness through his courage; he must be hostile even to the human beings whom he loves and to the institutions from whose womb he issued; he may spare neither human beings nor things, though he himself suffer [*mit leidet*] in hurting them; he will be mistaken for another [*verkannt*] and long be considered an ally of powers he abominates; he will, in view of the human limitations of his insight, have to be unjust, in spite of all his striving for justice [4].

One may ask why Nietzsche exposed himself to such wanton misconstruction, if he foresaw so clearly that he would be considered an ally of powers he abominated. The answer is apparently that he felt no choice but either to live in integrity, breaking with tradition, or to betray his conscience. To protect himself against misinterpretation, he always asked that people should read his words *"rück- und vorsichtig"* (M-V 5)—i.e., not only carefully but also looking before and behind, noting the context as well as his earlier and later works.

> If this writing is incomprehensible for anybody or will not go into his head, the fault, it seems to me, is not necessarily mine. It is plain enough, assuming—as I do assume—that one has

first read my earlier writings and not spared some trouble in doing this [GM-V 8].

In the end Nietzsche threw his pride to the winds and begged in the first paragraph of his preface to *Ecce Homo: "Above all, do not mistake me!"*

III

If the *Meditation* on Schopenhauer represents the consummation of Nietzsche's early philosophy and his last attempt to solve his value problem before he temporarily abandoned it to write in a different vein, it may be well to inquire once more concerning Nietzsche's concept of nature. The principle of life with which he started differed significantly from Lessing's "providence" and from Kant's "nature" by not being purposive. The notion of the improved *physis,* however, suggests that nature may have a purpose after all, and the exhortation to gain power to "aid the *physis*" seems to confirm this. It appears that Nietzsche thought natural events were governed by a purpose that requires our help to be fulfilled.

One need not conjecture on this point, for Nietzsche states his position clearly: the aim of culture and the aim of nature are one and the same.

> This is the basic idea of *culture* insofar as it assigns only one task to every single one of us: *to promote inside and outside of ourselves the generation of the philosopher, the artist, and the saint, and thus to work at the perfection of nature* [5].

Later in the essay, Nietzsche says quite expressly of nature: "That she wants to make the life of man significant and meaningful by generating the philosopher and the artist—that is certain in view of her own urge in need of redemption" (7). Nature thus has a purpose but is also herself in need of redemption; and man must aid her by perfecting himself and thereby redeeming nature. This account, of course, seems at best poetic. It does not appear to be based on empirical fact.

A closer examination of Nietzsche's point, however, reveals that he is trying to do no more than to describe experience. He is definitely not out to offer a romantic picture of the travails of nature, and the reference to "redemption"—a word that must have come readily to the mind of Wagner's young friend—is misleading. Nietzsche does not have in mind anything supernatural. By empirical observation, concentrating on art, philosophy, and religion, Nietzsche finds that humanity has not become "better" through history; i.e., he fails to find bigger and better artists and philosophers in his own time than, say, in the age of Plato or Leonardo. Yet it was shown in the second *Meditation* why "the *goal of humanity* cannot lie in the end, but only *in its highest specimens*" (9). In the third *Meditation*, this thought, too, is taken up again. The mass of men are essentially animals without any unique dignity, and "the goal of development" cannot, therefore, lie "in the mass of specimens or in their well-being" but only "in single great human beings." These, however, are as a matter of empirical fact clearly not "the last ones in point of time"—a view for which Nietzsche, here and elsewhere, has nothing but scorn—but are "apparently scattered and accidental existences" (6). The contrast Nietzsche later makes in *Zarathustra* between the overman and the *"last man"* (Z-V 5) further crystallizes this point. The *Meditation* also anticipates his later diatribes against utilitarianism: "here the ultimate aim is to be found in the happiness of all or of the most, and there in the development of large commonwealths." To Nietzsche all this is only a multiplication of zero by zero.

The question remains whether the universe as a whole has any purpose at all. Nietzsche may have shown to his own satisfaction that, *if* it has a purpose, it apparently fails to carry it out successfully as long as only "apparently scattered and accidental" great human beings are produced; he certainly has not demonstrated that there is any purpose at all. In fact, the naturalistic presumption would be that nature may well lack all purpose.

Nietzsche's lack of systematic commitments and premises, however, here permits him to be sufficiently candid to express a view that is not untrue to the phenomena confronting us. He really does not let "concepts, opinions, things past," or traditional views "step between himself and things" (7).

> The men with whom we live resemble a field of ruins of the most precious sculptural designs where everything shouts at us: come, help, perfect, . . . we yearn immeasurably to become whole [6].

Nothing is accomplished by discarding this experience as "mystic." A man with an open mind—and without any previous commitment to the opinion that nature is purposive or that it is not—might very well be led to the conclusion that is has a purpose which it is unable to accomplish completely. The question here is less whether Nietzsche is right than whether he is leaving empiricism and betraying his method by making supernatural assumptions. The answer to that limited and specific question is negative.

While Kant had declared in his essay on history, "Nature does nothing superfluous and is, in the use of means for her purposes [*Zwecke*], not squandering," Nietzsche writes: "The way of nature looks like squandering; . . . it proceeds . . . wastefully" (7).[11] Nature has purposes (*Zwecke*), but it is not *zweckmässig:* it does not proceed wisely to realize its purposes; its means are inadequate, wasteful, and inefficient. Hence man must help nature and work at his own perfection.

The plausibility of Nietzsche's view consists in its anthropomorphism. If we look at nature without prejudice, it seems that there is much which is too well designed to have been an accident, and much which is too ill designed to be explicable in terms of any fathomable purpose. Hence, Nietzsche concludes, nature is purposive but not entirely efficient in realizing its plans. This is the cosmological setting of his early philosophy.

The place Nietzsche would assign to natural selection deserves special mention. He grants that natural selection takes place, but he denies that it operates for "progress." Mediocrity seems more apt to survive than "the single higher specimens"—"that which is more unusual, more powerful, more complicated" (6). Hence natural selection will not generate bigger and better philosophers, artists, or saints, but only bigger and better brutes.

The point at which Nietzsche's early attempt to solve his value problem finally breaks down is this: how can he determine what specimens are the most valuable? How can he defend his assumption that artist, saint, and philosopher are the highest forms of life? He clearly denounces the proposition that what comes later in evolution is therefore more valuable, and he repudiates naked admiration for success. Is not the sanc-

---

[11] Cf. Goethe: " '*Nature does nothing in vain*' is an old Philistine slogan. Nature is eternally at work and alive, superfluous and squandering, in order that the infinite may ever be present because nothing can abide. In this I even believe that I come close to the Hegelian philosophy. . . ." (Letter to K. F. Zelter, August 13, 1831; cf. Eckermann, October 7, 1828.)

tion of his values thus reduced to that inner voice which prompts
him to perfect himself?

Nietzsche himself was not satisfied with this conclusion. He
did not wish to rely on any intuitive grasp of the purpose of
nature. He wanted a naturalistic value theory and a sanction
that would not be a poor substitute for God. He was in quest
of a standard and measure by which diverse values could be
judged. Therefore his early philosophy did not satisfy him. The
reconstruction of his early views, however, is no detour from
the best approach to his later works. Nietzsche himself never
renounced his early theories but only tried to strengthen them.
They are, in fact, nothing less than the clue to his later views,
which are so often misunderstood because his early philosophy
is ignored. His later writings are "plain enough, assuming—as
I do assume—that one has first read my earlier writings and
not spared some trouble in doing this" (GM-V 8).

Finally, it may be well to recall once more a few points that
are of special importance for Nietzsche's later thought. He accepted Darwin's doctrine concerning the lack of any cardinal
distinction between man and animals as incontrovertible empirical fact and tried to counter this "deadly" gospel with the new,
Nietzschean, assertion that man *can* rise above the beasts. He
granted that the factor of intelligence does not distinguish man
from all other animals and that most men's behavior is not
essentially different from animal behavior—notions which are
basic in much recent psychology. Our skills, crafts, and techniques can only raise us to the level of super-chimpanzees.
Nietzsche, however, defied Darwin, as it were, to find even
traces of art—which he distinguished from the crafts—or of religion and philosophy among the animals. If a technician is
only a super-ape, the same cannot be said of Plato. Some pursuits are supra-animalic, and the man who engages in them is a
truly *human* being and has a unique worth. The artist, saint, and
philosopher are representatives of true humanity and culture.

This triad recalls Hegel's subdivision of the realm of Absolute Spirit. Both philosophers consider art, religion, and philosophy man's most sublime pursuits. For Hegel, however, the great
turning point is that from the Philosophy of Nature to the
Philosophy of Spirit; in his *Encyclopädie,* the animals are in-

cluded in the Philosophy of Nature, while even primitive man is considered in the Philosophy of Spirit. For Nietzsche, on the other hand, the entire realm of Hegel's Objective Spirit, including the State, is still a part of nature. The State is only a more complicated version of the herd, and as long as man conforms he remains essentially an animal. The great turning point is, to Nietzsche's mind, that from Objective Spirit to Absolute Spirit, from the State to art, religion, and philosophy. Thus, while for Hegel the great cleft was that between animal and man, Nietzsche considers the gulf between the ordinary man, on the one side, and artist, saint and philosopher, on the other, the truly significant gap.

Nietzsche's doctrine is dangerous insofar as he affirms that the difference between man and man is more significant than that between man and animal. One would do scant justice to his thought, however, were one to forget that he began with the assumption that *all* men were essentially animals, and that he took over this assumption from the empirical sciences. He arrived at his supra-animalic triad only by looking for essentially human qualities, and it is thus no mere accident that he hit upon artist, saint, and philosopher. He searched for what he called "no-longer-animals" and not for super-brutes.

His insistence that truly human beings are not functions of any race, color, or creed, but widely scattered over the centuries and continents, is as characteristic as is his attack on the State. Nonconformity is the necessary condition of self-realization. The State is the devil who tempts and intimidates man into animal conformity and thus keeps him from rising into the heaven of true humanity; the Church is the Antichrist who has perverted Christ's original call to man to break with father and mother and become perfect: she has sold Christ to Caesar and become the chief accomplice of the State in compelling uniformity.

In the end, Nietzsche's early philosophy does not solve the problem of furnishing a naturalistic standard of values. The suggestion of a dialectical interpretation of health is not followed through; the supra-historical is recognized but not accounted for; and the problem of the value of culture remains puzzling. Nietzsche is consistently naturalistic, insofar as he insists that man need not break completely with his own animal nature to do the good and to create the beautiful. When he adds, however, that man should transfigure his *physis,* perfect himself, and aid nature, one must ask whether that, too, is naturalism—and Nietzsche fails to answer that question.

The dichotomy of two selves, an empirical self and a "true self," reappears in Nietzsche's account of nature: nature has a purpose but carries it out inefficiently and requires our aid. This dualism is mitigated by the conception of culture as another and transfigured *physis;* but one cannot be sure whether ultimately there are one or two basic principles, nor just how the relation of value and nature is to be understood. The problem can be expressed in terms of the Dionysian and Apollinian. Culture evidently requires both: Apollo must give form to Dionysus; man must organize the chaos and become a harmonious whole. Nietzsche, however, fails to explain the relation of these forces to each other. We are left to wonder whether they are both naturalistic principles, whether the Apollinian principle of individuation is supernatural, or whether both can perhaps be reduced to a more basic conception.

6

THE DISCOVERY OF THE
WILL TO POWER

When one speaks of *humanity*, the idea is fundamental
that this is something that *separates* and distinguishes
man from nature. In reality, however, there is no such
separation: "natural" qualities and those called properly
"human" are indivisibly grown together. Man, in his
highest and most noble capacities, is wholly nature and
embodies its uncanny dual character. Those of his abilities which are awesome and considered inhuman are
perhaps the fertile soil out of which alone all humanity
. . . can grow.—II, 369.

The basic difference between Nietzsche's earlier and later theories is that his final philosophy is based on the assumption of a
single basic principle, while the philosophy of his youth was
marked by a cleft which all but broke it in two. When Nietzsche introduced the will to power into his thought, all the dualistic tendencies which had rent it previously could be reduced to
mere manifestations of this basic drive. Thus a reconciliation
was finally effected between Dionysus and Apollo, nature and
value, wastefulness and purpose, empirical and true self, and
physis and culture.

While the study of Nietzsche's early works may reveal the
need for some modification, it does not explain why this change
should have consisted in an appeal to the will to power, nor
does it offer any sufficient clue to the meaning of this notorious
conception. The questions which arise in this connection are
best answered by a brief account of Nietzsche's discovery of the
will to power. Nothing could show better than this whether it is
primarily a perverse development of Schopenhauer's "will," an

early anticipation of Alfred Adler's version of psychoanalysis, a political notion, as Bäumler would have us believe—or something still different.

Frau Förster-Nietzsche recounts a story about the genesis of this conception which is apt to prejudice our understanding of it. She claims that her brother told her how, in the Franco-Prussian War of 1870/71, he saw a Prussian regiment attacking in spite of their evident fatigue, and that it was then that it occurred to him that life was essentially not a struggle for survival but a will to power.[1] The style and feeling, however, which characterize her enthusiastic description of the handsome soldiers and their flashing uniforms is quite remarkably at variance with all we find in Nietzsche's books and notes, while it is in tune with his sister's nationalism and feminine enthusiasm for uniforms. More important, of course, is the fact that Nietzsche did not write of a will to power, even in his notes, until almost ten years later—and then at first only to repudiate it.

The will to power did not spring from Nietzsche's head full grown. There is no point in his writings where it suddenly appears as a surprising inspiration, although no published work refers to it by name before its proclamation by Zarathustra. Rather it is possible—and important—to trace its gradual growth through Nietzsche's notes and books and thus to discover simultaneously what the relation of the will to power to psychology and politics might be and how we are supposed to know that there is this fundamental single principle.

I

The phrase "will to power" makes its first appearance in the notes of the late eighteen-seventies, not as the basic force of a monistic metaphysics but as one of two cardinal psychological phenomena: "Fear (negative) and will to power (positive) explain our strong consideration for the opinions of men" (IX, 297). This is but a variation of a theme struck earlier at the beginning of the third *Meditation*. There Nietzsche had sought to explain our deplorable tendency toward conformity by pointing out that either fear or laziness must be considered the most uni-

---

[1] *Das Leben Friedrich Nietzsches* (1895–1904), II, 682 f.

versal human trait. Now the same regrettable phenomenon is explained in terms of fear and the will to power.

Power here must evidently mean "worldly power" and social success, making friends and influencing people. Because men wish to have such power, they betray their destiny, fail to cultivate their *physis,* and conform. If this interpretation is correct, one should expect that Nietzsche scorned power, so understood, in his early period; and this expectation is fully borne out by the facts. In the drafts for *The Birth of Tragedy,* Nietzsche speaks of *"power* which is always evil" (III, 282); and at the end of the *Meditation* on Wagner he inquires: "Who of you will renounce power, knowing and experiencing that power is evil?" Nor are these merely random remarks, singled out to prove a point. They are entirely representative of Nietzsche's early views and are brought out with particular clarity in the last *Meditation,* that on Wagner. The young Wagner is pictured as imbued with a "sullen personal will, insatiably demanding *power and splendor"*; then his "craving for the highest power . . . is entirely transformed into artistic creativity"; and finally, "when he renounced success . . . and foreswore the thought of power, 'success' and 'power' come to him" (8).

When Nietzsche wrote this *Meditation* he had severe misgivings; and when *Human, All-Too-Human* appeared he was firmly convinced that Wagner had been thoroughly corrupted by his belated "success" and "power" and that, to maintain and increase them, he had made his peace with State and Church and bowed to public opinion. Wagner's retreat into conformity can only have strengthened Nietzsche's conviction—which perhaps was originally suggested to him, or at least significantly confirmed, by Burckhardt—that power, i.e., worldly power, is essentially evil. The note in which the will to power is first explicitly referred to, in an attempt to "explain our strong consideration for the opinions of men," is probably to be understood in terms of the Wagner experience. There is altogether no question but that the phenomenon "Wagner" had a significance for Nietzsche's thought comparable only to that of Goethe and Socrates, the Renaissance and classical Greece, Dionysus and the Crucified. In Wagner he found both the will to worldly power, the excessive ambition of which Nietzsche made so much in *The Case of Wagner* (6 ff.), and a suggestion of the possible transformation of such a will to power into artistic creativity. Wagner thus afforded him a singular opportunity for a first-hand study of the will to power—a point of departure for an induction, to speak scientifically, and the intensification of an everyday theme into a comprehensive symbol, to put it supra-historically.

The next book after the *Meditation* on Wagner represented a new direction in Nietzsche's thought: "the thinking about the human, all-too-human—or as the scholarly expression puts it: psychological observation" (MA I 35). His style now is aphoristic, and his books consist of a large number of analyses of various psychological phenomena—some with a bearing on his value problem, others in no way directly related to it. The irrational springs of human behavior are uncovered expertly, and the self-styled vivisectionist cuts mercilessly through prejudices and conventions to lay bare the hidden motivations of our actions. In the course of these investigations, which extend into his later works, Nietzsche frequently offers suggestions that one would today associate with psychoanalysis; e.g., "Laughter means: to rejoice at another's expense [*schadenfroh sein*], but with a good conscience" (FW 200). As a single more extensive example one may consider some observations on dreams.

> *The logic of the dream.* When one sleeps, the nervous system is constantly excited by manifold internal stimuli . . . the position of the sleeper, his blankets, influence his feelings variously . . . and all this excites by its unusualness the whole system, including the brain functions. Thus there are a hundred occasions for the mind to be surprised and to search for *reasons* for this excitation: the dream, however, is the *searching for, and the imagining of, the causes* for these excited feelings, i.e., the supposed causes. For example, if one ties two straps around one's feet, one may dream that two snakes are coiled around one's feet. . . . What is thus inferred to have been the near past becomes the present through the excited imagination. Thus everybody knows from experience how quickly one blends a strong sound—e.g., the tolling of bells or cannon shots—into his dream, i.e., how he explains them *ex post facto* through his dream, in such a way that he *supposes* that he experiences first the causal circumstances and then this sound. . . . I suppose: as man even now infers in dreams, mankind inferred for many thousands of years *also when awake;* the first cause that occurred to the mind to explain anything that required explanation sufficed and was considered the truth. . . . Dreams take us back again to distant conditions of human culture and put a means at our disposal for understanding them better [MA I 13].

. . . Our *dreams* have this very value and meaning: to *compensate* to a certain degree this accidental lack of "nourishment" during the day. Why was the dream of yesterday full of tenderness and tears, that of the day before jocular and exuberant, a former one adventurous . . . ? Why do I in this one enjoy indescribable beauties of music, why do I in another one float and fly with the rapture of an eagle up toward distant mountain peaks? These fictions, which give play to, and permit the discharge of, our drives of tenderness or jocularity or adventurousness, or our demand for music and mountains— and everybody will have his own better examples at hand— are interpretations of our nerve stimulations during dreams, *very free,* very arbitrary interpretations. . . . That this text, which after all generally remains much the same in one night as in another, is yet annotated so variously; that the inventing reason *imagines* such various *causes* for the same nerve stimulations today and yesterday—that is due to the fact that the prompter of this reason was a different one today from yesterday: another *drive* wanted to satisfy, exert, exercise, refresh, and discharge itself—today one drive is at its high tide, and yesterday it was another one. Waking life does not have this same *freedom* of interpretation as in dreams . . . but need I elaborate that our drives, when we are awake, also do nothing else than interpret nerve stimulations and posit "causes" according to their requirements? That between waking and dreaming there is no *essential* difference? . . . That even our moral judgments and valuations are only pictures and phantasies about a physiological process which is unknown to us . . . ? That all our so-called consciousness is a more or less fantastic commentary on an unknown, perhaps unknowable, but felt text? [M 119].

In the outbreaks of passion and in the fantasies of dreams and madness man rediscovers his own and mankind's prehistory [M 312; cf. MA I 12].

There is no need for any long comment on these observations. The quoted passages may serve to illustrate the tenor of some of Nietzsche's analyses insofar as they seem close to psychonanalysis. It should not be forgotten, however, that his aphoristic experimentalism reaches its height in this period and that he does not offer any systematic theory comparable to Freud's.[2] In fact, it will be seen later that the conception of "so-called conscious-

---

[2] Freud himself says in his *Selbstdarstellung,* after pointing out that he read Schopenhauer late in his life: "*Nietzsche,* the other philosopher whose premonitions and insights often agree in the most amazing manner with the laborious results of psychoanalysis, I have long avoided for this very

ness" as "a more or less fantastic commentary on an unknown
. . . text" is at odds with Nietzsche's later philosophy, or at least
with its main current. In the books now under consideration,
Nietzsche's open-mindedness and lack of any commitment to a
central thesis gives rise to a host of suggestive and fruitful observations—some of which will eventually serve as the basis of an
unpremeditated but impressive induction: that the basic psychological drive is the will to power.

There would be little sense in trying here to sample the
gems of *Human, All-Too-Human* or the *Dawn*; nor is there any
reason for showing in detail how Nietzsche, in a section on artists,
elaborates some insights about Wagner. In other sections he
deals with "the history of moral feelings," "religious life," "signs
of higher and lower cultures," and a number of other subjects
including "a glance at the State." Even when he returns to his
old value problem, however, he makes no attempt to indicate
the bearing of his observations on his previous theories, though
he suggests—as one would expect from the pervasive temper of
his work—that valuations are essentially rationalizations of our
interests: "A drive toward something or away from something
. . . without . . . a kind of . . . estimation of the value of the
goal does not exist in man" (MA I 32).

It is within this psychological framework that Nietzsche is led
to reintroduce power to explain various kinds of behavior:

> The reason why a powerful person is grateful is this: his bene-
> factor has . . . intruded into . . . [his] sphere. . . . It is a
> milder form of revenge. Without the satisfaction of gratitude,
> the powerful man would have shown himself powerless and
> would hence be considered so. Therefore every society of the
> good, i.e., originally of the powerful, posits gratitude as one of
> the first duties [MA I 44].

A brief explanation may clarify Nietzsche's point. Somebody does
something for me. There is an implication that I was powerless

---

reason. After all, I was less concerned about any priority than about the
preservation of my openmindedness [*Unbefangenheit*]." (*Gesammelte
Werke* [London 1948], XIV, 86.) Cf. *The Basic Writings of Sigmund Freud*
(New York, The Modern Library, 1938), 939. *Ibid.,* 103, Freud expresses
his admiration for Nietzsche's aphorism: " 'I have done that,' says my
memory. 'I could not have done that,' says my pride, and remains inexorable. Finally, my memory yields" (J 68).

Freud's other tributes to Nietzsche are cited in my *From Shakespeare
to Existentialism* (rev. ed., 1960), 323.

and needed his help. I am degraded in his eyes and in my own. Then I thank him, and the implication is reversed: he has done something for me, as if I were the powerful one and he my servant. In that sense, gratitude may be considered a mild form of revenge. More important: Nietzsche has explained a moral valuation as prompted by the will to power.

The next aphorism develops the suggestion that the good were originally the powerful. A "dual prehistory of Good and Evil" is sketched in terms of the diverse codes of the powerful and the powerless. The first juxtaposes Good and Bad; the latter, Good and Evil. The argument is terminated with the unpolemical conclusion that "our present ethics" is a development of the code of the powerful. When the same argument is repeated more elaborately and at far greater length in the *Genealogy* in 1887, "our present ethics" is pictured as heavily indebted to the morality of the powerless and oppressed or—to use Nietzsche's word—the slaves. The distinction between the powerful and the powerless, as here envisaged, is clearly a sociological one—not racial or biological—and it is suggested that being oppressed, which is here considered the equivalent of being powerless, may lead men to mistrust and hate everybody.

Proceeding quite unsystematically and considering each problem on its own merits, without a theory to prove or an ax to grind, Nietzsche reverts now and then to explanations in terms of what he was later to call a will to power. Speaking of pity, for example, Nietzsche observes that the effort of some neurotics to arouse pity is due to a wish *"to hurt":* when others suffer for their sake, they feel "that at least they still *have one power,* in spite of all their weakness, the power to hurt" (MA 1 50). Nietzsche's extensive polemic against pity is colored by the literal meaning of the German word, *Mitleid,* which has the same etymology as "sympathy" and means "suffering-with." To want pity is to want others to suffer with us. While Nietzsche, as a psychological observer, offers no evaluation, it is plain that he does not consider the neurotic's will to power admirable. The same may be said of another very short aphorism: *"Luke, 18:14 corrected.* He that humbleth himself wills to be exalted" (MA 1 87). Again, a will to power is recognized of which Nietzsche, by all indications, does not approve.

Beyond that, Nietzsche's "correction" of the ancient theological paradox, for which he would substitute a psychological paradox, is of great significance. An apparent negation of the will to power is explained in terms of the will to power. Even asceticism, humility, self-abasement, and renunciation of worldly power are perhaps motivated in this way. With this insight, the possibility of a psychological monism suggests itself: *all* psychological phenomena might be reducible to the will to power. Nietzsche, however, is not primarily in search of any basic principle, and he does not jump to this conclusion—yet.

It is thus apparent that Nietzsche approached the conception of a will to power from two distinct points of view. First, he thought of it as a craving for worldly success, which he repudiated as harmful to man's interest in perfecting himself. Secondly, he thought of the will to power as a psychological drive in terms of which many diverse phenomena could be explained; e.g., gratitude, pity, and self-abasement. The phrase "will to power" is not yet used, except in one note, and Nietzsche far from approves of this urge. While one cannot, on the basis of the evidence so far considered, make any sweeping statements about Nietzsche's philosophy, it seems worth insisting that, at least at first, Nietzsche used the will to power as a principle to explain behavior and did not picture it as a virtue. In fact, he used it generally to explain behavior he happened to dislike.

Among the aphorisms cited, there was only one in which power appeared as possibly good: in the "prehistory of Good and Evil" and the juxtaposition of the powerful and the oppressed. One may wonder, in that connection, about the relationship of power and the will to power. Is it possible that the will to power is essentially an urge of the impotent and that the powerful themselves have no will to power? Conceivably, one might think of power as good but of the will to power as a source of evil; conversely, one might think of the will to power as a source of good but of power itself as evil. Nietzsche's descriptive attitude bars any such judgments, but he clearly implies that the will to power exists both among the powerful—whose high esteem of gratitude Nietzsche would explain thus—and among the impotent, whose desire for pity Nietzsche construes as prompted by a will to power. The implication is that "powerful" and "powerless" are merely relative terms, and that the "powerful" and the "powerless" agree in desiring *more* power.

This view is confirmed by a note of that period: "The pleasure of power is explained by the hundredfold experience of displeasure at dependence and impotence [*Ohnmacht*]. If this experience is not there, then the pleasure is lacking, too" (IX, 398). Power is enjoyed only as *more* power. One enjoys not its possession but its increase: the overcoming of impotence. Since impotence is the equivalent of dependence, one might say that the achievement of independence is the source of pleasure. Nietzsche, however, says in the very next note: "One strives for independence (freedom) for the sake of *power,* not the other way around" (IX, 398). This note suggests that not independence but power is the source of pleasure. Nietzsche's thought seems to be this: man wants neither power nor independence—as such. He wants not freedom *from* something but freedom to act and realize himself. When speaking of power, Nietzsche, as a classical philologist, probably had in mind the conceptions of *dynamis* and *potentia.* Even closer is the relation of the will to power to Hegel's notion of spirit, which was conceived as essentially a striving for freedom[3]—and this parallel will have to be considered in some detail in a later chapter.

In *Human, All-Too-Human* and in the notes of that period —to summarize—Nietzsche sought to explain the following phenomena in terms of the will to power: our tendency to conform rather than to realize ourselves; the elevation of gratitude to the status of a virtue; the desire of neurotics—and perhaps also others —to arouse pity; Christian self-abasement; and the striving for independence and freedom. Of all these sundry manifestations of the will to power, Nietzsche probably approved only of the striving for freedom.

To the first volume of *Human, All-Too-Human* a second volume of *Vermischte Meinungen und Sprüche* was added in 1879, and in 1880 a third part appeared under the title *Der Wanderer und sein Schatten.* In spirit, these sequels are much like the first installment, though they add a liberal dose of new insights. They do not shed much new light on the conception of power, but it is noteworthy that Nietzsche introduces a distinction between "democracy as something yet to come" and "that which is even now so designated and distinguished from older forms of government only by driving with *new horses:* the roads are still the

---

[3] Cf., e.g., *Geschichtsphilosophie,* 44–47, 568 f.; *Aesthetik* I, 142.

same old ones, and the wheels are also still the same old ones."
While he evidently disapproves of contemporary democracies—
"Has the danger really decreased through *these* vehicles of the
welfare of nations?"—he seems more sympathetic toward that
truer democracy of the future which "wants to create and guarantee *independence* for as many as possible, independence of opinions, way of life, and business" (S 293). Nietzsche envisages the
eventual *"victory of democracy"* and the rise of a "middle class
that may *forget* socialism like a disease that has been weathered";
and he adds: "The practical result of this spreading of democrati-
zation will first be a European League of Nations" (S 292).

One further passage may be quoted here, written when Germany was at the zenith of her power:

> And perhaps the great day will come when a people, distin-
> guished by wars and victories and by the highest development
> of a military order and intelligence, and accustomed to make
> the heaviest sacrifices for these things, will exclaim of its own
> free will, "We break the sword," and will smash its entire mili-
> tary establishment down to its lowest foundations. *Rendering
> oneself unarmed when one has been the best-armed,* out of a
> height of feeling—that is the means to real peace, which must
> always rest on a peace of mind; whereas the so-called armed
> peace, as it now exists in all countries, is the absence of peace
> of mind. One trusts neither oneself nor one's neighbor and,
> half from hatred, half from fear, does not lay down arms.
> Rather perish than hate and fear, and *twice rather perish than
> make oneself hated and feared*—this must some day become the
> highest maxim for every single commonwealth, too [S 284].

II

Nietzsche's next work, the *Dawn,* furnishes a superb example of
his experimentalism. Not only does he speak of experimenting
(187, 453, 501, 547)—the book *is* an experiment. Prevalent moral
valuations form the subject; the subtitle reads "Thoughts about
Moral Prejudices"; and the implication is that current moral
valuations are nothing but prejudices. "With this book," Nietzsche writes later of the *Dawn,* "begins my campaign against
morality" (EH-M 1). In fact, the book contains one of Nietzsche's most sustained attempts at a "vivisection" of altruistic

ethics.[4] For the present, this may be ignored in favor of Nietzsche's attempt to substantiate his implicit hypothesis that psychological phenomena can be explained in terms of two key
concepts: fear and power. After Nietzsche in his previous work
had found that many different kinds of behavior can be so explained, he now tried to see how far he could get by using these
two concepts. The *Dawn* might therefore be considered as a final
test, a dress rehearsal, before the will to power is proclaimed as
Nietzsche's basic principle. Yet the *Dawn* does not contain any
mention of the will to power by that name, and the picture of
the dress rehearsal is misleading in one respect: Nietzsche evidently did not formulate an explicit working hypothesis which
he might then have proceeded to test by experiment before
maintaining it publicly. Instead he investigated his problems
without any clear notion of possible systematic implications.
While he tried to see how far he might get by reducing complex
and differentiated phenomena to fear and power, the full force of
his results did not strike him until later.[5]

In his next work, *The Gay Science*, Nietzsche still experi-
mented with the notion of power and did not yet expound any
monism nor any systematic psychological theory. The book also
contains the first tentative consideration of the conception of the
eternal recurrence of all events.[6] Then, suddenly, the implications of both the will to power and the eternal recurrence struck
Nietzsche's mind at once, like a flash of lightning, and in a

---

[4] M 63, 174, 214, 224, 289, 315, 334, 377, 385, 411, 516, 517, 549—and the
entire consecutive section M 131–148. The following notes of the same
period contain similar material: x, 385–93, 396, 399, 401, 408 f.

[5] This view of the *Dawn* is confirmed by Peter Gast "who was with Nietzsche
much of the time while the *Dawn* was written": "Nietzsche was . . . in
this book primarily concerned with two psychological problems: first, the
problem of *fear* . . . secondly, the problem of *power*. . . ." (editors' note,
x, 439) *Before* reading this, I noted the following aphorisms as carrying
out the experiment with fear: M 5, 26, 57, 104, 142, 173, 174, 220, 241,
250, 309, 310, 551—and these others for the experiment with power:
M 113, 128, 140, 146, 184, 189, 201, 204, 205, 215, 245, 248, 262, 271, 317,
348, 356, 360, 371, 548, 571. These two lists include all of the far fewer
aphorisms which Gast cited to illustrate his point. His observation may
therefore be considered a conclusive confirmation.

[6] The experiment with power is continued FW 13, 14, 18, 118, 119, 136,
137, though the name "will to power" occurs only in the Fifth Book
(FW 349), which Nietzsche appended to the second edition in 1887. Cf.
also FW 347, 370, 377 for references to power in the Fifth Book. The
recurrence is discussed FW 233, 285, 288, 341.

frenzied feeling of inspiration (EH-Z) he wrote his *Zarathustra*—the first published work to contain any mention of the will to power by that name—and there expounded both concepts.[7] From then on he considered it his task to work out the details of the insight he had first offered in the "dithyrambs" of *Zarathustra:* the universality of both the will to power and the eternal recurrence. Most of his interpreters have disregarded the conception of eternal recurrence, though it would seem that no author can be understood correctly as long as the very notion which he himself valued most extravagantly (G x 5; EH-Z 1) is ignored. While it is theoretically conceivable that the will to power and the eternal recurrence are mutually contradictory, no interpretation of the will to power can be considered satisfactory unless the question of its compatibility with its twin conception is at least considered in some detail. For they do not belong to different periods of Nietzsche's life or to different books and were evidently not considered mutually exclusive by Nietzsche himself.

Postponing discussion of the recurrence, one may note that in the *Dawn* power is still, no less than fear, a psychological phenomenon. The will to power, which appears frequently under different names, is considered "human, all-too-human" and not traced through the animal kingdom, nor taken to be a cosmic force. Even later, in *The Gay Science,* Nietzsche has only scorn for Schopenhauer's "unprovable doctrine of the *One Will*," no less than for his *"denial of the individual,"* his way of considering *"development* only an illusion," his *Schwärmerei* about the genius, and "the nonsense about *pity"* (FW 99). In fact, Nietzsche writes:

> Against him I urge these propositions: first, in order that there may be a will, a representation of pleasure or displeasure is required. . . . Third, only in intellectual beings is there pleasure, displeasure, and will; the vast majority of organisms has nothing of all this [FW 127].

In the *Dawn* Nietzsche does not celebrate or repudiate either power or fear: he uses both to explain phenomena and, while he does not pass judgment in so many words, presumably he considers both sometimes good and sometimes not. Thus it is "the great result of humanity to date" that we have shaken off

---

[7] Will to power: Z I 15; Z II 12, 20. Eternal recurrence: Z II 20; Z III 2, 3, 13, 16; Z IV 19.

that "constant fear of wild animals, of barbarians, of gods, and of our dreams" which haunts primitive man (M 5); but with our fear (*Furcht*) we have also lost our reverence (*Ehrfurcht*) for the incomprehensible, and the world has therefore all but lost its fascination for us (M 551).

Primarily, however, fear is nothing but our attitude toward power—or, in Nietzsche's own previous words, the negative aspect of our will to power. A privation of power gives rise to both fear and the will to power: fear is the negative motive which would make us avoid something; the will to power is the positive motive which would make us strive for something. Nietzsche does not yet conclude that, wherever there is fear, there is also a will to have the power to cope with what is feared. The two are still employed as separate principles.

For our present purpose, it will suffice to give one further example both of the regrettable and of the valuable results of fear. It explains not only conformity to the behavior of others—as the *Meditation* on Schopenhauer had suggested—but also the adoption of the valuations of others. First, people behave as if these valuations were their own, too, because they are afraid not to conform; then they get used to this pretense and "it becomes second nature." This is surely a common experience in countries taken over by totalitarian governments—but Nietzsche is thinking of early childhood. As children, we do not conform because the judgment of our elders is apt to be more rational than ours, but —according to Nietzsche—merely from impotence and fear (M 104).

Fear, however, is also a great teacher: the mother of our knowledge of man. Unlike love, which has "a secret impulse to see in another as much as possible of what is beautiful"—and which is gladly deceived about the true nature of another—fear "wishes to guess," to unriddle him; it prompts us to find out "what he can do, what he wants: to be deceived here would be a danger." Thus "fear has promoted the general insight about man more than has love" (M 309). That for fear one might substitute the concept of the will to power does not yet occur to Nietzsche; he does not infer that only our will to overpower the other one has prompted our knowledge.

We need not here examine, or even enumerate, all the phenomena that Nietzsche would explain, in the *Dawn*—and then in *The Gay Science*—as prompted by a will to power; for his psychology is of interest here primarily insofar as it clarifies the meaning of "power"—a word that is easily misconstrued. It will therefore be sufficient to list a few examples. There is, first, man's desire to find scapegoats, the quest of the weak and the impotent to find somebody upon whom they can look down and to whom they may feel superior (M 140); *Grosse Politik* (power politics) is prompted not only by the princes' and potentates' lust for power but also by a desire among "the lower strata of the nation" for a feeling of might (M 189); dishonesty in business, arson committed by those who wish to collect insurance, counterfeiting, and stock market speculation may all be prompted by a lust for money which, in turn, is wanted because it gives a feeling of power: the craving is the same as that which inspired previous generations when they "burnt Jews, heretics, and good books, and destroyed entire higher cultures, as that of Peru and Mexico":

> The means of the craving for power have changed, but the same volcano is still glowing . . . and what one did formerly "for God's sake" one does now for the sake of money . . . which *now* gives the highest feeling of power . . . [M 204].

The next aphorism, which contains an extensive eulogy of the Jews, contains an attempt to explain their usury in past centuries as an effort to achieve a feeling of power through the one occupation left to them: "for our self-respect depends on our ability to repay in kind both the good and bad." Even self-sacrifice may give an increased feeling of power, for one identifies oneself with a greater power, "be it a god or man," and glories in his might (M 145, 215).

Another type of behavior is explained in terms of the same paradox: if there should ever be a socialist state, it would enforce an unprecedented iron discipline—*"they know themselves"*—and the citizens would put up with their chains because "they are self-imposed, and the feeling of . . . *this* power is so young and charming to them that they would suffer anything for its sake" (M 184).

Napoleon is introduced: he "was annoyed because he spoke badly"; he decided, however, "to speak even worse *than he could* speak," for he did not want to be the slave of his shortcomings: he wanted to have the power to determine his manner of speaking (M 245).

Utilitarian behavior, such as kindness inspired either by the apprehension that unkindness would lead to an infraction of one's power or by the positive desire to inspire trust, is prompted by a will to power (M 248). And happiness is now taken to be essentially a feeling of power: its usual expressions are "giving, deriding, destroying—all three with one common basic drive" (M 356).

Suddenly it occurred to Nietzsche that the basic drive that prompted the development of Greek culture might well have been the will to power. He notes his conviction that the Greeks preferred power to anything "useful" and even to a good reputation (M 360); and the second mention of the "will to power"—by that name—occurs in the notes of that period and insists that the ancient Greeks frankly admitted their will to power (x, 414). This sudden association of the will to power with the Greeks was one of the most decisive steps in the development of this conception into an all-embracing monism.

Nietzsche had previously considered the contest (*agon*) the most fruitful concept for any analysis of Greek culture. He had thought not only of the rivalry of the ancient dramatists who vied with each other for the highest prize, but also of the Olympic games and the Greek gymnasium (II, 376); of Plato's effort to outdo the Sophists and the poets by composing more beautiful myths, speeches, and dialogues than they had ever conceived (II, 377); and of the Socratic dialectic, which he understood as a spiritual contest (VII, 191; M 544). Now it occurred to him that the contest itself was a manifestation of the will to power.

The will to power is thus not only the devil who diverts man from achieving culture, or a psychological urge that helps to explain diverse and complex types of human behavior: it is also envisaged as the basis of Greek culture, which Nietzsche then considered the acme of humanity. Instead of being associated primarily with neurotics who crave pity, with modern man's lust for money, with the burning of heretics and good books, with usury and counterfeiting, the will to power may now be envisaged as the basic drive of *all* human efforts. Philosophic discourse, the ancient tragedies and comedies, the Platonic dialogues, and the sculptures of the Periclean age are all understood in terms of the Greeks' will to outdo, excel, and overpower one another. Not only Athens and Sparta, and all the Greek city-states, but Aeschylus and Sophocles, Plato and Aristophanes, and all those who offered their speeches on love in the *Symposium* were competitors. Political and cultural achievements, art and philosophy are thus to be explained in terms of the will to power.

Nietzsche did not immediately recognize all these implications. Only in *Zarathustra* is the will to power proclaimed as the basic force underlying *all* human activities; and it is interesting to note that in Zarathustra's initial proclamation the culture of Greece is explicitly referred to and explained in terms of the will to power.

The philosophical significance of this monistic conception may be anticipated even now, if only by citing the first paragraph of Nietzsche's early fragment, *Homer's Contest* (1872):

> When one speaks of *humanity,* the idea is fundamental that this is something that *separates* and distinguishes man from nature. In reality, however, there is no such separation: "natural" qualities and those called properly "human" are indivisibly grown together. Man, in his highest and most noble capacities, is wholly nature and embodies its uncanny dual character. Those of his abilities which are awesome and considered inhuman are perhaps the fertile soil out of which alone all humanity . . . can grow [II, 369].

This fragment, in which Nietzsche had planned to develop the conception of the contest, was begun at about the time when *The Birth of Tragedy* was published. It has been shown how Nietzsche developed the notion of the "uncanny dual character" of nature in his *Meditations* and how this bifurcation threatened in the end to break his entire philosophy in two. The conception of the will to power points to a new emphasis on the continuity of nature and culture.

Nietzsche had not yet succeeded in establishing his thesis that the values of humanity were mere developments of our animal nature. The essay on *Homer's Contest* had remained a fragment, and the *Meditations* failed to prove this point. The psychological considerations that led Nietzsche to the conception of the will to power suggest the possibility of a new attempt to show how values can be generated out of nature. Before this account of the *Dawn* is concluded, however, two further points should be developed.

First, Nietzsche offers some more comments on the relation of power and the will to power.

> One should distinguish well: whoever still wants to gain the consciousness of power will use any means. . . . He, however,

who has it, has become very choosy and noble in his tastes
[M 348].

The point is that the will to power may be ruthless and a source
of evildoing, while power itself does not corrupt but ennobles
the mind. The powerful, as Nietzsche points out expressly, have
no need to prove their might either to themselves or to others by
oppressing or hurting others; if they do hurt others, they do so
incidentally in the process of using their power creatively; they
hurt others "without thinking of it." Only the weak man *"wishes
to hurt and to see the signs of suffering"* (M 371).

A good illustration of the manner in which a person who has
power, in Nietzsche's sense, may hurt another person incidentally
without the express wish of doing so, would be Goethe, whose
loves Nietzsche probably had to learn by heart, like most other
German students. Goethe—as German teachers like to point out
—broke Friederike's heart by lavishing his love upon her and
then not marrying her: here is one of the seeds of the Gretchen
tragedy. Goethe, however, had no thought of seeing the poor
girl suffer. Only the weak need to convince themselves and others
of their might by inflicting hurt: the truly powerful are not concerned with others but act out of a fullness and an overflow.

Nietzsche, of course, does not say that the powerful *should*
hurt others; he points out that *if* they hurt others they are not
motivated by the wish to hurt. There is, however, an implication
that impotence is dangerous for the human character: being oppressed and having to repress one's desires may lead to cruelty
and the desire to hurt. Impotence may thus be a source of poison,
and the possession of power may be a medicine: *"Medical Kit of
the Soul:* What is the strongest healing application?—Victory"
(M 571). This is not a doctor's prescription, as it were, but an im-
provisation from a "medical kit" *(Feld-Apotheke)*; it is a strong—
"the strongest"—medicine, and thus it is dangerous and not to
be prescribed generally.

The assumption is that the powerful and the impotent are
both imbued with the will to power, and that extreme or pro-
longed oppression and frustration may easily pervert this drive
and make the oppressed look for petty occasions to assert their
will to power by being cruel to others.

The *second* and final consideration about the *Dawn* is this:
we should ask expressly whether Nietzsche's conception of power
has not been whitewashed. We should face the question whether

Nietzsche did not, after all, have in mind political might. It so happens that the *Dawn* is quite unequivocal on this point. Three aphorisms will show quite definitely what Nietzsche had in mind.

The first of these three aphorisms may well be the most important one in the book and is entitled *"The Striving for Excellence."* The title suggests correctly that this aphorism marks the transition from the old conception of the contest to the new one of the will to power. The aphorism, moreover, constitutes one of Nietzsche's first sustained attempts to reduce practically all of human behavior to this single striving, in one uninterrupted analysis. He proceeds to do this in terms of a scale. At the bottom of the scale is the barbarian who tortures others; at the top, the ascetic who tortures himself.

> . . . Even when he who strives for excellence . . . wanted to make a delightful . . . impression, he did not enjoy this success insofar as he thus delighted his neighbor but insofar as he *impressed* himself on the soul of another, changed its form and ruled [*waltete*] over it according to his will. The striving for excellence is the striving to overwhelm [*überwältigen*] one's neighbor, even if only very indirectly or only in one's own feelings or even dreams. There is a long line of degrees of this secretly desired overwhelming, and a complete list of these would almost amount to a history of culture from the first still grimace-like barbarism to the grimace of . . . overrefinement. . . . The striving for excellence brings with it *for the neighbor*—to name only a few steps of this long ladder: tortures, then blows, then terror, then anguished amazement, then wonder, then envy, then laughing, then ridicule, then derision, then scorn, then the dealing of blows, then the inflicting of tortures: here, at the end of the ladder, stands the ascetic and martyr . . . [M 113].

The "history of culture" is thus to be explained in terms of man's will to overwhelm, outdo, excel, and overpower his neighbor. The barbarian does it by torturing his neighbor. In the light of Nietzsche's previous comments, he is essentially weak, else he would not need to inflict hurt. Nietzsche speaks of this as a low degree of the striving for excellence because he wishes to express that, *quantitatively,* we find little power at the bottom of the scale. Toward the middle of the scale, we find what might be called the normal degree of power: one seeks to evoke envy and admiration; one even seeks to elevate one's neighbor and derives a sense of power from doing so; one gives him joy and gaiety and lets him laugh, saying to oneself, as it were: I have the power to impress and delight him.

If our interpretation of the quantitativeness of these degrees were correct, it would follow that Nietzsche believed the ascetic to have a greater feeling of power than almost any other man; and this is fully borne out by the aphorism:

> Indeed, happiness—taken as the most alive feeling of power—has perhaps nowhere on earth been greater than in the souls of superstitious ascetics. This the Brahmins express in the story of the king Vishvamitra, who derived such strength from thousands of years of *penance exercises* that he undertook to build a new *heaven* [M 113; cf. GM III 10].

So serious is Nietzsche about this point—that ascetic self-torture is the source of the greatest possible feeling of power—that he concludes with a vision of God to develop the point more fully.

> Supposing that there were a God of love: what enjoyment for him to create *suffering* men and to suffer the . . . torture of looking upon them . . . What deliria of the divine ascetic are to be conjectured as he creates sin and sinners and eternal damnations and, beneath his heaven and throne, a tremendous site of eternal agony and of eternal sobbing and sighing! It is entirely impossible that the souls of Paul, of Dante, of Calvin . . . once penetrated the gruesome secrets of such voluptuousness of power . . . [M 113].

With this grotesque vision, the whole scale might begin all over again, as Nietzsche actually suggests. At the bottom was the barbarian who tortured his neighbor, at the top the ascetic who tortured himself; now one might conceive of an ascetic's torture of his beloved neighbor as a new form of self-torture.

This aphorism is of momentous significance. Nietzsche comes close to a solution of the problem that his early theory of values had been unable to solve, but he does not realize this and loses the key that might lead to the coveted answer. Nietzsche thinks of quantitative degrees of power as corresponding to various forms of behavior and of culture; and the saint—who was in his early philosophy, together with artist and philosopher, the most valuable human being—is considered the most powerful man. The barbarian, who is uncultured, is the least powerful. Power might thus be construed as the standard and measure of values. This would go well with Nietzsche's interpretation of health as the ability to overcome disease. For health he might substitute power. The artist's power consists in his ability to overcome disease and suffering. Here was at least a possible way of trying to cope with some of the problems of his early theory.

Nietzsche fails to see this and repudiates asceticism as a "grimace of overrefinement," i.e., a grotesque perversion. Both barbarian and ascetic are "grimaces," both are not representatives of true culture. The vision of the ascetic's torture of others —to make himself suffer—makes this clear.

Culture apparently is not the manifestation of the greatest power; it is somewhere along the middle of the scale. Nietzsche's repudiation of the barbarian, however, is clear, and political power was to his mind essentially a form of barbarism. This is expressly emphasized in the two aphorisms with which this account of the *Dawn* may be concluded.

> *Victory over Strength.* . . . Still one lies on one's knees before strength—according to the ancient habit of slaves—and yet, when the degree of *worthiness of being honored* is to be determined, only *the degree of reason in strength* is decisive: one must measure how far strength has been overcome by something higher and now serves that as its tool and means! [M 548].

The might of the German *Reich* does not impress Nietzsche. To bow before such strength is slavish. One might expect Nietzsche to base his repudiation on the assertion that only a weak nation finds it necessary to impress itself and others with barbarian brawn and armies, and that culture is a higher, i.e., a quantitatively greater, form of power. Instead Nietzsche refers to "the degree of reason in strength [*der Grad der Vernunft in der Kraft*]."

There is thus a strong suggestion of dualism: power appears almost as an evil principle, reason as the good. This repudiation of power as an evil principle becomes explicit in Nietzsche's denunciation of the German *Reich*. It is repudiated not because brawn is a manifestation of small power, but because power is a demon.

> *The Demon of Power.* Not need, nor desire—no, the love of power is the demon of man. One may give them everything— health, nourishment, quarters . . . —they remain unhappy . . . : for the demon . . . will be satisfied. One may take everything away from them and satisfy this demon: then they are almost happy. . . . Luther has already said this, and better than I,

in these verses: "If they take from us body, goods, honor, child, and wife: let it go—the *Reich* must yet remain to us!" Yes! Yes! The *"Reich!"* [M 262].

Luther, to be sure, had in mind the kingdom of God; Nietzsche, however, is *not* here considering Luther's words as an illustration of his own view that the Christian's sacrifice of body, goods, honor, child, and wife is really prompted by the desire for greater power in the kingdom of God beyond. Nietzsche is looking upon the German *Reich* of Bismarck, upon a nation thrilled by its love of power, upon a people willing to risk their bodies, their goods, and their children in war, a people who would "let go" even their "honor"—for the sake of the *Reich*. "Yes! Yes! The '*Reich*'!"

Nietzsche's position invites comparison with his repudiation of Rousseau in his third *Meditation:* his opposition is violent—but his right to that opposition is not quite clear. Perhaps the very passion of his repudiation was due in part to the fact that the *Reich* represented a position seemingly similar to his own and yet so completely opposed to his. Here was a frankly manifested will to power—but he did not mean that sort of power.

Thus Nietzsche seems to be relapsing into his early dualism. Instead of declaring that only the weak delight in brawn and that value can be measured in terms of the *quantitative* degree of power, Nietzsche introduces reason as his value standard. He speaks of power as the demon of man and proclaims that reason must control strength. There are two forces, one evil and the other good. The situation is reminiscent of Nietzsche's early philosophy. Still, the Dionysian forces of darkness are opposed to the sun god Apollo.

III

The choice of Zarathustra as his great protagonist may have been suggested to Nietzsche by his own dualistic tendencies. Here was the founder of a great dualistic religion, the prophet of light and darkness, Good and Evil, Ormazd and Ahriman.[8] Here was a religion that did not present its believers with an omnipotent and

---

[8] Gustav Theodor Fechner, *Zendavesta* (1851), had admittedly chosen the Persian title to give expression to his own dualistic conception of the day and night sides of the world.

omniscient God: here was a world-view much like that which Nietzsche himself had developed in the *Meditations* when he pictured nature as purposive but inefficient and in need of man's aid. Zarathustra, too, had told man of a purpose in nature (Ormazd) that would be able to win out in its struggle—*if* man would aid it.

Nietzsche, however, repudiated his earlier dualism through the very mouth of his Zarathustra.[9] Apparently, Dionysus defeats Apollo; the demon of darkness overpowers the restraining forces of the sun god; and reason is no longer recognized as the supreme principle and standard of values. This interpretation, however, would be only partly correct. To be sure, the self-styled Dionysian dithyrambs of *Zarathustra* (EH-Z 7) symbolize Nietzsche's departure from the Apollinian articulateness of his aphoristic style. It is further true that the will to power is proclaimed the one and only basic force of the cosmos. It remains to be seen, however, whether the conception of the will to power that is now evolved is really the Dionysian in a new guise, or whether it is not perhaps just as much the heir of Apollo as it is that of Dionysus.

Nietzsche had faced the choice between a dualism (of reason and will to power) and a monism (of only the will to power). The dualism was suggested in Nietzsche's declaration that only the degree of reason in strength could be the standard of valuation. The monism was suggested in Nietzsche's idea that quantitative degrees of power might be the measure of value. If one takes the example of Nietzsche's repudiation of the *Reich*, one can trace the lines his objections would have to take, according to which view he would embrace: as a *dualist*, he would say that the *Reich* was powerful, but that there was too little rationality in its might; as a *monist*, he would assert that the brawn of the *Reich* was actually an expression of weakness. The basic conception of Nietzsche's final theory of values is thus clear even now: qualitative differences between various modes of power are reducible to more basic quantitative differences; rationality is taken to be the

---

[9] Nietzsche himself remarked that his Zarathustra proclaimed a view that was the opposite of the real Zarathustra's. Nietzsche added that he chose Zarathustra as his protagonist because he was the first one to commit "the error": therefore, he had to be the first one to repudiate it. (EH IV 3) It seems to have gone unnoticed, however, *how close Nietzsche himself had come to the real Zarathustra's view*.

mark of great power; and with this crucial "qualification," *the quantitative degree of power is the measure of value.*

First of all, however, we must consider Zarathustra's proclamation of the will to power. The small number of passages containing any overt reference to it permit great brevity of exposition, while the fact that this is the first work where the "will to power" is introduced, and that Nietzsche prized this book more highly than anything else he wrote, makes it desirable not to skip these few passages.

Nietzsche first speaks of the "will to power" in the chapter "On the Thousand and One Goals." The chapter begins with moral relativism. Different nations have—this is the meaning of the title—different goals and moral codes. All of these, however, have one thing in common: they are creations of the will to power.

Nietzsche's difference with those who would rationalize the valuations of their own society is apparent. Against them he urges moral relativism, and—lacking any revelation—he cannot *a priori* assert the superiority of the values of his own society; nor can he judge, or even compare, the values of different societies unless they have something in common. Against the relativists, however, Nietzsche urges that there *is* a common element that makes possible comparative judgments of value about the moral codes of various societies.

> A table of virtues hangs over every people. Behold, it is the table of its overcomings; behold, it is the voice of its will to power. Praiseworthy is whatever seems difficult to a people; whatever seems indispensable and difficult is called good; and . . . the rarest, the most difficult—that they call holy.[10]

The will to power is thus introduced as the will to overcome *oneself.* That this is no accident is certain. The will to power is not mentioned again until much later—and then at length—in the chapter "On Self-Overcoming." After that, it is mentioned only once more in *Zarathustra.* The will to power is conceived of as the will to overcome oneself.

----

[10] The definition of the holy seems to have been influenced by the final words of Spinoza's *Ethics.* "Overcoming" as a translation of *Überwindung* —and "self-overcoming" for *Selbstüberwindung*—is admittedly inadequate, but self-surpassing, self-transcendence, and self-conquest would be worse though each suggests something of the connotation of the German word. The significance of Nietzsche's conception will be considered at length in the text.

Nietzsche asserts that moral goodness consists in doing what is difficult. To do the easy is not "morally good." He then proceeds as follows:

> Whatever makes it [a people] rule and triumph and shine, to its neighbor's awe and envy: that is to it the high, the first, the measure, the meaning of all things.

It might seem that besides self-overcoming Nietzsche thinks of overcoming one's neighbor. In his discussion of "the striving for excellence" in the *Dawn,* Nietzsche presented a scale of degrees of excellence, and the striving to arouse one's neighbor's awe and envy was placed nearer the bottom of that scale than the striving to arouse his admiration or to show one's power by elevating him. Now, while there is a suggestion of a contest between nations, each is trying to overcome *itself* to such a degree that it arouses its neighbors' awe and envy. In Nietzsche's vision the globe becomes a Greek gymnasium where all nations vie with each other, each trying to overcome itself and thus to excel all others.

A few sentences later, the Greeks are introduced as one of four historical illustrations; the others are, in that order, the Persians, the Jews, and the Germans:

> "You shall always be the first and excel all others: your jealous soul shall love no one, unless it be the friend"—that made the soul of the Greek quiver: thus he walked the path of his greatness.
>
> "To speak the truth and to handle bow and arrow well"— that seemed both dear and difficult to the people who gave me [Zarathustra] my name . . .
>
> "To honor father and mother and to follow their will to the root of one's soul"—this was the tablet of [self-] overcoming that another people hung up over themselves and became powerful and eternal thereby.
>
> "To practice loyalty and, for the sake of loyalty, to risk honor and blood even for evil and dangerous things"—with this teaching another people conquered themselves; and through this self-conquest they became pregnant and heavy with great hopes.

The greatness of Greece is interpreted in terms of the conception of the contest which, in turn, is now taken as reducible to a will to power. The Persians, like the Greeks, strove for both physical and moral power, here represented by truth-telling and arrow-shooting.

The Jews' honoring of father and mother, however, seems to be a striving for moral excellence only, not for physical power; yet of them alone Nietzsche says specifically that they became powerful. The Greeks had physical strength as well as "something higher" (M 548), and so did the Persians. Moral force alone, however, is sufficient to make a people a power to be reckoned with.

Nietzsche's comment on the Germans of Bismarck's *Reich* is interesting when considered in this light. It is perhaps impossible today to read his words without considering them prophetic.

Of course, Nietzsche's theory of values cannot ultimately rely on any world-order to see to it that moral force prevails, while physical force—if not controlled by morality—must perish. Any such superficial interpretation of history as a morally edifying success story is far indeed from Nietzsche's mind. He might, however, speak of his German contemporaries as manifesting a fundamental weakness by showing little moral force, and he might consider their valuations as prompted by a lack of true power.

Nietzsche's problem is still the same as ever: he distinguishes between power and true power, as he had earlier distinguished between nature and true nature and the empirical and the true self. His difference with Rousseau was that Rousseau spoke of nature and Nietzsche of true nature; his repudiation of the *Reich* comes down to this, that the *Reich* glories in its strength, which, however, is not true power, as Nietzsche sees it. To escape this dilemma, he would now posit a quantitative scale and consider "true" power as simply *more* power than, for example, the relatively small might of which his German contemporaries liked to boast.

Nietzsche would thus offer a novel solution for his earlier problems. Instead of assuming two qualitatively different principles, such as strength and reason, he would reduce both to a single, more fundamental force: the will to power. And the distinction of brawn and brains he would explain in terms of a quantitative difference between degrees of power. The conception of the will to power as essentially self-overcoming suggests further that Nietzsche's thought still moves along dialectical lines, as it did when he defined health as the ability to overcome disease: apparently, he would now broaden his earlier dialectical definition in an attempt to arrive at a general standard of values.

It is, however, far from plain what exactly is meant by "self-overcoming"; nor is it evident in what manner we could gauge quantitative degrees of power. These are problems which will require further analysis. Zarathustra's speech "On Self-Overcoming" does not offer any clear answers to these questions; rather, it introduces two further problems which may be considered briefly.

The first of these two new points does not seem puzzling at first glance. Nietzsche suggests that the pursuit of philosophy is prompted by the will to power. This is entirely consistent with his earlier view that artist, saint, and philosopher are the most truly *human* beings. He has since shown how the saint (ascetic) is one of the most powerful of men, and he would now add that the philosopher's excellence, too, corresponds to a similarly high position on the power scale. But Nietzsche raises a new and difficult question by suggesting that the will to truth is a function of the will to power.

> "Will to truth" you call it . . . ? A will to the thinkability of all being: this *I* call your will. All being you want to *make* thinkable: for you doubt, with well-founded suspicion, whether it is thinkable. Yet it shall yield and bend for you. . . . Smooth it shall become and serve the spirit as its mirror and reflection. That is your entire will . . . a will to power—also when you speak of good and evil and valuations [Z II 12].

It may seem to make the will to power more attractive that one can exert it by being a philosopher, without harming anyone; nor does Nietzsche's thought lack plausibility. Even as Alexander and Napoleon went out to conquer the world with their armed might, Aristotle and Hegel tried to subdue the entire cosmos, without cavalry and cannon, by sheer force of mind. This is not just Zarathustra's poetic proclamation but one of Nietzsche's characteristic declarations about the will to power. "Philosophy is this tyrannic urge itself, the most spiritual will to power" (J 9).

This conception, however, which—at first glance—seems to fit Nietzsche's philosophy so well by placing the philosopher at the pinnacle of the power scale, may yet be dangerous. By including truth within the confines of this theory of the will to power, he has perhaps called in a Trojan Horse that threatens his entire philosophy with ruin.

What Nietzsche intended was presumably a polemic against the view that had found eloquent expression in Hegel's famous declaration: "The initially hidden and precluded essence of the universe has no strength to resist the courage of knowledge." [11] These words, in which Hegel had meant to deny the doctrine of the thing-in-itself by claiming that the triumph of knowledge was complete and that no surd could escape its omnipotent grasp, seemed to Nietzsche to be proof of "Hegel's Gothic heaven-storming" (xvi, 82). Nietzsche insinuates that the world is *not* knowable. This may seem modest and unproblematic enough, yet Nietzsche's statement of his position invites criticism.

He looked upon himself as an experimental philosopher who wished to break with a tradition of "unlimited ambition." For the delusion of the metaphysicians that they might be able "to solve all with one stroke, with one word" and thus become " 'unriddlers of the universe,' " Nietzsche proposed to substitute "the small single questions and experiments" (M 547). Now one can hardly help inquiring whether his vision of the will to power is still an attempt to answer "small single questions" with an "experiment"—or an effort "to solve all with one stroke, with one word" and to unriddle the universe with a phrase. Nietzsche himself does not answer this or other criticisms as explicitly as one might wish; but it may be permissible to venture a reply which he might perhaps have offered in his defense. His own conception of the will to power is not "metaphysical" in that sense of the word which contemporary positivists would attach to it: it is not a mere phrase but, unlike Schopenhauer's "will," essentially an empirical concept, arrived at by an induction. The aphoristic works which preceded *Zarathustra* had sought to answer small single questions in an open-minded essentially unsystematic spirit. Now the time for a more comprehensive inference had come.

Another criticism is apparently more serious. Nietzsche asserts that any attempt to understand the universe is prompted by man's will to power. If so, it would seem that his own conception of the will to power must be admitted by him to be a creation of his will to power. Is not Nietzsche therefore in the predicament of Epimenides, the Cretan? If his assertion is correct, it is a fiction.

Nietzsche was not at his best with problems of this kind: he never worked out an entirely satisfactory theory of knowledge,

---

[11] *Geschichte der Philosophie,* I, 22.

and most of the relevant material remained in his notebooks and did not find its way into a more coherent presentation in his published works. Yet it seems necessary here to meet this criticism in the best possible way—for if Nietzsche's philosophy were shown at this point to be self-refuting and absurd, it might seem futile to consider it further.

First of all, Nietzsche's view is not as different from Kant's as it is from Hegel's: Kant, too, would have denied that the world "has no strength to resist the courage of knowledge." Thus Kant set himself the task of discovering those necessary forms of the human mind to which all phenomena—i.e., all that appears to the human mind—must necessarily conform and be subject. While phenomenal experience might be a vast fabrication of the human mind, this "fiction" must be considered necessary: it follows iron-clad rules and is not "subjective" in the sense that it would leave the individual any leeway. Our mind, says Kant, is so definitively constituted along the lines developed in his theory of knowledge that synthetic *a priori* judgments about all human experience, past, present, and future, are possible. While Kant's theory does not start out on the assumption that there is a God, he abstracts from the divine existence only histrionically, without really doubting it. Hence he is not driven to the conclusion that the human mind, including the faculty of reason, is a freak—and that the faith in God which, as he claims, is an inevitable postulate of practical reason, is perhaps merely due to a certain queerness of our constitution. Only the Darwinian doctrine of evolution lent any great impetus to such conclusions; but Kant's position came singularly close to them. As has been pointed out in a previous chapter, however, Kant did not think of the human reason as a naturalistic datum that might be studied scientifically; he still believed in a whole rational order—and the phrase so often used by him, "not only man but all rational beings," with its traditional suggestion that man shares reason with God and the angels, shows clearly how far Kant was from considering reason a mere peculiarity of *Homo sapiens*.

Nietzsche, coming after Darwin, felt impelled "to substitute for the Kantian question: 'how are synthetic judgments *a priori* possible?' another question: 'Why is the belief in such judgments *necessary*?' " And he even questioned that this belief was "necessary" in the sense of being required by the make-up of the human mind; instead he suggested "that for the sake of the survival of beings like ourselves such judgments must be *believed* to be true; though they might, of course, be *false* judgments for all that" (J 11).

More important: Nietzsche, who questioned the existence of God "existentially"—with all his heart and soul—could not anchor his own conception of the will to power in any divine ground. That, however, did not prevent him from conceiving of the will to power as a universal feature of the human constitution, whose fictions must be considered necessary (for man) because they are not subjective: they leave no leeway for individual differences between one man's thinking and another's. Nietzsche's Epimenidean predicament then appears in a new light. His theory of the will to power might be the one and only interpretation of human behavior of which we are capable when we consider the evidence and think about it as clearly as we can. Not only Nietzsche but mankind would then be in the position of the Cretan, and the dilemma—however ridiculous it might seem to the angel Gabriel—would be inescapable for us. This reply to an obvious and dangerous criticism is, of course, not to be found in Nietzsche's writings in this form, but the interpretation offered here is by no means superimposed upon him. It finds ample support in his writings and furnishes at least part of the necessary background for his occasional assertions that there "really" is no will, or that the will is "really" a fiction.

There is yet one final point about the will to power made in the chapter "On Self-Overcoming." Nietzsche claims that it is not only the basic urge of man but nothing less than the fundamental drive of all living beings: "Wherever I found the living, there I found the will to power."

> "Only where there is life, there is also will: not will to life but . . . will to power. There is much that life esteems more highly than life itself; but out of the esteeming itself speaks the will to power." Thus life taught me. . . .

Even this extreme generalization, the bold statement that all living beings are imbued with a will to power, is evidently offered in an empirical spirit. One may criticize Nietzsche for having performed an induction that is unconvincing; one may argue that he misconstrued his evidence or depended on insufficient data; one may scrutinize the terms "will" and "power" and inquire whether Nietzsche's view depends on certain ambiguities of these two words—one will yet have to admit that Nietzsche based his theory on empirical data and not on any dialectical ratiocination about Schopenhauer's metaphysics, as is so often supposed erroneously. The conclusion "Thus life taught me" is probably intended to stress that Nietzsche's insight is based on experience.

Of course, up to this point only some of Nietzsche's psychological evidence has been submitted; but if one wants to consider the data he adduced from the rest of nature, one must turn to his later writings. There one will find much further evidence as well as the still more extreme hypothesis that the will to power is the basic force of the entire universe. If all this should seem to contradict the view of the will to power developed in reply to the Epimenidean criticism, it may be suggested that the constitution of the human mind might conceivably require it to interpret not only human behavior but the entire cosmos in terms of the will to power. The most obvious objection at this point is, no doubt, that it seems empirically untrue that our minds are so constituted that, when we consider phenomena and think as carefully and cogently as we can, we are driven to assume that the will to power is the basic principle of the universe. This criticism seems not only relevant but, in the end, unanswerable. To evaluate this criticism and Nietzsche's position properly, it seems necessary, however, to accord a more systematic treatment to his final philosophy. By putting a number of questions to Nietzsche it will be possible to elicit the meaning of his later views better than could be done by proceeding further, book by book. For with *Zarathustra,* the discovery of the will to power as well as Nietzsche's philosophic "development" is completed; the gap between his early and late work has been bridged; and we may now ask whether the difficulties that arose in the context of his youthful dualism can be resolved through his monistic philosophy of power.

PART

III

Nietzsche's Philosophy
of Power

Denn alle Kraft dringt vorwärts in die Weite,
Zu leben und zu wirken hier und dort;
Dagegen engt und hemmt von jeder Seite
Der Strom der Welt und reisst uns mit sich fort:
In diesem innern Sturm und äussern Streite
Vernimmt der Geist ein schwer verstanden Wort:
Von der Gewalt, die alle Wesen bindet,
Befreit der Mensch sich, der sich überwindet.
　　　　　　　　—GOETHE, *Die Geheimnisse*

All force strives forward to work far and wide
To live and grow and ever to expand;
Yet we are checked and thwarted on each side
By the world's flux and swept along like sand:
In this internal storm and outward tide
We hear a promise, hard to understand:
From the compulsion that all creatures binds,
Who overcomes himself, his freedom finds.
　　　　　　　　—GOETHE, *The Mysteries*

7

MORALITY AND SUBLIMATION

I assess the *power* of a *will* by how much resistance, pain,
and torture it endures and knows how to turn to its advantage.—WM 382 (1888).

I

The central conception of Nietzsche's later thought, the will to
power, is introduced in Zarathustra's speech "On the Thousand
and One Goals": "A table of virtues [*eine Tafel der Güter*]
hangs over every people. Behold, it is the table of its overcom-
ings; behold, it is the voice of its will to power." This passage has
already been considered in passing in the preceding chapter,
but only now are we ready to consider some of its systematic implications—especially Nietzsche's conceptions of morality and of
sublimation. These in turn will make possible a proper estimation of the rest of his philosophy of power.

The passage cited suggests nothing less than a generic definition of morality, an attempt to crystallize the common essence of
all moral codes. Nietzsche himself, as we have seen, offers four
illustrations—namely, the codes of the Greeks, the Persians, the
Jews, and the Germans. And instead of stating any preference,
he stresses the common generic element, self-overcoming.

What is at stake is clearly something different from any attempt to develop a system of ethics. Even a very brief contrast
with Kant and Mill shows this. Kant insisted that man is not
morally good unless his conduct is marked by the total absence of
any psychological inclination and motivated solely by respect
for reason[1]—and Kant opposed all other views of morality as

---

[1] ". . . Without any inclination, solely from duty, only then does it have
genuine moral value." *Grundlegung,* section 1.

sheer perversions. John Stuart Mill, on the other hand, did not similarly repudiate Kant's ethics: rather he claimed that "to all those *a priori* moralists who deem it necessary to argue at all, utilitarian arguments are indispensable"—and adduced Kant's moral philosophy as his prime example.[2] To this extent at least, Mill—instead of opposing his own utilitarianism to other conceptions of morality—seems to have advanced it as a formulation of the essence of *all* moral codes.

Nietzsche's generic conception of morality is best understood in terms of a brief contrast with the rival utilitarian definition. (In Chapter 9, the pleasure principle and the power standard will be contrasted in more detail in a different context.) Mill could include Kant's ethics within the fold of utilitarianism only on the basis of a crucial misunderstanding of Kant.[3] For expediency was not a matter of concern for Kant at all: moral worth was, to his mind, solely a function of the rationality, i.e., consistency, of the maxim according to which an action was resolved. Any inconsistency, he thought, might be made explicit by universalizing the maxim and determining whether its universal adoption would give rise to a situation in which the maxim could no longer be applied. To the extent to which he did consider consequences, he was thus concerned not with their utility but only with a formal property: was the maxim self-defeating? Whether Kant's ethics is preferable to Mill's is not the question here, but as a *generic* definition of morality, utilitarianism would fail to include Kant's morality. Nor is Kant's the only one. The force of his ethics is due in large measure to the fact that he crystallized elements that had long been implicit in the Western religious tradition, which commanded man to do the good because God willed it, regardless of the consequences. And more recent studies in anthropology have brought to light a host of other moral codes that defy explanation in terms of expediency.

If actions inspired by love of God, fear of divine wrath, or a less clearly defined sense of awe should all be referred to ex-

---

[2] Mill, *Utilitarianism,* Chap. 1, paragraph 4.

[3] The same may be said of R. B. Perry's subsumption of Kant's conception of moral value under his own generic definition of value as "any object of any interest." Kant's view of value is not an instance of "Value as the Object of Qualified Interest," if interest is defined as a feature of the "motor-affective life." (*General Theory of Value,* 1926) For Kant the locus of moral and aesthetic value is in a setting defined by the total absence of any such interest.

pediency, then it might indeed be true that moral conduct is always "expedient." The word "expediency," however, is then given so wide a meaning that *all* conduct might well be called expedient and the distinguishing characteristic of moral conduct is lost. As a generic definition of moral goodness, the utilitarian definition must therefore be rejected.

Now one might well distinguish between the expediency of an act motivated by fear and the expediency of simply acting on impulse, but this distinction only confirms that expediency as such is not the essence of morality. There is another element that distinguishes the moral from the nonmoral—and this, says Nietzsche, is self-overcoming.

That Kant's ethic as well as, say, the Ten Commandments exhibits this characteristic seems clear; and the element of self-overcoming is no less essential to the utilitarian position. The force and plausibility of utilitarianism are inseparable from its insistence that the individual must overcome himself and subordinate his own interests to those of the greatest number. In so-called primitive moral codes, too, the element of self-control and the disciplining of the inclinations is invariably present. Self-overcoming may thus be considered the common essence of all moral codes, from "totem and taboo" to the ethics of the Buddha.

So general a statement should not be founded on induction alone, as only a fraction of the evidence could be surveyed here. Nietzsche's position can be established more firmly by considering the form a moral code would have to take to elude his generic definition. Such a code could not place any restraint on the individual and would have to permit him to act on impulse. While this position is conceivable, it would be in accordance with common usage to refuse to call it "moral." A man who adopted it might state his case thus: I repudiate morality and prefer to act on impulse.

This position should not be confused with classical Greek hedonism, which considered pleasure the aim of conduct but did not identify pleasure with the gratification of every impulse. Man was told to control his impulses for the sake of his ultimate happiness, which was conceived in refined and spiritual terms— usually as the pursuit of philosophy.

Wherever man is found he imposes restraints on himself; and it seems empirically sound to call man not only a "rational animal" but also a "moral animal." The two epithets are inseparable. The general concepts which are the characteristic function of reason involve the transcendence of the merely given, including impulse which can thus be criticized reflectively. Such self-criticism—i.e., man's critical reflection on his own intentions and actions—is the core of morality.

Of course, an action that is not impulsive is not necessarily good. If a crime was committed "in cold blood" that is not an extenuating circumstance. In such a case, however, the criminal has acted as a moral agent, and his act was in that sense moral—though morally evil. A small baby who acts on impulse, on the other hand, is not immoral but simply not a moral agent yet; and a man urging us to yield to our every impulse would be telling us neither to act morally nor immorally, but—as babies do, i.e., amorally.

That a generic definition of morality does not reveal whether particular acts are good or evil is only to be expected: for specific moral codes are not in agreement on such matters, and a generic definition can only crystallize what is common to all the members of the genus. Morality always consists in not yielding to impulses: moral codes are systems of injunctions against submission to various impulses, and positive moral commandments always enjoin a victory over animal instincts. Expediency, on the other hand, is no more than an important characteristic of some moral codes, conceivably of the best—but not, like self-overcoming, the very essence of morality itself.

Specific differences between particular moralities may be due to divergent conceptions not only of the aim and sanction, but also of the manner of self-overcoming. Thus the classical ideal was that reason should control the inclinations, while Kant insisted, as we have seen, that inclination must be overcome to such an extent that it may not even be a co-motive of action. Had Nietzsche developed his own earlier dualistic tendencies, he might now have spoken of reason's control over the will to power, of Apollo's victory over Dionysus, or of Ormazd's triumph over Ahriman. His repudiation of any such dualism through the mouth of his Zarathustra, however, rules out any such approximation of the classical and Kantian views. In fact, Nietzsche's monism raises the question as to how there can be any control whatever. Asked what in the world could overcome the will to power, Nietzsche would have to reply that there is no other principle besides the will to power, and that the will to power must therefore overcome itself. Thus the conception of self-overcoming gains an entirely new significance. But one may question whether it is still meaningful.

The demand that reason should overcome inclination, or that consideration for one's own future happiness or for the welfare of others should restrain our impulses, is easily comprehensible. In each case, we can point out how a man might have acted in a certain specified way, how he "overcame himself," and how he then acted differently. That seems much more difficult in the case of the alleged self-overcoming of the will to power. After all, the simile of overcoming—and we must not forget that the word is metaphorical—implies the presence of two forces, one of which overcomes the other. "Self-overcoming" is conceivable and meaningful when the self is analyzed into two forces, such as reason and the inclinations. Apart from such a duality, apart from the picture of one force as overcoming and controlling another, self-overcoming seems impossible.

One must therefore ask in all seriousness whether Nietzsche was possibly led astray by language and deceived by his own metaphorical expression. Perhaps the dualism he had repudiated was still in the back of his mind and vitiated his argument. Perhaps Nietzsche presupposed a duality of the Dionysian and Apollinian or, as in the *Dawn,* of strength and reason (M 548).

Those who have written about Nietzsche have rarely taken him seriously enough philosophically to ask such questions; and it is the great merit of Ludwig Klages' book on Nietzsche that he has, to some extent, made Nietzsche's problems his own and attempted to think them through. His conclusion, however, is untenable, though other authors have failed to refute Klages' critique and ignored his plausible objection to Nietzsche's philosophy.

Klages' fundamental objection is the one just outlined: Nietzsche's monism is held to be inconsistent with the *Überwindungsmotiv,* the theme of self-overcoming, which permeates his philosophy. In this conception of self-overcoming, Klages recognizes a Christian motif, incompatible with Nietzsche's profession of monism. It so happens that Klages would repudiate "the Christian in Nietzsche," [4] that he attacks Nietzsche's "Socratism," [5] and that he opposes the will to power as spirit (*Geist*) in disguise.[6] It is striking that one of the leading irrationalistic thinkers of our time should have repudiated the will to power as a Christian conception in disguise, finding in it a principle essentially opposed to irrationalism; but our concern here is only with Klages' assertion that Nietzsche was inconsistent, not with Klages' preference for one of the two allegedly contradictory positions.

Two entirely distinct problems now require careful consideration. First, we should ask how Nietzsche himself would picture the "overcoming" of the impulses: whether he meant that they should be extirpated, abnegated, controlled—or whether he had in mind yet another way of mastering them. Secondly, we must inquire how Nietzsche would deal with the special problem inherent in his monism, i.e., the problem of *self*-overcoming— and this question will be taken up in the next chapter. Neither of these two questions can be answered summarily. Each requires detailed consideration. Once both have been answered, however, the fundamentals of Nietzsche's philosophy will be clear.

II

Nietzsche proposed to explain all human behavior in terms of the will to power, and some of his earlier reductions have been presented in the last chapter. One may now quote him specifically: "our drives [*Triebe*] are reducible to the will to power" (XIV, 287). This is the result of Nietzsche's "small single questions and experiments" by which he penetrated human motivation far more deeply—so he thought—than any of the more systematic philosophers had done before him: they had all been impeded by the conventionally moralistic presuppositions of their systems:

> All of psychology to date remained stuck in moral prejudices and apprehensions: it did not dare go into any depths. To comprehend it [psychology] as the morphology and *theory of the evolution of the will to power,* as I do—that nobody has

[4] *Nietzsches Psychologische Errungenschaften* (1926), 196; chaps. IX, XI, XIV, XV *passim.*

[5] *Ibid.,* Chap. XIII.

[6] Cf. also Klages' *magnum opus: Der Geist als Widersacher der Seele,* 3 vols. (1929–1933).

come close to doing yet even in thought—insofar as it is permitted to recognize in what has so far been written a symptom of what has so far been kept secret [J 23; cf. XVIII, 339].

In 1872 Nietzsche had penned the sentence: "Those of his [man's] abilities which are awesome and considered inhuman are perhaps the fertile soil out of which alone all humanity . . . can grow" (II, 369). The essay, however, in which Nietzsche had sought to elaborate his meaning had remained a fragment; and it has been shown in previous chapters why he had not yet been ready to make good this ambitious claim. Now, however, after the discovery of the will to power, Nietzsche is ready to present the "doctrine of the derivability of all good drives from the bad" (J 23).

It is important to note that this "doctrine" does not entail the termination of Nietzsche's experimentalism:

In the end, not only is it permitted to make this experiment; the conscience of *method* demands it. Not to assume several kinds of causality until the experiment of making do with a single one has been pushed to its utmost limit (to the point of nonsense, if I may say so)—that is a moral of method which one may not shirk today—it follows "from its definition," as a mathematician would say. The question is in the end whether we really recognize the will as *efficient,* whether we believe in the causality of the will: if we do—and at bottom our faith in this is nothing less than our faith in causality itself—then we have to make the experiment of positing the causality of the will hypothetically as the only one. "Will," of course, can affect only "will"—and not "matter" (not "nerves," for example). In short, one has to risk the hypothesis whether will does not affect will wherever "effects" are recognized—and whether all mechanical occurrences are not, insofar as a force is active in them, will force, effects of will.

Suppose, finally, we succeeded in explaining our entire instinctive life as the development and ramification of *one* basic form of the will—namely, of the will to power, as *my* proposition has it; suppose all organic functions could be traced back to this will to power and one could also find in it the solution of the problem of procreation and nourishment—it is *one* problem— then one would have gained the right to determine *all* efficient force univocally as—*will to power.* The world viewed from inside, the world defined and determined according to its "intelligible character"—it would be "will to power" and nothing else [J 36].

One may doubt the cogency of Nietzsche's argument in places—one will have to admit that in the book that followed *Zarathustra*, Nietzsche still thought experimentally and not as a prophet or a legislator.

Of the many questions involved in Nietzsche's thesis, only one shall be considered in the present chapter. The problem of the causality of the will will be taken up briefly later on; and the question, not touched upon in our long quotation, how one and the same force can be the cause of so many diverse manifestations—a problem not unknown to philosophers and theologians of the past[7]—will be considered in the next chapter. At the moment, only the psychological problem shall be examined: not the *possibility* of *self*-overcoming, but the actual process of the overcoming of the impulses and the kind of control Nietzsche had in mind.

This process and control Nietzsche defines in a single word as—*sublimation*. It is almost incredible that Klages, who has written the only book that purports to present and analyze in detail Nietzsche's *psychologische Errungenschaften*, has ignored Nietzsche's conception of sublimation completely. Jaspers and Morgan, in the two most thorough and scholarly philosophic accounts of Nietzsche's thought, mention this conception—but give no recognition to its central significance for Nietzsche's later philosophy, nor do they mention that Nietzsche's conception anticipated Freud's.[8] Oehler's two-volume index to the works omits *sublimieren*. Under the circumstances it is perhaps not surprising that Brill should have claimed, in his Introduction to *The Basic Writings of Sigmund Freud*, that "sublimation" is "another term coined by Freud."[9] The founder of psychoanalysis himself, to be sure, had been more modest—not because he had

---

[7] Cf., e.g., St. Thomas Aquinas, *Summa Theologica*, I, 47, 1; Maimonides, *Guide of the Perplexed*, II, 22; *Meister Eckehart*, ed. Karrer (1923), 218. The same problem appears in Plotinus, sixth *Ennead*, IV. 6, in Neoplatonism generally, and especially in Nicolas de Cusa, *Dialogus de Genesi* (1447), entire, where the problem is put thus: *"quomodo Idem ipse est omnium causa: quae adeo sunt diversa et adversa."* Nietzsche's problem is not nearly so different from that of the Neoplatonic tradition as it may seem at first glance. This will become more apparent in the next chapter.

[8] Jaspers, *op. cit.*, gives only half a page of his comprehensive study to an exposition of sublimation. Morgan gives a little more space to it (*op. cit.*, 99 f., 128 ff., 180 f.). Somehow, not one of his quotations contains the word "sublimation," though some of the passages referred to in his footnotes do.

[9] Modern Library edition, *op. cit.*, 18.

read Nietzsche and found the term in his writings, but because the word is older than either Freud or Nietzsche. It was used even in medieval Germany as an adaptation of the Latin *sublimare;* and in modern times, Goethe, Novalis, and Schopenhauer employed it. Yet it was Nietzsche who first gave it the specific connotation it has today. Goethe had said that "human feelings and events" could not be brought upon the stage "in original naturalness"—"they must be wrought, prepared, sublimated." Novalis had written: "The coarse Philistine imagines the joys of heaven as a fair. . . . The sublimated one turns heaven into a magnificent church." "As the world is quasi a deposit of human nature, thus the world of gods is its sublimation. Both happen *uno actu.*" And Schopenhauer had spoken of "representations" as "sublimated into abstract concepts." [10] When Nietzsche first used the word in the first aphorism of *Human, All-Too-Human* (1878),[10a] he still intended the same meaning. In the second volume of the same work, however, he spoke of "sublimated sexuality" (95) and gave the word the connotation which is generally associated with it today.

This is altogether characteristic of Nietzsche's "coinages": the *Bildungsphilister,* the cultural philistine of the first *Meditation,* also had been known before, though not prominently, and Nietzsche only gave the term a new and lasting meaning. The same is true, as we shall see, of the *Übermensch.* One may add that Nietzsche uses the word sublimation on and off in his later writings (IX, 422, 437; M 202); that in a discussion of the Platonic Eros and the *Symposium* he refers to the "sublimated sex impulse" (XI, 259)—and that almost the same use is made of the word in a discussion of Christian love (J 189; cf. GM II 7); while in *The Will to Power* Nietzsche speaks of the artist's sublimation of his impulses (677), thus making clear the connection between Goethe's usage and the modern one.

The important issue, to be sure, is not who used what word

---

[10] Cf. Grimms' *Deutsches Wörterbuch,* art. *sublimieren,* where, however, Novalis and Freud are omitted, while Nietzsche is represented by a single reference, dated 1895, which gives no indication of the slight, but significant, shift in meaning the word underwent in his writings. Cf. also Paul Fischer, *Goethe-Wortschatz* (1929). The Novalis quotations are from *Blütenstaub,* fragments 77 and 96. Cf. also *Hegels theologische Jugendschriften,* ed. Herman Nohl, 308.

[10a] This is the only reference given for this term in Schlechta's *Nietzsche-Index* (1965).

when and how, but what it is that Nietzsche had in mind. There is always the danger of believing that a new term may solve an ancient problem, when actually no word or phrase can accomplish that much. Nietzsche, however, did not depend on the mere word "sublimation" but rather on the conception he sometimes—though by no means always—designated in this way. One should therefore inquire what happens when impulses are sublimated.

Nietzsche believed that a sexual impulse, for example, could be channeled into a creative spiritual activity, instead of being fulfilled directly. Similarly, the barbarian's desire to torture his foe can be sublimated into the desire to defeat one's rival, say, in the Olympic contests; it can even be sublimated into the rivalry of the tragedians who vie with each other for the highest prize, or into the efforts of a Plato to write more beautifully than the poets—and the entire Socratic dialectic could be construed as a sublimation of the same ancient striving to overwhelm one's foe.[11]

Can one properly speak of the sublimation of one and the same impulse? Instead of doing one thing, a man does another—and the continuity of the original impulse seems problematic. Now Nietzsche was definitely not one to speak glibly of the coarseness of the sex impulse, while recommending "simple" sublimation. There is a long aphorism in the *Dawn,* entitled *Selbst-Beherrschung und Mässigung ihr letztes Motiv,* "self-mastery and moderation as its ultimate motive"—though *Mässigung* would be best translated by a Greek word: Plato's *sophrosyne.* The aphorism begins: "I find no more than six essentially different methods to fight the violence of a drive"—and in the end Nietzsche summarizes:

> Thus: dodging the opportunities [for its satisfaction], implanting regularity in the drive, generating oversaturation and disgust with it, and bringing about its association with an agonizing thought—like that of disgrace, evil consequences, or insulted pride—then the dislocation of forces, and finally general [self-] weakening and exhaustion—those are the six methods [M 109].

Nietzsche does not confuse the last of these six methods with sublimation—one need only consider his account of it:

---

[11] Cf. the fragment *Homers Wettkampf* (ɪɪ, 367 ff.); the lecture on Heraclitus, ɪᴠ, 303; and ᴠ, 232; ᴠɪɪ, 191; M 113, 544; xɪ, 299; xɪᴠ, 129, 261, 263; G ɪɪ 8.

Finally sixth: whoever can stand it, and finds it reasonable, to weaken and depress his *entire* physical and psychical organization, will of course attain thereby also the goal of weakening a single violent drive: as do, for example, those who starve out their sensuality and thereby indeed also starve out and ruin their fitness and, not seldom, their mind [*Verstand*], like ascetics.

In other words, Nietzsche does not mistake self-mortification, or self-exhaustion by athletics or sports, for "sublimation."

It may seem that it is the fifth method that constitutes sublimation:

One brings about a dislocation of one's quanta of strength [*Kraftmengen*] by imposing on oneself an especially difficult and exacting task or by subjecting oneself intentionally to a new stimulus or delight and thus diverting one's thoughts and the play of physical forces into other channels.

Closer examination, however, shows that this fifth method can be re-enforced by the preceding four: and one may take it that sublimation, as conceived by Nietzsche, involves all of the first five methods. In a later passage, Nietzsche himself concludes:

One can dispose of one's drives like a gardener and cultivate . . . the seedlings of wrath, pity, brooding, and vanity as fruitfully and usefully as beautiful fruit on espaliers; one can do it with the good or the bad taste of a gardener and quasi in the French, or English, or Dutch, or Chinese manner; one can also let nature have its way and merely see to a little more tidiness and embellishment here and there . . . [M 560].

Now one may still press the point that "sublimation" covers up a logical confusion and that, if a man does one thing instead of another, a substitution takes place—and the original impulse is canceled or subdued, but not sublimated. This criticism might be relevant, if Nietzsche maintained that only the energy remains, while the objective of the impulse is changed: for the energy is as nondescript as Aristotle's matter, while the objective appears to define the very essence of an impulse. Nietzsche, however, insists—in conformity with tradition—that what remains is the essence and what is changed is accidental. He considers the will to power, which remains throughout, the "essence," while "all 'ends,' 'objectives,'" and the like, are merely accidental and changing attributes "of the one will," "of the will to power" (WM 675). In other words, not only the energy remains but also the objective, power; and those so-called objectives which are canceled are only accidental attributes of this more basic striving: they are, to use one of Nietzsche's favorite terms, mere "foregrounds." Thus Nietzsche's theory of sublimation avoids one of the most serious difficulties of its psychoanalytic equivalent—and an explicit contrast between the will to power and the sex drive may clarify this point.

When Nietzsche began to consider the will to power as possibly the basic human drive, he also thought of the sex drive; and in his notes one finds on the same two pages which contain the second and the third mention of the "will to power," in the order of Nietzsche's writings, also the following sentences:

> Sexual stimulation in the ascent involves a tension which releases itself in the feeling of power: the will to rule—a mark of the most sensual men; the waning propensity of the sex impulse shows itself in the relenting of the thirst for power.

> The reabsorption of semen by the blood . . . perhaps prompts the stimulus of power, the unrest of all forces toward the overcoming of resistances. . . . The feeling of power has so far mounted highest in abstinent priests and hermits (for example, among the Brahmins) [x, 414 f.].

One may also recall a famous epigram from *Beyond Good and Evil*: "The degree and kind of the sexuality of a human being reaches up into the ultimate pinnacle of his spirit" (75). Yet Nietzsche did not decide to reduce the will to power to a sexual *libido;* for sexuality is that very aspect of the basic drive which is canceled in sublimation and cannot, for that reason, be considered the essence of the drive. Sexuality is merely a foreground of something else that is more basic and hence preserved in sublimation: the will to power. The feeling of potency is essential, while its sexual manifestation is accidental; and thus the feeling of sexual potency can be sublimated into that ultimate feeling of power which the Brahmin king Vishvamitra derived "from thousands of years" of abstinence and self-control and which made him undertake "to build a new heaven" (M 113). Sexuality is not basic, though it *may* be base.

That sexuality need not be base, Nietzsche emphasizes constantly. In fact, much of his polemics against Christianity is based on his opinion that Christianity has tended to consider sexuality as necessarily base—an opinion that may seem merely perverse today but can be explained in terms of Nietzsche's interest in Paul, Augustine, and early Church history: the period on which his friend Overbeck was an expert. Instead of seeing that the sex drive might be sublimated, Christianity—according to Nietzsche—repudiated it (G v 1–4). Looking for a symbolic representation of this attitude—as Nietzsche always likes to do— he finds Jesus' dictum (Mark 9:43 ff.) that if a part of your body "offend thee" you should "cut it off."

> The logic is: the desires often produce great misfortune— consequently they are evil, reprehensible. A man must free him- self from them: otherwise he cannot be a *good* man—
> This is the same logic as: "if thine eye offend thee, pluck it out." In the particular case in which that dangerous "innocent from the country," the founder of Christianity, recommended this practice to his disciples, the case of sexual excitation, the consequence is, unfortunately, not only the loss of an organ but the *emasculation* of a man's character— And the same ap- plies to the moralist's madness that demands, instead of the restraining of the passions, their extirpation. Its conclusion is always: only the castrated man is a good man [WM 383; cf. A 45].

This contrast of the abnegation, repudiation, and extirpation of the passions on the one side, and their control and sublima- tion on the other, is one of the most important points in Nietz- sche's entire philosophy.

Nietzsche is ever insisting that for the Greeks "the *sexual* symbol was the venerable symbol *par excellence*" and that "only Christianity . . . has made something unclean out of sexuality: it threw *filth* upon the origin, upon the presupposition of our life" (G x 4).

> A dogma of the "immaculate conception" . . . ? *But with that conception is maculated* [A 34; cf. A 56].

> How can one put a book into the hands of children and women which contains that vile word: "to avoid fornication, let every man have his own wife, and let every woman have her own husband. . . . It is better to marry than to burn" [A 56].[12]

> The sex impulse can be base, but it is "capable of great refine- ment" [XI, 258 f.].

> Ecstasies are different in a pious, sublime, noble man, such as Plato, and in camel drivers who smoke hashish [XVI, 320].

---

[12] I Cor. 7:2, 9. The omission here is Nietzsche's.

III

Some of Nietzsche's ideas that have generally been misconstrued are comprehensible if only this contrast of sublimation and emasculation is taken into account. It is, for example, a common misconception that Nietzsche admired Cesare Borgia and glorified him.[13] Nietzsche found it ridiculous to consider a Cesare Borgia unhealthy in contrast to an emasculated man who is alleged to be healthy (J 197). When Nietzsche was criticized on that account, he clarified his point in another book, three years later (G IX 37). He now explained that he did not favor "the abolition of all decent feelings" but that he was not sure *"whether we have really become more moral."* Perhaps we have just become emasculated, and our failure to do evil is to be ascribed merely to our inability to do evil. Perhaps we are just weak. To be moral is to overcome one's impulse; if one does not have any impulses, one is not therefore moral. In other words, Cesare Borgia is not a hero, but—Nietzsche insists—we are no heroes either if our own impulses are merely too weak to tempt us. A few months later, in his last work, Nietzsche insisted once more that his point was merely that there was more hope for the man of strong impulses than for the man with no impulses: one should look "even for a Cesare Borgia rather than for a Parsifal" (EH III 1). Translators and interpreters have not always minded the *eher noch: "even* for a Borgia rather than a Parsifal." This *eher noch* leaves no doubt that Nietzsche considered Cesare Borgia far from admirable but preferred even him to the Parsifal ideal (cf. A 46, 61; WM 871).

Nietzsche believed that a man without impulses could not do the good or create the beautiful any more than a castrated man could beget children. A man with strong impulses might be evil because he had not yet learned to sublimate his impulses, but if he should ever acquire self-control, he might achieve greatness. In that sense, there is more joy in heaven over one repentant sinner than over ninety-nine just men—if the latter are just only because they are too feeble ever to have sinned.

---

[13] E.g., von Martin, *Nietzsche und Burckhardt,* 3rd rev. ed. (1945), 93, 119, 137 f. On p. 264 the author identifies Nietzsche's view of Cesare Borgia with "the will 'back to the animals'" and "back to the natural uncontrolled character of the 'animal-man.'"

There is a section in *The Will to Power* where this point is discussed at great length (WM 382–88). There Nietzsche insists throughout that we must "employ" (*in Dienst nehmen*) our impulses and not weaken or destroy them.

Instead of employing the great sources of strength, those impetuous torrents of the soul that are so often dangerous and overwhelming, and economizing them, this most shortsighted and pernicious mode of thought, the moral mode of thought, wants to make them dry up.

Overcoming of the affects?— No, if what is implied is their weakening and extirpation. But employing them: which may also mean subjecting them to a protracted tyranny (not only as an individual, but as a community, race, etc.). At last they are confidently granted freedom again: they love us as good servants and go voluntarily wherever our best interests lie.

Moral intolerance is an expression of weakness in a man: he is afraid of his own "immorality," he must deny his strongest drives because he does not yet know how to employ them. Thus the most fruitful regions of the earth remain uncultivated the longest:—the force is lacking that could here become master [383–85].

Nietzsche's few references to the "blond beast"—*blonde Bestie*—are to be understood similarly. The Borgia and the beast are both ideograms for the conception of unsublimated animal passion. Nietzsche does not glorify either of them. He derides emasculation and scorns the Church for having "hunted down" the Teutonic barbarians—"blond beasts"—only to put them behind bars in monasteries (G VII 2). This alleged historical process, however, is viewed supra-historically as an allegory or symbol of the extirpation of the impulses. The "blond beast" is not a racial concept and does not refer to the "Nordic race" of which the Nazis later made so much. Nietzsche specifically refers to Arabs and Japanese, Romans and Greeks, no less than ancient Teutonic tribes when he first introduces this term (GM I 11)—and the "blondness" obviously refers to the beast, the lion, rather than the kind of man. It may be well to add that, right after denouncing the Church for its alleged emasculation of these beasts, Nietzsche denounces the way in which the "Law of Manu" dealt with the outcastes, saying that "perhaps there is nothing that outrages our feelings more" (G VII 3), and concludes:

These regulations teach us enough: in them we find for once *Aryan* humanity, quite pure, quite primordial—we learn that the concept of "pure blood" is the opposite of a harmless concept [G VII 4].

The long exposition of the same ideas in the notes of *The Will to Power* culminates in the dictum: *"the Aryan influence* has corrupted all the world" (WM 142).

This conclusion may suggest that Nietzsche was something of a racist after all, though the very antipode of the later Nazi movement. As will be seen later on, however, this interpretation would be false; Nietzsche did not interpret history racially; and the violent dicta about "Aryan humanity" and "Aryan influence" must be understood as *ad hominem* arguments against contemporary racists. Nietzsche attacks them by saying that, if one were to accept such categories as Semitic and Aryan, the so-called Aryans would appear in the worst light. This notebook material is then introduced into a published work, the *Götzen-Dämmerung,* right after the criticism of the Christian Church—apparently because Nietzsche wanted to guard his critique of Christian practices against any misinterpretation by those who might claim that a "Semitic" religion had broken the fitness of the Teutonic tribes. *"Aryan* humanity," says Nietzsche, is even worse —and one may note that what he objects to so much is precisely the "Aryan" "concept of 'pure blood' " which was invoked by Manu—and might be invoked again some day—to justify or rationalize the oppression of "non-Aryans." In the *Genealogy,* in the other paragraph in which the "blond beast" is mentioned, Nietzsche is similarly careful to insist that "between the old Germanic tribes and us Germans there exists scarcely a conceptual relation, not to speak of a blood relation" (G I 11).

Nietzsche's over-all contention is crystallized in the title of that chapter in the *Götzen-Dämmerung* where the treatment of the "blond beasts" by the Church and of the outcastes by the Law of Manu is considered: "The 'Improvers' of Mankind." Nietzsche claims that the self-styled improvers have always tried to make man sick and to emasculate him. His polemics as well as a vast number of his positive assertions can be understood only in terms of his own ideas about the way in which the impulses should be "overcome": not by extirpation, but by sublimation.

Looking back on Nietzsche's early philosophy, one finds that an idea basic even then has now been strengthened and elaborated. The conception of "culture as another and improved physis," which was the culmination of the second *Meditation* and the leitmotif of the third, is now re-enforced by the more detailed account of sublimation. Nietzsche's difference with Rousseau—as the symbol of the "return to nature"—could now be restated in terms of the important distinction between abandonment to the impulses and sublimation. It becomes clear what it may mean to "organize the chaos" or to conceive of "culture as a harmony of living, thinking, appearing, and willing" (U II 10), and what the "transfigured *physis*" (U III 3) might be.

Our impulses are in a state of chaos. We would do this now, and another thing the next moment—and even a great number of things at the same time. We think one way and live another; we want one thing and do another. No man can live without bringing some order into this chaos. This may be done by thoroughly weakening the whole organism or by repudiating and repressing many of the impulses: but the result in that case is not a "harmony," and the *physis* is castrated, not "improved." Yet there is another way—namely, to "organize the chaos": sublimation allows for the achievement of an organic harmony and leads to that culture which is truly a "transfigured *physis*." [14]

---

[14] Only relatively few of the numerous passages in which Nietzsche develops the conception of sublimation have been referred to in the text. The following aphorisms are also relevant to this topic: S 37, 53; M 30, 110, 204, 502, 503; J 225, 229, 230, 260; GM III 8; G V 1–4; G IX 22; WM 255, 800, 801, 805, 806, 815, 820, 1025.

8

SUBLIMATION, *GEIST,* AND EROS

The Germans think that *strength* must reveal itself in hardness and cruelty; then they submit with fervor and admiration: they are suddenly rid of their pitiful weakness and their sensitivity for every naught, and they devoutly enjoy *terror.* That there is *strength* in mildness and stillness, they do not believe easily. They miss strength in Goethe . . . !—XI, 112.

The first question about self-overcoming has now been answered: Nietzsche pictured the triumph over the impulses in terms of sublimation. Ultimate clarification, however, must depend upon the solution of the second question, now to be considered: how is sublimation possible within the framework of Nietzsche's monism? If the assumption of two basic forces, one of which might overcome and sublimate the other, is rejected and we are faced literally with *self*-overcoming, it may seem that Nietzsche's conception is untenable. "Self-overcoming" is only a metaphor and involves two forces—and one may wonder whether Nietzsche was deceived by the word, or whether his earlier dualism was still in the back of his mind.

I

Now it is noteworthy that Nietzsche used another word side by side with sublimation: *Vergeistigung,* spiritualization (e.g., G v 1). Morgan notes both terms and explains that by "spiritualization" Nietzsche means "the marriage of *Geist* and passion." [1] Any such interpretation, however, must ignore Klages' pertinent

---

[1] *Op. cit.,* 128.

and incisive critique of Nietzsche, mentioned above. Nietzsche recognized only one basic principle, the will to power; and one must ask how passion and spirit can be accounted for in terms of this most fundamental drive. While a dualistic philosopher might readily permit their "marriage," Nietzsche must first require their credentials and investigate their origins; he must insist on knowing how they are related to the will to power. Eventually, he must account for sublimation solely on the basis of the will to power, having recourse to no other ultimate principle.

It may be well to ask once more why Nietzsche placed himself in so difficult a position, and why he would not accept the traditional dualism of reason and impulse. The answer is to be found not in sheer perversity but in Nietzsche's method. His monism was not derived from ratiocinations about Schopenhauer's metaphysics; rather he did not consider it legitimate to accept unquestioned the traditional belief in the supranatural status of reason. Having questioned God, he felt obliged also to question the supernatural origin of reason.

Empirical studies, moreover, had led him to assume that all human behavior could be explained in terms of the will to power. His own psychological observations, coupled with historical studies, especially of Greek and Renaissance culture—both perhaps under the influence of Burckhardt—and augmented, finally, by a sketchy knowledge of the natural sciences, had convinced Nietzsche that "the will to power is the most profound fact to which we penetrate." Now he concluded that not only our passions but also "our intellect" might well be interpreted as "an instrument" of the will to power (XVIII, 339). Intellect, reason, and spirit (*Geist*) all seemed to him to be manifestations of the same basic drive to which our passions were reducible.

The resulting doctrine is not, properly speaking, "irrationalism." It *is* "irrationalistic" insofar as the basic drive is not reason; it is *not* "irrationalistic," however, insofar as reason is given a unique status. In the sublimation of sexual impulses, the sexual objective is canceled. Rationality, however, is *sui generis,* and cannot be similarly canceled in the process of sublimation.

Reason and the sex drive are both forms of the will to power. The sex drive, however, is an impulse, and in yielding to it in its unsublimated form, man is still the slave of his passions and has no power over them. Rationality, on the other hand, gives man mastery over himself; and as the will to power is essentially the *"instinct of freedom"* (GM II 18), it can find fulfillment only through rationality. Reason is the "highest" manifestation of the will to power, in the distinct sense that through rationality it can realize its objective most fully.

While Nietzsche thus comes to the conclusion that reason is man's highest faculty, his view is not based on any other principle than the power standard. Reason is extolled not because it is the faculty that abstracts from the given, forms universal concepts, and draws inferences, but because these skills enable it to develop foresight and to give consideration to all the impulses, to organize their chaos, to integrate them into a harmony —and thus to give man power: power over himself and over nature. In human affairs, too, Nietzsche points out, reason gives men greater power than sheer bodily strength. Foresight and patience, and above all "great self-mastery" (which, under unfavorable circumstances, also makes possible dissimulation)—that is, according to Nietzsche, of the very essence of *Geist* (G IX 14).

This evaluation of *Geist* is so vital a point in Nietzsche's philosophy that one cannot overlook it without misapprehending Nietzsche's thought. The usual accounts begin with *The Birth of Tragedy*, where Nietzsche is alleged to have repudiated rationalism under the name of "Socratism"—many writers even believe that he considered the Apollinian "a bad thing," and then they proceed to scattered quotes from later works and jottings, disregarding the context of Nietzsche's thought and ignoring the fact that he had to account for reason in terms of the will to power. Nietzsche's conception of Socratism will be discussed in a later chapter; but his view of those who would repudiate reason is expressed aptly and unequivocally in a passage we have cited earlier. It makes one wonder what he would have thought of Heidegger's long critique of him (in *Holzwege*, 1950), which concludes: "Thinking begins only after we have experienced that reason, though glorified for centuries, is the most stiff-necked adversary of thinking." Here are Nietzsche's words:

> What is good-heartedness, refinement, and genius to me, when the human being who has these virtues tolerates slack feelings in his faith and judgments, and when the demand for certainty

is not to him the inmost craving and the deepest need—that which distinguishes the higher from the lower men. Among certain pious ones, I found a hatred of reason and appreciated it: at least they thus betrayed their bad intellectual conscience [FW 2; cf. FW 359].

Rationality "distinguishes the higher from the lower men." Nor is this a casual point in Nietzsche's writings. The identification of the hatred of reason with the bad intellectual conscience can be found everywhere in his books and notes; irrationality is ever a weakness in his eyes; and rationality, a sign of power. His entire attack on "systems" is based on his objection to the irrationality which he finds in the failure to question premises.

Much of his attack on Christianity is similarly based on what he took to be the Christian repudiation of reason and the glorification of the "poor in spirit." He ever insisted that "the first Church fought, as is well known, *against* the 'intelligent ones,'" and he concluded that it was for that very reason that the Church had to urge the extirpation of the passions and *"castratism"*: the people to whom the Church addressed itself simply lacked the power to control, sublimate, and spiritualize their passions; they were "poor in spirit." The lack of reason, intelligence, or spirit is a lack of power; and Nietzsche, far from repudiating these faculties, charged Christianity with the supreme crime of having deprecated them—and this not only in his "middle period," before the writing of *Zarathustra,* but even more vehemently in the *Götzen-Dämmerung,* on which the present account is based (G v 1).

Whether Nietzsche's attack on Christianity is tenable need not be discussed here. It is, however, pertinent to point out that Nietzsche himself was fully aware of the paradoxical nature of his objections. Perhaps the following epigram in the *Götzen-Dämmerung* is most eloquent of Nietzsche's recognition of this paradox: "The spiritualization of sensuality is called *love:* it is a great triumph over Christianity" (G v 3). This remark is revealing in another way, too; it shows what Nietzsche attacked as "Christian": not the Eros—which he associated with Plato's *Symposium* (XI, 259; GM III 8; XVI, 320; G IX 22 f.) rather than with the gospels—but the "revaluations of all values," the "slave rebellion in morals" (J 46, 195; GM I 7), and the glorification of the "foolish," the "weak," and the "base," for which he cited 1 Corinthians 1:27 ff. (A 45).

Nietzsche, the philosopher, considered philosophy "the most spiritual will to power" (J 9) and proposed to measure power and weakness in terms of man's willingness to subject even his most cherished beliefs to the rigors of rationality. Those who take refuge in irrationality, dogma, or systems based on unquestioned premises, seemed slack and weak to him. Again this point can be fully documented from the late works of 1888, and the *Antichrist* is quite as unequivocal in this respect as is the *Götzen-Dämmerung*: "The priest knows only one great danger: that is science" (A 49). By "science" Nietzsche means the willingness to question, to submit one's opinions to experiments, and to revise one's beliefs in the light of new evidence. Not to do this is a manifestation of irrationality, a weakness, and a lack of power.

The *Antichrist* is very clear regarding Nietzsche's affirmation of rationality and spirit: he repudiates Christianity for its alleged denunciation of these faculties, which he considers the highest manifestations of the will to power.

> Nature, *not* Manu, distinguishes the pre-eminently spiritual ones [*Geistigen*], those who are pre-eminently strong in muscle and temperament, and those, the third type, who excel neither in one respect nor in the other, the mediocre ones—the last as the great majority, the first as the elite [A 57].

Nietzsche's valuation of spirit is still the same as in the *Dawn,* where he rated reason higher than strength; now he values the power of the spirit higher than that of muscle and temperament. His standard, however, is different now. In the *Dawn,* reason was considered valuable as such, and strength was considered as having worth only insofar as it embodied reason (M 548). Now, as in all the later works, power is the sole standard, and rationality is valuable insofar as it is a manifestation of power. "The most spiritual [*geistigsten*] men" are "the *strongest* ones," as Nietzsche expressly declares (A 57).

It may appear as if this high valuation of rationality were contradicted by another passage in the *Antichrist*:

> Formerly, the proof of man's . . . divinity was found in his consciousness, in his "spirit." To become *perfect,* he was advised to draw in his senses, turtle fashion, to cease all intercourse with earthly things, to shed his mortal shroud: then his essence would remain, the "pure spirit." Here too we have reconsidered: the development of consciousness, the "spirit," is for us nothing less than the symptom of a relative imperfection

of the organism; . . . The "pure spirit" is a pure stupidity: if
we subtract the nervous system and the senses—the "mortal
shroud"—*then we miscalculate*—that is all! [A 14].

Nietzsche's own use of quotation marks indicates clearly that he
did not mean to repudiate the spirit, but only the "spirit," the
"pure spirit," that which man was supposed to find after giving
up his body. The entire polemic is thus in complete accord with
Nietzsche's conception of sublimation and his repudiation of
"castratism." The man who can develop his faculty of reason
only by extirpating his sensuality has a weak spirit; a strong
spirit need not make war on the impulses: it masters them fully
and is—to Nietzsche's mind—the acme of human power.

When Nietzsche, in the above quotation, speaks of consciousness in a somewhat deprecating manner, that may call for some
further comment. In the notes of *The Will to Power,* too, there
are similar comments:

> *Becoming conscious* is a sign that true morality, i.e., instinctive
> certainty of action, is going to the devil. . . . A virtue is *re-
> futed* with "in order to" [423].

> The great rationality in all moral education was ever that one
> tried to attain the *sureness of an instinct* . . . Indeed, this un-
> consciousness belongs to every kind of perfection: even the
> mathematician handles his combinations unconsciously [430].

Careful reading of such passages can leave no doubt that rationality is not deprecated. The mathematician who is able to handle
complicated calculations "unconsciously" is not "unconscious"
in the same manner as is, perhaps, an animal that acts on impulse. The "unconsciousness" that Nietzsche considers a sign
of power is what one might call an *attained* unconsciousness and
a state of perfect mastery. Nietzsche considers both the man who
acts on impulse and the man who deliberately counteracts his
impulses inferior to the man who acts rationally on instinct.[2]

This interpretation is further substantiated by the way in
which Nietzsche speaks of "instinct." In our discussion of Nietzsche's method, we pointed out how he declared that "by instinct"
he did not accept "rough-fisted answers," because he was "too
questioning" (EH II 1). This would be one good example of the

---

[2] This position is similar to that of Aristotle—hardly an irrationalist—and
the similarity is hardly accidental: the *Nicomachean Ethics* influenced
Nietzsche on several points.

manner in which rationality could become a matter of instinct: the truly rational man subjects all opinions to rational scrutiny; this has become his second nature.

Another good example can be found in that aphorism in the *Antichrist* in which Nietzsche declared that the spiritual men are the elite because they are "the *strongest* ones." Nietzsche's rather appealing picture of these higher men, of their natural "kindliness" and "graciousness," and of their manner of handling "the mediocre ones more tenderly than themselves," need not be analyzed here. It is, however, relevant to point out that he expressly says: "asceticism becomes in them nature . . . and instinct" (A 57). In other words, the truly rational man need not go to war against his impulses. If his reason is strong enough, he will naturally control his passions. He is, without being ostentatious, an ascetic—insofar as he does not yield to his impulses—but instead of extirpating them he masters and employs them.

In a note, Nietzsche develops his position in a manner which strikingly anticipates John Dewey's *Human Nature and Conduct*:

> The whole conception of the rank of the *passions:* as if it were right and normal to be led by *reason,* while the passions are considered abnormal . . . and nothing but *desires for pleasure.* Thus passion is degraded 1. as if it were only in *un*seemly cases, and not necessarily and always, that which activates; 2. insofar as it is taken to aim at something that has no great value, namely mere amusement.
>
> The misunderstanding of passion and *reason,* as if the latter existed as an entity by itself, and not rather as a state of the relations between different passions and desires; and as if every passion did not contain in itself its own quantum of reason [WM 387].

While the last point remains a suggestion, the opposition to the popular dualism of reason and passion, and to any deprecation of either of these, is one of the leitmotifs of Nietzsche's thought.

Nietzsche's doctrine differs from "irrationalism" inasmuch as it does not oppose reason to the basic principle of his philosophy: instead reason is pictured as the fulfillment of the will to power; and the irrational is not envisaged as something that is adverse to rationality but only as a weak form of rationality: it lacks the force, the rigor, and the power to be rational. The will to power is neither identical with reason nor opposed to it, but *potentially* rational.

Thus another point of Nietzsche's early philosophy is re-enforced: namely, the view of nature as purposive but inefficient. The processes of nature are not perfectly planned and thought out; we cannot say in truth that nature is entirely rational; but nature is not entirely irrational either, for it strives toward the development of rationality. Nature is nothing but the phenomenology of the will to power, and its craving for power cannot be fulfilled short of the development of reason.

Both impulse (passion) and reason (spirit) are manifestations of the will to power; and when reason overcomes the impulses, we cannot speak of a marriage of two diverse principles but only of the self-overcoming of the will to power. This one and only basic force has first manifested itself as impulse and then overcomes its own previous manifestation.

Klages' critique of Nietzsche now appears in a new light. Klages said in effect that a monistic metaphysics could not allow for an *Überwindungsmotiv,* i.e., for Nietzsche's insistence on overcoming. In other words, *self*-overcoming is impossible, inasmuch as overcoming always involves two forces, one of which overcomes the other. Now, however, it appears that there are two forces, but—and this is the crucial point—they are merely two manifestations of one basic force.

The question must hence be changed. Instead of asking whether it is legitimate to suppose that a force can overcome itself, one may grant that overcoming involves two forces. The question then becomes: can one force differentiate itself into two forces? With this problem we enter a new field: cosmology.

II

The decisive point of Nietzsche's cosmology, insofar as it concerns us, can be expressed in two words: Nietzsche was a *dialectical monist.* His basic force, the will to power, is not only the Dionysian passionate striving, akin to Schopenhauer's irrational will, but is also Apollinian and possesses an inherent capacity to give itself form. The victory of the Dionysian is thus not complete, and the will to power is a synthesis of Nietzsche's earlier two dualistic principles.

Nietzsche's position is best elucidated by comparing it, not with Schopenhauer's, as has generally been done, but with Hegel's; for there is a truly amazing parallel.[3] Each of the two men found a single word that epitomizes his entire dialectic; and the two words, though not identical, have literally the same meaning and can be analyzed into the same three distinct connotations.

Hegel's *"aufheben"* has been the despair of his translators. He was satisfied to remark that this word means both preserving and canceling;[4] his translators, however, were grieved to discover that it also means lifting up. Hegel apparently considered this the most obvious connotation and therefore did not mention it. At any rate, it was taken for granted that there is no English word with the same three meanings.[5]

Nietzsche's *"sublimieren"* has imposed no similar hardship on his translators, who could use the English "sublimating," which goes back to the same Latin root. The Latin word in question, *sublimare,* however, means—in German—*aufheben,* and Nietzsche's sublimation actually involves, no less than does Hegel's *aufheben,* a simultaneous preserving, canceling, and lifting up.

It has been shown how a sublimated impulse is preserved, canceled, and lifted up, and how Nietzsche does not incur the absurdities which would be encountered in an attempt to deny the Law of Contradiction. Sublimation is possible only because there is a basic force (the will to power) which is defined in terms of an objective (power) which remains the same throughout all "metamorphoses" (WM 657). This essential objective is preserved no less than is the energy, while the immediate objective is canceled; and the lifting up consists in the attainment of greater power.

This entire exposition could, of course, be repeated for Hegel's

---

[3] Löwith, *Von Hegel bis Nietzsche,* wants "to make really vivid the epoch from Hegel to Nietzsche," i.e., the period between these "two ends" (7); and in this he succeeds. There are also keen comments on both Hegel and Nieztsche, but no comparison along the lines suggested here.

[4] *Phänomenologie,* 94; *Logik,* 120; *Encyclopädie,* §81. Cf. my *Hegel,* sections 34 and 42.

[5] Cf. J. Loewenberg, *Hegel Selections,* xiii ff., and W. Lowrie's translation of Kierkegaard's *The Concept of Dread,* ix.

conception of *aufheben;* only Hegel's basic force is not the will
to power but spirit—not mind [6]—and its aim is freedom rather
than power. Further, it may seem that Hegel's *aufheben* is a
conceptual process, while Nietzsche's sublimation is a psychological notion. That there is a significant difference here is undeniable; but *aufheben* is not only conceptual and sublimation
not only psychological. Neither Hegel's spirit nor Nietzsche's
will to power can be restricted in such fashion: each is conceived
as, above all, the essence of the cosmos. *Aufheben* and sublimation are coextensive with these basic principles and are thus
essentially cosmic processes. They do not belong only in Hegel's
Logik or in Nietzsche's psychology, but are to be found wherever
the basic principle reveals itself—i.e., everywhere.[7]

---

[6] The translation of *Geist* as "mind"—as in J. Baillie's version of the
Phenomenology of the Mind (rev. ed., 1931)—is, I think, misleading and
unjustifiable, while "spirit" is both accurate and adequate. The untena-
bility of Baillie's translation of *Geist* as "mind" is best evidenced by his
own inconsistent use of "spirit" in many sections of his translation, where
"mind" would have been plainly absurd. Since the "Absolute" has generally been conceived as "mind" in Anglo-American Idealism, and since the
interpretation of Hegel's philosophy that is to be offered here depends
in part on this point, it is important to indicate just what is at stake.

"Mind" and "spirit" may appear to be synonyms, but Hegel's conception of *Geist* emphasizes those very features which distinguish spirit from
mind. This is especially evident in his assertion that the Greeks did not
know the principle of *Geist,* and that this was introduced only by
Christianity. (*Geschichte der Philosophie* I, 136. Hegel did not render
Anaxagoras' *nous* and Heraclitus' *logos* as *Geist.* Cf. also his exposition
of Plato's and Aristotle's thought, *ibid.,* vol. II.) He believed that the
Greeks had known the principle of mind, but not that of spirit—i.e.,
what he himself meant by *Geist.* Hegel's own conception was derived
from the *Heilige Geist* (Holy Spirit) which he considered as essentially a
living and creative force. (Cf. *Phänomenologie,* 27 ff., 570–601; and *Re-
ligionsphilosophie* I, 91, 99, 435; II, 226–47.)

Finally, attention may be called to the etymology of the word *Geist.*
Such considerations may often be misleading; in this particular case, however, a conceptual distinction between *Geist* and mind may be crystallized
in this manner. *Geist* and *spiritus*—like *pneuma* and the Hebrew *ruach,*
and unlike mind, *nous,* and *logos*—also connote breath and wind: they
are conceived as moving forces and as the essence of life. *Geist* is even
related to "yeast" and "geyser" and associated with the notion of a
ferment and an eruptive force. (Cf. R. Hildebrandt's article on *Geist* in
Grimm's *Deutsches Wörterbuch;* reprinted separately, Halle, 1926.)

[7] The overemphasis on Hegel's *Logik* has been coupled in Anglo-American
Idealism with the misconception of *Geist* as mind. The same two factors
have naturally also vitiated much Hegel criticism—notably William James'
in *A Pluralistic Universe.*

It is the very essence of the will to power to manifest itself in one way and then to sublimate its manifestations: the sublimation of the human impulses is only one such instance. Similarly, it is of the essence of Hegel's spirit to embody itself and then to *aufheben* its embodiments. In this respect, Hegel's and Nietzsche's philosophies are closely akin, and this affinity may be developed even further before the most important differences are considered. But first we must note that Nietzsche, too, used *aufheben* significantly in several passages (GM II 10 and III 27 and EH-GT 1 are especially noteworthy).

The will to power is the heir of Dionysus and Apollo. It is a ceaseless striving, but it has an inherent capacity to give form to itself. Because its way of manifesting itself in ever new guises is one of its most striking characteristics, Nietzsche speaks of its "Proteus nature" (XVI, 47; J 230). In overcoming or sublimating itself, it appears in a strange dual capacity. It is both that which overcomes (e.g., reason) and that which is overcome (e.g., impulse). In Aristotelian terms, it is both matter and form; in Hegel's, it is both "substance" and "subject." [8]

Hegel's account of this puzzle in the Preface of his *Phänomenologie* is helpful also in understanding Nietzsche's conception. Hegel repudiated Spinoza's God, Kant's thing-in-itself, and Schelling's Absolute for the same reason: they were all "substances" (matter) only and not also "subject" (form); theirs was an "inert simplicity" without any inherent necessity to give form to itself, to embody itself, and to become incarnate; and their manifold manifestations remained a mystery. Hegel compared these conceptions to "the night in which all cows are black."

Kant, to be sure, admitted that of such a surd there could be no experience; nor did he claim to know how the diverse manifestations of the thing-in-itself were to be accounted for. Hegel, however, contended that on Spinoza's, Kant's, and Schelling's assumptions the diversity of appearances could never have come about. Hence the ultimate reality *cannot* be an inert simplicity: we must start with experience and argue back from it, and the multiplicity of experience proves that reality cannot be an inert and simple "substance" (matter).

Hegel—and Nietzsche, who agreed with him in this respect

---

[8] For the following exposition of Hegel's polemics against his predecessors, including the quotes in the next paragraph, cf. *Phänomenologie*, 22 ff.

—rejected any monism that could not explain diversity any better than could, say, Thales' principle of water. If an over-simplification is pardonable when it is clearly marked as such and helps to crystallize an important point, one might conclude: *Nietzsche's will to power differs from Schopenhauer's will, much as Hegel's Absolute differs from that of his predecessors, Schelling's in particular.*

At the same time, both Hegel and Nietzsche insisted on a metaphysical monism. They assumed that metaphysical inquiry has not been pushed to the limits as long as a thinker is confronted with two or more principles. Ultimately, any duality has to be explained in terms of a single force. A critic might grant that, *if* the universe is to be explained in terms of a single force, that principle cannot be defined as an inert simplicity; yet he might object that the assumption that the cosmos can, and must, be reduced to one principle is due only to the Western heritage of monotheism. He might point out, in Nietzsche's own words, that "the Protestant minister is the grandfather of German philosophy" (A 10)—Nietzsche's included.

It would lead us too far astray here to examine the soundness of this basic assumption. Suffice it to crystallize its nature. One may then understand how neither Hegel nor Nietzsche was satisfied with an Absolute, or a God, who would be a mere demiurge, fashioning diversity after eternal patterns that would themselves be unaccounted for. Similarly, neither thinker would allow for any "matter" that might be opposed to the one and only absolute principle. Both thinkers postulated a single basic force whose very essence it is to manifest itself in diverse ways and to create multiplicity—not *ex nihilo,* but out of itself.

Hegel found the prototype of such a creative force in the Christian conception of the Holy Spirit, which he interpreted in his own characteristic fashion: God the Father must, without any external compulsion, become incarnate, embody himself, and thus become God the Son; in the Holy Spirit, however, God the Father and God the Son are one. Thus the spirit is a unity that is not an "inert simplicity," nor an "unstained self-identity," but essentially a process. By defining the Absolute as spirit, Hegel distinguished his own position from that of his predecessors.

Only when Hegel's Absolute is thus understood as essentially a creative force can the meaning Hegel himself attached to his *Logik* be understood. At the outset, Hegel describes that work as *"the exposition of God, as he is in his eternal essence before the creation of nature and of a finite spirit* [i.e., man]." [9] At the end of the work, Hegel declares that the Absolute Idea now *"decides . . . to release itself as Nature* freely *out of itself."* [10]

Hegel presented a further puzzle by assuring the reader that the movement of the concepts in the *Logik* is "not temporal, nor in any way whatever separate and distinct"; in fact, he claimed that the various concepts into which the understanding analyzes the one Absolute Idea are actually inseparably united in the Absolute. In the next paragraph, however, Hegel asserted that the Absolute Idea "is essentially a *process"* and not "restfully stable." [11]

The solution of these puzzles is that the spirit is charged with tension, as the heart of God might have been before the Creation —if only it were possible that there should ever have been a "before the Creation": for the spirit is essentially and ever creative; it is by its very nature in a state of tension that must "release itself."

Thus Hegel is not, at the end of his *Logik,* confronted with an unexpected transition to the Philosophy of Nature—as most of his interpreters have supposed, unless they have ignored the problem entirely. The entire *Logik* is an attempt—possibly a very bad one—to show how the spirit is so charged that it must ever "release itself." Hegel's *Logik* represents an attempt at an anatomy of creativity.

The Creation, however, is not accomplished and complete at any instant. Hegel took seriously, and gave a novel turn to, the Platonic suggestion that Time is the "moving image of eternity." [12] All that is created is, to his mind, a moving image of the eternal and timeless process of the concepts in the *Logik.* As each concept is inseparable from all the others—a mere moment in the tension of the Creator's heart—all that is created is an image of this instability and must perish. Moreover, even as the Absolute Idea of the *Logik* is nothing more, nor less, than the whole development of the concepts, so the spirit is "the bacchanalian whirl in which no member is not drunk; and

---

[9] *Logik,* I, 46.

[10] *Encyclopädie,* §244 (*"kleine Logik"*); cf. *Logik* III, 353.

[11] *Encyclopädie,* §§14 f., *et passim.*

[12] *Timaeus* 37.

because each, as soon as it detaches itself, dissolves immediately
—it [the whirl] is also transparent and simple repose." [13]

The spirit is only the whole process, and insofar as this is an
inseparable whole, the spirit is a unity. Even so, this unity is
never given all at once. The spirit, though it must ever become
incarnate, revealing itself in its creations, is never wholly there
at any one moment. This paradox can be best expressed in a
famous formulation of Whitehead's, if we take leave to substitute
"spirit" for his "Nature": "there is no spirit at an instant." [14]
In Hegel's own words—with which he closes his *Phänomenologie*
—the spirit is infinite, but "only out of the goblet of this realm
of [finite] spirits foams his infinitude for him."

In a way, this brief exposition of Hegel's conception of spirit
is, of course, a digression; but it throws light on Nietzsche's
conception of *self*-overcoming. To be sure, one might have tried
to explain this in terms of ancient philosophies, referring to the
Stoic conception of the *logos spermatikos,* to Plotinus' and
Proclus' systems, or to the later developments of Neoplatonism.
Some such historical comparison, however, seems called for to
counteract the common fallacy of considering the will to power
either as a monstrosity *sui generis* or merely as a development
of Schopenhauer's irrationalism. Actually, the metaphysics of the
will to power is a dialectical monism in which the basic force
is conceived as essentially creative.

One ancient philosopher, however, should be named expressly. Nietzsche and Hegel were at one in their high esteem
for Heraclitus. After our analysis, it can hardly seem surprising
that both thinkers admired the "dark" philosopher for the same
reason: their own absolute principles were not inert, or stable;
Hegel and Nietzsche expressly denied the peaceful self-identity of
the basic cosmic force and considered strife a definitive feature
of the "Absolute." [15]

---

[13] *Phänomenologie,* 45. Cf. my *Hegel* (1965), 424–29, or *Hegel Texts and Commentary* (1966), 70–73.

[14] *Nature and Life* (1934), 48.

[15] Cf. Hegel's declaration: "There is no sentence of Heraclitus' that I have not taken into my *Logik.*" What Hegel admires is that Heraclitus defined "the Absolute as process—as dialectic." (*Geschichte der Philosophie* I, 344 ff.) Cf. Nietzsche's lecture on Heraclitus (IV, 291–314) and the section on Heraclitus in *Die Philosophie im tragischen Zeitalter der Griechen* (IV, 173–88; also XIV, 109; J 204; XVI, 3 f., 7, 9, 70; WM 419; G III 2; and

The will to power is, as it were, always at war with itself. The battle between reason and impulse is only one of countless skirmishes. All natural events, all history, and the development of every human being, consist in a series of such contests: all that exists strives to transcend itself and is thus engaged in a fight against itself. The acorn strives to become an oak tree, though this involves its ceasing to be an acorn and, to that extent, self-overcoming. Man desires to be perfect and to have complete mastery of himself, though this involves a measure of asceticism and self-denial, and thus a kind of self-overcoming that seems essentially moral. Nietzsche's conception of morality has a cosmic setting.

Some of the vast differences between Hegel and Nietzsche are at bottom, due to divergent emphases. Hegel always stressed the result of the process, the synthesis, and the larger unit, while Nietzsche concerned himself primarily with the negative and with the individual. Hegel studied the self-realization of the spirit on the vastest possible scale. Beginning with the anatomy of the Creator in the *Logik*, he traced the career of his creative principle through the realm of nature, through anthropology and psychology (all in the *Encyclopädie*), through the whole process of world history (*Geschichtsphilosophie*), giving special attention to the manifestation of the spirit in the State (*Rechtsphilosophie*)—and he wound up with the histories of art, religion, and philosophy (in three cycles of lectures). Fully aware of the tragic fate of the individual, Hegel considered this relatively unimportant because he was more interested in the result of the process.[16] His antitheses, moreover, are often taken much less seriously than the positive stages of his expositions; and the element of strife, though omnipresent in his philosophy, has an almost histrionic quality at times.

Nietzsche, on the other hand, was more concerned with the individual and his attempts at self-realization. He excelled in his keen studies of individual states of mind, such as *ressentiment* and the ascetic attitude (GM)—and one may generalize that Nietzsche was, unlike Hegel, more of a psychologist than a his-

---

EG-GT 3. Karl Joel, *Nietzsche und die Romantik* (1905), 294, writes, after referring to Nietzsche's praise of Heraclitus: "Has ever a modern thinker spoken thus of an ancient one? Hegel perhaps . . . Hegel and Nietzsche! Here lies a problem yet to be solved." Perhaps we have, in the text, come close to the solution.

[16] Cf. especially *Geschichtsphilosophie,* 49 f. and 56–61.

torian. In the end his emphasis on individuality led him to the conception of a vast plurality of individual wills to power, and culminated in a monadological pluralism that shows many interesting parallels to that of Whitehead and, it would seem, of modern physics. A very brief outline of this monadology will be presented in the next chapter; but even now one might crystallize the contrast with Hegel by amending a previous suggestion and encumbering it with yet another oversimplification: as Nietzsche's relation to Schopenhauer resembles that of Hegel to Schelling, so Nietzsche's relation to Hegel somewhat resembles that of Leibniz to Spinoza.

Even more striking is Nietzsche's pre-eminent concern with the negative, which has led many readers to suppose—mistakenly —that he was a critic who would have preferred things to be different from the way they were. Any such interpretation, however, must perforce ignore his *amor fati.* "Nothing that is may be subtracted, nothing is dispensable" (EH-GT 2). "My formula for the greatness of a human being is *amor fati:* that one wants nothing to be different, not forward, not backward, not in all eternity" (EH II 10). If Nietzsche always appears as a critic, in spite of such declarations, there are primarily two reasons for this.

The first of these has been aptly epigrammatized by Nietzsche himself: *"Amor fati* is my inmost nature. This, however, does not preclude that I love . . . world-historical irony" (EH-W 4). In other words, though Christianity was in Nietzsche's eyes a *necessary* evil,[17] that did not prevent him from emphasizing that he considered it *evil.* Nietzsche—to use his own phrase—loved to insist on the world-historical irony (A 36) of the Church's complete perversion of Christ's gospel into its very opposite (U III 6; A entire).

The second reason why Nietzsche generally appears as the critic is this. Hegel thought of himself as standing at the close of an era, as the last great world-historical philosopher who tried to reconcile in a secular system the dogmata of Christianity and the heritage of Greek and modern philosophy. He tended to view his own philosophy as a fulfillment and *non plus ultra.*[18] Nietz-

---

[17] Cf. J-V; J 56, 60, 61, 62; GM III entire. Nietzsche did affirm and appreciate Christianity as necessary.

[18] Cf. especially: *Geschichte der Philosophie* III, 684–92; also *Rechtsphilosophie,* 36 f., and *Geschichtsphilosophie.* Cf. further Löwith, *Von Hegel bis Nietzsche,* 47–71.

sche, however, thought of himself as standing at the beginning of a new era, as the first philosopher to have really "uncovered" Christian morality, as the herald of an anti-Christian epoch. He was fully aware of the dubiousness of any such distinction: "To be the first here may be a curse; at any rate, it is a destiny" (EH IV 6).

If Nietzsche said No to the past, he said Yes to the future: the process as a whole he considered beyond criticism, as Hegel did. Again, Nietzsche himself summarized the point: "I contradict as has never been contradicted before and am nevertheless the opposite of a no-saying spirit" (EH IV 1).

The consequences of Nietzsche's differences with Hegel are of great importance. As stated above, one result may be found in Nietzsche's keen studies of individual states of mind: unlike Hegel, he was more of a psychologist than a historian. Another consequence of Nietzsche's emphasis on the negative and on the fate of the individual may be seen in the tremendous importance he attached to suffering and cruelty—the negative aspect of self-overcoming. It has been shown how Nietzsche pictured the ideal philosopher in the *Meditation* on Schopenhauer: "He destroys his earthly happiness through his courage; he must be hostile even to the human beings whom he loves and to the institutions from whose womb he issued; he may spare neither human beings nor things, though he himself suffers in hurting them" (4). These points need not be developed here at length: the importance of suffering will be discussed further in the framework of a contrast between power and pleasure; and the significance of "cruelty" against others will be considered later in the context of Nietzsche's repudiation of altruism and his valuation of friendship.

Nietzsche's valuation of suffering and cruelty was not the consequence of any gory irrationalism, but a corollary of his high esteem of rationality. The powerful man is the rational man who subjects even his most cherished faith to the severe scrutiny of reason and is prepared to give up his beliefs if they cannot stand this stern test. He abandons what he loves most, if rationality requires it. He does not yield to his inclinations and impulses and is willing to give up even his relatives and friends, if intellectual integrity demands it.

As an illustration, consider once more Nietzsche's admiration for Shakespeare's characterization of Brutus:

Independence of the soul—that is at stake here! No sacrifice can then be too great: even one's dearest friend one must be willing to sacrifice for it, though he be the most glorious human being, embellishment of the world, genius without peer [FW 98].

Freedom and independence cannot be had for nothing; and Nietzsche, throughout his writings, stressed the high price and the cruel sacrifice—not only, as Hegel tended to do, the glory of freedom attained.

Every smallest step in the field of free thinking, and of the personally formed life, has ever been fought for at the cost of spiritual and physical tortures . . . change has required its in-numerable martyrs. . . . Nothing has been bought more dearly than that little bit of human reason and sense of freedom that is now the basis of our pride [M 18].

One need not confine such references to the works of Nietz-sche's so-called "middle period," i.e., to books he wrote before *Zarathustra.* The theme of the entire third part of the *Genealogy* is that all truly worth-while human achievements so far, includ-ing most of art, religion, and philosophy, have involved asceticism and thus required man to be cruel toward himself and to suffer. The final aphorism states explicitly that, "except for the ascetic ideal," man's life has been animalic and meaningless. We have seen above that Nietzsche considered the mortification of the flesh a radical cure to which only the weak had to resort because they lacked the power to master their impulses and to employ them well. At the same time, Nietzsche realized that, before such power and perfect mastery could be attained, man generally had to be harsh with himself: what seems easy to us today may originally have required great sacrifices.

The moral laws that today come close to being part of the conscience of educated men and women everywhere were spread by prophets who risked death, by a philosopher who was sen-tenced to the hemlock, and by missionaries who were killed by barbarians. Discoveries that schoolchildren all but take for granted today were proclaimed by men who paid for them at the stake. Nor is such martyrdom imposed merely externally. One need only read Jeremiah's many anguished outcries to be re-minded that one pays dearly for being the Lord's prophet; and many a heretic who was burned publicly was only suffering once more, for all to see, what he had experienced a thousand times within his soul. His cruelty against himself may often have exceeded the tortures with which others rewarded him.

Recalling the previously given generic definition of morality, one may now add that man's conquest of his impulses, the triumph of reason, and—in one word—self-overcoming, always includes hardness against oneself. If cruelty is so understood—as the individual's attitude toward himself—one may well grant that "almost everything we call 'higher culture' rests on the spiritualization of, and giving depth to, cruelty" (J 229).

III

Why did Nietzsche call his basic principle a "will to power" rather than, say, an *"instinct of freedom,"* considering that he did equate the two? (GM II 18.) If the account here given of the will to power is correct, one may wonder why Nietzsche gave this force so unappealing a name. The answer is, to some extent, implicit in Nietzsche's critique of Kant and the university scholars and in his emphasis on suffering and cruelty.

Nietzsche was keenly aware of the negative aspects of the "instinct of freedom": those who are motivated by it, whether they be individuals or nations, shun no sacrifice and risk their lives, if need be. Often they do not shrink from violating the well-being of others, if it interferes with their aims; and independence is frequently to be had only after conflict and war.

Nietzsche had no mind to soft-pedal this element of egoism and strife. At the same time, he wished to make explicit his opposition to the Darwinistic conception of a "struggle for *existence.*" He contended that all living creatures, far from tending to preserve their existence, strive to enhance themselves, to grow, and to generate more life. For this end, Nietzsche believed, most living creatures are willing to risk their existence. In unusual circumstances of need, in *Notlagen,* a creature might have to exert a great effort merely to preserve its life. Nietzsche's prime examples of such exceptions are the chief protagonists of the striving for self-preservation and the struggle for existence: the "consumptive Spinoza"—whom he generally admired [19]—and the

---

[19] Nietzsche called Spinoza "the purest sage" (S 475), spoke of his thought as "a passionate soul-history" (M 481), named him with Plato and Goethe as a prototype of genius (M 497), designated his manner as "simple and

Darwinists who were brought up in overpopulated cities; but he insisted that "one should not mistake Malthus for nature" (FW 349; **G** IX 14).

Beyond that, Nietzsche also wished to counteract the ostrich prudery of his age. His belief that even a single compromise with the tastes of public opinion might lead a thinker eventually to lose his intellectual integrity invites comparison with Freud's attitude. Freud did not speak of the "erotic," which might have been more acceptable to his generation, but insisted on the more offensive "sex" impulse. Nietzsche and Freud both preferred terms that did not connote the sublimated manifestations at the expense of the more frequent and less cultured expressions of what they took to be a vastly underestimated drive.

> Why stroke the hypersensitive ears of our modern weaklings? Why yield even a single step . . . to the Tartuffery of words? For us psychologists this would involve a Tartuffery *of action.* . . . For a psychologist today shows his good taste (others may say his integrity) in this, if in anything, that he resists the shamefully *moralized* manner of speaking which makes all modern judgments about men and things slimy [GM III 19].

Nietzsche and Freud wanted to describe the significance of the drive in question; they were not exhorting men to act after a certain fashion. Speaking of sublimation, both tried to show how certain types of behavior could be explained, and how one striving might often be transformed into others. Least of all were they exhorting people to fulfill the desire in question in an unsublimated way. Nietzsche was not "endorsing" the will to power any more than Freud "endorsed" the sex impulse.

Nietzsche realized belatedly that his coinage, "the will to power," instead of being provocative, might be pleasing to those Germans who would think of nothing but the *Reich* (EH-W 1) —and in the fall of 1888 he sketched a preface for his planned book that was *not* used by his sister when she came to edit the relevant notes.

> *The Will to Power.* A book for *thinking,* nothing else: it belongs to those to whom thinking is a *delight,* nothing else. That it is written in German is untimely, to say the least: I

---

sublime" (FW 333), and honored him as one of his own spiritual ancestors (XIV, 109; XXI, 98). In Spinoza's philosophy, of course, Nietzsche accepted some elements and rejected others. Cf. pp. 139–140 above.

wish I had written it in French so that it might not appear as a confirmation of any *reichsdeutschen* aspirations [XIV, 373 f.].

The passage is reminiscent of the pathetic *"Above all, do not mistake me!"* in the Preface to *Ecce Homo*. Nietzsche begs his readers to keep in mind that he does not write to endorse a course of action. His book wants to stimulate *thought,* "nothing else"; and it is meant for people "to whom thinking is a *delight, nothing else"*—i.e., not a political program. The name "will to power" is too accurate to permit change—but if only it could be French to avoid misunderstanding! The Germans, in their "hebetation," have forgotten all but one meaning of "power" (*ibid.*).

Some of Nietzsche's reasons for calling his fundamental principle a "will to power" rather than an "instinct of freedom" or an Eros have been considered briefly; but did Nietzsche really have in mind something that might have been designated by these other terms? Two points may be developed in answer to this question.

First, the will to power is a striving that cannot be accurately described either as a will to affect others or as a will to "realize" oneself; it is essentially a striving to transcend and perfect oneself. Nietzsche's opposition to the conception of a will to live or of a desire for self-preservation is due to this insistence that nothing that is alive is sufficient unto itself. This is explicitly stated in *Zarathustra.*

> And life itself confided this secret to me: "Behold," it said, "I am *that which must always overcome itself.* Indeed, you call it a will to procreate or a drive to an end, to something higher, farther, more manifold: but all this is one. . . . Rather would I perish than forswear this; and verily, where there is perishing . . . there life sacrifices itself—for [more] power. . . . Whatever I create and however much I love it—soon I must oppose it and my love; . . . 'will to existence': that will does not exist. . . . not will to life but . . . will to power. There is much that life esteems more highly than life itself" [Z II 12].

Oscar Wilde, who agreed with Nietzsche that "all men kill the thing they love," wrote a short, one-page "poem in prose" that he entitled "The Artist." The artist wants to create a bronze image but finds no bronze in all the world except a previous work of his. He melts down his former creation to be able to use the bronze for his new work. This seemed to Nietzsche the essence of creativity and the way of all life.

There are insects among which the male dies after the act of copulation. Instead of seeking to preserve his life, he spends it— as Nietzsche would say—to enjoy the exercise of his potency and to gain immortality. This striving for immortality seemed important to Nietzsche. Oscar Wilde, in his prose-poem, called the new image for which the artist sacrificed his previous work, "The Pleasure That Abideth for a Moment." Nietzsche, however, associated the creative Eros with the yearning for immortality.

This point is better illustrated in terms of the human Eros than by reference to the self-sacrifice of the male insect. The quotation from *Zarathustra* refers to the "will to generation" as an instance of the will to power; but procreation seemed to Nietzsche merely one manifestation of the creative Eros, which could also manifest itself in many other ways. Nietzsche's development of this point is full of allusions to Plato's *Symposium,* which, almost certainly, suggested these ideas to him.[20]

Thus Nietzsche points out that most of the great philosophers were not married (GM III 7) and explains the matter as follows:

> As for the "chastity" of philosophers, finally, this type of spirit clearly has its fruitfulness somewhere else than in children; perhaps it also has the survival of its name elsewhere, its little immortality [GM III 8].

> Making music is another way of making children [WM 800].

Considering the martyrdom of many generations of early Christians, Nietzsche believed that they evidently were not seeking to preserve their lives but sacrificed these for "more life," for immortality, and for that ultimate power which Paul had promised them (I Cor. 6:3) when he foretold that they would judge even the angels (A 45). Nietzsche concluded that men were ever willing to forgo satisfactions and to give up even their lives, if only they could gain immortality, which he considered a supreme degree of power.

The *second* equally essential point regarding Nietzsche's conception of the will to power finds expression in the same chapter of *Zarathustra:*

---

[20] Cf. *Symposium,* 206 ff.

> All that is living is obeying . . . he who cannot obey himself is
> commanded . . . commanding is harder than obeying . . . Even
> when it [the living] commands itself: it must pay for its com-
> manding. It must become the judge, the avenger, and the victim
> of its own law. . . . What persuades the living that it obeys,
> commands, and exercises obedience even when it commands [it-
> self]? . . . the will to power.

Life, as Nietzsche sees it, is essentially dialectical. It is of the very
essence of the living that it denies itself the gratification of some
of its impulses, even that it sacrifices life itself, for more life and
power. In the passage from *Zarathustra,* this curbing of the impulses is pictured as an "obeying." All men obey certain laws,
and most of them obey laws that others command them to obey.
Children do this, and so do primitive men who submit to
medicine men, totems, and taboos; and Nietzsche believed that
most of his contemporaries were, in this respect, in the same class
with children and primitives. He also thought that the reason
why people obey the laws others impose on them is that they
want power. They believe that this is the way to get ahead and
become influential and successful; they fear that an infraction of
custom might cause society to retaliate and to diminish their
power.

Nietzsche assumed that only the weak need to rely on the rules
of others. Man, being unique by nature, should be able to
generate his own standards, if only he were powerful enough.

This point is best understood in terms of the contention that
the will to power is essentially a creative force. *The powerful
man is the creative man; but the creator is not likely to abide by
previously established laws.* A genuinely creative act contains its
own norms, and *every creation is a creation of new norms.* The
great artist does not stick to any established code; yet his work
is not lawless but has structure and form. Beethoven did not
conform to the rules of Haydn or Mozart; yet his symphonies
have form throughout: their form and law Beethoven created
with them.

Nietzsche's polemics against Philistine morality and against
Christian ethics are, at least in part, mere corollaries of his belief
that all established codes must ever be transcended by men who
are creative. This is one of the most significant connotations of
the phrase "Beyond Good and Evil." At any rate, Nietzsche ex-

pressed this point in the book to which he gave this title, using a bold paraphrase:

> Jesus said to his Jews: "the law was for servants. . . . What are morals to us sons of God!" [J 164].

As all these examples indicate, Nietzsche's opposition to established laws did not lead him to repudiate all discipline. In fact, Beethoven's code is not so different from Haydn's and Mozart's, and Jesus' could be pictured by him as a "fulfillment," rather than a denial, of the laws of Moses and the prophets. What Nietzsche had in mind was not a repudiation of all existing rules. On this point he was explicit, and his comments recall his earlier repudiation of Rousseau, in the third *Meditation*:

> It is the weak characters without power over themselves who *hate* the constraint of style . . . [and] are always out to form or interpret themselves and their environment as *free* nature—wild, arbitrary, fantastic, disorderly, astonishing [FW 290].

> The Germans have misgivings whether one credits them with passions; therefore they immediately make grimaces and excesses, *not* from the strength of the affect but to give themselves faith. Thus are even the passions in Richard Wagner [XI, 112].

Great power reveals itself in great self-mastery. While a weak state may kill off all dissenters, a strong state should be able to tolerate them. Nietzsche, who proposed to measure health in terms of the amount of disease with which an organism could deal successfully, also proposed "to measure the health of a society and of individuals according to how many parasites they can tolerate" (M 202). It is thus a weakness both to give in to one's impulses and to be arbitrary and wild and to resort to the extirpation of the impulses. Power reveals itself in that easy mastery and superiority which need not take refuge in such emergency measures. In the same aphorism where the "weak" are pictured as the "wild, arbitrary, fantastic, disorderly" ones, we find this picture of power:

> "Giving style" to one's character—a great and rare art! It is exercised by those who see all the strengths and weaknesses of their own nature and then comprehend them in an artistic plan until everything appears as art and reason. . . . It will be the strong and domineering natures who enjoy their finest gaiety in such compulsion, in such constraint and perfection under a law of their own.

This is the apotheosis of power, and there can be no question but that Nietzsche agreed with that ancient tradition which we can trace through continents and centuries to Laotze: that the man who conquers himself shows greater power than he who conquers others.[21]

> . . . I have found strength where one does not look for it: in simple, mild, and pleasant people, without the least desire to rule—and, conversely, the desire to rule has often appeared to me a sign of inward weakness: they fear their own slave soul and shroud it in a royal cloak (in the end, they still become the slaves of their followers, their fame, etc.). The powerful natures *dominate,* it is a necessity, they need not lift one finger. Even if, during their life time, they bury themselves in a garden house" [x, 412].

Because Nietzsche thought that the highest degree of power consists in self-mastery, he considered the ascetic one of the most powerful of men. From his early praise of the "saint" as, together with artist and philosopher, the only truly human being, we can trace Nietzsche's esteem of the ascetic through the *Dawn,* where it is claimed that no other type of man has achieved a greater feeling of power, to the third inquiry of the *Genealogy,* where man is considered to have been a mere animal—"except for the ascetic ideal." The asceticism of the most powerful men, however, consists in the sublimation of their impulses, in the organization of the chaos of their passions, and in man's giving "style" to his own character.

Nietzsche's emphasis on the suffering involved in self-perfection and on man's cruelty against himself is perhaps clearest in the second inquiry of the *Genealogy,* where he deals with the "bad conscience." Since he associated it closely with the Christian religion, it is doubly noteworthy that he insisted on the ultimate value of the "bad conscience."

> One should . . . not . . . think little of this . . . phenomenon merely because it is painful. . . . At bottom, it is . . . that very *instinct of freedom* (in my language: the will to power): only here the material upon which the form-giving and ravishing nature of this force vents itself is man himself, his . . . animalic . . . self—and *not . . . other men.* This secret self-ravishment, this artists' cruelty, this pleasure in giving form to oneself as a

---

[21] Lao-tze, section 33.

hard, recalcitrant, suffering material—burning into it a will, a critique, a contradiction, a contempt, a No—this . . . work of a soul that is willingly divided against itself and makes itself suffer—this whole *activistic* "bad conscience" has . . . been the real womb of all ideal and imaginative events and has thus brought to light an abundance of strange new beauty and affirmation— and perhaps *beauty itself.*—What would be "beautiful" if contradiction had not first become self-conscious, if the ugly had not first said to itself: "I am ugly"? [GM II 18].

This exposition furnishes an excellent illustration of Nietzsche's dialectic, of his keen emphasis on the negative, and of his ultimate recognition and affirmation of the value of the apparently negative. The will to power is a creative Eros—"the love of generation and of birth in beauty." [22] It may well be, however, that no thinker before Nietzsche has stressed so mercilessly the travail of such birth.

Nietzsche points out that man could not become conscious of the beautiful and the good without becoming conscious of the ugly and evil. To become powerful, to gain freedom, to master his impulses and perfect himself, man must first develop the feeling that his impulses are evil. This recognition is the essence of the bad conscience; man says to himself: my inclinations are damnable, and I am evil. At that point, man is divided against himself. There are two selves, as it were, one rational and the other irrational. The one self then tries to give form to the other; man tries to remake himself, to give "style" to himself, and to organize the chaos of his passions. His impulses are recalcitrant; man suffers and feels guilty; and he does violence to himself and ravishes his animal nature. Self-overcoming is not accomplished by a man's saying to himself: I would rather sublimate my impulses. First he must, as it were, burn a No into his own soul; he must brand his own impulses with contempt and become aware of the contradiction of good and evil.

Nietzsche would "remove the concept of sin from the world" (M 202). This phrase is one of the persistent motifs of his philosophy (M 148, 164; x, 426 f.; GM II 20). Ultimate power consists in controlling, sublimating, and employing one's impulses—not in considering them evil and fighting them. Before man can be reborn in beauty, however, he has to go through the suffering here described:

---

[22] *Symposium* 206 (Jowett).

It is a disease, the bad conscience—that is not subject to doubt
—but a disease as pregnancy is a disease [GM II 19].

This is Nietzsche's own conclusion of his argument about the bad
conscience: it is a necessary evil; it is the pregnancy through
which one must pass to be reborn in beauty.[23] When man is reborn, that state terminates: "Man has regarded his natural
propensities with an 'evil eye' all too long" (GM II 24).

Man has not only "physiological interests" in the things his body
requires and "psychological interests" in the things the individual
may consciously desire: he also has an "ontological interest"
common to all men. Yet while men share their physiological
interests because of their common physical make-up, they share
their ontological interest insofar as they all have both body and
spirit and find themselves in the same "ontological predicament."

A contemporary philosopher has suggested that "valuation
takes place only when there is something the matter . . . some
need, lack, or privation." [24] This is true, but contemporary discussions of value theory often take for granted that all our priva-
tions are due either to our bodily needs or to accidental individual experiences. It is overlooked that as human beings we
have ideals of perfection which we generally find ourselves unable
to attain. We recognize norms and standards of which we usually
fall short; we long for a triumph over old age, suffering, and
death; we yearn for perfection and immortality—and seem incapable of fulfillment. We desire to be "as gods," but we cannot
be so.

This "ontological" privation leads to "ontological" interests.[25]
The contrast between psychological and ontological interests
could of course be expressed in other terms—e.g., by criticizing

---

[23] Nietzsche speaks of the "reborn" (EH-Z 1) and often uses "pregnancy"
figuratively (e.g., M 552; FW 369; GM III 8)—presumably following out
the suggestions of *Symposium* 206 ff. and *Theaetetus* 148 ff. Cf. also these
references to Plato's Eros: XI, 259; XVI, 320; G IX 22 f. Nietzsche's dialectical appreciation of the negative is also evident in his assertion that the
Christian deprecation of sex brought about the sublimation of sexual
love into something spiritual (J 189).

[24] John Dewey, *Theory of Valuation* (1939), 34.

[25] Cf. my *Critique of Religion and Philosophy* (1958), section 97 on "Freud
and Aspiration" and 98 on "Man's Ontological Interest."

most contemporary schools of psychology as too narrow and too
"partial." The advantage of the phrase "ontological interest" may
be seen in its unpolemical and positive character, and it brings
out that what is desired is not the possession of an object, but a
state of being. Perhaps one could even construct a three-level
theory of values on the basis of the threefold conception of
"physiological," "psychological," and "ontological" interests; but
any such attempt would lead far beyond Nietzsche, who never
explicitly distinguished between these three. He did assert that
"through esteeming alone there is value: and without esteeming
the nut of existence would be hollow" (Z I 15); but he did not
develop any systematic interest theory of values. Yet his account
of man's ontological interest has no equal in the history of
Western thought since Plato offered his soul-stirring picture of
man's ontological predicament in his *Symposium.*

Nietzsche assumed that this predicament was characteristic of
the whole cosmos, and that all nature was pervaded by an Eros
he called the will to power. The acorn gives up its existence to
become an oak tree and thus to become more powerful. The
male insect sacrifices his life to beget offspring and thus to achieve
a form of immortality. In the Indian ascetics and the Christian
martyrs Nietzsche finds the same yearning for another state of
being. They all crave neither the preservation of their lives, nor
merely freedom from something, nor even power as a means to
accomplish some specific end: what they desire is power itself;
another life, as it were, richer and stronger; a rebirth in beauty
and perfection.

In *this* life, Nietzsche thinks, some artists and philosophers
come closest to this state of being, insofar as they may be able
to give style to their characters, to organize the chaos of their
passions, and to create a world of beauty here and now.

Nietzsche, however, was also aware that—more often than not
—the will to power manifests itself in more aggressive ways. The
weak, lacking the power for creation, would fain shroud their
slave souls in a royal cloak and, unable to gain mastery of themselves, seek to conquer others.[26] Men dedicate their lives to the

---

[26] Cf. Goethe's lines, at the beginning of the *Klassische Walpurgisnacht*
(*Faust II*):

> *For everyone who does not know*
> *How to control his inmost self would fain control*
> *His neighbor's will according to his own conceit.*

accumulation of riches; nations make wars to enslave other nations. Nature is not perfectly rational and does not efficiently fulfill her own longing for perfection. Recognizing this, Nietzsche speaks of the will to power; but he leaves no doubt that this drive is an Eros and can be fulfilled only through self-perfection.

9

POWER VERSUS PLEASURE

Without Contraries is no progression. Attraction and Repulsion, Reason and Energy, Love and Hate, are necessary to Human existence.

From these contraries spring what the religious call Good and Evil. Good is the passive that obeys Reason. Evil is the active springing from Energy. . . .

All Bibles or sacred codes have been the causes of the following Errors:

1. That Man has two real existing principles: Viz: a Body and a Soul.

2. That Energy, call'd Evil, is alone from the Body; and that Reason, call'd Good, is alone from the Soul.

3. That God will torment Man in Eternity for following his Energies.

But the following Contraries to these are True:

1. Man has no Body distinct from his Soul . . .

2. Energy is the only life, and is from the Body; and Reason is the bound . . . of Energy.

3. Energy is Eternal Delight.

Those who restrain desire, do so because theirs is weak enough to be restrained. . . .

He who desires but acts not, breeds pestilence. . . .

Joys impregnate, Sorrows bring forth. . . .

Joys laugh not! Sorrows weep not! . . .

Exuberance is beauty. . . .

These two classes of men are always upon earth, and they should be enemies: whoever tries to reconcile them seeks to destroy existence. Religion is an endeavor to reconcile the two. Note: Jesus Christ did not wish to unite, but to separate them . . . and he says: "I came not to send Peace, but a Sword." . . .

Opposition is true Friendship. . . .

One Law for the Lion and Ox is Oppression.

—WILLIAM BLAKE, *The Marriage of Heaven and Hell*

Nietzsche's philosophy of power entails the repudiation of the pleasure principle as a moral standard: human actions are to be evaluated in terms of their conduciveness to power, or—the same in Nietzsche's eyes—in terms of the power they manifest. For Nietzsche accepts the New Testament paradox: "whosoever hath, to him shall be given, and he shall have more abundance." Those whose actions express great power will develop their power through these actions. Our analysis of Nietzsche's conception of sublimation has shown that this does not mean that the "animal-man" is glorified. Nietzsche's power standard may be illuminated further by comparing it in some detail with the pleasure standard. If the preceding chapters have helped to destroy the presumption that Nietzsche's position is barbarous and obviously inferior, it will now become apparent that his own conviction of the obvious inferiority of the pleasure standard did not do complete justice to that position either. Nietzsche's critique of hedonism is based in part on untenable arguments—but an analysis of his reasoning will throw further light on his philosophy, which would appear in altogether too favorable a light if his errors were ignored. In the end, it will be seen that Nietzsche himself, while not a hedonist, was a proponent of what one might call the Good Life.

I

There is a sense in which it is a tautology that all men desire pleasure or happiness. At first glance, one might therefore wonder what is meant when Nietzsche is criticized for repudiating the pursuit of happiness: ". . . According to Nietzsche, men feel a life devoted to the pursuit of power to be a more satisfactory human life than a life devoted to the pursuit of happiness." [1] If men considered a life devoted to the pursuit of power to be most satisfactory, one might contend that this was their conception of the pursuit of happiness.

"Happiness" is, in other words, "elastic": men can enjoy this feeling in a great number of different ways, and it is conceivable that power gives them the greatest possible degree of it. On the other hand, it may be held—as the contrast of power and hap-

---

[1] Stace, *op. cit.*, 66.

piness in our quotation would suggest—that "happiness" means something more specific. In that case, it would not be a tautology that all men desire it, and this claim might actually be false. This consideration suggests that "happiness" has at least two different meanings: first, a man's happiness consists in the state he desires; secondly, happiness may be something more specific that possibly is not desired by all men.

To mark this important distinction, we shall call that state—not necessarily conscious—toward which a man strives, his *happiness;* and we shall define the term *pleasure* in a narrower sense, to refer to a conscious state. A little later on, a further distinction will have to be introduced, and "pleasure" will have to be defined in a still narrower sense—but until then it may suffice to distinguish happiness and pleasure in the manner indicated.

Nietzsche's first contention can now be summarized briefly: it is false that all men seek pleasure; as a matter of fact, their happiness consists in the possession of power. If it were suggested that Nietzsche thus pictured man in a degrading light, one might reply in the words of John Stuart Mill, merely substituting the word "powers" for "pleasures": it is not Nietzsche, but his accusers who "represent human nature in a degrading light; since the accusation supposes human beings to be capable of no powers except those of which swine are capable." [2] This retort crystallizes the fact that "power" and "pleasure" are both "elastic" terms.

Many of Nietzsche's critics are aware of the "elasticity" of pleasure, but not of that of power. Therefore they are open to *ad hominem* rebuttals when they claim that Nietzsche's conception of the will to power can mean only one of two things: either all human activity is a manifestation of it—in which case "power" loses all specific meaning—or "power" refers to something specific and "un-Christian." [3] Exactly the same could be said of the striving for happiness or pleasure. Certainly, the Gospels do not endorse the pursuit of either pleasure or power, unless these be defined in a spiritual sense: and of this both conceptions are equally capable.

Yet, one need not rely on any such retort *ad hominem,* for the dilemma is more apparent than real. Nietzsche does claim that all human activities are expressions of a will to power; yet "power"

---

[2] *Utilitarianism,* Chap. ii, paragraph 4.
[3] Stace, *op. cit.,* 292.

means something specific—and what Nietzsche has in mind is an empirical fact of nature and, as such, not contrary to Christian morals. Nietzsche insists that the way of nature is not the way of Christ, and the law of the jungle is not that of the Sermon on the Mount. So far, he does not contradict the Gospels at all. The crucial question is whether Nietzsche exhorted men to live as beasts do: that would indeed have been anti-Christian. As it happens, his view may well be anti-Christian, but certainly not in the manner suggested. Nietzsche is a naturalistic philosopher and does not consider flesh and spirit entirely discontinuous. In other words, he claims that man need not—and *cannot*—turn "against nature."

His thought on this question is epitomized in his polemics against the Stoics. In some respects, Nietzsche considered himself a Stoic (M 131, 546; J 237; EH-GT 3)—as he well might have—but he ridiculed their notion of living " 'according to Nature' " (J 9). He offered two comments. *First,* "Living—is that not precisely wanting to be other than this Nature?" In other words, nature and life are not stable norms but dialectical forces: they are, as Nietzsche sees them, processes of self-differentiation and self-overcoming. In that sense, living "according to nature" means trying to overcome nature.

Nature—and life, which is a natural process—do not maintain any status quo. They are continually in motion, striving toward self-transcendence. When man tries to master his animal nature and to sublimate his impulses, he is only exemplifying a striving that is essentially natural. Thus Nietzsche's *second* comment on the Stoics is this: "is not the Stoic, after all—a *piece* of Nature?" If he wishes " 'to live according to Life'—how could you *not* do that?" (J 9).

Thus Nietzsche agreed with the view developed in *The Winter's Tale* (IV, 3):

> Yet nature is made better by no mean,
> But nature makes that mean: so o'er that art,
> Which, you say, adds to nature, is an art
> That nature makes. . . . The art itself is nature.

Nietzsche—to summarize—would measure the value of conduct in terms of self-overcoming: this *Überwindungsmotiv* is, as Klages insists correctly, Christian. Nietzsche, however, assumed that he differed with Christianity on the question of the continuity of flesh and spirit, of nature and value.

"Power" means something specific for Nietzsche: self-overcoming. All natural events are manifestations of it, and it is not an anti-Christian notion. Even so, only the "elasticity" of power has been established, and no specific reasons have been given for Nietzsche's decided preference for this standard over the pleasure principle. It seems that he had, basically, two such reasons, and we shall consider these in turn.[4]

Nietzsche's first argument by which he seeks to establish the superiority of the power standard over the pleasure principle falls short of proving his point. In view of this, any exposition of this argument is, in a way, a digression. On the other hand, Nietzsche unquestionably attached great importance to these considerations, and we could skip them only at the cost of representing his philosophy in a false—and perhaps too attractive—light. His argument revolves around the status of consciousness and is thus relevant to his view of reason and to our contention that he was not, properly speaking, an irrationalist.

Nietzsche noted that there is a marked difference between the "elasticity" of power and pleasure. Pleasure is, at the most, coextensive with consciousness—perhaps it even requires self-consciousness—while power does not necessarily require any conscious state or feeling. We speak of power even in physics where consciousness and pleasure seem out of place.

In view of the fact that pleasure is, at the most, coextensive with consciousness, while power may be spoken of even beyond this realm, Nietzsche might have maintained that the feeling of pleasure is merely that conscious state which attends the possession of power, when this is accompanied by any feeling at all. This is, in fact, a point often made by him. From the *Dawn*—where Nietzsche first considered power at any length—to the last notes of 1888, we find him frequently identifying pleasure with

---

[4] Morgan, *op. cit.*, 117, in a footnote, enumerates eight arguments against hedonism, but they overlap, and the list, while faithful to Nietzsche's writings, is redundant.

the feeling of power[5] (M 146, 262, 439; FW 337; WM 693, 1023; A 2).

Yet even if pleasure were granted to be a mere "epiphenomenon" (XVII, 269) of the possession of power, one need not at all concede that, for that reason, man does not strive for pleasure. It is entirely conceivable that what man craves is this epiphenomenon. Nietzsche, however, denied that man strives for pleasure. His argument is based on a discussion of the status of consciousness—and fails to prove his point.

In a tentative outline for *The Will to Power,* Nietzsche jotted down: *"Not* for pleasure does man strive: but for power" (XIX 398). The note in which Nietzsche developed this point states: "To understand . . . what kind of a striving . . . life is, the formula must apply to trees and plants as well as to animals" (WM 704). These, however, strive to "expand, absorb, grow," or —in one word—*"for power."*

Briefly stated, Nietzsche claims not only that the feeling of pleasure is an epiphenomenon of the possession of power, but also that the striving for pleasure is, similarly, an epiphenomenon of the will to power which, in turn, is independent of consciousness. The contention is that human conduct must be explained in the same terms as the behavior of animals or even plants.

Nietzsche, instead of arguing for one conscious motive rather than another, here seems to reject all conscious motivation. This attack on mentalistic psychology has often been considered proof of Nietzsche's irrationalistic "physiologism"—but it can be understood correctly only in the context of Nietzsche's picture of the cosmos. The necessary background and setting can be sketched in with a few large strokes by a reference to what might well be called Nietzsche's *Physics:* a section in the notes of *The Will to Power* (618–39), written for the most part in 1885 and 1886, and not utilized in the composition of the many works Nietzsche published later. Like most of the notes Nietzsche failed to use, these conceptions were not fully thought through nor completely integrated with the rest of his philosophy. On the other hand, the attack on mentalistic psychology was published in the *Götzen-Dämmerung* and represents a more systematic statement of views

---

[5] This statement will require revision later when "pleasure" is defined in a narrower sense.

that recur throughout Nietzsche's writings, scattered here and there[6]—and it is best understood against the background of the fragmentary *Physics,* which might also be called Nietzsche's *Monadology.* Thus a very brief summary of the relevant notes seems in order.

The concepts of " 'empty space' and of lump-atoms" are untenable (WM 618). *"Pressure* and *push"* are derivative concepts that presuppose "things" and external relations (622). "There is no 'essence-in-itself'; (the *relations* . . . constitute the essence) . . ." (625). Causality and teleology imply each other and are both interpretations only (627). "There is no *after-one-another,* but only an into-one-another, a process in which the single moments that succeed each other do *not* condition each other as causes and effects" (631).

Perhaps one may interrupt this exposition to recall Goethe's: "men usually have only the concept of next-to-one-another, not the feeling of into-and-through-one-another [*In- und Durcheinander*], for one understands only what one can make oneself"; "the thinking man errs especially when he inquires after cause and effect; the two together make up the indivisible phenomenon." [7] The "Heraclitean" world-picture which Oehler and Bäumler consider proof of Nietzsche's irrationalism was derived, in the main, from Goethe, Hegel, and Leibniz—hardly "irrationalists."

To proceed with Nietzsche's "monadology": the *"subject"* is a fiction (632); there is only "a rearrangement of forces" and a change of "power quanta" (633).

> *Critique of Mechanism.* Let us here remove the two popular concepts, "necessity" and "law": the first introduces a false coercion, the second a false freedom into the world. "Things" do not behave regularly, according to a *rule:* there are no things (they are our fiction). . . . There is no law: every power draws its last consequence at every moment. . . . A power quantum is characterized by its effect [*Wirkung*] and by that which it resists. The adiaphorous is lacking, though it would be thinkable theoretically . . . Not self-preservation: every atom affects all being—it is thought away when one thinks away this radiation of power will. Therefore I call it a quantum of *"will to power":* thereby that character is expressed which cannot be thought away out of

---

[6] It also draws heavily on notes that the editors later included in *The Will to Power:* e.g., WM 41–44, 46, 334, 380, 470–92, 523–29, 545–52; cf. A 15.

[7] Letter to Zelter, March 28, 1804, and *Maximen und Reflexionen.*

the mechanical order, without thinking that order itself away.
. . . Mechanics as a doctrine of *motion* is already a translation
into the sense language of man [634].

We require "units" to be able to *calculate:* one must not suppose for that reason that there *are* such units. We have derived
the concept of the unit from our "ego" concept—our most ancient article of faith. . . . Two fictions: the concept of *motion*
(taken from our sense language) and the concept of the *atom*
(i.e., unit, derived from our psychical "experience") . . . No
things remain but dynamic quanta in a relation of tension to
all other dynamic quanta: their essence consists in their relation
to all other quanta, in their "affecting" [*"Wirken" auf*] them.
The will to power is neither a being nor a becoming, but a pathos
—it is the most fundamental fact from which becoming and affecting result [635].

The Greek *pathos* has a number of meanings: occasion, event,
passion, suffering, destiny—but we shall forgo any comparison
with Whitehead's philosophy of occasions and events, as an exposition of Whitehead would take us too far afield. Nietzsche's
"monadology" culminates in "a necessary perspectivism by virtue of which every force center—and not only man—construes
the whole rest of the world *from its own point of view* . . ." (636).

Nietzsche's approach to the problem of causality is further illuminated by a couple of notes incorporated in another section
of *The Will to Power:*

The question "why?" is always the question after a final cause,
after a "wherefor?" We have nothing resembling a "sense for
the perception of efficient causes." Thus *Hume* is right that only
habit (but not just that of the individual!) makes us expect that
one often observed process follows another. What gives us the
extraordinary firmness of our faith in causality, however, is not
the great habit . . . but our *inability* to *interpret* what happens
except as something that happens on *purpose*. It is the *faith* that
only what lives and thinks is *effective*—the faith in will and purpose; it is the faith that all that happens is a doing, and that all
doing presupposes a doer [WM 550].

The calculability of an event does not consist in the fact that
a rule is followed or a necessity obeyed, or that a law of causality
was projected by us into all that happens: it consists in the *recurrence of "identical cases."* There is not, as Kant supposed, a
sense of causality. One is surprised, one is disturbed—one desires
something familiar one can hold on to. As soon as something old
is pointed out in the new, we are calmed. The alleged instinct

for causality is merely the *fear of the unfamiliar* and the attempt
to discover something familiar in it—a search not for causes, but
for the familiar [WM 551].

Reconciling these two notes, one might point out that the
anthropomorphism criticized in the first of them might well be
characterized in terms of the second note—as a search for what
is familiar.

No extended analysis of these notes is required in the present
context. Even the brief sketch here given of Nietzsche's world-
picture makes it abundantly clear that Nietzsche did not attack
mentalistic psychology in order to establish the universality of
mechanistic causality—and that he did not espouse any "physiologism." He emphatically denied any dualism of cause and effect
as well as "the popular and entirely false opposition of soul and
body," which he had repudiated even in his first book (GT 21).
In fact, he tended toward an extreme form of the doctrine of internal relations—but the difficulties of this position may be safely
ignored here.

What concerns us is that Nietzsche's occasional insistence on
a reversal of cause and effect, which would seem to imply a deprecation of consciousness, must be understood as a polemical
antithesis against current prejudices. Nietzsche's writings are rich
in such antitheses; and his polemics frequently obscure his own
position. This will become clear as we now turn to consider
Nietzsche's attack on "spiritual causes" in the *Götzen-Dämmerung*
in the section (vi) which is entitled "The Four Great Errors." [8]

The first "error" consists in mistaking effects for causes—as
when we say that a people perished on account of their vices, instead of considering their vices consequences of the decadence of
which they died: "*first* example of my 'revaluation of all values':
a well turned out human being, a 'happy one,' *must* perform certain actions and shrinks instinctively from other actions. . . . In
a formula: his virtue is the *consequence* of his happiness" (G vi

---

[8] An earlier list of "Four Errors" appears in FW 115. The phrase was presumably suggested by Bacon's famous "Four Idols." The reference to
"idols" in the Preface to G points in the same direction; and although
the Preface still assumed that the work would be entitled "A Psychologist's Leisure," Gast insisted on "a more sumptuous, more resplendent
title," and Nietzsche finally chose *Götzen-Dämmerung* as an antithesis to
Wagner's *Götterdämmerung*. Nietzsche was interested in Bacon at that
time and suspected that Bacon had written "Shakespeare's" works (WM
848; cf. 468, and xvi, 331).

2). Here the word "revaluation" is used in a way that may have abetted the misapprehension that it meant the proposal of arbitrary antitheses to current valuations—but in fact it consists, here too, in a psychological insight: the weak who hope that their conformity to traditional morals may in the end ensure their happiness will, as a matter of fact, not find ultimate happiness; those, on the other hand, who have attained that happy state of being toward which we all strive will *eo ipso* be gracious and kindly. Happiness is envisaged less as a state of consciousness than as a state of being: as power.

The second "error" consists of the assumption of a "false causality" of "spiritual causes," such as "will," "consciousness," and "ego." The third "error" consists of the assumption of "imaginary causes" and may be illustrated by our invention of antecedents in dreams to explain a prior stimulus *ex post facto*. Nietzsche also names evil spirits and the construction of suffering as a punishment for sins as examples of "imaginary causes"—and one may here think of the Indian conception of karma or of the friends of Job who inferred that he must have sinned because they could not explain his affliction otherwise. The fourth "error," finally, consists in the assumption of a "free will." In view of the passages already cited, it hardly need be said that Nietzsche is not repudiating free will in favor of determinism. Rather he considers the popular notion of causality untenable and is convinced that the assumption of free will depends on it. Thus he entitles one of his notes: *"Toward an attack on [both] determinism and teleology"* (WM 552).

When Nietzsche speaks of mistaking effects for causes, he is—as Berkeley would have said—speaking "with the vulgar" and not strictly in accordance with his own philosophic position. Instead of saying, for example, that vices are a "consequence" of degeneration, he might have been better advised to speak of an "aspect"—but language and grammar force us in any case to propound the doctrine of "internal relations" in terms of "things" and "external relations," and such fault-finding may be pedantic. The crucial point is that Nietzsche—occasional polemical antitheses or popular expressions notwithstanding—did not deprecate consciousness in favor of physiological processes, but did criticize the conception of consciousness as a separate "thing," as an "entity" apart from the body, as a "spiritual cause."

Nietzsche envisaged man amidst nature: "the fatality of his essence is not to be disentangled from the fatality of all that which has been and will be" (G vi 8). Nature is neither teleologically aiming at a fixed goal or god, nor mechanistic and dead—nor does the vital force "explode" in unforeseeable directions; rather one may think of Goethe's dual conception of polarity and enhancement.[9] All of nature is imbued with a striving to overcome and transcend itself, and man cannot be extricated from this total picture.

Even if one were to grant Nietzsche his Goethean vision of the cosmos and the universality of the will to power, one might yet insist that value might have to be judged in terms of pleasure. Nietzsche's argument would prove the inferiority of the pleasure standard only if he were prepared to deny the efficacy of consciousness altogether. His view, however, precludes any deprecation of consciousness, which cannot be disentangled from the totality of human behavior. Nietzsche, moreover, makes much of the efficacy of consciousness. It has been seen how his very doctrine of the will to power encompassed the insight that this striving could never achieve ultimate fulfillment without availing itself of reason. In the discussion of the problems of race, later on, it will be seen how Nietzsche believed not only that our behavior could not be understood apart from its spiritual aspect, but even that biological heredity was incomprehensible if separated from man's spiritual life. Finally, he was convinced that his doctrine of eternal recurrence would have unequaled effects (xi, 183 ff.; FW 285, 341; xiv, 132; WM 1058).

Thus one need not charge Nietzsche with an Epimenidean fallacy, insofar as a philosopher who writes books to convince other people of the complete ineffectiveness of consciousness is ludicrous. While Nietzsche may have approximated such a ridiculous position in occasional scattered overstatements and antith-

---

[9] Cf., e.g., Goethe's comment to Kanzler von Müller (May 24, 1828) about "the intuition [*Anschauung*] of the two great driving forces of nature: the concept of *Polarität* and *Steigerung*—the one belonging to matter insofar as we think of it as material, the other insofar as we think of it as spiritual; the one is in everlasting attraction and repulsion, the other in ever striving ascent. But because matter never exists or can be effective without spirit, nor spirit without matter, matter, too, is able to enhance itself, just as the spirit won't let it be denied to itself to attract and repel."

eses against current prejudices, the context of his remarks and the structure of his philosophy as a whole leave no doubt that his position was not that unsound.

Historically, those remarks in which Nietzsche seemed to deprecate consciousness have been noted widely, while his high esteem of rationality has been largely ignored. Yet there are not, as it were, two Nietzsches—one an irrational "physiologist," the other a Platonist. Nietzsche's position is unambiguous and unequivocal, provided that one examines his philosophy as a whole. There are passages in his writings where he says, for example, "that all our so-called consciousness is a more or less fantastic commentary on an unknown, perhaps unknowable, but felt text" (M 119). Even such a statement, however, is immediately followed by examples which make it clear that what Nietzsche had in mind was merely a denial of any complete schism of body and soul.

> Suppose we note one day that somebody in the market place laughs at us as we pass: depending on whether this or that drive is just then at its height in us . . . and depending on the kind of man we are, it will be an entirely different experience . . . one seeks to start a fight about it; . . . another thinks as a consequence how ridiculous he is; and still another one is gratified that he has contributed to the gaiety and sunshine of the world.

> On a recent morning . . . a man collapsed . . . in front of me . . . ; all the women around screamed . . . ; I myself put him back on his feet. . . . I did the most obvious and rational thing and went on coldly. Suppose that one had told me the day before that tomorrow . . . somebody would collapse right next to me. . . . I should have suffered agonies of all sorts ahead of time and should not have slept that night and might, at the decisive moment, have done just what that man did, instead of helping him. For in the meantime any number of drives would have *had time* to imagine the experience . . .

Not the efficacy of consciousness, but the "popular" dualism of flesh and spirit, is denied. Thus Nietzsche writes elsewhere:

> Contentment protects even against colds. Has a woman who knew herself to be well dressed, ever caught cold? I am assuming that she was barely dressed [G 1 25].

In conclusion one may cite Nietzsche's version—published in 1881 —of what later became known as the James-Lange theory:

To understand another, i.e., *to reproduce his feeling in us,* we certainly do frequently go back to the *reason* for his . . . feeling and ask, for example: *why* is he sad?—in order then to become sad for the same reason; but it is much more usual not to do this and to generate the feeling in us through the *effects* which it . . . manifests in the other person: we reproduce the expression of his eyes, his voice, his gait, his posture. . . . Then a similar feeling originates in us as a consequence of an old association of movement and feeling which is drilled to run forward and backward [M 142].

The "forward and backward" is important: consciousness is no more deprecated than is the body, but their continuity is emphasized.

This is no purely academic question, but has important pedagogical and therapeutical implications. Thus psychoanalysis shows how physical symptoms or habits can be due to "feelings" and are curable through an analysis of these feelings, while John Dewey has always claimed, and conditioned-reflex therapy attempts to show, that feelings may be due to behavioral patterns. According to Nietzsche, both approaches are complementary. In other words, faith may beget action, but action may also beget faith.

Under these circumstances, Nietzsche's discussions of the status of consciousness fail to establish his thesis that value must be measured in terms of power rather than of pleasure. Even if the consciousness of pleasure were only an aspect of the possession of power, and even if the striving for pleasure were merely the conscious aspect of the will to power, the possibility would yet remain that this aspect is of considerable significance. In fact, we shall find that Nietzsche himself—in spite of the fact that he occasionally argued against the pleasure standard in this way—attached supreme significance to what *he* took to be the conscious aspect of that state of being he called power.

II

It now becomes necessary to distinguish between the conscious state Nietzsche himself associated with happiness and that other conscious state usually called pleasure. Only in that way can Nietzsche's second argument against the pleasure standard be expressed unequivocally—after his first argument, regarding conscious states in general, has been seen to fall short of proving his point. By a man's happiness we shall still understand the state—not necessarily conscious—that he desires; but while "pleasure" has so far been used in a comparatively wide sense to refer to a state of consciousness, we shall now define it more narrowly as a particular sensation that is marked definitively by the absence of any pain or discomfort. Nietzsche's second and crucial contention can then be formulated concisely: he did not repudiate the pursuit of happiness but claimed that the conscious aspect of that state for which man strives is not marked by the definitive absence of pain and discomfort—or more briefly, the state of consciousness man desires most is not pleasure.

It would, of course, be rash to conclude from this that Nietzsche claimed: what man enjoys most is suffering. Rather he insisted that man, by nature, strives for something to which pleasure and pain are only incidental. This position, which is sometimes held to be typically German, can actually be documented, almost at random, from the basic writings of Christianity and humanism.

The Gospels would seem to preach the doctrine that pain and pleasure are incidental to what man ought to strive for; and a good case might even be made out to substantiate the assertion that the Bible also considered self-perfection the ideal goal of human effort. Suffice it to add that the very document which speaks of the "pursuit of happiness" lists both "life" and "liberty" first; nor can there be much doubt as to which of these the author considered the *summum bonum*. He entitled his proclamation a "Declaration of Independence"—and even then thousands were renouncing pleasure and comfort and sacrificing their lives for liberty.

Nietzsche himself weakened his argument by occasional *bon mots*—well illustrated by the following epigram: "Man does *not* strive for pleasure; only the Englishman does" (G I 12). Such polemics obscure his basic contention; so do also his impassioned diatribes against Christianity, which have led many to believe that whatever is Christian is *eo ipso* not Nietzschean. Thus one of Nietzsche's critics holds that, "of course, self-sacrifice is a Christian, not a Nietzschean ideal." [10] We have tried to show that it is

---

[10] Stace, *op. cit.*, 224.

not only *a,* but nothing less than *the,* Nietzschean "ideal." In his keen appreciation of suffering and self-sacrifice as indispensable conditions of self-perfection, Nietzsche seems more "Christian" than most philosophers.[11]

Nietzsche differs with Christianity in his naturalistic denial of the breach between flesh and spirit, in his claim that self-sacrifice is the very essence of life, and in his paradoxical assertion— so well illustrated by his previously considered polemics against the Stoics—that man's attempts to sublimate his animal nature exemplify the very way of nature.

In *Zarathustra,* a suggestive definition of spirit (*Geist*) is offered: "spirit is the life that itself cuts into life" (Z II 8). This formulation is part of a long glorification of the spirit. Most of Nietzsche's interpreters and critics have ignored this paradox, while others—especially Bertram and Klages—have represented his thought as essentially schizophrenic. Any such view, however, does scant justice to Nietzsche's philosophy: he affirmed both life and spirit. If one decides in advance that one is good and the other bad, Nietzsche's doctrine may seem "ambiguous" (Bertram's thesis) or self-contradictory (Klages' allegation). Nietzsche rejected the premise that spirit came into the world in a supernatural way, and that a Christian God or a Klagesian devil was responsible for its "intrusion" into nature. He asserted that the spirit cuts into life, and that it is its function to counteract man's tendency to yield to his impulses; but he considered it an instrument used by life in its effort to enhance itself. Spirit is not opposed to life altogether, but directed only against one level of it. Its mission is not to destroy but to fulfill, to sublimate or—to use the expressions of the *Meditations*—to transfigure and perfect man's nature.

One cannot gain any adequate understanding of Nietzsche's repudiation of the pleasure principle by pigeonholing it—as is often done—as typically "Christian," "romantic," or "German." It must be viewed in the context of his philosophy. He envisages man amidst nature and sees him striving to perfect himself. Nietzsche finds in man and in all living creatures an Eros—or a

---

[11] R. B. Perry, *The Present Conflict of Ideals* (1918), 158, suggests that one would do better not to insist on Nietzsche's affinity with Christianity, because he himself was so eager to repudiate it. It seems important, however, to distinguish between those elements which Nietzsche attacked and those with which he agreed.

will to power—and ventures a "hypothesis from there to the total character of all being" (WM 689). Even if one does not consider this far-flung hypothesis well founded, one may yet admit—and this seems to be Nietzsche's only truly pertinent and potent argument against the pleasure principle—that the state man ultimately desires is not marked by the absence of pain and discomfort.

Again Nietzsche may be said to offer two arguments to prove this point—and only one is relevant. We shall consider the less pertinent argument first. Nietzsche makes much of the fact that, as he sees it, suffering is a necessary stage on the way to ultimate pleasure. One cannot have one without the other. Pleasure and pain are "twins" (FW 338); and "with the pleasure of Homer in one's soul, one is also of all creatures under the sun the one capable of the most suffering" (FW 302). Perhaps Nietzsche's comment on another aspect of Stoicism crystallizes this point most clearly: pleasure and pain are "so knotted together that whoever *wants* as much as possible of the one, *must* also have as much as possible of the other . . . The Stoics believed that this was so and were consistent in desiring as little as possible [of both]" (FW 2).

It may well be true that agony is the price of all birth, and travail the cost of creation; one may grant that all great pleasure can only be had after considerable suffering, and that those who are capable of the most extreme exultation are also most sensitive to anguish: yet it would not follow from all this that suffering possessed more than a merely instrumental value which is derivative from the value of the end toward which it is a means: pleasure. To prove his point, Nietzsche must clearly go a step further. He must claim not only that suffering is a necessary antecedent of all great pleasure, but he must further insist that happiness—i.e., that state which men desire—is not marked by the absence of discomfort and pain. This is, in fact, his position; it is his only truly pertinent argument against the pleasure principle; and it seems eminently worthy of consideration.

Using our distinction between "happiness" and "pleasure," we can say that happiness involves a measure of discomfort and pain. Nietzsche's own terminology is far from rigid or consistent, but on occasion he did make a clear distinction that closely parallels ours: *Glück* is marked by the absence of pain; *Lust* includes some pain (WM 696, 703). *"Lust"* is of course *not* the same as the

English "lust," but a term sometimes used by Nietzsche to connote that joy which exults in the face of suffering. He even goes to the extent of considering this joy a kind of suffering. This argument is not worked out; in two more or less dogmatic statements joy (*Lust*) is defined once as "a kind of pain" (WM 490), the other time as "a rhythm of little stimulations of displeasure [*Unlust*]" (WM 697).

Nietzsche comes closest to arguing this point in the following note:

> Pain is something different from *joy* [*Lust*]—I mean, it is *not* the opposite of joy. If the essence of "joy" has been designated correctly as a *plus-feeling* of power (and thus as a feeling of a difference and as presupposing comparison), the essence of "displeasure" [*Unlust*] is not yet defined thereby. The false opposites in which the people and—as a *consequence*—language believe, have always been dangerous foot fetters for the march of truth. There are even cases where a kind of joy is conditioned by a certain *rhythmic sequence* of little stimulations of displeasure: thus a very fast growth of the feeling of power, of the feeling of joy, is attained. This is the case, for example, in tickling and also in the sexual tickling in the act of coitus: thus we see displeasure acting as an ingredient of joy. It seems that a little inhibition is overcome and then immediately succeeded by another little inhibition that is again overcome—this play of resistance and victory—is the strongest stimulus of that total feeling of . . . overflowing power which constitutes the essence of joy. . . . Joy and pain are thus not opposites [WM 699].

Nietzsche here suggests not only that happiness does not exclude suffering but that joy may consist in what one might call a certain configuration in time of feelings of pain; and elsewhere he generalizes: "in all joy pain is included" (WM 658). More famous is a line from one of Nietzsche's poems in *Zarathustra* which may constitute an effort to give expression to the same point: *"Lust— tiefer noch als Herzeleid,"* joy—deeper yet than agony (Z IV 19).

In the writings of William James there is a passage that gives expression to a similar conviction and is possibly more persuasive because it calls attention less to our more limited aspirations than to our long-range hopes:

> Everybody must at some time have wondered at the strange paradox of our moral nature, that, although the pursuit of outward good is the breath of its nostrils, the attainment of outward good would seem to be its suffocation and death. Why does the paint-

ing of any paradise or utopia, in heaven or on earth, awaken such yearnings for . . . escape? The white-robed, harp-playing heaven of our sabbath-schools, and the lady-like, tea-table elysium represented in Mr. Spencer's Data of Ethics, as the final consummation of progress, are simply on a par in this respect—lubberlands, pure and simple, one and all. We look upon them from this delicious mess of insanities and realities, strivings and deadnesses, hopes and fears, agonies and exaltations, which form our present state, and *tedium vitae* is the only sentiment they awake in our breast. To our crepuscular natures, born for the conflict, the Rembrandtesque Chiaroscuro, the shifting struggle of the sunbeam in the gloom, such pictures of light upon light are vacuous and expressionless, neither to be enjoyed nor understood. If *this* be the whole fruit of the victory, we say; if the generations of mankind suffered and laid down their lives; if prophets confessed and martyrs sang in the fire and all the sacred tears were shed for no other end than that a race of creatures of such unexampled insipidity should succeed, and protract *in saecula saeculorum* their contented and inoffensive lives, why, at such a rate, better lose than win the battle, or at all events better ring down the curtain before the last act of the play, so that a business that began so importantly may be saved from so singularly flat a winding up.[12]

The insipid creatures in James' vision are similar indeed to Nietzsche's sarcastic conception of "the last man": "One has one's tiny pleasure for the day and one's tiny pleasure for the night— but one has a regard for health." "One herd: each wants the same, each is the same—and whoever feels different goes voluntarily into an asylum" (Z-V 5).

It would be pointless to call both James and Nietzsche "romantics." The question is whether, as long as we retain our human nature, a perfectly painless "heaven" would seem like a heaven to us—or whether such an abode would only be a subtle version of hell. In other words—to recall the conception of health as the capacity to overcome disease—can we define joy as essentially the overcoming of suffering? Perhaps one could define it not as the state attained at the end of suffering, in which case suffering would have merely instrumental value, but as the process of the overcoming itself—in which case joy would not be a passive sensation but rather the conscious aspect of activity. In fact,

---

[12] "The Dilemma of Determinism" (1884) in *The Will to Believe and Other Essays in Popular Philosophy* (1897), 167 f.

Nietzsche contends that happiness is a creative activity and that there is "in every action an *ingredient of displeasure* [*Unlust*]" (WM 694, 704). It may be objected that this is not true of every action, though Nietzsche might retort that only the discomfort accounts for, and stimulates, activity.

It might further be objected that the Nietzsche-James conception of happiness is essentially "Protestant," though Nietzsche might answer by citing the descriptions of heaven that he quotes in a different context as illustrations of *ressentiment:*

> For *what* is it that constitutes the bliss of this Paradise? We might even guess, but it is better to have it expressly described for us by an authority not to be underestimated in such matters, Thomas Aquinas, the great teacher and saint. *"Beati in regno coelesti,"* he says, meek as a lamb, *"videbunt poenas damnatorum, ut beatitudo illis magis complaceat.* [The blessed in the kingdom of heaven will see the punishments of the damned, in order that their bliss be that much greater.]" Or, if one would like to hear it in a stronger key, perhaps from the mouth of a triumphant Church Father adjuring his Christians to avoid the cruel pleasures of the public games—but why? "For the faith offers us much more"—he says, *De Spectaculis,* chs. 29 f.—"something much stronger; thanks to the Redemption, quite other joys are at our command; in place of athletes we have our martyrs; if we crave blood, we have the blood of Christ . . . But think of what awaits us on the day of his return, the day of his triumph!" and then goes on, the enraptured visionary . . . [GM I 15].

Tertullian's gory vision of the happiness of the blessed need not be cited here. It may be objected that such quotations lend one-sided emphasis to what one might call all-too-human elements in the writings of Christian fathers and saints. That is unquestionably true—though there is more material of this sort than is generally expected—and one need hardly stress that Nietzsche himself has only scorn for such visions of heaven. The relevant point here is merely that when happiness is not pictured as the process of a struggle against suffering or as a creative activity, it will nevertheless not be defined as a pure state of pleasure from which pain is completely absent: when the overcoming of suffering is not conceived in terms of one's own exertions, it is apt to take the form of one's own triumphant elevation over the suffering of others. That, of course, seems to Nietzsche the mark of petty weakness—as does any aspiration to find one's own power

through the oppression of others—and Nietzsche, admittedly
fond of world-historical ironies, makes the most of such passages
in Christian writers.

It might finally be urged that the conception of happiness as
a triumph over suffering, and especially the idealization of creative power, is characteristic at best of Western civilization only.
While it is impossible to offer any extended discussion of other
civilizations here, Hinduism and Buddhism cannot be ignored
entirely: for on the face of it, the conception of happiness—in the
sense here assigned to this word—as either Nirvana or a union of
Atman and Brahma seems the very antithesis of Nietzsche's
apotheosis of creativity. We must therefore ask whether the existence of hundreds of millions of Hindus and Buddhists does not
refute Nietzsche's contentions, though the answer will have to be
quite brief and stop short of any thorough analysis of the religions in question.

Acting the role of Nietzsche's advocate, one might point out
that Nietzsche's frequent emphasis on the superlative sense of
power among the Indian ascetics has considerable basis in fact.
A few quotations from the Gifford lectures of Archbishop Söderblom, a good authority on the comparative history of religion,
may illustrate this point:

> That these miraculous powers may be gained by means of the
> Yoga praxis the most enlightened Brahmans of the present day
> are themselves immovably convinced.
>
> Nor does the original Yoga system know of any celestial bliss, of
> which there are abundant descriptions elsewhere. It knows only
> of the feeling of freedom enjoyed by the released spirit.
>
> It was no mere chance that ascesis was called *tapas,* heat or heat-
> ing. Magical powers were sought thereby. The word *tapas* be-
> came the term for all kinds of self-torture and the superhuman
> power attained thereby. . . . Oneness with Brahman, originally
> "the power" and the power-filled sacrificial word . . .
>
> The Yogi . . . became dangerous to the gods. When they see
> him fast and mortify himself and produce "heat," *tapas,* they
> tremble, fearing for their power. He becomes their master. . . .
> Prayapati submits to self-castigation in order to gain strength to
> create.[13]

---

[13] *The Living God* (Gifford Lectures 1931, Oxford University Press 1933, reissued 1939), 41 f., 42 f., 48, 49 f. The first passage is quoted by Söderblom
from R. Garbe, "Yoga" E.R.E. II, 832–33.

But what of Buddhism? Did not the Buddha renounce all magical powers? Legend pictures his temptation by Mara, the tempter, who sought to dissuade him from taking the step to final blessedness—the story corresponds to Jesus' temptation in the desert—and Mara offered him dominion "over the four great continents and their two thousand attending isles." The Buddha-to-be, however, replied: "Mara . . . I do not wish for sovereignty. I am about to cause the ten thousand worlds to thunder with my becoming a Buddha." [14] The issue here is not one between power and Nirvana, but one between power and infinitely more power. What the ascetic, including even the Buddha, wants is not power that is of this world, power over men, or power over many countries, but cosmic power, world-shaking power—power even over the gods. ". . . The world shall be judged by you. . . . Know ye not that we shall judge angels?" (i Cor. 6:2 f.)

The Buddhist masses, Nietzsche's advocate might proceed, conceive of happiness not as Nirvana: they have their heavens and hells and their dreams of power, no less than do the Yoga ascetics. And if Nietzsche were pressed to admit that there are at least some who do yearn for the absolute extinction of all consciousness and for the utter negation of life, will, and activity, he might either retort that this was indeed a rare exception, an abnormality, a disease—in one word: decadence—or he might say that Nirvana was here conceived as the only chance to overpower life and suffering and that what is wanted here, too, is this ultimate and absolute triumph over the world. Just here—thus Nietzsche's defense might proceed to attack—power is wanted even at the price of consciousness; just here pleasure is not only incidental to ultimate happiness, but actually renounced altogether as incompatible with that highest power which man yearns for most.

Nietzsche himself might couple these assertions and say that only the decadent require so radical a cure, while the truly powerful need not escape into any Nirvana: they can win their triumph in this world and be creative. This emphasis on creativity reveals a certain limited validity even in Nietzsche's first argument, about conscious states in general. A powerful nature, says Nietzsche, "asks the devil whether it will be blessed—it has no such interest in pleasure . . . it is strength and action" (WM

---

[14] *Ibid.*, 89, quoted from Jataka, i, 63 (271).

781). More famous is the line in *Zarathustra:* "What matters pleasure! . . . I do not covet . . . pleasure, I covet my work." The reply to Zarathustra, who makes this assertion, crystallizes the point that the active life does not exclude a conscious aspect: "That you say as one who has more than enough of the good. Do you not lie in a sky-blue lake of pleasure?" (Z IV 1). If Nietzsche had accepted the terminology suggested above, we should have found Zarathustra lying in a sky-blue lake of joy.

Nietzsche, of course, does not propound or defend his own position in the manner here proposed;[15] and his argument suffers particularly from his failure to distinguish consistently between what we have called happiness, joy, and pleasure. This lack of terminological precision introduces confusion into his discussion of these problems—but while this is unquestionably a fault, one may add that Nietzsche shares it with most of the relevant literature. While the arguments of other writers are occasionally entirely invalidated by their illicit confusion of happiness and pleasure and their rash assumption that all men desire only pleasure—a criticism that has often been urged against Mill—Nietzsche's contention gains, rather than loses, from a terminological clarification. If happiness is defined as the state of being man desires; if joy is defined as the conscious aspect of this state; and if pleasure is defined as a sensation marked by the absence of pain and discomfort; then Nietzsche's position can be summarized quite briefly: *happiness is the fusion of power and joy*—and joy contains not only ingredients of pleasure but also a component of pain.

Nietzsche's objection to the pleasure standard means, in short, that happiness and pleasure are not identical; but he could not

---

[15] The defense proposed in the text is designed to meet a few of the most obvious objections, and to suggest that Nietzsche's position is worthy of serious consideration and not to be discounted rashly. A systematic and conclusive inquiry beyond this point is impossible within the present framework. It might, however, be well worthwhile to consider from this point of view the evidence adduced by Alfred Adler for a theory similar to Nietzsche's—or to examine the many phenomena in the field of child psychology that seem to fit Nietzsche's contentions, but were ignored by him because he had so little acquaintance with children. Finally, a critical comparison of Nietzsche's monistic theory of the will to power and Freud's later dualism might prove fruitful; for the phenomena that led Freud to postulate a death impulse could be dealt with in terms of Nietzsche's hypothesis.

formulate his point in just this manner because he had only one word for the two: *Glück*. This he deprecated in one sense, while in another sense he sought to determine its essential nature: "it is significantly enlightening to substitute for the individual 'happiness' (for which every living being is supposed to strive) *power*" (WM 688). When Nietzsche goes on to say that "joy is only a symptom of the feeling of attained power . . . (one does not strive for joy . . . joy accompanies; joy does not move)," he is committing what he himself would elsewhere brand as an important fallacy: he separates body and soul, flesh and spirit, the physical and the conscious, and comes close—to say the least—to deprecating the latter. In keeping with his own philosophic position, he should say that ultimate happiness consists in the inextricable fusion of power and joy.

Nirvana is not ultimate happiness but a substitute desired by some of the weak who are incapable of achieving that state of joyous power which they, too, would prefer if they had the strength to attain it. The pleasures of "modern man," finally, are even further removed from true happiness, which is not an aggregate of pleasures, nor any conglomeration of sensations, but a way of life. To be sure, such happiness is not the only thing appreciated for its own sake. Every pleasurable sensation, however trivial—the smell of a flower or the taste of cold water—is valued for its own sake. The indefinite addition of such pleasures, however, does not make for happiness: *vide, The Picture of Dorian Gray* or, as Nietzsche suggests, "modern man" (A 1).

Again one may think of the different kinds of interest we have distinguished. There are not only "physiological" and "psychological" interests in the useful and agreeable: man also has an "ontological" interest in another state of being—and Nietzsche "teaches us to differentiate between the real and apparent advancements of human happiness: how neither riches nor honors nor scholarship can raise the single one out of his profound discouragement over the worthlessness of his existence, and how the striving for these goals can receive meaning only from a high and transfiguring over-all aim" (U III 3).

While Nietzsche's repudiation of hedonism is emphatic, he himself may be called a proponent of the Good Life. His earlier philosophy had put him into the inconsistent position of exhorting man that he "ought" to live such a life. His conception of the will to power enables him now to say that the man who lives such a life is the powerful man, while the man who does not is weak—and if only he had the strength, he would live the Good Life, for it is what he, too, desires ultimately. In his frustration, however, the weak man either settles, *faute de mieux,* for some more or less petty form of power, such as that power over others which is found in positions of command, in bullying, or in crime —or he resigns himself to failure and dreams of greater power in another world. Such dreams may be highly spiritualized, but in many cases they include the hope that one will behold the downfall, or even the eternal tortures, of one's enemies.

Worldly power may thus cloak the most abysmal weakness; value cannot be measured in terms of "success," and it is precisely the dictator who is apt to be the slave of his passions. Nietzsche, of course, knew well the classical picture of the tyrant as the most slavish of men, in the eighth and ninth book of Plato's *Republic.* The ascetic, though lacking scepter and crown, seemed one of the most powerful of men to Nietzsche—but still more powerful is the man who need not resort to so radical a cure. As one should "measure the health of a society and of individuals according to how many parasites they can stand" (M 202), one must consider the man who is strong enough to maintain his mastery in the face of vehement passions as being more powerful than the ascetic who suppresses or extirpates his impulses. At the top of the power scale are those who are able to sublimate their impulses, to "organize the chaos," and to give "style" to their character.

The Good Life is the powerful life, the life of those who are in full control of their impulses and need not weaken them, and *the good man is for Nietzsche the passionate man who is the master of his passions.* The insistence that the good man is the passionate man distinguishes Nietzsche from the Stoic and—so he himself thought—from the Christian view. His insistence, on the other hand, that the good man masters his passions has been overlooked by the vast majority of Nietzsche's critics as well as by those who have, from time to time, cited him in defense of their own license.

In his early philosophy, Nietzsche had envisaged artist, saint, and philosopher as the supreme triad of humanity. Now he would still agree that these are the three types that have tried to rise above the mass of men, but he would evaluate them differently. The saint is now pictured as the man who has extirpated his passions and thus destroyed his chances of ever living the Good Life, while artist and philosopher employ their passions in spiritual pursuits and are the most nearly perfect of men; for the powerful life is the creative life.

Among philosophers it was, above all others, Socrates who was the perfect master of his passions—and Nietzsche's admiration for Socrates will be considered in detail later—while among artists Nietzsche found one closer to his own time. Near the end of the last work he himself published, he gave us a picture of the powerful man who leads the Good Life, and, as so often, Nietzsche chose a historical person to be his symbol:

> *Goethe*—. . . what he wanted was *totality;* he fought the mutual extraneousness of reason, senses, feeling, and will . . . he disciplined himself into wholeness, he *created* himself . . . Goethe conceived a human being who would be strong, highly educated, skillful in all bodily matters, self-controlled, reverent toward himself, and who might dare to afford the whole range and wealth of being natural, being strong enough for such freedom; the man of tolerance, not from weakness but from strength because he knows how to use to his advantage even that from which the average nature would perish; the man for whom there is no longer anything that is forbidden, unless it be *weakness,* whether called vice or virtue. Such a spirit who has *become free* stands amid the cosmos with a joyous and trusting fatalism, in the *faith* that only the particular is loathsome, and that all is redeemed and affirmed in the whole—*he does not negate any more.* Such a faith, however, is the highest of all possible faiths: I have baptized it with the name of *Dionysus* [G IX 49].[16]

The "Dionysian" of the *Götzen-Dämmerung* is no longer that of *The Birth of Tragedy.* In his early work, Nietzsche tended toward a dualistic metaphysics, and the Dionysian was conceived as a flood of passion to which the Apollinian principle of individuation might give form. In the "dithyrambs" of *Zarathustra*

---

[16] This conception of Goethe's "ascent to naturalness" is presented as a contrast to Rousseau's "return to nature." The phrase "reverent toward himself" refers to Goethe's distinction of four kinds of reverence—for what is above us, for what is beneath us, for our fellows, "and the supreme reverence, the reverence for oneself" (*Wilhelm Meisters Wanderjahre,* II, 1).

this opposition of the two gods was repudiated, and the will to power was proclaimed as the one and only basic force of the universe. This fundamental principle, which Nietzsche still called "Dionysian," is actually a union of Dionysus and Apollo: a creative striving that gives form to itself.

The Dionysian man is thus one who gives style to his own character (FW 290), tolerating his passions because he is strong enough to control them. In the light of our analysis of happiness one may further point out that the good man is not only powerful, but also possesses a unique state of consciousness. The Good Life does not consist in unconscious creativity but is crowned by what Nietzsche would call a Dionysian faith: the apotheosis of joy or—as Nietzsche sometimes calls it—*amor fati.*

Since the powerful man is able to redeem his every impulse and to integrate into the sublime totality of his own nature even "the ugly that could not be removed" (FW 290), assigning it a meaning and a redeeming function, he has the faith that in the macrocosm, too, the particular may have meaning in the vast totality of nature. Realizing that his own being is inextricably entangled in "the fatality of all that which has been and will be" (G VI 8), he knows that when he says Yes to his own being he also affirms the rest of the world; and as he would say of his own character, so he says of the cosmos: "Nothing that is may be subtracted, nothing is dispensable" (EH-GT 2).

The projection of one's feeling toward oneself upon a cosmic scale may seem to hinge on a metaphysical premise, but it can be defended empirically. That I am here, now, doing this—that depends on an awe-inspiring series of antecedent events, on millions of seemingly accidental moves and decisions, both by myself and many others whose moves and decisions in turn depended on yet other people. And our very existence, our being as we are, required that our parents had to choose each other, not anyone else, and beget us at the precise moment when we were actually begotten; and the same consideration applies to their parents, and to all our ancestors, going back indefinitely. Thus any affirmation of the present moment points far beyond the present—and it is a significant psychological corollary, on which Nietzsche frequently insists, that those who are dissatisfied with themselves usually project their dissatisfaction upon the world.

Power is the standard of value, but because this joyous feeling is inextricably connected with the possession of power, and where the one is found the other must be, too, Nietzsche can say:

> My formula for the greatness of a human being is *amor fati:* that one wants nothing to be different—not forward, not backward, not in all eternity. Not merely bear what is necessary, still less conceal it . . . but *love it* [EH II 10].

10

THE MASTER RACE

Maxim: to have intercourse with nobody who has any
share in the mendacious race swindle.—XVI, 374.

There is no "German culture," and there never has been
any—except in mystical hermits, Beethoven and Goethe
very much included!—LETTER TO OVERBECK, *May 21, 1884.*

It is well known that Nietzsche did not consider the Germans a
master race and that the following comment on the Poles represented his view of that people:

> The Poles I considered the most gifted and gallant among the
> Slavic people; and the giftedness of the Slavs seemed greater to
> me than that of the Germans—yes, I thought that the Germans
> had entered the line of gifted nations only through a strong
> mixture with Slavic blood [XI, 300].

If this note is representative of Nietzsche's views, it would seem
that he favored race mixture—and that the assertion, sometimes
made, that the Nazis had only to put Nietzsche's ideas into effect
may well be untenable. On the other hand, it is of course true
that the Nazis did quote Nietzsche in their own behalf and that
Nietzsche did speak of a master race.

This whole issue is of great importance not only for the
history of ideas but also for a proper understanding of Nietzsche's
philosophy. If one considers Nietzsche's conception of the Good
Life, for example, it appears that not all men are equally capable
of living in this way, of being good and creating the beautiful.
By definition, the valuable man is the powerful man, and the

weak man—it would seem—can do nothing to make himself powerful. Some people are more favored by nature than others. One may recall how Nietzsche had earlier seen himself compelled by Darwinism to deny any cardinal difference between man and animal, and how he had insisted—in an effort to restore some supra-animalic dignity to man—that artist, saint, and philosopher were the only truly human beings and thus more valuable specimens than the rest of mankind. Their greater value can now be interpreted in terms of their greater power—power being what all men desire. In other words, only some artists and philosophers —the saint has dropped out of the picture—fulfill the aspirations of humanity: they alone realize the state of being that the rest of mankind, too, desire and toward which they grope, more or less deliberately.

Even in the context of Nietzsche's early philosophy it was pointed out that this doctrine was dynamite insofar as it insisted that the gulf between some men and others is more significant than that between man and animal. At the same time, however, it was perfectly clear that Nietzsche looked to art, religion, and philosophy—and not to race—to elevate man above the beasts, and some men above the mass of mankind. The distinction is crucial, and while Nietzsche's doctrine is in any case "aristocratic," its relation to democratic philosophies depends on this point. If the value of a human being—and one should note that for Nietzsche all value is derivative from that of the individual and his state of being—were a function of race or indeed of anything purely biological, the consequences would be momentous: the chasm between the "powerful" elite and those others who are doomed to mediocrity would be fixed and permanent, even hereditary—and large masses of people, possibly whole nations, might be reliably determined to be inferior and possibly worthless "vessels of wrath fitted to destruction" (Rom. 9:22). On the other hand, if power—and the value of the human being—are construed not in terms of race, nor at all biologically, but in terms of artistic or philosophic creativity, the situation would be very different: the "powerful" and valuable specimens would be widely scattered over the centuries and continents and, as likely as not, unrecognized by their own contemporaries—this last qualification being fulfilled admirably by Nietzsche himself; no man could presume to know with any certainty who among his fellow men might be chosen and who damned; and all men might have to be treated with respect as potentially "truly human beings."

It is one of Nietzsche's most serious shortcomings—and has contributed seriously to his "influence"—that he failed to give any emphasis to this common human potentiality and did not consider the possibility that this potentiality might be quite sufficient to re-establish that "cardinal distinction between man and animal" which Darwin seemed to Nietzsche to have denied. Nor did Nietzsche stress the element of secrecy which surrounds the mystery of election and precludes man's ability to judge his fellows. On the other hand, Nietzsche was emphatic in not considering human worth a function of race—and this is the more remarkable in view of his extreme and enthusiastic admiration for classical Greek culture. For the myth of the master race seems to have developed out of certain Greek conceptions. Inspired by their own unique genius, the Greeks thought of themselves as a breed of masters, while considering all other peoples mere "barbarians," fit to be slaves—a notion confirmed even in the writings of Plato and Aristotle. It is well to call attention to Plato's "noble lie," but one certainly cannot infer from it that Plato recognized the fallacy of racism: at best he admits that he would be lying when telling the citizens of his "republic" that profound racial differences exist between them—but they are all Greeks! The cardinal distinction between Greeks and barbarians is taken for granted by Plato, too, though he does not accord it the same emphasis as Aristotle.[1]

These Hellenic seeds of the doctrine of the master race and

---

[1] Cf. Plato's *Republic* 414 f., 469 ff.; Aristotle's *Nicomachean Ethics* 1145a, 1149a; *Politics*, Book I. Arnold Toynbee censures Aristotle's position severely, while exonerating Plato by construing the "noble lie" as an admission of the fallacy of racism. (*A Study of History*, I, 249; III, 93 f.; VI, 246) In an amply documented monograph on *Hellenen und Barbaren: Aus der Geschichte des Nationalbewusstseins* (1923), Julius Jüthner shows how the often maligned Sophists proclaimed that all men were by nature equal, that no man was by nature a slave, and that Greeks and barbarians were made alike (17 f.), while Plato and Aristotle returned to ancient prejudices. Jüthner contends that "the average Greek was convinced that he was even physically different from the barbarians"—as different, in fact, as from the animals—and that comparison of the barbarians with animals was a "current commonplace" (7). Cf. also Hans Kohn, *The Idea of Nationalism: A Study in Its Origins and Background* (1944), Chapter II where this last passage from Jüthner is referred to in the context of an elaborate comparison of "Israel and Hellas."

the pseudo-scientific justification of slavery which the Greeks bestowed on us together with their tragedies and temples should not be confused with the basically different conception of the chosen people. It is not a mere coincidence that this conception was developed in the same book which gave the idea to the world that all men are descended from a single couple—brothers made alike in the image of one God. The notion of the chosen people is inseparable from the revelation which burns into memory that "thou wast a slave in the land of Egypt" and must therefore know how it feels to be oppressed; and it is based on a covenant which enjoins one law for citizen and stranger and commands that one should love the stranger as oneself. The chosen people were, from the beginning, essentially and definitively a spiritual group into which Gentiles could enter if they wished to be accepted into the covenant.[2]

This Biblical heritage—no less than the influence of the Stoics, the Enlightenment, and Goethe—barred Nietzsche from joining in with those of his contemporaries who were even then developing the modern Nordic version of the master-race myth —like Wagner, Gobineau, and Förster. Nietzsche's doctrine of election, to be sure, was not that of the Old Testament but strongly colored by his Protestant patrimony: though repudiating the religious framework of faith, dogmata, and sacraments, Nietzsche insists that it is the single one who is elected. And while in his discussions of the role of consciousness he occasionally deprecates its efficacy, Nietzsche is singularly unequivocal regarding the problem of race: he does not renounce spirit to glorify blood.

Much will be gained for the discussion of Nietzsche's view of race by focusing attention on two clearly stated themes that can be traced through almost all of Nietzsche's writings, from the *Meditations* to the notes of *The Will to Power* and *Ecce Homo*:

---

[2] The voluminous literature, beginning with the Bible itself, cannot be cited here; but it may be pertinent to call attention to the Book of Ruth, to the prophetic conception of eventual peace among all nations ("and they shall beat their swords into plowshares . . . nation shall not lift up a sword against nation . . ." Mic. 4:3) and to the extensive proselytizing which the Jews carried on in the ancient world: "ye compass sea and land to make one proselyte" (Matt. 23:15). See also my *Faith of a Heretic*, section 52.

the belief in the heredity of acquired characteristics and the conviction that race mixture might favor the attainment of culture—both in nations and in individuals. For obvious biographical and historical reasons Nietzsche's discussions of race revolve, more often than not, around the Jews; and this may help to cast into bold relief the differences between Nietzsche and the Nazis. Finally, the topic of this chapter affords an opportunity to sketch the methods by which Nietzsche has been "proved" to have agreed with the Nazis.

The theme of race mixture has already been suggested by the quote at the beginning of this chapter: German culture originated only after a "strong mixture with Slavic blood." Nietzsche liked to believe—though he was probably mistaken—that his last name indicated that he was himself of partly Polish descent and thus of mixed blood. It is characteristic that he sought to give this assumption a spiritual interpretation. In his praise of the Poles, part of which has been quoted, Nietzsche spoke of "the right of the Polish nobleman to overthrow, by his simple veto, the decision of a meeting," and he added that Copernicus made "only the greatest and most worthy use" of this privilege. In *Ecce Homo* Nietzsche proposed that he had inherited the spirit of the veto from his Polish ancestors (EH I 3). Like Kant,[3] Nietzsche conceived of himself as another Copernicus who had flatly contradicted all appearances (XI, 300) by tracing the most startling genealogies of beliefs that his contemporaries had taken for granted.

This self-interpretation is representative of the manner in which Nietzsche correlated his beliefs in the heredity of acquired characteristics and in the advantages of race mixture. He thought that diverse peoples had through their histories acquired and stored up various valuable characteristics, and he thought that the offspring of mixed races might be able to draw on the accumulated capital of many peoples.

In *Human, All-Too-Human*, Nietzsche states flatly that the son "uses the father's head-start and inherits his habits" (MA I 51). In a more famous aphorism of the same work, Nietzsche decried "nationalism" as "dangerous," advocated intermarriage between different nations, and expressed his hope for a "mixed race, that of the European man." After the ideal of the *"Good European"*

---

[3] *Kritik der Reinen Vernunft*, 2nd ed., xvi ff.

has been propounded in these terms, Nietzsche turns to a discussion of the Jews. What Nietzsche says of them may help to illustrate further how he assumed that what is acquired may be inherited, and that race mixture might make such accumulated capital available for a future European breed.

> The whole problem of the *Jews* exists only in nation states, for here their energy and higher intelligence, their accumulated capital of spirit and will, gathered from generation to generation through a long schooling in suffering, must become so preponderant as to arouse mass envy and hatred. In almost all contemporary nations, therefore—in direct proportion to the degree to which they act up nationalistically—the literary obscenity of leading the Jews to slaughter as scapegoats of every conceivable public and internal misfortune is spreading. As soon as it is no longer a matter of preserving nations, but of producing the strongest possible European mixed race, the Jew is just as useful and desirable an ingredient as any other national remnant [MA I 475].

At this point, one may wonder whether this passage can possibly be representative of Nietzsche's views, since it is after all a fact that the Nazis quoted him in their behalf. One must recall Bäumler's principle of Nietzsche exegesis: that the published works are a series of "poses," while the true Nietzsche appears only in the notes.[4] We shall soon see that the notes do not advocate racism either; and indeed it does not go too far to state that the Nazis were able to cite Nietzsche on racial questions only because they had another, not quite so openly admitted, principle of exegesis: that the complete sentences Nietzsche wrote down are masks of ideas that appear only in parentheses, subordinate sentences, and fragmentary quotations.

This may seem a harsh accusation, and we shall therefore proceed immediately to document it. Instead of choosing just any Nazi writer at random, we shall single out Oehler, whose perennial compilation of indices to Nietzsche's works can leave no doubt of his knowledge of their contents. Since he was, moreover, one of the chief representatives of the *Nietzsche-Archiv* and a co-editor of the collected works, his early abandonment of all accepted standards of scholarship, almost immediately after Hitler came to power, served as an invitation to other, less-well-

---

[4] *Nietzsche der Philosoph und Politiker*, 8, 63, *et passim.*

known "Nietzscheans" to help prove the contention that Nietzsche
was a precursor of Nazism.

Oehler's book, *Friedrich Nietzsche und die Deutsche Zukunft,*
is too fantastic to be cited here at any length. We are concerned
only with his proclamation: "To wish to give proof regarding
Nietzsche's thoughts, to establish that they agree with the race
views and strivings of the National Socialist movement would be
carrying coals to Newcastle." [5] It is representative of the manner
in which Oehler illustrates his point that he draws on the very
aphorism from *Human, All-Too-Human* (MA 1 475) from which
we have just quoted—although it would seem that the passage
cited by us reads almost like a deliberate denunciation of Hitler-
ism. It seems pro-Jewish, speaks of anti-Semitism as an "obscen-
ity," decries nationalism, and advocates intermarriage between
Jews and Germans. Oehler, however, cites this same aphorism:
"perhaps the young stock-exchange Jew is the most disgusting
invention of mankind." [6]

Oehler quotes correctly—but out of the following context:

> Unpleasant, even dangerous, qualities can be found in every na-
> tion and every individual: it is cruel to demand that the Jew
> should be an exception. These qualities may even be dangerous
> and revolting in him to an unusual degree; and perhaps the
> young stock-exchange Jew is the most disgusting invention of
> mankind. In spite of that, I should like to know how much one
> must forgive a people in a total accounting, when they have had
> the most painful history of all peoples, not without the fault of
> all of us, and when one owes to them the noblest man (Christ),
> the purest sage (Spinoza), the most powerful book, and the most
> effective moral law of the world. Moreover, in the darkest times
> of the Middle Ages, . . . Jewish free-thinkers, scholars, and phy-
> sicians . . . clung to the banner of enlightenment and spiritual
> independence. . . . We owe it to their exertions, not least of all,
> . . . that the bond of culture which now links us with the en-
> lightenment of Greco-Roman antiquity remained unbroken [MA
> 1 475].

Other Nazis have often admitted that Nietzsche differed with
Hitler on important points and have then tried to "explain" why
Nietzsche, fifty years before the advent of the Third Reich, could
not yet have known all the truth and nothing but the truth.
Bäumler's untenable contention, for example, that Nietzsche op-

---

[5] (1935), 86.
[6] *Ibid.,* 88.

posed the State and German nationalism only because the Second Reich had ignored him and because it was Christian, has been mentioned previously in the discussion of Nietzsche's third *Meditation*. Besides Oehler and Bäumler, Härtle should be mentioned as the author of an amazing book: *Nietzsche und der Nationalsozialismus* (1937). Here truth and falsity in Nietzsche's writings is distinguished clearly—and the formidable array of quotations may seem impressive to the uninitiated. The alleged pro-Nazi passages, however, are of the Oehler variety: clipped from a context in which they have a totally different meaning from that which they appear to have in Härtle's potpourri, they are frequently commented on with brazen irrelevancy; nor are omissions that pervert the sense always marked by the customary dots.[7]

---

[7] Unfortunately, Brinton is not sufficiently aware of the Nazis' unscrupulousness, and more than once he seems to have been trapped by the very men whom he hates most. One of his main theses is that Nietzsche was half a Nazi and half an anti-Nazi—and it is only with the first part of that claim that we should quarrel. Brinton's well-deserved prestige as a historian has lent his contention currency in wide circles, and it is therefore scarcely possible to omit any reference to his argument. His claim that Nietzsche was half a Nazi is supported mainly by section III of his chapter on "Nietzsche and the Nazis"—i.e., less than ten pages of his book—and what he offers are, for the most part, composite quotations which consist of lines picked from different contexts and put together in a manner that suggests a semblance of continuity. While it is plain that this was the only way in which the Nazis could quote Nietzsche, such a method could hardly establish the actual views of an author, even if the translations were always quite correct. The only point strictly relevant to the present argument is Brinton's claim that, while Nietzsche did have Jewish friends and said many nice things about the Jews, "most of the stock of professional anti-Semitism is represented in Nietzsche"—and Brinton even concludes that Nietzsche held the Jews responsible for "Christianity, Democracy, Marxism." (*op. cit.*, 215) A footnote (#19) is furnished to substantiate this claim by six references: (a) FW 301—in which the Jews are not mentioned; (b) G IV 26—but part IV has only six paragraphs, none of which deals with the Jews; (c) WM 184—a note for the *Antichrist* which will be discussed in the text; (d) WM 864—from which one may quote: "The anti-Semites do not forgive the Jews that the Jews have '*Geist*'— and money. Anti-Semites—Just another name for the 'underprivileged' ['*Schlechtweggekommenen*']"; (e) J 251—which is later cited by Brinton himself as containing a eulogy of the Jews: here anti-Semitism is branded as a "stupidity," a "befogging of the German spirit and conscience," a "disease" and an "infection"—and the Jews, "beyond any doubt the strongest, toughest, and purest race that now lives in Europe," are said to survive "because of some virtues which some today would like to brand as vices"—and Nietzsche concludes that intermarriage between German Gentiles and Jews should be encouraged, while "the anti-Semitic squallers" should be deported; (f) A 24–27—the *Antichrist* will be discussed in the

It would be cumbersome and pointless to adduce endless examples from Nazi works on Nietzsche to refute them each time
by referring to the context of Nietzsche's remarks. Suffice it to say
that neither Nietzsche's own unexpurgated writings nor the
tendentious anthologies that—with the exception of Frau Förster-
Nietzsche's pioneering efforts—made their appearance only years
after Hitler had come to power, enjoyed anywhere near the
circulation or attention with which they have been credited in
war-time magazine articles in the U.S. The Nazis derived their
racial doctrines from Dr. Hans F. K. Günther, who in turn made
no secret of his reliance on Plato's *Republic,* Gobineau, Chamberlain, Georges Vacher de Lapouge, Madison Grant, and Lothrop
Stoddard. Nor should one ignore the influence of the racial
policies followed in large parts of the United States upon the
Nazis' actions both in Germany and other countries.[8]

. . .

text. In conclusion one may ask: what of "the stock of professional anti-
Semitism"? At best, it appears in parentheses as an occasional concession,
while Nietzsche never leaves the slightest doubt about his own position.
And what of "Christianity, Democracy, Marxism"? This triad of what
Brinton ironically calls "the three great evils of modern civilization,"
implying clearly that Nietzsche thus refers to them, is not to be found
in any of the references, and Nietzsche never refers to Marx or Marxism.
The triad comes from Härtle, *op. cit.,* 50. From Härtle, too, comes the
reference to the nonexistent G IV 26 (*ibid.,* 48); for Härtle refers to the
Antichrist as "*Götzend.* IV"—and Brinton's second and sixth reference in
footnote #19 are thus redundant. In fact: all six references are from
Härtle—the erroneous FW 301 is a misprint for 361—and Brinton seems
to have taken the Nazis' word for it that Nietzsche was at least half a
Nazi; and he did not check the references he copied from Härtle.

In the paperback edition of his *Nietzsche* (1965), Brinton says in the
Preface: "I have not altered the text of the book at all, and have retained
as still fully appropriate the chapter on 'Nietzsche and the Nazis'" (vii).
The bogus references are still there. In a way this is odd because Brinton
read the above criticism before publishing two generous reviews of my
book in 1951; but by 1964, when he wrote the Preface, he may have
forgotten my criticisms. Cf. J 68: "'I have done that,' says my memory.
'I could not have done that,' says my pride, and remains inexorable.
Finally, my memory yields."

[8] Cf. Günther, *Platon als Hüter des Lebens: Platons Zucht- und Erziehungs-
gedanken und deren Bedeutung für die Gegenwart* (1928) and *Rassen-
kunde Europas* (3rd rev. ed., 1929) in which Madison Grant's *The Passing
of the Great Race or the Racial Basis of European History* (4th ed., 1923)
and Lothrop Stoddard's *The Rising Tide of Color against White
World-Supremacy* (1919), *The Revolt against Civilization: The Menace of
the Underman* (1924), *Racial Realities in Europe* (1925), and *Social Classes
in Post-War Europe* (1925) are cited frequently and prominently. Günther

To return to Nietzsche himself, whom we left writing *Human, All-Too-Human,* we shall now trace the development of his ideas about race to the last writings of 1888—keeping in mind the dual theme of Lamarckism and race mixture. In the *Dawn,* Nietzsche persists in his gigantic scheme for a future mixed breed and considers the advantages of an ingredient of Chinese blood (M 206). He also declares: "Probably there are no pure races but only races that have become pure, and these are very rare" (M 272). In developing this point, he claims that "mixed races always mean, at the same time, mixed cultures" and adds that they are "most often more evil, cruel, and restless." To draw the conclusion that Nietzsche therefore abominated mixed races[9] is, of course, to miss the very gist of his philosophy. One may recall how, at the end of the second *Meditation,* Nietzsche envisaged the genesis of Greek culture out of a veritable bedlam of Oriental civilizations —and it was in that context that he first used the phrase: *"to organize the chaos."* In fact, the aphorism in the *Dawn,* too, ends by holding out the Greeks as "the model of a race and culture that has become pure," i.e., a people who possessed the Apollinian power to organize the Dionysian chaos. There can be no question but that Nietzsche favored mixture of races and cultures, even if the mixed breed might often be "more evil, cruel, and restless": his whole philosophical position hinges on the view that only the weak fear chaos while powerful natures organize it. "One must yet have chaos in oneself to be able to give birth to a dancing star" (Z-V 5). Elsewhere Nietzsche speaks of creating a god out of one's "seven devils" (Z I 17). And he develops this point in *Beyond Good and Evil,* when speaking of the man who lives in "an age of disintegration that throws together and mixes different races" —a man "who has in his body the heritage of a manifold descent . . . i.e., opposite . . . drives and value standards":

> Yet if the opposition and war in such a nature act as one *more* stimulus and spur to life—and if, on the other hand, there has also been inherited and bred, besides its powerful and irreconcilable drives, the proper mastery and subtlety in the waging of

also applauds President Harding's reference to Stoddard's *The Rising Tide of Color* in a speech on Oct. 26, 1921, and the American immigration laws, "which are designed to promote the desired North-West European immigration, to check the undesired South and East European immigration, while immigration from Asia, as well as that of human beings of inferior quality, is prohibited altogether" (325).

[9] Oehler, *op. cit.,* 86 f.

war against oneself, i.e., self-control . . . : then originate those
magical, incomprehensible, and unfathomable ones, those enigmatic men predestined for victory and seduction, whose most
beautiful examples are Alcibiades and Caesar (to whom I should
like to join that *first* European according to my taste, the Ho-
henstaufen Frederick II)—and among artists perhaps Leonardo
da Vinci [J 200].[10]

In *The Gay Science* (99), Nietzsche explicitly names Lamarck
to defend him against Schopenhauer, while in a later note (XVI, 9)
he describes Hegel and Lamarck as the proponents of a truer
doctrine of evolution than Darwin's. "Darwin has forgotten the
spirit," Nietzsche explains later (G IX 14). It is apparent that even
in his last period—for we have begun to cite the notes and works
written after *Zarathustra*—Nietzsche repudiated "physiologism."
Against Darwin he urged the Lamarckian doctrine of the heredity
of acquired characteristics—the very doctrine the Nazis never
tired of branding as a Bolshevistic lie because, as they frankly
admitted, it would invalidate their whole racism. Actually, Darwin had invoked this conception, too, although he had considered
natural selection more important.

Most contemporary biologists, of course, reject Lamarckism.
In the present context, however, the decisive point is that Nietzsche was faithful to his own repudiation of any strict division of

---

[10] Nietzsche's admiration for these four men invites comment. He felt
charmed by what he took to have been Leonardo's singularly undogmatic
mind and "supra-Christian vista"—and while he preferred the revolutionary Michelangelo to Raphael, he considered Leonardo's open-minded
calm and "supra-European" horizon evidence of even higher rank (XVI,
51 f.; XVII, 317 f.; WM 380).

Frederick II, German Emperor from 1215 to 1250, was admired by
Nietzsche as an enemy of the Church (A 60; EH-Z 4) who was of mixed
blood and cultivated "Moorish-Oriental enlightenment" (XVI, 356). There
may have been personal overtones, too. Christened "Friedrich Wilhelm,"
Nietzsche had dropped the "Wilhelm." Now he thought that in his medieval namesake he had discovered the outright antithesis of all the connotations of his own original name: the emperor had not even lived in
Germany—and though his reasons had been quite different, Nietzsche
apparently felt that the contempt for nationalism and traditional religion,
and the love of the South and enlightenment were common to his hero
and himself.

Nietzsche's admiration of Caesar—which also has personal overtones
—will be considered in some detail in the next chapter, while the
enigmatic reference to Alcibiades—in a place where one might expect
the mention of Socrates—is perhaps explained at the end of our last
chapter.

flesh and spirit and that he insisted that the two could be understood only in their inextricable togetherness. No process of human life, including heredity, could be understood in terms of the body alone. Yet historically it has been Nietzsche's fate that his insistence that man's spiritual life cannot be understood completely apart from his body has been emphasized out of all proportion and thoroughly misunderstood because his concomitant insistence that man's physical life cannot be understood apart from the spirit was ignored.

The assumption, upheld in much of the literature, that Nietzsche's work can be divided into three periods in such a manner that each turning point is the equivalent of a radical change of mind, is untenable. To be sure, Nietzsche himself suggested that he had gone through three stages on his *"way to wisdom"* (XVI, 36 f.); and he expressed the same thought in a Zarathustric parable (Z I 1). These three periods are accounted for when one distinguishes Nietzsche's early philosophy, the extreme experimentalism of the aphoristic works in which the will to power was discovered, and his final outlook. The notion, however, that Nietzsche sympathized with the Enlightenment, admired Socrates, despised nationalism, and advocated race mixture only in his middle period, while he later broke with this tradition, became a racist, espoused a "physiologism," and came close to Nazism, is entirely unwarranted.

In view of Nietzsche's extreme version of the doctrine of internal relations, his Lamarckism—to which he always remained faithful—may be taken to mean that there really are no purely spiritual characteristics or qualities that are acquired accidentally: there is no body here, no spirit there, nor are there any accidents. Man is what he thinks no less than what he does, and his religion and philosophy are of his very essence no less than is his physique. In any case, there is no break here between his earlier and later writings.

In the Fifth Book of *The Gay Science*, for example, which was written after *Zarathustra*, Nietzsche denounces "nationalism and race hatred" as a "scabies of the heart and blood poisoning" for which he is "by far not 'German' enough, as the word 'German' is used today"; he is "too well informed" and "in race and descent too manifold and mixed" "to share the thoroughly mendacious [*verlognen*] racial self-admiration and perversion which today displays itself in Germany as a sign of German outlook and seems doubly false among the people of the 'historical sense' " (FW 377). Nietzsche—just as in his "middle period"—further states that he prefers to be a *"good European"* and an heir of the "European spirit." Toward the end of the aphorism, he declares—as so often—that the very habits of "integrity, without any reservations," which Christian morality has bred in us through the course of centuries, are among our noblest heritages and force us to make a clean break with religious dogmata, which we can no longer accept without compromising our intellectual honesty. One would be hard pressed to show that this means a break with the "enlightened" spirit of *Human, All-Too-Human.*

From *Beyond Good and Evil,* we have already cited the passage on men of mixed blood and the praise of the medieval Emperor Frederick II. In the same work Nietzsche summarizes his belief in the heredity of acquired characteristics.

> One cannot erase out of the soul of a man what his ancestors have done most eagerly and often. . . . It is not at all possible that a man should *not* have in his body the qualities and preferences of his parents and ancestors—whatever appearances may say against this. This is the problem of race [J 264].

This passage bears out the assertion that for Nietzsche this was a corollary of his view of the mind-body problem. The two are so inextricably entangled with each other that "it is not at all possible" to explain heredity by ignoring the spiritual life of man, "whatever appearances may say against this." Nietzsche's definition of a people *(Volk)* is consistent with this view; he emphasizes not the blood but the common experience: "When men have lived together for a long time under similar conditions (of climate, soil, danger, needs, and work), then there *comes to be . . .* a people" (J 268).

One may wonder about the conception of master-morality and slave-morality which is introduced in *Beyond Good and Evil* (260) and discussed further in the *Genealogy* (1). It is noteworthy that these two slogans play a comparatively small role in Nietzsche's writings and that—Gobineau's allegedly decisive influence on Nietzsche notwithstanding—they are *not* interpreted racially.[11]

---

[11] Curt von Westernhagen, *Nietzsche, Juden, Antijuden* (Weimar, n.d.[1936]), 29, aptly describes Nietzsche's relation to Gobineau: "he has used the terminology of the man who has brought the doctrine of race to support his own doctrine of un-race. In spite of certain popular superficial analogies, an expert like Schemann therefore designates Gobineau and Nietzsche

What Nietzsche is concerned with is the contrast of those who have power and those who lack it (cf. MA I 45), and he investigates it by contrasting not individuals but groups of people. The distinction therefore tends to become sociological, as the consequences of oppression are considered. While the discussion is stained by its decidedly polemical design, one should keep in mind that *it does not follow from Nietzsche's "vivisection" of slave-morality that he identifies his own position with that of the masters:*[12] he means to be descriptive, and though his polemic may create a presumption that he approves of the masters, their morality does not coincide with his own ethics. That the "blond beast" is not a racial concept either, that it specifically includes the Arabs and the Japanese (GM I 11), and that it is an ideogram Nietzsche used to symbolize the people who have strong animal impulses which they have not yet learned to master—that has been shown in a previous chapter.

In the *Götzen-Dämmerung* Nietzsche proceeds, a year later, to counteract possible misconstructions of these notions of *Beyond Good and Evil* and the *Genealogy*. While he goes to the extent of calling Christianity "the *anti-Aryan* religion par excellence" and "the revaluation of all Aryan values"—thus employing terminology later used by the Nazis—he denounces *"Aryan* humanity" in the very same paragraph (G VII 4). Manu's provisions for the oppression of the outcastes, who were alleged to be of inferior race, are held up to scorn—"perhaps there is nothing that outrages our feelings more" (G VII 3)—and Nietzsche concludes that "we learn that the concept of 'pure blood' is the opposite of a harmless concept." Anti-Semitism is denounced as ever (G I 19); German nationalism is repudiated thoroughly (G VIII entire); and Nietzsche goes out of his way to leave no doubts among his compatriots as to what he does *not* mean by power:

One pays heavily for coming to power: power *makes stupid.* The Germans, once called the people of thinkers—do they still think

—with complete justification—as 'antipodes.' " Westernhagen's careful account of Nietzsche's race views differs from other Nazi studies by being scholarly and candid—and, significantly, he concludes that Nietzsche must be repudiated in the name of National Socialism. Cf. also L. Schemann, *Gobineau, Eine Biographie,* 2 vols. (1913–16), *Gobineau und die Deutsche Kultur* (1934), 62 ff., and *Deutsche Klassiker über die Rassenfrage* (1934), 37 ff.

[12] This is recognized by Josiah Royce in his sympathetic and perceptive article on "Nietzsche" in *Atlantic Monthly,* March 1917, 330.

at all today? The Germans are now bored with the spirit, the
Germans now mistrust the spirit. . . . *Deutschland, Deutschland
über alles,* I fear that was the end of German philosophy [G VIII
1; cf. G I 23].

This people has deliberately made itself stupid . . . [G VIII 2].

Culture and State—one should not deceive oneself about this—
are antagonists: *'Kultur-Staat'* is merely a modern idea. One lives
off the other, one thrives at the expense of the other. All great
ages of culture are ages of political decline: what is great cultur-
ally has always been unpolitical, even anti-political. Goethe's
heart opened up at the phenomenon of Napoleon—it closed up
at the "Wars of Liberation." At the same moment when Germany
comes up as a great power, France gains a new importance as a
cultural power [G VIII 4].

All this is clear and unequivocal, but what are we to make of
the attack against Christianity as "anti-Aryan"? This cannot be
understood entirely until one turns to Nietzsche's *Antichrist,*
written immediately upon the completion of the *Götzen-Dämmerung.* The *Antichrist* is the apotheosis of Nietzsche as a po-
lemicist—although it has not generally been understood at what
this polemic was aimed. This is not the place to examine Nietzsche's repudiation of Christianity; but the book is also an important document for Nietzsche's racial views. The Nazis sought
to find in it a primarily anti-Semitic doctrine: Christianity, it
seemed, was here repudiated in view of its Semitic origins. Even
Overbeck, who read the manuscript after Nietzsche had become
insane, was amazed at Nietzsche's vehement invective against the
Jewish founders of Christianity—and Overbeck concluded that
Nietzsche's anti-Christianity must have been motivated anti-
Semitically at bottom.[13] Such an interpretation, however, is
"structure-blind."

Nietzsche denounces many things in his *Antichrist*—none
more vigorously than anti-Semitism; e.g., "An anti-Semite certainly is not any more decent because he lies as a matter of principle" (A 55). Nor should we forget that most anti-Semites have
always been self-styled Christians. The Nazis constitute a very
notable exception, but the success of their anti-Semitic propaganda would hardly have been possible had it not been for the
preparatory work of a previous generation of "Christian" anti-

---

[13] Bernoulli I, 362.

Semites. It was this generation, of which Wagner and Förster were notable spokesmen—and whose heritage Chamberlain passed on to Rosenberg—that Nietzsche turned against in his *Antichrist*. To be sure, Nietzsche insists upon the importance of the Jewish origins of Christianity—but only to deny that Judaism was, as it were, the manure pile on which the white lily of Christianity happened accidentally to make its first appearance, as Wagner and Förster claimed, and as generations had believed before them. And in his fervor for polemical antitheses, Nietzsche goes to the extent of claiming that Jesus "called the people at the bottom, the outcastes and 'sinners,' the *pariahs* within Judaism, to negate the dominant order" (A 27). Completely reversing the claims of the professional anti-Semites, he pictures Christianity as the miscarriage of Judaism and finds no expression low enough to describe the early Christians. That is the meaning of Nietzsche's assertion:

> I touch here only upon the problem of the genesis of Christianity. The *first* principle for its solution is: Christianity can be understood only in terms of the soil out of which it grew—it is *not* a movement of opposition against the Jewish instinct, it is its very consequence itself [A 24].

Christianity is envisaged as the dross of Judaism; and Nietzsche, commenting on Luke 6:23—"for in the like manner did their fathers unto the prophets"—can exclaim: "Impertinent rabble! They compare themselves to the prophets, no less" [A 45].

Nietzsche's attitude—however perverse—is perfectly consistent with his comparative evaluation of the Old and the New Testament. The Old Testament is "the most powerful book" (MA I 475) for which Nietzsche has the highest admiration:

> The Jews have experienced wrath differently from us and pronounced it holy: for they have seen the sullen majesty of man, joined with which it manifested itself, in their own midst at a height that a European is not able to imagine; they have formed their wrathful holy Jehovah after their wrathful holy prophets. Measured against them, the great wroth ones among the Europeans are quasi second-hand creatures [M 38].

> In the Jewish "Old Testament" . . . there are men, things, and speeches in so grand a style that Greek and Indian literature have nothing to compare with it. One stands with awe and reverence before these tremendous remnants of what man once was, and will have sad thoughts about ancient Asia and its protruding

little peninsula, Europe, which wants by all means to signify, as
against Asia, the "progress of man." . . . The taste for the Old
Testament is a touchstone of "greatness" and "smallness." . . .
To have glued this New Testament, a kind of rococo of taste in
every respect, to the Old Testament to form one book . . . that
is perhaps the greatest audacity and "sin against the spirit" that
literary Europe has on its conscience [J 52; cf. J 250].

I do not like the "New Testament." . . . The *Old* Testament—
that is something else again: all honor to the Old Testament!
I find in it great human beings, a heroic landscape, and
something of the very rarest quality in the world, the in-
comparable naïveté of the *strong heart;* what is more, I find a
people. In the New one, on the other hand, I find nothing but
petty sectarianism, mere rococo of the soul, mere involutions,
nooks, queer things, the air of the conventicle, not to forget an
occasional whiff of bucolic mawkishness that belongs to the epoch
(*and* to the Roman province) and is not so much Jewish as Hel-
lenistic. Humility and self-importance cheek-by-jowl; a garrulous-
ness of feeling that almost stupefies; impassioned vehemence, not
passion; embarrassing gesticulation . . . [GM III 22].

In *Nietzsche contra Wagner,* composed shortly after the *Antichrist,* a passage from *Human, All-Too-Human* is cited—and
eight words are added:

Only in Handel's music did there resound . . . the Jewish-heroic
trait that gave the Reformation a trait of greatness—the Old
Testament become music, *not* the New [NCW IV; MA II 171].

When the *Antichrist* is considered in this setting, in the context of Nietzsche's thought, it becomes perfectly clear that Nietzsche's anti-Christianity was not motivated anti-Semitically at
bottom and that he did not develop a racial interpretation of
history. In *Ecce Homo,* moreover, the budding anti-Semitic
historiography of the new *Reich* is expressly denounced together
with German nationalism generally (EH-W).

There is no point in indulging in endless redundancies by
citing more examples. Suffice it to say that the notes—which
Bäumler so decidedly prefers to the books—are entirely at one
with the finished works. Here, too, Nietsche could be quoted in
support of Nazism only when passages were torn from their context. Thus Oehler quotes correctly from the notes of Nietzsche's
last years: "No *new* Jews any more! And keep the doors toward

the East closed!" [14] But Oehler fails to mention that Nietzsche himself put these words within quotation marks and proceeded: "—thus a wise consideration might counsel the German Jews themselves" because it is "their task to grow into the German character," and continued immigration would impede the process of intermarriage and assimilation (XVI, 371).

In the same notes, we find this passage:

> . . . The dignity of death and a kind of *consecration* of passion has perhaps never yet been represented more beautifully . . . than by certain Jews of the Old Testament: to these even the Greeks could have gone to school! [XVI, 373; cf. J 52].

This, from Nietzsche, would seem *non plus ultra;* the fact that the same note also refers to "the dangers of the Jewish soul" is not surprising: a man without fierce passions cannot represent the "consecration of passion," and to Nietzsche no triumph seems possible without dangers. Another aphorism, published in *Beyond Good and Evil,* offers a more elaborate contrast of Jews and Greeks, completely reversing the racists' cliché that the Jews are endowed merely with a genius for adaptation:

> There are two kinds of genius: one that above all begets and wants to beget, and another that likes to be fertilized and to give birth. And just so there are among people of genius those to whom has fallen the woman's problem of pregnancy and the secret task of giving form, maturing, and perfecting—the Greeks, for example, were a people of this kind, and also the French— and others who must fertilize and become the cause of new orders of life—like the Jews, the Romans and, asked in all modesty, the Germans? [J 248].

Questionable, as is so much that Nietzsche says on problems of this sort, but not entirely improvised for polemical purposes: the conception of the Greeks, for example, is plainly a development of Nietzsche's earlier ideas about their Apollinian genius.

In the notes of *The Will to Power,* one finds Nietzsche saying: "A lot is said today about the *Semitic* spirit of the *New Testament*: but what is called Semitic is merely priestly." He goes on to say that this so-called "Semitism" is nowhere worse than in the Law of Manu (WM 143). Subjected to a flood of racist propaganda—from his family, Wagner, his publisher Schmeitzner,

---

[14] *Op. cit.,* 89.

and the men who sent him the *Anti-Semitic Correspondence* in which he first saw the otherwise ignored Zarathustra hailed as the "divine man"—Nietzsche always struggled against this poison. It is not surprising that he should occasionally have availed himself of racial categories in framing his rebuttals in his notes, and that he should have used such words as "Aryan" and "Semitic." It is also in the notes of *The Will to Power* that we encounter the master race—and it is characteristic of Nietzsche's situation that the application of this term to the "Aryans" should have found its way into the very note in which he planned to prove that the Old Testament and Islam are in no way inferior to "Aryan" religions (WM 145). Even here the "Aryans" are not *the* master race but merely *eine Herrenrasse*—and it is characteristic of Nietzsche's refusal to identify his own position with that of the "masters" that he should have criticized them so vehemently in the very same context:

> *Toward a critique of the Manu Law Book.* The whole book is founded on the holy lie. . . . We find a species of man, the priestly, which feels itself to be the norm, the high point and the supreme expression of the type man: this species derives the concept "improvement" from itself. It believes in its own superiority, it wills itself to be superior in fact: the origin of the holy lie is the *will to power.* . . .
>
> Power through the lie—in the knowledge that one does not possess it physically, militarily—the lie as a supplement to power, a new concept of "truth."
>
> It is a mistake to suppose an *unconscious and naive* development here, a kind of self-deception— Fanatics do not invent such carefully thought-out systems of oppression— The most cold-blooded reflection was at work here; the same kind of reflection as a Plato applied when he imagined his "Republic." . . .
>
> We possess the classic model in specifically *Aryan* forms: we may therefore hold the best-endowed and most reflective species of man responsible for the most fundamental lie that has ever been told— That lie has been copied almost everywhere: *Aryan influence* has corrupted all the world [WM 142].

It seems abundantly plain that Nietzsche did not identify his own views with the "masters" any more than with the "slaves" —and it is characteristic that the term "master race" reappears elsewhere in *The Will to Power* to designate a future, internationally mixed, race of philosophers and artists who cultivate iron self-control (WM 960). To be sure, this conception, too, was not thought through, and—though jotted down at the time of *Beyond Good and Evil*—it was not published by Nietzsche.

One may conclude this argument by citing four short epigrams that are representative of the notes of this period:

> Value of anti-Semitism: to drive the Jews to set themselves higher goals. . . .
>
> Contra Aryan and Semitic. Where races are mixed, there is the source of great cultures.
>
> How much mendacity [*Verlogenheit*] and morass is involved in raising racial questions in the medley Europe of today!
>
> Maxim: to have intercourse with nobody who has any share in the mendacious race swindle [xvi, 373 f.].

These epigrams summarize much of Nietzsche's thought about these problems. Until the very end he considered racism a maze of lies, and believed that race mixture was the source of great cultures and that social penalization might well result in a redoubled spiritual effort.[15] Now as ever, he insisted that the Jews had through their history accumulated characteristics that made it desirable that they should become an ingredient of a future mixed race (xvi, 374) and that anti-Semitism was "the lowest level of European culture, its morass" (xvi, 391). Though he sometimes employs racial terminology, the main current of his thought is definitely "contra Aryan and Semitic" and concerned with culture, not with race—and culture was to Nietzsche not a function of race, nor of anything merely physical, but something that involves the whole man, body and spirit; and even insofar as it draws upon heredity, it must take into account the spirit no less than the body.

Nietzsche's assumption that acquired characteristics are inherited may well be indefensible, and some of the nice things he says about the Jews are perhaps as wrong as some of his parenthetical concessions to the anti-Semites. What is important here is merely that Nietzsche's views are quite unequivocally opposed to those of the Nazis—more so than those of almost any other prominent German of his own time or before him—and that these views are not temperamental antitheses but corollaries of his

---

[15] These Nietzschean ideas are shared by Toynbee. Cf. Toynbee's "law that the geneses of civilizations require contributions from more races than one" (*op. cit.*, I, 278 and 239 ff.); his elaborate attempt at a refutation of racism (*ibid.*, 207–27); and his conception of the "stimulus of penalizations" (II, 208–58).

philosophy. Nietzsche was no more ambiguous in this respect than is the statement that the Nazis' way of citing him represents one of the darkest pages in the history of literary unscrupulousness.

Finally, we must consider the meaning of Nietzsche's conception of *Zucht und Züchtung*. Once—just once—he had considered using this phrase as the title of the fourth and last part of *The Will to Power*—and Frau Förster-Nietzsche later chose this draft when *she* edited *The Will to Power*, because *Zucht und Züchtung* seemed to her a natural meeting ground for Förster and Nietzsche. The two words cannot be translated with complete accuracy: they suggest discipline and breeding—the latter both in the sense of education and of "breeding" animals. The word "cultivation"—another meaning of *Züchtung*—would more clearly suggest the link with Nietzsche's conception of culture, but it would not bring out Nietzsche's hopes for a future mixed race. The term "breeding"—with its dual connotation—is probably closest to what Nietzsche had in mind.

> What I want to make clear by all the means in my power:
>
> a. that there is no worse confusion than the confusion of breeding with taming: which is what has been done— Breeding, as I understand it, is a means of storing up the tremendous forces of mankind so that the generations can build upon the work of their forefathers—not only outwardly, but inwardly, organically growing out of them and becoming something stronger [WM 398].

The conception hinges on the assumption that flesh and spirit are inseparable and that power—which involves reason no less than passion—can be accumulated and inherited (WM 440, 646). Nietzsche thinks that one might be able to breed "will, responsibility" and other qualities of character and says plainly that such characteristics are what he has in mind when speaking of "a *stronger race*" (WM 898). But the notes of *The Will to Power* contain very little material about "breeding"—and the fourth part deals hardly at all with what the sister's title promises: there simply were not enough relevant notes.

Nietzsche speaks of "a doctrine" as being "strong enough to have the effect of *breeding*," and in the same note jots down:

(. . . To strive for the fullness of nature by coupling opposites: race mixture to this end). The new courage—no *a priori* truths (*those* were sought by those who were accustomed to faith!) but *free* submission to a dominant thought which has its time, e.g., time as a property of space, etc. [WM 862].

Hardly "physiologism"—nor very well thought through. These are mere notes, however, and in his published works Nietzsche included little that related to "breeding"—and when he used such terminology at all, he used it far more circumspectly than in his notes.

The breeding [*Zucht*] of suffering, of *great* suffering—do you not know that only *this* breeding has created all exaltations of man so far? The tension of the soul in misfortune that breeds [*an-züchtet*] its strength . . . and whatever was given to it of depth, . . . spirit, . . . greatness: was it not given to it . . . through the breeding of great suffering? [J 225].

If one looks for a philosophic precedent for Nietzsche's strange concern with breeding, one will have to seek it not in his German predecessors but in Plato—though Nietzsche was rather more explicit in emphasizing the function of the spirit in heredity, for which he cited Lamarck. In conclusion, let us consider an aphorism that has not always been construed correctly:

There is only nobility by birth and blood [*nur Geburtsadel, Ge-blütsadel*]. (I am not referring to the little word *"von"* and the Gotha Almanac: parenthesis for asses.) Where there is talk of "aristocrats of the spirit," there is usually no lack of reasons for keeping something secret; it is, as is well known, a motto among ambitious Jews. For spirit alone does not make noble [*adelt nicht*]; rather something is required *to make noble the spirit.* What is required therefor? Blood [*Geblüt*] [WM 942].

In his "parenthesis for asses," Nietzsche would seem to have made it abundantly clear that he was not referring to any socially acknowledged "nobility"—so clear, in fact, that Härtle omits the parenthesis, without marking the omission, when he quotes these lines.[16] Nor does Nietzsche say that "blood" makes men noble. He merely says that "spirit alone" is insufficient—a point taken into full consideration throughout the present exposition.

It may nevertheless seem disturbing that Nietzsche speaks of

---

[16] *Op. cit.,* 55.

"blood." Unquestionably, however, "blood" was not to Nietzsche's mind a biologistic conception any more than "breeding." Nietzsche assumed that—as Goethe put it in one of the poems of his *Divan*—"whoever cannot account to himself for a heritage of three thousand years" lacks nobility. Culture, unlike riches, cannot be acquired from one day to another: it requires tradition. What Nietzsche means by "blood" is well illustrated by another note: "When I speak of Plato, Pascal, Spinoza, and Goethe, then I know that their blood rolls in mine" (xxi, 98). Elsewhere, Nietzsche jotted down: "My ancestors: *Heraclitus, Empedocles, Spinoza, Goethe*" (xiv, 109).[17]

To be sure, tradition could not be acquired by a perfunctory reading of the classics—but it could be acquired by hard study involving not only the "pure spirit" but an entire way of life. It is therefore characteristic that Nietzsche hesitated to publish his remarks on "breeding," and that in his last work he spoke of *Selbstzucht*, i.e., of giving breeding to oneself (EH-U 1 3). He abandoned the title *Zucht und Züchtung* as soon as he had written it down, and only his sister chose later to perpetuate it. Nietzsche's own subsequent plans for the last part of his *magnum opus* omit any reference to these words: they stress "overcoming" (xviii, 345); and his last outlines introduce the conception of eternal recurrence (xviii, 348 ff.).

---

[17] Andler devotes the whole first volume of his six-volume *Nietzsche* to these *"précurseurs"*: Goethe, Schiller, Hölderlin, Kleist, Fichte, Schopenhauer, Montaigne, Pascal, La Rochefoucauld, Fontenelle, Chamfort, Stendhal, Burckhardt, and Emerson. Nietzsche did admire most of these men; and Hölderlin, intoxicated with love of ancient Hellas and insane at thirty-two, invites comparison with Nietzsche—and it seems to have been from him that Nietzsche derived his enthusiasm for Empedocles. But apart from Goethe and Schopenhauer—and perhaps Burckhardt—none of the men chosen by Andler seem as important for Nietzsche's thought as Heraclitus, Socrates, Plato, Aristotle, the Stoics, Spinoza, Kant, Hegel, Heine, Darwin, and Dostoevsky.

11

OVERMAN AND ETERNAL RECURRENCE

My formula for the greatness of a human being is *amor fati:* that one wants nothing to be different—not forward, not backward, not in all eternity.—EH II 10.

Nietzsche's philosophy of power culminates in the dual vision of the overman and the eternal recurrence. The two conceptions have seemed contradictory to many readers, and most interpreters of Nietzsche's thought have simply disregarded the recurrence. In view of Nietzsche's own conviction that the two ideas belonged closely together and that the doctrine of recurrence was the climax of his whole philosophy, the usual approach must be considered perilous. The present exposition of Nietzsche's philosophy, on the other hand, allows for an understanding of both conceptions in their intimate relation, and it obviates any lengthy argument: for the two ideas will be seen to fit quite naturally into the setting we have provided.

I

First of all, one may note that Nietzsche did not coin the word *Übermensch.* The *hyperanthropos* is to be found in the writings of Lucian, in the second century A.D.[1]—and Nietzsche, as a classical philologist, had studied Lucian and made frequent reference to him in his *philologica.* In German, the word had been used by Heinrich Müller (*Geistliche Erquickungsstunden,* 1664),

---

[1] *Kataplous* 16.

by J. G. Herder, by Jean Paul—and by Goethe, in a poem (*Zueignung*) and in *Faust* (Part I, line 490), where a spirit scorns the frightened Faust who has conjured him and calls him *Übermenschen*.[2] It is therefore characteristic that the young Nietzsche first applied the term to Byron's Manfred—not to Byron himself, as Oehler claims in his index (XXIII, 233)—and that Nietzsche calls Manfred an *"Übermenschen* who controls spirits" (I, 38), thus closely paralleling Goethe's usage. Goethe himself is mentioned on the next page.

Of course, Nietzsche later gave the term a new meaning—but one easily overlooks the connotation the word had for him, and the English "superman" is misleading. Nietzsche's conception depends on the associations of the word *über*. In the third *Meditation* he had inquired as to how the individual might be able to give meaning to his life, lest his "existence" remain "a thoughtless accident." His answer had been, in effect, that you should realize your own true self; and the question had then arisen how you can know this true self. This problem was solved by the suggestion that you might consider your "educator" and meditate upon those of his features which you have always loved most. You should then envisage "your true self [which] does not lie deeply concealed within you but immeasurably high over you [*über dir*]" (I).

An aphorism in *The Gay Science* suggests the connection between this ideal self over us and the overman. Nietzsche here denounces monotheism for preaching the existence of one *Normalgott* as a single norm which suggests somehow that there is also a *Normalmensch*: a norm to which all men must conform and a bar to the development of individuality. It was the advantage of polytheism, Nietzsche contends, that it allowed for a *"multiplicity of norms."* Hence it also "first allowed for individuals; here the right of individuals was honored for the first time" (FW 143). The argument seems questionable: we have seen that Nietzsche himself amply recognized elsewhere how remarkable the Old Testament is for its portraits of great individuals—and he even wrote that "Greek and Indian literature have nothing

---

[2] One may also note that Goethe already had entitled one of his poems *Dythyrambe,* and that it was from him that Nietzsche borrowed the title for his Proem to *The Gay Science: Scherz, List und Rache;* Goethe had subtitled his work by that name *Ein Singspiel,* Nietzsche subtitled his: *Vorspiel in deutschen Reimen.*

to compare with it" in this respect (J 52). The passage in *The Gay Science* evidently does not represent Nietzsche's considered opinion of monotheism—but its importance lies in the fact that he proceeds to applaud "the invention of gods, heroes, and *Übermenschen* of all kinds, as well as *Neben-* and *Untermenschen,* dwarfs, fairies, centaurs, satyrs, demons, and devils." The *Nebenmenschen,* the creatures living alongside man, may be the dwarfs, the fairies, and the centaurs; the *Untermenschen* are presumably the satyrs, demons, and devils; while the *Übermenschen* of this aphorism seem to be the gods, the demigods, and heroes of the ancient Greeks. To Nietzsche these *Übermenschen* appear as symbols of the repudiation of any conformity to a single norm: antitheses to mediocrity and stagnation. As he himself had tried to break with conformity in order to realize his own unique individuality—looking for an "educator" in whose most beloved features he might behold his ideal self "immeasurably high above"—the Greeks envisaged their ideal individualities in their *Übermenschen.* This aphorism is significant because it contains one of the few references to the overman before *Zarathustra* and was written just before that work.

In *Zarathustra,* the overman makes his first important public appearance—together with the eternal recurrence and the will to power, which had not been fully developed either before Zarathustra expounded them. Zarathustra's first speech to the people begins with the words: "I teach you the *Übermenschen.* Man is something that should be overcome [*überwunden*]. What have you done to overcome him?" (Z-V 3).

Klages, in his chapter on the *Überwindungsmotiv,* makes a point worth quoting in this connection: "Altogether, *Zarathustra* is an enraptured and uncanny exegesis of the proposition '*über.*' Over-fullness, over-goodness, over-time, over-kind, over-wealth, over-hero, to over-drink—those are a few out of the great number of over-words, some of which are newly coined and some of which are used over again—and they are just as many variations of the one exclusively meant: overcoming." [3] This observation seems sound. The *Übermensch* at any rate cannot be dissociated from the conception of *Überwindung,* of overcoming. "Man is something that should be overcome"—and the man who has overcome himself has become an overman.

---

[3] *Op. cit.,* 204.

It matters little that Zarathustra declares elsewhere:

> Never yet has there been an overman. Naked I saw both the greatest and the smallest man. They are still all-too-similar to each other. Verily even the greatest I found all-too-human [Z II 4].

The question is merely whether a Goethe became truly perfect, or whether even he was, in some respects, "all-too-human." This consideration, however, does not affect the interpretation of the *Übermensch* as the man who has overcome himself.

This is not the customary exegesis of the "superman." The allegories Zarathustra uses in his first speech have led most readers astray:

> What is the ape to man? A laughing-stock or a painful embarrassment. And man shall be just that for the overman [Z-V 3].

> Man is a rope, tied between beast and overman—a rope over an abyss [Z-V 4].

Man as a rope—that is a picture of what we have called man's "ontological predicament": he lives, as it were, between two worlds and reaches out for ideals he cannot attain short of crossing an apparently insuperable abyss. "In man there is both *creator* and creature" (J 225), the human and the all-too-human, the superhuman and the animalic.

That is also the clue to the chapter "Of Child and Marriage." Zarathustra begins his sermon: "I have a question for you alone, my brother"—it is still *Die Frage an den Einzelnen,* the question for the single one, or perhaps better: for two single ones. Nietzsche's whole point in this chapter is that there are two kinds of marriage: that between creatures and that between creators; that between those who are fleeing themselves, their task, and their loneliness, and that between—two single ones.

> Are you the victorious one, the self-conqueror, the commander of your senses . . . ? Or is it the animal and need that speak out of your wish? Or loneliness? Or lack of peace with yourself? Let your victory and your freedom long for a child. You shall build living monuments to your victory and your liberation [cf. A 56, p. 223 above].

It is in this context that Nietzsche says: *"Nicht nur fort sollst du dich pflanzen sondern hinauf"*—you should propagate yourself not only onward but upward: procreation need not be a senseless continuation of an essentially meaningless story and an addition of more and more zeros—it can really be a creation. Nietzsche proceeds:

> What child would not have cause to weep over its parents? Worthy I deemed this man and ripe for the sense of the earth: but when I saw his wife, the earth seemed to me a house for the senseless. Indeed, I wished that the earth might tremble in convulsions when a saint mates with a goose. This one went out like a hero in quest of truths, and eventually he conquered a little dressed-up lie. His marriage, he calls it.

Marriage, as Nietzsche sees it, is all too apt to be the supreme temptation for man to betray his call; but he does not, for that reason, deprecate marriage altogether. Although "for the most part two animals find each other," marriage *can* be creative and "holy": namely, when two single ones meet—two who have *become* single ones by overcoming the duality of the inward and the outward, thought and action, ideal and reality. Even if they have not yet attained this state of being, but come together to aid each other in this supreme effort, mutually intensifying the "longing for the overman," eager that their children should not only represent another generation but surpass them, their marriage is a true marriage, and they have something to live for together: educating themselves, each other, and their children.

An optimistic age found its own belief in endless progress symbolized by Nietzsche's "superman." Nietzsche himself, however, claimed that only "scholarly oxen" could have construed his conception Darwinistically (EH III 1). This vehement expression, while typical of his last books, seems unjustified in view of the plain fact that the symbolism of *Zarathustra* invites misunderstanding. Yet Nietzsche had long insisted that his books could not be understood correctly if read hastily; he had pleaded in his prefaces that they should be studied *"rück- und vorsichtig,"* not only carefully but also with an eye to what comes before and after, "with mental reserve, with doors left open, with delicate fingers and eyes" (M-V 5). And he had claimed that his writings were clear enough "assuming—as I do assume—that one has first read my earlier writings and not spared some trouble in doing this" (GM-V 8).

In the second *Meditation,* Nietzsche had already declared: "The *goal of humanity* cannot lie in the end but only *in its highest specimens"* (9). In the third *Meditation* he had claimed that "the goal of development" could be found only "in single great human beings" who are not "the last ones in point of time" but "apparently scattered and accidental existences" (6). And he had even approximated the similes of *Zarathustra* when he claimed that only *"the philosophers, artists, and saints"* are "truly *human* beings and *no-longer-animals"* (5). Apparently Nietzsche expected that his readers, recalling these passages, would not construe the similes of ape and rope in any different fashion. The unphilosophic and inartistic mass remain animalic, while the man who overcomes himself, sublimating his impulses, consecrating his passions, and giving style to his character, becomes truly human or—as Zarathustra would say, enraptured by the word *über*—*super*human. This point is further illustrated by Nietzsche's later use of the phrase "human, superhuman" (FW 382; EH-Z 2). This is, of course, a variation of the earlier "human, all-too-human" with which Nietzsche had intended to brand our animal nature. The "human, superhuman" then refers to our true self, and the "superman" is the one who has transfigured his *physis* and acquired self-mastery.

Having looked back, one may now test this exegesis by becoming *"vorsichtig"* and looking to Nietzsche's later works. At the beginning of the *Antichrist* we find Nietzsche explaining himself as follows:

> The problem I thus pose is not what shall succeed mankind in the sequence of living beings (man is an end [*Ende*]), but what type of man shall be *bred,* shall be *willed,* for being higher in value. . . . Even in the past this higher type has appeared often —but as a fortunate accident, as an exception, never as something *willed.* . . . From dread the opposite type was willed, bred, and *attained:* the domestic animal, the herd animal, the sick human animal—the Christian.
>
> Mankind does *not* represent a development toward something better or stronger or higher in the sense accepted today. "Progress" is merely a modern idea, that is, a false idea. The European today is vastly inferior in value to the European of the Renaissance: further development is altogether *not* according to any necessity in the direction of elevation. . . . In another sense, success in individual cases is constantly encountered in the most widely different places and cultures: here we really do find a *higher type* that is, in relation to mankind as a whole, a kind of overman. Such fortunate accidents of great success have always been possible and *will* perhaps always be possible [A 3, 4].

Here is one of the few hints in Nietzsche's finished works of his ideas about "breeding"; he charges Christianity with having bred only conformity and mediocrity and with having thwarted the development of single superior individuals—"the church sends all 'great men [*Menschen*]' to hell, it fights *against* all 'greatness of man' " (WM 871; cf. A 5); and Nietzsche repudiates the modern notion of progress in the very same breath in which he speaks of the overman—to say that he has existed many times in the past. The conception is the same as in the third *Meditation:* "apparently scattered and accidental existences" (U III 6). In *Ecce Homo,* this exegesis of the overman is reiterated and explicitly distinguished from prominent misconstructions:

> The word "overman," as the designation of a type of supreme achievement, as opposed to "modern" men, to "good" men, to Christians and other nihilists—a word that in the mouth of a Zarathustra, the annihilator of morality, becomes a very pensive word—had been understood almost everywhere with the utmost innocence in the sense of those very values whose opposite Zarathustra was meant to represent—that is, an "idealistic" type of a higher kind of man, half "saint," half "genius."
>
> Other scholarly oxen have suspected me of Darwinism on that account. Even the "hero worship" of that unconscious and involuntary counterfeiter, Carlyle, which I have repudiated so maliciously, has been read into it [EH III 1].[4]

One may wonder just how Nietzsche's conception differs from Carlyle's hero worship—and perhaps even more who these "fortunate accidents of great success," the overmen of the past, may have been. Both questions may be answered briefly. Carlyle, as a historian, finds that great men make history, that society depends on hero worship, and that without heroes there can be only anarchy, which he abhors. For Nietzsche, the overman does not have instrumental value for the maintenance of society: he is valuable in himself because he embodies the state of being for which all of us long; he has the only ultimate value there is; and

---

[4] Nietzsche's crucial difference with Carlyle's hero worship (cf. FW 347; G IX 1, 12; A 54) is overlooked by Eric Bentley, *A Century of Hero-Worship: A Study of the Idea of Heroism in Carlyle and Nietzsche with Notes on other Hero-Worshippers of Modern Times* (1944). Bentley is too intent on psychologizing Nietzsche—and he makes too much of Carlyle's and Nietzsche's common quest for a father substitute—to do justice to Nietzsche's philosophical position.

society is censured insofar as it insists on conformity and impedes his development (cf. G. ıx 44).

Therefore, Napoleon is not appreciated as the instrument that brought about the termination of revolutionary anarchy, but the revolution is appreciated as the instrument that made possible Napoleon: "The revolution made possible Napoleon: that is its justification. For a similar prize one should have to desire the anarchical crash of our entire civilization." This is the hyperbolic formulation of a note, used to illustrate Nietzsche's point: "The *value* of a human being . . . does not lie in his usefulness: for it would continue to exist even if there were nobody to whom he could be useful" (WM 877).

Napoleon is often praised by Nietzsche, though he ridicules him on occasion: "For Napoleon was like such a paper eagle. When one removed the lights from behind him, he was only miserable paper and was put into a nook!" (xxı, 19) What Nietzsche admired in Napoleon, however, were not his military triumphs or his imperial crown.[5] Rather he found in Napoleon the antithesis of the German "Wars of Liberation," of the resurgence of German nationalism, and—besides Goethe—the greatest modern symbol of his own ideal: the Good European.

> In all the more profound and comprehensive human beings of this century, the total tendency underlying the enigmatic workings of their soul was, at bottom, to prepare the way for this new *synthesis* and to anticipate, experimentally, the European of the future. Only in their foregrounds or in weaker hours, as in old

---

[5] Typical not only of one author's misconstruction of Nietzsche's philosophy to fit a psychological pattern, but also of a widespread misapprehension, is Reyburn's contrast of the virtuous and sickly Nietzsche, who "had sipped his chocolate at the village inn when the gay dogs drank their beer!" and his "adolescent" passion for great conquerors. Nietzsche's "principle is quite clear, and we can easily supply other examples for ourselves. Genghis Khan was a mightier conqueror than Napoleon," and thus the "death and carnage" spread by his hordes were a small price for his presence on earth; for "Nietzsche is quite definite on this point. The value of the great man is inherent in himself . . ." (*Nietzsche,* 412 f.). What is overlooked is merely that Nietzsche did not consider the Khan a "great man."

In fact, what Nietzsche admired were not, strictly speaking, "great men," but "great human beings"—*grosse Menschen,* as he himself writes. And instead of speaking of "the value of the great man" as "inherent in himself," he says that "the value of a human being . . . does not lie in his usefulness." Greatness, as conceived by Nietzsche, entails superior humanity, and that is also the connotation of *Übermensch.*

age, they belonged to the "fatherlandish" ones—they were merely taking a rest from themselves when they became "patriots." I am thinking of human beings like Napoleon, Goethe, Beethoven, Stendhal, Heinrich Heine, and Schopenhauer [J 256; XVI, 375].

. . . When Napoleon wanted to bring Europe into an association of states (the only human being who was strong enough for that!), they botched everything with their *"Wars of Liberation"* and conjured up the misfortune of the insanity of nationalities (with the consequence of race fights in such long-mixed countries as Europe!) [XVI, 368].[6]

The Napoleon whom Nietzsche admired was the *"ens realissimum"* or, as Hegel had called him, the "world-soul," who had, at the turn of the century, inspired men like Beethoven and Goethe (G IX 49). "Goethe's heart opened up at the phenomenon of Napoleon—it closed up at the 'Wars of Liberation' " (G VIII 4). "What is certain is that it was not the 'Wars of Liberation' that made him look up more cheerfully, any more than the French Revolution; the event on whose account he *re-thought* his *Faust,* yes, the whole problem of 'man,' was the appearance of Napoleon" (J 244). What Nietzsche admired was not Napoleon's prowess on the battlefield, but what Napoleon had made of himself.

Courage before the enemy is one thing: having that, one can yet be a coward and an indecisive muddle-head. Thus Napoleon judged with respect to the "most courageous man" known to him, Murat . . . [FW 169].

In the end, however, Nietzsche did not consider Napoleon an *Übermenschen.* In the *Genealogy* he called him "this synthesis of *Unmensch* and *Übermensch,"* evidently not charmed by Napoleon's inhuman qualities; and in the notes of *The Will to*

---

[6] Cf. the first book of Heine's *Romantische Schule,* where Napoleon is pictured as *der grosse Klassiker* and contrasted with *die kleinen Romantiker*—and especially the following passage: "the patriotism of the German . . . consists in this that his heart becomes narrower . . . that he hates the alien, that he does not want any more to be a citizen of the world, a European . . . there began the shabby, plump, and unwashed opposition against an outlook which is the most splendid and holiest thing Germany has produced, namely against that humaneness, . . . that cosmopolitanism to which our greatest spirits, Lessing, Herder, Schiller, Goethe, Jean Paul—to which all educated people in Germany had always done homage."

The Hegel quotation in the next sentence above is from a letter, dated October 18, 1806, translated in my *Hegel* (1965), 316; Anchor Books edition (1966), 318.

Power one finds this explanatory statement about Napoleon: "he himself, however, had been corrupted by the means he *had* to employ, and had *lost* the *nobility* of his character" (WM 1026).

Caesar came closer to Nietzsche's ideal—but in him, too, it was not the military or political successes that Nietzsche looked to, but the embodiment of the passionate man who controls his passions: the man who, in the face of universal disintegration and licentiousness, knowing this decadence as part of his own soul, performs his unique deed of self-integration, self-creation, and self-mastery. Nietzsche looked to the "Julius Caesar [who] defended himself against sickliness and headaches by tremendous marches, the most frugal way of life, uninterrupted sojourn in the open air, and continuous exertion" (G IX 31). One gathers that Caesar was one of Nietzsche's "educators."

> The highest type of free man should be sought where the highest resistance is constantly overcome: five steps from tyranny, close to the threshold of the danger of servitude. This is true psychologically if by "tyrants" are meant inexorable and fearful instincts that provoke the maximum of authority and discipline [*Zucht*] against themselves; most beautiful type: Julius Caesar . . . [G IX 38].

Tyranny over others is not part of Nietzsche's vision, though the failure to indulge in it is no virtue unless one has the power to become a tyrant and refrains deliberately. The ideal is "the Roman Caesar with Christ's soul" (WM 983).

The *Übermensch*—even if one considers Nietzsche's reverence for Napoleon and Caesar, rather than his admiration for Socrates and Goethe—does not introduce a new conception into the account here given of Nietzsche's philosophy: he is the "Dionysian" man who is depicted under the name of Goethe at the end of the *Götzen-Dämmerung* (IX, 49). He has overcome his animal nature, organized the chaos of his passions, sublimated his impulses, and given style to his character—or, as Nietzsche said of Goethe: "he disciplined himself to wholeness, he *created* himself" and became "the man of tolerance, not from weakness but from strength," "a spirit who has *become free.*"

II

When the *Übermensch* is thus understood, the conception not only does not conflict with the doctrine of eternal recurrence, but the essential connection between the two ideas becomes clear. As a matter of fact, the seedlings of the two can be found close together even before *Zarathustra:* in the second *Meditation* —although Nietzsche expressly repudiated the Pythagorean doctrine of eternal recurrence in that very work.

One may note first of all that Nietzsche did not consider his own later doctrine "absolutely unique, snatched from the pure air of the Engadine." [7] As a classical philologist, he had become acquainted with it at an early date. In his "Lectures on the Pre-Platonic Philosophers," he had referred to the recurrence in his exposition of Pythagorean philosophy (IV, 352); and in the second *Meditation* he referred to it again (2). Later, after he had himself become "the teacher of the eternal recurrence" (G x 5), he stated expressly:

> The doctrine of the "eternal recurrence," i.e., of the unconditional and infinitely repeated circular course of all things—this doctrine of Zarathustra *might* in the end have been taught already by Heraclitus. At least the Stoics, who inherited almost all their principal ideas from Heraclitus, show traces of it [EH-GT 3].[8]

And in the notes of *The Will to Power,* Nietzsche writes: "I have found this idea in earlier thinkers" (1066).

Not all of these "earlier thinkers" belong to classical antiquity, and apparently Heinrich Heine, whom Nietzsche admired fervently, was one of them. In one of Heine's books which Nietz-

---

[7] Brinton, *op. cit.,* 76.

[8] Knight, *op. cit.,* 106, comments, after citing this passage: "This is inexact; and it is probable that the inexactitude is intentional." He then adduces evidence to show that Heraclitus believed in cycles, though perhaps not "that things will . . . repeat themselves. And of course Heraclitus may have taken that last step—though no evidence survives to prove it" (108). This would seem to corroborate Nietzsche's words, but Knight claims that he has shown Nietzsche to have been not only "inexact" but—"insincere" (111). Knight also claims that Nietzsche did not wish to admit his debt to the Stoics, "whom he rarely mentions" (107), although Nietzsche went to the extent of calling himself the "last of the Stoics" (J 227; cf. M 131, 546). Knight further accepts the Darwinistic misinterpretation of the overman and then argues that Nietzsche was not "an optimist in the proper sense of the term"—and while this is surely true, Knight infers from this that Nietzsche was inconsistent and insincere (181). In the end, Nietzsche was not a philosopher but "a critic and a stylist" (189).

sche owned, we find the following passage:[9] ". . . And she answered with a tender voice: 'Let us be good friends.'—But what
I have told you here, dear reader, that is not an event of yesterday or the day before. . . . For time is infinite, but the things in
time, the concrete bodies, are finite. They may indeed disperse
into the smallest particles; but these particles, the atoms, have
their determinate number, and the number of the configurations
that, all of themselves, are formed out of them is also determinate.
Now, however long a time may pass, according to the eternal laws
governing the combinations of this eternal play of repetition, all
configurations that have previously existed on this earth must yet
meet, attract, repulse, kiss, and corrupt each other again. . . .
And thus it will happen one day that a man will be born again,
just like me, and a woman will be born, just like Mary—only that
it is to be hoped that the head of this man may contain a little
less foolishness—and in a better land they will meet and contemplate each other a long time; and finally the woman will give
her hand to the man and say with a tender voice: 'Let us be

---

[9] The passage was first cited in the *Frankfurter Zeitung*, April 18, 1899,
and then again by H. Lichtenberger, *La philosophie de Nietzsche* (4th
ed., 1899), 189. Lichtenberger referred the passage to *Sämtliche Werke*,
ed. Ernst Elster, III, 542 (*Reise von München nach Genua, Lesarten*), and
commented: "*Il ne figure pas dans les éditions anciennes de Heine, et
Nietzsche ne l'a pas connu.*" Bernoulli, *op. cit.*, I, 448, points out that
"this is an error. The passage is found in *Letzte Gedichte und Gedanken
von H. Heine*, Hamburg, 1869, ed. Adolf Strodtmann . . . and it might
very well have come to Nietzsche's attention." Bernoulli, too, overlooked
that Nietzsche actually possessed the book which is listed as #440 in
"Friedrich Nietzsches Bibliothek" (by Elisabeth Förster-Nietzsche) in
Bücher und Wege zu Büchern (1900), ed. Arthur Berthold.

Nietzsche also owned E. Dühring, *Kursus der Philosophie* (1875), which
contains another reference to the recurrence (84). Dühring denies the
possibility of eternal recurrence, and R. Steiner concluded that Nietzsche's
doctrine was a mere antithesis (*Gegenidee*) to Dühring's. ("Die 'soge-
nannte' Wiederkunft des Gleichen von Nietzsche" in *Das Magazin für
Litteratur*, 1900.) Psychological and historical causation, however, is
certainly more complex.

Thomas Mann, finally, when he suggests that Nietzsche's doctrine may
have been a *Lesefrucht* from the devil's dialogue with Ivan Karamazov
(*Neue Studien*, 89), overlooks that Nietzsche did not read Dostoevsky
until early in 1887. (Cf., e.g., his letter to Overbeck, February 23, 1887:
"A few weeks ago, I did not even know Dostoevsky's name. . . . A fortu-
itous reach in a bookstore . . .") Nor does Nietzsche ever seem to have
read *The Brothers Karamazov*.

For a detailed account of Nietzsche's reading of Dostoevsky, see my
edition of the *Genealogy*, the commentary on GM III 15 and 24.

good friends.' " The details of the theory, as here stated, are as similar to Nietzsche's later version of it as the playful context is dissimilar from that provided by Nietzsche's philosophy. In fact, only the significance of the doctrine in the framework of Nietzsche's thought is novel.

Returning to the second *Meditation* (2), where Nietzsche repudiated the Pythagorean doctrine of recurrence, we find that the point of his critique was merely that events do not, and cannot, recur within the span of known history—and about this he never changed his mind.[10] The second *Meditation* contains the germs not only of the later conception of the *Übermensch* but also of Nietzsche's own version of the recurrence.

One should recall the description of the supra-historical point of view. From this perspective, one "does not envisage salvation in the process, but . . . the world is finished in every single moment and its end [*Ende*] attained. What could ten new years teach that the past could not teach?" (1). This passage—and indeed the whole conception of the supra-historical—represents the ground out of which the later doctrine of eternal recurrence grew, just as the *Übermensch* developed out of the insight that "the *goal of humanity* cannot lie in the end [*Ende*] but only in *its highest specimens*" (9). Both conceptions depend on Nietzsche's denial of indefinite progress—of what Hegel called the Bad Infinite[11]—and they suggest the possible infinite value of the moment and the individual.

Nietzsche himself insisted on the close relationship of both conceptions (XIV, 110, 178 ff.); and only the common evolutionary misconstruction of the overman involves an inconsistency with

---

[10] Therefore, Löwith's conception of "The Repetition of Classical Antiquity at the Peak of Modernity as the Historical Meaning of the Doctrine of Eternal Recurrence" (Chapter IV of *Nietzsches Philosophie der Ewigen Wiederkungt des Gleichen*) is untenable, quite apart from the fact that Löwith shares the common prejudice that Nietzsche wanted to go back beyond Socrates to the pre-Socratics. The doctrine of recurrence grew out of the supra-historical outlook and has no "historical meaning" of this sort. Insofar as Nietzsche's attitude was not supra-historical but historical, his approach was dialectical and somewhat similar to Hegel's: he accepted the actual course of events as necessary and "would not have anything be different—not forward, not backward, not in all eternity." (EH II 10). "Nothing that is may be subtracted" (EH I 2)—and Nietzsche certainly did not want to subtract the historical development from antiquity to his own time and "go back."

[11] *Encyclopädie* §94 f.; cf. §60.

the doctrine of eternal recurrence. Nietzsche's vehement scorn of the idea of progress as "modern" and "false," his belief that the men of ancient Greece and of the Renaissance were far superior to his own contemporaries, his insistence that the highest specimens were widely scattered over continents and centuries, his reference to the scholarly oxen who suspected him of Darwinism—all these and many other passages were simply overlooked.

The doctrine of the eternal recurrence of all things has actually been referred to previously—as the Dionysian faith. The man—Nietzsche chose Goethe as his representative—who has organized the chaos of his passions and integrated every feature of his character, redeeming even the ugly by giving it a meaning in a beautiful totality—this *Übermensch* would also realize how inextricably his own being was involved in the totality of the cosmos: and in affirming his own being, he would also affirm all that is, has been, or will be (G IX 49). Elsewhere, Nietzsche notes: "Thereupon Zarathustra related, *out of the joy of the Übermensch, the secret* that all recurs" (XIV, 180).

In his "Drunken Song," too, Nietzsche related his conception of the eternal recurrence to the feeling of joy analyzed above as the conscious aspect of the possession of power, as the faith of the overman. One may cite part of Nietzsche's exegesis of the last two lines:

> Doch alle Lust will Ewigkeit—
> Will tiefe, tiefe Ewigkeit.
> [Z III 15; Z IV 19]

Explaining the meaning of "all joy wants eternity—wants deep, wants deep eternity," Nietzsche brings out the relation between "joy" and eternal recurrence:

> Pain, too, is a joy. . . . Have you ever said Yes to a single joy? . . . then you said Yes, too, to *all* woe. All things are entangled, ensnared, enamored. If ever you wanted one thing twice, if ever you said "you please me, happiness! Abide, moment!" then you wanted back *all*. All anew, all eternally, all entangled, ensnared, enamored—oh, then you *loved* the world. Eternal ones, love it eternally and evermore: and to woe, too, you say: go, but return! *For all joy wants—eternity!*

. . . You higher men, do learn this, joy wants eternity. Joy wants the eternity of *all* things, *wants deep, wants deep eternity!* [Z IV 19].

This is the ultimate apotheosis of the supra-historical outlook, the supreme exaltation of the moment. Negatively, the doctrine of eternal recurrence is the most extreme repudiation of any deprecation of the moment, the finite, and the individual—the antithesis of any faith in infinite progress, whether it be evolution, Faust's unbounded striving,[12] or the endless improvement of the human soul in Kant's conception of immortality. It is the antithesis, too, of any faith in another world; it is the creed of one whose message began: "I beseech you, my brothers, *remain faithful to the earth* and do not believe those who speak to you of other-worldly hopes" (Z-V 3).

Those who would make a romantic out of Nietzsche have usually discounted his conception of the recurrence altogether, called it a "deceptively mocking mystery of delusion," [13] and insisted that he moved "the goal beyond all that had been achieved into the unachievable." [14] Actually, the conception of the overman is inseparable from that of the recurrence; and together they give expression to Nietzsche's fundamental anti-romanticism —as may be shown briefly by referring to Arthur O. Lovejoy's analyses of romanticism.[15] Friedrich Schlegel, for example, actually contrasted the classical *System des Kreislaufes* which conceives history "as a movement that returns upon itself in repeated cycles" with the modern, romantic system of infinite progress (*System der unendlichen Fortschreitung*) (212). And Novalis celebrated what he himself described as "the annihilation of the

---

[12] This is alluded to in the quotation from the "Drunken Song": "you please me, happiness! Abide, moment!" Nietzsche, of course, recognized the difference between Goethe and Faust, and knew such passages as: "ever hold fast to the present . . . every moment is of infinite value, for it is the representative of a whole eternity" (Eckermann, Nov. 3, 1823). Cf. also Goethe's "cheerful overlooking of the mobile earthly happenings that ever recur in circles and spirals" (letter to Zelter, May 11, 1820), and my essay on "Goethe's Faith and Faust's Redemption," in *From Shakespeare to Existentialism*.

[13] Bertram, *Nietzsche*, 12.

[14] E. Gundolf, *op. cit.*, 32.

[15] *Essays in the History of Ideas*, The Johns Hopkins Press, 1948. Page references are given in parentheses in the text. I have translated the German quotations.

present and the apotheosis of the future which is truly a better world." Lovejoy comments: "Preoccupation with supersensible realities and a feeling of the illusoriness of ordinary existence was thus often held to be a distinctive trait of Romantic art, on the ground that Christianity is an otherworldly religion"; and he goes on to quote A. W. Schlegel: "in the Christian view, the contemplation of the infinite has annihilated the finite; and life has become a world of shadows, life has become night" (246). Lovejoy remarks that "in German Romanticism between 1797 and 1800 there grew up . . . *both* an 'apotheosis of the future' and a tendency . . . towards the medieval. A belief in progress and a spirit of reaction were, paradoxically . . . nurtured for a time in the same minds," (252). The common and characteristic element may be found in the repudiation of the finitude of the present moment—while Nietzsche, herein the heir of Goethe, glorifies exactly this in his dual conception of overman and recurrence.

The suggestion that the eternal recurrence is to be construed as essentially similar to Kant's Categorical Imperative[16] is misleading. It is maintained that the man who believes in the recurrence will act in such a manner that he could wish his act to recur eternally. In the first place, however, Kant never meant to appeal to our psychological disposition. He believed that certain maxims were self-contradictory, and that this contradiction would become explicit when one envisaged the consequences of the universal adoption of such maxims. Our emotional reaction to the consequences was of no concern to him. The man who believes in the recurrence, on the other hand, would be deterred from certain actions—if at all—only by his affective response to the consequences. Secondly—and this is surely more important for an understanding of Nietzsche's doctrine—Nietzsche was not primarily a moral philosopher at all, but supremely interested in the sphere of "Absolute Spirit": he was concerned, above all, with the artist, the philosopher, and the man who achieves self-perfection—the last having taken the place of the saint. Particular actions seemed much less important to Nietzsche than the state of being of the whole man—and those who achieve self-perfection and affirm their own being and all eternity, backward and forward, have no thought of the morrow. They want an eter-

---

[16] Cf. Oscar Ewald, *Nietzsches Lehre in ihren Grundbegriffen: Die Ewige Wiederkunft des Gleichen und der Sinn des Übermenschen* (1903), 62 *et passim*, and Simmel, *op. cit.*, 247 ff.

nal recurrence out of the fullness of their delight in the moment. They do not deliberate, absurdly, how they should act to avoid unpleasant consequences—knowing all the while that whatever they are about to do has already been done by them an infinite number of times in the past. Thus Nietzsche could pointedly contrast the Dionysian faith of Goethe with the philosophy of *"Kant, the antipode of Goethe"* (G IX 49) and conclude his work: "I, the last disciple of the philosopher Dionysus—I, the teacher of the eternal recurrence" (G x 5).[17]

One may yet wonder why Nietzsche, having conceived of the will to power and the overman, able to look back upon many a keen psychological insight as well as a comprehensive philosophy, should have preferred to think of himself as the teacher of the eternal recurrence. Why did he value this most dubious doctrine, which was to have no influence to speak of, so extravagantly? For it is plain that none of his other ideas meant so much to him. The answer must be sought in the fact that the eternal recurrence was to Nietzsche less an idea than an experience—the supreme experience of a life unusually rich in suffering, pain, and agony. He made much of the moment when he had this experience (EH-Z) because to him it was the moment that redeemed his life. Beginning with *The Birth of Tragedy*, Nietzsche had inquired how life might be "justified." His first answer, proposed several times in his first book, had been: "Only as an aesthetic phenomenon is the world justified." This solution had still been somewhat academic; and even the analysis of Greek tragedy and the suggestion that the Greeks enjoyed life, in spite of their suffering, as "at bottom . . . powerful and joyous" (GT 7) had been offered, as it were, by a distant observer. It was not until August 1881, near Sils Maria, "6,000 feet beyond man and time," that the thought came to Nietzsche that the man who per-

---

[17] This is overlooked by Albert Schweitzer when he writes: "Compared to the Brahmanic superman, Nietzsche's is a miserable creature. The Brahmanic one is superior to the whole world, Nietzsche's only to human society." "This is what is so petty and so extremely timely about Nietzsche's philosophy: it treats only of man and society and does not know the problem of man and world" (*Die Weltanschauung der Indischen Denker*, 1935, 26 and 185). Ananda Coomaraswamy, on the other hand, in his "Cosmopolitan View of Nietzsche" in *The Dance of Siva* (1924), stresses the parallels between Nietzsche and the Oriental religions. Strange in view of the title of his book is his omission of any reference to Zarathustra's conception of the dancing god, which invites comparison with the Indian Dionysus, the Siva Nataraja (Z I 7).

fects himself and transfigures his *physis* achieves that happiness toward which all men grope, and feels a supreme joy which obviates any concern with the "justification" of the world: he affirms it forward, backward, and "in all eternity." "Not merely bear what is necessary, still less conceal it . . . but *love* it" (EH II 10).[18]

It is noteworthy that Nietzsche also says that this feeling of joy, this *"amor fati,"* is his "formula for the greatness of a human being." Power is still the standard of value—but this joy is the conscious feeling that is inextricably connected with a man's possession of power. Conversely, the man who experiences this joy is the powerful man—and instead of relying on heavenly powers to redeem him, to give meaning to his life, and to justify the world, he gives meaning to his own life by achieving perfection and exulting in every moment.

This is also the meaning of one of the first passages—written before *Zarathustra*—in which the recurrence is referred to:

> How, if some day or night, a demon were to sneak after you into your loneliest loneliness and say to you: "This life, as you now live it and have lived it, you will have to live once more and innumerable times more; and there will be nothing new in it, but every pain and every joy and every thought and sigh . . . must return to you—all in the same succession and sequence—even this spider and this moonlight between the trees, and even this moment and I myself. The eternal hourglass of existence is turned over and over—and you with it, a dust grain of dust!" Would you not throw yourself down and gnash your teeth and curse the demon who spoke thus? Or have you once experienced a tremendous moment when you would have answered him: "You are a god, and never did I hear anything more godlike!" If this thought were to gain possession of you, it would change you as you are, or perhaps crush you. The question in each and everything, "do you want this once more and innumerable times more?" would weigh upon your actions as the greatest stress. Or how well disposed would you have to become to yourself and to life to *crave nothing more fervently* than this ultimate eternal confirmation . . . ? [FW 341].

It is easy to see how this aphorism gave rise to the misapprehension that the recurrence represents an analogy to Kant's Categorical Imperative. This passage was taken to show that the doc-

---

[18] The similarity to Spinoza and the Stoics is obvious—and not accidental.

trine was intended to require man to ask himself constantly: "Do you want this once more and innumerable times more?" That, however, is not the meaning of Nietzsche's conception of "the greatest stress." As ever, he is not concerned with particular actions but with the individual's state of being. Man is to ask himself whether his present state of being is such that he would have to answer the demon with impotent anger and gnashing of teeth, or whether he could say: "Never did I hear anything more god-like!" If he is one of those who are still imperfect and unredeemed, if he still finds that the demonic doctrine all but drowns his soul in dread, then it might serve him as the greatest possible stimulus to his "will to power" and to his yearning for that joyous affirmation of himself and life which would enable him "to crave nothing more fervently than this ultimate eternal confirmation."

This interpretation is also corroborated by another aphorism in *The Gay Science:*

> *Excelsior!* ". . . there is no reason any more in what happens, no love in what will happen to you; no resting place is any longer open to your heart where it has only to find and to seek no longer; you resist any ultimate peace, you want the eternal recurrence of war and peace: man of renunciation, all this you want to renounce? Who will give you the strength for this? Nobody yet has had this strength!" There is a lake that one day refused to flow off and erected a dam where it had hitherto flowed off: ever since, this lake has been rising higher and higher [285].

The problem is plainly not one of devising a criterion for particular acts but, insofar as it concerns our behavior at all, to provide an incentive for man to raise his state of being (cf. FW 335), to cross the cleft from the animals to true humanity—or, in Nietzsche's word, to become an overman.

This explains also why Nietzsche thought that his doctrine might be a decisive factor in "breeding": "A doctrine is required, strong enough to have the effect of *breeding:* strengthening the strong, paralyzing and breaking the world-weary" (WM 862; cf. 1053). The weak, who are able to stand life only by hoping for kingdom, power, and glory in another life, would be crushed by this terrifying doctrine, while the strong would find in it the last incentive to achieve perfection—or if they had attained this state already, the doctrine would merely coincide with their own Dionysian faith.

Thus Nietzsche does occasionally speak of "natural selection" —but in his conception of it "the spirit" is *not* "forgotten," as it is in biologistic constructions (G IX 14), and "breeding" is at least as spiritual as it is physical. One would go wrong, however, if one assumed that Nietzsche had devised his doctrine specifically as a factor in a "breeding" scheme. The eternal recurrence was not meant to be a "noble lie," and it has been seen that Nietzsche had the greatest scorn for such unholy means. On the contrary, Nietzsche thought that his doctrine of eternal recurrence was "the *most scientific* of all possible hypotheses" (WM 55).

If science assumes a finite amount of energy in a finite space and an infinite time, it might follow that only a finite number of configurations of the power quanta were possible. In that case, either an end state must be reached or the same configurations must eventually be repeated and recur eternally. If an end state could be reached—and no beginning of time is posited— the end state must have been reached by now: but empirically that is not the case, and there is still change. Therefore, Nietzsche concluded, the doctrine of the eternal recurrence of the same—at great intervals—must be considered "the *most scientific of all possible hypotheses*" (WM 55, 1062 ff.).

The criticism, which has been made, that Nietzsche's doctrine requires the additional assumption—not recognized by him— "that neither space nor time are continuous" [19] is unfounded. It depends on reading into the "identity" between an event and its repetition a meaning plainly not intended by Nietzsche. If "power quanta" rearrange themselves continually, as he thought that they did (WM 618–39), the possibility arises that they repeat the same patterns.

It may seem odd that this "most scientific" hypothesis has found no acceptance among scientists. This is not the place to go into scientific questions, but one may note that Nietzsche concluded his own reflections about possible proofs of his "hypothesis" by saying:

> This conception is not, as it stands, a mechanistic one: for if it were, then it would not stipulate an infinite recurrence of identical cases, but a final state. Because the world has not reached this, mechanism must be considered an imperfect and merely provisional hypothesis [WM 1066].

---

[19] Morgan, *op. cit.*, 287.

The hypothesis that the universe is "running down" would have seemed "mechanistic" to Nietzsche, and less scientific than his own, because—if no beginning in time is posited, and space and energy are considered finite—the universe should have long completed this process.

Simmel has offered a very elegant refutation of Nietzsche's attempted proof of the eternal recurrence of the same events. Even if there were exceedingly few things in a finite space in an infinite time, they would not have to repeat the same configurations. Suppose there were three wheels of equal size, rotating on the same axis, one point marked on the circumference of each wheel, and these three points lined up in one straight line. If the second wheel rotated twice as fast as the first, and if the speed of the third wheel was $1/\pi$ of the speed of the first, the initial line-up would never recur.[20]

In his books, of course, Nietzsche never offered any proof of his doctrine: it is only in his notes that we encounter these attempts; and his reasons for not publishing a proof presumably included his own sense that his efforts were inadequate. But while the references to this doctrine in his writings stress the experience of believing it, it is important to note that Nietzsche thought that the eternal recurrence might be implied by modern science; it appeared to him in the same light in which a later generation received the theory that the universe is "running down"; and he thought of it as "the most extreme form of nihilism." *"Duration* coupled with an 'in vain,' without aim and end [*Ziel und Zweck*], is *the most paralyzing* thought." "Let us think this thought in its most terrible form: existence as it is, without sense and aim, but recurring inevitably without a finale of nothingness: '*the eternal recurrence'* " (WM 55). The doctrine means that all events are repeated endlessly, that there is no plan nor goal to give meaning to history or life, and that we are mere puppets in an absolutely senseless play. The eternal recurrence is the epitome of "a tale told by an idiot, full of sound and fury, signifying nothing." In a note for *Zarathustra*, Nietzsche wrote: *"After the vision of the overman*, in a gruesome way the doctrine of the *recurrence:* now *bearable!"* (XIV, 110; cf. 179).

---

[20] *Op. cit.,* 250 f. See also Milič Čapek's article on "Eternal Return" in the *Encyclopedia of Philosophy*, where this point is not made and Simmel is not listed in the Bibliography.

Nietzsche believed not only that his doctrine was a meeting place of science and philosophy—he also thought he had succeeded in creating a synthesis of the philosophies of Heraclitus and Parmenides, of the dynamic and the static world-pictures, of being and becoming: "That *all recurs* is the most extreme *approach of a world of becoming to one of being.*" Nietzsche's doctrine would *"impress* upon becoming the character of being" (WM 617). In the moment it would find eternity.

In his deprecation of any faith that pins its hopes on the future, Nietzsche—in 1888—went to the extent of writing two notes, both entitled *Anti-Darwin:*

> There are no *transitional forms.* . . . Every type has its *limits:* beyond these there is no evolution. . . .
>
> *My general view.—First proposition:* man as a species is not progressing. Higher types are indeed attained, but they do not last. The level of the species is *not* raised.
> *Second proposition:* man as a species does not represent any progress compared with any other animal. The whole animal and vegetable kingdom does not evolve from the lower to the higher—but all at the same time, in utter disorder, over and against each other. The richer and more complex forms—for the expression "higher type" means no more than this—perish more easily: only the lowest preserve an apparent indestructibility. The former are achieved only rarely and maintain their superiority with difficulty; the latter are favored by a compromising fruitfulness.
> Among men, too, the higher types, the lucky strokes of evolution, perish most easily as fortunes change. They are exposed to every kind of decadence: they are extreme, and that almost means decadents.
> The brief spell of beauty, of genius, of Caesar, is *sui generis:* such things are not inherited [WM 684].
>
> . . . That the higher organizations should have evolved out of the lower has not been demonstrated in a single case. . . . I do not see how an accidental variation offers an advantage [WM 685].

This is hardly Nietzsche's considered position. It seems to be at odds with earlier notes about "breeding," and one may wonder whether the formulation "Man as a species does not represent any progress compared with any other animal" is compatible—in this form—with Nietzsche's central conclusion that value is measured objectively "by the quantum of increased and *organized power*" (WM 674—in 1888—*et passim*). Of course, such notes represent no more than drafts for a statement that was probably intended to obviate misconstructions of the overman. Man—even the mediocre specimen—is in a sense more powerful than other species; but Nietzsche has little thought of power over others, and mankind as a whole does not represent to his mind an advance over other animals, any more than reptiles seem to him "superior" to fish. He has in mind the "fortunate accidents"—Socrates or Caesar, Leonardo or Goethe: men whose "power" gives them no advantage in any "struggle for existence" —men who, even if they outlive Mozart, Keats, or Shelley, either leave no children, or in any case no heirs. Yet these men represent the "power" for which all beings strive—for the basic drive, says Nietzsche, is not the will to preserve life but the will to power—and it should be clear how remote Nietzsche's "power" is from Darwin's "fitness." Moreover, the sharp antitheses of these notes underline the fact that Nietzsche's dual vision of overman and recurrence glorifies the moment—"all simultaneously" —and not progress.

Once more Nietzsche's view may be compared with that of Hegel, Germany's foremost philosopher of development. Nietzsche—and at first glance this may seem surprising—denounced his "educator" Schopenhauer for his "unintelligent wrath against Hegel," whose conception of development he had failed to appreciate (J 204). This is the more remarkable in view of Nietzsche's strong aversion to Hegel's fusion of philosophy with Christian dogma.[21] Yet the passage about the brief duration of the genius can be almost exactly duplicated from the works of Hegel —only that he cites Alexander and Achilles as examples, and not Caesar.[22] Indeed one may wonder why Nietzsche should have introduced the Roman who died in his fifties rather than the Hellenic youths—but in his later writings where Nietzsche referred to the "Dionysian" to designate the mastery of passion, not its

---

[21] Goethe had felt no less of an aversion to this fusion, although he, too, had admired Hegel's philosophy in other respects and been personally fond of Hegel. (Cf. Letter to Zelter, Jan. 27, 1832, and Conversations with Eckermann, Feb. 4, 1829.)

[22] *Encyclopädie* §258 *Zusatz*.

wanton flood, he sought the classical representation of self-discipline among the ancient Romans (the Greeks *"cannot* mean to us what the Romans do" [G x 2]).

Whatever Hegel said of Alexander and Achilles, it may yet seem that his entire system was founded on belief in progress. This is, no doubt, the aspect of his thought that is best known: the "development" of Hegel's categories in the *Logik,* the frequently absurd construction of world-history,[23] and the claim that his own system was, so far, the culmination of the history of philosophy. Yet Hegel not only said that the superior individual does not endure while the mediocre lasts, but also conceived of the "way of the spirit" as a "circle that returns into itself"; he spoke of philosophy as a *Kreislauf* or as a "circle" and defined "development" itself not as a line but as a "circle that returns into itself." [24] One may also recall his frequent contrast of the "bad infinity" that denotes indefinite progress and the "true infinity" that is best represented by a circle.[25] These conceptions may appear to be at odds with Hegel's exoteric philosophy of development, but the apparent inconsistency can be resolved— perhaps best by using as examples the history of art, religion, and philosophy.

Since Hegel's revolutionary lectures on these subjects—his history of philosophy was the foundation on which E. Zeller, J. E. Erdmann, and Kuno Fischer built—it has become a truism that

---

[23] Hegel's remarks on the United States, however, are discerning. Far from claiming that world history would culminate in Prussia, Hegel hailed the United States as the land of the future and expected it to enter world history, decisively, after its frontiers were conquered.

[24] *Phänomenologie,* 613; *Logik* I, 75; *Rechtsphilosophie* §2 *Zusatz; Geschichte der Philosophie* I, 56.

[25] "This determination of the true infinite cannot be accomplished by the *formula* [Schelling's] of the *oneness* of the finite and the infinite which we have already criticized. Such *oneness* is abstract, motionless self-identity. . . . The infinite, however, is . . . *becoming* . . . and thus also *being there [Dasein].* . . . It *is* and *is there,* now; it is present. Only the bad infinite is the beyond because it is only the negation of the finite which is posited as *real* . . . as something that is only negative it is even meant to be *not there;* it is meant to be unattainable. This unattainability, however, is not its exaltation but its defect. . . . The untrue is the unattainable. . . . The picture of progress into infinity is the straight *line* . . . which goes *out* into the indefinite. The picture of the real infinite . . . is the circle . . . which is closed and entirely present" (*Logik* I, 173).

they are to be understood in terms of development. What is often overlooked—and what Hegel himself frequently ignored in the detailed execution of his lectures, though in principle he was aware of it—is that any such approach is one-sided and thoroughly misleading if not balanced by another idea. The Baroque and Rodin's sculptures can be viewed as developments of Michelangelo's later style, and Proclus' and Plotinus' speculations are developments of Plato's insights: yet not only does it fail to follow that the later is superior, but there is a sense in which Plato's thought and Buonarotti's sculptures are *non plus ultra*—and their full appreciation would, as it were, "reveal all." This is, of course, the supra-historical perspective, which employs later developments only as a commentary to aid the understanding of what went before: so viewed, the history of Western philosophy is indeed—in Whitehead's phrase—a series of footnotes to Plato. The cosmos, so conceived, becomes a universe of monads; events are timeless symbols that reflect each other; and the meaning that is progressively revealed in history "for us" is actually completely given in each moment.[26] This is, in fact, the very core of Hegel's vision, though he himself seems often to lose sight of it when he treats what has gone before merely as stepping stones.

It may be well to illustrate this point at least briefly by citing Hegel's lectures on the philosophy of history. In the introduction —which, like most of Hegel's introductions, is superior to the execution of the program which follows—Hegel says expressly: "When, for example, we see a man kneel and pray before an idol, and this object is objectionable to reason, we can yet hold fast to his feeling . . . [which] has the same values as that of the Christian . . . and as that of the philosopher who immerses himself in eternal truth. . . ." "The religiousness and the ethics of a limited life—of a shepherd or a peasant—in its concentrated inwardness and its limitation to a few very simple circumstances . . . has infinite value, and the same value as the religiousness and ethics of a cultivated cognition and an existence rich in the extent of its relations and actions. This inward center . . . remains untouched by, and is removed from, the loud noise of world his-

---

[26] Cf. Leopold von Ranke's classical formulation: "Every epoch is immediate to God, and its value rests not at all on that which issues from it, but in its existence itself, in its own self." *Epochen der Neueren Geschichte* (1888), 5.

tory." [27] While these passages are of crucial significance for any proper estimation of Hegel's philosophy of history, it is plain that Hegel himself failed to stress this sufficiently.

Nietzsche is plainly guilty on opposite grounds. He turns a profound and valid insight into an exclusive "doctrine"—and he might be criticized in the very words he used to pass judgment on Christianity: he "transformed the symbolic into crudities" (WM 170). Yet his doctrine of eternal recurrence is not an arbitrary antithesis to the Christian conception: Nietzsche returns to the world-picture of an era that had not yet felt the impact of Micah or Isaiah, nor experienced how "the festivals of the eternal periodicity of life are changed into celebrations of God's deeds." [28] He returns to the visions of Pythagoras, Heraclitus, the Stoics, and the Buddhists—seeing no other alternative to the conception of history as the development in time of the one God's will, and convinced that contemporary mechanism was still founded on the Biblical assumption of an absolute beginning and end of events.

One can grasp Nietzsche's conception of "Dionysian" joy while feeling that the more explicit "doctrine" transforms a fruitful notion into a rigid crudity. One should remember, however, that the doctrine of the eternal recurrence—as distinguished from the profound experience of joy that comes to the overman —was presented by Nietzsche not as a dogma but as a hypothesis, true to his method. And if one may judge from Goethe's last letter to his friend, the composer Karl Friedrich Zelter, one may conclude that Nietzsche's fundamental intuition would have won him the approval of two of his greatest compatriots: "Fortu-

---

[27] *Die Vernunft in der Geschichte: Einleitung in die Philosophie der Weltgeschichte,* ed. Lasson (1917), 28 and 88. The whole section on "Der Wert des Individuums," 84–89, is pertinent to the subject under discussion. Cf. also G. Lasson, *Hegel als Geschichtsphilosoph* (1920), especially the section on "Zeit und Ewigkeit,"172–77; e.g.: "One might suppose that . . . those who lived later had a definite advantage over earlier generations. . . . But that is not Hegel's opinion. . . . Thus the individual has one side according to which he is not drawn into the stream of historical life, but is as it were immediately related to the absolute spirit" (173). "Peace and conciliation of opposition do not lie in the distance of an infinite process as an ideal yet to be reached, but are already inwardly present at every moment of the whole course of history" (174).

[28] G. van der Leeuw, *Religion in Essence and Manifestation* (transl. J. E. Turner, 1938), Chap. 84, 3.

nately, the character of your talent depends on the tone, i.e., on the moment. Since a succession of consecutive moments is, however, always a kind of eternity, it was given to you to find permanence in the transitory and thus to satisfy fully not only me but also the spirit of Hegel, insofar as I understand it."

PART

IV

Synopsis

Has one understood me?—*Dionysus versus the Crucified*—

—EH IV 9

12

NIETZSCHE'S REPUDIATION
OF CHRIST

In truth, there was only *one* Christian, and he died on
the cross.—A 39.

The most serious Christians have always been well disposed toward me.—EH 1 7.

In a now famous conversation, Goethe retorted: "I pagan? Well,
after all I let Gretchen be executed and Ottilie [in the *Elective
Affinities*] starve to death; don't people find that Christian
enough? What do they want that would be more Christian?" [1]
The sarcasm of this brief rebuttal crystallizes—more clearly than
Nietzsche's excessive polemics—the contrast between the original
"glad tidings" (evangel) and the resentful bourgeois morality that
purports to be Christian even while it insists on throwing the first
stone.

Nietzsche's repudiation of Christ cannot be understood—any
more than can Kierkegaard's *Attack on Christendom*—unless one
distinguishes between contemporary Christianity and the original
gospel; and Nietzsche further differentiates between Jesus of
Nazareth and the Christ of the creeds. Discrimination between
these conceptions makes possible a clear and systematic exposition of Nietzsche's views. And Nietzsche's position is so intimately
related to the rest of his thought that his philosophy cannot be
fully understood apart from it.

---

[1] *Goethes Gespräche,* ed. F. von Biedermann, II (1909), 62. Elsewhere Goethe
referred to himself as an "old pagan" and exclaimed: "We want to remain
pagans. Long live paganism!" (*Ibid.,* 354 and 396.)

We shall begin by considering Nietzsche's conception of Jesus, whom he respected—although what he has to say of Jesus is designed to shock any devoutly Christian reader. Then we shall analyze Nietzsche's repudiation of faith in Christ and see how his critique throws light on his over-all view of truth, reason, and faith. Finally, Nietzsche's opposition to Christian morality must be considered—and this involves not only an account of his critique; one must also ask what Nietzsche proposed to put in its place.

I

Most famous among Nietzsche's pronouncements about Jesus is his epigram: "In truth, there was only *one* Christian, and he died on the cross." Nietzsche himself went on:

> The "evangel" *died* on the cross. What has been called "evangel" from that moment was actually the opposite of that which *he* had lived: *"ill* tidings," a *dysangel* [A 39].

While it is evident that Nietzsche would make a sharp distinction between the message of Jesus and the creed of the disciples, it would be quite false were one to conclude that Nietzsche accepted the original "glad tidings." They serve him as a welcome contrast and antithesis to later Christianity, and he takes pleasure in pointing to the "world-historical irony" of this juxtaposition —but he is critical even of Jesus himself.

Nietzsche's attitude depends on his conception of Jesus—and this conception is not only heretical theologically, but does not recommend itself on purely historical grounds. This is not the place for a comparative study or evaluation of various conceptions of Jesus—only Nietzsche's view must be outlined briefly because his attitude toward Jesus is incomprehensible apart from it.

Nietzsche offers two pictures of Jesus: one from the outside— a polemical attempt at reconstructing history—and one from the inside—an equally polemical attempt at reconstructing what Nietzsche provocatively calls "the *psychology of the Redeemer"* (A 28). The *external* perspective leads to the following vision:

> I fail to see against what the rebellion—as whose cause Jesus has been understood or *misunderstood*—may have been di-

rected, if it was not a rebellion against the Jewish church—church exactly in the same sense in which we use the word today. It was a rebellion against "the good and the just," against "the saints of Israel," against the hierarchy of society—*not* against its corruption, but against caste, privilege, order, and formula; it was the *disbelief* in "higher men," the *No* to all that was priest or theologian. But the hierarchy which was thus questioned, even if only for a moment, was the lake-dwelling on which alone the Jewish people, amid the "water," could continue to exist, the hard-won *last* chance of survival, the residue of its independent political existence. An attack on this was an attack on the deepest instinct of a people, on the toughest life-will that has ever existed in any people on earth. This holy anarchist, who summoned the people at the bottom, the outcastes and "sinners," the *pariahs* within Judaism, to negate the dominant order—using language, if the Gospels could be trusted, that today, too, would still lead to Siberia—was a political criminal insofar as political criminals were at all possible in an *absurdly unpolitical* community. This brought him to the cross: the proof for this is the inscription on the cross. He died for *his* guilt. All evidence is lacking, however often it has been claimed, that he died for the guilt of others [A 27].

This is Nietzsche's very deliberate antithesis to the Christian tradition, designed to give offense to Christian readers. It does not represent Nietzsche's own estimate of Jesus—and he immediately goes on to say: "A completely different question is whether he was at all conscious of any such opposition."

This question Nietzsche answers in the negative. Jesus' own sense of his mission is not even touched upon by any contemplation of external repercussions. What is needed therefor is a picture of "the psychological type of the Redeemer":

Renan, that buffoon in *psychologicis,* has introduced the two most inappropriate concepts possible into his explanation of the Jesus type: the concept of *genius* and the concept of the *hero.* . . . But if anything is unevangelical it is the concept of the hero. Just the opposite of all wrestling, of all feeling-oneself-in-a-struggle has here become instinct: the incapacity for resistance becomes morality here ("resist not evil"—the most profound word of the Gospels, their key in a certain sense), blessedness in peace, in gentleness, in not *being able* to be an enemy. What are the "glad tidings"? True life, eternal life has been found—it is not promised, it is here, it is *in you:* as a living in love, in love without subtraction and exclusion, without regard for station. Everyone is the child of God—Jesus definitely presumes nothing for himself alone—and as a child of God everyone is equal to everyone. To make a *hero* of Jesus! And even more, what a misunderstanding is the word "genius"! Our whole concept, our cultural concept of "spirit," has no meaning whatever in the world in which Jesus lives. Spoken with the precision of a physiologist, even an entirely different word would still be more nearly fitting here [A 29].

In the version of the *Antichrist* published by Nietzsche's sister after he had become insane, the "entirely different word" was omitted; and one may presume that she, like most other readers, must have seen nothing in this word but blasphemy. On the other hand, the word in question would have made explicit Nietzsche's reference and the authority on whom he relied "in *psychologicis*": Dostoevsky—"the only psychologist, by the way, from whom I learned something" (G IX 45). In another passage in the *Antichrist* that was not expurgated, Nietzsche speaks of "this queer and sick world into which the Gospels introduce us —a world out of a Russian novel in which the scum of society, nervous diseases, and 'childlike' idiocy seem to give each other a rendezvous," and concludes:

> It is regrettable that no Dostoevsky lived near this most interesting decadent—I mean somebody who would have known how to sense the very stirring charm of such a mixture of the sublime, the sick, and the childlike [A 31; cf. W Epilogue].

Even without the still more offensive explicitness of the censored passage—which reads, "the *word idiot*" [2]—it seems plain that

---

[2] This was first revealed in print by Hofmiller, "Nietzsche," 82, in an attempt to prove that Nietzsche must have been insane when he wrote it. The association with Dostoevsky went unnoticed. While Nietzsche never mentions *The Idiot*, he freely owns how deeply he was impressed by Dostoevsky after discovering him early in 1887—and it was in the following year that the word "idiot" assumed a sudden significance in Nietzsche's writings.

When editing previously published passages for inclusion in NCW, he inserted "idiot" in sections 2 and 3 (cf. W 5; G II 7; A 11, 26, 42, 51, 52, 53; EH-W 2; WM 154, 431, 437, 734, 800, and 808); and his letters to Brandes and Strindberg, Oct. 20 and Dec. 7, 1888, also suggest that he associated the word with Dostoevsky. He may not have read the whole novel, but seems to have been acquainted with the central conception.

Some very striking parallels in Dostoevsky's and Nietzsche's works are admittedly not reducible to any influence. Thus "The Pale Criminal" in *Zarathustra* I reminds us instantly of Raskolnikov, and Thomas Mann actually takes it for a deliberate portrait of Dostoevsky's hero (*Neue Studien,* 78)—but it appeared in print in 1883. In the case of *The Idiot,*

Nietzsche conceived of Jesus in the image of Dostoevsky's *Idiot*.

This conception of the Redeemer is the clue both to Nietzsche's reverence for Jesus and to his critique: his whole attitude toward Jesus hinges upon the "something" he "learned" from Dostoevsky. Nietzsche was, of course, aware of the discrepancies between his picture and that found in the Gospels; but he thought that any differences could be explained in terms of the psychology of the disciples and first followers. And he insisted that some features might have been accurately preserved, "however crippled or covered up by alien traits—as the type of Francis of Assisi is preserved in his legends in spite of their being legends" (A 29). In conclusion one may cite Nietzsche's conception of the death of Jesus:

> This "bringer of glad tidings" died as he had lived, as he had *taught—not* to "redeem men" but to show how one must live. This *practice* is his legacy to mankind: his behavior before the judges, before the catchpoles, before the accusers and all kinds of slander and scorn—his behavior on the *cross*. He does not resist, he does not defend his right, he takes no step to ward off the worst; on the contrary, *he provokes it*. And he begs, he suffers, he loves *with* those, *in* those who do him evil. *Not* to resist, *not* to be angry, *not* to hold responsible—but to resist not even the evil one—to *love* him [A 35].

Nietzsche's evaluation depends on his notion of the facts. He had come to the conclusion that one must "estimate the *power*

---

however, the evidence is of quite another sort: cf. especially A 31, cited in the text above.

Incidentally, Thomas Mann also errs in thinking that Nietzsche nowhere mentions Tolstoi (*ibid.*)—cf. GM III 26, A 7, and WM 82, 434, 1020. On the other hand, it has been claimed that the picture offered in the *Antichrist* of the original gospel is simply "taken over" from Tolstoi's *My Religion*. (E. Hirsch, "Nietzsche und Luther," *Luther-Jahrbuch* 1920/21, 98.) Indeed, Tolstoi declares in Chapter I that the words "Resist not evil" were to him "the key that opened all the rest"; and the image of the key reappears in A 29, cited above. But one must ignore the whole context and point of Nietzsche's sentence to find here an instance of plagiarism—or even of agreement—as Hirsch does. Yet Hofmiller, *Friedrich Nietzsche*, 34 f., accepts without reservation Hirsch's account. Schestow, *Tolstoi und Nietzsche* and *Dostojewski und Nietzsche* offers comparisons without going into questions of influence.

Tolstoi's interpretation of the original gospel seems to have made a profound impression on Nietzsche (see also A 38, quoted below at the beginning of section II); but Nietzsche, unlike Tolstoi, found the original gospel, too, unacceptable.

of a *will*" (and thus also the worth of a man) "by how much resistance, pain, and torture it endures and knows to turn to its advantage" (WM 382). Here was indeed endurance almost beyond belief, but complete indifference to advantage. Here was serenity but not self-control—for there was nothing to be controlled. "Here we find blessedness in peace, in gentleness, in not *being able* to be an enemy" (A 29). This was not Nietzsche's ideal of the passionate man who controls his passions—nor, of course, an embodiment of the extirpation of the passions which Nietzsche associated with later Christianity—but a childlike state of freedom from the passions. In the *Antichrist* Nietzsche thus speaks of a "case of delayed . . . puberty" (A 32), and Zarathustra already had proclaimed:

> He died too early; he himself would have recanted his teaching had he reached my age. Noble enough was he to recant [I 21].

In the chapter in *Zarathustra,* as well as in the picture of Jesus before his judges, a deliberate contrast is intended—and it will be shown later that Nietzsche himself "received the decisive thought" about how he ought to live from the behavior of another man before his judges.

II

Nietzsche's repudiation of Christ—as distinguished from Jesus—is not tempered by reverence or restraint. In the past his vehement opposition to Christian morality has distracted attention from his equally impassioned critique of the Christian "faith," but this critique is a focal point of Nietzsche's thought and was so considered by Nietzsche himself. Hence we cannot pass it by in silence without sacrificing an accurate estimation of his philosophic position.

It may be well to distinguish two major phases of Nietzsche's critique of faith in Christ and to epitomize them briefly as *faith versus action* and *faith versus reason.* Under the first heading one may consider first of all Nietzsche's prophetic indignation against the hypocrisy of those who—to use Elijah's words—limp on both legs:

> Where has the last feeling of decency and self-respect gone when even our statesmen, . . . anti-Christians through and

through in their deeds, still call themselves Christians today and attend communion? . . . *Whom* then does Christianity negate? *What* does it call "world"? That one is a soldier, that one is a judge, that one is a patriot; that one resists; that one sees to one's honor; that one seeks one's advantage; that one is *proud*. . . . What a *miscarriage of falseness* must modern man be that he is *not ashamed* to be called a Christian in spite of this [A 38].

Here Nietzsche opposes "faith" as that which modern man professes hypocritically without having a thought of doing anything about it—except going to communion. The point is expressed even more sharply in *The Will to Power*:

The Christians have never practiced the actions Jesus prescribed to them; and the impudent garrulous talk about the "justification by faith" and its supreme and sole significance is only the consequence of the Church's lack of courage and will to profess the *works* Jesus demanded. The Buddhist does not act like the non-Buddhist; the *Christian acts like all the world* and has a Christianity of ceremonies and *moods* [WM 191].

Nietzsche is not satisfied with insisting on the sharp antithesis of evangel and Church which the Reformers had stressed—and the picture, occasionally encountered in the literature, of Nietzsche as essentially "a Protestant preacher" is misleading, though certain passages in his writings are of course reminiscent of the early Luther:

The *Church* is precisely that against which Jesus preached [WM 168].

That mankind lies on its knees before the opposite of that which was the origin, the meaning, the *right* of the evangel, that in the concept "Church" it has pronounced holy just that which the "bringer of the glad tidings" felt to be *beneath* and *behind* himself—one would look in vain for a greater example of *world-historical irony* [A 36].

Nietzsche, however, is determined to include Luther in his accusations, and his attack on Luther's *sola fide* and on Luther's great example, Paul, is even more impassioned than his diatribes against the Church—quite apart from the fact that by "Church" he means Protestantism no less than Catholicism.

The "justification by faith" seems to Nietzsche an inversion of Jesus' evangel. He never tires of insisting that the legacy of Jesus was essentially a practice, and he is convinced—presumably by Dostoevsky—that "even today *such* a life is possible, for *certain* human beings even necessary: genuine original Christianity will be possible at all times" (A 39). The Christian religion, however, seems to him to be founded on Paul's denial of this proposition—a denial that Nietzsche would explain by saying that Paul knew that for *him* such a life was not possible. Nor was it possible for St. Augustine, Luther, or Calvin. Paul is for Nietzsche *"the first Christian"* (M 68); the discoverer of faith as a remedy against the incapacity for what one deems to be right action; the man who made it possible for pagans the world over to persist in their own way of life while calling themselves Christians.

Without Paul, "there would be no Christendom." Unable to fulfill even the Jewish law—not to speak of Jesus' so much more demanding way of life—he conceived of faith in Christ as a substitute. This was his "escape" and "the perfect revenge" against the law and those who were able to follow it. Paul had the same experience which Luther had centuries later when he realized his inability "to become the perfect man of the clerical ideal in his monastery" and "one day began to hate the clerical ideal and the pope, and the saints, and the whole clergy, with a true and deadly hatred, all the more the less he could own it to himself" (M 68). This concomitance of "escape" and "revenge"— "faith" as a way out of one's inability "to get rid of one's sins" and faith as a screen for fanatical hatred—that seems to Nietzsche the essence of "the Christianity of Paul, Augustine, and Luther" (XVI, 323 f.). And that is, to his mind, the most incredible inversion of the gospel.

Confronted with the "most gruesome paradox" of "the cross, which was generally reserved for the rabble," the disciples reacted with hatred against the dominant order and began to assume that Jesus, too, had been a rebel against *"dominant Jewry."*

> Until then this warlike, this no-saying, no-doing trait in his image had been *lacking;* even more: he had been its opposite. Evidently, the small community did *not* understand the main point, the exemplary character of this kind of death, the freedom, the superiority *over* any feeling of *ressentiment* . . . His disciples were far from *forgiving* this death—which would have been evangelic in the highest sense. . . .

The cross became the turning point: "Precisely the most unevangelic feeling, *revenge,* came to the top again. . . . One needed 'retribution,' 'judgment' "—as if these were not the very things the evangel had denied; and the "kingdom of God" was now construed "as a judgment over the enemies," "as the final act, as a promise," while "the evangel had been precisely the presence, the fulfillment, the *actuality* of this 'kingdom.'" Along with the evangel, the figure of Jesus was inverted into its very opposite when the early Christians "carried the whole contempt and bitterness against the Pharisees and theologians into the type of the master" (A 40).

Nietzsche concludes that Paul alone made it possible for these resentful people to consider themselves Christians. Paul substituted faith in Christ for the Christlike life:

> What has been called "evangel" from that moment was actually the opposite of that which *he* had lived: *"ill* tidings," a *dysangel.* It is false to the point of nonsense to find the mark of the Christian in a "faith," for instance, in the faith in redemption through Christ: only Christian *practice,* a life such as he lived who died on the cross, is Christian [A 39].

> The "glad tidings" was followed on its heels by the *very worst:* that of Paul. In Paul was embodied the opposite type of that of the "bringer of the glad tidings": the genius in hatred, in the vision of hatred, in the inexorable logic of hatred [A 42].

The conception that "God had given his son for the forgiveness of sins, as a *sacrifice,*" "the *trespass sacrifice*—moreover in its most revolting, most barbarous form—the sacrifice of the guiltless for the guilty": this seems to Nietzsche "gruesome paganism"—and faith in this, a travesty on the evangel.

> From now on there enters into the type of the Redeemer, step by step: the doctrine of judgment and return, the doctrine of death as a sacrificial death, the doctrine of the *resurrection* with which the whole concept of "blessedness," the whole and only actuality of the evangel, is conjured away—in favor of a state *after* death!—Paul . . ." [A 41].

The kingdom of God, Nietzsche agrees, is in the hearts of men—and when it is sought in another life, the central insight of Jesus seems to him to be betrayed. Beyond that even, the conception of another life seems fateful to Nietzsche, and one may perhaps distinguish three reasons. None of them, to be sure, purports to refute the doctrine of the resurrection, nor does Nietzsche argue about that point at all. He considered the conception of the resurrection one of those impressive "symbols" that had been transformed into "crudities" by being made into dogmas (WM 170). That the dogma cannot be proved, Nietzsche takes for granted; and under the circumstances he feels entitled to an agnostic attitude, metaphysically. Psychologically, however, he is concerned with the state of mind which this doctrine has engendered or confirmed.

First, the conception of a life after death has historically furnished the basis for the deprecation of this life. The expectation of perfection in another world has made men condone their imperfection in this world. Instead of striving to become perfect here and now, as Jesus had exhorted them to do, they put their trust in the distant future.

Secondly, the deprecation of this world could be carried to the extent of a complete disvaluation of anything a man might do in this life—and this aspect of the Christian faith made it possible for Christianity "to turn the mills of the State's forces" (U III 6). Thus Luther's impassioned disvaluation of the secular realm furnished the philosophic basis for his repudiation of monastic life and celibacy, for his occasionally fierce deprecation of all moral effort, and for his doctrine of absolute obedience to the authorities of *this* world. They simply did not seem to him to have the same importance as the Church against which he himself had rebelled. The doctrine of two worlds thus becomes almost a symbol of a double standard. There is a Christian world where one will be perfect and in which one must have faith, and there is a pagan world, which one perceives all around oneself, where one cannot be perfect and where those "who have faith and know that their sins are borne by Christ are just." [3] Faith takes the place of action: instead of perfecting oneself, one has faith that Christ was perfect—and meanwhile there is a Church that, instead of insisting that man leave father and mother and break with conformity, insists that man conform to the Church in matters of faith and to the State in matters of action. Jesus' "Render to Caesar the things that are Caesar's" appeared to Nietzsche as an expression of the sublime indifference felt by those absorbed in the task of self-perfection. Luther's doctrine, on the other hand, seemed to him an escape from this very task and a complete inversion of the gospel.

---

[3] Luther, *Sämtliche Schriften*, ed. cit., VI, 634; see also IV, 1593; VII, 166; IX, 1133; XII, 1406.

The third point, finally, is that the conception of the resurrection furnished the setting for a new doctrine of retribution—of revenge and reward. This is strongly brought out in Nietzsche's vitriolic comments on a number of quotations from the Gospels:

> I give some examples of what these little people put into their heads, what they *put into the mouth* of their master: without exception, confessions of "beautiful souls":
> "And whosoever shall not receive you, nor hear you, when ye depart thence, shake off the dust under your feet for a testimony against them. Verily I say unto you, It shall be more tolerable for Sodom and Gomorrha in the day of judgment, than for that city" (Mark 6:11)—How *evangelic!* . . .
> "Whosoever will come after me, let him deny himself, and take up his cross, and follow me. For—" (. . . Christian morality is refuted by its *For's:* its "reasons" refute . . .) Mark 8:34. . . .
> "For if ye love them which love you, *what reward have ye?* . . ." (Matt. 5:46)—Principle of "Christian love": it wants in the end to be *paid* well.
> "But *if ye* forgive not men their trespasses, neither will your Father forgive your trespasses" (Matt. 6:15)—Very compromising for said "Father" . . . [A 45].

Thus the conception of the resurrection made possible a new doctrine of retribution. And Nietzsche charges that the Christian "faith" made it possible for men not only to persist in their unchristian behavior, but also to indulge their lust for revenge by hoping for the eventual torture and destruction of their persecutors. Nietzsche's reference, in this context, to Tertullian and Aquinas (GM I 15) has already been cited in a previous chapter. He may also have had in mind Paul's admonitions: "Bless them which persecute you: bless, and curse not. . . . Avenge not yourselves, but rather give place unto wrath: for it is written, Vengeance is mine; I will repay, saith the Lord. Therefore if thine enemy hunger, feed him; if he thirst, give him drink: for in so doing thou shalt heap coals of fire on his head" (Rom. 12:14 and 19–20).

Although Paul is partly quoting from the Old Testament —and many readers would construe such passages as a relapse into Judaism, while finding the Christian spirit in Paul's hymn on charity—Nietzsche considers Christian precisely the revaluation of the evangel by the addition of a most unevangelic promise. On the other hand, Paul's "song in honor of charity is nothing Christian," according to Nietzsche, but a flaring up of "the eternal flame" of Judaism (WM 175). At first glance, this may seem only perverse—yet it is not sheer spite but understandable as coming from a man whose whole conception of historical Christianity hinges on Luther. For although Luther claimed to have derived his version of the gospel from St. Paul's Epistles, and though he went to the extent of repudiating the Epistle of James in the name of Paul, he did not accept the second half of Paul's pronouncement: "And now abideth faith, hope, charity, these three; but the greatest of these is charity" (I Cor. 13:13). On the contrary, Luther taught consistently that "although charity is . . . a beautiful . . . virtue, faith is infinitely much greater and more sublime"; and Luther's writings abound in statements like this: "the sophistic doctrine of faith that receives its true character only through charity . . . is from the Devil and confuses us into Turkish and Jewish errors." [4]

To be sure, Luther did not mean to repudiate love and works of love, however many extreme passages one could quote from his works almost at random. He had insisted that "Faith alone, without any works, makes just before God"—but he had also taught that "He does not have a truthful faith in whom the works of love do not follow faith." [5] On superficial examination, he seems to contradict himself, especially when he asserts that "Faith without works, i.e., a sentimental thought, a mere delusion and dream of the heart, is false and does not justify." Luther's point, however, is that what *justifies* is the faith—not the charity or the works it engenders—but he also believes and insists that faith *does* engender these. Thus he says on the same page: "We, too, say that faith without works is worth nothing and useless. This is understood by the Papists and zealots to mean that faith without works does not justify." [6] It is as if the works of love, and love itself, were mere inefficacious epiphenomena of the faith that alone makes just, "and one should reject and

---

[4] *Ibid.*, IV, 2061; I, 948. The German word for "charity" in Nietzsche, Luther, and the New Testament is *"Liebe."* Concerning St. James, see *ibid.*, XIV, 105.

[5] *Ibid.*, XVI, 1688 f. and IX, 635; cf. IV, 223; XI, 1460; XIV, 89; XIX, 1470; XXII, 454.

[6] *Ibid.*, IX, 210. The quotation from Luther that immediately follows in my text is from *ibid.*, I, 947.

repudiate the harmful notion of faith that receives its true character only through charity, since it gives and credits all to charity
but takes all from faith."

Such passages in Luther must be kept in mind if one wants
to understand Nietzsche's apparently paradoxical assertion that
charity is Jewish and not Christian, and that the essential characteristic of historical Christianity is faith. And this faith appears
to him as the antithesis of the Christian practice:

> "Faith" was at all times, for example in Luther, only a cloak, a
> pretext, a *screen* behind which the instincts played their game
> —a shrewd *blindness* about the dominance of *certain* instincts.
> "Faith"—I have already called it the characteristic Christian
> *shrewdness*—one always *spoke* of "faith," but one always acted
> from instinct alone [A 39].

Again, a note from *The Will to Power* is, if possible, still more
emphatic:

> . . . Faith . . . The background is a deep conviction of Luther
> and his like of their incapacity for Christian works—a per-
> sonal fact shrouded by an extreme mistrust whether *every kind*
> of action is not altogether sin and from the Devil: so that the
> value of existence is transferred to single high tension states
> of *inactivity* (prayer, effusion, etc.). In the end he would be
> right: the instincts expressed in the whole activity of the Reform-
> ers are the most brutal there are [WM 192].

A Luther—this seems to be Nietzsche's point—*cannot* live
like Dostoevsky's Prince Myshkin: hence the "conviction of
Luther and his like of their incapacity for Christian works";
hence also Nietzsche's final judgment "in the end he would be
right." If Luther is, in physique, temperament, and character,
the incarnate antithesis of Dostoevsky's Prince, the other Reformers—men like Calvin or John Knox—were no Myshkins
either.

With this consideration in mind, Nietzsche can also turn
against Luther's assertion that the Christian faith will produce
Christian charity and Christian works:

> Still this fundamental error is propagated through Protestant
> teachers: that only faith matters and that out of faith works
> must follow necessarily. This is simply not true . . . [M 22].

Luther's and Calvin's faith—not to speak of John Knox and
Cotton Mather, or of Torquemada and Loyola—did not enable

them to lead a Christlike life: rather it was, Nietzsche thinks, an escape from, and a screen for, "their incapacity for Christian works." In his few references to Calvin, Nietzsche invariably refers to his fanatical "cruelty," which he infers less from the burning of Servetus than from Calvin's doctrines of predestination and eternal damnation (MA I 101; M 113; GM II 7); and the many passages in which Luther appears associate him almost always with wrath and hatred and coarseness. The German Reformation is envisaged as *"Der Bauernaufstand des Geistes"*— the peasants' revolt of the spirit (FW 358; cf. 97; GM III 22; XVI, 327, 353, 388).

III

In this conception of the "peasants' revolt," Nietzsche's critique of faith as opposed to action meets with his critique of faith as opposed to reason—and we shall now consider the second major phase of Nietzsche's repudiation of faith in Christ: *faith versus reason*. Of the two, this may well be the more crucial and significant for Nietzsche's thought—and its bearing on Nietzsche's alleged irrationalism and romanticism should be obvious. As a matter of fact, this aspect of Nietzsche's anti-Christianity has usually been ignored together with the whole heritage of the Enlightenment, which is so essential to Nietzsche's philosophy that it cannot be subtracted without perverting the central import of his thought.

> *The Temptress.* Honesty is the great temptress of all fanatics. What seemed to Luther to approach in the form of the Devil or a beautiful woman, and what he warded off in that uncouth manner, was probably honesty and perhaps in rarer cases even truth [M 511].

This brief aphorism, quoted in full, may seem to be no more than an inspiration of malice. One cannot understand what Nietzsche means if one has not read Luther:

> Whoever wants to be a Christian should tear the eyes out of his reason. . . .

> Reason and the wisdom of our flesh condemn the wisdom of the word of God.

Here [in matters of faith] you must part with reason and not
know anything of it and even kill it; else one will not get into
the kingdom of heaven.[7]

What Nietzsche opposes is, in other words, any doctrine of
double truth. For any *credo quia absurdum est* and for any
sacrificium intellectus, Nietzsche has only scorn—and he frequently gives vent to it throughout his writings. He even proposes an alteration of this famous phrase into *credo quia ab-
surdus sum* (M 417).

With the German Reformation, however, the double standard seems to Nietzsche to have become victorious. "Definition
of Protestantism: the partial paralysis of Christianity—*and* of
reason" (A 10). The new emphasis on faith means not only the
negation of the Christian *practice* but also the partial paralysis
of reason. " 'Faith' as an imperative is the *veto* against science"
(A 47). Nietzsche does not only have in mind the natural sciences
but also what he considers the wanton falsification of history—
an important theme in the *Antichrist*—and the almost diametri-
cal opposition to the standards of his own field, philology:

> *The Philology of Christianity.* How little Christianity educates
> the sense of honesty and justice can be seen pretty well from
> the writings of its scholars: they advance their conjectures as
> blandly as dogmas and are hardly ever honestly perplexed by
> the exegesis of a Biblical verse. Again and again they say, "I
> am right, for it is written," and the interpretation that follows
> is of such impudent arbitrariness that a philologist is stopped
> in his tracks, torn between anger and laughter, and keeps ask-
> ing himself: Is it possible? Is this honest? Is it even decent?
> What dishonesties of this sort are still perpetrated from Prot-
> estant pulpits today, how . . . *the art of reading badly* [is] for-
> mally inculcated upon the people—all this will be underesti-
> mated only by those who go to church either never or always. In
> the end, however, what are we to expect of the after-effects of
> a religion that enacted during the centuries of its foundation
> that unheard-of philological farce about the Old Testament?
> I refer to the attempt to pull away the Old Testament from
> under the feet of the Jews—with the claim that it . . . *belongs*
> to the Christians as the *true* Israel, while the Jews had merely
> usurped it. And now the Christians yielded to a rage of inter-
> pretation and interpolation, which could not possibly have been
> accompanied by a good conscience. However much the Jewish

---

[7] *Ibid.,* v, 452; v, 528; vII, 985 f.

scholars protested, everywhere in the Old Testament there were supposed to be references to Christ and only to Christ, and particularly to his cross. Wherever any piece of wood, a switch, a ladder, a twig, a tree, a willow, or a staff is mentioned, this was supposed to indicate a prophecy of the wood of the cross. . . . Has anybody who claimed this ever *believed* it? [M 84].

For Nietzsche there is no excuse for a double standard—for one set of principles for the exegesis of the Bible and another for the interpretation of other ancient texts. If the Christian approach to the Old Testament is at odds with the usual standards of philological or historical research—so much the worse for it.

The success of such double standards depended, according to Nietzsche, on the fact that the men who were most vocal in shaping Christianity were *ungeistig:* reason was not their strength. In antiquity the slaves of the Roman Empire, among whom Christianity first made spectacular progress, lacked the mental capacity for intellectual integrity and thus brought about "a revaluation of all ancient values": they could not appreciate their masters' "freedom from faith . . . 'Enlightenment' enrages: for the slave wants the unconditional, he understands only the tyrannical" (J 46). At the end of the Middle Ages, the Lutheran *Bauernaufstand* (peasants' revolt) parallels the ancient *Sklavenaufstand* (slaves' revolt). At this point, Nietzsche prefers the scholastic repudiation of any conflict of faith and reason to Luther's Protestantism:

> One wants to go *back* through the Church fathers to the Greeks, from the North to the South, from the formulas to the forms. . . . Arabesques, flourishes, Rococo of scholastic abstractions— still better . . . than the peasants' and plebes' reality of the European North, still a protest of higher spirituality against the peasants' war and plebes' revolt that became master of the spiritual tastes in the North of Europe and had its leader in the great "unspiritual man," in Luther [WM 419].

Luther is *ungeistig,* he deprecates reason, and he is therefore nowhere at all compared to Montaigne (XVI, 33). And from this point of view, Nietzsche—who notes elsewhere that "the Protestant minister is the grandfather of German philosophy" (A 10)[8]

---

[8] Cf. Heine's conception of "German philosophy" as the "daughter" of "the Protestant church," in Book 1 of *Die Romantische Schule.* Other parallels to Nietzsche in Book 1 include the conception of the Renaissance as a "far more effective" protest against the Church than Luther's, and above

—says: "in this respect German philosophy is a piece of Counter-Reformation" (WM 419). Both statements contain some truth: Leibniz' *Theodicy* is not only a product of German Protestantism, it is also a sustained protest against the doctrine of double truth, against any bifurcation of faith and reason, against any depreca-tion of *Geist;* and in Hegel—according to his own pronounce-ments, Germany's most Protestant, most Lutheran philosopher—the opposition to any dualism of faith and reason, the antithesis to any deprecation of reason, and the triumph of *Geist* reaches its height. What Nietzsche opposes are Leibniz's and Hegel's con-cessions to faith; what he applauds as "a piece of Counter-Reformation" is their rehabilitation of reason.

It is interesting to note that Kant, whose distinction of theo-retical and practical reason was a variation on the old theme of reason and faith, also believed in two worlds, one phenomenal and one noumenal, and in the immortality of the human soul in the "other," noumenal, world. Hegel, on the other hand, who vigorously denied any dualism of faith and reason, also rejected any doctrine of two worlds—and his attitude toward the popular doctrine of immortality is well illustrated by Heine's anecdote: "Altogether the conversation of Hegel was always a kind of monologue, sighed forth by fits and starts in a toneless voice. The baroqueness of his expressions often startled me. . . . One beautiful starry-skyed evening, we two stood next to each other at a window . . . and I talked of the stars with sentimental enthusiasm and called them the abode of the blessed. The master, however, grumbled to himself: 'The stars, hum! hum! the stars are only a gleaming leprosy in the sky.' For God's sake, I shouted, then there is no happy locality up there to reward virtues after death? He, however, staring at me with his pale eyes, said cuttingly: 'So you want to get a tip for having nursed your sick mother and for not having poisoned your dear brother?' " [9] The doctrine of two lives and worlds is a symbol of a double standard. There is, as it were, one world to be known by reason and another to be believed in by faith. There is, in Luther's words, "the wisdom of our flesh" and "the wisdom

---

all Heine's estimate of the medieval *Parsifal* as the essence of "romanti-cism," and of *Tristan and Isolde* as the "most beautiful poem of the Middle Ages"—precisely Nietzsche's later evaluation of the two Wagnerian operas.

[9] *Geständnisse (Sämtliche Werke,* Original-Ausgabe 1862, XIV, 278 f.).

of the word of God." Nietzsche, like Hegel, denied any such dualism.[10]

In his attack on faith as opposed to reason, Nietzsche made two points deserving special emphasis. First, conviction is no proof of truth. Any reference to the martyrs' blood is irrelevant in questions of truth:

> To prove a conviction is quite senseless; rather, it is important to prove that one has a right to be so convinced. Conviction is an objection [*Einwand*], a question mark, a *défi* . . . [XVI, 318; cf. WM 377, 456].

And Nietzsche concludes this note with a very emphatic parenthesis, accentuated by three exclamation points: "a very popular error: having the courage of one's convictions; rather it is a matter of having the courage for an *attack* on one's convictions!!!"

Writing up these ideas in the *Antichrist*, Nietzsche includes some epigrams that have become famous:

> Every conviction has its history . . . it *becomes* a conviction after *not* having been one for a long time, and after scarcely having been one for an even longer time. . . . In the son, that becomes conviction which in the father still was a lie. By lie I mean: wishing *not* to see something that one does see; wishing not to see something *as* one sees it. . . . The most common lie is that with which one lies to oneself; lying to others is relatively an exception. Now this wishing-*not*-to-see what one does see, this wishing not to see *as* one sees, is almost the first condition for all who are *party* in any sense: of necessity, the party man becomes a liar. German historiography, for example, is convinced that Rome represented despotism and that the Germanic tribes brought the spirit of freedom into the world: what is the difference between this conviction and a lie? [A 55].

"*Grosse Geister*," says Nietzsche, "are skeptics"—not party men. "Zarathustra is a skeptic" (A 54). Perhaps Nietzsche had failed

---

[10] This may be further evidence of Nietzsche's—and Hegel's—fundamental anti-romanticism: thus Lovejoy observes in the chapter "Coleridge and Kant's Two Worlds" (*op. cit.*, 275): "here—as in the most representative German Romantic writers—we see that one characteristic thing in the so-called Romantic influence was a revolt against naturalism, an ethical and metaphysical dualism, a philosophy of two worlds" (cf. *ibid.*, 246 ff.).

to make this plain enough when he wrote his *Zarathustra* some years before. "Strength and that *freedom* which issues from the force and over-force of the spirit [*Geist*] *prove* themselves by *skepsis*. . . . Convictions are prisons." They are criticized much as Nietzsche criticizes systems:

> Freedom from all kinds of convictions, to be *able* to see freely, is part of strength. . . . Conviction as a *means*. . . . Great passion uses and uses up convictions, it does not succumb to them—it knows itself sovereign. Conversely: the need for faith, for some kind of unconditional Yes and No, this Carlylism, if one will forgive me this word, is a need born of *weakness*. The man of faith . . . is necessarily a dependent man—one who cannot posit *himself* as an end . . . does not belong to *himself*, he can only be a means; he must be *used up*, he requires somebody to use him up. His instinct gives the highest honor to a morality of self-abnegation. . . . The man of faith is not free to have any conscience at all for questions of "true" and "untrue": to have integrity on *this* point would at once destroy him. The pathological condition of his perspective turns the convinced into fanatics—Savonarola, Luther, Rousseau, Robespierre, Saint-Simon—the opposition-type of the strong spirit who has become *free*. Yet the grand pose of these *sick* spirits, these epileptics of the concept, makes an impression on the great mass—the fanatics are picturesque; man prefers to see gestures rather than to hear *reasons* [A 54; cf. WM 457, 963].

If these quotations suggest Nietzsche's line of attack against adducing conviction as a proof, one may now turn to consider his equally outspoken attack on the presumption that what is useful or makes happy must be true. In his insistence that happiness and unhappiness are completely irrelevant to the truth of a proposition, Nietzsche is opposed not only to Pascal, the old Schelling, and Kierkegaard—who are fellow precursors of German existentialism—but also to William James. "Happiness and virtue are no arguments," nor should one forget "that making-unhappy and making-evil are just as little counter-arguments. Something might be true, though it were in the highest degree obnoxious and dangerous" (J 39). But if reason cannot decide the issue—is it not then "reasonable" to embrace that alternative which would be more conducive to our happiness? Do we not have a "right to believe"? Says Nietzsche: "Reason, the *right* of reason, does not extend that far" (A 10). Blessedness and pleasure are no proofs under any circumstances—"so little that it almost furnishes a counter-proof or in any case provokes the utmost suspicion against 'truth' when feelings of pleasure take part in the discussion of the question: 'what is true?' " Moreover Nietzsche doubts that there is any "pre-established harmony" between truth and pleasure:

> The experience of all severe, of all profoundly inclined spirits teaches the *opposite*. At every step, one has to wrestle for truth; one has had to surrender for it almost everything to which the heart, to which our love, our trust in life cling otherwise. That requires greatness of soul: the service of truth is the hardest service. What does it mean after all to have *integrity* in matters of the spirit? That one is severe against one's heart, that one despises "beautiful sentiments," that one makes of every Yes and No a matter of conscience! Faith makes blessed: *consequently*, it lies.
>
> That faith makes blessed under certain circumstances, that blessedness does not make of a fixed idea a *true* idea, that faith moves no mountains but *puts* mountains where there are none: a quick walk through a *madhouse* enlightens one sufficiently about this [A 50–51].

According to Nietzsche, utility, and even conduciveness to the preservation of life, is equally irrelevant to truth.

> How many people still make the inference: "one could not stand life if there were no God!" (or as they say in the circles of the Idealists: "one could not stand life if it lacked the ethical significance of its ground!")—consequently there *must* be a God (or an ethical significance of existence)! . . . what presumption to decree that all that is necessary for my preservation must also really *be there!* As if my preservation were anything necessary! [M 90].

> We have fixed a world for ourselves in which we can live—by assuming bodies, lines, planes, causes and effects, motion and rest, form and content: without these articles of faith nobody now could stand life. By that, however, they are still not at all proved. Life is no argument; among the conditions of life might be error [FW 121; cf. 110].

> A belief [*Glaube*] may be a necessary condition of life and *yet be false* [WM 483; cf. 487, 493, 497, and J 11].

Nietzsche's attitude is similar to Vaihinger's—and different from that of many Pragmatists—insofar as he insists that, though the intellect is an instrument, its figments should be frankly labeled as fictions. Utility, however great, is no argument for truth. [11]

The question arises, of course, from what point of view the fictions of the intellect could possibly be criticized and found out to be only fictions. With Kant, Nietzsche believes in reason's capacity for self-criticism—and the fictions in question may be found either to be self-contradictory or to contradict each other. To be bold in offering such criticisms is part of the service of truth.

> *To what extent we, too, are still pious.* In science, convictions have no rights of citizenship . . . only when they decide to descend to the modesty of a hypothesis, of a provisional experimental point of view, of a regulative fiction, may they be granted admission and even a certain value . . . though always with the restriction that they remain under police supervision, under the police of mistrust. Yet does this not mean . . . : only when a conviction *ceases* to be a conviction may it attain admission to science? Would not the discipline [*Zucht*] of the scientific spirit begin with this, no longer to permit oneself any convictions? Probably this is the case: but one must still ask whether, *in order that this discipline could begin,* there must not have been a conviction to begin with—and even such a commanding and unconditional one that it sacrificed all other convictions for its own sake. It is clear that science, too, rests on a faith; there is no science "without presuppositions." The question whether *truth* is needed must not only have been affirmed in advance, but affirmed to the extent that the principle, the faith, the conviction is expressed: *"nothing* is needed *more* than truth, and in relation to it all else has only a second-rate value."

Nietzsche then inquires whether "this unconditional will to truth" is "the will *not to let oneself be deceived"* or "the will *not to deceive."* He decides in favor of the second alternative.

---

[11] Thus one cannot agree with Barzun when he asserts at the end of a brilliant chapter on "Nietzsche contra Wagner" (in *Darwin, Marx, Wagner,* 1941) that Nietzsche, after consistently attacking romanticism "in his early and middle periods," was in the end "brought back to a new romanticism," resorted to "the primacy of faith," and "became a Pragmatist" (333). *The Will to Power,* to which Barzun offers a general reference, without citing any particular passage, does not support this view (cf., e.g. WM 172, 192, 253, 377, 445–57, 483, 487, 493, 497, 593, 920, 963, 1041), nor does it always represent Nietzsche's final position, as its fragments antedate the *Antichrist* and other late works.

Not letting oneself be deceived really means not deceiving one-self—and "I will not deceive *myself*" is really included in the decision "I will not deceive." Moreover, Nietzsche explicitly seeks to refute the suggestion that this decision is founded on utility.

> What do you know in advance of the character of existence to be able to decide whether the greater advantage is on the side of the unconditionally mistrustful or of the unconditionally trusting? Yet if both are required, much trust *and* much mis-trust: whence might science then take its unconditional faith, its conviction on which it rests, that truth is more important than anything else, even than any other conviction? Just this conviction could not have originated, if both truth *and* un-truth showed themselves continually to be useful, as is the case. Thus the undeniably existing faith in science cannot owe its origin to such a utility calculus but must rather have originated *in spite* of the fact that the inutility and dangerousness of the "will to truth," of "truth at any price" is proved to it con-tinually.

Nietzsche concludes that the "will to truth," not being founded on considerations of utility, means—"there remains no choice—'I will not deceive, not even myself': *and with this we are on the ground of morality.*"

Nietzsche goes further: "appearance, error, deception, dissimu-lation, delusion, self-delusion" all aid life; life "has always shown itself to be on the side of the most unscrupulous *polytropoi*":[12] is not then the "will to truth" a mere "quixotism"? No, says Nietzsche—it is something rather more terrifying, "namely a principle that is hostile to life and destructive," perhaps even "a hidden will to death."

> But one will have gathered what I am driving at: namely that it is still a *metaphysical faith* upon which our faith in science rests—that even we devotees of knowledge today, we godless ones and anti-metaphysicians, still take *our* fire, too, from the flame that a faith, thousands of years old, has kindled: that Christian faith, which was also the faith of Plato, that God is truth, that truth is divine [FW 344].

---

[12] The wily and versatile; literally, the much-turned, much-traveled. *Poly-tropos* is an epithet applied to Odysseus in the first line of the *Odyssey*, and while there is no good equivalent for it in English, there are two in German: *viel-gewandt* and, even better, *viel-verschlagen*.

That is the conception of the author of *The Gay Science,* written
years after *Zarathustra;* that is how Nietzsche considers himself
"still pious"; that is Nietzsche's faith.[13]

---

[13] In a chapter on "Religious Psychology," which deals mainly with the
Genealogy, Danto argues for a different interpretation of Nietzsche's
attitude toward truth, and in two footnotes he takes issue with me
(*op. cit.,* 187, 191 f.). But the level of his argument borders on the incredible. His book abounds in quotations, and he states that "The translations, despite a merely adequate German, are all my own" (14). Adequate
for what? Danto does not realize that the second part of the *Genealogy*
deals with the "bad conscience": he thinks *schlechtes Gewissen* means
"bad consciousness" (164, 180)—a blunder not to be found in any previous
translation of Nietzsche. The German words sprinkled through the text
are almost invariably wrong, and those that appear several times are
misspelled consistently. The translations abound in serious mistakes and
omissions that are not indicated: on pages 189–94 I checked the nine
quotations set off in slightly smaller type, and every single one of them
is disfigured by important mistranslations or unacknowledged omissions,
or both. These omissions range from a few crucial words to nine lines.
An extended reply to this kind of misreading of Nietzsche would be
useless. But three points can be made briefly.

First, he leans largely on GM III 24 ff. and on FW 344, which is
quoted in GM III 24. In my commentary on the *Genealogy* I have offered
a detailed interpretation of these sections and, without mentioning
Danto, demonstrated that his interpretation is untenable. For Nietzsche's
own asceticism see also, e.g., EH–V 3, EH I 8, EH II 9.

Second: The other passage about which Danto takes issue with me
is G IX 14. Here (187) he follows the lead of Hanna's *Lyrical Existentialists* (167) in not quoting Nietzsche's parenthesis, which shows that the
reading urged against me is wrong. Both men also ignore FW 2, cited on
the same page of my Chapter 8, section I, and indeed all the evidence I
present. (Thomas Hanna, whose book deserves even less consideration than
Danto's—see my review, listed in the Bibliography—actually charges me
with "a failure to grasp the notion of the will to power as an inner
asceticism whose activity is one of stylization" (166), and then presents
as his own discovery what I developed, e.g., in Chapter 8, section III,
of this volume; toward the end of Chapter 9; and at the end of section I
of Chapter 11.)

Third: It is pointless to base interpretations of Nietzsche on a few
snippets from his writings, paying no attention to the context—this is
deliberate in Danto's case (19)—or to what Nietzsche says elsewhere on
the same subject.

If Danto's avowed attempt to link Nietzsche with analytic philosophy
were not so timely, and if he were not a respectable philosopher, one
might simply ignore his book. But when a reputable writer strays out
of his field, most readers have no way of telling that the book exceeds
the author's competence. Danto's book ranks well below Brinton's
Nietzsche and Karl Popper's notorious reading of Hegel, with which
I have dealt elsewhere.

Thus Nietzsche scorns any utilitarian or pragmatic approach to truth and insists that those who search for it must never ask whether the truth will profit or harm them—and yet he considers the will to truth a form of the will to power. If his position should seem inconsistent, the apparent contradiction vanishes as soon as one recalls the crucial difference between Nietzsche's conception of power and Bacon's or Hobbes'. To Bacon, knowledge meant power over nature, and truth could thus be utilized as a means to new comforts. For Hobbes, too, power was essentially a tool, an instrument, a means for security. Nietzsche, on the other hand, values power not as a means but as the state of being that man desires for its own sake as his own ultimate end. And truth he considers an essential aspect of this state of being. Self-perfection and ultimate happiness are not compatible with self-deception and illusion. Petty pleasures may depend on illusions, and truth may spell discomfort and suffering—but renouncing truth for that reason would be a sign of weakness and preclude our attainment of that state of being short of which we can never find lasting and surpassing happiness.

When Nietzsche describes the will to truth as "a principle that is hostile to life and destructive," he is entirely consistent with his emphatic and fundamental assertion that man wants power more than life. And—though this is rarely recognized and greatly embitters the irrationalistic Klages, who is one of the few who have interpreted Nietzsche correctly in this matter—Nietzsche does *not* condemn *Geist* and the passion for truth but declares truth to be "divine." Power is a state of being for which man willingly risks death and from which he excludes himself if he "tolerates slack feelings in his faith and judgments" (FW 2). Untruth, in short, is weakness; and truth is power—even if it spells death.

These are points on which Nietzsche is quite emphatic. He insists that error, however advantageous for life, remains error (J 4, 34); and he suggests that

> the strength of a spirit might be measured according to how much of the "truth" he would be able to stand—more clearly, to what degree it would *need* to be watered down, shrouded, sweetened, blunted, and falsified [J 39; cf. WM 1041; EH-V 3].

Toward the end of the *Genealogy,* finally, where Nietzsche works up to the conclusion that the "ascetic ideal" alone has given man's life meaning, he quotes parts of the aphorism *To what extent we, too, are still pious,* emphasizes the ascetic element in the "will to truth," and adds:

> Whoever feels that this has been stated too briefly should read the section of *The Gay Science* entitled: "To what extent we, too, are still pious" [GM III 24].

This aphorism, then, on which such emphasis has been placed here, is not a casual one that Nietzsche himself might later have forgotten. He considered it an important statement of his position, and it is the basis of his polemic against faith as opposed to reason. When he was twenty, he had written his sister: "if you wish to strive for peace of soul and pleasure, then believe; if you wish to be a devotee of truth, then inquire." The self-styled Antichrist still sees himself as a devotee of truth—*ein Jünger der Wahrheit*—and rejects the Christian faith as incompatible with the moral demands of this vocation. And insofar as Christianity teaches "that God is truth, that truth is divine," and that simple pleasures must be sacrificed to "ascetic ideals," Nietzsche concludes that "Christianity *as dogma* has perished of its own morality" (GM III 27). He continues: "Christianity *as morality* must also perish now. We stand at the threshold of this event." And it is to Nietzsche's repudiation of Christian morality that we must turn now.

IV

Nietzsche himself hailed the "ruin" of Christian morality as "that great spectacle in a hundred acts which is reserved for the next two centuries in Europe, the most terrible, most questionable, and perhaps also the most hopeful of all spectacles" (GM III 27). Perhaps some readers would censure less the content of Nietzsche's prophecy than its emotional overtones: Nietzsche's vision of "new *barbarians*" may seem realistic, but hardly hopeful. Any such criticism, however, would be wide of the mark, for Nietzsche's prophecy has really not come true. What he expected was not a relapse into ancient paganism or a world-historical atavism, but a "new Enlightenment" (XIV, 282, 289 ff.; XVIII, 337). His expectations concerning the fate of the Jews are revealing in this respect: "When Christianity is once destroyed, one will become *more appreciative of the Jews"* (XVI, 403).[14] Nor is his picture of the "new barbarians" particularly barbarous: "One always sees only the weakening, pampering effects of the spirit which make for sickliness; but now there will come

$$\begin{matrix} \text{new} \\ \textit{barbarians:} \end{matrix} \left\{ \begin{matrix} \text{the cynics} \\ \text{the experimenters} \\ \text{the conquerors} \end{matrix} \right\} \begin{matrix} \text{a combination of spiritual supe-} \\ \text{riority with well-being and ex-} \\ \text{cess of strength" [WM 899].} \end{matrix}$$

Nietzsche distinguished between the barbarians who come from "the depth" and *"another kind of barbarian* who comes from the height" (WM 900). If we have seen the one kind, we certainly have not seen the other. Nor need we rely on a mere note for this crucial distinction:

> I, too, speak of a "return to nature," although it is really not a going back but an *ascent.* . . . *Goethe*—not a German event but a European one: a magnificent attempt to overcome the eighteenth century by a return to nature, by an *ascent* to naturalness [G IX 48 f.].

The contrast of Rousseau and Goethe is, as we have seen, one of the leitmotifs of Nietzsche's thought—and he is misunderstood when one forgets his conception of sublimation and the difference between the Dionysian he glorified in his last writings and the Dionysian he had earlier contrasted with the Apollinian.

While Nietzsche repudiated the mortification of the flesh, which he associated with Christianity, he did not propose to mortify the spirit. In fact, one of his principal contentions against the Christian faith was precisely that it seemed to him to deprecate reason. What Nietzsche envisaged was "a combination of spiritual superiority with well-being and excess of strength"— something very much akin to Heine's vision of Shakespeare: "Shakespeare is at the same time Jew and Greek . . . spiritualism and art have interpenetrated in him . . . and unfolded into a higher totality. Is perhaps such a harmonious fusion of these two elements the task of our whole European civilization?" [15] Nietzsche's conception of Goethe is fundamentally similar:

---

[14] Heine was a better prophet in this respect: "When Satan, that sinful pantheism, once becomes victorious, . . . then there will draw up over the heads of the poor Jews a storm of persecution that will far outdistance even their former sufferings" (*Shakespeares Mädchen und Frauen: Porzia*).

[15] *Heinrich Heine über Ludwig Börne,* Book II (Letters from Helgoland), July 29.

He sought help from history, natural science, antiquity, and also Spinoza, but, above all, from practical activity. . . . He did not retire from life [as, according to Nietzsche, Christianity had taught men to do] but placed himself in the midst of it. . . . What he wanted was *totality:* he fought the mutual extraneousness of reason, senses, feeling, and will. . . . Goethe conceived a human being who would be strong, highly educated, skillful in all bodily matters, self-controlled . . . the man of tolerance, not from weakness but from strength [G IX 49].

Mens sana in corpore sano, the new barbarian, Goethe, the passionate man who is the master of his passions—that is Nietzsche's ethic and his critique of Christian morality, as he understood it, in a nutshell.

Nietzsche's impassioned attack on Christian morals, however, and his own ethic which is so often misunderstood, require a more comprehensive analysis than has so far been offered—and this shall be attempted now. Friedrich Jodl, in his standard work on the history of ethics, represents a common attitude when he confines himself to Nietzsche's repudiation of altruism and construes it merely as a reaction against Schopenhauer's morality of pity or "a caricature of Darwinian ideas." [16] This interpretation is surely false. Nietzsche's critique of altruism deserves more consideration than this, and it has a significant affinity with the ethics of Plato, Aristotle, the Stoics, Spinoza, and Kant. In the Gospels, too, there is much that seems close to Nietzsche in this respect. It may well be that any ethic in which the highest good is the individual's state of being—whether that be self-control, self-perfection, or the attainment of the kingdom of God—entails some deprecation of any overly great concern about others (A 20). Nietzsche himself was keenly aware of his historical precedents and, far from feigning any novelty, he often stressed this respectable tradition.

We shall begin our analysis by documenting this last assertion, and then go on to consider Nietzsche's position, concentrating on his praise of friendship and his repudiation of neighbor-love and pity. It will be seen that what he condemns as "neighbor-love" is not at all what sincere Christians mean by that term, and that Nietzsche himself concedes that he is opposed to only

---

[16] *Geschichte der Ethik,* vol. II (2nd rev. ed., 1912), 495.

one kind of pity. His vehement attack is not directed against the Christian virtues as such. As a matter of fact, it has already been shown in our discussion of faith and action how he respected that practice which he considered Jesus' true legacy. What he denounces is not sincere Christianity, but insincere Christianity —those who are unchristian in their practice but nevertheless profess Christianity, as well as those who superficially seem Christian in their practice but whose motivation and state of mind are essentially unchristian. We are thus led on to a discussion of Nietzsche's famous conception of *ressentiment*, and in view of its great significance for Nietzsche's whole philosophy and psychology we shall pause to consider some of its ramifications as well as its historical derivation. Finally, it will become apparent that Nietzsche's opposition to Christian morality, no less than his opposition to the Christian faith, is reducible to the contrast between strength and weakness: in the last analysis, it is a question of power. Nietzsche proposes that "the strength of a spirit might be measured by how much of the 'truth' he would be able to stand," and "to what degree it would *need* to be watered down, . . . and falsified" (J 39), and he charges that the Christian faith is a refuge of the weak. Similarly, he condemns Christian morality as a morality of the weak.

In *Ecce Homo,* Nietzsche introduces his own interpretation of the *Dawn:* "With this book begins my campaign against *morality.*" (In the concluding lines of this self-interpretation, he himself explains that by "morality" he means only one type of morality.) If one then turns to the *Dawn* and reads his detailed critique of altruism (M 131–48), one finds that Nietzsche begins with a reference to the ancient moralists:

> *The moral fashions.* . . . These greatest wonders of classical morality—Epictetus, for example—did not know anything of the now customary glorification of thinking of others and living for others. In view of our moral fashion, one would have to call them flatly immoral; for they fought with all their energies *for* their ego and *against* sympathy for others (especially sympathy for their suffering and moral shortcomings). Perhaps they would reply to us: "If you have such a boring and ugly object in yourselves, by all means do think more of others than of yourselves" [M 131].

The issue here is plainly one not of selfishness versus decency but of self-perfection versus running away from oneself.

In the following aphorisms, too, Nietzsche seeks to make the same point, still referring to his predecessors. Against Schopenhauer's cult of pity he cites Kant:

> Kant still stands outside this movement: he teaches expressly that we must be insensitive to the suffering of others, if our good deeds are to have any moral worth—and Schopenhauer, mightily enraged, as one will readily understand, calls this a manifestation of Kant's bad taste [M 132].

Then Spinoza is alluded to:

> Pity [*Mitleiden*], insofar as it really induces suffering [*Leiden*], . . . is a weakness as is any losing oneself to a *harmful* affect [M 134].

There is no need for many more quotations to show how Nietzsche himself did not think of his critique of altruism as anything new or sensational. One may clinch the argument by citing the Preface of the *Genealogy:*

> This modern philosophers' predilection for, and overestimation of, pity is really something new: it was precisely on the unworthiness of pity that the philosophers had agreed until now. I name only: Plato, Spinoza, La Rochefoucauld, and Kant— four spirits as different from each other as possible, but united in one respect: in the deprecation of pity [GM-V 5].

Thus it is a sheer fallacy to consider Nietzsche's opposition to altruism as an essentially evolutionistic novelty, as a mere temperamental reaction against Schopenhauer, or as a monstrous example of "Egotism in German Philosophy." Nietzsche thought that almost all the great philosophers of the past, from Plato to Kant, had agreed that *self*-perfection was the goal of morality.

It may be urged that, even so, self-perfection is perhaps best sought not in seclusion, nor through exclusive preoccupation with oneself, but in community with others. This was exactly what Nietzsche himself proposed, and he took his cue, as he did so often, from the ancient Greeks. In the notes for *The Birth of Tragedy*, Nietzsche blamed Socrates for the fact that the classical Greek theories of ethics did not evolve any higher conception than that of friendship (III, 201). By the time he wrote the *Dawn*, however, he had begun to discover the possible meaning of friendship:

> *Friendship.* . . . In classical antiquity, friendship was experienced deeply and strongly. . . . In this consists their headstart before us: we, on the other side, have developed idealized love between the sexes. All the great virtues of the ancients were founded on this, that *man* stood next to *man,* and that no woman could claim to be the nearest, the highest, or . . . the only one whom he loved. . . . Perhaps, our trees do not grow so high because of the ivy and the vines [M 503].

In Nietzsche's next work, *The Gay Science,* we find a passage that establishes the transition from this aphorism to *Zarathustra:*

> . . . If one considers, finally, that the whole rest of the world seems . . . pale and worthless to the lover who is prepared to make any sacrifice, to disturb any order, and to disregard any other interest; then one may indeed marvel that this wild greed and injustice of love between the sexes has been so glorified and deified . . . yes—that one has taken from this love the conception of love as the opposite of egoism, although it is perhaps the most candid expression of egoism . . . [the omission includes a reference to the Greeks]. There is apparently, here and there on earth, a kind of continuation of love where this greedy desire of two persons for each other has given way to a new craving and greed, a *common* higher thirst for an ideal that stands above [*über*] them: but who knows this love? who has experienced it? Its true name is *friendship* [FW 14].

It seems as if Nietzsche had purposely left behind our entire civilization to travel back through the centuries to ancient Athens to join the company at Plato's *Symposium.* Perhaps no other modern philosopher has tried so hard to re-experience the spirit of Socrates and his disciples.

In *Zarathustra,* finally, the conception of friendship is presented full grown. The "common higher thirst for an ideal above" has become a common "longing for the *Übermenschen*" (Z I 14): friendship is a means toward the self-perfection of two human beings. There is a chapter "On the Friend," and another "On Neighbor-Love": "not the neighbor I teach you, but the friend" (Z I 16).

If Nietzsche had not always enjoyed polemics, he might have presented his ideas in terms of a repudiation of one sort of love and an affirmation of another kind of love. Instead he renounced Christian love for the sake of Greek friendship. Nevertheless the chapter "On Neighbor-Love" reads almost like an exegesis of a key sentence in the Sermon on the Mount, and Nietzsche clearly circumscribed this text deliberately: "Ye have heard that it hath been said, Thou shalt love thy neighbor, and hate thine enemy. But I say unto you, Love your enemies" (Matt. 5:43 f.). Nietzsche's chapter ends: "My brothers, neighbor-love I do not teach you: I teach you love of the farthest." Elsewhere, Zarathustra says: "Do love your neighbors as yourselves—but first be such as *love themselves*" (Z III 5).

What Nietzsche is repudiating is that kind of neighbor-love which is only man's "bad love of himself." The theme of the chapter is that "you flee to your neighbor from yourselves and would like to make a virtue of that"; "you cannot stand yourselves and do not love yourselves enough." The love of those who have not learned to stand solitude, or who "invite a witness when [they] wish to speak well of" themselves is not a virtue but simply a weakness; nor do they profit their neighbors.

What Nietzsche attacks is not the spirit of the Sermon on the Mount but Philistine morality. Love is usually not unselfish; it is often the escape of two immature persons neither of whom has learned to be alone or to make something of himself. Love, however, can be fruitful if two persons strive together to perfect themselves and each other. Such a relationship seems to Nietzsche the highest possible relationship between two human beings.

To be sure, if a friend whom one loves in this manner should suffer, one will suffer with him [*Mitleiden*]. It occurs to Nietzsche, however, that it might be better to "hide this feeling under a hard shell" (Z I 14).

> But if you have a suffering friend, be a resting place for his suffering, but a hard bed, as it were . . . : thus will you profit him best. And if a friend wrongs you, then say: "I forgive you what you did to me; but that you have done it to *yourself*— how could I forgive that." Thus speaks all great love: it overcomes even forgiveness and pity . . . all great love is even beyond all pity: for it still wants to—create the beloved. "Myself I sacrifice to my love, *and my neighbor as myself*"—thus runs the speech of all creators. But all creators are hard [Z II 3; cf. M 46].

The best that a friend can do for a friend is to help him to gain self-mastery. And that cannot be done by commiserating with him or by indulging his weaknesses. "The foe *will* not—the friend *must* not spare [*Es* will *der Feind—es* darf *der Freund nicht schonen*]," as Goethe says in *Tasso* (I. 2) where this theme is prominent. Later in the play (IV, 4), Goethe elaborates:

> True friendship manifests itself denying
> At the right time, and love will often grant
> A harmful good when it heeds more the will
> Of the demanding one than his well-being.

And in yet another scene (IV, 2) Goethe employs the metaphor of the doctor which Nietzsche was to use so often:

> Spare not the sick man, dear physician! Give
> The medicine to him and do not think
> If it be bitter. Whether he recover,
> That do consider, good and clever friend!

In short, Nietzsche thought that friends should be educators to one another; and educators must not be sentimental.

According to Nietzsche, pity is bad both for those who feel it and for those who are being pitied. It is bad for the pitied because it does not help them toward happiness and perfection and well-being. It even degrades, for pity includes a measure of condescension and sometimes even contempt. We do not pity those we admire (M 135; FW 338). Moreover, the pitying one rarely understands the "whole inner sequence" and the "entire economy of the soul": "he wants to *help* and does not realize that there is a personal necessity of suffering." A religion that preaches pity assumes that suffering is bad; it is in that sense a *"religion of comfortableness."* Self-perfection, however, is possible only through suffering, and the ultimate happiness of the man who has overcome himself does not exclude suffering. Hence Nietzsche says to the pitying ones: "How little you know of man's *happiness,* you comfortable and good-natured ones!" (FW 338).

Pity is also bad for those who feel it:

> How is it possible to stay on one's *own* path? Always someone crying calls us aside; our eye rarely sees a case where it does not become necessary to leave our own task immediately. . . . There is even a secret seduction in all this . . . : just our "own path" is too hard . . . and too far from the love and gratitude of others . . . we do not at all mind escaping it [FW 338].

Pity is not unselfish; all our conduct is selfish, and we cannot help that. Pity, however, is our *bad* love of ourselves, while the

Eros for the friend and toward our own self-perfection is a superior love. There is a passage in *Beyond Good and Evil* that crystallizes this point:

> In man *creator* and *creature* are united. . . . And . . . *your* pity is for the "creature in man," for that which must be formed, broken, forged, torn, burned, . . . and purged—for that which necessarily *must* and *shall* suffer. And *our* pity—do you not grasp for whom our *converse* pity is, when it protests against your pity as against the worst of all pamperings and weaknesses? Thus it is pity *versus* pity [J 225].

These lines are from the same aphorism in which Nietzsche explains how suffering "breeds" strength and depth of soul and how "spirit" and "greatness" are born of it.

The preachers of pity see only the "creature" in man, only his animal nature; they lack respect for man's potential dignity, for the "creator" in him—and they have no notion either of perfecting themselves or of helping others to become strong and great. One recalls Goethe's letter to Frau von Stein (June 8, 1787): "Also, I must say myself, I think it true that humanity will triumph eventually, only I fear that at the same time the world will become a large hospital and each will become the other's humane nurse." If only men would instead try to make the most of themselves, the world might be a better place to live in: "Because so much is done for others, the world is so imperfect" (x, 401). In this polemic against pity, Nietzsche is probably not ranged against Jesus:

> *Type of my disciples.* To those human beings *in whom I have a stake,* I wish suffering, being forsaken, sickness, maltreatment, humiliation—I wish that they should not remain unfamiliar with profound self-contempt, the torture of self-mistrust, and the misery of the vanquished: I have no pity for them because I wish them the only thing that can prove today whether one is worth anything or not—*that one endures* [WM 910].

There arises a crucial question: what of those who cannot hold out and would be crushed by such agonies instead of being reborn, refined as gold? It is of central significance that Nietzsche himself makes a sharp distinction in this respect between the powerful with whom he is especially concerned and the less favored specimens who are not capable of such refinement. Even in his *Antichrist* we find him saying that nature has divided men into three groups—the most spiritual [*geistigsten*] being the elite:

The most spiritual men, as the *strongest,* find their happiness where others would find their destruction: in the labyrinth, in hardness against themselves and others, in experiments. Their joy is self-conquest: asceticism becomes in them nature, need, and instinct. Difficult tasks are a privilege to them; to play with burdens that crush others, a *recreation.* Knowledge—a form of asceticism. They are the most venerable kind of man: that does not preclude their being the most cheerful and the kindliest [A 57].

Hardness against oneself and one's friends is essential for those who would educate and perfect themselves and their friends— but hardness against those who would not be able to stand such treatment is, says Nietzsche, entirely unpardonable:

> *When the exceptional human being treats the mediocre more tenderly than himself and his peers, this is not mere courtesy of the heart—it is simply his duty* [A 57].[17]

In his determination to be unequivocally emphatic on this point, to leave no doubt that *this* is not the issue on which he differs from Christianity, Nietzsche uses—and italicizes—a word that does not come to his lips easily: "duty." In fact, one may wonder whether Nietzsche—purposes of emphasis apart—is really entitled to this word. In his defense it may be said that he takes consideration for the weak to be the spiritual man's duty toward himself: he owes it to himself. One may also recall a much earlier note: " 'Duty' means: wanting a goal not for the sake of something else but for its own sake" (x, 379). Graciousness is part of "power," as Nietzsche conceives it—an element of that happiness for which all beings strive. Man wants to be gracious, for its own sake; but only *"the fewest"* may "represent happiness, beauty, and graciousness on earth": "they are the most spiritual men" and "in them alone graciousness is not a weakness" (A 57).

Nietzsche accorded ample recognition to the fact that there are benevolent other-regarding impulses. One may recall a passage from the *Dawn,* cited already in a different context, where he

---

[17] Italics supplied. How wrong one can go by considering *The Will to Power* Nietzsche's last work is well illustrated by the fact that, as published by the sister, it contains a note explaining "What is *noble?*" which reads in part: "the conviction that one has duties only toward one's peers" (WM 943). Not only is this a mere note—but it is dated three years before the *Antichrist,* and, unlike the note entitled *Type of my disciples* (written in 1887), it was not included in his own plan for the distribution of his notes among the four parts of a draft which he penned toward the end of 1887.

reflected on a man's having collapsed in the street in front of him: had Nietzsche known about this on the day before, he says, he would have spent a sleepless night, experiencing all sorts of agonies in advance (M 119). There is no need to amass further evidence for an assertion that seems to be in complete accordance with all the known facts: Nietzsche was fully aware of the exist- ence of such impulses and did not consider them necessarily sickly or bad. Like Kant, however, he saw no moral worth what- ever in indulging inclinations. Morality means to him mastery of the impulses: "My humanity does *not* consist in sympathizing with man but in *standing* that I sympathize with him. My hu- manity is a perpetual self-overcoming" (EH 1 8). Until we have achieved self-mastery and self-perfection, we should be best advised to concentrate on this—by far the most important— task, instead of scattering our efforts. Running off to help others would likely be a weakness, psychologically: giving alms to others is easier than making something of oneself.

V

Nietzsche thus attacks only one kind of pity and neighbor-love, and this is not the kind which is "Christian" in the ideal sense of that word. In fact, Nietzsche may seem to be merely perverse when he uses the word "neighbor-love" in connection with those who "invite a witness when [they] wish to speak well of" themselves. His critique, however, is in keeping with his concep- tion of the philosopher's mission: he believes that, ever since Socrates, the greatest philosophers have always "uncovered how much hypocrisy . . . was concealed under the best honored type of their contemporary morality" (J 212). What he attacks, in other words, is the state of mind that frequently hides behind the respectable façade of Christian virtue; and of the motives Nietzsche discusses in this context, the one he emphasizes most is *ressentiment*. This is one of the key conceptions of Nietzsche's psychology and the clue to many of his philosophic contentions, and we shall now consider it in detail.

To be kindly when one is merely too weak and timid to act otherwise, to be humble when any other course would have unpleasant repercussions, and to be obliging when a less ami- able gesture would provoke the master's kick or switch—that is the slave's morality, making a virtue of necessity. And such "morality" may well go together with impotent hatred and immeasurable envy, with *ressentiment* which would like nothing better than revenge—a chance to outdo the master's insults and "better the instruction." The graciousness of slaves who crave a heaven from which they will behold their masters frying in the flames of hell—that is to Nietzsche's mind no virtue. In the strong, however, and "in them alone, graciousness is not a weakness."

> Of all evil I deem you capable: therefore I want the good from you. Verily, I have often laughed at the weaklings who thought themselves good because they had no claws [Z II 13].

To have claws and not to use them, and above all to be above any *ressentiment* or desire for vengeance, that is, according to Nietzsche, the sign of true power; and this is also the clue to his persistent critique of punishment.[18] These themes are developed in the chapters "On the Adder's Bite" and "On the Tarantulas" in *Zarathustra,* and in a section in *Ecce Homo.*

> But if you have an enemy, do not requite him evil with good, for that would put him to shame. Rather prove that he did you some good. And rather be angry than put to shame. And if you are cursed, I do not like it that you want to bless. Rather join a little in the cursing. And if you have been done a great wrong, then quickly add five little ones: a gruesome sight is a person single-mindedly obsessed by a wrong. . . . A little revenge is more human than no revenge. . . . It is nobler to declare oneself wrong than to insist on being right—especially when one is right. Only one must be rich enough for that. I do not like your cold justice; and out of the eyes of your judges always look the executioner and his cold steel. Tell me, where is that justice which is love with open eyes? Would that you might invent for me the love that bears not only all punishment but all guilt! Would that you might invent for me the justice that acquits everyone, except him that judges! . . . How can I give each his own? Let this be sufficient for me: I give each my own [Z I 19].

Much of this is surely closer to the gospel than what Nietzsche is attacking. But what of the sentence, "A little revenge is more human than no revenge at all"? Nietzsche assumes that the little revenge would allow the offended person to get his

---

[18] Cf. M 202, 236, 252, 366; FW 321; GM II 10.

grievance out of his system, while no revenge at all would mean that the afflicted would henceforth be consumed by *ressentiment.* This is expressly stated in *Ecce Homo,* in a passage that develops similar ideas.

> It also seems to me that the rudest word, the rudest letter are still more benign, more decent than silence. Those who remain silent are almost always lacking in delicacy and courtesy of the heart. Silence is an objection; swallowing things leads of necessity to a bad character—it even upsets the stomach. All who remain silent are dyspeptic.
>
> You see, I don't want rudeness to be underestimated: it is by far the *most humane* form of contradiction and, in the midst of effeminacy, one of our foremost virtues.
>
> If one is rich enough for this, it is even a good fortune to be in the wrong. A god who would come to earth must not *do* anything except wrong: not to take the punishment upon oneself but the *guilt,* would be divine [EH 1 5].

The last sentence became the central inspiration of Sartre's *The Flies.* First in an article (see Bibliography) and then in *Tragedy and Philosophy,* I have dealt in detail with Nietzsche's immense influence on this play. Sartre's most obvious difference with the Greek poets who had used the same story—Homer, Aeschylus, Sophocles, and Euripides—is, of course, that in all of their versions Orestes kills Aegistheus and Clytemnestra to avenge his father, while Sartre's Orestes is not motivated by revenge. This opposition to revenge is Nietzschean, too, and expressed most emphatically in Zarathustra's chapter "On the Tarantulas":

> For *that man be delivered from revenge,* that is for me the bridge to the highest hope, and a rainbow after long storms. The tarantulas, of course, would have it otherwise. "What justice means to us is precisely that the world be filled with the storms of our revenge"—thus they speak to each other. "We shall wreak vengeance and abuse on all whose equals we are not"—thus do the tarantulas vow. "And 'will to equality' shall henceforth be the name for virtue; and against all that has power we want to raise our clamor!" You preachers of equality, . . . your most secret ambitions to be tyrants thus shroud themselves in words of virtue. Aggrieved conceit, repressed envy—perhaps the conceit and envy of your fathers—erupt from you as a flame and as the frenzy of revenge. . . . They are like enthusiasts, yet it is not the heart that fires them—but revenge . . . to be a judge seems bliss to them. But thus I

counsel you, my friends: Mistrust all in whom the impulse to
punish is powerful. . . . Mistrust all who talk much of their
justice! Verily, their souls lack more than honey. And when
they call themselves the good and the just, do not forget that
they would be pharisees, if only they had—[worldly] power. My
friends, I do not want to be mixed up and confused with others
[Z II 7].

The difference between Nietzsche's ethics and what he himself took to be Christian ethics is not ultimately reducible to
different forms of behavior or divergent tables of virtues: it
revolves primarily around the agent's state of mind or, more
basically, his state of being. Nietzsche's critique of the morality of
ressentiment is thus not an arbitrary addition to his philosophy,
but an integral part of it. It is, for example, closely related to
his previously mentioned contrast of the "Dionysian" and the
"romantic," and to his repudiation of the latter. To show this,
and to elucidate the significance of Nietzsche's conception of
ressentiment, it seems best to cite Nietzsche's own words at some
length.

> *What is romanticism?* . . . At first, I approached the modern
> world . . . *hopefully.* I understood . . . the philosophic pessi-
> mism of the nineteenth century as if it were the symptom of a
> greater strength of thought, of more daring courage, and of a
> more triumphant *fullness* of life, than had marked the eight-
> eenth century, the era of Hume and Kant. . . . Similarly, I
> interpreted German music as if it were an expression of a
> Dionysian powerfulness of the German soul . . . I mistook at
> that time—both in philosophic pessimism and in German mu-
> sic—what was their true character: their *romanticism.* What
> is romanticism? Every art and every philosophy may be con-
> sidered a remedy and aid in the service of growing and strug-
> gling life: they always presuppose suffering and sufferers. But
> there are two kinds of sufferers: first, those who suffer from
> the *overfullness of life* and want a Dionysian art . . . and then
> those who suffer from the *impoverishment of life* and seek
> . . . redemption from themselves through art and knowledge,
> or intoxication, convulsion, anaesthesia, and frenzy. To this
> dual need of the *latter* corresponds all romanticism in art and
> knowledge, . . . Schopenhauer as well as Richard Wagner, to
> name those most famous and most definite romantics whom
> I *misunderstood* at first. . . . Those who suffer most and are
> poorest in life would need mildness, peacefulness, and good-
> ness most . . . and, if possible, also a god who would really
> be a god for the sick, a "savior" . . . Thus I gradually learned

to understand . . . the "Christian" who is essentially a romantic—and my eye became ever sharper for that most difficult *backward inference* in which the most mistakes are made
—the backward inference from the work to the maker, from
the deed to the doer, from the ideal to him who *needs it,* from
every way of thinking and valuing to the *craving* behind it
that prompts it. Regarding all aesthetic values I now avail
myself of this main distinction: I ask in every single case, "Is
it hunger or overflow that has here become creative?" . . .
The desire for *destruction,* change, and becoming can be an
expression of overfull, future-pregnant strength (my term for
this is, as one knows, the word "Dionysian"); but it can also
be the hatred [i.e., *ressentiment*] of the misdeveloped, needy,
underprivileged [*des Missratenen, Entbehrenden, Schlechtweggekommenen*] who destroys, who *must* destroy, because the
existing, and even all existence, all being, outrages and provokes
him. To understand this feeling, one should closely examine
our anarchists. The will to *eternize* also requires a dual interpretation. First, it can come from gratitude and love: an art
of this origin will ever be an art of apotheoses—dithyrambic
perhaps with Rubens, blissfully jesting with Hafiz, bright
and benign with Goethe, and spreading a Homeric light and
glory over all things (. . .[19]) But it can also be that tyrannic
will [i.e., *ressentiment*] of one who is seriously ailing, struggling,
and tortured . . . who as it were revenges himself on all things
by impressing on them . . . and burning into them *his* image,
the image of *his* torture. The latter is *romantic pessimism*
in its most expressive form, whether as Schopenhauerian volun-
tarism or as Wagnerian music: romantic pessimism, the last
great event in the fate of our culture. (. . . there *could* still be
quite another kind of pessimism, one that is classical . . . only
that the word "classical" antagonizes my ears—it is far too
trite. . . . I call this pessimism . . . *Dionysian* pessimism) [FW
370].

The basic distinction here is that between two states of being: the
"overfullness of life" and the "impoverishment of life," power
and impotence. Both may express themselves in superficially

---

[19] The omitted phrase reads: "(in this case I speak of *Apollinian* art)."
This parenthesis is missing in the otherwise almost identical draft for
this passage in WM 846. It has been omitted above because Nietzsche,
as a matter of fact, does *not* speak of "Apollinian" art in such cases:
in his other late works he consistently refers to it as "Dionysian." The
insertion of the parenthesis was plainly an afterthought, suggested by the
possibility of a neat conceptual symmetry—but inconsistent even with its
immediate context: *vide* the "dithyrambic" Rubens and Hafiz.

similar ways—but Nietzsche would judge the expressions not according to appearances but in the light of their psychological origins. And the Christian faith and morality are—he claims— no less than romantic philosophy and art, or anarchism, or, as he suggests elsewhere (GM II 11), anti-Semitism, expressions of a deeply rooted *ressentiment*.

This conception of *ressentiment* is not—as is sometimes supposed—entirely original with Nietzsche. The antecedents of the idea may be sketched very briefly insofar as they help to throw light on Nietzsche's meaning. Heine's contrast of *Hellenes* and *Nazarenes*—one of the persistent motifs of his writings—is probably the most important precedent. And it is noteworthy that Heine's own famed irony was *not* considered "romantic" by Nietzsche, but "Dionysian"—the expression of strength, not of *ressentiment:*

> The highest conception of the lyric poet, *Heinrich Heine* gave to me. I seek in vain in all the realms of thousands of years for an equally sweet and passionate music. He possessed that divine sarcasm [*Bosheit*] without which I cannot imagine perfection. I estimate the value of human beings, of races, according to the necessity by which they cannot conceive the god apart from the satyr. And how he handles his German! It will be said one day that Heine and I have been by far the foremost artists of the German language—at an incalculable distance from everything mere Germans have done with it [EH II 4] [20]

This passage is not merely a polemical antithesis to anti-Semitic evaluations of Heine. It was Heine's irony—and not the essentially different, pointedly equivocal and inconclusive, irony of the German romantics—that served Nietzsche as a model. It was from Heine that he learned much about the nuances of "divine" sarcasm and about the handling of the German language; perhaps Nietzsche's prose owes more to him than to any other German writer. And the agonized poet who celebrated the beauty of life in overflowing verses from what he called his

---

[20] In connection with this prophecy, one may cite Thomas Mann: "Of his [Heine's] works I have long loved the book on Börne most. . . . His psychology of the Nazarene type anticipates Nietzsche. . . . And incidentally, this book contains the most magnificent [*genialste*] German prose prior to Nietzsche." ("Notiz über Heine," 1908, reprinted in *Rede und Antwort*, 1922, 382.) *Heinrich Heine über Ludwig Börne* may have been the model for *The Case of Wagner,* and for the title *Nietzsche contra Wagner.*

Matratzengruft (mattress tomb) apparently seemed a paragon of power to Nietzsche, and not a romantic.

To return to the conception of *ressentiment,* it is Heine's interpretation of Börne's hatred of Goethe that is most relevant: "the little Nazarene hated the great Greek. . . . I say Nazarene to use neither the expression 'Jewish' nor 'Christian,' although both expressions are synonymous for me and are used by me not to designate a faith but a character . . . as opposed to 'Hellenes,' with which word I also do not designate a particular people but a bent of the spirit and a way of looking at things . . . all men are either Jews or Hellenes—men with ascetic, picture-hating drives that crave spiritualization, or men with a life-loving [*lebensheiteren*] . . . and realistic character. Thus there have been Hellenes in German ministers' families and Jews who were born in Athens. . . . Börne was wholly a Nazarene; his antipathy to Goethe proceeded straight from his Nazarene disposition; and his later political exaltation was grounded in that uncouth asceticism and that thirst for martyrdom which is so often found among republicans, which they call republican virtue, and which is so little distinguished from the early Christians' craving for suffering. . . ." [21]

Here one may find the inspiration of many of Nietzsche's remarks about pagans and Christians—the clue to such statements as "Raphael said Yes, Raphael *did* Yes; consequently Raphael was no Christian" (G IX 9), or "pagans are all who say Yes to life" (A 55). The remark about the republicans—Heine himself was of course one of the most prominent liberals of his day—was also elaborated, overelaborated, by Nietzsche. And Heine's analysis of the little Nazarene's hatred of the great Greek is the psychology of *ressentiment, in nuce.*

In their evaluations of the New Testament, however, Heine and Nietzsche differed decisively. While Heine writes, much like Nietzsche, "all of mankind strove ever after, *in imitationem*

---

[21] *Heinrich Heine über Ludwig Börne,* Book I. Of the many passages in which Heine expressed similar ideas, only the concluding verses of his last poem, "Für die Mouche," need be mentioned: here the bifurcation of mankind is reiterated, and the line, "Ever will truth struggle against the beautiful," seems a deliberate antithesis to Keats' romantic identification of truth and beauty, and essentially at one with Nietzsche's conception of truth as an "ascetic ideal." The poem ends, in Heinesque fashion, as the "I-a, I-a" of an ass awakens the poet—and this may possibly have helped to inspire Z IV 17.

Christi, for the mortification of the body and a suprasensible union with the absolute spirit," Heine does not therefore condemn the Gospels: "From the Old Testament I sometimes leap into the New. . . . What holy ground does your foot step on here! At such reading one should take off one's shoes." [22] Nietzsche, on the other hand, writes: "one does well to put on gloves when reading the New Testament. The proximity of so much uncleanliness almost forces one to do this" (A 46). Each quotation is entirely representative of its author's views: Heine's sarcasm and criticism stopped short of the Gospels, while Nietzsche's reach their incredible climax precisely in his comments on the New Testament. But while he charges the early Christians, including the authors of the Gospels, with the most hateful lust for revenge, he sharply distinguishes between the disciples and their master: they failed to "understand the main point, the exemplary character of this kind of death, the freedom, the superiority over any feeling of *ressentiment*" (A 40).

VI

Goethe, who served Heine as the prototype of the Hellene, served Nietzsche as the model of that paganism which he opposed to Christianity: here was the "new barbarian"—the overman with the "Dionysian faith." Goethe, especially in his *Venetian Epigrams*

---

[22] It would be altogether false were one to infer from the preceding that "Jew" and "Christian" are opprobrious terms in Heine's writings. In fact, his long eulogy of Moses invites comparison with Nietzschean passages: "May God forgive me this sin, but sometimes it seems to me as if this Mosaic God were only the reflected splendor of Moses himself, to whom he looks so similar . . . in wrath and love [cf. M 38 on p. 299]. . . . Formerly, . . . I did not forgive the legislator of the Jews his hatred against all pictures . . . I did not see that Moses . . . possessed the true artistic spirit . . . [which] was, as in his Egyptian compatriots, directed only towards the colossal and indestructible. But he did not, like the Egyptians, form his works of art of brick and granite . . . he took a poor shepherds' tribe and out of it created a people that was also to defy the centuries . . . [cf. Nietzsche: ". . . conquering and dominating natures in search of material to mold. Prometheus . . ." (WM 900)]. "I see now that the Greeks were only beautiful youths; the Jews, however, were always men, . . . martyrs who gave the world a god and a morality and fought and suffered on all the battlefields of thought [cf. Nietzsche: XVI, 373 on p. 301, and MA I 475 on p. 299]" (*Geständnisse, Werke, ed. cit.,* XIV, 294 ff.).

(52 and 66),[23] had even surpassed Nietzsche's later blasphemies about the cross; and hence Nietzsche declares: "One must feel about the cross as Goethe did" (WM 175). Moreover, the repudiation of the "Nazarene" can be traced back to Goethe: this name had been associated with a romantic school of painting that Goethe abominated, and he had actually spoken of the "infamous manner of the Nazarenes" [24] and, on several occasions, denounced them as weak and sickly. The fusion of Christianity and Teutonism, religion and nationalism, which developed out of German romanticism was as abhorrent to Goethe as Wagner's revival of this ideology was to Nietzsche. And Goethe's estimate of the romantics themselves, and of their religiousness, turned on what he took to be their essential weakness, dissatisfaction with themselves, and envy of those superior to them.

Thus he complained in 1823 of having had to witness "for more than twenty years"—the date suggests the beginnings of the German romantic movement—what he describes as "the shallow dilettantism of the age which seeks a false foundation in antiquarianism and fatherlandishness, and a weakening element in bigotry—an atmosphere in which noble women, half-knowing benefactors, and poor amateurs are so happy to meet; where a hollow jargon of clichés one has contrived sounds so sweetish; where a shroud of maxims one has tailored for one's own miserable body, will be so nobly becoming; and where, gnawed at daily by consumption, one is sickly from that insecurity which is born of unsureness and must, simply to live and peter on, lie to oneself most ignominiously." [25]

---

[23] Included as #8 and 12 in my *Twenty German Poets*, Modern Library, 30–33. Cf. also Goethe's statement: "the painful torture wood, the most disgusting thing under the sun, no reasonable human being should strive to exhume . . ." (Letter to Zelter, June 9, 1831. Goethe himself intended these letters for publication "as a kind of leaven . . . to incommode the prevalent spiritless political newspaper existence," as he put it in the letter of Nov. 23, 1831. Cf. Oct. 31, 1831, and Jan. 3, 1832.)

[24] Conversation with Müller, June 18, 1926 (Biedermann).

[25] Letter to Zelter, Aug. 24, 1823. The above passage contains such coinages as *Altertümelei, Vaterländerei, unvermögende Versuchler,* and *fortzuwebeln.* I have rendered the last two as "poor amateurs" and "peter on," and may add that *unvermögend* means both impotent and impecunious. And I have used six words to render Goethe's single *Unsicherheit.* Finally, Goethe's and Heinrich Meyer's joint manifesto against *Neu-deutsche religiös-patriotische Kunst,* which is to be found in the *Sophien-Ausgabe* of Goethe's works, expresses similar sentiments.

380   NIETZSCHE: PHILOSOPHER, PSYCHOLOGIST, ANTICHRIST

Still closer to Nietzsche, and to Heine's analysis of Börne, is Goethe's portrait of the Schlegels: "The brothers Schlegel were and are . . . miserable men all their life long: they wanted to represent more than was granted them by nature. . . . Therefore they have done much damage in art and literature. From their false doctrines . . . which preconized . . . egoism coupled with weakness, the German artists and dilettantes have not recovered yet. . . . Friedrich Schlegel finally suffocated from his rumination [*Wiederkäuen*] of ethical and religious absurdities which he would have liked to spread during the course of his uncomfortable life, wherefore he fled into Catholicism. . . . Closely considered, the interest in Indian things was also merely a *pis aller.* They had sense enough to see that they could not do anything brilliant in the German, Latin, or Greek field. . . . I had enough to do with myself; what did I care about others! . . . The envy at seeing so many more effective talents coming up . . . could not possibly let the mind of this good man [A. W. Schlegel] attain to any good will." [26]

Nietzsche quoted from this passage in *The Case of Wagner:*

> What Goethe would have thought of Wagner? Goethe once asked himself what danger confronted all romantics: the romantics' fatality. His answer is: "to suffocate of the rumination of ethical and religious absurdities." Briefer: *Parsifal* [W 3].

And Goethe's formulation, "egoism coupled with weakness" is the very essence of Nietzsche's conception of romanticism. Finally, it was already pointed out at the end of Chapter 4 that Nietzsche developed his later contrast of the romantic and Dionysian out of Goethe's famous dictum: "The classical I call the healthy and the romantic the sick" (cf. S 217).

Nietzsche's repudiation of Christian morality cannot be understood any more than can his critique of romanticism, unless one keeps in mind that his own positive conception of the Dionysian was derived from Goethe's classical ideal—and not from the German romantics.[27] Nietzsche speaks of

---

[26] Letter to Zelter, Oct. 20, 1831. Cf. also this remark about the Schlegels and Tieck: "In Spinoza we can look up what is the matter with these gentlemen: it is envy." (Conversation with Sulpiz Boisserée, Aug. 3, 1815.) In a complete history of the concept of *ressentiment*, Spinoza would of course deserve an important place. Cf. also Nietzsche's reference to the representativeness of "the hatred of Novalis against Goethe." (XVII, 367.)

[27] This misconception was propagated by Joel, Bertram, Thomas Mann,

My fight against *romanticism* in which Christian ideals and
Rousseau's ideals mingle together with a longing for the bygone era of priestly-aristocratic culture, for virtù, and for
"strong human beings" . . . a false and imitative kind of
stronger humanity that esteems extreme states generally and
sees in them the symptom of strength ("cult of passion" . . .
furore espressivo, not from fullness but *dearth*). . . . Stifter
and Gottfried Keller are signs of more strength and inner well-
being . . . [WM 1021].

The German romantics themselves had conceived of the "romantic"—to cite A. W. Schlegel—as something "peculiarly modern,
not formed after the models of [classical] antiquity," and defined
its "character" as a "fusion of the ancient German with the later,
i.e., Christianized, Roman." [28] It is a commonplace that Nietzsche held no brief either for the "ancient German" or for the
Christian—and that he preferred ancient Greece to both. It is less
well known that Nietzsche distinguished his own position sharply
not only from the romantic glorification of the Middle Ages,[29]

Langer, and others. Joel later decided that Nietzsche, while a romantic,
was also an embodiment of the Baroque. (*Wandlungen der Weltanschauung* II, 1934.) The appropriateness of such categories is questionable
in principle—and in this instance the label is plainly misleading. Leibniz
—the one "Baroque" philosopher whom Nietzsche does resemble, both in
his monadologic conception of the cosmos and in his emphatic opposition
to any doctrine of double truth—marks the transition from the Baroque
to the Enlightenment; and the parallel hinges on this fact.

[28] *Vorlesungen über schöne Litteratur und Kunst* (Berlin, 1801–04; ed.
Minor, 1884), III, 7 and 17—quoted by Lovejoy, *op. cit.,* 190, who proves
that the early German romantics conceived of romanticism as an antithesis
to the classical, and did not derive their conception from Goethe's *Wilhelm
Meister* (*Roman, romantisch*), as Haym had suggested.

[29] One of the earliest examples of this is Novalis' *Christenheit oder Europa*.
Even so, the "romantic" Nietzsche interpretations have often suggested
that Novalis and Nietzsche were profoundly similar. It is true that Novalis,
too, took his philosophy very seriously and sought to live it—but his
philosophy was quite different: he himself called it "magic idealism."
His romantic glorification of night and death, his decision to "die his
philosophy," and the lover's singing himself to death at twenty-eight
resemble the consummation of Wagner's *Tristan and Isolde,* but invite
a contrast with Nietzsche's "Dionysian" glorification of life and the "great
noon." In the three volumes of Novalis' "fragments" (these do not include
his unfinished works, like *Ofterdingen,* but only his aphorisms), there are
some lines that seem very close to Nietzsche. The two men, however, are
basically quite different, and the context usually reveals the superficiality
of such parallels. An example may illustrate this point. Novalis: "Charcoal
and diamond are *one* material, and yet how different! Should not the
same be the case with man and woman? We are clay, and women are

but also from any longing "for virtù and for 'strong human beings' "—and many an interpreter has read into Nietzsche the very " 'cult of passion' " and "*furore espressivo, not* from fullness but *dearth*" which he himself denounced. While Nietzsche repudiated Christianity and the Christian elements in romanticism, *this* was not the alternative he proposed instead.

As a matter of fact, the position of the allegedly Heraclitean and irrationalistic Nietzsche is to be found—superbly formulated—in Aristotle's *Nicomachean Ethics:* "the good man ought to be a lover of self, since he will then act nobly, and so both benefit himself and aid his fellows; but the bad man ought not to be a lover of self, since he will follow his base passions, and so injure both himself and his neighbours." [30] Nietzsche is not exhorting the mass of men to renounce traditional restraints. He denounces what he considers Wagner's typically romantic libertinism as *"Freigeisterei der Leidenschaft* (Rousseau's aim)" (WM 106); and he writes: "One must not let oneself be seduced by blue eyes and swelled bosoms: *there is nothing romantic about greatness of soul"* (WM 981).

"Greatness of soul" is a translation of Aristotle's *megalopsychia.* And as Aristotle's conception apparently made a tremendous impression on Nietzsche, whose opposition to Christianity can scarcely be seen in proper perspective apart from Aristotle's ethics, it seems necessary to quote at least in part the relevant passage from the *Nicomachean Ethics:*

> A person is thought to be great-souled if he claims much and deserves much. . . . He that claims less than he deserves is small-souled . . . the truly great-souled man must be a good man. . . . Greatness of soul seems . . . a crowning ornament of all the virtues. . . . Great honours accorded by persons of worth will afford [the great-souled man] pleasure in a moderate

---

. . . sapphires which also consist of clay" (*Fragmente des Jahres 1798,* #1218). Nietzsche: " 'Why so hard—the kitchen coal once said to the diamond: are we not closely related?' Why so soft? oh my brothers . . . are you not my brothers? . . . all creators are hard. . . . Become hard!" (Z III 12). The dreamy Novalis worships women, beauty, and iridescence; Nietzsche, hardness. Both men make much of suffering—but Novalis celebrates its voluptuous passivity—*"ein Stachel der Wollust"* (*Hymnen an die Nacht*)—and prizes it as a foretaste of death, while for Nietzsche it is the great stimulus of life and creativity.

[30] 1169a, transl. H. Rackham, Loeb Classical Library.

degree: he will feel he is receiving only what belongs to him, or even less, for no honour can be adequate to the merits of perfect virtue, yet all the same he will deign to accept their honours, because they have no greater tribute to offer him. Honour rendered by common people and on trivial grounds he will utterly despise, for this is not what he merits. . . . He therefore to whom even honour is a small thing will be indifferent to other things as well. Hence great-souled men are thought to be haughty. . . . The great-souled man is justified in despising other people—his estimates are correct; but most proud men have no good ground for their pride. . . . He is fond of conferring benefits, but ashamed to receive them, because the former is a mark of superiority and the latter of inferiority. He returns a service done to him with interest, since this will put the original benefactor into his debt in turn, and make him the party benefited. The great-souled are said to have a good memory for any benefit they have conferred, but a bad memory for those which they have received (since the recipient of a benefit is the inferior of his benefactor, whereas they desire to be superior). . . . It is also characteristic of the great-souled men never to ask help from others, or only with reluctance, but to render aid willingly; and to be haughty towards men of position and fortune, but courteous towards those of moderate station . . . and to adopt a high manner with the former is not ill-bred, but it is vulgar to lord it over humble people. . . . He must be open both in love and in hate, since concealment shows timidity; and care more for the truth than for what people will think; . . . he is outspoken and frank, except when speaking with ironical self-depreciation, as he does to common people. He will be incapable of living at the will of another, unless a friend, since to do so is slavish. . . . He does not bear a grudge, for it is not a mark of greatness of soul to recall things against people, especially the wrongs they have done you, but rather to overlook them. He is . . . not given to speaking evil himself, even of his enemies, except when he deliberately intends to give offence. . . . Such then being the great-souled man, the corresponding character on the side of deficiency is the small-souled man, and on that of excess the vain man [IV: 3; *ed. cit.*].

One may sympathize with Bertrand Russell's comment: "One shudders to think what a vain man would be like" [31]—but Aristotle's answer is very simple and contained in the same para-

---

[31] *A History of Western Philosophy* (1945), 176.

graph: "He that claims much but does not deserve much is vain."
Aristotle thus condemns vanity without in the least praising
meekness or humility; and many of the provocative ideas he expresses so unprovocatively and dryly are fashioned into polemical
arrows in Nietzsche's works, especially in *Zarathustra*.

Nietzsche's debt to Aristotle's ethics is thus considerable, and
it is quite unjustifiable to infer from Nietzsche's disagreement
with Aristotle's theory of tragedy that Aristotle meant little or
nothing to him—or that the only Greek philosophers whom he
admired were the pre-Socratics. In his own mind, he seems to
have distinguished clearly between Aristotle's ethics and aesthetics; witness the following lines: "I honor Aristotle and honor
him most highly—but he certainly did not hit the nail, not to
speak of hitting it on the head, when he spoke of the ultimate
aim of Greek tragedy" (FW 80).

Aristotle's portrait of the "great-souled" man was undoubtedly
influenced by Socrates, particularly by his behavior before his
judges, in the *Apology*, though this seems to have gone unnoticed.
Here is a striking instance of the manner in which personality
sometimes becomes a crucial influence in the history of ideas—
and another link between Socrates and Nietzsche.

To return to Nietzsche's conception of greatness of soul, he
insists that "greatness of soul cannot be separated from greatness
of mind [*geistiger Grösse*]. For it involves *independence;* and
without greatness of mind this should not be permitted, as it
causes mischief" (WM 984). And in a crucial passage, he explains:

> Hatred against mediocrity is unworthy of a philosopher: it is
> almost a question mark concerning his *"right* to philosophy."
> Just because he is the exception, he must protect the norm and
> encourage self-confidence in all the mediocre [*hat er die Regel
> in Schutz zu nehmen, hat er allem Mittleren den guten Mut
> zu sich selber zu erhalten*] [WM 893; cf. A 57].

Nietzsche's point is *not* that the happiness of the weak should
be sacrificed to that of the strong, but that the weak are incapacitated for ultimate happiness. Only the strong attain that happiness which all men want. How much would a Schlegel or Börne
prefer to be a Goethe; how much would the slave rather not
have to rely on his dreams of other-worldly retribution; how

much happier would each be if he were better favored in this world! To be sure, says Nietzsche, "for the mediocre, being mediocre is his happiness" (A 57), and he would be unhappy if treated with the same hardness which the most spiritual men accord themselves. Ultimate happiness, however, that which man wants most, is represented only by "the fewest." Thus the *Antichrist* begins:

> Let us face ourselves. We are Hyperboreans; we know very well how far off we live. "Neither by land nor by sea will you find the way to the Hyperboreans"—Pindar already knew this about us. Beyond the north, ice, and death—*our* life, *our* happiness. We have discovered happiness, we know the way, we have found the exit out of the labyrinth of thousands of years. Who *else* has found it? Modern man perhaps? "I have got lost; I am everything that has got lost," sighs modern man. *This* modernity was our sickness: lazy peace, cowardly compromise, the whole virtuous uncleanliness of the modern Yes and No. . . . Rather live in the ice than among modern virtues and other south winds! We were intrepid enough, we spared neither ourselves nor others; but for a long time we did not know where to turn with our intrepidity. We became gloomy, we were called fatalists. *Our fatum*—abundance, tension, the damming of strength. We thirsted for lightning and deeds and were most remote from the happiness of the weakling, "resignation." In our atmosphere was a thunderstorm; the nature we are became dark—*for we saw no way*. Formula for our happiness: a Yes, a No, a straight line, a goal [A 1].

One may doubt that Nietzsche attained ultimate happiness: the *Antichrist,* while large portions of it are surprisingly sober and philosophical, is elsewhere singularly lacking in self-mastery and graciousness. The frenzied vehemence of many passages seems far from the majestic calm and the mature repose of Nietzsche's "most spiritual men"—of Socrates or Goethe. That, however, is a biographical question: what counts in this context is that Nietzsche was convinced that modern man was failing in his pursuit of happiness, that modern man was far from the state that he— like all men—longed for most, and that this happiness consisted in a state Nietzsche called "power."

Nietzsche's critique of modern man, of romanticism, and of Christianity is thus the negative counterpart of his philosophy of power. Nietzsche understands all three as forms of weakness—

sickness, dearth, and *ressentiment* are key terms in his criticism—
and as he has come to identify happiness with power, he contends
that those who lack such power as he has in mind cannot find
ultimate happiness.

VII

Before we conclude this account of Nietzsche's repudiation of
Christianity, we must consider Nietzsche's alleged glorification of
war. When he condemns "lazy peace," in our last long quotation,
it is surely not a question of the interpreter's "gentleness" or
"toughness" whether he takes Nietzsche to advocate war or not.
And one may generalize that in most of his notorious remarks
about "war," notably including the chapter "On War and Warriors" in *Zarathustra,* the word is used metaphorically. It should
be noted that this chapter is immediately followed by Nietzsche's
attack on the State as "The New Idol" and that Nietzsche is
plainly not speaking of soldiers.

> And if you cannot be saints of knowledge, at least be its war-
> riors. They are the companions and forerunners of such saint-
> hood. I see many soldiers: would that I saw many [such] war-
> riors! "Uniform" one calls what they wear: would that what it
> conceals were not uniform! You should have eyes that always
> seek an enemy—*your* enemy. . . . You should seek your en-
> emy and you should wage your war—for your thoughts. And
> if your thought be vanquished, your honesty should still find
> cause for triumph in that. You should love peace as a means
> to new wars—and the short peace more than the long. . . .
> Let your work be a struggle, let your peace be a victory.

"You should love peace as a means to new wars—and the short
peace more than the long," has often been cited out of context to
show that Nietzsche was a fascist. Nietzsche, however, is surely
not speaking of "war" in the literal sense any more than he is
speaking of soldiers. It is the quest for knowledge that he discusses, and he evidently believes that it need not be an entirely
private affair: it can be a contest, as it was in Socrates' day; and
the goal might be truth rather than winning an argument.
Hence one might triumph even in defeat. To be sure, one must
rest even in one's fight for truth, but such "peace" should give us

greater strength when we renew the struggle: it is a mere means. Happiness is found not in complacency but in joyous activity.

The same considerations apply to the shocking lines that follow the above quotation: "You say, it is the good cause that hallows even war? I say to you: it is the good war that hallows any cause." The idea is similar to that expressed in Dewey's epigram: "Men do not shoot because targets exist, but they set up targets in order that throwing and shooting may be more effective and significant." [32] Nietzsche, like Dewey, does not regard activity, exertion, and competition as essentially evil and hence justifiable as means only, but says, as it were: If this is not happiness, what is?

Nietzsche's choice of the word "war," which has prompted so much misunderstanding, suggests further—deliberately, no doubt —that innocuousness is not essential, and that one should not be squeamish about being injurious. The quest for knowledge, as Nietzsche likes to remind his readers, entails frequent disagreement with others and, at least in some fields of study, an occasional disregard not only for one's own feelings but also for those of others. In such cases it may of course be said that the good cause of truth hallows such offensiveness, while Nietzsche's dictum goes further in condoning the good war regardless of the cause. In the light of some of the material discussed earlier in this and other chapters, it appears that Nietzsche was so strongly opposed to any concessions to the "hypersensitive ears of our modern weaklings," and so eager not to "yield even a single step" (GM III 19), that he came to consider a disregard for the proprieties and sentiments of his contemporaries as good in itself. The atmosphere of his time seemed to him opposed to an uncompromising and uninhibited commitment to truth, and anything that would change that atmosphere might be welcome. The Greeks attained greatness through competition; could we hope to attain it through conformity and "lazy peace"?

To be sure, there are passages in which Nietzsche speaks of wars to come, meaning literally wars, and—with *amor fati*— seems glad of it; but even then he points out that men "throw themselves with delight into the new danger of *death* because they think that in the sacrifice for the fatherland they have at long last that long sought permission—the permission *to dodge their goal:*

---

[32] *Human Nature and Conduct* (1922), 226.

war is for them a detour to suicide, but a detour with a good conscience" (FW 338).

In that respect, war is classed with the altruism of the weak who find in it an escape from their hard task of self-perfection. In the end, Nietzsche—believing that "the time for small politics is gone," that "the next century will bring the fight for the dominion of the earth—the *coercion* to great politics"—hopes that the vast wars to come will bring to an end nationalism and "the comedy" of the existence of many states: he envisages "such an increase of the menace of Russia" that Europe will be forced, in self-defense, to become "One Europe" (FW 362; J 208). "The era of national wars" itself is but an *"entr' acte"*— a necessary evil, a period that "may indeed help such an art as Wagner's to a sudden glory, without thereby guaranteeing it a *future"*; in fact, "the Germans themselves have no future" (NCW IV).

The philosophically significant passages about "war," however, do not refer to the breakdown of diplomacy between nations any more than did Heraclitus' famous epigram: "War is the father of all things." It was from him that Nietzsche borrowed his unfortunate simile—the word "war"—but his meaning seems as clear as, and indeed quite similar to, such words of Jesus as these:

"Think not that I am come to send peace on earth: I came not to send peace, but a sword" (Matt. 10:34).

"I am come to send fire on the earth; and would that it were already kindled!" (Luke 12:49).

"Suppose ye that I am come to give peace on earth? I tell you, Nay; but rather division" (Luke 12:51).

". . . He that hath no sword, let him sell his garment and buy one" (Luke 22:36).

Here, too, the problem whether what is meant is war, arson, and swords, is solved by the context—for example: "For I am come to set a man at variance against his father, and the daughter against her mother . . . He that loveth father or mother more than me is not worthy of me: and he that loveth son or daughter more than me is not worthy of me. And he that taketh not his cross, and followeth after me, is not worthy of me" (Matt. 10:35, 37–38).

Self-perfection involves non-conformity and not what Nietzsche calls the "lazy peace, cowardly compromise, the whole virtuous uncleanliness of the modern Yes and No" (A 1). It would be perverse to claim that Nietzsche means to condemn "peace" and advocate "war."

Pity and altruism must be curbed by those who want to perfect themselves; but Nietzsche—his own Hyperborean loneliness notwithstanding—thinks that friendship may ease the way. Here man does not flee from himself or exert his will to "power" cheaply by indebting others to him. In friendship man can sublimate his jealousy into a keen spiritual competition, and the friends may vie with each other to make something of themselves that will delight, inspire, and spur on the other. "You cannot turn out too beautifully for your friend: for you shall be to him an arrow and a longing for the *Übermensch*" (Z I 14). The friend is less likely to shirk the task of self-perfection than are those who profess to love their neighbors. The weak man's love of his neighbor, carried to extremes, might be represented by those wealthy philanthropists whose personalities are no asset to the world. Nietzsche, however, exalted the friend:

> I teach you the friend in whom the world stands completed, a bowl of goodness—the creating friend who always has a completed world to give away [Z I 16].

> Physician, help yourself: thus you help your patient too. Let this be his best help that he may behold with his eyes the man who heals himself [Z I 22].

The man who has perfected himself has more to offer others than riches: he can give himself.

One recalls Goethe's conception of "two friends of the kind who always in turn enhance each other";[33] and above all one may think of the Greeks. The general practice of completely ignoring Nietzsche's exaltation of friendship[34]—though his critique of altruism cannot be correctly understood apart from this—has gone together with the false assumption that Nietzsche was decisively influenced by, and loved, only the *pre*-Socratic Greeks. Yet what Nietzsche probably tried to recapture more than anything else was the spirit of Socrates and his disciples—and when he writes

---

[33] Letter to Zelter, Oct. 30, 1824.
[34] Cf. even Jaspers, *op. cit.*, and Morgan, *op. cit.*

in one of his last works that "one does not *learn* from the Greeks —their way is too foreign" (G x 2), he seems to sum up the desperate failure of this effort. Failure or no—Nietzsche's repudiation of Christ cannot be fully understood apart from Nietzsche's admiration for Socrates.

13

NIETZSCHE'S ADMIRATION
FOR SOCRATES

. . . received the decisive thought as to how a philosopher
ought to behave toward men from the apology of Socrates:
as their physician, as a gadfly on the neck of man.—IV, 404.

Nietzsche's admiration for Socrates is a focal point of his thought
and reflects his views of reason and morality as well as the image
of man he envisaged. His critics and interpreters have been persistently preoccupied with his critique of Socrates, and it has
become a dogma, unquestioned and unexamined, that Nietzsche
repudiated Socrates. At best, it is admitted that his attitude was
"ambiguous," but no systematic inquiry has been made concerning Nietzsche's admiration for Socrates. Such a study, however—
and it is attempted in this chapter—leads to a reinterpretation of
The Birth of Tragedy and a new understanding of *Ecce Homo*,
and it throws new light on Nietzsche's entire philosophy, from his
first book to his last. It gives a concrete illustration, sadly lacking
in the voluminous Nietzsche literature, of his dialectic; it brings
to light the unequaled impact on his mind of the irony and ceaseless questioning of Socrates; and it shows how Nietzsche, for
whom Socrates was allegedly "a villain," [1] modeled his conception of his own task largely after Socrates' apology.

I

The prevalent impression of Nietzsche's attitude toward Socrates
depends partly on a misconstruction of his first book, which was

---

[1] Brinton, *op. cit.*, 83.

written, for the most part, during the Franco-Prussian War and
published in 1872. Its origin is thus reminiscent of that of Hegel's
first book, the *Phenomenology,* which was completed in Jena in
1806 while the French took the city. *The Birth of Tragedy* also
resembles Hegel's work in its fundamentally dialectical conception. Though Nietzsche's uneven style brings out the negative
and critical note most strongly, he was not primarily "for" or
"against": he tried to comprehend. In a general way, his dialectic
appears in his attitude toward his heroes. Like Oscar Wilde, he
thought that "all men kill the thing they love"—even that they
should kill it. Thus he explained his love of *Carmen* by calling
attention to "Don José's last cry on which the work ends: 'Yes! *I*
have killed her, *I*—my adored Carmen!'* Such a conception of love
(the only one worthy of a philosopher) is rare: it raises a work of
art above thousands" (W 2). We find no similar commentary on
Othello—but it is against this background that we must understand Nietzsche's great admiration for Shakespeare's portrait of
Brutus.

> Independence of the soul—that is at stake here! No sacrifice
> can then be too great: even one's dearest friend one must be
> willing to sacrifice for it, though he be the most glorious human
> being, embellishment of the world, genius without peer . . .
> [FW 98].

Friedrich Gundolf has pointed out, in two books on Caesar
and on Shakespeare, that Nietzsche read his own "sacrifice" of
Wagner into this drama. Nietzsche's relationship to Wagner, however, is merely the most striking instance of his dialectic. He pictured the second, negative, stage of his own development—and
of any quest for independence and freedom—as a deliberate
renunciation of all one has previously worshiped: old friends and
values are given up in a "twilight of the idols" (XVI, 37). If one
considers Nietzsche's attitude toward Schopenhauer, one finds the
same break: the Brutus crisis. The category "What Nietzsche
Hated" [2] is thus inadequate; and we shall now see how the inclusion of Socrates in it is quite untenable.

In *The Birth of Tragedy,* Socrates is introduced as a demigod,
the equal of Dionysus and Apollo, man and myth at once. Nietzsche has propounded his thesis of the origin of Greek tragedy out
of the "Dionysian" and the "Apollinian"; he has described the

---

[2] *Ibid.,* Chapter IV.

great dramas of Aeschylus and Sophocles, and finally the Euripidean attack on these giants. "Euripides, too, was . . . a mask only: the deity who spoke out of him was not Dionysus, nor Apollo, but . . . Socrates" (GT 12). While Socrates is pictured, in the following pages, as the embodiment of that rationalism which superseded tragedy, his superhuman dignity is emphasized throughout. Reverently, Nietzsche speaks of the "logical urge" of Socrates: ". . . in its unbridled flood it displays a natural power such as we encounter to our awed amazement only in the very greatest instinctive forces" (13). He speaks of sensing "even a breath of that divine naïveté and assurance of the Socratic direction of life" and of the "dignified seriousness with which he everywhere emphasized his divine calling, even before his judges" (13). Nor have there been many since Plato who have described Socrates' death with more loving poetry:

> That he was sentenced to death, not exile, Socrates himself seems to have brought about with perfect awareness and without any natural awe of death. He went to his death with the calm with which, according to Plato's description, he leaves the Symposium at dawn, the last of the revelers, to begin a new day, while on the benches and on the earth his drowsy table companions remain behind to dream of Socrates, the true eroticist [13].

Nietzsche's conception of Socrates was decisively shaped by Plato's *Symposium*[3] and *Apology,* and Socrates became little less than an idol for him. To reconcile this patent fact with the established notion that Nietzsche's attitude was hateful, some of the more careful students of Nietzsche's work have postulated a distinction between "Socratism," which he is then said to have detested, and the personality of Socrates himself.[4] Some such distinction is indeed required—but its validity depends on the definition of Socratism; and the view that Nietzsche merely admired the man Socrates while hating the outlook he embodied is untenable. Even a cursory inspection of §15 of *The Birth of Tragedy* shows this quite conclusively—and this section marks

---

[3] When Nietzsche graduated from school, he designated the *Symposium* his "*Lieblingsdichtung.*" (Cf. his *curriculum vitae* in E. Förster-Nietzsche, *Das Leben Friedrich Nietzsches* I, 109.)

[4] Cf. Hildebrandt, *Nietzsches Wettkampf mit Sokrates und Plato* (1922). Here a chronological analysis of Nietzsche's writings is offered, but GT 15 is ignored. A similar view had been suggested earlier (1918) by Bertram, *op. cit.*, who had, however, avoided any final clarity.

the climax and conclusion of Nietzsche's long analysis of the problem of Socrates. The original manuscript ended with §15; the remainder of the work, which consists of the "timely" application of the previous analysis to Wagner's work, was—as Nietzsche later regretted (GT-V)—added as an afterthought.[5] Nevertheless, interpreters have almost invariably ignored §15—and on this depends not only Brinton's construction but also Morgan's: *"The Birth of Tragedy* not only formulates the antinomy between knowledge and life: it presages Nietzsche's solution . . . suggesting that the antagonism between Socratism and art may not be necessary."[6] Actually, Nietzsche starts out with the antithesis of the Dionysian and the Apollinian; and their synthesis is found in tragic art. Then Socrates is introduced as the antithesis of tragic art. The antagonism is not one which "may not be necessary." Rather, Nietzsche persistently concerned himself with what he accepted as necessary; and because Socratism seemed necessary to him—he affirmed it. Like Hegel, Nietzsche sought to comprehend phenomena in their necessary sequence; that is part of the significance of his *amor fati.*

In fact, Nietzsche asks explicitly: "Perhaps art is even a necessary corollary and supplement of science?" (GT 14). In the next sentence, he replies: ". . . it must now be said how the influence of Socrates . . . again and again prompts a regeneration of *art"* (15). Far from merely presaging a solution, Nietzsche then tries systematically to show how the "sublime metaphysical delusion" of Socrates is that very instinct which leads science ever again to its own limits—at which it must necessarily give way to art. Socratism—i.e., the rationalistic tendency—was not arbitrarily

---

[5] The original manuscript, entitled *Socrates und die Griechische Tragödie,* was published in 1933.

One of Rilke's comments on *The Birth of Tragedy,* written in 1900 but not published until 1966 (see Bibliography), is very perceptive: "It seems to me that the accident of Wagner is to be blamed for the fact that N immediately applied his insights and hopes, which suit the German character so little, to this occasion, which was nearest at hand (too near!); this detracts greatly from the final third of the book. This damage is far greater than his use of Kantian and Schopenhauerian terminology. If Schopenhauer's conception of music in particular did much to advance N's purpose, the immediate application of everything to Wagner's creations spells disappointment: one does not *wish* that all these lofty promises are supposed to have been *already* fulfilled; above all, one believes that the author of the book is himself well qualified (*as a poet*) to make the attempt at a 'resurrection of Dionysus' " (1174 f.).

[6] *Op. cit.,* 264.

injected into the Greek mind by Socrates; it was "already effective before Socrates" and "only gained in him an indescribably magnificent expression" (14). What—Nietzsche asks in the end— would have happened to mankind *without* Socratism? He finds

> in Socrates the one turning point . . . of world history. For if one were to think of this whole incalculable sum of energy . . . as *not* employed in the service of knowledge, . . . then the instinctive lust for life would probably have been so weakened in general wars of annihilation . . . that suicide would have become a general custom, and individuals might have experienced the final remnant of a sense of duty when . . . strangling their parents and friends: . . . [15].

This is the final vision of *The Birth of Tragedy*—except for the appended application to Wagnerian opera. Unrestrained pessimism would not only fail to produce great art, but it would lead to race suicide. The Socratic heritage, the elemental passion for knowledge, must "by virtue of its own infinity guarantee the infinity" and continuation of art (15).

In the picture of the "theoretical man" who dedicates his life to the pursuit of truth, Nietzsche does not only pay homage to the "dignity" of Socrates, but his own features mingle with those of his ideal (15). Socratism is still envisaged as the necessary antithesis of tragedy; but by ensuring the continued development of culture, it makes possible an eventual synthesis of art and philosophy, even as tragedy itself was a synthesis of Apollo and Dionysus. The new synthesis, of course, cannot be anti-Socratic; and one may note that Nietzsche pictures it—another attempt at a self-portrait—as "an 'artistic Socrates' " (14).

In the end, consider Nietzsche's own estimate of *The Birth of Tragedy*:

> It smells offensively Hegelian, and the cadaverous perfume of Schopenhauer sticks only to a few formulas. An "idea"—the antithesis of the Dionysian and the Apollinian—translated into the realm of metaphysics; history itself as the development of this "idea"; in tragedy this antithesis is *aufgehoben* into a unity; and in this perspective things that had never before faced each other are suddenly juxtaposed, used to illuminate each other, and *comprehended* [*begriffen*] [EH-GT 1].[7]

---

[7] Oehler in his very influential book on *Friedrich Nietzsche und die Vorsokratiker* (1904), 28, claims that the early Nietzsche "was completely under the influence of Schopenhauer" and hence a pessimist, and therefore

In the summer of 1872, in 1873, and in 1876, Nietzsche, then a professor at the University of Basel, lectured on "The Pre-Platonic Philosophers." His lectures (IV, 245–364) substantiate what has here been said about his attitude toward Socrates. First of all, the significant conception of the "pre-*Platonic*" philosophers (which so pointedly includes Socrates) has been unjustifiably ignored in Oehler's book on *Nietzsche and the Pre-Socratics*; and practically all later interpreters have relied on Oehler's account of Nietzsche's relation to the ancient Greeks. The only English book that gives a detailed account of Nietzsche's "connection with Greek literature and thought" even goes to the extent of re-christening the lectures altogether, referring to them as *The Pre-Socratics*.[8]

Actually, Nietzsche quite specifically includes Socrates: "Socrates is the last one in this line" (1). In his lecture on Heraclitus, Nietzsche says further that three of the pre-Platonics embody the "purest types: Pythagoras, Heraclitus, Socrates—the sage as religious reformer, the sage as proud and lonely truth-finder, and the sage as the eternally and everywhere seeking one" (1). One may suspect that Nietzsche must have felt a special kinship to the ever seeking Socrates. In any case, the lecture on Socrates leaves little doubt about this self-identification. Socrates is celebrated as "the first philosopher of *life* [*Lebensphilosoph*]": "Thought serves life, while in all previous philosophers life served thought and knowledge" (17). Even then, Nietzsche was writing his "untimely" essay on the "Use and Disadvantage of History for Life." Written in 1873, it appeared in 1874.

---

had to repudiate optimistic Socratism. While the literature has, for the most part, followed Oehler, Troeltsch, *Der Historismus und seine Probleme* (1922), 499 ff., recognized Nietzsche's elaborate dialectic and hence found in *The Birth of Tragedy* "more Hegel than Schopenhauer," though he did not consider Nietzsche's attitude toward Socrates.

[8] Knight, *op. cit.,* 18. To the inaccuracies that Knight accepts uncritically from Oehler, Bertram, and Frau Förster-Nietzsche he adds many errors of his own; e.g., we are told that "only once does Nietzsche praise" Plato (57) and that "Nietzsche was undoubtedly influenced, in his Superman theories, by . . . Kierkegaard" (138 f. and 58). Yet Nietzsche's writings abound in tributes to Plato (who exerted a decisive influence on Nietzsche's thought); while the "Superman theories" were developed long before 1888, when Nietzsche first heard of Kierkegaard (from Brandes), too late to become acquainted with his ideas. Knight, however, follows Bertram in admitting—amid many inconsistencies—that Socrates influenced Nietzsche's conception of the ideal philosopher.

His admiration for Socrates, however, prevented him no more than the Platonic Alcibiades from stressing the physical ugliness of Socrates no less than his plebeian descent. His flat nose and thick lips, and his alleged admission that nature had endowed him with the fiercest passions, are all emphasized on the page preceding the praise of the *Lebensphilosoph*.[9]

The lecture draws heavily on the *Apology*: wisdom consists in seeing the limitations of one's own knowledge; Socrates, living in poverty, considered it his mission to be a gadfly on the neck of man; "life without such inquiries is no life." The irony of Socrates receives special emphasis. We may quote parts of the final tribute:

> Thus one must consider his magnificent apology: he speaks before posterity . . . he wanted death. He had the most splendid opportunity to show his triumph over human fear and weakness and also the dignity of his divine mission. Grote says: death took him hence in full magnificence and glory, as the sun of the tropics sets . . . with him the line of original and typical *"sophoi"* [sages] is exhausted: one may think of Heraclitus, Parmenides, Empedocles, Democritus, and Socrates. Now comes a new era . . . [10].

The prevalent view of Nietzsche's repudiation of Socrates ignores these lectures completely; yet the fragments of that period reiterate the same profound admiration. Beyond question the most important of these is *Philosophy in the Tragic Era of the Greeks,* which Knight identifies with "pre-Socratic philosophy," concluding that Socrates must have been conceived as the great villain.[10] Yet the essay, like the lectures, is based on the conception of "the pre-Platonic philosophers as a group that belongs together and to which alone I intend to devote this study" (2); and Nietzsche speaks of "the republic of geniuses from Thales to Socrates" (2).

---

[9] Ignoring this, Oehler, *op. cit.*, 28 ff., 31 f., assumes that Nietzsche's later insistence on Socrates' features and descent is proof of his hatred. The literature has generally followed Oehler.

[10] *Op. cit.*, 23, 58. Knight depends on Oehler, who, while granting that Nietzsche himself attached supreme importance to this fragment, assumed that Nietzsche was concerned with the pre-Socratic only (*op. cit.*, 123). The same assumption is at least implicit in Löwith, *Nietzsches Philosophie der Ewigen Wiederkunft des Gleichen,* 110, and Hofmiller, *Friedrich Nietzsche,* 15. The latter even claims that, in the realm of classical philology, Nietzsche was not at all interested "in Plato and Aristotle, but exclusively in the pre-Socratics" (12).

Of the many quotations that might be added, we shall adduce only two from the lectures on "The Study of the Platonic Dialogues" (IV, 365–443). Here the *Apology* is celebrated as "a masterpiece of the highest rank" (I 2), and later Nietzsche adds:

> Plato seems to have received the decisive thought as to how a philosopher ought to behave toward men from the apology of Socrates: as their physician, as a gadfly on the neck of man [II, 11].

Even then, in the spring of 1873, Nietzsche began, but did not complete, an "untimely" essay on "The Philosopher as the Physician of Culture" (*Der Philosoph als Arzt der Kultur*, VI, 65–74). Apparently, Nietzsche himself derived his picture of the ideal philosopher from the *Apology*, and Socrates became his model.

II

After what has been said so far, one may suspect that the point must be at hand where Nietzsche's passionate admiration should have been shaken by a "Brutus crisis"—a deliberate attempt to maintain "independence of the soul" by turning against the idolized Socrates. In a fragment, sketched late in 1875, we actually find an enumeration of three brief points regarding "Socratism" which is abruptly terminated by the sentence:

> Socrates, to confess it frankly, is so close to me that almost always I fight a fight against him [VI, 101].

Now we have previously admitted that some distinction must indeed be made between Nietzsche's attitudes toward Socrates and Socratism, although it is false to say that Nietzsche abominated Socratism, if the latter is taken to mean the outlook Socrates embodied.

Quite generally, Nietzsche distinguishes between (a) men whom he admires, (b) the ideas for which they stand, and (c) their followers. Only in terms of some such categories can one understand Nietzsche's complex attitude toward Jesus, Christianity, and Christendom. Similarly, Nietzsche admired Schopenhauer; respected but criticized Schopenhauer's philosophy; and despised the followers who made his "debauches and vices . . . a matter of faith" (FW 99). Nietzsche admired Wagner and felt drawn to much of his music; but he abominated the ostentatiously Christian nationalists and anti-Semites who congregated in Bayreuth —and his critique of Wagner might be epitomized by saying that he accused Wagner of having become a Wagnerian (EH-MA 2).

Nietzsche's fight against Socrates thus takes two forms: denunciations of his epigoni and respectful criticisms of his own doctrines. The critical period begins, characteristically, with a brief note in which the pre-Socratics and the post-Socratics are contrasted and the increasing concern with happiness after Socrates is deplored (vi, 104). The attack on the epigoni is also foreshadowed by the conception of Alexandrian culture which we find in the closing pages of *The Birth of Tragedy*—but Nietzsche distinguished between the *Lebensphilosoph* Socrates and the mediocrity who knows only the palest pleasures and lacks any conception of life or passion.

Socrates, while definitely a decisive "turning point" in history, is the very embodiment of Nietzsche's highest ideal: the passionate man who can control his passions. Here, as in Goethe, he found a man who had "given style to his character" (FW 290) and "disciplined himself to wholeness" (G IX 49). Such men, however, live, more often than not, on the threshold of what Nietzsche called decadence; and they perform their great deed of self-creation and integration on the verge of destruction and disintegration (cf. x, 412).

Even Schopenhauer does not come up to this ultimate standard. Against both him and Kant, Nietzsche levels the charge that they failed to achieve any true integration of life and learning: "Is that the life of sages? It remains science . . . Socrates would demand that one should bring philosophy down to man again" (vii, 21). The notion that Nietzsche repudiated his earlier view of Socrates as the "theoretical man," when he now described his philosophy as "practical," rests on a basic misunderstanding. There is no new positivistic and pro-Socratic period in which Nietzsche gives up his previous conceptions. Throughout, Socrates is admired for his integration of the theoretical and practical: in the earliest writings he is both the "theoretical man" and the *Lebensphilosoph;* now he is "the theoretical man" who "would rather die than become old and feeble in spirit" (vii, 198).[11]

---

[11] Hildebrandt, *op. cit.*, who would distinguish the anti-Socratic "theoretical" construction and the pro-Socratic "practical" interpretation, overlooks these and many similar passages.

Socrates is thus the very incarnation of the ideal Nietzsche opposes to his contemporary "Alexandrianism"; and in the essay on Schopenhauer, in the *Untimely Meditations,* Socrates is enlisted on Nietzsche's side: "the conditions for the origin of genius have *not improved* in modern times, and the aversion to original men has increased to such a degree that Socrates could not have lived among us and would not, in any case, have reached the age of seventy" (U III 6).

From Nietzsche's next work, *Human, All-Too-Human,* where Socrates is often referred to with unqualified approval and the notions of the gadfly and the divine calling are still prominent, we shall cite only a single passage:

> *Socrates:* If all goes well, the time will come when, to develop oneself morally-rationally, one will take up the *memorabilia* of Socrates rather than the Bible, and when Montaigne and Horace will be employed as precursors and guides to the understanding of the simplest and most imperishable mediator-sage, Socrates. . . . Above the founder of Christianity, Socrates is distinguished by the gay kind of seriousness and that *wisdom full of pranks* which constitutes the best state of the soul of man. Moreover, he had the greater intelligence [S 86].

Such passages would seem to render absurd any claim that Nietzsche hated Socrates. Oehler, however, has suggested—and most of the literature has followed him—that Nietzsche's writings are to be divided into three stages of which the second, with its enlightened views, represents a temporary departure from true Nietzscheanism. This untenable dogma was intended to explain away Nietzsche's break with Wagner, his repudiation of nationalism and racism, and his vision of the "Good European." All the ideals of Nietzsche's so-called "middle period," however, can also be found in his later writings and actually receive their most extreme formulation in the last works of 1888. State worship, for example, is denounced in the essay on Schopenhauer in the "early" period; in the aphorisms of the "middle" period; then, even more vehemently, in the chapter "On the New Idol" in *Zarathustra;* and finally in *Götzen-Dämmerung* and *Ecce Homo.*[12] Just as persistent are his antiracism, his appreciation of the Enlightenment—and his admiration for Socrates.

---

[12] Those who would consider Nietzsche's condemnation of the State as somehow anti-Socratic may well be reminded of Socrates' dictum in the

The *Dawn* is the first of Nietzsche's books in which a respectful critique of Socratic doctrines can be found. Socrates and Plato, though they were "great doubters and admirable innovators," shared that "deepest error that 'right knowledge *must be followed* by right action' " (M 116; cf. M 22).

In *The Gay Science* Nietzsche's admiration for Socrates reaches its apotheosis. The genuine simplicity of the dying Socrates is celebrated once more (FW 36), his war on ignorance and unthinking acceptance of the opinions of others is lauded (FW 328), and Nietzsche declares: "I admire the courage and wisdom of Socrates in all he did, said—and did not say" (FW 340). This affirmation, though unqualified, is not blind—and the very same aphorism ends with the words: "we must overcome even the Greeks." As a dialectical thinker, Nietzsche affirms as necessary and admires even what must be overcome. His admiration does not arrest his thinking, and his critique does not detract from his admiration. In his own historical situation, Socrates acted as wisely and courageously as was then possible; but in the same passage Nietzsche claims that Socrates was a pessimist who "suffered life" as a disease. This is what must be overcome—and the following aphorism contains one of the first statements of the conception of

---

Apology: "if I had engaged in politics, I should have perished long ago, and done no good to either you or to myself. . . . No man who goes to war with you or any other multitude, honestly striving against the many lawless and unrighteous deeds which are done in a state, will save his life; he who will fight for the right, if he would live even for a brief space, must have a private station and not a public one" (31 f., Jowett). Even in the *Republic*, where the Platonic Socrates describes the ideal City, he concludes: "perhaps there is a pattern set up in the heavens for one who desires to see it and, seeing it, to found one in himself. But whether it exists anywhere or ever will exist is no matter; for this is the only commonwealth in whose politics he can ever take part" (592, Cornford). Nietzsche, to be sure, did not believe in Plato's heaven or his Theory of Forms— but he assumed that Socrates had not believed in them either; and in their opposition to any existing form of government, and perhaps also in their deprecation of business and democracy, both Plato and Nietzsche seem to have considered themselves heirs of Socrates. The scattered notes of Nietzsche's last years in which he toys with notions of breeding philosophers and with a caste system in which nature herself distinguishes between the predominantly spiritual ones (*Geistige*), the warriors, and the mediocre mass, are obviously inspired by the *Republic*, no less than are the notes in which Nietzsche suggests that military discipline must be part of the philosopher's education. Yet who among all the great philosophers was a soldier's soldier—except Socrates?

eternal recurrence. With this ultimate affirmation of life, Nietzsche would overcome pessimism; but this doctrine obviously bars any idiosyncratic repudiation.

Zarathustra, Nietzsche's next work, contains no explicit mention of Socrates; yet two of its chapters cannot be properly understood apart from Nietzsche's admiration for Socrates: "On the Friend" and "On Free Death." Nietzsche's scornful words about love of one's neighbor are known well enough, but the key sentence of the chapter "On Neighbor-Love" should not be ignored:[13] "Not the neighbor do I teach you but the friend."

Nietzsche's high esteem for the Greeks is a commonplace; but it has been assumed that he wanted to return to the pre-Socratics, while his great debt to Socrates, Plato, Aristotle, and the Stoics has been overlooked.[14] In his attempt to surpass the Sermon on the Mount, Nietzsche goes back to the Socratics. Thus we find an epigram at the end of the first part of *Zarathustra* (quoted again in the preface to *Ecce Homo*): "The man who seeks knowledge must be able not only to love his enemies but also to hate his friends." One is immediately reminded of Aristotle's excuse for his disagreement with Plato (*Nicomachean Ethics* 1096a): it is a "duty, for the sake of maintaining the truth, even to destroy what touches us closely" since "piety requires us to honor truth above our friends." Nietzsche goes beyond Aristotle by urging his

---

[13] In this respect, Jodl's *Geschichte der Ethik* is at one with Morgan, *op. cit.;* while Santayana, in his *Egotism in German Philosophy,* actually writes: "it is remarkable how little he learned from the Greeks . . . no sense for friendship . . ." (121 f.).

[14] Thus Oehler ignores Nietzsche's dialectic, his ceaseless questioning, his irony, his discourse on love of one's educator, his conception of sublimation with its incessant allusions to the *Symposium,* his development of Plato's notion of *sophrosyne,* his eulogy of friendship and free death, his *amor fati,* etc. A just recognition of Nietzsche's debt to the pre-Socratics need not entail the claim that Nietzsche despised the later Greeks. Like Oehler's later book on *Friedrich Nietzsche und die Deutsche Zukunft* (1935), his *Friedrich Nietzsche und die Vorsokratiker* depends on a tendentious selection of fragmentary quotations, torn from their context. Oehler's earlier book, however, ends with a quotation which, while supposed to justify the attempt to trace Nietzsche's spiritual ancestry, is actually amusingly at odds not only with Oehler's *furor Teutonicus,* but also with his central thesis that Nietzsche's preference for the pre-Socratics entailed a repudiation of Socrates and Plato: ". . . In that which moved Zarathustra, Moses, Mohammed, Jesus, Plato, Brutus, Spinoza, Mirabeau—I live, too. . . ."

own readers: "One repays a teacher badly if one always remains a pupil only" (Z I 22). Like Socrates, Nietzsche would rather arouse a zest for knowledge than commit anyone to his own views. And when he writes, in the chapter "On the Friend," "one who is unable to loosen his own chains may yet be a redeemer for his friend," he seems to recall Socrates' claim that he was but a barren midwife.

Nietzsche's emphatic scorn for those who would abandon their own path to follow another master, and his vision of a disciple who might follow his master's conceptions beyond the master's boldest dreams are thus no longer enigmatic. We can also understand the episode in Nietzsche's biography when he was looking for such a disciple—just one, not twelve. A "Nietzschean," however, whether "gentle" or "tough," is in a sense a contradiction in terms: to be a Nietzschean, one must not be a Nietzschean.

Nietzsche's hymn on "dying at the right time," in the chapter "On Free Death," has stumped his interpreters: for he obviously does not have in mind suicide. Jesus, moreover, is named explicitly as one who died a "free death," but "too early" and "too young," and not "at the right time." A close reading of the chapter, however, and a comparison with the many passages in which Nietzsche speaks of Socrates' death leave no doubt that we are confronted with another juxtaposition of Socrates and Christ. Nietzsche's general failure to equal his hero could hardly be illustrated more frightfully than by his own creeping death.

In the preface to *Beyond Good and Evil,* Nietzsche's next work, we are told that the influence of Socrates, though it may well have been a corruption, was a *necessary* and fruitful ingredient in the development of Western man: "let us not be ungrateful . . ." We must keep this programmatic preface in mind when we read Nietzsche's violent objection to the Socratic identification of the good with the useful and agreeable, "which smells of the plebes" (190). Although Socrates, "that great ironist, so rich in secrets," recognized the irrational component of moral judgments, his influence led to the misconception that reason and instinct aim naturally for the good (191).

A later passage shows conclusively that Nietzsche has not really changed his mind about Socrates: he is still the ideal philosopher. Short of the value-creating philosopher of the future

who has never yet existed—and does not live today (211) [15]—
there is none greater than Socrates.

> The philosopher, as a *necessary* man of tomorrow . . . always
> had to find himself, in opposition to his today. . . . Hitherto
> all these extraordinary promoters of man, who are called phi-
> losophers, and who rarely have felt themselves to be friends of
> wisdom, but rather disagreeable fools and dangerous question
> marks, have found their . . . hard, unwanted, inescapable task
> . . . in being the bad conscience of their time. By applying the
> knife vivisectionally to the very *virtues of the time* they be-
> trayed their own secret: to know of a *new* greatness of man
> . . . Each time they have uncovered how much hypocrisy,
> comfortableness, letting oneself go and letting oneself drop
> . . . were concealed under the most honored type of their
> contemporary morality. . . . At the time of Socrates, among
> men of fatigued instincts, among the conservatives of ancient
> Athens who let themselves go . . . *irony* was perhaps neces-
> sary for greatness of soul—that Socratic sarcastic [*boshaft*] as-
> surance of the old physician and plebeian who cut ruthlessly
> into his own flesh, as well as into the flesh and heart of the
> "nobility," with a glance that said unmistakably: "Don't try to
> deceive me by dissimulation. Here we are equal." Today, con-
> versely, when only the herd animal is honored and dispenses
> honors in Europe, and when "equality of rights" could all too
> easily be converted into an equality in violating rights—by that
> I mean, into a common war on all that is rare, strange, or
> privileged, on the higher man, the higher soul, the higher duty,
> the higher responsibility, and on the wealth of creative power
> and mastery—today the concept of "greatness" entails being
> noble, wanting to be by oneself, being capable of being differ-
> ent, standing alone, and having to live independently. . . . To-
> day—is greatness *possible?* [212].

Nietzsche realizes that the greatness of Socrates is indubitable,
while his own greatness is problematic. The model philosopher
is still a physician, but the gadfly has turned into a vivisectionist.
The passage also throws light on Nietzsche's aristocratic tendencies. In an age in which there was a "nobility" that deemed itself superior without living up to its exalted conception of itself,
greatness could manifest itself in the bold insistence on a fundamental equality. In our time, however, equality is confused with
conformity—as Nietzsche sees it—and it is taken to involve the
renunciation of personal initiative and the demand for a general

---

[15] In J 44, Nietzsche expressly calls himself a mere "herald and precursor"
of the "philosophers of the future."

leveling. Men are losing the ambition to be equally excellent, which involves as the surest means the desire to excel one another in continued competition, and they are becoming resigned to being equally mediocre. Instead of vying for distinction, men nurture a *ressentiment* against all that is distinguished, superior, or strange. The philosopher, however, must always stand opposed to his time and may never conform; it is his calling to be a fearless critic and diagnostician—as Socrates was. And Nietzsche feels that he is only keeping the faith with this Socratic heritage when he calls attention to the dangers of the modern idealization of equality, and he challenges us to have the courage to be different and independent. In the modern world, however, is that still possible?

In the *Genealogy of Morals,* Socrates is mentioned only once:

> What great philosopher hitherto has been married? Heraclitus, Plato, Descartes, Spinoza, Leibniz, Kant, Schopenhauer—these were not. . . . A married philosopher belongs *in comedy* . . . and that exception . . . the *sarcastic* [*boshaft*] Socrates, it seems, married *ironically* just to demonstrate *this* proposition [III, 7]

Eight *great* philosophers are named; only one is a pre-Socratic, though others could have been added easily—and Socrates and Plato are both included.

The posthumously published notes of Nietzsche's last years have sometimes been invoked to prove assertions about Nietzsche that are at odds with the published works. As a matter of principle, it should not be forgotten that the notes, including those which the editors chose to publish as *The Will to Power,* are mostly the scribblings Nietzsche jotted into his notebooks during his long walks—and at night. They cannot balance the lectures and the books; and most of them, including again the material published in *The Will to Power,* appear in Nietzsche's later books, often in a form and a context that yield an unexpected meaning.

In any case, the notes contain no departure from Nietzsche's previous position. Side by side with occasional tributes to the philosophers "before Socrates" (WM 437; XVI, 3, 4), we find, for example, these sentences:

> Some ancient writings one reads to understand antiquity: others, however, are such that one studies antiquity *in order* to be

able to read *them*. To these belongs the *Apology*; its theme is supra-Greek . . . [XVI, 6].

Nietzsche's references to the ugliness and plebeian descent of Socrates are as continuous with the earlier works as the tributes to his irony and integrity.

The passages about Socrates in *The Will to Power* deal primarily with his alleged decadence (429–32, 437, 441–43, 578). But, as we have seen, Nietzsche explains in the Preface of *The Case of Wagner*: "I am no less than Wagner a child of this age, that is, a *decadent;* but I comprehended this, I resisted it. The philosopher in me resisted." Wagner, it seems, resembled the Athenians who let themselves go, while Nietzsche emulates Socrates, the model philosopher: "What does a philosopher demand of himself, first and last? To overcome his time in himself, to become 'timeless.'" This conception of the decadent philosopher who cannot cure his own decadence but yet struggles against it is developed in the *Götzen-Dämmerung*. Like his first book, it contains an extended treatment of what Nietzsche now calls "The Problem of Socrates";[16] and one may generalize that the works of 1888, for all their hyperboles and for all their glaring faults, represent more sustained analyses than any of Nietzsche's works since *The Birth of Tragedy*. However strained and unrestrained they are, they contain some of Nietzsche's most fruitful and ingenious conceptions.

In his chapter on "The Problem of Socrates," Nietzsche recalls the ugliness, plebeian descent, and decadence of Socrates and adds—in a sentence which we shall have to recall later: "Socrates was the buffoon [*Hanswurst*] who *made others take him seriously*" (5). He is also said to have "fascinated" the contest-craving Greeks by offering them a new kind of spiritualized dialectical contest, and—as in *The Birth of Tragedy*—he is considered a great "erotic" (8). Far more significant is the fact that, just as in Nietzsche's first book, Socratism is considered dialectically as something necessary—in fact, as the very force that saved Western civilization from an otherwise inescapable destruction. Socrates "understood that all the world *needed* him—his means, his cure, his personal artifice of self-preservation" (9): "one had only *one* choice: either to perish or—to be *absurdly rational*"

---

[16] Knight, *op. cit.*, 128, erroneously declares this chapter to be part of the *Genealogy*.

(10). In this way alone could the excesses of the instincts be curbed in an age of disintegration and degeneration; Socratism alone could prevent the premature end of Western man. Yet "to *have to* fight the instincts—that is the formula for decadence" (11). Socratism itself is decadent and cannot produce a real cure; by thwarting death it can only make possible an eventual regeneration which may not come about for centuries. Socrates himself realized this: "In the *wisdom* of his courage to die," he recognized that for himself no ultimate cure was possible—except death (12).[17]

III

Ecce Homo was Nietzsche's last work and in many ways the culmination of his philosophy. Much of it can be understood only in terms of a juxtaposition which we have previously encountered: Christ versus Socrates. As Nietzsche assures us in the *Antichrist,* he reveres the life and death of Jesus—but instead of interpreting it as a promise of another world and another life, and instead of conceding the divinity of Jesus, Nietzsche insists: *Ecce Homo!* Man can live and die in a grand style, working out his own salvation instead of relying on the sacrifice of another. Where Kierkegaard, at the outset of his *Fragments,* poses an alternative of Christ, the Savior, and Socrates, the Teacher, and then chooses Christ and revelation, Nietzsche, as ever, prefers Socrates: man's salvation is in himself, if anywhere. Like Kierkegaard—and unlike some "humanists" today—Nietzsche felt that this position entailed a decisive break with Christianity. In any case, it does not involve any departure from Nietzsche's "middle" period. He still considers himself the heir of the Enlightenment: at the end of *Ecce Homo* he cites Voltaire's *"Écrasez l'infâme!"*

This vehement polemic is not incompatible with the *amor fati* stressed in *Ecce Homo.* Thus we are told in the first part:

---

[17] Not only Hildebrandt, *op. cit.,* 57–59, assumes that this chapter contains another "hateful" repudiation of Socratism, but even Klages, *op. cit.,* 181, takes for granted Nietzsche's "passionate repudiation of Socrates . . . in GT and G"—and that in a chapter in which Klages accuses (!) Nietzsche of "Socratism," i.e. of not having been sufficiently irrational. Neither author offers any analysis of the text of G.

"Nothing that is may be subtracted, nothing is dispensable" (2); and in the second part Nietzsche elaborates: "My formula for the greatness of a human being is *amor fati:* that one wants nothing to be different—not forward, not backward, not in all eternity" (10). If this attitude is not markedly different from Hegel's, Nietzsche's attitude toward Christianity certainly is. Yet both men define their own historical significance in terms of their relation to Christianity. Owing to this, each considers himself, in Nietzsche's words, a destiny. Hegel thought his system reconciled in an essentially secular philosophy the dogmata of Christianity and the heritage of ancient and modern philosophy. He saw himself standing at the end of an era as a fulfillment. Nietzsche answered his own question, "why I am a destiny," by claiming that he was the first to have "uncovered" Christian morality. He believed that after him no secular Christian system would be possible any more; and he considered himself the first philosopher of an irrevocably anti-Christian era. "To be the first one here may be a curse; in any case, it is a destiny" (6). His anti-Christianity, therefore, does not seem to him essentially negative. He is no critic who would have things be different: he lives at the beginning of a new era, and things *will* be different. "I contradict as has never been contradicted before and am yet the opposite of a no-saying spirit" (1).

All this shows the essential continuity of Nietzsche's thought, no less than does his reiteration in the first chapter that he, as well as Socrates, is decadent. In his discussion of *Zarathustra,* Nietzsche ascribes to the overman that "omni-presence of sarcasm [*Bosheit*] and frolics" which he evidently associated with Socrates; and in speaking of *The Case of Wagner* Nietzsche emphasizes his own love of irony. Yet not one of these points is as important as the fact that *Ecce Homo* is Nietzsche's *Apology.*

Brinton remarks incidentally—though, in conformity with almost the entire literature, he fails to discuss *Ecce Homo*—that it "is not apologetic." [18] This, of course, is the basis of our comparison with the *Apology*—that masterpiece for whose sake one studies antiquity. The heading of the first chapter, "why I am so wise," recalls the leitmotif of the *Apology.* Socrates, after claiming that he was the wisest of men, had interpreted his wis-

---

[18] *Op. cit.,* 65. Hildebrandt, in his discussion of Nietzsche's attitude toward Socrates, does not even mention *Ecce Homo.*

dom in terms of the foolishness of his contemporaries, who thought they knew what they really did not know, and in terms of his own calling. Nietzsche answers his own provocative question in terms of "the disparity between the greatness of my task and the smallness of my contemporaries" (EH-V 1). His wisdom, he claims, consists in his opposition to his time—and we have seen that he felt close to Socrates in this respect.

The second question, "why I am so clever," is similarly answered: "I have never pondered questions that are none" (1). Again one recalls the *Apology*, where Socrates scorns far-flung speculations; he confined his inquiries to a few basic questions of morality.

The third question, "why I write such good books," receives a more startling reply: "There is altogether no prouder nor, at the same time, more subtle kind of book: here and there they attain the ultimate that can be attained on earth—cynicism" (3). We are reminded of that Socratic "wisdom full of pranks which constitutes the best state of the soul of man," and of the "sarcastic assurance" of the "great ironist" who vivisected the virtues of his age. Nietzsche concedes that a cynic may be no more than an "indiscreet billy goat and ape," but even so he considers "cynicism the only form in which mean souls touch honesty" (J 26). His position here depends, as it often does, on the conviction that superficially similar forms of behavior may be expressions of profoundly different states of mind: "In sarcasm [*Bosheit*] the frolicker and the weakling meet" (Z 1 10); it may be an expression of *ressentiment* or of greatness of soul. Thus Nietzsche expressly associates cynicism with the "new barbarians" who combine "spiritual superiority with well-being and excess of strength" (WM 899). And in a letter to Brandes, on November 20, 1888, he says: "I have now written an account of myself with a cynicism that will become world-historical. The book is called *Ecce Homo. . . .*" [19]

In the *Götzen-Dämmerung*, Socrates had been called a buffoon: now "buffoon" and "satyr" (a term the Platonic Alcibiades had used to picture Socrates) become idealized conceptions.

---

[19] Morgan, *op. cit.*, 133 f., writes: "I am unable to account for Nietzsche's extraordinary valuation of *cynicism.*" The present analysis would indicate that it is to be accounted for in terms of Nietzsche's admiration for Socrates. In *Ecce Homo* he tried to outdo Socrates' request for maintenance in the Prytaneum (*Apology* 36).

Nietzsche, too, would be a satyr (EH-V); he praises Heine's "divine sarcasm without which I cannot imagine perfection" and calls him a satyr; and on the same page he says of Shakespeare: "what must a man have suffered to find it so very necessary to be a buffoon" (EH II 4). In the end, Nietzsche says of himself: "I do not want to be a saint, rather a buffoon. Perhaps I am a buffoon" (EH IV 1).

We may conclude by considering a passage from *Beyond Good and Evil* (295) which is quoted in *Ecce Homo* (III 6). Originally Nietzsche had claimed that he was here describing Dionysus—and indeed this is a picture of him whom Nietzsche has in mind when he writes, in the last line of his last book: "Has one understood me?—*Dionysus versus the Crucified*—"

Who is "Dionysus"? Nietzsche encountered the death and resurrection of a god in both Orphism and Christianity; but the rebirth of Dionysus seemed to him a reaffirmation of life as "indestructible, powerful, and joyous," in spite of suffering and death, while he construed the crucifixion as a "curse on life," and recalled that Goethe already had spurned the cross.[20] When "Dionysus" absorbed the Apollinian, and the reaffirmation of life assumed the meaning of passion sublimated as opposed to passion extirpated, Goethe became Nietzsche's model, and he "baptized" Goethe's faith "with the name of *Dionysus*" (G IX 49). Beyond doubt, the title *Ecce Homo* refers not only to Pilate's famous words about Jesus, but also to the exclamation with which Napoleon greeted Goethe: *Voilà un homme!* When Nietzsche had first cited this phrase (J 209), he had been unable to suppress the comment: "that meant, 'But this is a *man!* I had expected a mere German.' " *Ecce Homo* suggests a larger contrast: Goethe versus Christ, "*Dionysus versus the Crucified.*"

Nietzsche, however, is not thinking of Goethe alone. In *Beyond Good and Evil* already, "Dionysus is a philosopher" (295); and while Nietzsche prefaces the quotation in *Ecce Homo,* "I forbid, by the way, any conjecture as to whom I am describing in this passage," we need not conjecture if we remember that Nietzsche called Socrates the "Pied Piper of Athens"—in *The Gay Science,* right after saying: "I admire the courage and wisdom of Socrates in all he did, said—and did not say" (340).

---

[20] GT 7; WM 1052; WH 175. Cf. p. 379.

The genius of the heart, as that great hidden one has it . . .
the Pied Piper . . . whose voice knows how to descend into
the depths of every soul. . . . The genius of the heart . . .
who teaches one to listen, who smooths rough souls and
lets them taste a new yearning. . . . The genius of the heart
. . . who divines the hidden and forgotten treasure, the
drop of goodness . . . under the . . . thick ice. . . . The genius of the heart from whose touch everyone goes away richer,
not having found grace nor amazed, not as blessed and oppressed by the goods of another, but richer in himself . . .
opened up . . . less sure perhaps . . . but full of hopes that as
yet have no name [J 295].

The last lines may be true of Nietzsche, too—and he goes on
to call himself a disciple of this "Dionysus" and, in a later passage, also a Pied Piper (G-V). Yet he fell so pitifully short of
Socrates' serenely mature humanity that his very admiration
invites comparison with the mad, drunken Alcibiades in the
Symposium, who also could not resist the fascination and charm
of Socrates. And if we seek an epitaph for Nietzsche, we might
do well to couple his hymn on the genius of the heart with the
words of the Platonic Alcibiades:

I have been bitten by a more than viper's tooth; I have known
in my soul . . . that worst of pangs . . . the pang of philosophy
which will make a man say or do anything. And you . . . all
of you, and I need not say Socrates himself, have had experience
of the same madness and passion in your longing after wisdom.
Therefore, listen and excuse my doings . . . and my sayings.
. . . But let profane and unmannered persons close up the doors
of their ears.

EPILOGUE

Nietzsche's Heritage

> Virtually everything my generation discussed, tried to think through—one might say, suffered; one might also say, spun out—had long been expressed and exhausted by Nietzsche, who had found definitive formulations; the rest was exegesis.
> —GOTTFRIED BENN, "Nietzsche—nach 50 Jahren"

Nietzsche is perhaps best known as the prophet of great wars and power politics and as an opponent of political liberalism and democracy. That is the idol of the "tough Nietzscheans" and the whipping boy of many a critic. The "tender Nietzscheans," on the other hand, insist—quite rightly—that Nietzsche scorned totalitarianism, denounced the State as "The New Idol" (Z I 11), and was himself a kindly and charitable person; but some of them infer falsely that he must therefore have been a liberal and a democrat, or a socialist. We have tried to show that Nietzsche opposed both the idolatry of the State and political liberalism because he was basically *"antipolitical"* (EH I 3) and, moreover, loathed the very idea of belonging to any "party" whatever.

It is this protestant Nietzsche who does not conform to any party line—the "gadfly" who would follow "the truth into all hide-outs" and die rather than cease philosophizing—whose heritage we now want to consider in closing. A comprehensive study of his heritage would of course require another book and painstaking analyses of such diverse movements as psychoanalysis, existentialism, and Nazism, of Scheler's and Klages' conceptions of *ressentiment* and Hartmann's *Ethik,* Spengler's construction of history and Thomas Mann's novels, George

Bernard Shaw, and a host of others. All that can be attempted in this Epilogue is a summary of a very few points.

There is something shrill about much of Nietzsche's writings: he delights in antitheses to what is current; it is as if he were swimming against the stream for its own sake; and he makes a sport of being provocative. Even if one does not agree with him, one may yet value this aspect of Nietzsche's thought—if only on the grounds suggested by John Stuart Mill in his essay *On Liberty*: "if there are any persons who contest a received opinion, . . . let us thank them for it, open our minds to listen to them, and rejoice that there is some one to do for us what we otherwise ought, if we have any regard for either the certainty or the vitality of our convictions, to do with much greater labor for ourselves." [1]

Nietzsche's manner, however, is apt to obscure his basic intentions. His opposition to the Sermon on the Mount is more obvious than what he would put in its place: "If you have an enemy, do not requite him evil with good, for that would put him to shame. Rather prove that he did you some good" (Z I 19). He seems to condemn neighbor-love and morality altogether and lacks the patience to make clear that his criticism is directed only against certain types of these; and he speaks of "war" even when he is evidently thinking of strife, of "power" rather than "self-perfection," and of the "Dionysian" rather than the "classical." He insists that "War and courage have done more great things than neighbor-love" (Z II 18) and leaves it to the context to show that he is concerned with strife and exertion generally rather than armed conflict between nations—and that by neighbor-love he means the ineffectual pastime of sterile souls who flee their task of self-perfection. He goes out of his way to emphasize that "great things" must be "fought" for and that it takes courage to win independence, for individuals as well as nations—and he fails to place equal emphasis on the point, no less important for any real understanding of his philosophy, that "Thoughts that come with doves' feet guide the world" (Z II 22 and EH-V 4) and "the greatest events—those are not our loudest but our stillest hours" (Z II 18). Some "great things" may have issued from wars; but "the greatest events" are the experiences of those stillest hours when we are creative, absorbed, and heedless of society.

---

[1] Chapter II.

Rembrandt painting one of his self-portraits has no thought of his neighbor; he neither loves him nor plots against him—he is a creator.

> Little do the people comprehend the great, that is the creating. But they have a mind for all . . . actors. . . . Around the inventors of new values the world revolves. . . . But around the actors revolve the people and fame . . . The actor has spirit but little conscience of the spirit. Always he has faith in that with which he inspires the most faith—faith in himself! Tomorrow he has a new faith and the day after tomorrow a newer one. . . . To overthrow—that means to him: to prove. To drive to frenzy—that means to him: to persuade. And blood is to him the best of all reasons. . . . Far from the market place and from fame happens all that is great: far from the market place and from fame, the inventors of new values have always dwelt [Z I 12].

The personal experience of the contrast of Bayreuth and Sils Maria has here become the occasion for a more general insight —and the contemporary reader of this passage is less likely to think of Wagner than of his most notorious admirer. The positive significance of the passage may be seen in the fact that Nietzsche's philosophy is indeed a sustained celebration of creativity—and all genuine creation is, as we have tried to show, a creation of new values and norms. Nietzsche's reference to "inventors" of new values, however, is misleading insofar as "invention" may suggest deliberate contrivance; and it has been shown that Nietzsche's "revaluation" was not intended as such.

Nietzsche failed to distinguish sharply enough between that internal criticism of "contemporary virtue" which is properly the revaluation, and that creation of new norms which is characteristic of all creativity—whether it be Michelangelo's or Beethoven's, Shakespeare's or Goethe's. The confusion may have been due in part to the fact that one man—whom Nietzsche supremely admired—represented both the critical and the creative function in the highest degree: Socrates. He was not only the "gadfly" of Athens and the "vivisectionist" of contemporary conceit and hypocrisy; he also created his own character and embodied new values which generations of philosophers after him sought to explicate in their ethics. One may think of Plato, Aristotle, the Cynics and Cyrenaics, the Stoics and the Epicureans.

Nietzsche himself—however short he fell of equaling his hero in other respects—was not a mere critic of "timely" valuations either; he, too, conceived a new picture of man—"new" not only to his own age, but also in its rich psychological detail and in its ramifications. And in that sense it may be said in the end that he did offer new values—if only implicitly, after the manner of great artists and creators, "away from the market place." There is a sense in which every great individual is an embodiment of new norms, an incarnate value-legislation, and a promise and challenge to posterity. Nietzsche himself saw this, and this insight inspired his "monumentalistic" or "supra-historical" approach to history. And this is a significant aspect of his heritage.[2]

---

[2] It was further developed by Stefan George's disciples. While some of them perversely denied this insight to Nietzsche in their contributions to the Nietzsche literature, claiming that he had envisaged such individuals only as unattainable goals, other members of the Circle composed studies of the very men whom Nietzsche himself had held up as examples: Caesar, Frederick II, Shakespeare, Napoleon, Goethe. In these books, especially in those by F. Gundolf, we recognize Nietzsche's heritage; and they are, on the whole, closer to his spirit than is Spengler's approach to history, although Spengler says in his preface to *Der Untergang des Abendlandes* that he owes "everything" to Goethe and Nietzsche. What he did owe to Nietzsche, besides the conception of culture as "the unity of the artistic style in all the expressions of the life of a people" (U I 1), is well brought out by a passage in *The Will to Power*:

"That mankind has to solve a total task, that it as a whole moves toward some goal—this very . . . arbitrary notion is still very young. . . . It is no whole, this mankind: it is an indissoluble multiplicity of ascending and descending life processes—it does not have a youth and then a maturity and finally an old age. Rather the layers cut through each other and lie above each other—and in a few millennia there may yet exist younger types of man than we can discover today. Decadence, on the other hand, belongs to all epochs of mankind: everywhere there are decay and waste materials; it is a life process itself, the secretion of the forms of decline and offal" (WM 339).

Spengler accepts Nietzsche's denial of the unity of history; but on the level of the various independent cultures that he posits, he reinstates all the propositions Nietzsche denies. Thus Nietzsche's central point—namely, that the individual is not the pawn of any historical process—is given up. To Nietzsche, as to Goethe, the individual had been a revelation. Spengler's willful use of persons and events, on the other hand, issues from a lack of any such respect for the individual. And this perversion of the "suprahistorical" outlook leads to Spengler's falsifications of history. His biologism, his use of the "Apollinian" as the name of one particular culture, and his romantic glorification of the "Faustian" are essentially different from Nietzsche, who, incidentally, grew more and more contemptuous of Faust and, unlike Spengler, recognized the crucial difference between Goethe and his creature. In short, Nietzsche's denial of the unity of history was a fruitful antithesis to Lessing, Hegel, Comte, etc., and this heritage was developed by Spengler, but richly blended with un-Nietzschean elements.

A book on "The Development of the Nietzsche Picture in Germany" [3] distinguishes between the early interpretations—and one may add that many of the later studies present much the same picture—where Nietzsche appears in a "blood red light" as the ruthless individualist and admirer of Cesare Borgia; a second stage that emphasizes Nietzsche's *Kulturphilosophie*; a third phase that discovers in Nietzsche "the great antipode of Schopenhauer," the victor over the *fin de siècle,* and "The Dionysian Yea-Sayer to Life"—and finally, after the "entr'acte" of the George Circle's interpretations, Nietzsche emerges as "The Metaphysician." Without going into the question of the adequacy of this analysis, one may concede that some of the major interpretations have here been epitomized.

The "blood red" interpretation is surely untenable; it is easily refuted by reference to Nietzsche's conception of sublimation—and we have dealt with it in detail in the preceding chapters. The picture of Nietzsche as a great metaphysician appeared together with the conception of Nietzsche as a *Politiker:* not only are both theses defended together in the same book by Bäumler, but they are based on the same principles of exegesis—namely, the concentration on fragments and notes which are willfully arranged to yield a "system" that is quite remote from Nietzsche's own intentions.[4] Nietzsche's philosophy of culture and his "Dionysian" affirmation of life, on the other hand, are indeed highlights of his thought. "Culture," however, is for Nietzsche inseparable from education; his primary concern is with the attainment of culture. And the "Dionysian faith," *amor fati,* is—according to Nietzsche—the state of mind that accompanies such culture as he envisages. It is the faith of those who are above any *ressentiment* because they affirm not only their own being but also all existence, the faith of Spinoza and Goethe.

"*To educate educators! But the first ones must educate themselves!* And for these I write" (VII, 215). To educate educators—

---

[3] Gisela Deesz, *Die Entwicklung des Nietzsche-Bildes in Deutschland* (1933).
[4] *Ibid.,* 86, Deesz says in her discussion of Bäumler's *Nietzsche der Philosoph und Politiker:* "The second part, which deals with Nietzsche as a political philosopher . . . appears to us more as a hypostatization of Bäumler's own political ideals . . . than as a representation of Nietzsche's position in such matters." She overlooks that the same consideration applies to the first part of the book.

that might have been Stefan George's motto; yet the poet and
his Circle failed to understand Nietzsche's own "education" beyond his break with Wagner, which, as we have seen, they construed as "apostasy"—and George himself became "the Master,"
like Wagner. This is overlooked when George (and Spengler) are
pictured as mediators between Nietzsche and the Nazis. George
influenced Nazism precisely where he differed from Nietzsche.
(And this is also true of Spengler.[5]) Inasmuch as the George
Kreis evolved a *Führerprinzip* and a party line,[6] it stood opposed
to Nietzsche's heritage—quite consciously and deliberately opposed to it, as George's previously cited poem on "Nietzsche"
shows: Nietzsche's Socratic protestantism and chronic heresy, so
utterly irreconcilable with any form of totalitarianism, were rejected in favor of "constraint within a circle." The Circle, of
course, was to represent a *cultural* elite; and George, with his
fastidious passion for refinement, never came to terms with the
Nazis. (Neither did Spengler.) In 1933, when he was offered the
presidency of the *Deutsche Dichterakademie* and given the chance
to become the much-sought-for poet laureate of Hitler Germany,
he sent one of the many Jewish members of the Circle to inform
Goebbels of his refusal [7]—and emigrated to Switzerland. When
he died in December 1933, two brothers, Counts Stauffenberg,
kept a death watch over his body. They kept his memory alive,
and one of them commemorated the tenth anniversary of his
death with a cycle of poems.[8] A year later, on July 20, 1944, the
other brother planted the famous bomb that was meant to kill
Hitler. As a corrective to the cliché that Stefan George was a
link between Nietzsche and Hitler, one is tempted to say that
George transmitted Nietzsche's heritage to von Stauffenberg.
Actually no such formula does justice to the complexities of
historical influence: hardly any educated German after 1900 was
not somehow "influenced" by Nietzsche, for it is the mark of a
truly great personality that it subtly affects the whole atmosphere
and climate of contemporary life—a change no one can escape

---

[5] See note 2 above.

[6] Cf. especially F. Wolters, *Herrschaft und Dienst* (1909), and, for George's
imperious attitude toward his disciples and concrete instances of insistence
on a "party line," E. Salin, *Um Stefan George* (1948), *passim.*

[7] Stefan George, *Poems*, transl. Valhope and Morwitz (1943), 10.

[8] *Der Tod des Meisters: Zum Zehnten Jahrestag* (published 1948).

altogether.[9] Perhaps it is therefore more to the point to observe
that George and his Circle never appropriated Nietzsche's insight
into the basic antinomy of beauty and truth, art and philosophy,
illusion and dedication;[10] that they never accepted his uninhibited passion for truth; that they signally failed to develop his
insight that education is, in the end, "a question for the single
one."

This leitmotif of Nietzsche's life and thought—the theme of the
antipolitical individual who seeks self-perfection far from the
modern world—has of course not gone entirely unnoticed. We
encounter it, for example, without Nietzsche's polemical flour-
ishes, in the work of Hermann Hesse. This German poet who,
even before the First World War, left Germany for the seclusion
of the Swiss Alps, like Nietzsche, developed this motif in his
novels, from *Demian* and *Siddhartha* to the *Glasperlenspiel* (after
which he was awarded the Nobel Prize)—and this last book also
advances a Nietzschean idea that should be cited here:

> I know that in the not distant future many Germans will feel
> as I do: the desire to live for one's education free from politics,
> nationality, and newspapers. . . . There must yet be circles as
> the monastic orders were, only with broader contents. . . . Ed-
> ucation through the State's education is to be scorned [VII,
> 383 f.; cf. 355 f.].

The vision of this early note recurs toward the end:

> What has been *spoilt* through the abuse of the church: . . .
> the *"monastery"*: temporary isolation . . . a kind of deepest
> concentration on oneself and self-recovery—to avoid not "temp-
> tations" but "obligations" . . . away from the tyranny of
> stimuli and influences that condemns us to spend our strength
> in reactions, and does not permit us any more to let it *ac-
> cumulate* to the point of *spontaneous activity*. (One should
> observe our scholars closely: they have reached the point where

---

[9] See my "Goethe and the History of Ideas," *Journal of the History of
Ideas,* October 1949; revised version in my *From Shakespeare to Existentialism.*

[10] This Nietzschean theme of *Geist* was developed by Thomas Mann, who
also explored in his novels, from *Tonio Kröger* to the Joseph stories, the
Nietzschean notion that "the [physically] weak have more spirit. One
must need spirit to acquire spirit" (G IX 14).

they think only "reactively," i.e., they must read before they can think) [WM 916].

In the present book Nietzsche's philosophy has been stressed far more than his literary genius or that dimension of his work which inspired many of the greatest writers of the twentieth century: Thomas Mann no less than Hesse; Rilke as well as Gottfried Benn; André Malraux and André Gide; Jean-Paul Sartre and Albert Camus; George Bernard Shaw, W. B. Yeats, and Eugene O'Neill. With Nietzsche's immense influence on Rilke and Sartre I have dealt elsewhere; Thomas Mann, Benn, Gide, Camus, and Shaw have written essays on Nietzsche (for these seven men see the Bibliography); Gide also speaks of Nietzsche again and again in his Journals; Malraux drew on Nietzsche's life in *La Lutte avec l'ange* and Mann in *Doktor Faustus*; and O'Neill paid tribute to Nietzsche when accepting the Nobel Prize[11] and often stressed his great debt to him.[12] With the exception of Sartre, these men were not primarily interested in philosophy, but they grasped many of Nietzsche's central concerns better than most philosophers have done. And they also responded to Nietzsche as a man.

Discoveries about Nietzsche's impact on major figures continue. It was only after Freud's death that Ernest Jones revealed, in *The Life and Work of Sigmund Freud* (II, 344 and III, 460), how highly Freud had thought of Nietzsche. Martin Buber was in his eighties when he mentioned in his "Autobiographical Fragments" (see Bibliography) that as a youth he had translated Part I of *Zarathustra* into Polish. And in 1968 the first volume of Chaim Weizmann's letters (Oxford University Press) showed how the man who led the Zionist movement and become the first President of Israel had mentioned Nietzsche repeatedly in his letters to his future wife; e.g., August 3, 1902: "I am sending you Nietzsche: learn to read and understand him. This is the best and the finest thing I can send you." And March 14, 1901: "Lichtenberger's paper on Nietzsche was not good at all. The

---

[11] Arthur and Barbara Gelb, *O'Neill* (1962), 814.

[12] *Ibid.*, 121 f. (for further references see the Index); Croswell Bowen, *The Curse of the Misbegotten* (1959), 39 and especially 168 f.; Barrett H. Clark, *Eugene O'Neill: The Man and His Plays* (1947), 25 and 84; and *O'Neill and His Plays: Four Decades of Criticism*, ed. Oscar Cargill, *et. al.* (1961), 399 ff. and 408–14. Cf. also Drimmer's dissertation, listed in the Bibliography.

French are incapable of understanding Nietzsche. They are too superficial for a revaluation of all values. Moreover this fellow Lichtenberger seems to have strong nerves, and this is a handicap in studying Nietzsche."

Nietzsche's conception of the will to power is not primarily a metaphysical principle: Nietzsche's central concern is with man, and power is to him above all a state of the human being. The projection of the will to power from the human sphere to the cosmos is an afterthought—an extreme conjecture that is not substantiated by the evidence and is at variance with Nietzsche's own critical principles.

The will to power is the backbone of Nietzsche's philosophy —but one should not accept Santayana's picture of Nietzsche: "the meaning he chiefly intended . . . wealth and military power"; "To be trained and harnessed [is] an accession of power detestable to Nietzsche." [13] Wealth and military might were never signs of great power to Nietzsche's mind; and he realized fully that power involves self-discipline: this is, in fact, the central point of his conception.

> *One thing is needful.* "Giving style" to one's character—a great and rare art! It is exercised by those who see all the strengths and weaknesses of their own natures and then comprehend them in an artistic plan until everything appears as art and reason, and even weakness delights the eye. Here a large mass of second nature has been added; there a piece of original nature has been removed: both by long practice and daily labor. Here the ugly that could not be removed is hidden; there it has been reinterpreted and made sublime. . . . It will be the strong and domineering natures who enjoy their finest gaiety in such compulsion, in such constraint and perfection under a law of their own; the passion of their tremendous will relents when confronted with stylized, conquered, and serving nature; even when they have to build palaces and lay out gardens, they demur at giving nature a free hand. Conversely, it is the weak characters without power over themselves who *hate* the constraint of style . . . they hate to serve. Such spirits . . . are always out to interpret themselves and their environment as *free* nature—wild, arbitrary, fantastic, disorderly, . . . only in this way do they please themselves. For one thing is needful: that a human being *attain* his satisfaction

---

[13] *Egotism in German Philosophy*, 108 f.

with himself . . . only then is a human being at all tolerable
to behold. Whoever is dissatisfied with himself is always ready
to revenge himself therefor; we others will be his victims . . .
[FW 290].

This aphorism is a faithful reflection of much of Nietzsche's
thought. It epitomizes his contrasts of Goethe and Rousseau, his
praise of Socrates and Caesar, his repudiation of romanticism,
and his admiration for the Enlightenment. He considered the
hatred of self-discipline a sure mark of weakness; and any *ressentiment,* a manifestation of the frustrated will to power of those
who cannot attain satisfaction with themselves. *"One thing is
needful"*—namely, "that a human being attain satisfaction with
himself," recreate himself, and become a "single one" by giving
style to his character.

One may recall Kant's definition of enlightenment: *"Enlightenment is man's emergence from his self-incurred minority. Minority* is the incapacity for using one's understanding without
the guidance of another. And this minority is *self-incurred* when
it is caused by the lack, not of understanding, but of determination and courage to use it without the guidance of another.
Sapere aude! Have the courage to avail yourself of your own
understanding—that is the motto of the Enlightenment." The
early Nietzsche agreed with Kant—also that "Laziness and cowardice are the causes why such a large portion of humanity . . .
like to remain minors their life long, and why it becomes so easy
for others to pose as their guardians." [14] Soon however, he lost
the optimism of some of the men of the Enlightenment; he gave
up all hope for his own people and for mankind, and addressed
himself only to single human beings: "Not to the people let
Zarathustra speak, but to companions. . . . To lure many away
from the herd, for that I have come" (Z-V 9).[15] And as Nietzsche
considered Goethe's Conversations with Eckermann "the best
German book," he may have consciously emulated Goethe's dic-

---

[14] *Beantwortung der Frage: Was ist Aufklärung?* Cf. Chap. 5, I, of this
edition.

[15] This is insufficiently appreciated by M. Havenstein, who also underrates
Nietzsche as a philosopher, though his book on *Nietzsche als Erzieher*
(1922) was the first that made this conception (EH-U 3) the leitmotif of an
interpretation. Cf. p. vii: "Nietzsche . . . is not primarily a thinker and
poet, but an educator, an educator of his nation and mankind [*Volks- und
Menschheitserzieher*]."

tum: "My things cannot become popular; whoever thinks of that or exerts himself to that end is in error. They are not written for the mass but for single human beings who want and seek something similar and move in a similar direction." [16] To be sure, toward the very end of his life, when, unlike Goethe, he had gained little or no recognition, he sought frantically to attract attention. And the incredible influence which his ideas have exerted since then, testifies that he did have something to say to all men. Even so, he addressed his works primarily to the few—as an educator. And like Socrates he did not wish to convert them to any metaphysics of his own, but said in essence:

"Become who you are!"

Nietzsche's relationship to existentialism and to analytical philosophy has come to be of special interest in recent years. Jaspers, Heidegger, and Camus have written about Nietzsche, but the full measure of his influence on their thought still remains to be explored. Camus' last novel, *The Fall,* for example, is a veritable case history of the will to power of the weak who, as a last resort, derive a sense of superiority from their insistence that they are unworthy and guilt-ridden—adding that they are better than other men who refuse to admit that they are no less guilty. Elsewhere I have tried to demonstrate Nietzsche's influence on Sartre's *The Flies,* but more comprehensive studies of the debts various "existentialists" owe to Nietzsche might illuminate their works.

In many ways Nietzsche is close to what one might call the temper of existentialism. He fused philosophy and psychology, he took a special interest in what Jaspers later called *Psychologie der Weltanschauungen,* he wrote of the death of God, he discussed nihilism and alternative attitudes toward an absurd world, he was a penetrating literary critic, and he mobilized the resources of literature to communicate his philosophy. Nevertheless, there is also a strong positivistic streak in Nietzsche's thought, and it has not gone entirely unnoticed that he bears some similarities to Wittgenstein. But a good study of this aspect of Nietzsche's philosophy is still needed.

It was widely taken for granted at one time that positivistic

---

[16] Oct. 11, 1828.

elements could be found only in Nietzsche's so-called middle period. Actually, the late works, written after *Zarathustra,* are full of relevant passages; e.g., *"language* . . . will continue to talk of opposites where there are only degrees" (J 24; J 16 and 17 are no less pertinent). Or take the fifth book of *The Gay Science,* published a year later, where Nietzsche speaks of "epistemologists who have got stuck in the snares of grammar (the metaphysics of the people)" (FW 354). Or "the seduction of language (and of the fundamental errors of reason that are petrified in it) which conceives and misconceives all effects as conditioned by something that causes effects, by a 'subject' " (GM I 13). In *Twilight of the Idols,* finally, the whole of Chapters III, IV, and VI is of the greatest interest in this context.[17]

Nevertheless, we should resist the fashionable tendency to assimilate German philosophers by claiming that they really said what some recent British and American philosophers have said, too. If we admit what is foreign and different only after showing to our satisfaction that it is not different or new after all, we gain nothing, and we destroy all incentives for studying non-English texts.

In at least two obvious ways Nietzsche was decisively different from practically all analytic philosophers. First, he was far from suggesting that ordinary language has some special authority—let alone, that religious language does—and that only philosophers have been misled by language, while simpler people and common sense are more nearly right. Philosophers, he thought, should pay more attention to language—not in order to learn from its implicit wisdom but rather to discover how from childhood we have been misled. Secondly, Nietzsche was at least as close to existentialism as he was to analytical philosophy; and thus he may help to remind us how both movements are one-sided and partial. Nietzsche was not a member of, and cannot be claimed by, any school or movement. He offered fascinating ideas and theories, but he also taught "the courage for an *attack* on one's convictions" (xvi, 318).

---

[17] See also S 33 and the many passages listed in the Indices to my new translations under "language," "perspective," etc.

APPENDIX

Nietzsche's "Suppressed" Manuscripts[1]

I

Since the eighteen-nineties there has been considerable discussion about the adequacy of the editing of Nietzsche's late works, and occasionally bitter polemics about suppressed material have appeared in German newspapers and periodicals as well as in a few books. In the mid-fifties the controversy was revived in the wake of a new three-volume edition of Nietzsche's works, edited by Karl Schlechta,[2] but the acrimonious debate was not very illuminating, and the sensational claims that traveled across the ocean were largely misleading. More and more often it was asked how reliable our printed texts are; also, what new revelations may be expected from unpublished manuscripts. I shall try to answer both questions.

The discussion will revolve largely around *Friedrich Nietzsches Werke des Zusammenbruchs,* by Erich F. Podach, who makes sensational claims about *The Antichrist* and, above all, *Ecce Homo,* and who wants to supersede all previous editions of these works, including Schlechta's.[3]

---

[1] This essay appeared originally as an article in the *Journal of the History of Philosophy,* II, 2 (October, 1964), 205–25, under the title "Nietzsche in the Light of His Suppressed Manuscripts." The notes were also published in 1964, but those marked with an asterisk represent additions published now for the first time. Section X is also new.

[2] *Werke in drei Bänden* (1954–56).

[3] My article was completed before two reviews of Podach's book appeared in *The Philosophical Review,* April 1964, pp. 282–85, and in *The Journal of Philosophy,* April 23, 1964, pp. 286–88. Both reviews are by Henry Walter Brann; both accept uncritically Podach's editing and Podach's

II

Erich Podach holds a unique place in the Nietzsche literature: nobody else has contributed five genuinely important books. Yet Podach is not a philosopher, and he has never shown any profound understanding of Nietzsche's thought. The point is that all of his books make use of unpublished documents. His study of *Nietzsches Zusammenbruch* (1930) was translated into English in 1931. *Gestalten um Nietzsche* (1932)[4] is his most interesting book and deserves to be translated: it offers chapters on Nietzsche's mother, Rohde, Gast, Bernhard and Elisabeth Förster, and Julius

claims; and both add original errors. Brann says that Podach tells "the amazing story of the most brazen literary fraud committed in recent times," and he quotes Podach as saying that "Nietzsche is the most brazenly falsified figure of recent literary and cultural history with regard both to his life and to his works." (The last sentence is rendered into smoother English in *The Philosophical Review*, and the two reviews are slightly different.) I shall try to show how Podach and Brann themselves have contributed to this "amazing story" by trying to convince us that one of Nietzsche's best books was not written by him.

* In October 1965, Brann, who was mentioned only in this footnote and in one sentence in footnote 7, published a four-page "Reply to Walter Kaufmann" in *Journal of the History of Philosophy*, and gave the impression that my essay had consisted in large part of a "vitriolic assault" on him. Brann's review, in June 1952, of my *Nietzsche* had begun: "In literature to the frightening extent of about 1,000 volumes, this book is by far the most objective and the best informed. It is the most intelligent analysis of Nietzsche's thought and influence yet written." (*The Jewish Forum*, XXXV, 5) Brann continued in that vein and did not chide my comparison (in Chap. 13, section III) of *Ecce Homo* with Socrates' *Apology*. In his "Reply" of 1965, however, he says: "to compare this pseudo-autobiography with Goethe's *Dichtung und Wahrheit* and Plato's *Apology* [as I do in section IV, below] is a literary blasphemy unmatched in the annals of philosophical and literary criticism. One has to be rather naïve to fall for this mishmash of violent half-truths [i.e., *Ecce Homo*] . . ." Brann's "Reply" concludes, on the same page (250): "why does he [Kaufmann] choose to make his criticisms in such an emotionally charged, *ad hominem* manner?"

Notes 7 and 8 below give at least some idea of what one would be up against if one wanted to oblige Brann by cataloguing and correcting all his "original" errors. Regarding *Ecce Homo*, I can now refer to my new translation, with introduction and commentary (1967).

4 Both title page and copyright notice say 1932, but in the list of the author's previous books that appears opposite the title page of his fifth volume the date is given as 1931. In the jacket blurb 1932 is given correctly, but another date is wrong.

Langbehn. In 1937 Podach published *Der kranke Nietzsche: Briefe seiner Mutter an Franz Overbeck,* and after that *Friedrich Nietzsche und Lou Salomé.* All of these volumes are revelant to the biography of Nietzsche; but the last of them is now completely dated by Binion's *Frau Lou* (1968) (see note 13 below).

The fifth book aims to offer philologically reliable texts of *Nietzsches Werke des Zusammenbruchs,* i.e., *Nietzsche contra Wagner, Der Antichrist, Ecce Homo,* and *Dionysos-Dithyramben.* All of these were first published after Nietzsche had become insane (in January 1889), and while no philosophically important changes were made, the early editors were not greatly concerned about philological exactitude.

Nietzsche contra Wagner, for example, as published first in 1895 and reprinted many times since, differs quite strikingly from the final version of which Nietzsche himself was reading proofs in January, 1889, when he collapsed. Yet a very few copies of the original version were actually printed in 1889. This version contained a third chapter, "Intermezzo," deleted in 1895 and ever since, and this, a page and a half long, ended with the poem variously called, in later collections of Nietzsche's verse, "Venice" or "Gondola Song." The reason for this omission was not at all sinister. Nietzsche was working on several books late in 1888. Initially, this section formed part of *Ecce Homo;* then he inserted it in *Nietzsche contra Wagner;* then he wrote his publisher that after all he preferred to move it back into *Ecce Homo;* but when soon thereafter he received proofs of *Nietzsche contra Wagner* that included this section he did not delete it. He even made some slight corrections in it. The editors included it in *Ecce Homo,* with the corrections Nietzsche had made in the proofs. Moreover, the 1889 edition ended with the poem "Von der Armuth des Reichsten," but this, too, was omitted in 1895 and in all subsequent editions. Instead it was included in the *Dionysos-Dithyramben.* Here, too, Nietzsche's intentions were unclear. Poems concluded both *Nietzsche contra Wagner* and *Ecce Homo,* but on January 1 Nietzsche sent the publisher a postcard and on January 2 a telegram, requesting the return of the poems to him. The first edition of *Ecce Homo* (1908) included the poem originally intended for it; all later editions did not. In any case, there was no conspiracy to suppress these poems: they were printed in 1891, along with four others, to be published together with Part ɪᴠ of *Thus Spoke Zarathustra,* under the title *Diony-sos-Dithyramben*. In 1898, when Nietzsche's sister first published his *Gedichte und Sprüche,* the chapter called "Dionysos-Dithyramben" contained nine items (instead of six) and included three poems from the fourth part of *Zarathustra,* in Nietzsche's own subsequent revision.

Unquestionably, the early editors were not philologists; and in the nineties Nietzsche did not seem to merit critical editions. His books had been failures commercially and did not yet command a scholarly audience. Nietzsche was still living, hopelessly insane (he died in 1900); and any emphasis on his shifting intentions during the last weeks of 1888 when he was writing his last books must have seemed likely to discredit these books. The editors believed in the value of these books at a time when Nietzsche's importance was still far from assured, and they could argue in good faith that they were doing the best they could do under the circumstances.

When the *Historisch-Kritische Gesamtausgabe* of Nietzsche's *Werke* and *Briefe,* begun in 1933, was abandoned during the war, after publication of four volumes of letters and five of "works," all chronologically arranged, it had not even reached Nietzsche's first book, much less his last works. All we got instead was Karl Schlechta's edition of Nietzsche's *Werke in drei Bänden* (1954–56), and this, though plainly much less complete than quite a number of previous editions, was very widely hailed as philologically adequate. After all, Schlechta had worked in the Nietzsche archives in the thirties, and his third volume offered a *Philologischer Nachbericht* (1383–1432). Podach shows that Schlechta's edition is not as sound as it might and should have been: while Schlechta assumed that the archives in Weimar, in East Germany, could no longer be consulted after the war, Podach did work in Weimar to prepare his edition, and he is extremely scornful of Schlechta.[5]

Indeed, Podach quotes seven pages (418–25) from a review of

[5] The archives are now housed with the Goethe and Schiller archives and were also consulted, in the summer of 1959, by Frederick R. Love whose *Young Nietzsche and the Wagnerian Experience* (1963) I reviewed in *Journal of the History of Philosophy,* III, 2 (October 1965).

* The archives also furnished me the facsimiles of Nietzsche's manuscripts that I included and discussed in my edition of *The Will to Power* (1967).

the third volume of the *Historisch-Kritische Gesamtausgabe* of the *Werke* that he contributed to a Swiss newspaper in 1935, to show how utterly inadequate Schlechta's work was even then.[6] It was the publication and widespread success of Schlechta's three-volume set that prompted Podach's publication of his new book.

At first Podach intended to write a critical review for the *Deutsche Rundschau*; but while he was at work on that, photostats of manuscripts that he had requested from Weimar convinced him that Schlechta's inadequacies far surpassed anything that could be set straight in an article: something like the new book was required. At this point Podach's own words must be quoted: "This compelled the author once again to occupy himself intensively not only with Nietzsche, which in any case is not one of the pleasant things in life, but also with the Nietzsche literature which is, with few exceptions, insufferable. But in the long run it was not possible to pass over in silence a literary deception of such dimensions" (431).

This book, then, is not a labor of love. Its inspiration is negative, and in the 150 pages contributed by the editor we can distinguish two different polemical thrusts. The most brilliant pages are once again, as in *Gestalten um Nietzsche,* the devastating quotations from men the author despises, along with his vitriolic comments. Here one may single out particularly the members of the *Wissenschaftliche Ausschuss* that supervised, at least nomi-

---

[6] Podach's central charge is that the 166-page apparatus at the end of the volume, though extremely scholarly in appearance, "leaves totally unclear what in [Nietzsche's] notes is, on the one hand, original or the result of his studies—in brief, more or less his own—and what is merely something he read. Above all, the postscript does not fulfil the duty of showing from where Nietzsche got his quotations. . . . The inclination is palpable to ascribe to Nietzsche original sources where in fact he merely used second- or third-hand sources. In short, already with its third volume the edition has become Nietzsche-apologetic" (419). Schlechta was the editor of Nietzsche's "philosophical notes"; and by taking p. 392 as an illustration which he analyzes in detail, Podach demonstrates "the superficiality of these Kant studies" with which Schlechta had credited Nietzsche. Then he scores against H. J. Mette who, in the same volume, printed as a poem by the young Nietzsche a poem by Theodor Storm (1817–1888), published in 1851, that the young Nietzsche had copied. The errors are plain, but it is doubtful whether Schlechta's, any more than Mette's, were prompted by apologetics.

nally, the publication of the Historical-Critical *Gesamtausgabe* (412 ff.),[7] and two interpreters of one of Nietzsche's poems (360 ff.), especially Volkmann-Schluck,[8] a philosophy professor

---

[7] Those discussed and quoted by Podach include C. G. Emge, Oswald Spengler, Walter F. Otto, Martin Heidegger, and Hans Heyse. H. W. Brann's remarks about the committee and the *Gesamtausgabe,* in the penultimate paragraph of his above-mentioned piece in *The Philosophical Review,* misrepresent not only the facts but also Podach's claims.

＊ In his "Reply" Brann questioned the last sentence of this note. What he had said was: ". . . a whole group of quite renowned scholars, among whom we find such names as Martin Heidegger and Oswald Spengler, tried to compile a forty-volume edition of Nietzsche's works designed to prove that the author of *Zarathustra* had been an early pioneer of Nazism" (284). This characterization of (a) the *Historisch-Kritische Gesamtausgabe* and of (b) Heidegger's and (c) Spengler's interest in it is utterly misleading—as are the implications for (d) the two men's conceptions of Nietzsche and (e) Spengler's relationship to the Nazi regime.

[8] His little opus, *Nietzsches Gedicht "Die Wüste wächst, weh dem, der Wüsten birgt . . ."* (1958, 42 pp.), is probably the funniest item in the whole Nietzsche literature. If it were not for compelling external evidence, one might assume that this is a dead-pan parody of Heidegger; but Heidegger considers Volkmann-Schluck one of his ablest and most promising disciples (or at least did on Easter Sunday, 1953, in a conversation with me), and the book looks, from the outside, too, like several of Heidegger's own essays which were brought out by the same publisher.

There are only two prerequisites for the thorough enjoyment of this interpretation: one must have read some of Heidegger's own late essays, and one has to know Nietzsche's poem, which the author kindly reprints at the outset. (For an English translation of the almost identical earlier version of the poem that forms part of *Zarathustra* IV, see *The Portable Nietzsche,* 416 ff.) The oddest feature of Volkmann-Schluck's hyper-professorial and solemn exegesis is that it shows no inkling of the whimsical humor of the poem. Like his master, the author never shows a trace of a sense of humor: but why, then, did he have to tackle this particular poem? I give only two very brief illustrations: *"Von welcher Art der Zustand ist, in dem sich der Schatten Zarathustras befindet, sagt vor allem die 5. Strophe: er ist aus der noesis durch die Kluft hindurch in die aisthesis gefallen. Seit Plato bewegt sich das Denken . . ."* (18). *"Das Zweibeinige und Einbeinige betrifft zunächst das Verhältnis zur Zeit"* (26). It is to be hoped that the author can be persuaded to publish similar commentaries on Christian Morgenstern's *Galgenlieder.* Meanwhile, it is one of the merits of Podach's big book that he has called our attention to this little one.

＊ In his "Reply" Brann says: "Kaufmann feels obliged to defend the man because he is a professor of philosophy, and because Heidegger has called him his ablest and most promising disciple. Does Heidegger loom as a philosophical authority in Kaufmann's eyes? Has he forgotten that Heidegger became a supporter of Hitler? . . . Kaufmann, who should

and Heidegger disciple. In the last case, Podach's critique is couched in a parody of the professor's Heideggerian prose.

Once again, Podach has made a contribution to our understanding of German *Kulturgeschichte*: as in some of the portraits in his *Gestalten,* he shows us the corruption of the intellectual atmosphere. His recounting of the failings of so many editors is at times chilling. And this is deliberate. Podach is appalled by the new legend that the philosopher's sister can be blamed for everything; and though in the 'thirties he was one of her leading opponents and repeatedly made use of previously unpublished materials to expose her distortions, he now defends her in places without retracting his earlier charges—defends her against those who suggest that she alone lacked integrity, as if dozens of professors and editors had not compromised themselves wretchedly, too.

The other polemical thrust is directed against Nietzsche. Podach's dislike of the man to whom he has devoted five books is not only openly expressed on the last page of the fifth book, in the passage last quoted; it is also in evidence here and there —especially in his treatment of *The Antichrist* and *Ecce Homo.*

Podach's version of *Nietzsche contra Wagner* follows the edition of 1889 and holds no surprises for anyone fortunate enough to have seen one of the exceedingly few copies of that. And Podach's treatment of the *Dionysos-Dithyramben* does not call for detailed discussion: his main point is that there never was a *Druckmanuskript,* there only were two handwritten copies, neither ready for the printer; and Schlechta's version is, according to Podach, high-handed and contains such mistakes as taking the break at the bottom of a page for the end of a stanza—with dire results for Volkmann-Schluck's exegesis. But *The Antichrist* and *Ecce Homo* require detailed attention.

III

Podach's version of *The Antichrist* differs from most previous editions in two respects. First, he restores words that had been

---

know better, overlooks a typical weakness of German academics, namely, their complete lack of humor" (248).

Holy Aristophanes!

For my views about Heidegger see, e.g., Chaps. 17 and 18 of *From Shakespeare to Existentialism* and my article on "Existentialism and Death" in *The Meaning of Death* (1959), ed. Herman Feifel.

omitted in three places when the book was first published in 1895. These words are also found in Schlechta's edition, and, in two cases out of the three, in the English translation of *The Antichrist* in *The Portable Nietzsche*.[9] Indeed, the deleted words were published by Josef Hofmiller in 1931.[10]

In section 29 three words were deleted in all editions until 1954: "the word *idiot*." Hofmiller made this public to show that Nietzsche was insane when he wrote *The Antichrist*. In fact, the phrase is one of many indications that Nietzsche's image of Jesus was decisively influenced by Dostoevsky's portrait of Prince Myshkin in *The Idiot*.[11]

In section 35 a few lines were omitted after ". . . he loves with those, in those, who do him evil" and before "*Not* to resist, *not* to be angry. . . ." They read:

The words to the *malefactor* on the cross contain the whole evangel. "That was truly a godlike man, 'a child of God,'"

[9] Selected and translated, with an introduction, prefaces, and notes, by Walter Kaufmann (1954).

[10] "Nietzsche" in *Süddeutsche Monatshefte*, November 1931, 73–131. This was the lead article, and Hofmiller was a respected critic. But to see Podach and Schlechta in perspective, it is not irrelevant that the banner headline on the January 1932 issue read "*Die jungen Mädchen von heute*"; and on the February issue, "*Homöopathie*." Ironically, the same issue that began with Hofmiller's "Nietzsche" also contained a short article "Ulrich von Wilamowitz-Moellendorff": the scholar whose first important publications were two polemics (1872 and 1873) that sought to destroy Nietzsche's reputation, on the heels of the publication of *The Birth of Tragedy*, had died September 25, 1931. That article began, "The greatness of this worthy, whose star has just sunk under the horizon . . ." and ended: "But we, to whom it was granted to turn our eyes toward him while living and, at the sight of such greatness, to feel strengthened and educated, want at least to try . . . to fix the 'image of the worthy' also for later generations." Hofmiller on Nietzsche ended: "What, then, remains of Nietzsche? Enough remains. . . . The critic and diagnostician of the time remains. The moralist remains, taking that word in its French, not its German sense. . . . What will remain longest of all are the three works of his middle period: *Human, All-Too-Human* and *The Dawn*, and *The Gay Science*. What will remain are *les plus belles pages*. . . . Details will remain: observations, ideas, thoughts, moods, maxims, and reflections, insofar as and because they are independent of his supposed system. What will remain is the artist; the poet will remain."

In his most recent, sixth (!) book on Nietzsche (see section IX below) Podach himself quotes this passage and introduces it by saying that the answer which he himself has been giving for over thirty years was best formulated by Hofmiller in 1931.

[11] See Chap. 12, n. 2, above.

says the malefactor. "If you feel that"—replies the Redeemer—
"then you are in Paradise, then you, too, are a child of God."

This was presumably omitted because it is not found in the
Gospels this way. But the reaction to this deletion was surely as
misguided as the deletion itself. Hofmiller crowed that the words
"are still today suppressed by the editors because they are not
right. 'Truly this was the Son of God!' is said not by the malefactor but by the centurion, and only after the Savior has died
(Matt. 27:54). The words of the malefactor (Luke 23:40) are
importantly different. What is characteristic of this kind of criticism of religion is its naïve dilettantism" (94 f.). Podach takes a
far dimmer view of Nietzsche than Hofmiller did. But this kind
of criticism only shows that *they* are dilettantes—and prigs besides. A scholar in the field of German philosophy would surely
know that Hegel's numerous quotations from Goethe and Schiller
are frequently inexact and evidently always from memory, and
that Kant's criticism of his predecessors, like Aristotle's, leaves
much to be desired. And what a common failing it is to recall a
Gospel passage inaccurately! Of course, Nietzsche should have
checked it; but he was trying feverishly to finish several books—
and this was the sort of thing that his young friend Gast, who
got one set of the proofs, had full authority to delete. Hence it
is misleading to speak of "suppression."

What is surprising is that there are so few such mistakes or
lapses in spelling or syntax. Podach makes much of the fact that
at one point in *Ecce Homo* Nietzsche wrote "Cagliari" instead of
"Chiavari," although the two towns are "two and a half degrees
of latitude" apart! Hundreds of professors whose eyesight, health,
and working conditions are beyond compare with Nietzsche's do
far worse—even men who pride themselves on their carefulness
and who quite lack Nietzsche's high-strung artistic temperament.

The last restoration: in the final paragraph of section 38 some
editions have "a prince" instead of "a young prince." The word
"young" was apparently omitted in 1895 because it seemed to
make the reference to the young Kaiser Wilhelm II too obvious
and possibly actionable. But this word was long restored in
Kröners Taschenausgabe, and Schlechta, too, has it though he
elicits Podach's scorn for confessing his inability to discover the
deletion in section 38.

Finally, Podach's version also includes some new material at
the end of *The Antichrist*: a one-page "Law Against Christianity"

(*Gesetz wider das Christentum*) that comprises seven "propositions," and then a concluding quotation from *Zarathustra*: section 30 from the chapter "On Old and New Tablets" (*Twilight of the Idols,* finished a few weeks earlier and published in January 1889, concluded with section 29).

To begin with the quotation, Podach (403) corrects Nietzsche: "not as Nietzsche indicates, *Zarathustra* III, p. 90 (The Hammer Speaks) but III, p. 30 (On Old and New Tablets)." But here it is Podach who errs: in the first edition of *Zarathustra,* section 30 is found on p. 90 of Part III, as indicated by Nietzsche. The title "The Hammer Speaks" is not found there for either section 29 or section 30, but was evidently meant to be added before the quotation, as it had been in *Twilight.*

Why were the "Law" and the quotation omitted from all editions before Podach's? The "Law" is so shrill that it plainly weakens the book, and the quotation is somewhat irrelevant and anticlimactic. Nietzsche seems to have added both as a momentary and ill-advised afterthought. But unlike the three deletions in the text which, according to Podach, are due "with a probability verging on certainty, to the printer or publisher" (403), the omission of the "Law" and the quotation was due, *pace* Podach, also with a probability verging on certainty, to Nietzsche himself.

Podach seems to have included this material for the very reason for which some early editors might have felt tempted to suppress it if it had formed part of the manuscript: he plainly wishes to compromise Nietzsche. Now this matter of the "Law Against Christianity" calls for two comments.

First, one would expect that a man who writes a book like *The Antichrist,* which is exceedingly shrill in many places, must very probably have penned still shriller passages. Finding an example should cause no surprise, and if Nietzsche in his last days really had placed such a page at the end instead of discarding it, this would in no way alter the value of the book we know.

Second, it seems plain that Podach's procedure at this point does not reflect Nietzsche's final intentions. Podach found the "Law" in the *Ecce Homo* file but argues from the pagination and the contents that these pages were really intended for *The Antichrist* (77–80). While his argument is convincing, it shows no more than that these pages were at one time meant to conclude *The Antichrist,* but the "Law" was quite evidently not found at the end of this manuscript but rather among Nietzsche's notes.[12] Even upon finishing Podach's Preface to his version of *The Antichrist,* a critical reader must conclude that it is most probable that Nietzsche removed the "Law" from *The Antichrist* and then, instead of filing or destroying it, left it lying around. By the time one reaches p. 400, this surmise becomes a certainty. Here we find a concession in small print which is neither hinted at nor referred to in the Preface: the page in question "is covered with a crust of glue; it was evidently formerly glued shut or covered up with a page glued over it—probably a measure Nietzsche took to keep secret his world-historical laws up to the moment of their promulgation. As a matter of fact, the page escaped Overbeck. The text is missing in the copy he made of *The Antichrist.*" In sum, Podach's inclusion of the "Law" at the end of *The Antichrist* can be supported only by the guess, in small print on p. 400, that Nietzsche pasted over this text to keep it secret. This guess, however, is not merely extremely tenuous; Podach's procedure at this point is far more unscrupulous than dozens of offenses for which he chides earlier editors.

Podach's respect for Overbeck's scholarly and human integrity is evident in all of his books, and he never questions that Overbeck copied what was there to be copied. The "Law" plainly was not there at the end of the manuscript. As if this were not enough, it appears that something was pasted over it; but Podach assumes, without argument, that a blank page was pasted over it to keep the text secret—although the *Ecce Homo* manuscript abounds in instances where changes were made by pasting the new version over the old one.

IV

Podach's attempt to debunk Nietzsche reaches its climax in his editing of *Ecce Homo.* He quotes Nietzsche's letter to Gast of November 13, 1888, with the news that *Ecce Homo,* begun

---

[12] Cf. H. J. Mette's "Sachlicher Vorbericht" in *Historisch-Kritische Gesamtausgabe, Werke,* I, xlix; also published separately as *Der handschriftliche Nachlass Friedrich Nietzsches* (1932), 17. Here these pages are catalogued as part of the *Ecce Homo* file, and Mette says that they were definitely not sent to the printer and presumably were found in the *Nachlass.*

October 15, was finished November 4, and comments that Nietzsche's "reliability in matters relating to himself was never very
great" (166). We are assured that *"Ecce Homo* was finished
neither November 4 nor on any other day . . ." (169)—which is
a half-truth.

There seems to be no reason—and Podach adduces none—for
doubting the following information provided by Professor Raoul
Richter in his scholarly postscript to the first edition of the book
(1908). Since this was a limited edition and the postscript has
never been reprinted, these points merit a fairly detailed statement.

Nietzsche apparently did finish *Ecce Homo* on November 4,
1888, and before the middle of the month he sent the manuscript
to his publisher, Naumann, to get it printed and published. In
a letter of November 20, he mentions additions to Georg Brandes;
and then he also mentioned the additions to his publisher. On
a card, postmarked November 27, he asked Naumann to return
"the second part of the MS . . . because I still want to insert
some things." He explained that he meant "the whole second
half of the MS, beginning with the section entitled '*Thus Spoke
Zarathustra.*' I assume that this won't delay the printing for even
a moment, as I shall send back the MS immediately. . . ." On
December 1, he acknowledged receipt of the second half but requested the return of the whole MS, including the additions: "I
want to give you a MS as good as the last one, at the risk that I
have to be a copier for another week." The next day he wrote
Gast that he had asked the MS back once more. On December 3,
Naumann wrote Nietzsche that he was returning the MS, but
"copying it once more I do not consider necessary; I merely should
especially recommend that you read the proofs carefully, although
I shall make a point of doing likewise." Evidently, then, *the MS
struck Naumann as finished, clear, and printable.* On December
6, Nietzsche telegraphed Naumann: "MS back. Everything re-
worked [*umgearbeitet*]." And on the 8th, Nietzsche wrote Gast:
"I sent *Ecce Homo* back to C. G. Naumann day before yesterday
after laying it once more on the gold scales from the first to the
last word to set my conscience finally at rest."

Then Nietzsche hesitated whether *Nietzsche contra Wagner*
or *Ecce Homo* should appear first. He had worked on both books
during the same time, and both represented attempts to preclude
misunderstandings of his outlook and what he stood for. He was

thinking of having *Ecce Homo* appear simultaneously in German and in English and French translations and, though he had given some thought to the question of the translators, this would clearly involve a delay of up to a year. On December 15, he decided in favor of publishing *Nietzsche contra Wagner* first, but on the same day the publisher dispatched the first installment of the proofs of *Ecce Homo,* sending one set to Nietzsche and another to Gast, and on the eighteenth the second installment was sent to both men. On the twentieth Nietzsche sent his publisher a card, and then also a telegram, expressing the wish to see *Ecce* published first after all; the same day he also requested the publisher to move the "Intermezzo" from *Nietzsche contra Wagner* to *Ecce Homo,* as originally planned.

The path we have been following is sinuous, but for all that the development seems clear, and nothing suggests that there was no finished manuscript. The week from December 27 to January 2—the last week before Nietzsche's collapse—adds a few final twists. On the twenty-seventh Nietzsche wrote his publisher: "Much obliged for the zeal with which the printing progresses. I have returned, ready for the printer, both the second install-ment of the proofs of *Ecce* and the two installments of *N. contra W.* . . . Everything considered, let us publish in the year 1889 *The Twilight of the Idols* and *Nietzsche contra Wagner.* . . . *Ecce Homo,* which must be turned over to the translators as soon as it is finished, could not in any case be ready before 1890 to appear simultaneously in all three languages. For the *Revalua-tion of All Values* [i.e., *The Antichrist*], I do not yet have any date in mind. The success of *Ecce Homo* will have to precede it. That this work is ready for the printer I have written you."

On the twenty-ninth, Nietzsche sent the publisher "the poem which should conclude *Ecce Homo.*" On the twenty-second he had first mentioned the idea of including this poem in *Ecce* in a letter to Gast, but then he had referred to its possible insertion between two chapters. On the thirtieth Nietzsche sent his pub-lisher a postcard requesting the insertion of one sentence in the "Intermezzo." On January 1, he sent another card asking the pub-lisher to return the poem to him once more, and on January 2, finally, he sent Naumann a telegram requesting the manuscripts of the two final poems—possibly because he had decided to con-clude neither *Ecce* nor *N. contra W.* with a poem.

It is for publishers to say whether many authors are that

much trouble. I suspect that a few who quite lack Nietzsche's genius are. Certainly, very few complete so many books in one year: *The Case of Wagner, Twilight of the Idols, The Antichrist, Ecce Homo,* and *Nietzsche contra Wagner*—few great writers have produced five comparable works in such a short time. Under the circumstances, Nietzsche's excitement, his indecision about the most effective order of publication for the last two titles, and his changes of mind about various details are far from surprising. What *is* surprising is Podach's attitude toward *Ecce Homo.*

Podach claims, as we have seen, that the book was not really finished—and he prints the manuscript with Nietzsche's many editorial directions, such as requests to insert or move passages; he prints alternative versions of the same passage, one after the other; he indicates where something has been pasted over and prints both the latter version and the former. All this is valuable up to a point, and we are in the editor's debt for letting us see easily what it took him considerable work to find out. What is unfortunate is Podach's manifest conviction that all this serves to debunk the book and its author.

Indeed, Podach makes his version look more chaotic than the original manuscript version, in at least one important respect: "I have not indicated where whole sections in 'the final manuscript' [*im 'Druckmanuskript'*] are crossed out. Here some of the texts show plainly that they are variants or preliminary versions, while in other cases it cannot be decided whether N or Gast has deleted them" (408). On purely philological grounds, Podach's procedure seems wholly unjustifiable. Why should preliminary versions that have been crossed out and superseded be printed as if they had been neither crossed out nor superseded, leaving it to the reader to make a choice where the author made his choice over seventy years before? Since the publisher evidently found that the manuscript sent to him was printable and did not need copying over—and thus apparently did not contain alternative versions of the same passages—the suggestion that in some cases it cannot be decided whether Nietzsche or Gast eliminated the variant versions seems implausible. But even if this should be true in some cases, the philologically correct procedure would surely be to indicate the final version in all cases, to relegate variants to an appendix or at most to footnotes, and to indicate in which cases there is room for doubt whether the deletions were effected by Nietzsche's hand.

The way a writer works and the way his books look shortly before they are finished—or even the way a patient publisher is willing to send them to the printer—the follies an author narrowly avoids and his momentary indecision about two ways of putting a point—all this should not shock a reasonably sophisticated reader, and it certainly could not shock anybody who has gone through remotely similar processes, whether as a writer or as an editor or publisher. But Podach shows once again, and more blatantly than ever before, how little feeling he has for the man to whom he has devoted five books and from whose name his own literary reputation is inseparable.

Podach's characterization of *Ecce Homo* (205 ff.), which he dislikes intensely, is exceedingly unperceptive and invites parodies in the form of similar exposés of other great works of literature. While there is no need to discuss that, the last sentences of his long introduction to the text deserve to be quoted and criticized:

> [We] must renounce an illusion that has become dear. The hitherto familiar *Ecce Homo* does not exist. But now we have access to that which has been preserved of *Ecce Homo* as Nietzsche wrote it. . . . All this belongs to *Ecce Homo*. . . .

> An "*Ecce Homo*" is not a writing that may be edited. . . . It is not permitted to borrow titles from the Bible and from Cardinal Newman [Nietzsche really did not do the latter], to proclaim that one wishes to say what one is and how one became, and then to employ the art of *mise en scène* when it comes to the confession of character and life and, in spite of all assurances, to shrink from an undisguised self-portrait.

> Genuine confessions are irrevocable. They do not permit crossing out, nor cancelled passages, nor secrets that are held back. Then only will it be shown what is mask and original image, joke and seriousness, histrionics and self-illumination, abandonment to myth and persevering will to truth and reality.

Podach plainly fails to understand the difference between notes a man might take to show them to his psychoanalyst and works like Goethe's *Dichtung und Wahrheit* and Plato's *Apology*. *Ecce Homo* is obviously modeled on Goethe and Socrates, and the title of the first chapter, "Why I am so wise," points back to Socrates' claim, in his immensely unapologetic "apology," that he was the wisest of men—not because he was so exceedingly wise but because his contemporaries were so incredibly stupid.

Borrowing titles from the Bible is permitted to everyone, including ephemeral writers who do not brook comparison with Nietzsche, and is not a privilege that entails special rules. In literature and philosophy crossing out is always permitted, and cancelled passages suggest that the author has done some work instead of merely serving up his stream of consciousness. The dichotomy of joke and seriousness frequently breaks down in great works of literature: again one may recall the *Apology*; also Goethe's *Faust* and much of the best literature of the twentieth century, including Gide and Kafka, Sartre and Wittgenstein, and some fine contemporary German writers. One of the reasons why so much of the literature about Kierkegaard and Nietzsche is so wide of the mark is that most of the contributors utterly lack the mordant humor of those two.

Most of the men who have written about Nietzsche and Kierkegaard have really found these men utterly uncongenial, though few have said this as plainly as Podach has on the last page of his fifth book on Nietzsche. Now it may seem that likemindedness, temperament, and even the range of a writer's emotional and intellectual experience are altogether irrelevant when the points at issue do not concern appreciation or over-all interpretation but philological accuracy. Yet while this would be nice, it plainly is not so, and it is by no means the least interesting point about Podach's book that it shows this so clearly.[13]

---

[13] Another minor illustration of Podach's bias: while he cites hardly anything from the Nietzsche literature which, as we have seen, he finds "with few exceptions, insufferable" (431), he singles out Ernest Newman's *The Life of Richard Wagner*, Vol. 4, as "important for the knowledge of Nietzsche's relations with Wagner" (11; cf. 393), and he relies uncritically on A. H. J. Knight's *Some Aspects of the Life and Work of Nietzsche* (407). For a detailed critique of Newman's treatment of Nietzsche's relations with Wagner, see Chap. 1, section II, above. Use of the index will show how utterly unreliable Knight's book is and how wrong it is on the point on which Podach cites it. Newman accepted the unscrupulous book by Bäumler, the leading Nazi interpreter of Nietzsche, as a "masterly epitome of Nietzsche's thinking" (335), and he was, as I put it in 1950, "apparently unaware of the full extent of Knight's indebtedness to Frau Förster-Nietzsche, Richard Oehler (her nephew), and Bertram, of Knight's many 'original' factual errors, and of Bäumler's near-perfect perversion of Nietzsche" (p. 40, above). How then can one explain Podach's honorable mention of, and reliance on, Newman and Knight? Their books

V

Here a word about the facsimiles of manuscript pages and notes is in order. Podach has made it very difficult to match up the plates with the pages in the text on which transcripts are offered: one has to hunt for references to the plates in the last thirty pages. But when one does make comparisons, it appears that his vaunted fidelity to the manuscripts is by no means unexceptionable, though he is vitriolic about the slightest errors of previous editors.

He claims that he indicates where words have been crossed out but in fact often fails to do this,[14] and there are other small deviations.[15] On Plate XII, we are given a facsimile of a six-line note which is characterized in the text as one of Nietzsche's "intimate conversations with himself" (176): it is not a draft and evidently dredged up only to compromise its author. In this note, a word crossed out in the manuscript is printed without any indication that it was crossed out; nor does Podach indicate that one word was underlined; and the printed version breaks off without any punctuation while the manuscript ends with three dots. It would also seem that Podach has deciphered some things that clearly cannot be deciphered with any certainty. The point here is not merely or mainly that his contempt for all previous editors is ill-taken, nor is it only that Podach's fidelity to the manuscripts cannot be sustained: his ideal of historical-critical fidelity is questionable. This last claim must surely sound extreme and unreasonable, but a single example may suffice to show what is meant.

It will be best to turn again to *Ecce Homo,* and Plate XVI, already cited, will do. Even if Podach's printed version did not fail in the respects just noted, it would still fall short by not in any way indicating well over a dozen inserts Nietzsche made

---

share a contempt for Nietzsche and an abundance of easily avoidable errors that place him in a bad light.

* Binion shows in *Frau Lou* how the same bias vitiates Podach's untenable account of Nietzsche's relation to Lou and Paul Rée. Cf. Chapter 1 above, note 28.

[14] Cf. Plates VI and XVI with 156 f. and 254 ff. In the latter instance only a single deletion is indicated, in the last line.

[15] E.g., Plate XVI, line 5.

on the manuscript page, ranging in length from one or two words to a line. These afterthoughts and attempts to improve his style are surely more interesting than Podach's occasional indications that something has been crossed out and can no longer be read.

Would a really faithful critical edition be worth the trouble? It would certainly do more harm than good if those who bought or read it agreed with Podach and his publisher that all previous editions belonged "in the junk room for editorial-literary manipulations. . . ." (These words appear on the jacket, but Podach himself says as much and makes very unjudicious use of the word "manipulation.") More volumes of facsimiles, reproduced large enough for reading and accompanied by pertinent information, would be most welcome as throwing light on Nietzsche's working habits; but they can no more take the place of the finished works than his drafts and notes could. Moreover, judicious use of manuscript materials of this sort will always require judgment as well as honesty, and in such cases judgment depends on some congeniality and a deliberate empathy. At the point where the scholar's work approaches the detective's, a refusal to put oneself in one's subject's place and the insistence on hostility unmitigated by sympathy can be ruinous.

In the fifties, Schlechta reacted against the popular overvaluation of *The Will to Power:* he was not content to tell his readers, as others had done before him, that the material known under this title consisted merely of some of the notes Nietzsche had jotted down in the period from 1884 to 1888, the systematic arrangement being due to editors who never stopped to consider which notes Nietzsche had long put to use in his later books and which notes he had not used because he probably was not satisfied with them; no, Schlechta claimed that he reprinted the material in the order in which it was found in Nietzsche's notebooks. Perhaps the day will come when others will discover that here and there he did not really follow the sequence in the notebooks as accurately as he thought he did.[16] But how much does this really matter? Since Nietzsche sometimes put notes in the back, or on right-hand pages, first, the order was admittedly not chrono-

---

[16] The day has come: see 202–06 in Podach's sixth book on Nietzsche (see section IX below). *Ibid.*, 8, Podach says that "Nietzsche as a rule used his notebooks from back to front."

* For the discoveries I made in connection with my own edition of *The Will to Power* (1967), see section X, below.

logical, and Schlechta's presentation is simply chaotic and makes *The Will to Power* almost unreadable.

The sister's edition, for all the absurd pretensions that this was Nietzsche's systematic *magnum opus*, at least had the virtue that one could find at a glance where there were a lot of notes about art or Christianity or epistemology. To be sure, Nietzsche's thought defies neat systematization; still this edition was useful for those who realized that these were merely notes, and in the two best editions an appendix listed the approximate date of composition for every single note—information not given in Schlechta's three-volume set. In sum, Schlechta tried to all but destroy the material along with the sister's pretensions.

Now Podach has tried to do much the same with *Ecce Homo:* he has succeeded in giving us a text that almost everybody will find utterly unreadable. Such reactions against the old Nietzsche legends and decades of abuses are certainly understandable, but they obviously overshoot the mark. Of course, Podach has not literally destroyed *Ecce Homo:* we can still read the old version and then compare it with Podach's, and for the wealth of new information he gives us we can be grateful to him.

VI

Some of this information is incidental and not directly concerned with the books of 1888. One example may illustrate this. Podach describes how Nietzsche's sister forged a letter—an interesting addition to Schlechta's long discussion of her forgeries.[17] The letter, written by Nietzsche to his sister toward the end of October, 1888, no longer exists; all that has survived in the archives is a copy in the sister's hand, with her notation: "Original burnt at my mother's request, end of 1896." There is no reason to believe that the mother had anything whatever to do with this. The copy is incomplete:

> Omissions are marked in the copy by . . . , in the printed version by [— — —]. The published version differs strikingly from the copy in two places. In the third paragraph the printed text omits after "I except Germany; only there have I had *ugly* experiences": "because—this I have very often written to you— the Germans are the meanest people!—[*das gemeinste Volk*]."

---

[17] *Werke,* III, 1409-23.

In the fourth paragraph, on the other hand, the published version offers more than the copy, which merely says: "Our new Kaiser, however, pleases me more and more: his latest move is that he has taken a very sharp stand against anti-Semitism [*die Antisemiterei*] and the *Kreuzzeitung* [a rightist, anti-Semitic paper]. Do likewise, my brave Llama [Nietzsche's nickname for his sister, who had married an anti-Semitic leader]! . . . . ." For the benefit and edification of Wilhelmian Nietzscheans, the five dots were replaced in the published version by the tribute: "The will to power as a principle would surely make sense to him."

This little revelation (163) gives a fair indication of the interest of long-suppressed information that can be brought to light by work in the Nietzsche archives. Nietzsche's sister suppressed some remarks directed against herself, her husband, Richard Wagner, the Germans, Jesus, and Christianity; also some remarks that directly or indirectly impugned his health and might suggest that his last works were products of insanity. No doubt, some remarks about Jesus and Christianity invited suppression for this last reason no less than on account of the offense they would give.

We can distinguish the following motives for suppression: (a) to shield the objects of Nietzsche's attacks, particularly when these were people still living (this includes clearly indicated omissions in his letters, as published under the sister's supervision); (b) to shield Nietzsche against avoidable enmities and against the imputation that he must have been out of his mind long before he collapsed in January, 1889; (c) to keep from public knowledge what her brother had written to her and about her. To illustrate this last category, a single example from Schlechta's third volume (1421) will suffice: "between a vengeful anti-Semitic goose and myself there can be no reconciliation." To bolster her own authority as her brother's best interpreter, she did not even shrink from forgeries, as Schlechta has shown in considerable detail.

Almost all of this trickery, however, is confined to Nietzsche's letters—and is philosophically quite uninteresting. The sister did not invent letters: she published as addressed to herself what Nietzsche had in fact written to others, particularly to their mother; and a few such letters which were printed as letters to the sister were in fact composed out of snippets from letters and drafts for letters to others. All this is fascinating for the student of Nietzsche's relation to his sister and for those interested in her character; yet it is amazing how little it adds to the portrait available in 1950.

The publication of yet further remarks about the sister and her husband, about Wagner and the Germans, or about Jesus and Christianity could hardly hold many important surprises; I doubt that it holds any. A writer who finished a book a year from 1872, when he was 27, until 1887, fifteen years later, excepting only 1875 and 1877 (but he finished two in 1873, and two in 1883)—and who completed five volumes in 1888—has hardly failed to bear testimony of his views, and we need not rummage through his letters and his *Nachlass* to find out what he thought. Letters and notes certainly add something to the total picture, and because Nietzsche was never wholly satisfied with his epistemological reflections, for example, some of his tentative ideas are found only in his notes. Elsewhere, too, it is interesting to compare the notes with the finished works or to supplement our understanding of the man by reading his letters.

What is unusual about the forgeries in the letter Podach cites (quoted above) is that here for once the sister interpolated a philosophically relevant sentence, suggesting that Nietzsche thought—as in fact he surely did not—that young Kaiser Wilhelm would understand the conception of the will to power. But even here the evidence in Nietzsche's books, and also in his notes, is so overwhelming that no serious student was ever taken in by this contemptible ruse. While this little interpolation may have helped to make Nietzsche palatable to admirers of the Kaiser, and while it certainly helped to buttress the sister's stupid misinterpretation of the will to power, it has long been plain that her interpretation was untenable. So one had to assume that this sentence, if genuine, must have been meant ironically: the will to power as a principle might appeal to him, although he certainly would not understand it. The works of that period leave no doubt whatsoever about Nietzsche's positions, and if his attitude toward the German Empire of his day were open to criticism one could at most object that he was too utterly contemptuous and vitriolic. Let anybody who doubts that read *Twilight,* Chapter 8 ("What the Germans Lack"), or *Nietzsche contra Wagner,* or *Ecce Homo.*

Knowing the sister's history and prejudices, one did not have to doubt the authenticity of either these books or *The Antichrist.*

They represent such merciless attacks on almost everything that had been dear to her before she became her brother's keeper that it was perfectly plain that they spoke his mind. Indeed, one might ask: what more could anyone want?

Podach, though he keeps caviling at the errors of previous editors, really performs a service he has no wish whatever of doing us: he confirms conclusively that Nietzsche's "Werke des Zusammenbruchs" were not disfigured in any important way. Nothing that has come out of recent research on Nietzsche's manuscripts requires us to change in the slightest the picture of Nietzsche's thought that was available when World War II ended.

VII

It has been noted before that Podach, like Hofmiller, is a dilettante, and this is relevant both to the tone of their claims and to the now widely accepted image of the Nietzsche manuscripts and the Nietzsche editions we know. Consider the case of Hegel, as neither Hofmiller nor Podach has done. Hegel himself wrote four books, but his "works" comprise twenty volumes in Glockner's *Jubiläumsausgabe* (not counting the two-volume biography and the four-volume *Hegel-Lexikon,* which form part of this edition), and the critical edition of the "works" in Meiner's series, the admirable *Philosophische Bibliothek,* was to comprise over thirty volumes, but was never finished.

Ever since the decade following Hegel's death, in 1831, when the first edition of his collected works was published, most of the volumes were taken up by Hegel's lectures on the philosophy of history, the philosophy of art, the philosophy of religion, and the history of philosophy, and two of Hegel's books were greatly expanded (one of them from one volume to three volumes) by additions, clearly indicated, which were taken from the lectures. Hegel, as we know from his students, lectured slowly, as if he were dredging up his thoughts from immense depths, and this encouraged some of his students to try to write down his every word. But he gave the same lecture courses several times, and they were somewhat different every time. During these years when he lectured in Berlin his system changed, and the second edition of the system (*Encyclopädie der philosophischen Wissenschaften*), published by Hegel himself in 1827, was not only about twice as long as the first edition of 1817 but also so importantly different as to be practically a new book; and then Hegel published a revised third edition in 1830. In assigning their additions to the sections of the third edition, which had not yet appeared when Hegel gave the lectures on which these additions were based, the students naturally had to take liberties. And since they did not wish to omit the best formulations or particularly striking pages in publishing the works based entirely on lecture notes, they had to conflate notes taken several years apart. Necessarily, the transitions often had to be supplied by the editors, and the resultant "works" were never presented, even orally, by Hegel himself in the form in which generations have read and studied them. Not only are the words occasionally those of his students and not his own—a fact admitted in the Prefaces but not indicated specifically in the texts—but the train of thought is not really his: ideas developed and formulated many years apart stand side by side on the same page without any warning. Yet some of the editors were professors, and the whole edition was considered a triumph of *Pietät* and scholarship, not only in Germany but also in the English-speaking world where the image of Hegel was formed at least as much by some of the lecture courses, especially those on the philosophy of history, and by the additions to the "Lesser Logic" (i.e., the first part of the *Encyclopedia*) as by Hegel's own words. To be sure, this is not as it should be, and the point here is not to defend Hegel's editors; it is rather to see the editing of Nietzsche's works in perspective.

The early Hegel editors were excited about the master's philosophy, which some of them also developed in their own works, and they felt that they owed it to the deceased as well as to their contemporaries to make available to a broader public the stimulating ideas that he had presented in his lectures. It was still in a similar spirit that Georg Lasson, in the first quarter of the twentieth century, began to publish critical editions: he supplied often excellent prefaces, immensely helpful footnotes, and variant readings at the end; and in the case of the lectures, he consulted Hegel's own manuscripts.

At the end of his 1907 edition of Hegel's first book, the *Phänomenologie des Geistes* (1807), Lasson says of the first reprinting of that book in the collected works, in 1832:

> Moreover, Joh[ann] Schulze, to make the text easier to read, effected many small transpositions, as well as changes and ad-

ditions of words which in a few places alter the sense slightly and in others are dispensable—and which, even where they seem useful, ought to have been marked as departures from the original text. Otherwise, the printing of this edition was careful [523].

The next edition—the only other one before Lasson's—was less careful and marred by several small omissions, up to two lines in length. Lasson lists all these divergencies, and thousands of students found their way to Hegel through his green volumes.

When Johannes Hoffmeister took over, this contagious enthusiasm disappeared: he was not a philosopher but, like Schlechta and Mette who were laboring over Nietzsche during the same period, a man who had made it his job to edit the definitive historical-critical edition—for the record, as it were.[18] As it happened, neither of the two historical-critical projects got at all far.

It would be wrong, then, to see the development from 1889 to Podach's edition of *Friedrich Nietzsches Werke des Zusammenbruchs* as a long battle in which the truth finally wins out over sneaky manipulations. To be sure, Nietzsche's sister did build a legend [19] and committed some forgeries. But there is also another aspect to this story: it brings to mind the young Nietzsche's somewhat scornful reflections on the growth of Alexandrianism as well as his dictum in *Ecce Homo:* "In my case, too, the Germans will do all they can to make an immense destiny bring forth a mouse. So far they have compromised themselves in my case; I doubt that they will do any better in the future" (EH-W3).

VIII

One final question remains: has not Podach shown, as he has plainly tried to do, that the author of *The Antichrist* and *Ecce Homo* was not entirely sane? In reply to this, I have criticized Podach's procedures in detail. But suppose it were said: however that may be, Nietzsche was not so sane as the foregoing pages suggest, and his letters in December, 1888, contain many more incriminating passages than have been quoted here. In answer to that, two things need to be said.

---

[18] See my *Hegel* (1965), sections 52–53.
[19] See the "Prologue: The Nietzsche Legend," above. But the legend should be distinguished from Gast's editorial services to Nietzsche.

First, similar passages abound in his earlier letters, too, and it is not possible to draw any sharp line in this continuum, except after his collapse in the street, early in January, 1889. For a few days he sent meaningful and moving, but evidently insane, cards and letters; then the rest was silence. Consider this portion from a letter that Schlechta prints (III, 1420 f.). It was written in May 1884, and another long quotation from it will be found in Chapter 1, above, near the end of section III. Nietzsche is referring to his *Zarathustra,* which was meeting with no response whatsoever:

> . . . Who knows how many generations will have to pass to produce a few human beings who will recapture in feeling, in all its depth, *what* I have done! And even then the thought still terrifies me how unqualified and totally unsuited people will one day invoke my authority. But this is the agony of every great teacher of mankind; he knows that under certain circumstances and accidents he *can* become a calamity for humanity as well as a blessing. Well, I myself will do everything to avoid facilitating at least all too crude misunderstandings. . . .

This is hardly meek; neither is it insane. If the ideas were utterly out of touch with reality, one might speak of megalomania; as it is, Aristotle's word, *megalopsychia,*[20] is rather more fitting.

Second, the whole notion of possibly discrediting Nietzsche's late works by proving from manuscripts and letters that he was not entirely sane is altogether inappropriate. A parallel may show this better than any argument: it is uncomfortably like trying to discredit Van Gogh's late paintings by pointing out that he was not altogether sane when he created them. As it happens, he was not, and some of them were done while he was in an asylum. To be sure, this is not altogether irrelevant to an appreciation: it adds poignancy to know under what strains he worked and how desperately he tried to cling to his creative work, painting to the last. And if anyone failed to see this by looking at the canvases, the biography would convince him that in these works there is no showmanship, no concern with what might sell, no gimmick. Nietzsche lacked the single-minded purity of Van Gogh and had a more complex and versatile mind. The point is not

---

[20] *Nicomachean Ethics,* IV:3. ". . . a person is thought to be great-souled if he claims much and deserves much."

to show that his character closely resembled Van Gogh's; rather, that a sound judgment of the quality of their late works must obviously be based on a study of the finished works themselves.

Those who want to determine the rank of *The Antichrist* or *Ecce Homo* will find it more pertinent and illuminating to compare them with the writings of Voltaire and Shaw than to look for sensational discoveries. But in whatever light we look at them, these books hold their own.

IX

Podach's sixth Nietzsche book—"a glance into Nietzsche's notebooks" [21]—came to my attention too late to be considered in the body of this article. In any case, it is Podach's least interesting book. The lack of organization is striking. The quotations from the notebooks are generally not in quotation marks, nor are they set off typographically from Podach's comments and his ten interlarded "excursuses." Of course, no careful reader need ever be in doubt whether Nietzsche or Podach is speaking. But this is hardly the way to publish the *Nachlass*. And it is doubly ironical that an author who aims to debunk Nietzsche should secure an audience by so closely following the example of Nietzsche's sister: sprinkling generous quotations from hitherto unpublished material into an otherwise unimportant book.

There is little or nothing here that would command an audience if it were not for the fact that Podach prints, e.g., the passages that, when Nietzsche's and Overbeck's correspondence was published in 1916, were deleted to avoid embarrassment to persons then still living (184–90). But Podach's commentary is absurd: he claims that these passages in Nietzsche's letters to his best friend illustrate Nietzsche's "immoderate public [*sic!*] criticism of his friends" and says they were suppressed "because they violently contradict the legend contrived by the sister, of the noble and ideal friend Nietzsche who supposedly suffered so from the ignoble behavior of his friends" (184).

Podach's "methodical idea of considering the drafts for titles and plans as indicators of the state and character of Nietzsche's

---

[21] *Ein Blick in Notizbücher Nietzsches: Ewige Wiederkunft, Wille zur Macht, Ariadne: Eine schaffensanalytische Studie mit 4 Abbildungen* (1963).

writings" (10) is flimsy: even after finishing a book, many writers still consider many alternative titles. And Podach's claim that "Thus it appears that the great writer to whom we are indebted for aphorisms of high philosophical esprit was not a philosopher" (10 f.), certainly cannot be established by a glance into Nietzsche's notebooks. This claim does not rest on new discoveries but on Podach's conviction that philosophy must be systematic. Indeed, the sentence just quoted is followed by the words: "His personality and his spiritual organization were not those of a systematic thinker." We did not need hitherto unpublished notes to discover that.

As usual, Podach makes some minor contributions, e.g., he presses some further criticisms against Schlechta's editing of the *Nachlass*.[22] But Podach shows as little understanding of Nietzsche's philosophy as ever,[23] almost completely ignores philosophically interesting discussions of Nietzsche, and above all fails to see that Nietzsche's philosophy has to be studied and evaluated on the basis of his books.

X

While preparing new translations, with commentaries, of five of Nietzsche's works and of *The Will to Power,* since this article was originally published in 1964, I discovered to my surprise that Schlechta's edition of Nietzsche's works in three volumes is far more unreliable than I had thought.

The first edition of *Beyond Good and Evil* (1886) differs slightly from all subsequent editions, though it is the only one Nietzsche himself published. Schlechta says unequivocally in his long Philological Postscript that his text is that of the first edition of 1886 (III, 1387), but in fact he consistently reproduces the text of the later editions, evidently unaware of the fact that there are differences. (The discrepancies are indicated in my edition.)

In the last section on *The Birth of Tragedy* in *Ecce Homo* (EH-GT 4) Nietzsche comments on several passages from his

---

[22] 199–209. This final "excursus" also takes issue with some passing remarks I made about Schlechta in an article, "Deutscher Geist heute," in *Texte und Zeichen* (1957): I was too kind though not as laudatory as Podach suggests.

[23] The last two paragraphs on p. 35 furnish a striking example.

Meditation on Wagner and furnishes page references—which Schlechta converts into references to various pages in *The Birth of Tragedy* in his own volume I.

Finally, although Schlechta claims (III, 1393) that his arrangement of *The Will to Power* is "faithful to the manuscripts and chronological," it is neither. He does not even take into account the scores of deviations from the manuscripts that are indicated in an appendix in the edition of 1911: he reproduces the familiar text. His innovations are merely that he abandoned the old title and the systematic arrangement, to which the publishing house of Kröner claimed copyright.[24]

It would be tedious to discuss Schlechta's handling of the *Nachlass* beyond this point, but in his "Bibliography (*Revised 1965*)" Brinton says of Schlechta's edition, which he misdates, that it is "A thorough edition, the best now available, especially for the *Nachlass*." [25] And Danto—also in 1965—relies on this "superb edition" and cites the *Nachlass* according to Schlechta, under the impression that he has done away with "the notorious editorial liberties taken with Nietzsche's literary estate by his sister and those directly responsible to her in the Nietzsche Archives." Only four of Danto's *Nachlass* references are to another edition—"the Leipzig edition (1901) of Nietzsche's works because I could not locate them in Schlechta—the promised index to his edition has not appeared as yet" (324). This is quite a muddle. In fact there are at least eight different editions published in Leipzig (see the Bibliography, below), and Danto's four references are to volume XII of the first edition of the so-called *Grossoktavausgabe*, which was soon superseded by a greatly superior second edition in which volume XII was redone com-

---

[24] One would expect *Der Wille zur Macht* to be in the public domain, like Nietzsche's other writings, but Kröner admits that the arrangement was the editorial creation of Peter Gast and Nietzsche's sister. Under German law, copyright is retained for sixty years after the death of the author—or, in this case, the editors.

For more details about Schlechta's editions, see the Appendix to my edition of *The Will to Power* as well as the many other references to Schlechta in that volume and in my other translations (all of them have indices).

[25] *Op. cit.*, 253. The whole Bibliography is astounding: on 252–53 alone there are over a dozen outright mistakes; and the summary that ascribes to Klages' "important book" a view of Nietzsche diametrically opposed to that which Klages actually defends with great skill (258) is unfortunately typical, not only of the Bibliography.

pletely. Schlechta's index (1965) is totally irrelevant: *nothing* in volume XII was included in Schlechta's edition. Not only did he omit most of the material that is to be found in the first five volumes of the *Historisch-Kritische Gesamtausgabe,* but he also left out the equivalent of eight volumes of philosophically interesting *Nachlass* material that is included both in the second edition of the *Grossoktavausgabe* and in the *Musarion* edition of the works. Indeed, of the notes and fragments of the eighteen-eighties Schlechta included *only* what Gast and the sister had chosen to include in *Der Wille zur Macht,* and he copied their text, "editorial liberties" included.

Even as Schlechta's four volumes (including index) cannot replace the far more complete editions that comprise, respectively, 19 and 23 volumes, his selection of 278 letters cannot take the place of the many volumes of letters published previously, though he includes a few letters not printed before as well as interesting information about the way Nietzsche's sister published—as though they were addressed to herself—letters, drafts for letters, and mosaics pieced together from drafts for letters to others. There is material in volume III that is of interest to scholars, and Schlechta is *not* to be blamed for the fact that some Americans have mistaken a popular edition "in three volumes" for an adequate basis for scholarly work.

Neither Schlechta nor Podach has made any discoveries that have a bearing on Nietzsche's philosophy. Both have an animus against Nietzsche, partly because they cannot help associating him with the Nazis' use of him. In this respect they resemble Brinton, who may be allowed the final word: "Nietzsche's opponents generally have not been of the intellectual calibre of his supporters" (257).

FOUR PREVIOUSLY UNPUBLISHED LETTERS:

Commentary and Facsimile Pages*

Nietzsche's life and character have probably excited more interest than those of any other philosopher. Thomas Mann drew inspiration from both for his *Doctor Faustus,* André Malraux embodied an episode from Nietzsche's life in *La Lutte avec l'ange,* and Stefan George, Christian Morgenstern, and Gottfried Benn each wrote more than one poem on him.

Hence a good deal of attention has always been focused on Nietzsche's letters, although they contain scarcely any philosophy. The various German collections of the letters are spread over fifteen volumes, but many letters still await publication. In the following pages I want to illuminate Nietzsche's character with the help of four hitherto unpublished Nietzsche letters.

His finest letters are exceedingly personal. Many people write letters mainly in order to write, and then address them to someone almost as an afterthought. Nietzsche wrote in his notebooks when he wanted to try out ideas; and when he succeeded in giving adequate form to his thoughts he put them into his books. His letters usually show a pervasive awareness of the person whom he is addressing and speak to *him,* not to the public or posterity. Hence many of Nietzsche's letters are of no great interest except to those who are concerned with establishing some small point about his life, but *some* letters illuminate his relationships to others and show us vividly how he felt.

Our first letter was addressed to Karl Hillebrand (1829–1884), a scholar and literary critic to whom the *Encyclopaedia Britannica,* eleventh edition, devoted half a column. Hillebrand "became involved, as a student in Heidelberg, in the Baden revolutionary

---

* These leters are reproduced on pages 464–476.

movement, and was imprisoned in Rastatt. He succeeded in escaping and lived for a time in Strassburg, Paris—where for several months he was Heine's secretary—and Bordeaux." He took a doctorate at the Sorbonne, became a professor at Douai, resigned his chair and went to Italy when the Franco-Prussian War broke out in 1870, and died in Florence. "His essays, collected under the title *Zeiten, Völker und Menschen* (Berlin, 1874–1885), show clear discernment, a finely balanced cosmopolitan judgment and grace of style." Thus, the *Encyclopaedia*. The collection mentioned includes three review-essays on Nietzsche's first three *Unzeitgemässe Betrachtungen*—Nietzsche's earliest books, except for *The Birth of Tragedy*. Like most of Nietzsche's works, the "Untimely Meditations" met with very little response. Here is Nietzsche's letter to Hillebrand, written in April 1878:[1]

> *Hochverehrter Herr*
> after a winter of severe illness, my health is waking up again and I am enjoying your four volumes *Völker, Zeiten und Menschen,* delighted as if they were milk and honey. O books that exhale a *European* air and not nationalistic nitrogen! How good for the lungs! And then: I'd like to see the author who could equal your candor and benevolent sense of justice—/or rather: I shall exert myself to discover all authors—but how few they'll be!—who come *close* to you in these great virtues.— How grateful I am to you for collecting these essays! Otherwise you might almost have escaped me, for I read neither newspapers nor magazines and altogether, living on the edge of blindness, read (and write) *very little.* This reminds me that you have spoken of my writings, too: of all the comments on them that have come to my notice, yours are by far the *only* ones that have truly delighted me. For here it is clearly *superiority* (in experience and taste and a few other things) that passes judgment, and if only he that is judged is no fool he will takes sides *against himself* with genuine pleasure. And how gladly one *learns* from you!
>
> > Cordially grateful and devoted,
> > Dr. Friedrich Nietzsche
> > University of Basel, Switzerland
>
> Don't take amiss a philologist's pedantry: it is *das Sophisma,* not *der Sophismus*—please forgive me!—

---

[1] The manuscript belongs to the Princeton University Library. A stroke (/) indicates the end of a page.

Our second letter was written five and a half years later, after Nietzsche had finished the third part of *Zarathustra,* which appeared in 1883, and before he wrote the fourth part the following winter in Nice and Mentone. He sent the letter from Mentone in late November 1883, to Paul Lanzky. In 1884, only forty copies of *Zarathustra* IV were printed, privately, but no more than seven were actually distributed among friends. Lanzky got one of the seven; so did the music critic Fuchs, to whom the last of our four letters was written.

Since Lanzky was one of the few who were close to Nietzsche during his last creative years, it is not surprising that Nietzsche mentioned him in five of his letters to Peter Gast, in nine to Franz Overbeck, and in sixteen to his mother and sister, not counting three with which the sister tampered before publishing them. While it has thus long been possible to reconstruct Nietzsche's relation to Lanzky by turning to these three published collections, not one of Nietzsche's letters to Lanzky has been published, and the comprehensive survey of Nietzsche's known letters in the first volume of the *Historisch-Kritische Gesamtausgabe* of the letters (1938) indicates that the Nietzsche Archive in Weimar owned only three *drafts* for letters and one draft for a postcard to Lanzky.

On December 26, 1883, Franz Overbeck received a letter from Nietzsche which contains this passage:

> There is a new human being who may have been given to me at the right time: his name is Paul Lanzky, and he is so devoted to me that he would like to tie his destiny to mine as soon as possible. Independent and a friend of solitude and simplicity, 31 years old, with a philosophical disposition, even more of a pessimist than a skeptic—he is the first to address me in his letters as *Verehrtester Meister!* (which aroused the most diverse feelings and memories). . . .[2]

Nietzsche was then thirty-nine, and earlier that year Richard Wagner had died, whom his admirers had been in the habit of calling *Meister.*

In November 1884 Nietzsche wrote his mother and sister from Mentone:

---

[2] Cf. the letters to mother and sister, Dec. 25, 1883, and to Gast, March 5, 1884.

Imagine: meanwhile Herr Lanzky waited for me one whole week in the *pension de Genève* (Nizza); I heard about it two days too late. Then he left for Ajaccio. A touching letter from him reached me today.[3]

A few days later, November 28, Nietzsche wrote them:

After my last card, until today, a severe attack. Today exhausted.— The Corsican affair is settled: Herr Lanzky will come back from there and spend the winter with me in the same *Pension.* (The result of letters and telegrams.) I will and must stick to Nizza for the sake of my future "colony," which now seems more possible to me (I mean: sympathetic people to whom I can present my philosophy). So alone as I have been here or in the Engadine, I am always sick.

Our hitherto unpublished letter is evidently one of the letters Nietzsche mentions here. The manuscript[4] comprises three small pages, written very neatly:

Mein lieber Herr Lanzky,
Malheur! You have left a couple of days too early—but that you have come to Nizza pleases me greatly, and I might even carry my gratitude so far as to come to Corsica now. Send me, immediately if/that is possible, a few details about the How and Where in Ajaccio—addressed here, Mentone, *pension des Etrangers.*

I am not well just now; but walking bravely and making plans for the future of man shall get me over that. Not counting a few attacks of impatience and rudeness./

Again: I feel *cordially* delighted to have heard from you again.

Faithfully yours,
Dr. Friedrich Nietzsche
Prof.

N.B. Give it a try and come to the pier Sunday morning, Nov. 30: perhaps I'll be *there.*

That is the author of *Zarathustra,* about to write the fourth and last part. A few passages from the later letters about Lanzky may round out the picture. December 4, 1884, Nietzsche wrote mother and sister:

Herr L. . . . came back immediately when I telegraphed him: *Venez pour Nice. Votre ami N.* He telegraphed back: *Je*

---

[3] Nietzsche's sister seems to have tampered with the first part of this letter but not with this paragraph (see *Werke,* ed. Schlechta, III, 1417).
[4] Owned by the author.

serai à Nice mercredi. Votre bien heureux Lanzky.— He has some notion who I am. On the whole, however, to say it in French: *il m'ôte la solitude, sans me donner la compagnie.*— So nothing will come of *Zarath. IV* this winter.[5]

On December 21, Nietzsche wrote mother and sister:

> Lanzky is not cheerful enough for me. But he takes a lot of trouble and bears with me, though occasionally I cannot bear things any longer without becoming rude. . . .
>
> Please send me, for Lanzky's sake, Rohde's pamphlet about *The Birth of Tragedy* (bound in brown leather) . . .
>
> I am sending you an essay Lanzky has written about me, not that I feel like praising it but only because it is the first longish essay about me. That it appeared in a provincial Hungarian journal is another example of the stupidity and clumsiness of my publisher.

The following day Nietzsche wrote Overbeck:

> Then Herr Paul Lanzky lives in my *pension,* a great admirer: formerly editor of the *Revista Europea,* thus *in summa* a journalist. But yesterday when he gave me a long essay about me (printed in a Hungarian journal!), I had no choice but to do what I had done last year with Dr. Paneth,[6] also a great admirer and worshipper: namely, to oblige him not to write about me. I do not have the least wish to see a new kind of Nohl, Pohl and "Kohl" [7] sprout up around me—and prefer my absolute concealment a thousand times to being together with mediocre enthusiasts.

The following month, Nietzsche wrote Overbeck in the same vein: "Lanzky, a considerate man who is very devoted to me, but not somebody to be together with for a long time. I'd prefer even a buffoon!" And February 12, 1885, he wrote mother and sister:

---

[5] The French might be translated thus: "Come to Nice. Your friend N."— "I'll be in Nice Wednesday. Your happy Lanzky."— "He takes away my solitude without giving me company."

[6] About Dr. Paneth, who in 1884 wrote a lot about Nietzsche to his friend Sigmund Freud, see my *From Shakespeare to Existentialism,* Chap. 16, section 3.

[7] K. F. L. Nohl and R. Pohl were ardent Wagnerians who wrote a great deal about their master; *Kohl* means drivel or twaddle as well as cabbage. The same unholy trinity is encountered in *Ecce Homo,* in section 2 of the discussion of *Human, All-Too-Human.* For further details see my commentary on that passage in my version of *Ecce Homo.*

Tomorrow Herr Lanzky leaves me, a very decent man who nevertheless impressed on me again the value and necessity of solitude for me. I shall watch out lest I lose another winter in this way. To be sure, I have every reason to be very grateful to him for many signs of good will and consideration; but one thing is a hundred times more important to me than anything else.

A week later, Nietzsche expressed similar ideas to Overbeck:

I have been through a lot; having the very decent Lanzky here (who will leave next Monday) has helped me over a great deal. But on the other side of this account I might say that I have learned how much I still need complete solitude for a good long while (say, five years!). There is too much in me that still wants to grow ripe and come together; the time for "disciples and a school" *et hoc genus omne* has not come yet.

March 21, 1885, Nietzsche wrote his mother and sister:

You see, I am more cheerful again; the most essential fact is probably that Herr Lanzky is gone. A man who deserves the greatest respect and very devoted to me—but what do those two things matter to me? To me he means what I call by such names as "overcast" or "German weather." In fact, nobody now living means a great deal to me; the human beings I like have been dead for a long, long time; e.g., Abbé Galiani or Henri Beyle or Montaigne.

The following November *Zarathustra,* Part IV was completed and privately printed, and Nietzsche wrote his mother from Florence:

The day after tomorrow we (i.e., Herr Lanzky and I) retreat into the wood-, mountain-, and cloister-solitude of Vallombrosa, not at all far from here. The best room is being prepared for me; we'll have quiet; the place is famous: Dante and Milton have glorified it, the latter in his description of paradise.

In December Nietzsche wrote Overbeck that he was once again "experimenting with places to live":

It must be possible eventually to find something independent and suitable for me; but I doubt more and more that I'll find it. Hence I need people who look after me. The unpractical side of my nature, being half blind, and on the other hand being anxious, helpless, discouraged as a consequence of my ill health, often fixes me in situations that almost kill me.

Almost seven years of solitude and for the most part truly a dog's life because I lacked everything necessary for *me.* I thank heaven that nobody has really witnessed it at close range (except Lanzky, who is still utterly beside himself about it).

On January 9, 1886, Nietzsche wrote Overbeck:

> I have every reason to be grateful that a man like L., a remarkably noble and fine character, albeit unfortunately no "intellect"—crossed my path: in the long run he will probably become something like my "practical reason," my counsel for home economics, health, etc.

Finally, Nietzsche wrote Gast on December 9, 1888, less than a month before his total collapse, that he had finished his final revision of *Ecce Homo,* and

> The day before yesterday, Strindberg wrote me his first letter —the first letter with a world-historical accent ever to reach me. He has some idea that *Zarathustra* is a *non plus ultra.*

Nietzsche feels elated. He has also received a letter from a female admirer in St. Petersburg; Georg Brandes is lecturing about him in Copenhagen; Nietzsche has just sent *Twilight of the Idols* to Hippolyte Taine and hopes for a French translation; perhaps Miss Helen Zimmern will do some English translations (she actually did translate *Beyond Good and Evil* later on); and Lanzky is mentioned again later, in the same letter to Gast:

> Dear friend, I want to get back all copies of the fourth part of *Zarathustra* in order to secure this *ineditum* against all accidents of life and death (I read it recently and almost died of emotion). If I publish it after a few decades of world-historical crises—wars!—only then will the right time have come. Please strain your memory to determine who has copies. My memory yields: Lanzky, Widemann, Fuchs, Brandes, probably Overbeck.

This final reference to Paul Lanzky may give some idea of Nietzsche's solitude during his last years. Paul Heinrich Widemann was a young composer and friend of Gast's. Brandes had discovered Nietzsche and corresponded with him, but they never met.

Before we turn to Fuchs, let us consider the third of our four unpublished letters. This was addressed to Nietzsche's publisher, E. W. Fritzsch:[8]

---

[8] The manuscript belongs to the Houghton Library, Harvard University. The postscripts are written in the margins.

Sils Maria, Oberengadin
Switzerland, 29 Aug. 86

Lieber und werther Herr Fritzsch,
Here is the Preface for the *new* edition of *The Birth of Tragedy*. Given this very meaty Preface which provides so much orientation, you can launch this book once more—it even seems very important to me that this should be done. All signs indicate that during the next years people will pay a good deal of attention to my books (inasmuch as I am, if I may say so, by far the most independent thinker of this time who thinks in the great style more than anyone else); people will *need* me and make all kinds of/ efforts to get at me, to understand and "explain" me, etc. To forestall the worst mistakes, nothing seems more useful to me (apart from *Beyond Good and Evil,* which has just appeared) than the *two* prefaces I took the liberty of sending you: they indicate the way I went—and, quite seriously, if I myself do not offer a couple of hints how I am to be understood, the worst stupidities are bound to happen.

I cannot judge to what extent it might be advisable or inadvisable commercially and from a publisher's point of view to bring upon the market simultaneously several books by the same author. What is essential is that as a prerequisite for the understanding of my *Zarathustra*/ (an unparalleled event in literature *and* philosophy *and* poetry *and* morality, etc., etc. You may believe me, you lucky owner of this *Wundertier!*) *all* of my earlier writings must be understood seriously and profoundly; ditto, the necessity of the sequence of these writings and of the development that finds expression in them. Perhaps it would be equally useful to issue now, immediately, also the new edition of *The Birth* (with the "Attempt at a Self-Criticism"). This "Attempt," together with the "Preface to *Human, All-Too-Human,*" provides genuine enlightenment about me—and the very best preparation for my audacious son, Zarathustra./

In December I hope to be able to continue with the prefaces—in Nizza where so far I have never lacked courage and inspiration around that time of year. Namely, *Hum., All-Too-Hum.,* second volume (comprising *Mixed Opin. and Maxims* and *The Wanderer*), 2. *Dawn,* 3. *Gay Science.*

I think you know, my dear Herr publisher, how much courage and inspiration is required precisely for such prefaces? and in addition even more "good will"—

Let us assume that by next spring all my works, insofar as they are in your hands, will be ready for another flight with new "wings." For these prefaces shall be *wings!* (Only the 4 *Untimely Medit.* I want to leave as they stand: that is why I have considered it necessary to call attention to them very definitely in the postscript that I sent you recently for the Preface to *Hum., All-Too-Hum.*)—Hoping for a brief reply to this address,

Your most devoted Dr. Nietzsche, Prof./

Please be good enough to tell me something about the prices of the books that are to appear next. Hermann Credner[9] once told or wrote me that Schmeitzner's prices had been the greatest obstacle on my way to date./

A separate little volume of nothing but prefaces would be a sin against good taste. The dreadful little preface-word "I" is tolerated only on condition that it is not encountered in the book that follows: it is justified only in a preface.—/

Sept. 1: Just now letter and proofs arrived. Has the postscript (sent to you by registered mail) not reached you yet? Lest everything be delayed, I ask you to drop it (not to print it). But this "Self-Criticism" more than ever!

This letter does not need to be placed in the context of other letters. Nietzsche's works were duly reissued with his new prefaces, and that for the new edition of *The Birth of Tragedy* is a masterpiece. So far from singing his own praises, the self-criticism leaves nothing to be desired in sharpness; perhaps no other great writer has ever dealt so harshly with one of his own works in a preface.

Eventually, in *Ecce Homo,* Nietzsche did commit the sin against good taste of which he writes here. The reviews of his own books in that work are assembled under the chapter heading "Why I Write Such Good Books"—but are redeemed by an abundance of insight and wit.

Our fourth unpublished letter is addressed to Dr. Carl Fuchs in Danzig. Fuchs (1838–1922) received his doctorate at Greifswald with a dissertation entitled *Präliminarien zu einer Kritik der Tonkunst* (1870, "Prolegomena for a Critique of Music"). He was a concert pianist and conductor before he became organist at the Petrikirche in Danzig and from 1887 until 1920 also music critic of the *Danziger Zeitung.* For many years he also served as organist for the synagogue, but according to the *vita* appended to his dissertation he was a Protestant (and his mother's maiden name was Stechert). He published several books on music and

---

[9] A publisher in Leipzig, discussed in a letter to Overbeck, July 20, 1888.

in 1904 received the title of professor. Some of Nietzsche's letters to him were printed in *Gesammelte Briefe,* vol. I (1900), but this letter fills an interesting gap in our knowledge of Nietzsche. On July 20, 1888, Nietzsche wrote Overbeck:

> Dear friend, nothing has improved, neither the weather nor my health—both remain *absurd.* But today I'll tell you of something that is still more absurd: Dr. Fuchs. Recently he has sent me a whole literature (including one letter of twelve large crowded sheets!). In the process I have slowly turned into a hedgehog, and my old mistrust is complete again. His egoism is so clever and on the other hand so anxious and unfree that nothing avails him—neither his great talent nor the fact that there is a lot in his nature that is *genuinely* artistic.

The account of Fuchs is long and detailed; all of it was omitted when the letter was printed in *Friedrich Nietzsches Briefwechsel mit Franz Overbeck* (1916)—the omission was indicated, but there was no way of telling how very long it was. Now, however, the German text is readily accessible in the third volume of Schlechta's edition of the *Werke* (1302 ff.). It will suffice here to cite the end of Nietzsche's comments on Fuchs.

> He is also the organist at the synagogue in Danzig. You may imagine how he made fun of the Jewish services in the *dirtiest* way (but he allows himself to be *paid* for it!!).
>
> Finally, he wrote me a letter about his *descent,* with so many digusting and indecent indiscretions about his mother and his father that I lost my patience and in the rudest manner forbade him to send me such letters. I am not in the least inclined to allow my solitude to be disturbed by the contingency of letters.— So far have we come. Unfortunately I know this kind of man too well to be able to hope that this will be the end.

Schlechta does not include in his selection Nietzsche's postcard to Overbeck, July 26, 1888, which was printed in 1916 and begins: "Dear friend, another word regarding Dr. F. He has meanwhile answered my letter—excellently, not merely cleverly." The very next day Nietzsche wrote Gast to send Fuchs a copy of Part IV of *Zarathustra,* and on the twenty-ninth he informed Fuchs of this, "as a sign that everything between us is all right again."

Our letter is the one Nietzsche mentioned to Overbeck— the one he described as a sample of his rudest manner:[10]

---

[10] It is owned by the author.

Wednesday, July 18, 1888

Lieber Herr Doctor,

Don't feel annoyed, but from sheer necessity I must resist your letters. It is altogether forbidden to me to hear such *privatissima, personalissima:* their effect on me is, I dare not say what—it would sound too medical. For just a moment put yourself into the place of one who has my *Zarathustra* on his soul. Once you have comprehended what exertion it has cost me to gain some sort of equilibrium vis-à-vis the whole fact of man,/ you will also comprehend the extreme caution with which I now approach all human intercourse. I want once and for all not to know many things any more, never to hear many things any more—at this price I may perhaps endure.

I have given men the most profound book they own, my *Zarathustra*: a book that confers such distinction that whoever can say, "I have understood six sentences in it, that is, lived through them" thus belongs to a higher order of mortals.— But how one has to atone for that! pay for that! it almost corrupts/ one's character! The gulf has become too great. Ever since, I really do nothing any more but buffooneries to remain master over an intolerable tension and vulnerability.

This between us. The rest is silence.

Your friend
Nietzsche.

Hochverehrter Herr

nach neuer Müller schwerer Erkrankung genieße ich jetzt im Mor-
gendämmern der Gesundheit Ihre
vier Bände „Völker Zeiten und
Menschen" und freue mich darüber
wie als ob es Milch und Honig wäre.
O Bücher, auf denen eine euvegä-
ische Luft weht und nicht der lieben
nationale Riechstoff! Wie das den
Lungen wohltut! Und dann: ich
möchte den Autor sehen, der Ihnen
an Unbefangenheit und wohlwollender
Gerechtigkeit — dann gleichkäm —

oder vielmehr: ich will nicht berechnen,
alle Lesovan — die wenige werden
aber sein! — Niemand zu lesen, die
Ihnen in betreff jener hohen Tu-
genden nahe kommen. —

Wie danke ich Ihnen, daß Sie
diese Aufsätze gesammelt haben!
Sie wären mir leicht fast ganz
entgangen, da ich weder Zeitungen
noch Zeitschriften lese und überhaupt,
der Nähe der Verbindung wegen, sehr
wenig lese (und schreibe)

Viel wundert mich daran, daß Sie
auch über meine Gedichte gesprochen
haben: ist ihr bei mir das Einzige,
was mir von dem, was mir von Nachspielen

über denselben bekannt geworden ist, wirklich Freude gemacht hat. Denn eine vortheilt erscheint die Überlegenheit (im Erfahren und Geschmack und manchen andern Dingen —), da ergreift der Beobachter, wenn er kein Narr ist, mit Vergnügen gegen sich selber Partei. Und wie gern man von Ihnen lernt!

Von Herzen dankbar und
ergeben

Dr Friedrich Nietzsche
(Universität Basel (Schweiz))

Übrigens darf dem Philologen eine Pedanterie nicht: es heisst „das Doctissimus", nicht
der Doctissimus" — ich bitte um Verzeihung! —
„

Mein lieber Herr Lautsky,

Malheur! Sie sind ein paar Tage zu früh abge=
reist — aber dass Sie nach
Nizza gekommen sind, ge=
fällt mir sehr, ich könnte
meine Dankbarkeit dafür unter
Umständen ja, weit drüben,
jetzt nach Corsica zu kom—
men. Haben Sie mir, wenn

möglich sogleich, um paar
Tagesstunden über das „Hin
und Her" in Ajaccio —
Dieser adressirt, Mentone
pension des Etrangers.

Ich befinde mich gerade nicht
gut, dagegen Spaziergehen
und Schlaf-Machen für die
Menschen-Zukunft soll mich
darüber hinweg bringen. Leichte
Anfälle von Ungeduld und
Grobheit abgerechnet.

Nochmals: es ist mir herz-
lich angenehm, von Ihnen
wieder gehört zu haben.

Treulich

Dr. Friedrich Nietzsche
Prof

NB. Kommen Sie doch, versuchs-
weise, Sonntag den 30 Nov. mor-
gens an den Hafen:- vielleicht bin
ich schon da.

Sils-Maria, Oberengadin
Schweiz. 29 Aug. 86.

Lieber und werther Herr Fritzsch,

Hier folgt die Vorrede zur neuen Ausgabe der "Geburt der Tragödie": Sie
bekommen auf diese sehr inhaltreiche und
gründlich orientirende Vorrede hin das
Buch noch einmal neu drucken
lassen, — es scheint mir sogar von größ-
tem Nutzen, dass dies geschieht. Alle
Anzeichen sprechen dafür, dass man sich
in den nächsten Jahren viel mit meinen
Sachen beschäftigen wird (— insofern ich,
mit Verlaub gesagt, bei meinem der
unabhängigste und im großen Stile den-
kendste Denker dieser Zeit bin —): man
wird mich nöthig haben, und alle möglichen

Sollten Sie mir zufällig etwas über die Drucke der früheren aufzuzählen bitte mir! Hiermit danke ich
dafür sein Schweizerisches Werk das größte Hindernis verursachen, ist das mir schwer ein Maße Da-
Maße.

Versuche, mir beizukommen, mich zu ver-
stehen, zu „erklären" usw. machen. Um
den gröbsten Fehlgriffen vorzubeugen, scheint
mir (abgesehn von dem eben erschienenen
„Jenseits von Gut und Böse") nichts nützlicher
als die beiden Vorreden, welche ich mir
erlaubte, Ihnen zu übersenden: sie deuten
den Weg an, den ich gegangen bin —
und, wahrhaftig geredet, wenn ich selber
nicht ein paar Winke gebe, wie man
mich zu verstehen hat, so müssen die größe-
ren Dummheiten passiren. —
Ich kann nicht beurtheilen, ob es eben so
geschäftlich und buchhändlerisch rathsam
oder unrathsam ist, Bücher derselben Cur-
[illegible] zugleich auf den Markt zu bringen.
Das Wesentliche ist, dass nun die Voraus-
setzungen für das Verständniss des Zarathustra

1 Seite (bin bitte durch d. Bogen ein. Ist der Verfasser („hinausgeschrieben" an Sie adressirt; und nicht in Ihren Händen: nun nicht leicht zu verzögern, bitte ich ihn zu lassen (also nicht so drucken) ihm so mehr eben d. Selbstkritik!

zu haben (— eine Sammlung über Gedanken in der Litteratur und Philosophie und Poesie und Moral usw. usw. Sie dürfen mirs glauben, die glücklichsten Lesestunden dieser Mußestunden! —) Alle meine früheren Schriften werden sich und mich verstehen zu müssen; eingeschlossen die Nothwendigkeit und der Auseinanderfolge dieser Schriften und der in ihnen sich ausdrückenden Entwicklung. Vielleicht ist es ebenfalls nützlich, sogleich jetzt für die neue Ausgabe der Geburt "mit dem Versuche einer Selbstkritik") aus zu Händen. Dieser "Versuch", zusammengehalten mit der Vorrede von Menschl. Allzu-menschliches") ergiebt nun manche Aufklärung über mich — und die allerbeste Vorbereitung für meinen vorausgehenden Sohn Zarathustra.

Im Dezember hoffe ich mit den Vorreden fortfahren zu können: nämlich in Nizza, wo es mir bisher niemals, zu dieser Zeit, an Muth und Inspiration gefehlt hat.

1) Menschl. Allzum. Erster Band (nebst Vorrede)
2) Morgenröthe.   „Verm. M. u. Spr." und „der Wanderer"
3) Fröhl. Wissenschaft

Ich denke, Sie müssen, lieber Herr Verleger, mir meinen Muth und Inspiration gerade zu solchen „Vorreden" noch gut? Und außerdem noch mehr „guter Mölle"? —

Nehmen wir an, daß bis zum Frühjahr meine ganze Litteratur, so weit sie in Ihren Händen ist, zum neuen Fluge fertig und neu beflügelt" ist. Denn diese Vorreden" sollen flügel sein! (Nur die 4 angezeigten Übersetzungen will ich lassen, wie sie sind: deshalb habe ich, in dem zuletzt übersandten Nachtrag zur Vorrede sie Menschl. Allzum., sehr bestimmt auch sie aufmerksam

[left margin:] zu machen für nöthig befunden) — (ein zarte Zukunft fühlen vielleicht eingeweihte Dr. Nietzsche 1888

Mittwoch, den 18. Juli 1888

Lieber Herr Doctor,

Wenn Sie nicht böse, erlaube ich Ihnen
mich, nachzudrängen, gegen Ihren Brief
zur Wehre. Es ist mir vollkommen
verboten, dergleichen privatissima, ja,
sonatissima anzuhören; das mich
auch mir, ich mag, mich zu sagen ein —
es klänge zu medizinisch. Versuchen
Sie doch einen Augenblick in die Um-
stände zu setzen, der meinen Character
auch der Sache hat. Wenn Sie vorsich-
tigen haben, werden Bücher ab mir ge-
bracht, zur ganzen Wissenschaft Mensch
mir ungefähre Gleichgewicht in ver-
                                    langen,

… verzichten, ja auf die extreme Vorsicht
verzichten, weil ich jetzt jeden
menschlichen Verkehr behandle. Ich will,
ein für alle Mal, jede Verleumdung nicht
mehr wissen, jede Verleumdung nur mehr
hören — über diesen Punkt halte ich
es unerschütterlich aus.

Ich habe den Menschen das tiefste
Buch gegeben, das sie besitzen,
meinen Zarathustra: ein Buch,
das dermaßen ausgezeichnet, daß
wer sagen kann „ich habe sechs
Sätze davon verstanden, das heißt
erlebt" damit zu einer höheren
Ordnung der Menschen gehört. —
Aber wie man das büßen muß!
abgeßen muß! es ruiniert einmal

Ihr Charakter! Die Lücke ist zu groß geworden. Ich denke seitdem, …………… und ………………, um über eine ……………… Mannes ……………… Euer zu ……………

Sind ……… und … der ………
………………
Ihr Freund
……………

BIBLIOGRAPHY

and Key to Abbreviations

I. *Nietzsche's Books, with a Key to the Abbreviations Used in the Present Volume.*

II. *Nietzsche's Collected Works in German.*

III. *Additional Material Not Included in the Collected Editions.*

IV. *Nietzsche's Correspondence in German.*

V. *Nietzsche in English.*

VI. *Works About Nietzsche.*

I. NIETZSCHE'S BOOKS, WITH A KEY TO THE ABBREVIATIONS USED IN THE PRESENT VOLUME

Die Geburt der Tragödie (The Birth of Tragedy)	GT	1872	III
Unzeitgemässe Betrachtungen (Untimely Meditations)	U		
I. *David Strauss, der Bekenner und Schriftsteller* (David Strauss, the Confessor and Writer)		1873	VI
II. *Vom Nutzen und Nachteil der Historie für das Leben* (Of the Use and Disadvantage of History for Life)		1874	VI
III. *Schopenhauer als Erzieher* (S. as Educator)		1874	VII
IV. *Richard Wagner in Bayreuth*		1876	VII
Menschliches, Allzumenschliches	MA		

(Human, All-Too-Human)

I.		1878	VIII
II. *Vermischte Meinungen und Sprüche* (Mixed Opinions and Maxims)		1879	IX
Der Wanderer und sein Schatten (The Wanderer and his Shadow)	S	1880	IX
Die Morgenröte (The Dawn)	M	1881	X
Die Fröhliche Wissenschaft (The Gay Science) Book V (§§343–383) added in 1887.	FW	1882	XII
Also Sprach Zarathustra (Thus Spoke Zarathustra) Parts I and II, 1883; III, 1884; IV, 1885 —first public edition of Z IV, 1892.	Z		XIII
Jenseits von Gut und Böse (Beyond Good and Evil)	J	1886	XV
Zur Genealogie der Moral (On the Genealogy of Morals) Three inquiries.	GM	1887	XV
Der Fall Wagner (The Case of Wagner)	W	1888	XVII
Die Götzen-Dämmerung (The Twilight of the Idols) Ten chapters.	G	1889	XVII
Der Antichrist (The Antichrist)	A	1895 *	XVII
Ecce Homo Four chapters; also ten sections on the above titles: EH–GT; EH–U; etc.	EH	1908 *	XXI
Nietzsche contra Wagner Ten chapters.	NCW	1895 *	XVII
Der Wille zur Macht (The Will to Power) 1067 sections.	WM	**	XVIII– XIX

Prefaces (*Vorreden*) are abbreviated "V"; e.g., GT–V.

These works are cited by the abbreviations given above and by the numbers of the aphorisms or sections—which are the same in all editions, regardless of language.

All other references are to the Musarion edition of the *Gesammelte Werke* (23 vols., 1920–29). The arrangement of the Musarion edition is chronological; thus every reference reveals at a glance the approximate date of the passages referred to, except that vol. XXI contains autobiographical sketches of all periods.

To facilitate the determination of the dates of all passages cited in the present book, the above list shows both the dates of the first editions of Nietzsche's books and the volume of the Musarion edition in which they are to be found. Often these volumes contain notes and fragments of the same period to which the book belongs. Vol. I contains *juvenilia* not included in previous editions of the works; II, IV, and V, philological material of the Basel period; XI, by-products of M and FW; XIV, material roughly contemporaneous with Z, while notes of the last years are found mostly in XVI and in WM (XVIII and XIX). Nietzsche's verse is offered in chronological order in XX.

The following changes in the second editions of Nietzsche's books are worthy of note. GT: 1st ed. was entitled *Die Geburt der Tragödie aus dem Geiste der Musik*; a 2nd ed. (1878), published while the 1st ed. was still in print, contained some changes; and in 1886 a Preface was added to the remaining copies of both editions, and the title was changed to *Die Geburt der Tragödie Oder Griechentum und Pessimismus.* MA: 1st ed., with dedication "To the Memory of Voltaire, in Commemoration of [the 100th anniversary of] his Death, May 30, 1878" and a motto from Descartes "In Place of a Preface"; 2nd ed. (1886) without both of these, but with a Preface, and with MA II and S as vol. II, also with a new Preface. M: 2nd ed. with Preface, 1887. FW: see the Key to Abbreviations above; an appendix of poems (*Lieder des Prinzen Vogelfrei*) was also added in 1887. Some very minor discrepancies between the first edition of J (the only one Nietzsche himself supervised) and all subsequent editions are pointed out in my commentary on my translation (see section v below).

An asterisk (*) after the date in the above list indicates that the first edition appeared after Nietzsche had become insane. The three books in question are discussed at length in the Appendix to the present volume, and in the case of EH, I may also refer to my translation with commentary (listed under V below). Nevertheless, I see no reason to delete the two paragraphs on this subject that appeared in the original edition of my *Nietzsche* in 1950:

In A and EH slight changes were effected by Gast and Nietzsche's sister. Cf. Friedrich Nietzsche, *Werke und Briefe: Historisch-Kritische Gesamtausgabe,* Munich, Beck, 1933–42, *Werke* I, vii–cxxii; e.g., xlv: "The previous editions of *The Antichrist* contained occasional corrections by Gast and are not quite unobjectionable: in sections 29, 35, and 38, for example . . . sometimes single words, and sometimes a few sentences, are missing." And a number of deviations from Nietzsche's manuscript in all previous editions of EH are listed on pages xlvii–xlix. Cf.

also Hofmiller, "Nietzsche," 83 and 94. According to the notes at the end of the first and second editions of WM, in the *Grossoktavausgabe* of the works, a number of words and passages were also omitted from the notes published as WM. The *Historisch-Kritische Gesamtausgabe* proceeds chronologically and stops short even of Nietzsche's first book (GT); thus it cannot be resorted to in order to make up for these defects of all previous editions.

Under these circumstances, any work on Nietzsche might seem merely provisional, pending the publication of all hitherto suppressed words and sentences. Such an inference, however, would be unwarranted. The principles which guided Gast and Frau Förster-Nietzsche in making omissions are very plain—from their published Nietzsche interpretations, from the explanations which accompany some of the omissions (WM), from the context, and from the nature of those censored passages which have been published from time to time; e.g., by Hofmiller and Podach. Some unkind comments on Frau Förster-Nietzsche, Richard Wagner, anti-Semitism, the German *Reich,* and Christianity were suppressed; but there is no reason whatever for believing that the hitherto withheld material includes anything of significance that would have corroborated Frau Förster-Nietzsche's version of her brother's thought. It is therefore quite unlikely that future editions of Nietzsche's works will necessitate any radical revision of an interpretation which does justice to the material so far published.

The Will to Power has been marked with two asterisks (**) in the above list because it is not really one of Nietzsche's books but rather a posthumously published selection from his notebooks. For the history of its publication, see section I of the Prologue, above; II, 2b in the Bibliography, below; and above all my translation with commentary, listed under V, below.

II. NIETZSCHE'S COLLECTED WORKS IN GERMAN

The title of editions 1–6 is *Nietzsches Werke.* For Nietzsche scholars, 2b, 8, and, within its very narrow limits, 9 are the only reasonably adequate editions. Although 10 and 11 contain some interesting material, they cannot replace 2b or 8. Those with a more casual interest in Nietzsche will find 7 most convenient: except for the editorial postscripts, vols. 70–78 are adequate for most purposes. When 12 is completed, it will contain more material than any previous edition.

1. *Gesamtausgabe,* ed. Peter Gast. Leipzig, Naumann, 1892 ff. Discontinued after vol. V.

2. *Grossoktavausgabe,* ed. by various editors under the general supervision of Elisabeth Förster-Nietzsche—the turnover being due in
large measure to disagreement about the methods to be followed
in publishing the *Nachlass,* i.e., notes, fragments, and other MS
material not published by Nietzsche himself. The early volumes
were published by Naumann; later the edition was taken over by
Kröner, Leipzig.
   a. First ed.: 15 vols., 1894–1904. Vols. I–VIII contain Nietzsche's
   books; vols. IX–XV the *Nachlass.*
      It was in vol. VIII (1895) that A and NCW were first pub-
   lished.
   b. Second ed.: 19 vols., 1901–13.
   Section I (vols. I–VIII), 1905–10; *Werke* (books).
   Section II (vols. IX–XVI), 1901–11: *Nachlass.*
   Section III (vols. XVII–XIX), 1910–13: *Philologica.*
      The last section, which contains articles, lecture notes, and
   other materials that reflect Nietzsche's career as a classical philologist, was first added in the second edition, and at the same time
   section II was revised extensively: only vols. XIII and XIV
   remained unchanged. Vols. IX and X (1903) and XI and XII
   (1901) were "completely remodeled," and the former vol. XV
   (1901), which had contained the first edition of WM, was sup-
   planted by a complete rearrangement in two vols., XV (1910)
   and XVI (1911). The new vol. XV also contained EH, which had
   never before been included in a collected edition.
      In 1926, Richard Oehler's index was added as vol. XX, but
   this index does not cover section III.
3. *Kleinoktavausgabe,* 16 vols., Leipzig, Kröner, 1899–1912.
   This edition agrees, page for page, with 2b, but lacks the *Philologica* and is smaller in size.
4. *Taschenausgabe,* 11 vols., Leipzig, Kröner, 1906 (vol. XI, 1913).
   Selections from the *Nachlass* are included in the volumes which
   contain the works of the same period.
      It was in volumes 9 and 10 that the second revised edition of
   WM (see 2b, above) was first published, but without the scholarly
   apparatus of the 1911 edition.
5. *Klassiker-Ausgabe,* 9 vols., Leipzig, Kröner, 1919.
   This edition contains only the books and WM.
6. *Dünndruck-Gesamtausgabe,* 6 vols., Leipzig, Kröner, 1930.
   This thin-paper ed. contains the books, WM, and a selection from
   the *Nachlass* of the Basel period. In 1931 two more volumes of
   Nachlass material were added, under the title *Die Unschuld des
   Werdens* (the innocence of becoming), ed. Alfred Bäumler.

7. *Kröners Taschenausgabe,* vols. 70–78 and 82–83, contains the same material as 6; but these very handy volumes can be bought separately, and vol. 170 (1943) contains Richard Oehler's index for this edition.

  a. *Sämtliche Werke in zwölf Bänden,* 12 vols., Stuttgart, Kröner, 1964–65, is a reprint of the preceding edition: vols. 70–78, 82–83, and 170 comprise 12 vols. But in this edition WM is no longer presented as one of Nietzsche's books: the title page adds *Ausgewählt und geordnet von Peter Gast unter Mitwirkung von Elisabeth Förster-Nietzsche* (selected and arranged by Peter Gast with the aid of Elisabeth Förster-Nietzsche); and in a postscript (pp. 711–15) to his editorial afterword (pp. 699–711) Alfred Bäumler deals with *"Der Nachlass und seine Kritiker"* (The *Nachlass* and its critics), attempting a reply to Karl Schlechta and Erich Podach. It is noteworthy that on the title page of vol. 78 (1930) of edition 7 above, no credit was given to Gast and Nietzsche's sister.

8. *Gesammelte Werke, Musarionausgabe,* 23 vols. Munich, Musarion Verlag, 1920–29.

  Books, *Nachlass,* and *Philologica* are arranged in a single chronological sequence; a new volume of *juvenilia* is added as vol. I; and Oehler's index, which covers the *Philologica,* too, comprises half of volume XXI (names) and all of vols. XXII and XXIII (subjects).

9. *Werke und Briefe: Historisch-Kritische Gesamtausgabe,* 9 vols. Munich, Beck, 1933–42. Discontinued after 5 vols. of *Werke* and 4 vols. of *Briefe* had appeared. The arrangement is chronological, and the "works" do not include any of Nietzsche's books but cover only the period from 1854, when Nietzsche was 10, to 1869. But H. J. Mette's discussion of the MSS in *Werke,* I, xxxi–cxxvi, is of interest also regarding the MSS of Nietzsche's later works. For the letters see IV, 5 below.

10. *Werke in drei Bänden,* ed. Karl Schlechta, 3 vols. Munich, Carl Hanser, 1954–56.

  Vols. I and II contain all of Nietzsche's books, as well as the so-called *Dionysos-Dithyramben* (some of the late poems); vol. III, a selection from the *Nachlass,* including a wretched rearrangement of WM, as well as 278 letters, a chronology (pp. 1359–82), and a Philological Postscript (pp. 1383–1432). For some criticisms of this edition, see the Appendix, above, and my editions of *Beyond Good and Evil, Ecce Homo,* and *The Will to Power.* The selections from the *Nachlass* are inadequate for scholarly purposes. In 1965 a fourth volume was added: *Nietzsche-Index.* Like Oehler's earlier indices, this is very helfpul but incomplete even as far as proper names are concerned.

    a. *Werke in zwei Bänden,* ed. Ivo Frenzel, 2 vols. Munich, Carl Hanser, 1967. Based on the preceding edition and marred by the same inaccuracies. U I, U III, MA II, S, M, and NCW are omitted altogether, along with all of vol. III, except for a few early autobiographical sketches. The editorial matter is new and includes some explanatory notes at the end.

11. *Friedrich Nietzsches Werke der Zusammenbruchs* by Erich F. Podach (Heidelberg, Wolfgang Rothe, 1961) seeks to supersede all previous editions of NCW, A, EH, and *Dionysos-Dithyramben,* and is particularly scornful of Schlechta's edition. For a detailed critique of Podach's editing see the Appendix, above, as well as my editions of *Ecce Homo* and *The Will to Power.*

12. *Werke: Kritische Gesamtausgabe,* ed. Giorgio Colli and Mazzino Montinari, about 30 vols., Berlin, De Gruyter, 1967 ff. The *International Nietzsche Bibliography* (1960; see VI, A, below) does not list any contributions by either of the two editors, and vols. 1–3 of Division IV—the first to be published—are unimpressive.

III. ADDITIONAL MATERIAL NOT INCLUDED IN THE COLLECTED EDITIONS

1. *Vorstufen der Geburt der Tragödie* (stages on the way toward *The Birth of Tragedy*), 3 vols. Leipzig, Hadl, 1926–28.
    a. *Das Griechische Musikdrama* (the Greek music drama, lecture, 1870), 1926.
    b. *Sokrates und die Tragödie* (Socrates and tragedy, lecture, 1870), 1927.
    c. *Die Dionysische Weltanschauung* (the Dionysian world view, essay, 1870), 1928.

2. *Socrates und die Griechische Tragödie: Ursprüngliche Fassung der Geburt der Tragödie aus dem Geiste der Musik,* ed. H. J. Mette. Munich, Beck, 1933 (original version).

3. *Lieder für eine Singstimme mit Klavierbegleitung* (songs for a voice with piano accompaniment); vol. I of *Musikalische Werke von Friedrich Nietzsche,* ed. Georg Göhler. Leipzig, Kistner and Siegel, 1924.

4. *Hymnus an das Leben, für gemischten Chor und Orchester* (hymn to life, for mixed choir and orchestra). Leipzig, Fritzsch, 1887 (text by Lou Salomé).

5. *Friedrich Nietzsches Randglossen zu Bizets Carmen* (Friedrich Nietzsche's marginal glosses to Bizet's *Carmen*), by Hugo Daffner. Regensburg, Bosse, no date (1912).

6. Nietzsche's marginal glosses to Guyau's *Esquisse d'une Morale sans Obligation ni Sanction* (sketch of an ethic without obligation or sanction; 1885), in a 25-page appendix to the German edition of F. M. Guyau, *Sittlichkeit ohne "Pflicht."* Leipzig, Klinkhardt, 1909.

7. *Der Werdende Nietzsche: Autobiographische Aufzeichnungen* (Nietzsche in the process of becoming: autobiographical sketches), ed. E. Förster-Nietzsche. Munich, Musarion, 1924.

8. *Mein Leben: Autobiographische Skizze des jungen Nietzsche* (my life: an autobiographical sketch of the young Nietzsche; written September 18, 1863). Frankfurt am Main, Moritz Diesterweg, 1936. Facsimile on pp. 5–12; printed transcript on pp. 13–15.

9. *Mein Leben, Mein Lebenslauf: 1861, 1863, 1864* (my life, the course of my life). Berlin, W. Keiper, 1943. Four sketches in facsimile only, pp. 7–31. The second of these is identical with 8 above, but the eight pages of the original are reproduced on seven pages: the first six lines of the third page are printed as if they had been found at the bottom of the second page, etc. Although Nietzsche plainly states that he was born October 15, 1844, both editions state that he was 19 when he wrote *Mein Leben* in September, 1863.

10. *Ein Blick in Notizbücher Nietzsches: Ewige Wiederkunft, Wille zur Macht, Ariadne: Eine schaffensanalytische Studie mit 4 Abbildungen* (a glance into Nietzsche's notebooks: eternal recurrence, will to power, Ariadne: a study in the analysis of creation, with 4 illustrations—i.e., facsimiles), by Erich F. Podach. Heidelberg, Wolfgang Rothe, 1963. For a brief discussion, see section ix of the Appendix, above.

11. See Roos in VI, below.

IV. NIETZSCHE'S CORRESPONDENCE IN GERMAN

1. *Friedrich Nietzsches Gesammelte Briefe* (Friedrich Nietzsche's collected letters), 5 vols. (the 5th actually consists of 2 vols. with continuous pagination). The first eds. of vols. I–III were published by Schuster and Loeffler, Berlin and Leipzig, 1900–05; those of vols. IV–V, by the Insel-Verlag, Leipzig, 1908–09, which also published the later editions of I–III.

Vol. I contains letters to Carl von Gersdorff, Frau Marie Baumgartner, Otto Eiser, Frau Louise Ott, Gustav Krug, Paul Deussen,

Carl Fuchs, Reinhart von Seydlitz, Karl Knortz—and in later editions also to Wilhelm Pinder, Theodor Muncker, Theodor Opitz, Heinrich Romundt, Frau Vischer-Heussler, Frau Pinder, and Freifrau von Seydlitz.

Vol. II contains correspondence with Erwin Rohde.

Vol. III contains correspondence with Friedrich Ritschl, Jacob Burckhardt, Hippolyte Taine, Gottfried Keller, Heinrich von Stein, Georg Brandes, Hans von Bülow, Hugo von Senger, and Malwida von Meysenbug.

Vol. IV contains letters to Gast. (Gast's letters to Nietzsche were published separately: *Die Briefe Peter Gasts an Friedrich Nietzsche,* 2 vols., Munich, Verlag der Nietzsche-Gesellschaft, 1923–24.)

Vol. V contains letters to Nietzsche's mother and sister—but some of the letters "to the sister" are not authentic: several were really written to the mother, while others are composed of drafts for letters directed to others (see Friedrich Nietzsche, *Werke in drei Bänden*, ed. Karl Schlechta, vol. III, Munich, Carl Hanser, 1956, pp. 1408 ff.; also Schlechta's selection of 278 letters, *ibid.*, pp. 929–1352).

2. *Nietzsches Briefwechsel mit Franz Overbeck,* ed. C. A. Bernoulli and Richard Oehler. Leipzig, Insel, 1916. See also IV, 7, below.

3. Elisabeth Förster-Nietzsche, *Wagner und Nietzsche zur Zeit ihrer Freundschaft.* Munich, Müller, 1915; translated by C. V. Kerr, with an introduction by H. L. Mencken, as *The Nietzsche-Wagner Correspondence.* London, Duckworth, 1922.

4. Karl Strecker, *Nietzsche und Strindberg, mit ihrem Briefwechsel.* Munich, Müller, 1921.

5. *Werke und Briefe: Historisch-Kritische Gesamtausgabe* (see II, 9, above) offers 4 vols. of letters (Munich, Beck, 1938–42) which span the period from 1850 to 1877. *Briefe,* vol. I, pp. xii–lviii, offer a detailed and valuable survey of the whereabouts of all Nietzsche letters of which the Nietzsche Archive had any knowledge at that time. This survey also lists letters published in periodicals and in biographical works. Many letters are privately owned and as yet unpublished.

6. *Werke in drei Bänden,* ed. Karl Schlechta, vol. III, pp. 929–1352: see II, 10 and IV, 1, vol. V, above.

7. Podach's *Blick in Notizbücher Nietzsches* (III, 10, above), pp. 184–90, contains passages that, when IV, 2, was published in 1916, were deleted to avoid embarrassment to persons then still living.

8. *Briefe: Kritische Gesamtausgabe,* ed. Giorgio Colli and Mazzino Montinari, about 15 vols., Berlin, De Gruyter, 1969 ff. See II, 12, above.

V. NIETZSCHE IN ENGLISH
A. The Oscar Levy Translations

1. *The Complete Works of Friedrich Nietzsche,* 18 vols., ed. Oscar Levy. New York, Macmillan, 1909–11; reissued by Russell & Russell, New York, 1964.
2. *Selected Letters of Friedrich Nietzsche,* ed. Oscar Levy, transl. A. M. Ludovici. New York and Toronto, Doubleday, Page, 1921.

These translations, none of them by Dr. Levy himself, represent an immense labor of love but are thoroughly unreliable. None of the translators were philosophers, few were scholars. Mistakes abound, and it is impossible to form any notion of Nietzsche's style on the basis of these versions. Thomas Common's translation of *Zarathustra,* which replaced Alexander Tille's earlier attempt, is particularly inadequate but held the field until 1954, while Common's attempt to render *The Case of Wagner* was superseded by A. M. Ludovici's.

Common and Ludovici did more of these translations than anyone else, and in his Preface to the final revised edition Oscar Levy called Ludovici "the most gifted and conscientious of my collaborators." But in that same rev. ed., to give a mere two examples, Ludovici has "cosmopolitan" where Nietzsche has "cosmological"; and where Nietzsche says, "Ibsen has become very clear to me," Ludovici says: "Ibsen has become very German." Before 1914, Ludovici wrote three books about Nietzsche, but the items listed under his name in VI, B, below, are more revealing.

B. The Walter Kaufmann Translations

Between 1954 and 1967 all but four of Nietzsche's works appeared in new translations, edited by Walter Kaufmann. The translations of the *Genealogy of Morals* and *The Will to Power* are by Kaufmann and R. J. Hollingdale jointly. All the other translations are by Kaufmann alone, who also contributed introductions and copious notes.

1. *The Portable Nietzsche.* New York, Viking, 1954; paperback ed., with the same pagination, 1958. Contains new translations of four complete books:

> *Thus Spoke Zarathustra*
> *Twilight of the Idols*
> *The Antichrist*
> *Nietzsche contra Wagner*

and of selections from Nietzsche's other books, his notes, and his letters, as well as 60 pages of editorial material, including a brief commentary on every chapter of *Zarathustra*.

1.a. *Thus Spoke Zarathustra* has also been issued separately in paperback, New York, Viking, 1966.

2. *Basic Writings of Nietzsche,* New York, Modern Library Giant, 1968, contains all of the material in 2.a, b, and c, with a new introduction.

2.a. *Beyond Good and Evil,* with commentary. New York, Vintage Books (paperback), 1966.

2.b. *The Birth of Tragedy* and *The Case of Wagner,* with commentary. New York, Vintage Books (paperback), 1967.

2.c. *On the Genealogy of Morals* and *Ecce Homo,* with commentary. New York, Vintage Books (paperback), 1967.

3. *The Will to Power,* with commentary. New York, Random House, 1967; Vintage Books (paperback), 1968.

4. *Twenty German Poets: A Bilingual Collection.* New York, Random House, 1962; reprinted in the Modern Library (New York), 1963. Includes eleven poems by, and three about, Nietzsche.

C. Other Translations

There are many other versions of single works, but no one else has translated more than two or three, and none of the major works has been rendered into English by another philosopher.

Kaufmann's *Zarathustra* (1954), the third English version in over sixty years and the first to dispense with Victorian archaisms, such as "spake" and "thou" with its attendant verb forms, was followed rather closely by two other modern versions; but neither Marianne Cowan (Chicago, Gateway Editions [paperback], Henry Regnery, 1957) nor R. J. Hollingdale (Harmondsworth and Baltimore, Penguin Books [paperback], 1961) departs from Kaufmann's interpretations.

Marianne Cowan's versions of *Beyond Good and Evil* (1955) and *Philosophy in the Tragic Age of the Greeks* (1962) have also appeared as Gateway paperbacks.

Francis Golffing's distinctly contemporary versions of *The Birth of Tragedy* and *The Genealogy of Morals* (Garden City, N.Y., Anchor Books [paperback], 1956) depart radically from earlier translations of these works, but often also from the originals. The accent is on freedom, and there are striking omissions.

The third *Meditation* has been translated by J. W. Hillesheim and Malcolm R. Simpson, *Schopenhauer as Educator* (Chicago, Gateway Editions [paperback], Henry Regnery, 1965).

Nietzsche: Unpublished Letters, transl. and ed. by Kurt F. Leidecker,

New York, Philosophical Library, 1959, offers a selection of 75 items from Schlechta's selection of 278 letters (II, 10, above). Some of these 75 letters have appeared previously in better English translations; Leidecker's versions are as unreliable as his preface, nor does he provide any notes to explain allusions. Reviewed by Walter Kaufmann in *Philosophy and Phenomenological Research*, XXI, 2 (December, 1960), 275 f.

My Sister and I is a crude forgery: see under Kaufmann in VI, below.

D. What is Needed

The Oscar Levy translations include all of Nietzsche's books, the Walter Kaufmann translations do not include U, MA, S, M, and FW. While these works are less important than GT and the later works, beginning with Z, they all need to be redone. So far, however, only U III has been redone.

It would be foolish to insist on a rigid sequence of priorities, but on the whole it seems safe to rank these books in inverse chronological order. Certainly, FW is much the most important of the lot: philosophically, Book V, added in 1887, belongs with the later works, and the volume is also outstanding stylistically. A new version of FW is what is needed most; and after that, M.

Selections from MA, S, M, and FW, in new translations, may be found in 1 above; but a set of all of these books in scholarly translations that capture something of Nietzsche's literary brilliance would constitute an important and delightful contribution.

Eventually, it would be desirable also to have one or more well-translated and edited volumes of letters. Thus far, however, many interesting letters have not yet been published in German; and a good selection of those made available in the original would have to draw on approximately 15 vols. The editor, moreover, would have to be thoroughly at home in Nietzsche's works and life. Everything considered, then, it would be plausible to translate all of Nietzsche's books first.

VI. WORKS ABOUT NIETZSCHE

A. Bibliography

International Nietzsche Bibliography, ed. Herbert W. Reichert and Karl Schlechta. Chapel Hill, University of North Carolina Press, 1960. Arranged by languages—27 of them, from Bulgarian to Vietnamese—this is by far the most comprehensive bibliography ever attempted, though it is far from complete. Ephemeral articles, encyclopedias, histories, and reference works were excluded deliberately, and some items that should have been included escaped the editors' attention; 3973 items are listed, including translations of items that are listed both under the original language and again under the languages of the translations. In spite of some faults, this bibliography supersedes all earlier efforts.

B. Some Works about Nietzsche

In the Bibliography of the original edition of my *Nietzsche,* I included only works by authors referred to in the preceding pages. I have greatly expanded the Bibliography, adding (1) titles cited in the new edition but not formerly; (2) studies that have appeared since 1950 but are not cited above; (3) a very few authors of older items that are not cited.

Still, three-quarters of the authors listed are mentioned above—the Index shows where. Many are discussed at length or repeatedly, and those who read all the notes on an author will often find that they approximate a critical review. An asterisk (*) indicates some outstanding examples.

The primary purpose of this part of the Bibliography still is to furnish information about books discussed above; but it should also serve two other purposes. First, it should give some idea of the range of Nietzsche's influence: see, e.g., Benn, Bianquis, Buber, Camus, Deesz, Drimmer, Ellis, Gide, Heidegger, Hesse, Jaspers, Jung, Mann, Rilke, Rukser, Seidler, and Shaw.

Secondly, the list shows who has written on various specialized topics. It is interesting to note that relatively few books concentrate on Nietzsche's philosophy. Among these, the writings of *Jaspers* and *Vaihinger, Morgan* and *Hollingdale, Simmel* and *Klages* are likely to prove most helpful and stimulating to students; but the last two have not been translated. In addition to these, Del Negro, Eisler, and Granier have dealt specifically with Nietzsche's theory of knowledge.

ANDLER, CHARLES. *Nietzsche: Sa vie et sa pensée.* 6 vols. Paris, Bossard, 1920–31.

ANDREAS-SALOMÉ, LOU. *Friedrich Nietzsche in seinen Werken.* Vienna, Konegan, 1894; 3rd ed., Dresden, 1924.

———. *Lebensrückblick,* ed. Ernst Pfeiffer. Zurich, Max Niehaus, and Wiesbaden, Insel-Verlag, 1951. Binion's book on her, listed below, demonstrates her unreliability.

*BÄUMLER, ALFRED. "Bachofen und Nietzsche" (1929), "Nietzsche"

(1930), and "Nietzsche und der Nationalsozialismus" (1934)—all in *Studien zur deutschen Geistesgeschichte.* Berlin, Junker and Dünnhaupt, 1937.

———. *Nietzsche der Philosoph und Politiker.* Leipzig, Reclam, 1931.

———. Postscripts to *Kröners Taschenausgabe* of Nietzsche's works (II, 7 in the listing above).

———. See also under Hofmiller below.

BARZUN, JACQUES. "Nietzsche contra Wagner," in *Darwin, Marx, Wagner.* Boston, Little, Brown, 1941; rev. ed., Garden City, N.Y., Anchor Books (paperback), 1958.

BENN, GOTTFRIED. "Nietzsche—nach 50 Jahren (1950)," in *Frühe Prosa und Reden,* Wiesbaden, Limes Verlag, 1950, pp. 253–68. Reprinted in vol. I of *Gesammelte Werke,* Wiesbaden, Limes Verlag, 1959.

———. Three poems: "Sils Maria" (first publ., 1933), "Turin" (1936), and "Turin" (1958), in *Gedichte: Gesammelte Werke in vier Bänden: Dritter Band.* Wiesbaden, Limes Verlag, 1960, pp. 153, 177, and 465. The author was one of the leading poets of his generation (cf. V, B 4, above), but his Nietzsche poems are not among his best.

BENTLEY, ERIC R. *A Century of Hero-Worship: A Study of the Idea of Heroism in Carlyle and Nietzsche with Notes on Other Hero-Worshippers of Modern Times.* Philadelphia and New York, Lippincott, 1944.

BERNOULLI, CARL A. *Franz Overbeck und Friedrich Nietzsche: Eine Freundschaft.* 2 vols. Jena, Diederichs, 1908. Important for Nietzsche's biography. Elisabeth Förster-Nietzsche sued and obtained a judgment so that some letters were blacked out in almost all copies.

*BERTRAM, ERNST. *Nietzsche: Versuch einer Mythologie.* Berlin, Bondi, 1918 (7th rev. ed., 21,000 copies, 1929). French transl. by R. Pitrou, Paris, Rieder, 1932.

BIANQUIS, GENEVIÈVE. *Nietzsche en France: L'influence de Nietzsche sur la pensée Française.* Paris, Alcan, 1929. Bibliography on pp. 119–26.

BINION, RUDOLPH. *Frau Lou: Nietzsche's Wayward Disciple.* With a Foreword by Walter Kaufmann. Princeton, Princeton University Press, 1968. Supersedes all previous studies of Lou Andreas-Salomé and of her relationship to Nietzsche.

BLUNCK, RICHARD. *Friedrich Nietzsche: Kindheit und Jugend.* Munich and Basel, Ernst Reinhardt, 1953. Good biography up to 1869.

BORLAND, HAROLD H. *Nietzsche's Influence on Swedish Literature, With Special Reference to Strindberg, Ola Hansson, Heidenstam and Fröding.* Göteborg, Göteborgs Kungl. Vetenskaps-och Vitterhets-Samhälles Handlingar, VI, A, vol. VI, 3, 1956. 177 pp., including bibliography and index.

BRANDES, GEORG. *Friedrich Nietzsche.* Transl. from the Danish by A. G.

Chater. London, Heinemann, 1914. Four essays by the critic who "discovered" Nietzsche, dated 1889, 1899, 1900, and 1909.

* Brann, Hellmuth Walther. *Nietzsche und die Frauen.* Leipzig, Meiner, 1931.

———. "A Reply to Walter Kaufmann," in *Journal of the History of Philosophy,* III, 2 (October 1965), pp. 246–50. Discussed in the Appendix, above. Like the three book reviews listed in note 3 of the Appendix, this is signed: Henry Walter Brann.

* Brinton, Crane. *Nietzsche.* Cambridge, Mass., Harvard University Press, 1941; New York, Harper Torchbook [paperback] with new preface, epilogue, and bibliography, 1965. In the new edition, the numerous errors of the original edition remain uncorrected, but in a short Preface Brinton disowns the chapter, "Nietzsche in Western Thought." The rev. bibliography adds serious new errors.

———. Reviews of the original ed. of Kaufmann's *Nietzsche* in *Saturday Review,* January 13, 1951, and *Germanic Review,* XXVI (October 1951), 239–40.

Buber, Martin. "Autobiographische Fragmente," in *Martin Buber,* eds. Paul Arthur Schilpp and Maurice Friedman. Stuttgart, Kohlhammer, 1963, pp. 8–11 and 34. "Autobiographical Fragments," in *The Philosophy of Martin Buber,* eds. Paul Arthur Schilpp and Maurice Friedman. La Salle, Ill., Open Court, and London, Cambridge University Press, 1967, pp. 12 f.

———. "Ein Wort über Nietzsche und die Lebenswerte," in *Kunst und Leben,* Berlin, December 1900. An encomium of about one thousand words, written after Nietzsche's death.

Camus, Albert. "Nietzsche et le nihilisme," in *L'homme révolté.* Paris, Gallimard, 1951, pp. 88–105. "Nietzsche and nihilism," in *The Rebel,* transl. by Anthony Bower. New York, Vintage Books (paperback), 1956, pp. 65–80.

Cohn, Paul. *Um Nietzsches Untergang: Beiträge zum Verständnis des Genies, mit einem Anhang von Elisabeth Förster-Nietzsche: Die Zeit von Nietzsches Erkrankung bis zu seinem Tode.* Hanover, Morris, 1931.

Coomaraswamy, Ananda. "Cosmopolitan View of Nietzsche," in *The Dance of Siva: Fourteen Indian Essays.* New York, Sunwise Turn, and London, Simpkin, Marshall, Hamilton, Kent, 1924.

*Danto, Arthur C. *Nietzsche as Philosopher.* New York, Macmillan, 1965.

Deesz, Gisela. *Die Entwicklung des Nietzsche-Bildes in Deutschland* (dissertation, Bonn). Würzburg, Triltsch, 1933.

Del Negro, Walter. *Die Rolle der Fiktionen in der Erkenntnistheorie Friedrich Nietzsches.* Munich, Rösl, 1923. Vol. 5 in the series "Bausteine zu einer Philosophie des 'Als-Ob,'" ed. Hans Vaihinger (see below) and Raymund Schmidt.

DEUSSEN, PAUL. *Erinnerungen an Friedrich Nietzsche.* Leipzig, Brockhaus, 1901.

DREWS, ARTHUR. *Nietzsches Philosophie.* Heidelberg, Winter 1904.

DRIMMER, MELVIN. *Nietzsche in American Thought: 1895–1925.* Ph.D. thesis, University of Rochester (N.Y.), 1965; Ann Arbor, Mich., University Microfilms, 727 pp., including bibliography, pp. 634–727.

EISLER, RUDOLF. *Nietzsches Erkenntnistheorie und Metaphysik: Darstellung und Kritik.* Leipzig, Hermann Haacke, 1902. One of the few monographs on Nietzsche's theory of knowledge. The author is better known for his philosophical dictionaries.

ELLIS, HAVELOCK. "Nietzsche," in *Affirmations.* London, Walter Scott, 1898, pp. 1–85. Second ed. with a new preface, Boston and New York, Houghton Mifflin, 1915, pp. 1–85.

EWALD, OSCAR. *Nietzsches Lehre in ihren Grundbegriffen: Die Ewige Wiederkunft des Gleichen und der Sinn des Übermenschen.* Berlin, Hofmann, 1903.

FAIRLEY, BARKER. "Nietzsche and Goethe" and "Nietzsche and the Poetic Impulse," in *Bulletin of the John Rylands Library.* Manchester, 1934 and 1935 (XVIII, 298–314; XIX, 344–61).

FIGGIS, JOHN. *The Will to Freedom or the Gospel of Nietzsche and the Gospel of Christ.* New York, Scribner, 1917.

FINK, EUGEN. *Nietzsches Philosophie.* Stuttgart, Kohlhammer, 1960.

*FÖRSTER-NIETZSCHE, E. *Das Leben Friedrich Nietzsches.* 2 vols. in 3. Leipzig, Naumann, 1895–1904.

———. *Der junge Nietzsche.* Leipzig, Kröner, 1912.

———. *Der einsame Nietzsche.* Leipzig, Kröner, 1914.

———. Engl. transl. of the last two titles as *The Life of Nietzsche,* 2 vols., 1912–15: vol. I. *The Young Nietzsche,* transl. by A. M. Ludovici; vol. II. *The Lonely Nietzsche,* transl. by P. V. Cohn.

———. *Friedrich Nietzsche und die Frauen seiner Zeit.* Munich, Beck, 1935.

———. "Friedrich Nietzsches Bibliothek," in *Bücher und Wege zu Büchern.* Ed. Arthur Berthold. Berlin and Stuttgart, Spemann, 1900 (contains a list of the books Nietzsche owned).

FREUD, SIGMUND. Discussion of "Nietzsche: '*On the Ascetic Ideal*' (Section 3 of *Genealogy of Morality*)," Scientific Meeting on April 1, 1908, in *Minutes of the Vienna Psychoanalytic Society,* vol. I: 1906–08, ed. Herman Nunberg and Ernst Federn, transl. M. Nunberg. New York, International Universities Press, 1963, pp. 355–361. The discussants include not only Freud but also Alfred Adler and Otto Rank.

———. Discussion of "Nietzsche's *Ecce Homo,*" Scientific Meeting on

October 28, 1908, in *Minutes of the Vienna Psychoanalytic Society,* vol. II: 1908–10, ed. Herman Numberg and Ernst Federn, transl. M. Nunberg. New York, International Universities Press, 1967, pp. 25–33. The discussants include not only Freud but also Alfred Adler and Otto Rank.

*GEORGE, STEFAN. "Nietzsche" in *Der Siebente Ring.* Berlin, Bondi, 1907.

————. "Einer stand auf . . ." in *Der Stern des Bundes.* Berlin, Bondi, 1914. The original texts and verse translations of both poems are included in *Twenty German Poets* (V, B 4, above).

GIDE, ANDRÉ. "Lettres à Angèle," XII (dated December 10, 1898), in *Prétextes,* Paris, 1903; nouvelle édition, augmentéen, Paris, Mercure de France, 1913, pp. 166–82. Not included in the English *Pretexts.* German transl. by Dieter Bassermann in *Ariadne, 1. Jahrbuch der Nietzsche Gesellschaft,* Munich, 1925, pp. 110–21: "Nietzsche, Brief an Angèle."

GRANIER, JEAN. *Le Problème de la Vérité dans la philosophie de Nietzsche.* Paris, Editions du Seuil, 1966.

GUNDOLF, ERNST. *Nietzsche als Richter unserer Zeit.* (Sein Amt. The same volume also contains Hildebrandt's essay, listed below.) Breslau, Hirt, 1923.

GUNDOLF, FRIEDRICH (brother of Ernst). Section on Nietzsche in *Caesar im Neunzehnten Jahrhundert.* Berlin, Bondi, 1926. Gundolf's references to Nietzsche in his other books are also noteworthy and have had some influence.

HÄRTLE, HEINRICH. *Nietzsche und der Nationalsozialismus.* Munich, Eher (Zentralverlag der NSDAP), 1937.

HANNA, THOMAS. *The Lyrical Existentialists.* New York, Atheneum, 1962.

Reviewed by Walter Kaufmann in *The New York Times Book Review,* March 11, 1962: "Appalling lapses in scholarship, logic, and style abound."

HAVENSTEIN, MARTIN. *Nietzsche als Erzieher.* Berlin, Mittler, 1922.

HEIDEGGER, MARTIN. "Nietzsches Wort 'Gott ist tot' " in *Holzwege.* Frankfurt am Main, Klostermann, 1950.

————. "Wer ist Nietzsches Zarathustra?," in *Vorträge und Aufsätze.* Pfullingen, Neske, 1954. Transl. by Bernd Magnus, in *Lectures and Addresses.* New York, Harper and Row, 1967.

————. *Nietzsche.* 2 vols. Pfullingen, Neske, 1961. Lectures held at the University of Freiburg, 1936–40, on The Will to Power as Art, The Eternal Recurrence, and The Will to Power as Knowledge (vol. I); on The Eternal Recurrence and The Will to Power, and on European Nihilism, followed by essays on Nietzsche's Metaphysics (1940), The Place of Nihilism in the History of Being (1944/46), Metaphysics as the History of Being (1941), Drafts for a History of Being as Metaphysics (1941), and How Memory Penetrates Metaphysics (1941) —all in vol. II. One of the major efforts—certainly the bulkiest one— of the later Heidegger: important for those who want to understand Heidegger.

HELLER, ERICH. "Burckhardt and Nietzsche" and "Nietzsche and Goethe" and "Rilke and Nietzsche," in *The Disinherited Mind.* Philadelphia, Dufour and Saifer, 1952. For a critique of the very stimulating Rilke essay see the chapters, "Nietzsche and Rilke" and "Art, Tradition, and Truth" in the first book listed under Kaufmann, below.

————. "The Importance of Nietzsche" and "Wittgenstein and Nietzsche," in *The Artist's Journey Into the Interior and Other Essays.* New York, Random House, 1965; New York, Vintage Books [paperback], 1968.

HESSE, HERMANN. *Zarathustras Wiederkehr: Ein Wort an die deutsche Jugend.* Berlin, Fischer, 1919. Reprinted in *Krieg und Frieden,* Zurich, Fretz, 1946.

* HILDEBRANDT, KURT. *Nietzsches Wettkampf mit Sokrates und Plato.* Dresden, Sybillen, 1922.

————. *Nietzsche als Richter unserer Zeit* (Sein Schicksal. Cf. E. Gundolf above). Breslau, Hirt, 1923.

————. *Wagner und Nietzsche: Ihr Kampf gegen das Neunzehnte Jahrhundert.* Breslau, Hirt, 1924.

————. *Gesundheit und Krankheit in Nietzsches Leben und Werk.* Berlin, Karger, 1926.

HILLEBRAND, KARL. "Einiges über den Verfall der deutschen Sprache und der deutschen Gesinnung" (review of U I, September 1873), "Ueber historisches Wissen und historischen Sinn" (review of U II, June 1874), and "Schopenhauer und das deutsche Publikum" (review of U III, November 1874) in *Zeiten, Völker und Menschen,* vol. II: *Wälsches und Deutsches.* Berlin, Robert Oppenheim, 1875.

HIRSCH, EMANUEL. "Luther und Nietzsche," in *Luther-Jahrbuch.* 1920/ 21 (II/III, 61–106).

*HOFMILLER, JOSEF. "Nietzsches Testament" (1902) and "Nietzsche und Rohde" (1903), in *Versuche.* Munich, Süddeutsche Monatshefte G.m.b.H., 1909.

————. Hofmiller-Bäumler polemics, in *Süddeutsche Monatshefte,* XXVIII, 536, 607 f., 685 f., 758 ff., and XXIX, 58 f.

————. "Nietzsche," in *Süddeutsche Monatshefte,* 1931 (XXIX, 73–131).

————. *Friedrich Nietzsche.* Hamburg-Bergedorf, Stromverlag, no date (written in 1932 and based on the above "Nietzsche," without, however, superseding it entirely).

HOLLINGDALE, R. J. *Nietzsche: The Man and His Philosophy.* Baton Rouge, Louisiana State University Press, 1965. Sympathetic, informed, and well written, this is the best biography in English; but the account of Nietzsche's relationships to Lou Salomé and Paul Rée is dated by Binion's book. Nietzsche's philosophy is discussed in the context of his life.

HORNEFFER, ERNST. *Nietzsches Lehre von der Ewigen Wiederkunft des Gleichen und deren bisherige Veröffentlichung.* Leipzig, Naumann, 1900. See also Steiner, below.

HUBBARD, STANLEY. *Nietzsche und Emerson.* Basel, Verlag für Recht und Gesellschaft, 1958.

*JASPERS, KARL. *Nietzsche: Einführung in das Verständnis seines Philosophierens.* Berlin and Leipzig, De Gruyter, 1936 (2nd ed., 1947, "unchanged," but with a new preface). Transl. by Charles F. Wallraff and Frederick J. Schmitz, *Nietzsche: An Introduction to the Understanding of His Philosophical Activity.* Tucson, University of Arizona Press, 1965.

Reviewed by Walter Kaufmann in *Saturday Review,* May 22, 1965, 86–88.

For a detailed critical discussion, also of the next item, see the first book listed under Kaufmann, below.

———. *Nietzsche und das Christentum.* Hameln, Verlag der Bücherstube Fritz Seifert, n.d. ("This essay was written as the basis for a lecture which was delivered . . . May 12, 1938. It is here printed without any changes or additions. . . .") Transl. by E. B. Ashton, *Nietzsche and Christianity.* Chicago, Gateway Editions, Henry Regnery, 1961. A miniature version of the approach encountered in Jaspers' big *Nietzsche.*

———. "Kierkegaard und Nietzsche" in *Vernunft und Existenz.* Groningen, J. W. Wolters, 1935. Transl. by William Earle in *Reason and Existenz.* New York, Noonday Press, 1955. Reprinted in Walter Kaufmann, *Existentialism from Dostoevsky to Sartre.* New York, Meridian Books [paperback], 1956, pp. 158–84.

JOEL, KARL. *Nietzsche und die Romantik.* Jena and Leipzig, Diederichs, 1905 (also contains "Nietzsche und die Antike").

———. Section on Nietzsche in *Wandlungen der Weltanschauung,* vol. II. Tübingen, Mohr, 1934.

JUNG, CARL G. *Psychologische Typen.* Zurich, Rascher, 1937. (Chapter III: "The Apollinian and the Dionysian"). Transl. by H. Godwin Baynes, *Psychological Types.* New York, Pantheon, 1959.

KAUFMANN, WALTER. "How Nietzsche Revolutionized Ethics," "Nietzsche and Rilke," "Art, Tradition, and Truth," "Philosophy versus Poetry," and "Jaspers' Relation to Nietzsche," in *From Shakespeare to Existentialism.* Boston, Beacon Press, 1959; rev. ed., Garden City, N.Y., Anchor Books (paperback), 1960.

————. *Hegel.* Garden City, N.Y., Doubleday, 1965; Garden City, N.Y., Anchor Books (paperback), 2 vols., 1966.

————. *Tragedy and Philosophy.* Garden City, N.Y., Doubleday, 1968. Includes criticisms of Nietzsche's ideas about tragedy, and supersedes the article listed next.

————. "Nietzsche Between Homer and Sartre: Five Treatments of the Orestes Story," in *Revue Internationale de Philosophie,* No. 67 (1964), pp. 50–73. Demonstrates Nietzsche's immense influence on Sartre's *The Flies.*

————. Articles on Nietzsche in *Encyclopedia Americana, Encyclopaedia Britannica, Collier's Encyclopedia, Grolier Encyclopedia, The Encyclopedia of Philosophy,* and in *The Concise Encyclopedia of Western Philosophy and Philosophers,* ed. J. O. Urmson.

————. Exposés of *My Sister and I* as a forgery, falsely attributed to Nietzsche, in *Milwaukee Journal,* February 24, 1952; in *Partisan Review,* vol. XIX, 3 (May/June 1952), 372–76; and of the rev. ed. in *The Philosophical Review,* vol. LXIV, 1 (January 1955), 152 f.[1]

————. Reviews of books by Hanna, Jaspers, Lea, Löwith, Love, Steiner, and Thompson are listed under those names; review of Leidecker is listed under V, C, above.

————. See also the introductions and commentaries in the translations listed above under V, B.

*KLAGES, LUDWIG. *Die Psychologischen Errungenschaften Nietzsches.* Leipzig, Barth, 1926.

* KNIGHT, A. H. J. *Some Aspects of the Life and Work of Nietzsche and particularly of his Connection with Greek Literature and Thought.* Cambridge, Cambridge University Press, 1933.

KNIGHT, G. WILSON. *Christ and Nietzsche: An Essay in Poetic Wisdom.* London and New York, Staples Press, 1948.

LANGE-EICHBAUM, WILHELM. *Nietzsche: Krankheit und Wirkung.* Hamburg, Lettenbauer, 1946. A psychiatrist's attempt to prove beyond a doubt that Nietzsche's insanity was due to syphilis and that his influence was due to his insanity.

LANGER, NORBERT. *Das Problem der Romantik bei Nietzsche.* Münster, Helios, 1929.

---

[1] In 1965 the late David George Plotkin came to Princeton to explain to me that he was the author not only of several books published over his own name and over the pseudonym, David George Kin, but also of some books attributed to others. He gave me a long handwritten and signed statement, describing how, for a flat fee paid him by the publisher, he had written *My Sister and I.*

Lea, F. A. *The Tragic Philosopher; A Study of Friedrich Nietzsche.* New York, Philosophical Library, 1957. An attempt to do what Hollingdale did much better, eight years later.

Reviewed by Walter Kaufmann in *The Philosophical Review,* LXVII, 2 (April 1958), 274–76.

Lichtenberger, H. *La philosophie de Nietzsche.* Paris, Alcan, 1898 (4th ed., 1899). Transl. by J. M. Kennedy, *The Gospel of Superman,* Edinburgh and London, T. N. Foulis, 1910; new ed. with new preface by H. L., 1926.

*Löwith, Karl. *Kierkegaard und Nietzsche oder Philosophische und Theologische Überwindung des Nihilismus.* Frankfurt am Main, Klostermann, 1933.

———. *Nietzsches Philosophie der Ewigen Wiederkunft des Gleichen.* Berlin, Die Runde, 1935. Rev. ed., Stuttgart, Kohlhammer, 1956.

———. "Burckhardt und Nietzsche"—Chapter 1 of *Jacob Burckhardt: Der Mensch inmitten der Geschichte.* Lucerne, Vita Nova, 1936.

———. *Von Hegel bis Nietzsche.* Zurich and New York, Europa, 1941. Transl. by David E. Green, *From Hegel to Nietzsche.* New York, Holt, 1964; Garden City, N.Y., Anchor Books (paperback), 1967. By far the best of Löwith's historical studies, this volume is organized by topics, each of which is broken down into sections devoted to different writers, in chronological order. There are eight sections on Nietzsche, including discussions of his views of Goethe and Hegel; his relation to the Hegelians of the forties; his attempt to overcome nihilism; his conception of herd man and lead animal; his conception of labor; his critique of education; his conception of the overman; and his critique of Christian morality and culture.

Reviewed by Walter Kaufmann in *Union Seminary Quarterly Review,* XXI, 2, 2 (January 1966), 266 f.

———. "Nietzsche's Revival of the Doctrine of Eternal Recurrence," in *Meaning in History.* Chicago, University of Chicago Press, 1949.

———. "Zu Schlechtas neuer Nietzsche-Legende," in *Merkur* 126 (August 1958), pp. 781–84.

Love, Frederick R. *Young Nietzsche and the Wagnerian Experience.* Chapel Hill, University of Carolina Press, 1963. A good monograph that takes into account Nietzsche's compositions, including unpublished items in the archives in Weimar. It is full of pertinent, but untranslated, German quotations. The break with Wagner is not included. Love shows how Nietzsche never was "a passionate devotee of Wagnerian music."

Reviewed by Walter Kaufmann in *Journal of the History of Philosophy,* III, 2 (October 1965), 284–86.

Ludovici, Anthony. "Hitler and Nietzsche," in *The English Review,*

LXIV, 1 (January 1937), 44–52, and 2 (February, 1937), 192–202. "It seems fairly obvious that there must be a strong Nietzschean influence in National Socialism, if only because of the powerful breath of pre-Socratic Hellenism which has prevailed in Germany ever since the N.S.D.A.P. seized the reins of government" (44). "I happened to be one of the English guests of honour present when that statement was made [by Hitler, at the Reichsparteitag in Nürnberg], and I applauded it" (46).

———. See also Förster-Nietzsche and V, A, above.

MANN, THOMAS. "Rede über Nietzsche" in *Bemühungen*. Berlin, Fischer, 1925.

———. "Nietzsches Philosophie" and "Dostojewski—Mit Maassen," in *Neue Studien*. Stockholm, Bermann-Fischer, 1948.

———. Both essays have also been published in English: *Nietzsche's Philosophy in the Light of Contemporary Events*. Washington, Library of Congress, 1948.

———. *The Short Novels of Dostoevsky*, with an introduction by Thomas Mann. New York, Dial Press, 1945.

MARTIN, ALFRED VON. *Nietzsche und Burckhardt: Zwei Geistige Welten im Dialog*. 3rd rev. ed., Basel, Reinhardt, 1945.

MÖBIUS, PAUL J. *Über das Pathologische bei Nietzsche*. Wiesbaden, Bergmann, 1902 (rev. ed., Leipzig, Barth, 1904, in vol. v of Möbius, *Ausgewählte Werke*).

* MORGAN, GEORGE A., JR. *What Nietzsche Means*. Cambridge, Mass., Harvard University Press, 1941; New York Torchbooks (paperback), 1965.

*NEWMAN, ERNEST. *The Life of Richard Wagner*, vol. IV: 1866–83. New York, Knopf, 1946.

NICHOLLS, R. A. *Nietzsche in the Early Work of Thomas Mann*. Berkeley and Los Angeles, University of California Press, 1955.

NOLTE, ERNST. "Marx und Nietzsche in Sozialismus des jungen Mussolini" in *Historische Zeitschrift*, vol. 191 (1960), pp. 249–335.

*OEHLER, RICHARD. *Friedrich Nietzsche und die Vorsokratiker*. Leipzig, Dürr, 1904.

———. *Friedrich Nietzsche und die Deutsche Zukunft*. Leipzig, Armanen, 1935.

PANNWITZ, RUDOLF. *Nietzsche und die Verwandlung des Menschen*. Amsterdam, Akademische Verlagsanstalt Pantheon, 1943. Written in 1939.

———. "Nietzsche-Philologie?" in *Merkur*, November 1957, pp. 1073–87. Attack on Schlechta's edition of WM. Answered by Schlechta (see below).

*PODACH, ERICH F. *Nietzsches Zusammenbruch: Beiträge zu einer*

Biographie auf Grund unveröffentlichter Dokumente. Heidelberg, Kampmann, 1930. Transl. by F. A. Voigt, *The Madness of Nietzsche,* New York, Putnam, 1931.

————. *Gestalten um Nietzsche, mit unveröffentlichten Dokumenten zur Geschichte seines Lebens und seines Werks.* Weimar, Lichtenstein, 1932. Chapters on Nietzsche's mother, Rohde, Gast, Bernhard and Elisabeth Förster, and Langbehn.

————. *Der Kranke Nietzsche: Briefe seiner Mutter an Franz Overbeck.* Vienna, Bermann-Fischer, 1937.

————. *Friedrich Nietzsche und Lou Salomé: Ihre Begegnung 1882.* Zurich and Leipzig, Niehans, n.d. This book is dated by Binion's study, listed above.

————. See also the two books listed above under II, 11 and III, 10.

REINHARDT, KARL. *Nietzsches Klage der Ariadne.* Frankfurt am Main, Klostermann, 1936. The author was a very prominent classical philologist, but this essay, sharply criticized by Podach in III, 10, above, does him no credit.

REYBURN, H. A. *Nietzsche: The Story of a Human Philosopher.* London and New York, Macmillan, 1948 (a German edition was published in 1946).

RILKE, RAINER MARIA. Marginal comments on GT, probably written in March 1900, in Berlin; published for the first time in Rilke's *Sämtliche Werke,* VI, Frankfurt am Main, Insel-Verlag, 1966, pp. 1163–77; includes a poem of 12 lines, dated March 18, 1900.

See also Heller and Kaufmann, above.

ROHDE, ERWIN. *Afterphilologie: Zur Beleuchtung des von dem Dr. phil. U. v. Wilamowitz-Möllendorf herausgegebenen Pamphlets "Zukunftsphilologie!"* Leipzig, Fritzsch, 1872.

ROOS, CARL. *Nietzsche und das Labyrinth.* Copenhagen, Gyldendal, 1940. Nietzsche's early Empedocles fragments are printed in an appendix.

ROSENBERG, ALFRED. *Friedrich Nietzsche.* Ansprache bei einer Gedenkstunde anlässlich des 100. Geburtstages Friedrich Nietzsches am 15. October 1944 in Weimar. Munich, Eher (Zentralverlag der NSDAP).

ROYCE, JOSIAH. "Nietzsche," in *Atlantic Monthly,* March 1917, pp. 321–31. A sympathetic and perceptive article, "found among the posthumous papers of Professor Royce."

RUKSER, UDO. *Nietzsche in der Hispania.* Bern and Munich, Francke, 1962. A comprehensive study of the reception of Nietzsche in the Spanish-speaking world. The bibliography, 1888–1962 (pp. 358–69), is said to include everything published about Nietzsche in Spanish; it also includes some non-Spanish items.

SALIN, EDGAR. *Jacob Burckhardt und Nietzsche.* Basel, Verlag der Universitätsbibliothek, 1938.

SALOMÉ, LOU. See Andreas-Salomé, Lou, above.

SALTER, WILLIAM MACKINTIRE. *Nietzsche, the Thinker.* New York, Holt, 1917.

SANTAYANA, GEORGE. *Egotism in German Philosophy.* New York, Scribner, no date (chapts. XI–XIII).

SCHESTOW, LEO. *Tolstoi und Nietzsche* (transl. from the Russian by N. Strasser). Cologne, Marcan-Block, 1923.

———. *Dostojewski und Nietzsche: Philosophie der Tragödie* (transl. by R. von Walter). Cologne, Marcan, 1924.

SCHEUER, O. F. *Friedrich Nietzsche als Student.* Bonn, Albert Ahn, 1923.

* SCHLECHTA, KARL. *Der Fall Nietzsche: Aufsätze und Vorträge.* Munich, Carl Hanser, 1958. The last essay is a reply to Pannwitz's attack (see above). Wolfram von den Steinen criticized Schlechta's book and defended Pannwitz in *Merkur* 126 (August 1958), 772–80. See also Löwith, above, who criticized Schlechta in the same issue of *Merkur,* and II, 10, above.

SEIDLER, INGO. "Das Nietzschebild Robert Musils" in *Deutsche Vierteljahrsschrift für Literaturwissenschaft und Geistesgeschichte,* 39, 3 (1965), pp. 329–49.

SHAW, GEORGE BERNARD. Reviews of Engl. transl. of *Nietzsche contra Wagner, &c.*" by Thomas Common, 1896, and of *"A Genealogy of Morals and Poems,"* transl. by William Haussman and John Gray, and of *Zarathustra,* transl. by Alexander Tille, all 1899, in *Saturday Review,* April 11, 1896, pp. 373 f., and May 13, 1899, Supplement, iii.

SIMMEL, GEORG. *Schopenhauer und Nietzsche: Ein Vortragszyklus.* Leipzig, Duncker and Humblot, 1907.

SONNS, STEFAN, *Das Gewissen in der Philosophie Nietzsches* Winterthur, P. G. Keller, 1955. Dissertation, Zurich, University of Zurich. Includes comparisons with Paul Rée's writings.

SPITTELER, CARL. *Meine Beziehungen zu Nietzsche.* Munich, Süddeutsche Monatshefte, 1908.

*STACE, WALTER T. *The Destiny of Western Man.* New York, Reynal & Hitchcock, 1942 (2nd ed., 1947—"The only change . . . is the insertion of the new chapter on Russian communism.")

STEINER, RUDOLF. *Friedrich Nietzsche: Ein Kämpfer gegen seine Zeit.* Weimar, Felber, 1895. The second edition (Dornach, Schweiz, Philosophisch-Anthroposophischer Verlag am Goetheanum, 1926) also contains "Friedrich Nietzsche im 'Lebensgang' Rudolf Steiners" (1924) and "Die Philosophie Friedrich Nietzsches als psycho-pathologisches

Problem," "Friedrich Nietzsches Persönlichkeit und die Psycho-Pa-
thologie," and "Die Persönlichkeit Friedrich Nietzsches: Gedächtnis-
rede"—all 1900. Transl. by Margaret Ingram deRis, *Friedrich Nietzsche: Fighter for Freedom*. Englewood, N.J., Rudolf Steiner Publications, 1960.

    Reviewed by Walter Kaufmann in *Chicago Review*, XIV, 3 (Au-
tumn-Winter, 1960), 115–16. These essays are hopelessly dated, in part
by the far more interesting polemics listed next; and the translation
occasionally changes the meaning completely.

———. "Das Nietzsche-Archiv und seine Anklagen gegen den bisherigen
Herausgeber [Kögel]" in *Das Magazin für Litteratur*, 1900 (LXIX,
145–58; consists of "I. Die Herausgabe von Nietzsches Werken" and
"II. Zur Charakteristik der Frau Elisabeth Förster-Nietzsche"). Reply
by E. Horneffer, "Eine Verteidigung der sogennanten 'Wiederkunft
des Gleichen' von Nietzsche," *ibid.*, pp. 377–83. Reply by Steiner,
ibid., pp. 384–89, 401–04, 425–34.

STEKEL, WILHELM. "Nietzsche und Wagner: Eine sexual-psychologische
Studie zur Psychogenese des Freundschaftsgefühles und des Freund-
schaftsverrates" in *Zeitschrift für Sexualwissenschaft*, IV, 1917.

STROUX, JOHANNES. *Nietzsches Professur in Basel*. Jena, Frommannsche
Buchhandlung, 1925.

THIEL, RUDOLF. *Die Generation ohne Männer*. Berlin, Paul Neff, 1932.

THOMPSON, R. MOTSON. *Nietzsche and Christian Ethics*. New York,
Philosophical Library, 1951. A medley of popular errors.

    Reviewed by Walter Kaufmann in *The Philosophical Review*,
LXI, 4 (October 1952), pp 595–99.

TILLICH, PAUL. "Nietzsche and the Bourgeois Spirit," in *Journal of the
History of Ideas*, 6 (1945), pp. 307–09.

TÖNNIES, FERDINAND. *Der Nietzsche-Kultus: Eine Kritik*. Leipzig, Reis-
land, 1897.

VAIHINGER, HANS. *Nietzsche als Philosoph*. Berlin, Reuther and Reich-
ard, 1902.

———. *Die Philosophie des Als-Ob*. Leipzig, Meiner, 1911. Transl. by
C. K. Ogden, *The Philosophy of 'As if.'* New York, Harcourt Brace,
1924. The chapter on "Nietzsche and His Doctrine of Conscious
Illusion (The Will to Illusion)" (pp. 341–62), remains one of the most
interesting studies in any language of Nietzsche's theory of knowledge, but see note 6 in Chapter 4, above. Cf. also Del Negro, above.

*VOLKMANN-SCHLUCK, K. H. *Nietzsches Gedicht "Die Wüste wächst,
weh dem, der Wüsten birgt . . ."* Frankfurt am Main, Klostermann,
1958.

VUILLEMIN, J. "Nietzsche Aujourd'hui," in *Les Temps Modernes*, 6, 67

(May 1951), pp. 1921–54. A detailed comparison of the original edition of the present volume with the Nietzsche interpretations of Jaspers, Heidegger, and Löwith.

WEIGAND, WILHELM. *Friedrich Nietzsche: Ein psychologischer Versuch.* Munich, Franz'sche Hofbuchhandlung, 1893.

WESTERNHAGEN, CURT VON. *Nietzsche, Juden, Antijuden.* Weimar, Duncker, no date (1936).

WILAMOWITZ-MÖLLENDORF, U. VON. *Zukunftsphilologie! Eine Erwiderung auf Friedrich Nietzsches "Geburt der Tragödie."* Berlin, Bornträger, 1873.

———. *Zukunftsphilologie. Zweites Stück: Eine Erwiderung auf die Rettungsversuche für Friedrich Nietzsches "Geburt der Tragödie."* Berlin, Bornträger, 1873. For some discussion, see V, B2b, above.

WILLIAMS, W. D. *Nietzsche and the French: A Study of the influence of Nietzsche's French reading on his thought and writing.* Oxford, Blackwell, 1952.

WRIGHT, WILLARD H. *What Nietzsche Taught.* New York, Huebsch, 1915.

ZEITLER, JULIUS. *Nietzsches Ästhetik.* Leipzig, Hermann Seemann Nachfolger, 1900.

INDEX

The exceptionally fine index for the original edition (1950) was prepared by Dr. John Rawls, then an instructor at Princeton, now Professor of Philosophy at Harvard. In the second edition (1956) it was unfortunately replaced by an index of names only, in order to save space. The present index is based on Rawls' work, and I welcome this opportunity to thank him again.

I am profoundly indebted to Sonia Volochova, who has adapted and greatly expanded the old index.

For references to Nietzsche's works see Nietzsche; m stands for mottoes; n for notes.